PARALLEL of LIFE & ART

Alison & Peter Smithson.
46 LIMERSTON ST.
SW·10·

Not Quite Architecture

M. Christine Boyer

Not Quite Architecture

Writing around Alison and
Peter Smithson

The MIT Press
Cambridge, Massachusetts
London, England

This publication is made possible in part through a grant from the Barr Ferree Foundation Fund for Publications, Department of Art and Archaeology, Princeton University.

© 2017 Massachusetts Institute of Technology

All rights reserved. No part of this book may be reproduced in any form by any electronic or mechanical means (including photocopying, recording, or information storage and retrieval) without permission in writing from the publisher.

This book was set in Helvetica Neue Pro by the MIT Press. Printed and bound in Canada.

Library of Congress Cataloging-in-Publication Data

Names: Boyer, M. Christine, author.
Title: Not quite architecture : writing around Alison and Peter Smithson / M. Christine Boyer.
Description: Cambridge, MA : The MIT Press, 2017. | Includes bibliographical references and index.
Identifiers: LCCN 2016024880 | ISBN 9780262035514 (hardcover : alk. paper)
Subjects: LCSH: Smithson, Alison, 1928–1993—Written works. | Smithson, Peter, 1923–2003—Written works. | Architecture, Modern—20th century.
Classification: LCC NA997.S57 B69 2017 | DDC 724/.6—dc23 LC record available at https://lccn.loc.gov/2016024880

10 9 8 7 6 5 4 3 2 1

To Max Risselada and Dirk van den Heuvel,
without whom this book would not have
been possible

Contents

Preface ix
Acknowledgments xv

1 Compromising Modernism: Architectural Polemics in Postwar England 1
2 A History of Beginnings: Alternate Routes for a Younger Generation of Architects 37
3 Thoughts Touching Everything 75
4 Messages from America 113
5 Fashionable Modernity 157
6 Vehicles of Desire 195
7 Team 10: Keeping the Language of Modern Architecture Alive 231
8 Retrospective Ruminations 259
9 Landscapes of Lyrical Appropriateness 293
10 The "Sensibility Primers": Revenge of the Picturesque 329
11 The Fictional Smithsons: Autobiographical Accounts 359

Notes 397
Index 465

Preface

Not Quite Architecture engages the writings of English architects Alison Smithson (1928–1993) and Peter Smithson (1923–2003) in the context of post-World War II discussions about architecture and urbanism.[1] The Smithsons were ringleaders of the New Brutalism following their winning design for Hunstanton School (1949–1954), members of the Independent Group that defined English Pop Art (1952–1956), co-planners of the tenth and last CIAM[2] conference (1956), and part of Team 10 (1953–1981). They built only a few buildings and exhibition structures, but wrote copiously from the early 1950s until their respective deaths, creating a considerable body of work that includes not only books but many articles, lectures, and unpublished manuscripts.

This book delves into the five decades of Alison and Peter Smithson's writings and retrospective ruminations stored in archives in the Loeb Library, Graduate School of Design, Harvard University; the Netherlands Architectural Institute (NAi), Rotterdam; and a private collection (the Smithson Family Collection) in England. After first setting the scene, it focuses on the unknown writings and theoretical revisions of Alison and Peter Smithson. It is more than a book on the Smithsons' writings, however, for it considers the setting around them—the context in which concepts and practices such as Townscape Analysis, New Brutalism, English Pop Art, and the discourse of Team 10 took place.

The story told by *Not Quite Architecture* begins with the editorial policy of *Architectural Review* (*AR*), which advocated Townscape Analysis as an urban design strategy for postwar reconstruction of towns and cities. Architectural critic Reyner Banham believed that this policy, which applied English Picturesque principles to urban areas badly damaged by bombs or unsightly development, embodied debased English habits of compromise and sentimentality. The Smithsons, as provocateurs of New Brutalism, also raised a banner in protest against Townscape Analysis and warred against the controversial Picturesque forces *AR* was promoting. Yet on the day their cluster design for the Economist Building (1962) was revealed—so Banham claimed—the architectural struggle against the Picturesque was lost. The Smithsons were not amused: Banham, they objected, was like a mere war correspondent, while they were true combatants in the struggle for New Brutalism. His dispatches from the front got the emotions right but not the details. Only those in the fight rightly understand the "Brutalist blockage" deployed by aesthetic controllers, moral regulators, and British bureaucrats.

Beyond analyzing the Townscape policy of *AR* and the Smithsons' position with respect to New Brutalism, this book explores the development of a cluster of urban concepts set down by the Smithsons in articles published in *Architectural Design* (*AD*) in the 1950s and examines the thought of two generations of Pop Art devotees as expressed in *ARK*, the student-run magazine of the Royal College of Art in the 1960s. And besides theorizing and writing, the Smithsons were involved with CIAM meetings from 1953 on and in the formation of Team 10, of which Alison was self-appointed "stirrer and stimulator." Debates within Team 10 were often discordant, as individual members sought by different means to keep alive the language of modern architecture. I review these debates and Alison's methods of shaping their record, including the development of a graphics of communication and a series of lectures she offered in the 1980s on the myth and inheritance of Team 10.

During the 1970s, when the Smithsons had little or no paying architectural work, they wrote extensively. These writings, they professed, were a means to identify and define ideas so that when the time came to build, distance had been put between the initial impulse and a project's fulfillment. Their written ideas, they believed, would eventually transmute into built form. Nevertheless, they wandered into fields ordinarily considered "not quite architecture,"[3] such as fashion design, communication graphics, multievocative ideograms, picturesque perceptions, and children's books. They were intensely concerned with the "responsibility" of the architect to ensure the quality of place, to build with lyrical appropriateness, to arrange architectural objects into a composite order, and—as both inheritor and passer-on of that language—to extend outward the language of modern architecture to other climates, lands, and cultures.

Meanwhile, Alison had already begun in the 1950s to write and obsessively rewrite a series of novels. These include several unpublished manuscripts, called by her "sensibility primers," intended to reenergize architectural ideas. These revolved around subjects as diverse as imperial India, the ground in which the Bauhaus took root, and a memory game played on a map of Paris. Other novels interweave quasi-autobiographical stories about a young woman being a magazine editor or an international correspondent, or a young girl's dreams of achieving a life of action, love, and importance.

The Smithsons had the knack of seamlessly blending work, travel, and childrearing. They reveled in trips by motorcar and an impressively diverse range of creative activities (not all successful by commercial or critical standards): they wrote children's stories, celebrated ephemeral events in the city, and taught design studios focused on pavilions, idylls, and enclaves. As they went about their attempt to renew the language of modern architecture, they reached back to their own childhood romances of picturesque landscapes from northern England: sloping hillsides, spoil heaps, stone walls, hedgerows. They drew on their personal connections to beloved cities of Edinburgh and Bath as both remembrancers and continuers. "We were people picking up and quizzically turning things over in our hands, reconsidering everything."[4]

Everything seemed to touch on everything else—so much so that an accounting of their many activities spirals up and around layers of projects, groups of words, composites of ideas—pausing, then turning back before again springing forward. One of Alison's figures for their approach to renewing architectural language was embroidery, the needle moving away from and back to a canvas provided by the Heroic Period of modern architecture, each motion tracing in the air considerations from two generations' inheritance.[5]

She and Peter believed passionately that architects must recognize (not mimic) architectural precedents and the spirit of place. Reflection upon the "idea-so-far"—the "idea" of an architectural site as evolved in its prior history of ideas—was identical in her mind to a "place-response" urbanism in which what already exists on-site is reassessed in the "coming-into-being" of the work in hand or the idea in mind. Thus, writing and drawing alternated, the ephemeral and the permanent intertwined, the graphic work and built work intermixed—always extending ideas outward toward built form.[6]

The Smithsons faced in two temporal directions at once: wanting to respect tradition, that is, their inheritance from the Modern Movement of architecture, yet also wanting to be innovative, open to change, projecting into the future. Their practice of looking backward while moving forward was transformative, allowing them to reposition their architectural projects within a discourse of continuity and inheritance rather than of rupture and revolution. Uninterested in breaking with their modern predecessors, they drew from Le Corbusier an unshakable general precept: architecture without social intention is empty and meaningless.[7] Peter Smithson called the application of this view "socioplastics"—urbanism through architecture—an idea that would change and reenergize CIAM discourse.[8]

In the Smithsons' retrospective ruminations, project after project was given an English identity, a softer touch, and a layered approach at variance with Brutalism's more strident notes. Indeed, it became clear to them that the English Picturesque tradition had influenced their way of thinking and working from the start. After all, they said, there is a ha-ha at Hunstanton School. The English Picturesque tradition grew ever more dominant, more explicit, more apparent in their architectural language of connective forms and extended modes of inhabitation, laying them open to Banham's angry charge of collaborating in "the revenge of the Picturesque."

Early on, the Smithsons consciously developed their writings and architectural projects as ad hoc reactions to the situation "as found"—images, materials, junk in the streets, advertisements, fashionable clothes—recycling this flotsam and jetsam as art. But a shift in their thinking took place over time. In the 1950s they had evaluated the situation "as found" and concluded that the motorcar, sound-producing equipment, appliances, and affluence had changed the pattern of inhabitation though not the visible expression of houses or communities. By the 1970s, their view of the landscape from a moving vehicle prompted the growth of a new sensibility, new ways of seeing, new forms of identification between individual and place. They began to think ecologically, to seek a connection to nature, learning to live more "sweetly" on the ground. This sensitivity to nature informed their "climate registers," which demonstrated how man, machine, and the environment interacted, and led them to think about ephemeral "events," light-touch decorations of the urban scene.

The recycling of bits and pieces in a manner lightened by whimsy was fundamental to the Smithson style. For example, Alison also liked to make scrapbooks and collages—

Preface

bits and pieces of material taken "as found" and glued into compositions without hierarchy. Only the connection, the juxtaposition, the "and," was important. Likewise in the Smithsons' writings, characterized by a kind of connective association of interactive loops, one concept blurs with another, one event transforms into another. This style of montage writing valorizes change, not static representation; it points not to the interpretation of imagery, to representational content, but to blurring boundaries, overlap, coupling materials. And it often makes the writings and projects of Alison and Peter Smithson difficult to decipher, for they do not fit into specified categories or sort into hierarchical arrangements. Consider, for example, the following excerpt, in which the precise meaning remains elusive: "We have to *know-instinctively* to be at peace, to sense rather than to see: and this means that we have to raise the individual items or elements above themselves, shifting sideways the emphasis of their bare selves, to the level that they recess together and subtly serve as *signs* to help us know how to *behave* in our buildings, guide how we want to live as a society in our cities."[9]

How to Read a Building

Writings, both published and unpublished, notes on scraps of paper, diagrams and photographs—all form part of the historical archive of architecture. As Derrida claimed, however, "*every* archive … is at once *institutive* and *conservative* … it keeps, it puts in reserve, it saves, but in an unnatural fashion."[10] And so for some, texts in the architectural archive—the narrations surrounding a building—are more important than the actual building or site. Visitors to the Villa Savoye, the architectural historian Panayotis Tournikiotis claims,

> pay homage to the historical fact—that is, to the fact that has been recorded in the established historical texts and is illustrated in the official albums of modern architecture. It is as if the visitors were still seeing, on the site, the first photograph of the project, as if they were recognizing it as recorded in Le Corbusier's *Oeuvre Complète* and as reproduced in the histories. … No discovery, no revelation, can be made on the spot.[11]

For others it is the image—the representation of architecture in the mass media—that is of prime importance in the story of modern architecture. On this view, without *L'Esprit Nouveau* there would be no Le Corbusier.[12]

While accepting that architectural magazines have indeed been important in spreading the "word" of modern architecture, and that during wars architecture by necessity passes largely through books, *Not Quite Architecture* takes a different slant on the materiality of history, on the encounter between persons and objects, landscapes, animals, roads, climate, and buildings. Language, the experience of objects, time, and tradition—all become entangled one with another, requiring a flexible, associative, and many-layered form of reading. The published article or photo of the built work takes us only so far. The endless swirl of technological and other cultural contexts, the private letter, the scribbled scrap, the old history book glued full of images, the spinning of a child's tale—all these may be received words in a language that must be read as fully as possible if we are to best understand architectural history—and most especially that of postwar England, where architects like the Smithsons deliberately plugged into the richest available range of cultural encounters. The Smithsons' philosophy of the situation "as found" may be a starting point for such a rereading of architectural history.

Their approach to the built work of Le Corbusier was step-by-step, tentative: "Nervous, not knowing what we would find; nervous as to how a stranger would be received; nervous, not wanting to be disappointed."[13] To their amazement they discovered that many of Le Corbusier's villas from the 1920s still, in the 1950s, bore traces of their original color; and that his villas were situated in nature, and taught how "to think in the beyond," that is, included in their compositions space outside the confines of house and garden. Site visits provided "a personal revelation, a discovery; something almost too personal to be shared. To possess the experience was to possess part of 'Corb'."[14] At the time of Le Corbusier's death in 1965, Peter made a photojournal of his own visits to all the "built-work" from the *Oeuvre Complète*, adding the age of Le Corbusier when each building was constructed, the date when Peter's photograph was taken, the dates of various other visits, and Peter's age at the date of "first confrontation."[15] He first visited the Villa Savoye, for example, in 1950, when he was 27, and Le Corbusier was 44 when the Villa was built. The space between the initial act and the later visit left room for thought; something ineffable remained in the air.

The personal archives of Alison and Peter Smithson contain many unpublished articles and manuscripts, lectures unresolved and still being worked on at the authors' deaths, even a "magic box" (so labeled) filled with ideas and a scrapbook carefully wrapped for protection; but can a book about their writings delve into personal meanings not quite formulated or developed into a shared vocabulary? Is all this material meant for the public eye, or is its exhumation one of those unnatural acts that an archive engenders? One gesture by the Smithsons makes it appear that even these ideas were, in fact, meant for public distribution: almost all their archived documents, both public and private, are meticulously numbered and collated, with the apparent intent of being placed in an archive. For example, in the box labeled "AMS Lectures as Evolved" is a manuscript entitled "A History of Three Natures of Layering." This carries the identification marks "3NL 1–9" and "AMS December 1981" at the end of the manuscript, while the right-hand corner of each page carries the mark "3NL" and an appropriate page number. Other writings in other boxes are similarly marked: "Noah's Ark" is referenced "NOASARC 1–21." Not all the archived lectures and manuscripts are so meticulously labeled, in whatever box or whatever version, but most are, with dates of rewritings and subsequent editions noted.[16] There is a great deal of systematization here, hinting at hopes of eventual publication, or at least consultation.

This curious but helpful attention to archival mechanics, unappreciated by outside eyes during the authors' lifetime, is an example of the Smithsons' habit of being private and public simultaneously, neither one nor the other. During a 2001 interview with Kester Rattenbury, Peter Smithson disavowed didactic intent: "What Alison and I write is for oneself. You write about the insights you have. You think, 'well, maybe, if they're useful to me, they might be useful to somebody else'—but never intentionally to influence or instruct."[17] Yet *Team 10 Primer*, the unpublished "sensibility primers," and most of the Smithsons' other projects have obvious pedagogical intent.

Perhaps the explanation is more interesting than mere inconsistency. Writing, for the Smithsons—always an inward-looking act, in their case often unpublished as well—was a tool of architecture, a demonstration of architectural thought, a way to evolve narrative frames for public consumption in built form. The composite order and voided space of the Economist Building, for example, were taken from or extended into layers of thought about voids in the house/patio, holes in the city, and the space in between. And so thinking and making swirled around—or spiraled into and out of—the discourse of Team 10, where projects were examined, debated, extended. Ideas were rethought over time; generations of architectural ideas reinterpreted, reenergized, made worthy of passing on.

Yet struggle as we will, ideas retain an ineffable, immaterial, and stubbornly private aspect. Even so with built forms. Once a project is constructed, something arises from the walls, the voids, the site, is released into the air to speak an unspoken language—something that is "not quite architecture." The "as found" debris of urban streets, childhood memories of enclosures and idylls, the celebratory decorations of holidays and special events—these, too, though they quicken built spaces, are not quite architecture. Something below the surface, where imagination flows free of the confines of rational thought, bubbles up into the formation of new sensibilities, responsibilities, ways of inhabiting place, of moving lightly through space.

The Smithsons' writings navigate this emotional terrain, speaking into the void in full acknowledgment of the indeterminacy of words released into the air. There is something about architecture that cannot be said, something that cannot be transmuted into printed word, focused photograph, built form. Every house is a haunted house; and around every building, however deliberate its design or brutal its materiality, lingers that which is not quite architecture.

Acknowledgments

This book is indebted to the staff of the archives at the Het Nieuwe Institut, formerly the Netherlands Architectural Institute (NAi), Rotterdam; The Special Collections at the Frances Loeb Library, Harvard University; and Marquand Library, Princeton University. It is grateful for permission to access The Smithson Family Collection, UK. Larry Gilman, David Stewart, and Gillian Beaumont have provided careful editing.

Some of chapter 2 is based on the essay "An Encounter with History: The Postwar Debate between the English Journals of *Architectural Review* and *Architectural Design* (1945–1960)," published in Max Risselada, ed., *Team 10: Between Modernity and the Everyday* (Delft: TU Delft, 2003), 135–163. And some material of chapter 7 is drawn from the essay "Keeping the Language of Modern Architecture Alive," published in Max Risselada, ed., *Team 10: Keeping the Language of Modern Architecture Alive* (Delft: TU Delft, 2006), 32–71, as well as an essay entitled "The Team 10 Discourse: Keeping the Language of Modern Architecture Alive and Fresh," in Max Risselada and Dirk van den Heuvel, eds., *Team 10: In Search of a Utopia of the Present 1953–1981* (Rotterdam: NAi Publishers, 2006), 264–270.

WESTMINSTER REGAINED

Panorama of the Westminster precinct

1

2

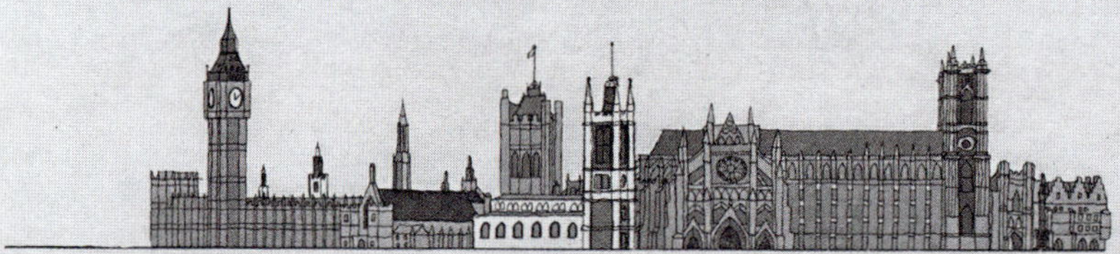

3

4

5

6

7

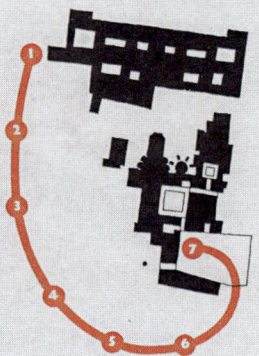

The view of a town as a piece of moving scenery hardly enters the head of the man in the street, yet for the man in the street especially this is usually what the town is—a moving set. Several factors militate against this view. First, the visual nerve for a variety of reasons is extraordinarily inactive in the urban individual. Secondly it is hard for those who enjoy the pleasure of seeing for its own sake to indulge their peculiarity without danger to life and limb. The particular sequence of views shown here are, as it were, " stills," taken from the uninterrupted sequence of views which would unfold themselves if a keen eye was allowed freedom to take the walk shown in red on the map above (the positions from which the " stills " are taken are numbered). This walk, on which it is essential to get a certain distance from the objects viewed, cannot of course be taken without the observer wading at enormous risk through an avalanche of fast-moving traffic. A visual experience, therefore, in which every shade of white and grey, subtle contrasts of shadow and light, and a series of objects, the towers, masts, roofs and spires of Westminster, which continually reassemble in a really miraculous variety of " compositions," cannot be enjoyed single-mindedly because the area has not been developed as a homogeneous unity as, for instance, the Oxford college is developed. Yet this scene in fact rivals Oxford and is of the same collegiate character. As a piece of urban landscape it can hold its own with the most illustrious examples in the world—the Place de la Concorde, the Piazza del Popolo or even the Piazza San Marco. The map on the next page shows what it is that prevents us from getting the full enjoyment and use out of it. In the pages that follow, proposals are put forward that show how, with surprisingly few changes, we could reveal and preserve a national monument, which for sheer visual genius cannot be equalled anywhere.

1

Compromising Modernism: Architectural Polemics in Postwar England

Prologue

In the early 1950s, controversy escalated in British architectural circles over the meaning and methodology of the English Picturesque as it was then being extended to towns and cityscapes in postwar England.[1] The editorial staff of the *Architectural Review* (hereafter, *AR*) had for some years advocated the "Picturesque" as an urban design methodology, but art historian Peter (Reyner) Banham, along with many members of the younger generation of architects, waved the standard of the "New Brutalism" that had first been unfurled by Alison and Peter Smithson. In a 1968 retrospective attack, he charged that the *Review* cohort had "thrown principle to the wind and espoused the most debased English habits of compromise and sentimentality."[2] He even demanded an apology from *AR*. None was given.

Provoking both sides, Banham maintained that although Alison and Peter Smithson had been the first aggressors against *AR*'s position, they had all too soon surrendered to the troops of the Picturesque. On the very day the Smithsons' "cluster" design for the Economist Building (London St. James's, 1959–1962) was put forward, Banham asserted, an already weakened New Brutalism had died.

The Smithsons, unsurprisingly, were not amused. Banham, they retorted, was a mere "war correspondent," not (like them) a true combatant, so his reports from the Front got the emotions right but not the facts: "For there is still another level for which only the combatants have access, a kind of locked-on and locked-in knowledge of the roles people actually played rather than the roles they appeared to play which get mentioned in the dispatches."[3] One had to be a veteran combatant in order to possess an accurate knowledge of the commitments made by New Brutalists against all types of stops, controls, and regulations—including those erected by Banham himself.[4]

1.1
"Panorama of the Westminster Precinct," drawings by Gordon Cullen.
"The view of the town as a piece of moving scenery hardly enters
the head of the man in the street, yet for the man in the street
especially this is usually what the town is—a moving set." The editor
and Gordon Cullen, "Westminster Regained: Proposals for the
Re-planning of the Westminster Precinct," *AR* 102 (November 1947), 161.

But what had the battle over the English Picturesque really been about? Even to its participants, the answer was not always clear. Since confusion reigns within the literature over who were the compromisers of modernism and why, and what was actually written about the Picturesque and New Brutalism, I begin this book by reviewing the editorial policy of *AR* and exploring the deep roots of the English Picturesque tradition, as these purport to be exposed in its pages. I then turn to the writings of Alison and Peter Smithson in order to understand how they became advocates not only of New Brutalism but of the English Picturesque, its apparent opposite. I shall argue that Peter and Alison Smithson, while indeed radical innovators, were also quintessentially English architects, making peace with an inheritance drawn from the English Picturesque and the English landscape as they extended their design features to embrace such notions and concepts as "ordinariness," "the *as found*," "lyrical appropriateness," "place-response," "climate registers," "sensibility primers," "idylls," and "enclaves," among other similar and purportedly non-Brutalist concepts.

I. Tempering Modernism in Wartime at the *Architectural Review*

Postwar Reconstruction

Planning for postwar reconstruction had begun at the height of the Blitz in the spring of 1941, and was integral to Britain's war aims. Boosted by the dazzling rhetoric of the Beveridge Report (December 1942), which promised to eradicate the five evils of want, squalor, greed, poverty, and disease once the war was over, planning gained quickly in popularity.[5] But what would reconstruction planning actually mean, especially for architects? Would it be the cutting edge of modernity, the work of a body of experts with informed opinions steering a course toward an equitable, democratic, high-technology future? Or would it mean answering the desires of the common soldier, who dreamed of the stability of England's prewar past and longed to live in comfortable suburbs, when he returned from the war?[6] This controversy had not been resolved by the war's end, and postwar architects and planners remained caught in it. Should they make a clean sweep of all that was familiar and homey, or respect traditional human-scale townscapes wherever these had survived the ravages of time and bombs?

Between the two world wars, Britain had experienced slow economic and demographic growth, as well as little increase in vehicular circulation. Thus, in this period the architectural community, though steeped in late-nineteenth-century Garden City ideals promoted by Ebenezer Howard and interpreted by Raymond Unwin, Barry Parker, and Patrick Abercrombie, gained little direct hands-on experience in the replanning of towns. But by 1945, the UK was Europe's most crowded country and the capital, London, Europe's largest city as well as the world's third most crowded conurbation (after Singapore and Hong Kong). Aerial bombing had all but eradicated the centers of Coventry, Plymouth, Exeter, and Bristol, but no British city had suffered more than the capital, especially in the Blitz of 1940–1941 and in the strikes by Hitler's "retaliation weapons" in 1944–1945.[7] By the end of the war, the buildings occupying 30 percent of the overall acreage of the City of London (the ancient central core, which included the modern financial district) and over 20 percent of the East End borough were destroyed. Nearly half a million houses in the London metropolitan region were rendered uninhabitable and another 25 million seriously damaged. Housing needs were acute, further exacerbated by the approximately one million persons having moved to Greater London during the war.[8] The pressure for architectural solutions was thus immense. Architects had to learn quickly how to guide postwar reconstruction and redevelopment, in addition to coping with burgeoning demographics, and attempting to resolve the housing crisis unleashed by World War II.

Few architects had been active modernists before the war. However, in the ten years of reconstruction that followed, a debate between modernism and tradition was joined, at least as perceived by architectural journals. A forthright encounter with architectural history was viewed as arguably the best way forward. Were architects to heed the man in the street, tempering their modernism with historical references to respect and cater to his tastes, or could the heroic dynamism of the so-called Modern Movement of the post-World War I period be reclaimed, and its lessons redeployed?

I shall explore this debate between modernism and tradition, especially as famously revealed in the pages of *AR* and later in a different way in *Architectural Design* (hereafter, *AD*), in chapter 2. By 1955, for a number of architects, the debate was essentially over. Modernism had become the style of choice for local authorities, industries, businesses, and private clients, so that modernist schools, flats, and industrial and public buildings were being built up and down the country.[9] Yet for others, the pull of nostalgia and the old picturesque townscapes, not to mention villagescapes, remained strong and never completely vanished.

The architectural mouthpiece for English modernism before and after World War II was the monthly *AR*, owned and proprietarily edited by Hubert de Cronin Hastings. Owing in part to the war itself, *AR*'s supporting editorial "staff" included, at various times, John Betjeman, James M. Richards, Nikolaus Pevsner, and Osbert Lancaster, backed up by artists John Piper, Lancaster, Paul Nash, and Gordon Cullen, and photographers M. O. Dell and H. L. Wainwright.[10] Hastings suggested that pseudonyms be deployed, perhaps to divert attention from *AR*'s ambivalent advocacy of "modernism": he wrote as Ivor de Wolfe, Richards as James MacQuedy, and Pevsner as Peter F. R. Donner. Richards became assistant editor in 1935, went to war in 1942–1946, and assumed full editorship (as part of an advisory board) from 1946 to 1970.[11] While Richards was away on war duty, Pevsner was made the editorial right-hand man. Together, Pevsner and Hastings began to study and promote the picturesqueness of English towns and villages, tempering the earlier and more strident modernism.[12] Starting in the early 1940s, Pevsner (trained in Germany as a historian) began to assemble his thoughts on picturesque townscape

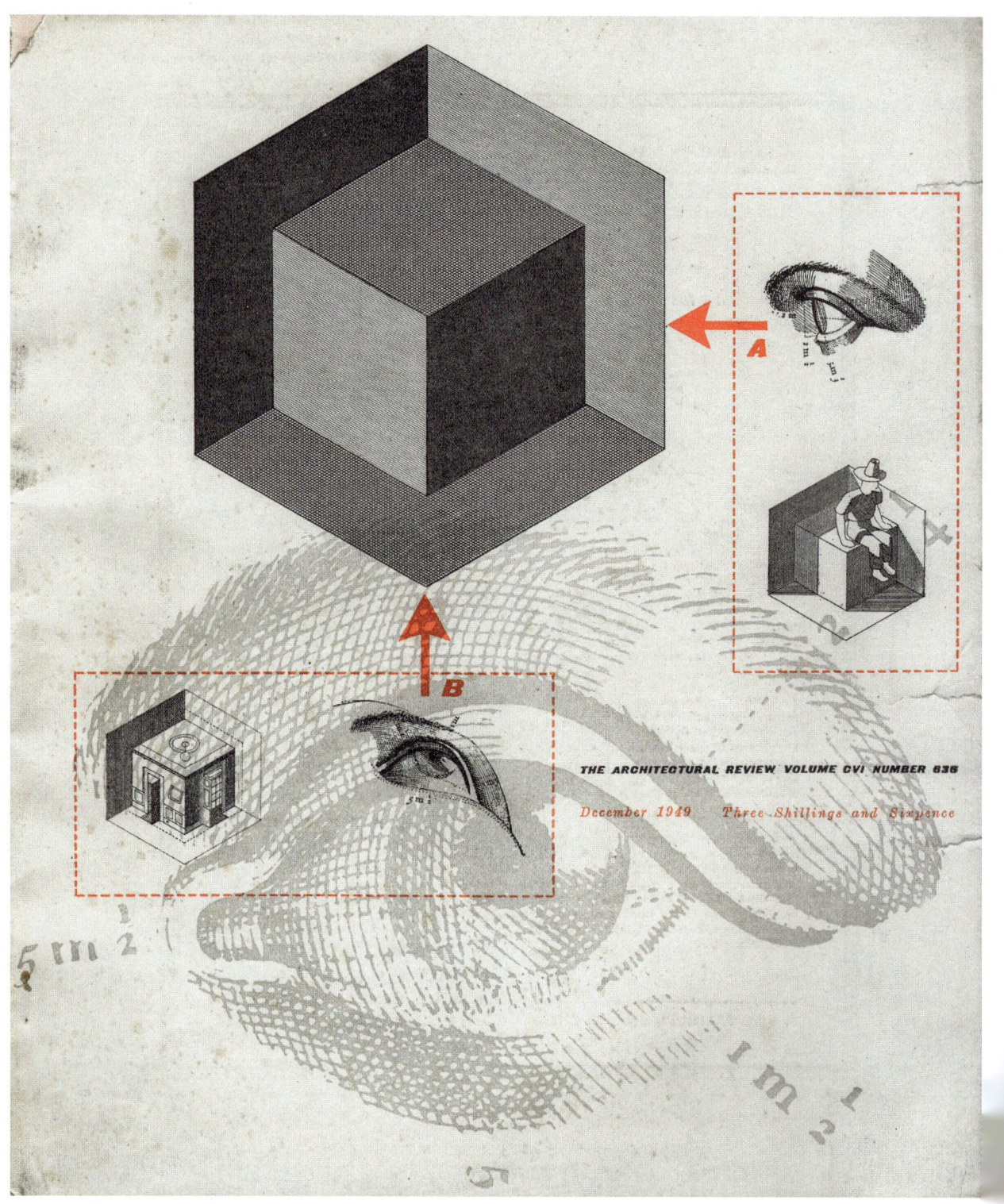

planning into a manuscript, stressing the links between modernism, the Picturesque theory of the eighteenth century, and English national identity.[13] This remained unpublished until 2010, but it offers insight into the postwar debate on what modernism would bring to English cities and towns.[14] Richards contributed to this townscape discussion while on war duty in Cairo, a thought-provoking reversal of his prewar advocacy of modern architecture.

From the vantage of 1971, however, Richards claimed that the battle for modernism had been won, because "we are all modernists now, though what that means I am not sure that we know, nor whether what it means any longer matters."[15] Nonetheless, what modernism meant had certainly appeared to matter in the 1940s and 1950s, that period when architects and planners ardently debated how English cities in need of repair from bombs, neglect, and postponed investment during six long years of war might be rebuilt. Reconstruction, *AR* maintained, was an opportunity to usher in a visionary new world of modern architecture across England. Yet *AR* always declined to take a hard modernist line, instead modulating its approach with large doses of vernacular architecture, the Picturesque, yielding a sense of Englishness, and of English cultural traditions.[16] It soft-pedaled modernism, seeking to collage old with new in creative ways.[17] *AR*'s makers thought that recalling English traditions while engaging reconstruction and the modern would ensure continuity of a progressive sort, as opposed to a "tabula rasa" approach redolent of Le Corbusier's "architecture or revolution." Rediscovery of the Picturesque, a deluge of Townscape Analysis, and a firm reeducation of the eye thus came to characterize *AR*'s editorial policy from the 1940s into the 1970s.[18] As it would editorialize in 1947, surveying the magazine's first fifty years and looking forward to the next half-century: "Once again, this is an opportunity to maintain the continuity of tradition and show that historical precedent can be used constructively, not as an escape."[19]

1.2
Gordon Cullen's cover of *AR* 106 (December 1949), "Townscape Casebook" issue ("eye" changed perspective = changed perception).

This was a shift from the 1920s, when *AR* had undertaken to support modern architecture's move across the Channel to Britain from its Continental base. But by the mid-1930s, a vexing ambivalence had arisen that was to persist through the war and beyond. Could England somehow be both modern *and* traditional? The later well-known and often contentious John Betjeman, assistant editor of *AR* until succeeded by J. M. Richards in 1935, promoted his own contextual modernism tempered by an abiding interest in preservation and regional variety. In 1934, he began to edit the Shell Guides to England's counties, drawing attention to Georgian and early Victorian architecture and pointing out the evils of over-restoration.[20] There was, he argued, a deep connection between physical places and the personalities of peoples: "the chapel architecture of the nineteenth century is not denominational but racial … the buildings are essentially local and vary with the districts."[21]

Very possibly the war itself had kept Britain from making a full break with its English past, as John Betjeman claimed in *English Cities and Small Towns* (1943). Aerial bombing

> built up affection for the old towns of England among those many who formerly thought little about them. … These old towns of England are numerous enough to survive a decade of barbarian bombing, but their texture is so delicate that a single year of over enthusiastic "postwar reconstruction" may destroy the lot.[22]

The word "reconstruction" needed to be contained between quotation marks because it was a piece of un-English jargon cutting abstractly across historic texture.

Betjeman would continue to argue, later joined by Ian Nairn in his essay "Outrage" (*AR*, June 1955), for a connection between England's people and England's landscapes. "Subtopia"—a neologism that Nairn created from "suburb" and "utopia"—smudged over the vital difference between town and country, erased distinctiveness of place, steamrolled individuality, and caused everything to appear dully uniform.[23] Fighting back, the individual observer should see and feel each local area intimately, and thus be able to make his own decision about projected change. The integrity of both site and spectator are thus saved: "In trying to keep intact the identity of your environment you will maintain your own as well."[24]

"Englishness," particularly for Betjeman but also for many others, involved feeling at home in a specific place, identification with particular towns and landscapes, and a distaste for modern industrial society and suburban standardization. England was on these terms an unassuming nation, a land of ordinary, modest, honest, straightforward people held together by a number of unstated assumptions, rights, and obligations.

Thus, well before the war was over, England had begun to fuss with and worry over the future character and texture of postwar society. A divergence appeared to loom. Would this future England be economically and politically impoverished after losing its imperial grip, yet somehow remain a nation of autonomous and freethinking individuals, self-aware and humanistically literate? Or would it morph fatally into an energized, rationalized mini-America of technocrats and crassly commercial and spiritually bankrupt mass consumers? Any debate between traditional and modern architecture was contained within this larger either-or.[25]

Enlarging Visual Life

Under Richards's editorial guidance and as prompted by Hastings, AR selected a middle way in this determined and drawn-out debate: tradition and modernity might be related to each other, and without resorting to pastiche. Postwar reconstruction could work together with a sense of place—if architects but heeded how England's traditional towns and villages had grown and changed, mixing tradition with newness as they developed. Richards traveled throughout Britain keeping an intuitively critical eye on such "vernacular" forms as lighthouses, canal locks, and Victorian pubs. The painter John Piper, whose spirited illustrations adorned many pages of AR, accompanied Richards on some of these "topographical expeditions." Likewise in 1939, Piper began a series of "topographical" essays for AR that recorded and interrogated some of the English vernacular artifacts witnessed on these landscape journeys—shopkeepers' signs, inland canals, farmers' markets, and the like—as vehicles of "Englishness."

Richards and Piper influenced each other, for they both took to heart the message these vernacular forms relayed. Piper's first piece in the series, "The Nautical Style," described the gaiety, color, and delightful shapes of weather-beaten functional objects such as bollards, buoys, and lighthouses, which made seaside architecture evocative and sometimes nostalgic—full of simplicity yet lots of fun.[26] In the 1940s he continued to write whimsical articles extolling the surface treatments and textures of popular forms, offering these objects as buffers against wartime melancholy at the moment when London's landscape was being transformed by underground air raid shelters, removal of street signs, and imposition of blackout orders, its streets strewn with rubble and its squares and houses ravaged by bombs. The surreal cityscape of bits and pieces of past and present provided ample grist for Piper's mill as he promoted, and, if it could be said, embellished—as virtually all British media did, in that period—the "will-to-war" among the civilian population.[27]

Richards, too, took to heart the message of his traveling companion. In general, vernacular objects and structures, signs, steps, bridges, even suburbs, were accepted by the editors of AR as visual reminders of the past and as fundamental connectors to offset the universalizing tendencies of modern architecture. In 1950, they labeled this policy the "Functional Tradition" and considered it the building block of townscape design.[28]

Assigned in 1942 to the Ministry of Information in Cairo, in exile from the English countryside, Richards began his nostalgic and influential *Castles on the Ground: The Anatomy of Suburbia* (1946), in which he extolled commonplace vernacular architecture and its enduring qualities.[29] He began by describing that image of "home" the ordinary Englishman dreams of when at war, away on a business trip, or living in rented rooms in the middle of town: an idyllic suburban villa. This architectural type was held in disdain by "people of taste," who deem it a "citadel" of debasement and vulgarity,[30] yet the "suburban environment is the choice of people who know what they like, and the architecture of the suburb may be called a true contemporary vernacular."[31] Such attraction to ordinary modernity might seem an aberration by architects, yet suburbia was a modern aesthetic that allowed romance and fantasy to flourish—unlike modern architecture. Modern architects, Richards argued, had never been able to develop and keep a "common touch," incapable of appreciating a contemporary vernacular rooted in people's everyday instincts—"the suburban style"—now spreading over English hill and dale.[32] Yet if democracy means anything, it must mean paying attention to the expressed preferences of the majority; modern architects must not only build "castles in the air" but attend to what already exists—suburbia's "castles on the ground."[33]

Richards went on to describe the characteristic features of this "suburban style."[34] First, it was an ad hoc world, invented rather than evolved. Second, it was concerned with scenic effects that were not strictly architectural, especially the presentation of an enclosed world from which all other worlds were excluded. Inside this synthetic refuge suburbia harbored its own infinite variety of concealments and surprises, grudgingly revealing hidden aspects around a bend in the road or a glimpse into a domestic interior. Any sense of the whole was offset by attention to intricate detail—hewing to the stimulus of the particular as an abstract world of generalities rolled by.[35] All these characteristics, as Richards noted, were close kin to the English Picturesque tradition.[36]

As editor in chief, Richards held AR to the task not only of educating architects about the need to respect the public's tastes, but also of educating the general public about the changing world of architectural ideas. The quality of the built environment, both modern and traditional, was too important to be left to chance; the architect must learn about the public's needs and desires, the public about architectural thinking. In 1971, looking back over his career with AR, Richards described the proper role of an architectural magazine:

> An architectural magazine can be looked at as a bridge, carrying traffic in both directions. It can help to span the distance between architects and the public they serve, on the one hand by informing the public about architecture's potentialities, objectives and techniques, and on the other by giving architects a better understanding of the public's needs and discontents.[37] … Unless architects can sell their wares to a wide public by persuading it that they can contribute to the enrichment of life, as well as to the appreciation of art, the revolution of the 1930s will have been in vain.[38]

Architects have a moral responsibility to offer the public lectures on how to visualize its built environment, having been trained to create order, to arrange disparate elements into a pleasing pattern and insert these into a structural framework, to see constructively:

> Above all he [the architect] has been trained to have an eye—not only an eye for aesthetic nuances, but one that enables him to construct a picture of what the future world will actually be like; a world which the voices of technological and social improvement, in which he and he alone is simultaneously involved, are combining to bring about.[39]

Training the eye, both professional and public, was a moral obligation that Richards accepted wholeheartedly. Following Piper's lead, his explicit policy was to surprise the eye of the reader with unexpected images from a variety of sources. Thus, in the postwar decades *AR* experimented with layouts, typefaces, and the treatment of images. Richards claimed that the motive of the magazine's innovations was not "simply pride in its own craft; they have been based on the desirability of using visual images—just as an architect does—to establish moods and reflect the spirit of the occasion; to arrest the eye and accustom it to take nothing for granted."[40]

Townscape Analysis

In 1947 Gordon Cullen became first the assistant art editor and soon enough preeminent draftsman of *AR*, responsible for translating its ideas about the picturesque into images. He developed a distinctive "serial vision," of perspectival drawings from several points of view that would take the spectator on an imaginary spatial trajectory. This process inevitably showed what a town or place actually looked like, including sidewalk clutter, surface treatment, signage, shop windows, and what we now call "street furniture." His graphic effects mixed the painterly, the poetic, and the practical to organize jumbles of a particular locality's artifacts, buildings, and streets into a visual coherence—what came to be known as "townscape."

The magazine's insistent style, largely crafted by Cullen, attracted critical attention. In 1959, Joseph Rykwert, for example, described *AR* as "probably the most striking architectural publication appearing anywhere in the world."[41] With its "ship-shape look," "close print," and "colored pages," it gave readers the impression that each and every issue was packed with solid ideas and coverage of recent works and projects. *AR*'s international reputation, Rykwert formulated, was primarily due to Cullen, whose "photographic eye" trimmed the field of vision to its most arresting and striking passages.

Yet Rykwert's judgments were not meant to flatter: he deeply disapproved. *AR*, he charged, was addicted to surface treatment, and to avoidance of any deeper analysis. Putatively promoting town planning, *AR* restricted its vision to the visual paraphernalia of Townscape Analysis—traffic signs, street furniture, and advertisements. The issues were inherently trivialized: "the people look like dolls, the buildings like models, the landscapes positively dinky."[42] If readers examined *AR*'s policies since World War II, Rykwert maintained, they would find much about "pleasing decay" and the use of color and textured materials in picturesque English villages, but little about how to solve the

1.3

Gordon Cullen, "Serial Vision," in *The Concise Townscape* (New York: Van Nostrand Reinhold, 1961, 1971 edn.), 17.

problems of postwar reconstruction, especially for London. (But note that Pevsner and Hastings, as we shall see later, insisted that their picturesque approach was eminently part of a "functional tradition," respecting as it did the evolved, organic functionality of a place. The "functional tradition" in building, planning, ornamentation, and materials, they argued, was the basis for townscape design, creating a dialogue between local vernaculars and modern architecture.)

This flawed vision, as Rykwert interpreted it, was conceived during the war, when *AR* rediscovered the "Picturesque"—the eighteenth-century school of art theory founded by Sir Uvedale Price (1747–1829)—and proceeded to apply it to reconstruction planning.[43] Its problems were evident in its informal "Programme for London" (June 1945)—visually lush, but saying nothing about how to alleviate pervasive traffic problems and dysfunctional land use.

AR's artistically "woolly" schemes, Rykwert complained, continued through the 1950s, for instance in its campaign against "subtopia," which it initiated in a special issue called "Outrage" in June 1955 (followed by "Counter-Attack" in June 1957). Rykwert claimed (oddly in error) that *AR* had defined "subtopia" as "making an ideal of suburbia," when in reality the author of these articles, Ian Nairn, was critical of the spread of suburbia and sprawl. Rykwert groused that *AR*, as usual, concerned itself with symptoms, not underlying causes, restricting its attention to such superficial objects as "wirescapes" and traffic signs. Finally, he laid the blame for *AR*'s superficial approach to the disasters spawned by unregulated suburban development squarely on Richards's scandalous *Castles on the Ground*, which wrongly claimed that it "is no use trying to impose a strange new style on any public, since architecture will lose its meaning for the public if it changes faster than the popular demand for it."[44]

Rykwert was no advocate of popular taste. As for words "ending in '-scape' and others coined in the *Review*," he was priggishly alarmed: "[O]ne can only hope they will not pass into the language permanently, but they do filter through every now and then, with horrible results."[45]

Although his criticism was confused, at times even begrudgingly approving in a perverse fashion, Rykwert assisted in constructing an alternative view of postwar reconstruction that was taken further by various writers in the pages of *AD* in the 1950s. Yet, importantly, he overlooked the role that self-imposed wartime censorship may well have played in shaping *AR*'s editorial policy of tempered modernism and visual education. British propaganda sought to promote action that would win the war on all fronts; this included maintaining civilian morale or will-to-war while giving the enemy little feedback on the reality of bombing's devastation. London was indeed a target, and it was essential that its civilians stand firm until victory had been achieved. Thus, citizens' fears were inked out and discussions of postwar reconstruction relentlessly deployed instead. *AR* determined to withhold comment on destruction caused by the Blitz, heroically excused in an editorial of 1941 to the effect that: "the best service [*AR*] could perform was to try and maintain the cultural values of peace-time lest these become submerged in the expediencies of war-time, with its distorted values."[46]

AR's emphasis on the Englishness of Picturesque town planning principles should undoubtedly be seen in this context. Britain was fighting for its way of life, customs, and traditions, including its architectural monuments and beloved townscapes.[47] That *AR* continued to pursue its policy of tempered modernism throughout the 1950s and 1960s reflects a widespread awareness that World War II had been "the people's war." It had been a war fought by the man in the street, and he might not understand the abstract geometries of modern architecture. *AR*'s editors felt a sense of moral obligation to keep in touch with architects and other readers; to link the users of buildings to place and time, an aim expressed in its willingness to consider popular taste, lifestyles, and desires. It was *AR*'s intent, as advocated by John Piper, J. M. Richards, Nikolaus Pevsner, and Hubert de Cronin Hastings, to find an alternative, less dour aesthetic than mere modernism alone.

This wartime compromise was somewhat offset after Reyner Banham joined the editorial staff in 1952 as part-time literary editor, becoming a full-time assistant executive editor from October 1959 to November 1964.[48] He saw *AR* as rather stuffy, its editorial policy as controlled by fuddy-duddies, and its tempered modernism liable to offend a younger generation of architects, home from the war and eager to battle for the cause of modern architecture. Yet *AR* offered Banham tantalizing exposure to the often world-famous architects who stopped by its Queen Anne's Gate offices: he took the job.

He had trained in part as an engineer and was apprenticed during the war to the Bristol Aeroplane Company, and so brought an up-to-date understanding of technology and materials to the magazine. Critical of *AR*'s compromising tendencies and Pevsner's theories of the English Picturesque—and perhaps also because Pevsner was his dissertation advisor and so there was "need" for conflict—Banham offered as antidotes to nostalgia and tradition not only science and technology, including information and communication theories, but American popular culture.[49]

Nevertheless, Townscape Analysis remained *AR*'s premier editorial campaign from its initial beginnings in the 1940s, through its advocacy of Townscape casebooks in the 1950s, and into the 1960s, when it would be criticized for wielding too great an influence over the discourse and practice of British architecture.[50] After Banham left *AR* in 1964 to teach at the Bartlett School of Architecture and Pevsner was absorbed in the 1960s with production of *Buildings of England*, *AR*'s editorial policy increasingly expressed the influence of the owner, Hastings, who had masterminded the Townscape campaign from its initiation in 1942.[51] Facing financial problems, Hastings tried in 1969 to increase circulation with a series of special issues titled "Manplan,"[52] with huge photographic essays accompanied by lengthy texts suggesting solutions to England's visual ills. Yet *AR*'s financial position only worsened and Richards, though he had had nothing to do with the ill-advised Manplan project, was let go in 1970. Hastings made a final (unsuccessful) attempt in 1971 to boost circulation with a special issue on "Civilia, the End of Sub Urban Man." He retired in early 1973, bringing both the editorial campaign of Townscape Analysis and the ad hoc collaboration between Hastings, Pevsner, and Richards to an end.[53]

II. The Fashioning of Townscape Analysis

The English Picturesque

That *AR* promoted the will-to-war by tempering modernism has been mentioned. But what did "tempering" actually mean, and why was Englishness or national identity the battleground for an architectural debate over "modernism" and "reconstruction" after the war? To address these questions, we need to look more critically at the policy promoted by *AR* in the 1940s and 1950s as it developed its theory of the Englishness of Townscape Analysis.

When Richards left *AR* for the Middle East in 1942, Nikolaus Pevsner filled in as a temporary editor in chief. As a resident alien he was unlikely to be called up for service—indeed, he suffered internment as an "enemy alien" for three months in 1940. Given his background in university art history, a discipline almost nonexistent in England, Pevsner could be relied upon to temper modernism with a dose of history and tradition. He was supervised by the executive editor of *AR*, Hubert de Cronin Hastings, who now took a stronger hand in directing editorial policy.

Ill at ease with the purist attitude of prewar modernism and the architectural elite's perpetual quest for novelty, Hastings wanted *AR* to look for directions that architecture and a more humanized urbanism might take when peace returned. He and Pevsner believed that a so-called sensibility to "visual planning"—that eventually became Townscape Analysis—was the route to take, and began in the early 1940s to publish pieces advocating this view under Hastings's pseudonym, Ivor de Wolfe, as well as Pevsner's real name and also his own pseudonym, Peter F. R. Donner.[54] Their developing sensibility entailed the creation of a pleasing picture of a town or city, and they advocated this perspective in an editorial campaign directed to a visual reeducation of the eye.[55]

Writing as Peter F. R. Donner, Pevsner began in 1942 to discuss domestic design in a regular feature titled "Treasure Hunt." This took readers on picture-book architectural quests for out-of-the-ordinary gems to reveal the instructive qualities of Victorian and post-Victorian structures, which in spite of being everywhere were seldom appreciated. Nineteenth-century urban vernacular, Pevsner suggested, deserved attention for its pursuit of the ornamental and fantastic. In other writings, he exposed his readers to the remarkable tradition of architectural "pattern-books" of the eighteenth and nineteenth centuries, arguing that architectural magazines might be able to play much the same role in forming the opinions of today's architects and their clients.[56] He was making the point that now-forgotten architectural styles and "pattern-book" rules accounted for a good part of the developing formula of the contemporary "Picturesque."

These investigations led Pevsner in 1944 to reconsider the art of the English landscape, which he termed the nation's greatest and most characteristic aesthetic achievement.[57] He wished to examine the roots from which English landscape had sprung. Why had it been created by the English and not the French, why did it develop from 1710 to 1730, and why was it conceived by the same men who pursued a rigid and formal architectural style? Was there a lesson to be learned here about how the picturesque and the austere, the traditional and the modern, could sit down together?

None but English theorists, Pevsner argued—William Temple, Joseph Addison, and Alexander Pope—had ever "dreamt of applying their notion of nature to the actual nature that surrounds us … with a vague equation of nature, reason and universal order."[58] Their idea of "following nature" established a completely new sense of beauty based on irregularity and fancy, effects composed (apparently) without art or effort. This soon developed into the notion of the *Picturesque*: the worship of visible harmony, temperance, and ease—"the state corresponding in ethics to 'simple, plain-look'd Virtue'"[59] (taking a phrase from Shaftesbury's *The Moralists*, 1711).

Yet Pevsner was eager to point out that "nature" and "reason"—roughly corresponding to the picturesque and the modern—were compatible from the start in this pairing. The eighteenth century had been an age not only of landscape gardening but of rapidly advancing physics, including discoveries with telescope and microscope; and while the advocates of the picturesque might have exiled mathematics from the garden, they admired them in the universe.[60] Indeed, reason was to these thinkers part of nature, not its opponent. Neo-Palladian building and the English garden coexisted, real and surreal not standing so far apart. "Whig is the first source of the landscape garden," Pevsner wrote, "the philosophy of rationalism the second."[61]

Earlier in 1944, Pevsner had written a summary of and commentary on Sir Uvedale Price's *Essays on the Picturesque* (1794).[62] It was Price who first suggested the term "Picturesque" for that quality which should add "visual delight," and stressed the stimulating power and piquancy of sudden contrasts. "The two opposite qualities of roughness and of sudden variation, joined to that of irregularity, are the most efficient causes of the picturesque,"[63] where "roughness," Price taught, conveys irritation, animation, spirit, and variety. In twentieth-century translation, Pevsner offers "abruptness" for "roughness" and "stimulus" for "irritation." As for "variety," Pevsner takes great delight in emphasizing that it is a "great and universal source of pleasure. … To visual stimulus by piquant contrast we have thus to add variety, intricacy and the raising of curiosity—in short, the unexpected, unforeseeable in all its aspects"[64] (i.e., the "accident"). "It is one of Price's most important discoveries," Pevsner avers, "to have recognised the claims of the aesthetically questionable for a place in a picturesque composition."[65]

But how to use Price's lessons on the "picturesque," visual delight, sudden variation, contrast and accident, and imitation and originality; to teach the contemporary improver a lesson or two? Price's principles were first proffered with a view to the conditions of a country estate, not to an urban pattern. Is there something to be learned from the etymological relationships between "painter," "picture," and "picturesque" that might be applied to the problems of urban planning? Pevsner digs deeper into Price's writings:

> The painter as the visual type, physiologically and psychologically speaking, reacts more intensely than other types to impressions of sight. Hence he is the one to tell how a sketch of scenery, rural or urban, can be converted into a landscape, that is a piece of three-dimensional art, planned to give visual pleasure ... that the landscape gardener, whether he knows it or not, works like a painter.[66]

Here is the lesson Price could teach the twentieth-century improver, even if few architects, much less laymen, were currently susceptible to "the pictorial approach to urban scenery."[67] Nevertheless, Pevsner fought shy of particulars, merely noting that the "truth of Price's sentences for council housing and council flats need not be specifically emphasized. ... The application of these passages [of Price] to the problems of urban planning is evident."[68] He concludes: "As we can go for enlightenment to Leonardo, or Goethe, or van Gogh, so we can take our problems of visual planning to Price and be certain of answers well worth pondering."[69]

The Art of Urban Landscapes

The Town and Country Planning Ordinance, passed in 1945, accorded local authorities power to designate blitzed and derelict sites as reconstruction areas. These powers were increased in 1947, as all development and land use changes were in that year declared subject to local planning permission. In its postwar role as bridge builder, *AR* thus set out to educate those who lacked the architect's eye to the pitfalls of muddle and defeat should policies imposed by town councils go unchallenged by informed architect-citizens. To this end, from the late 1940s well into the 1950s *AR* published a concordance of principles for urban design. The perceived guidelines for Townscape Analysis were exemplified by Gordon Cullen's ten-page "Townscape Casebook" of 1949.[70] Attention to townscape details would, it was claimed, expand "the architect's range of perception: from the individual building to the relationship between buildings, from the consideration of limited architectural values to the consideration of values related to the whole environment."[71]

J. M. Richards believed that *AR*'s postwar policy of focusing on historical monuments would help its readership to a better understanding of the role of old buildings in the modern town, and of local history. Continuity with the past must be respected.[72] Pevsner also developed these lessons, under Hastings's tutelage, after discovering the theory of the English Picturesque in the early 1940s. He and Hastings revived the arcane word *Sharawaggi* (rhymes with "stodgy") to underscore their notion of the English Picturesque, unfurling it on behalf of "that Picturesque landscaping tradition to which England owes its most personal aesthetic character."[73]

A 1944 editorial most likely written by Hastings, "Exterior Furnishing or Sharawaggi: The Art of Making Urban Landscape," confessed that the use of this peculiar term was provocative and would no doubt antagonize many readers.[74] Yet the gesture was called for because the simple, ordinary man understood more about his visual surroundings—had a better instinctive grasp of Sharawaggi—than did the modern architect; furthermore, he knew that the architects' creed of functionalism had failed to satisfy his own needs. To discern the ordinary man's desires and to incorporate these into a simple, pleasurable design strategy was the challenge *AR* wished English architects to embrace as a set of revived or at least reapplied conventions.

Advocating a newly revived postwar attention to "Englishness," Pevsner informed an audience at the Architectural Association in November 1945 that he was not a Londoner, not an architect nor a planner, or even a true-born Englishman. Nevertheless, he said he was working for *AR* first because he had become "mixed up in a campaign for the re-establishment of certain principles of visual planning,"[75] and second because he had had good opportunities to travel about the country over the last dozen or so years, and had discerned certain features about English town planning that differed from its Continental counterpart. He saw that characteristics of English planning at its best were the traditional groupings (and variety of plans and buildings) in the buildout over time of collegiate layouts at Oxford and Cambridge: "the variety and intricacy of the grouping and the varied sky-line by their very lack of symmetry and formality have a peculiar quality that strikes everybody coming to this country for the first time and seeing what planning was like here in the past."[76] These reflected a sense of Englishness. The work of Picturesque planning brought "pleasure to the eye" as a spectator walked through a city or town: variety, contrasts, incongruities in skylines, accidental effects, intricacy of details, and a bold mixing of old and new. Yet the architect must hold to certain principles, for the English Picturesque is not equal to a mere asymmetrical arrangement that leaves the rest to chance. The basics had been laid down long before:

> If … you take the principles which were formulated a hundred and fifty years ago, the principles of variety, of intricacy, of the connection of a building with nature, of advance and recess, swelling and sinking, and of contrasts of texture, you will find that a great many of these principles are principles which you would apply to the idiom which has developed during the last twenty to thirty years.[77]

The Picturesque tradition should, Pevsner argued, be applied to the entire reconstruction of the area around and precinct of St. Paul's Cathedral in London, as *AR* had proposed in 1946, turning it into a pedestrian domain (except for service roads) and excluding all fast-moving traffic.

The picturesque was not a mere "romantic escape," but particularly fitted the modern spirit of the age: renew the theory of the Picturesque, Pevsner insisted, and full-blown principles for reconstruction would make their appearance. It would, moreover, be eminently more English to treat each site "on its own merit"—a principle referred to in the mid-eighteenth century as tolerance in action, and today called "functionalism." Treated thus "functionally," planning and architecture must follow a subtle system of rules that would serve to endow them with a quality of the "informal," which is at the same time "the practical"—and "the English."[78]

Confusion frequently surrounds the term "functional." For the editors of AR the word denoted the vernacular object, built or otherwise, and traditional modes of planning, namely those practices governed by such tacitly accepted design principles once employed by wheelwrights or locksmiths. The editors were to some degree winging it here in order to insert a link between vernacular forms and modern objects, between traditional and modern planning principles. For the confirmed modernist, on the contrary, the term "functional" sets up a relationship between form and "function" together with an obligation to research users' needs so as to reach efficient and affordable architectural solutions. "Form follows function"—the modernist creed—had come to mean designing with the latest materials and technology to produce the simplest, most efficient forms.

Joseph Rykwert, once again as already noted, criticized AR's 1945 London plan as the artifact of a nonfunctional, visual-only planning ideology. AR's editors nonetheless defended it on their own terms as a "functional" city plan—that is, a "functional build-up of the scene without any preconceived intellectual pattern."[79] London, they claimed, was a "conglomerate" city composed of differences, and the lesson the modern architect has got to learn is that planning is an "art of compromise … by which apparently incompatible purposes and apparently incongruous forms, and hopelessly antipathetic people, come up for reconciliation."[80] Such is what AR's townscape campaign referred to as "the greater functionalism" able to marshal control over differing, even rival visual standards.

1.4 and 1.5 (following pages)
Illustrations by architect Hugh Casson for St. Paul's reconstruction. Some of the buildings Casson envisages for St. Paul's precinct "are modern ones, but for the purpose of the argument they might equally well be banker's Georgian, since it is not the buildings but the spaces between them, and the oblique, multifocal effects which can be obtained by an imaginative build-up of these spaces, large and small, that he is concerned with here." "A Test Case—The Precinct of St. Paul's," AR 97 (June 1945), 189, 190.

Constructive Compromise

Pevsner pursued his personal advocacy of picturesque Townscape Analysis well into the 1950s,[81] but Hastings was almost certainly the instigator behind *AR*'s long-term promotion of that program. His 1945 essay "The English Planning Tradition and the City" underlines the link between English townscape and English identity, and defines the notion of "constructive compromise."

> A timid preservationist attitude aimed at mere street improvement falls as short of what is required as the fantasies of the brave-new-worlders. Constructive compromise is what the genius loci calls for, not tabula rasa.[82]
>
> London has grown functionally, is an organism evoked largely without conscious control, a product of competing interests, from building speculators to pressure groups. The nature of an organism so evolved, though informal in the sense it doesn't fill out any preconceived intellectual pattern, is what we call functional, has, if it is lucky, what we mean by functional form.[83]
>
> Thus it was precisely *because of their functional approach* that modern architects have rediscovered picturesque theory. It is precisely *because of their functional approach* that they appreciate, unlike most academic architects, that London is a product of the picturesque impulse.[84]

With the advent of peace, *AR* reiterated that it had a responsibility to educate the public's vision as well as the eye of the architect himself. A 1947 editorial signed by the entire editorial-cum-advisory staff—Richards, Pevsner, Lancaster, and Hastings—noted the fact that "running through and linking [all the aims of the publication] together is the aim of visual re-education."[85] Over its first fifty years, *AR* held to a policy of not discussing policy; now it broke that silence to declare that its prime purpose had been to provide the raw material of architectural history by collecting within its pages the most interesting buildings of the time, wherever they appeared. For its next half-century, the publication planned to extend the discussion of architectural history to diverse types of buildings and topics that orthodox readers might find disturbing. *AR* would in the future thus be engaged in rehabilitating what might be seen as "frivolous subjects" such as Victorian merry-go-rounds, rustic-styled railway stations, lighthouses, and gin palaces, though aware that the intended exercise might irritate erudite readers.

Hastings was at pains to sketch out and promote "a way of looking at the world that is perennially English."[86] In editorial comments prefacing his 1949 "Townscape: A Plea for an English Visual Philosophy Founded on the True Rock of Sir Uvedale Price," he stated:

> while every teacup gets itself documented by some famous expert, the greatest question our society has to face, involving the way of life for the whole community, goes by default, isn't even put down for discussion, just because there are no terms to discuss it with. That question is, of course, the question of our whole physical surroundings as perceived by the eye—in short, landscape.[87]

In Hastings's revealed opinion, the English "eye," the English landscape, and the English national identity represent a historical and cultural continuum. This "perennial visual philosophy could revolutionize our national contribution to architecture and town-planning by making possible our own regional development of the International style, as a result of our own self-knowledge—technics given in marriage to psychology."[88]

This visual approach propounded by the Picturesque abhors grand theories and principles, preoccupied as it is with independent details, facilitating their fulfillment and freedom—and, by mutual differentiation, is intended to achieve a higher synthesis. This was the approach that Townscape Analysis would aspire to apply in the visualization of English towns and cities.

But with no grand theory, how could such analysis hope to proceed? In answer, Hastings provided the offer of a "case-book" and called on "the true radical … to begin the long business of establishing visual planning precedents (not principles), by the collection of individual examples of civic design."[89] Just as English common law has matured out of the proliferation of cases, or precedents, a modern aesthetic will grow from the application of innumerable individual judgments—likewise as a species of precedents. "[T]his is the only way an English visual tradition can be reborn. A mass of precedents gone over creatively to make a living idiom."[90] A retraining of the eye by the contemplation of innumerable particulars and their notation would be required.

III. Training Radical Vision: The Illustrators of Townscape Analysis

An Urban Surrealism

In a 1944 editorial, "Exterior Furnishings or Sharawaggi," Hubert de Cronin Hastings argued that without

> a visual policy a physical planning policy is a kind of monstrosity. So we proposed a simple thesis. That England has a traditional way of seeing things which was brought into full consciousness, and raised to an art, in Picturesque theory and practice, known in the eighteenth century as the Modern Manner.[91]

This erstwhile "Modern Manner," never till now applied to urban landscape, was to be explicated by *AR* via simple rules and casebook examples. Whatever the name it went under—Sharawaggi, the Picturesque, Townscape Analysis, or the Functional Tradition—here was an aesthetic sensibility apt to reconcile (by means of contrast, concealment, surprise, and process of counterweighting) those superficial antagonisms of shape that betoken the livelihood and the livability of any vital democracy. The often ignored virtues of incompatibility—presented as a fundamental national characteristic—must be brought to consciousness and applied henceforward to the urban scene.

Thus *AR* began its outline of a set of principles and conventions (based on numerous precedents) that it continued to elaborate over the next decade and a half into the full-blown art of Townscape Analysis. Hastings set forth two tenets pertaining to what amounted to an "aesthetic faith": first, each example of the art of Townscape required absorption by a painter's eye, thus yielding a mental sketch of its qualities. Additionally, it became the painter's actual duty to turn that eye on the contemporary scene, as found in town and city. Thus, such artists employed by *AR* as John Piper, Paul Nash, and Christopher Wood were the first to depict a music hall, a Victorian pub, an electrical pylon, or a wildly Gothic four-cornered lamppost as counterpart of the grotto, tumbledown cottage, or sunken lane deployed in eighteenth-century Picturesque landscapes. Most contemporary architects, Hastings admitted, would be quick enough to charge any such recommendations with blatant reactionism or flippancy, but such responses only opened the profession to chastisement for ignoring Uvedale Price's dictum that any object may be ugly in itself, yet in a suitable context exhibit aesthetic possibilities.

With the actual war nearing its climax, Hastings drew ideological battle lines against his three antagonists: Garden City advocates, Bauhausian revolutionaries, and the newly prominent County Council regulators.[92] The first might understand coziness but be incapable of taking in the urban scene; the second were said not to tolerate anything old, and might do more to destroy than to create; and the third were seen as addicted to neo-Georgian architecture and always insisted on the maximum widening of roads. There must, then, be a compromise, namely "the English form of synthesis." Everything must be tempered and given its chance to exist within the inconsistency of urban Sharawaggi—an inconsistency rendering the English contemporary townscape more casual and humane, better suited to an actual day-to-day reality.

But *AR*'s editors did not wish to risk thorough alienation of the modern architect. In the event, and so as to make Sharawaggi palatable to avant-gardists, they turned to coopting some of the milder among Surrealism's fantastical visual juxtapositions. Surely modernist architects could sympathize—for had not the Surrealists themselves set out to make people see functionally incoherent objects in convincing visual relationships? These assume the very principles behind *AR*'s attachment to the awful and the odd, in follies such as Seaside Surrealism and super-follies such as nineteenth-century suburbs, the pattern-books of the early nineteenth century, and, most of all, the camouflage patterns of wartime shapes and colors. Might not this confabulation of ghastly shapes and vernacular forms be assimilated to the visual pleasures of surrealistic and fantastical gestures?[93]

Townscape Case Studies

In the aftermath of the war, Hastings, in his 1949 article entitled simply "Townscape," proposed a direct analogy between Townscape design and English common law, built up as the latter was by logically arguing from the precedents (set by prior cases). He called upon the talented architectural draftsman Gordon Cullen to further the analogy by way of a running compendium, or what came to be known as the "Townscape Casebook," intended pictorially to describe the diversity of elements required for Townscape

Analysis.[94] Cullen held there were two ways of looking at the physical environment of roads, bridges, buildings, vegetation, paving, and whatnot—namely, the associational and the objective. "As far as the urban scene goes it is nearly always the former, hardly ever the latter. There is no Art of the ensemble, and no terminology to isolate and communicate our feelings."[95] He gathered materials from earlier articles in *AR* and classified them under headings "designed to suggest the type of vision—the particular exercise of the eye—needed to apprehend them."[96] These rubrics included, among others, "eye as fandancer," "eye as netter," "eye as movie camera," "eye as exterior decorator," "eye as matchmaker," "eye as sculptor," "eye as painter," "eye as traffic cop," and "eye as poet." These "vistas"—as they amounted to—did not take on the role of principles, nor were they to be followed as "crib sheets" but, rather, as aids to a particular kind of visual sensibility.[97] Thus, Cullen's designation of the "eye as fandancer" likened vistas to the ephemeral female poses conjured by this term. By contrast, the caption under a photograph of the gardens at Versailles laconically noted that this "Grandiose Vista … to many people … is synonymous with Civic Design. It looks its best from the air, its worst from the ground."[98] Juxtaposed was a "Screen Vista" offering a more sustained contact with environment, trees, and bollards said to reveal a pattern in common with games, dances, or the rituals of courtship.

In terms of a concrete method and procedure, the advent of Gordon Cullen's "Townscape Casebook" brought *AR*'s policy of "re-educating the eye" to the fore. An editorial comment published in January 1947, marking *AR*'s fiftieth anniversary, had been prophetic. It was said to be the role of *AR* to take note of architectural events from the neo-Georgian revival style to the Modern Movement: "But what is of even greater augury for the future is the endeavour, running throughout the story, to re-establish the supremacy of the eye."[99] The campaign sought to subordinate abstract theories to the insight of the "seeing eye" as the final arbiter of the juxtapositions and interpolations that Hastings was convinced must constitute the contemporary townscape. It was no doubt he who also wrote: "the REVIEW has a 'call', a call of quite a low-class, evangelical kind. It does not set out to lead a political or moral or even a social revolution. … The REVIEW has another job to do, in its own way no less revolutionary— … which may be described by the words, *visual re-education.*"[100] Painters and photographers used their eyes, and architects must now learn anew from them how to see. Indeed, "[u]nderlying the whole of the REVIEW's apparently diffuse and disjointed articles on landscape and townscape is this master-proposition of the importance of the pursuit of visual life."[101]

IV. The Functional Tradition: J. M. Richards

The Next Step Forward

If Hastings himself from the start, and the historian Pevsner over time as "resident archivist," were *AR*'s primary promoters of the English Picturesque as the foundation of its

Townscape Analysis, Richards, who served *AR* for well over thirty years (the longest of any of its editors, beginning in 1937), was the chief exponent and moderator of its modernist vector, and thus also eventual transformer of its "functionalist" tradition. As proprietor, Hastings's interest naturally lay in forming the editorial policy of *AR*, and Pevsner's in architectural history, as yet a burgeoning discipline and one without proper academic credentials. While Richards was trained as an architect, he never practiced but remained a journalist and produced a number of highly regarded books, including accounts of a humanized vernacular style. Together, articles and books contributed enormously over time to the building of a bridge of communication between the architect and the man in the street. Above all, his writing needs to be set collectively in the broadest possible context of postwar architectural practice—the debate concerning the pursuit of modernism, and the reconstruction and eventual expansion of Britain's towns and cities.

Facing the initiation of the Cold War in 1948 and a threat of nuclear warfare, *AR* nonetheless decided to spurn fatalism. It began 1950 with a special number devoted to the renewal of the "functional tradition" so as to embrace "the next step forward."[102] Boldly the editors proclaimed that a "lively, virile and enjoyable architecture, and the determination to have it" would somehow be capable of altering the shape of future events—in a way that would "render the atom bomb redundant."[103] The next fifty years were to succeed in re-creating a semblance of the architect's formal vision of a physically humane environment. And since *AR* believed architecture to be properly apprehended through the eye, it promised thus to commence the next half-century with a new study of the visual implications of its Townscape policy, as outlined over the war years by Hastings and Pevsner.

Having made a tour of some visually promising English towns, *AR* discovered that good townscapes depend not only on the architect and the planner, in their necessary professional roles, but even more fundamentally

> on a number of imponderable relationships, of shape and siting certainly, but also of detail—of things like road surfaces, road signs, railings, awnings, lettering, symbols, signals, colours, textures—upon objects conceived anywhere but on the town planner's drawing board—upon decisions made by officials who are as anonymous as the results their decisions bring about.[104]

It was these anonymous, visually unidentified elements of the urban scene, along with the forgotten and unacknowledged routines and formulas that brought them into being, which must be collected, analyzed, and elevated to consciousness.[105] All this, as the "components" of a "Functional Nexus," was painstakingly assembled under Gordon Cullen's direction into the archival Casebook referred to earlier as having begun at the end of 1949. The whole method was to represent an extension of the Functional Tradition, which meant designing with attention honed to the most suitable materials and processes—and with an eye to new performance standards that held up to the scrutiny of specific criteria.

These same principles, unexpressed, have unconsciously controlled the forms evolved by countless generations of blacksmiths, masons, wheelwrights, millwrights and shipwrights. This is the Functional Tradition. This is the living tradition from which each successive generation can learn and has learned, and our generation is no exception.[106]

1.6
J. M. Richards, "The Discipline of Functionalism," *AR* 107, special issue "The Functional Tradition" (January 1950), 8.

Two months later, Richards had begun to further clarify the meaning of the Functional Tradition in his article entitled "The Next Step?" that set forth architecture's course for the ensuing second half of the twentieth century. Over the past fifty years, he explained, architects had come to respond to the strong admonition of the architect William Lethaby, a lifelong socialist, to develop and to apply in their work convictions on many of the more burning issues of the times.[107] By and large, Richards concluded, the profession of architecture had thereby achieved a measure of social consciousness, with its members having now assumed the role of sociologists, economists, and even politicians. They came at last to concern themselves with solving the problems of the modern world, albeit too often in a utopian manner. Yet with all that, they had still somehow forgotten, he cautioned his readers, that the traditional task of the architect was to bring order and urbanity into a disorganized world. The solutions in hand were unlikely to be deferred while architects studied the problem referring everything back to first principles, or demanded a rational explanation for every item of a new brief, or for that matter mistrusted affording pleasure in architecture for pleasure's sake.

> But though modern architecture has come to stay, the way forward is not clear. The present is a moment of crisis, not any longer because we need modern architecture but because we have got it.[108]

What direction, then, should architects take to develop their art? Richards takes for granted that scientific planning and techniques must form the functional basis. But "functionalism"—as we have seen above—is a term having signified the most various things at different times. The word was a useful battle cry for the Modern Movement of the 1920s, and later it also proved a useful paradigm as deployed over against "formalism," once modernism seemed to ossify into a "style." But the time was fast approaching when functionalism, still an invaluable base, would itself in turn be reduced to a species of formalism. Richards warned that if architects failed to understand how "functionalism" had been a transitory achievement, it would all too soon be fossilized. The problem was that the "functional school did not evolve the kind of language that allows architecture to operate as a means of communication."[109] In line with AR's overall editorial policy, Richards stood convinced that architecture must have meaning for others besides architects; it must reach beyond the establishment of pure form and be part of the life of the times. It must communicate with the man in the street.

Richards goes on to seek alternative paths architects could follow, ways to graft tradition onto modernity while remaining in touch with vital sources of popular response. Bridges and farm buildings, jetties and lighthouses, common built objects of seaside and countryside—and all the items AR had been extolling since the 1930s—are evidence of the deep roots of modern architecture. Thus, Richards believes, the next step could be taken in any one of three different directions.

> First is a maximum exploitation of mechanization, which leads toward a more profound study of general characteristics that can be standardized. A second path is conscious humanization. This implies more assured concentration on organic and visual aspects, not only a building's technical essentials, and will lead toward a greater regional differentiation and exploitation of the genius loci. The third path is that of monumentality. Properly, buildings become monumental when they have something monumental to say, when they are reflections of the times that produce them.[110]

With these three paths in view, Richards offers a conditional next step:

> Beyond the functionalism of the general, which is concerned with establishing principles, there is a logical next step, the functionalism of the particular. There is therefore no call to abandon functionalism in the search for an architectural idiom capable of the full range of expression its human purposes require; only to understand that functionalism itself, by its very nature, implies the reverse of what it is often allowed to imply: not reducing everything to broad generalizations—quality in architecture belongs to the exact not the approximate—but relating it ever more closely to the essential particulars of time and place and purpose. That is the level on which humanity and science meet.[111]

V. The Festival of Britain (May 3–September 30, 1951)

A Tonic to the Nation

Most of *AR*'s forays into the revival of the English Picturesque, the promotion of a national art of Townscape Analysis, and the transformed definition of the "functional tradition" took place during the six years when the Labour government, having won a landslide victory in July 1945, prepared for the Festival of Britain. This was intended as the centenary of the Great Exhibition of 1851 and a celebration of Britain's survival of World War II. In 1951, England apparently had little to celebrate. It still suffered from austerity imposed by war debts and American loans. Rationing of basic goods such as food, coal, sugar, paper, and items of clothing remained compulsory (as it would until 1954). The Iron Curtain had been drawn since 1945, Russia had tested its first atomic bomb in 1949, and the Korean War had begun in June 1950. In this atmosphere, plans for the Festival leaned toward the nostalgic and nationalistic rather than the original and futuristic.

The initial proposal, sent to Parliament in December 1947, proclaimed that the celebration would be a "national display illustrating the British contribution to civilization, past, present and future, in arts, in science and technology, and in industrial design."[112] It would attempt to boost morale in order to hold on to all that was best in national life, a goal expressed by Geoffrey Fisher, the Archbishop of Canterbury, in the epigraph of the Festival's *Official Book* (1950):

SOUTH BANK

A SPECIAL NUMBER OF THE ARCHITECTURAL REVIEW FOR AUGUST 1951   VOLUME CX   NUMBER 656   FIVE SHILLINGS

1.7
"The Cover. The South Bank exhibition may be regarded as the first modern townscape, not only by virtue of the fact that its buildings and furnishings are designed in the contemporary idiom throughout, but equally because its layout represents that realization in urban terms of the principles of the Picturesque in which the future of town planning as a visual art, assuredly lies. … The cover, with a diorama showing the Houses of Parliament, Whitehall Court and St. Paul's superimposed on a plan of the exhibition, emphasizes this significant aspect of the South Bank achievement. It was designed by Gordon Cullen and D. Dewar Mills." "South Bank Exhibition," *AR* 110 (August 1951), 1.

> The chief and governing purpose of the Festival is to declare our belief in the British way of life. ... It is good at a time like the present so to strengthen, and in part to recover our hold on all that is best in our national life.[113]

It was hoped the Festival would be a pedagogical showcase of how to build a better Britain, from the design of household items to neighborhoods and homes.[114] Gerald Barry, editor of *News Chronicle*, was selected as Director General of the Festival in 1947. He called for Festival celebrations that should be "gay and entertaining—not precious or 'highbrow'—There is no reason either now, or still less, in 1951, to be afraid of being amused."[115] As a journalist, Barry was an excellent choice to publicize the Festival, keep to strict deadlines under pressure, and communicate clearly the Festival's message. He had a talent for extracting headlines and captions from complicated narratives. What the British people needed after war years of regimentation and continued rationing, he argued, was a fling. The Festival would be "a tonic to the nation."[116]

A war-damaged site in the South Bank area of London, divided by the Hungerford Bridge over the Thames, was chosen for the Festival. Following Barry's directives, it would narrate a consecutive story of the British people and the land they lived in and by. Upstream of the bridge, it would tell the story of the Land and what the British had derived from it; downstream it would unfurl the story of the People and their domestic surroundings.[117] Hugh Casson, already mentioned as one of *AR*'s visual planners, was appointed Director of the Festival's Council for Architecture, Town Planning, and Building Research.[118] Thirty structures, built in a variety of modernist idioms and enclosed in their own landscaped enclaves (including the Skylon and the Dome of Discovery, beacons for the future), would offer the public lessons in modern architecture and planning.[119]

Landscape and townscape became metaphors for national character, carrying out an official rhetoric of unanimity and stability. A London guidebook (May 1951) claimed that the Festival was "designed to cater 'for all the reasonable needs of the intelligent visitor, from townscape to tea'."[120] A Festival guidebook produced in association with *Architects' Journal* claimed that it was "the greatest architectural event of the post-war years" and

> the first full-scale example of modern architecture doing a popular job ... *because* it is doing the job for the man-in-the-street, not the aesthete in his ivory tower or the financier behind his high wall; *because* ... for the very first time in history it is trying to create a still greater thing than architecture, a modern *background*, a twentieth century urban environment.[121]

No wonder Richards believed that the Festival "was the physical embodiment of the townscape policy of *Architectural Review*. Non-monumental, non-axial, informal spaces with changes in level."[122]

A Hard-Edged Modernism

AR's special edition on the Festival appeared just a month after the second postwar CIAM meeting (Hoddesdon, England, July 7–14, 1951), convened to discuss "the core/coeur of the city." J. M. Richards spoke to the conferees, again advocating his policy of tempering modernism with good chunks of the Functional Tradition.

> The town centres we build are an expression of our own culture. … Our interest in what has gone before thus takes two forms: appreciation of the atmosphere the past has created and visual awareness of the physical objects—in the shape of spaces and buildings—it has left behind it. The first is not so much aesthetic as a psychological form of apprehension, for it must not be forgotten that only an architect himself has the habit of applying strictly aesthetic standards to what he sees. To the inhabitants of the town—for whose benefit the Core exists—it is not primarily a work of art, to be apprehended as an aesthetic experience, but a collection of symbols and familiar assembly of objects having certain associations and reviving certain memories—since the *Core is the repository of the community's collective memory.*[123]

Stressing the role Townscape Analysis had played in planning the South Bank site of the exhibition, Richards pointed out to the conferees how the structures of old London, seen from across the Thames, acted as a backdrop to the Exhibition:

> Without compromising the modernity of the exhibition they were incorporated into the same picture and given fresh significance by the part they had in it. … For in this scenic use of exhibition buildings, the intrinsic merit of the buildings themselves is largely irrelevant. The colour, outline, scale and texture they possess can be used by the planner with a discriminating eye to provide a foil to the architecture he himself has the opportunity to contribute, to bring out the latent character of every place, and intensify its functional significance. He can help each generation, instead of being inhibited by the past, to see it with its own eyes and endow it with fresh significance.[124]

Thus a tempered modernism, with its collage of old and the new, background and foreground, had been absorbed into the Exhibition's own townscape. True, it was a modernism devoid of the vitality and energy of its heroic precedents; yet Hugh Casson, the Festival's Director of Architecture, believed "it made people want things to be better and to believe that they could be."[125]

In the view of a younger generation, the Festival was a very mixed success at best. Among these young postwar architects were Alison and Peter Smithson, their allied practice bellwether of a new group of architects and designers. Percy Johnson-Marshall, who was at the time working for the London County Council, where the Smithsons were briefly employed in the School Division (1949–1950), later recalled:

The Festival of Britain absorbed modern architecture into the show. It was a very British way to behave, but it did not suit everyone. There were already others, of whom the Smithsons are the best known, who wanted to regain a harder edge. I stress the word *regain*. They were not mere iconoclasts. They believed in the importance of history and were passionately keen to rekindle that spark that the masters like Corb and Mies had ignited. To a real extent they were reaching back to move forward. Certainly they were young, but there were older people who agreed with them and also younger people who didn't.[126]

Writing twenty-five years after the event, Reyner Banham minimized the impact of "the Festival Style," that triumph of the Council of Industrial Design, editors of *AR*, and other guardians who kept the Festival's "mythography" alive well into the 1960s, but only as a "fossilized survival." "Influence wise," Banham claimed, "the Festival died a-borning," except of course for the dominance of Townscape principles of design.[127]

AR in the 1930s had stood staunchly for modernism, but by the 1950s, Banham claimed, its position of compromise was a drawback to a younger generation. The Englishness of the Picturesque movement, development of Townscape casebooks, outrage over the loss of craftsmanship in the Functional Tradition, praise of the anonymous vernacular object and the "suburban style"—none of these was accepted by a new generation as sufficient to educate the eye to face an increasingly affluent society of mounting consumer desires. A stream of loaded symbols and images, seen first in Britain in imported American magazines and then on television, made all *AR*'s attempts appear parochial, sentimental, and compromised.[128]

Still, *AR* had not just conjured the picturesque English landscape out of thin air as a cipher for national identity or a durable reminder of national character. Instead, *AR*'s editorial policy of the 1940s and 1950s transposed this most time-honored of visual metaphors to the manmade townscape. In so doing, *AR* urged what had survived of a formerly cohesive built environment to operate chiefly as a site of memory—one profoundly mediated by visual representation. Yet this very townscape was after the war caught up between the growing appeal of American-style fashion, new advertising, and burgeoning mass media on the one hand. On the other stood the agencies of a "New Britain," including the ubiquitous borough councils—tyrants, as *AR* envisioned them, who invaded and destroyed wherever and whatever they could.

To conjoin English national identity visually with new awareness of the presence of her network of traditionally cobbled together towns and cities had inevitably wrought a self-compromising stance, now both inherently vulnerable—and doubly untenable—in a postwar climate of rapid growth and change. Unlike the stiff upper lip *AR* had maintained in the face of war, and in particular during the Blitz, the magazine's persistently Townscape-limited vision might well now appear to render what had been very real loss and fear in more dubious and suspect elegiac tones.

VI. Conclusion

As mid-twentieth-century legend proposes (largely in the form of Banham's early, unabashedly polemical tracts and other later writings, which architectural historians too often mistake for objective factual description), the younger generation of architects, home from the war, stood betrayed and abandoned by AR's editorial policy, which now threw "principle to the wind and espoused the most debased English habits of compromise and sentimentality."[129] They accordingly saw the Picturesque as

> one of the historically contributing causes to the visual disorders of suburbia, and [was] to be scorned. So combat was joined between a barely middle-aged architectural "Establishment" armed with a major magazine, and a generation of battle-hardened and unusually mature students.[130]

It did not take long, in line with Banham's version of the scenario, for the Picturesque group to win over some of the opposition, even formerly strident partisans of New Brutalism, evinced by the treasonous new Economist Building (1959–1962) by Alice and Peter Smithson in London, just south of Piccadilly. The Smithsons, having paved the way for topographical notions in their "Cluster City" (AR, November 1957), put these ideas into play in the Economist's site plan. To Banham, "Cluster City" was receptive of AR's neo-Picturesque pronunciations, if only since the Smithsons had defined a "cluster" as a made place, proclaiming that it is "the built form of place that identifies the people."[131] This might almost appear to, but did not, echo Betjeman's far more simplistic sentiments. But the scuffle was not over, at least for the cantankerous—if still young but opinionated—Banham, who wrote:

> if the Picturesque has triumphed once again as a pragmatic technique of site planning, it is still unacceptable to most thinking British architects as an aesthetic discipline, and the battles of the early nineteen-fifties are still being fought.[132]

But what if lines of battle had never been so clearly drawn as Banham makes out? What if memory and topography are intimately linked in work by the Smithsons—without the least retreat from orthodox modernity, or even from the classical, into some putative undergrowth of a facile and Picturesque sentimentality?

I will argue in the following chapters that contrary to a widely credited narrative, Alison and Peter Smithson had never been stridently anti-Picturesque to begin with. Nor did they refuse to acknowledge the traditions of predecessors, or to accept less than a full ethical responsibility for place and people. It was Banham, rather, who freely defined what was and was not, according to his view, "New Brutalism," and now and again vented his disappointment at the "revenge of the Picturesque." I will make the case that Alison and Peter Smithson were in fact eminently English architects, always susceptible to the English Picturesque and to consideration of the landscape and site (place) and how it operates as a locus of memory; and that this susceptibility gave rise to that "lyrical appropriateness" set forth in the extended language of their buildings, assuring the profundity of their connection to place. The Smithsons were against regulations and controls of all kinds—what they referred to as "British Blockages." But from the start, they were, and remained, open to characteristic British influences, including the existing landscape and functional tradition: notably, the northern landscapes of their childhood, the industrial feats of the nineteenth century, and the culture of the ordinary "man in the street."

Glancing ahead, we easily observe that over five decades of writing, the Smithsons' architectural projects were continually redefined as each idea was fitted to a cohesive discourse of continuity and inheritance. Initial intentions, they believed—the pre-language of forms—only later became apparent. Upon reflection, then, project after project of the Smithsons was given a more "English" identity, a softer touch, and a more layered approach substantially at variance with New Brutalism's rougher textures and tones.

I characterize the Smithsons' thought process of looking back over their architectural and ideational inheritance as a chain of "retrospective ruminations." These resulted in major shifts, especially in 1963 and 1968–1978, proposing a new sensibility toward the land and its traditions—a sense of being at home in a place called "England." They used every medium at their disposal to express a special view of mid-century "Englishness," including built works, writing, lectures, exhibitions, drawings, scrapbooks, movies, and—more outlandishly—clothing, flags, and banners.

Was this really, as Banham decried it, "the revenge of the Picturesque"? Was it just more "compromised modernism," no better than the curious and purportedly doomed backward gaze of *AR*? Or was it rather the manifestation of a unique sensibility, always present in the Smithsons' built work and their writing, to unconscious associations that strengthened with time, ripening eventually in the course of a rich joint career into an architecture of superbly "lyrical appropriateness"?

To Alison and Peter themselves, it seemed clear that the English Picturesque had influenced thought and work from the start—and hardly, let it be said, for the worse.

4 ARCHITECTURAL DESIGN
April 1957 Volume XXVII Price 3/6

2

A History of Beginnings: Alternate Routes for a Younger Generation of Architects

The culture of particular form is approaching its end
The culture of determined relations has begun
Piet Mondrian[1]

Prologue

Although he was an advocate of English Townscape Analysis, J. M. Richards's opening words in *Modern Architecture* (1939) laid down an important new direction that postwar architects might follow. He drew attention to modern architecture as a social art:

> The words "modern architecture" are used here to mean something more particular than contemporary architecture. They are used to mean the new kind of architecture that is growing up with this century as this century's own contribution to the art of architecture; the work of those people, whose number is happily increasing, who understand that architecture is a social art related to the life of the people it serves, not an academic exercise in applied ornament.[2]

The idea that modern architecture was a social art was strongly supported by like-minded British architects who established the Modern Architectural Research Group (MARS group) (1933–1957). The group served as the British branch of the Congrès International d'Architecture Moderne (CIAM) and hosted the CIAM meetings in Bridgwater (1947) and Hoddeson (1951).

2.1
The April cover of *AD* (1957) juxtaposes a few Brutalist images: "the machine in its newest and most potent manifestation, emblem of mass production; the Eastern housing pattern which provided the impetus for cluster planning and for the search for new kinds of order in cities; the cinema image of violence, awareness of our realities and of mass communications. Overall is the concern with Man, his place in rapidly changing societies and his equally important relation to old-fashioned reality, the earth, the sun and his neighbour."

Many members of the MARS group taught at the Architectural Association (AA), were on the council of the Royal Institute of British Architects (RIBA), and held key positions in government departments. In particular they staffed the London County Council's (LCC) Housing Division set up in 1950 under the direction of chief architect Robert Matthew. Housing was a uniquely "modern architectural" problem as advocated by CIAM and evidenced in the built work of Le Corbusier. Le Corbusier had a strong influence on architects in postwar Britain. He lectured at the AA in 1947 and in 1953, the year he won RIBA's Royal Gold Medal, he exhibited his art at the Institute of Contemporary Arts (ICA), and he was present at both CIAM meetings held in Britain.

Le Corbusier's Unité d'Habitation (completed in 1952) became a model for the work of the LCC's Housing Division. Robert Matthew spoke at RIBA's Gold Medal presentation, claiming that Le Corbusier's urbanism was

> nothing less than a new affirmation of the Rights of Man, the Rights of Man in terms of sun, light, space, quiet, trees and grass. … These studies [in the functions of the city] knitting together the technological possibilities of building with radical solutions to … the seemingly intractable problems of traffic circulation, have for long now been recognized as a fundamental contribution to twentieth century town planning technique. Even some of the world's largest bureaucracies [no doubt referring to the LCC] have not been entirely impervious to these ideas.[3]

An emerging generation of architects, younger than the *AR* group extolling the charms of the English Picturesque, formed an overlapping network of colleagues in postwar London. Some of them, including John Voelcker, William (Bill) Howell, and Alan Colquhoun, continued their education, interrupted by military service, at the AA, where they made their first contact with modern architecture. After graduation they were among the young group of architects employed by the LCC's Architects' Department. Voelcker, the Howells, the Smithsons, and St. John Wilson were participating members of MARS by 1953, and hence followed CIAM activities. Reyner Banham and St. John Wilson shared adjoining houses in Primrose Hill, and Wilson was a member of a group, which included Richard Hamilton, James Stirling, John McHale, Magda Cordell, and Colquhoun, gathering from time to time on Sunday mornings at the Banhams' home. Denys Lasdun and Theo Crosby worked in the office of the early advocates of modern architecture Maxwell Fry and Jane Drew. Crosby shared a flat in Doughty Street with the Smithsons, and during the 1950s he attended evening classes at the Central School of Arts and Crafts, where he met Richard Hamilton, Eduardo Paolozzi, and the graphic artist Edward Wright. And so the network grew and overlapped, gathering strength in their mutual advocacy of modern architecture.

Yet who was going to publicize their agenda on architecture and art? *AR* was a well-established magazine of great repute. Even if it published sentimental articles on Townscape and the English Picturesque, nevertheless its articles were written by an elite group of architectural critics, and its audience of readers was numerous and widespread. By the mid-1950s, *Architectural Design* (*AD*) became the preferred mouthpiece of the younger generation of architects eager to express their vision of a new postwar British modernism.[4] By opening its pages to the Smithsons and their followers, who articulated their opinions on New Brutalism, the failures of CIAM, and its replacement by Team 10, the editors of *AD* knew they were publishing the neo-avant-garde architects of the postwar generation. They hoped to thereby boost their popularity and number of readers.

That *AD* became the major channel for a younger generation of architects and readers was mainly due to its editor Monica Pidgeon's "unflaggingly adventurous, occasionally fiery, spirit and knack for spotting new talent."[5] She ghosted for its editor, Tony Towndrow, while he was employed by the Ministry of Public Works during World War II, and became editor when he departed for Australia in 1946.[6] A female editor was not to the owners' liking, however, for it would not ensure advertisers' confidence; hence, they required that the name of a male architect such as Denys Lasdun be placed on the masthead as "consultant" along with hers.[7]

Pidgeon saw that the latest technical architectural information, as well as CIAM conferences and the Union Internationale des Architectes (UIA), were adequately covered. She attracted the talents of Theo Crosby, who joined *AD* as technical editor in 1953.[8] He was given free rein to experiment with graphic design and to publish work that interested him on modern architecture and art. Under this duo the magazine prospered and grew, continually at the forefront of cultural thought and design. When Crosby left *AD* in 1962, he was followed as technical editor in 1962–1964 by Kenneth Frampton and in 1964–1975 by Robin Middleton. The same year Pidgeon left to become editor of *RIBA Journal*.

Crosby had an eye for colorful and imaginative covers and visually demanding illustrations. This knack, together with Pidgeon's attention to information-jammed pages, also helped to increase *AD*'s popularity and circulation. He was especially concerned with fine-tuning the relationship between the high and popular arts, and examining the impact of mass communication and information theory on architecture.[9] Familiar with many members of the so-called Independent Group that gathered at the Institute of Contemporary Arts in the early 1950s, he saw that *AD* gave them adequate coverage.[10]

Consequently there were a variety of overlapping paths to follow for a younger generation of architects eager to rebuild postwar London as a new modern city: one was to design housing following the rational proportions of Le Corbusier's "Modulor," another was to engage in the activities of MARS group and CIAM, and a third, intertwined with the other two, was to fully explore what advocacy of architecture as a social art truly meant. Peter Smithson would enigmatically label this "socio-plastics"—calling for an architectural form to match the spirit of the times; an architecture of social and moral commitment. It is to these alternative paths that we now turn.

I. Different Paths to Follow for Postwar Reconstruction and Design Methodology

Following the Steps of Le Corbusier

If *AR*'s outspoken advocacy of Townscape Analysis had not been bad enough for the younger generation of architects, in 1954 Pevsner took one of their idols to task in the pages of *AR*. There he proclaimed that

> If one looks at the work of the pioneers of twentieth century architecture, say as early as about 1925, Gropius's Bauhaus or better still Le Corbusier's Stuttgart houses of 1927 and his Centrosoyus project of 1927, … do they not show that, albeit unconsciously, the modern revolution of the early twentieth century and the Picturesque revolution of a hundred years before had all their fundamentals in common … ? That is the functional function of the Picturesque, meaning the Varied, the Intricate, the On-its-own-Merit in the twentieth century.[11]

In accord with the editorial policy of *AR*, Pevsner felt that "no other aesthetic theory fits the demands of modern architecture and planning as well as that of [Uvedale] Price and [Payne] Knight."[12]

Many younger architects, such as St. John Wilson, Howell, and the Smithsons, disagreed.[13] Le Corbusier's modular system of proportion and his brand of rationalism were the banners they unfurled for the cause of modern architecture. They were no doubt in agreement with Alan Colquhoun's 1954 letter published in *AR*.[14] "The explicit aim of the modern movement," Colquhoun wrote, "was to find the sources of a style proper to the twentieth century." Since "the Picturesque movement was clearly connected with 'Historicism,' any purely eclectic attitude towards style must fail to define the modern movement."[15] The new role for modern architecture was to be didactic, to reveal the link between architectural form and function for a specific time. Pevsner might lump together the architecture of Palladio, Edwin Lutyens, and Le Corbusier according to their Picturesque qualities, but

> each has a content that escapes definition in those terms and it is precisely this content, linking each work with its own age, which would interest a modern architect. … Not to admit the didactic element in modern architecture is to make nonsense of it. But once this didactic element is admitted no purely visual "theory" basing itself on the universal validity of forms independent of structure and function appears to be adequate. It is because this fact has been lost sight of that so much Post War British architecture is effete and superficial.[16]

Pevsner replied that he was saying nothing more than that both the Picturesque and the Modern movements expressed a theoretical system in which these same categories [i.e., free grouping, mixture of materials, differentiation of vehicular traffic and pedestrian paths, the interaction between landscape and buildings] were understood and appreciated in their aesthetic value, even if the English system was developed in terms of lawn and lakes and trees rather than of stone and streets and trees.[17]

This opening debate was soon followed by Pevsner's Reith Lectures on the BBC in October and November 1955, "The Picturesqueness of English Art," published in book form in 1956. This was Pevsner's culminating contribution, drawn from his detailed research notes on the English Picturesque, which he had been studying since the early 1940s (see chapter 1).

There would be an outcry from the "anti-picturesque generation," as Reyner Banham labeled those he assumed were arch protestors of the revival of the English Picturesque and its Townscape proponents. His own manifesto on "New Brutalism," published in *AR* a month after Pevsner completed his Reith Lectures, calls New Brutalism, not Townscape design, "our first native art-movement" in the postwar period. In a rather self-serving manner, he professed:

> One cannot begin to study the New Brutalism without realizing how deeply the New Art-History has bitten into progressive English architectural thoughts, into teaching methods, into the common language of communication between architects and between architectural critics. ... The New Brutalism has to be seen against the background of the recent history of history, and, in particular, the growing sense of the inner history of the Modern Movement.[18]

As far as architectural history is concerned, Theo Crosby remembered there were many discussions about history and precedents at the ICA, which moved the younger set of architects to travel to see historic buildings themselves. "Ours was a history of beginnings," embarking on an adventure to discover alternative routes. "We went to see Alberti, Brunelleschi and Michelangelo; Palladio rather than Bernini."[19] Since foreign travel allowance was limited to £50 in the 1950s, it took a great deal of ingenuity to plan these excursions. Reyner Banham also reminisced about these travels:

> ... the kilometres we must have tramped around the suburbs of Paris and Amsterdam, the millions of francs the concierges and caretakers must have accepted in bribes to let us in! Outside of the business of design itself, history was the most turbulently active of the mental disciplines immediately adjacent to architecture—.[20]

The Smithsons were part of this fanning-out of travelers to see the relics of modern architecture and its classical precedents. In the late 1980s, Peter Smithson ruminated on his and Alison's first confrontation with the work of Le Corbusier:

> When we first visited Le Corbusier's houses from the nineteen twenties in the nineteen fifties (earliest visit, Villa Savoye: A. S. 1948; A. + P., 1950) many houses still bore traces of their original colour, especially Pessac (1956).
>
> Although we knew about Le Corbusier's polychromy from plates in a loose-leaf-folder cahier in our architectural school's library, the faded reality was something amazing—as the discovery of traces of colour on Greek temples must have been for the first generation of architect-excavators in the early nineteenth century. … In a sense we were excavating modern, for by the nineteen fifties, the Heroic Period had disappeared.
>
> Everything we found there was a revelation and it was a personal revelation, a discovery; something almost too personal to be shared. To possess the experience was to possess part of "Corb."[21]

Peter Smithson believed that from

> Le Corbusier's work and writings from this period a general precept is unshakably adhesed [sic] to our generation—that an architecture without social intention is empty.
>
> For Alison and I [sic], Le Corbusier did the work a true architect was
> obliged to do—
> urbanism, travel
> architecture, theory
> exhibitions, polemic furniture, looking again at history
> art works, ephemera (graphics, etc.).
>
> We have followed.[22]

As discussed below, this juxtaposition architectural practice–theory speaks in general to the 1950s search for a route that led toward the humanization of architecture and its "social intention."

In this effort, the pages of *AD* offered the Smithsons full scope for their developing ideas. Between 1953 and 1975, *AD* published 168 articles written by or about the work and interests of the Smithsons.[23] Peter Smithson remembered the 1950s as a period of great hope:

> To purify our ideas we made:
> Projects
> Essays
> Exhibition at full-scale.
>
> We had an architectural magazine open to us for publication of essays and projects and we had Team X (people of like minds and similar objectives).[24]

The Classical Tradition

For a brief time in the 1940s and early 1950s, many young architects were re-asking an ancient question made freshly pertinent by Le Corbusier's writings on the "Modulor" (his anthropocentric scale of proportions): was there a universal system of proportions, based on the body and mathematics, that could be extended to contemporary design?

Since many of the postwar generation of architects, mentioned above, were working in LCC's architectural department in charge of designing schools or housing estates, they wanted to find methods of design that would lower the cost of construction and provide an ordering unit or module for a building that could be repetitively applied.[25]

After Le Corbusier lectured on the "Modulor" and the Golden Section at the AA's centenary celebration in 1947, and with the translation of his *Le Modulor* (1948) into English (as *The Modulor*) in 1954, many of these younger architects believed that Le Corbusier's theories, not to mention his exemplary Unité d'Habitation in Marseille (1947–1952), vindicated the notion that building systems, prefabricated elements, and standardized parts could achieve a heightened aesthetic appeal if guided by a proportional system based on the human body and additive mathematical components. An order so produced could offer, in a word, beauty.

Just as important in this discourse on classical proportions was Rudolf Wittkower's *Architectural Principles in the Age of Humanism*, partly published in the *Journal of the Warburg and Courtauld Institutes* in 1949 and reworked in book form in 1951. By a scholar of Italian Baroque art, this small book was a diversion from his main body of work, but focused attention on the societal meaning of proportion theory.

Wittkower opened and closed his text with the following claims: Renaissance architects, all of whom had close ties to humanist circles, had been concerned with the meaning of classical trends of thought, and this should be of great interest to young architects today, who may well provide new solutions to these ancient problems.[26] Students of Wittkower's who were advancing toward these solutions included Colin Rowe, Joseph Rykwert, and Alan Colquhoun. Geometric rigor and proportional systems stemming from Vitruvius and Alberti offered something to hold on to in the struggle not only against the English Picturesque but also against extreme Functionalism and the leftover purities of the Machine Aesthetic.

The humanism of the Renaissance, which Wittkower so elegantly detailed, served as a call to order: a return to basic principles intrinsic to the discipline of architecture as an intellectual practice. Yet one reviewer, A. S. G. Butler, called Wittkower's book "difficult, dull and unrewarding," in need of simpler exposition and clearer diagrams. Butler's review brought the following response from the Smithsons: "Dr. Wittkower is regarded by the younger architects as the *only* art-historian working in England capable of describing and analysing buildings in spatial and plastic terms and not in terms of derivation and dates; and this is no insular phenomenon."[27] This rebuttal was the Smithsons' first attempt, Peter claimed, to put thoughts on design methodology into published form. "But from then on you will find records of thought processes, and later on, the process of writing opens to the future. That's not retrospective—it's prospective."[28]

Peter Smithson averred in 1978 that Wittkower's 1949 book "confirmed, and deepened for life, a direction we had already taken; for, our first real building (designed 1949–1950)—the School at Hunstanton—had been, through some inner compulsion, as regularly bayed and as strictly organized as we could make it."[29] He went on to claim that it was an unnoticed art-historical fact that the postwar generation of architects was fascinated with centrist geometries, with squares, circles, diagonals; and the key differences among their designs lay in how they blunted these geometric perfections. "In the architecture of this generation therefore, the symmetry appears as a convenience, like the string on a neatly tied parcel. … The sound and sensible way to wrap something up."[30]

In 2001 Peter once again recalled how classicism had been recycled in the postwar period into the process of design:

> [I]t dawned on me that you [can] examine classicism as modes of operation, rather than as images you can see. For me, classicism is central to my thought. It is a result of ten years or so of looking at all Le Corbusier structures and another ten years looking at Mies van der Rohe buildings and then ten or fifteen years of looking at all the Doric temples and classical Greek towns. I make it sound very serious, but in fact that was how we spent our holidays.[31]

Thus the humanization of architectural practice and an aesthetic system appealing to the intellect were taught to the younger generation by both *Architectural Principles in the Age of Humanism* and *The Modulor*. Ruth Olitsky and John Voelcker, reviewing both books, argued as follows in "Form and Mathematics" (*AD*, October 1954):

> Both books are concerned, broadly speaking, with interpretations of man's place in the physical universe. The first explicitly, through meticulous historical documentation; the second implicitly, through the development of mind and idea. Each book illuminates the significance of the other, and through them both it becomes possible to see the origins of many issues which are very much alive amongst architects at the present time.[32]

Le Corbusier's "Modulor" system of proportions, the reviewers noted, was an instrument of measure derived from the figure of man and mathematical theory.

> Le Modulor, because of its deep affinity with the classical tradition, or if only because it has caught the imagination of architects, provides a cosmological symbol, that is to say a symbol for existing ideas about space and time with respect to man. … The enigma of the present time lies in the fact that there is no generally accepted and

shared formal language. The formal tradition must be invoked, for it is only through its language that the symbol may symbolize, that the mathematics can be used, and that architects can once again make the physical universe, or at least a small part of it, an intelligible place to live in.[33]

Not everyone was going to agree. John Summerson, for instance, attacked the younger generation's search for architectural principles on which to rest a theory of modern architecture in a lecture delivered in May 1957 at the Royal Institute of British Architects (RIBA).[34] Architectural design and architectural theory, he argued, do not always develop in tandem: many changes in style are not reflected in theory, and vice versa.

> So we must bear in mind about theory that it is an historical process with a life of its own in its own medium of words and that there is no question either of principles being abstracted wholly from practice or of practice being necessarily a reflection of theory. This makes a pretty big hole in the proposition called "A theory of modern architecture." But it brings us nearer to a realistic view of what we are discussing.[35]

In a printed response, Peter Smithson was not entirely in agreement. He believed he had constructed a theory-practice cycle:

> This cycle is being pedalled along and both wheels, practice and theory, revolve simultaneously. ... [E]verything starts with a revolution. There is an existing thing against which discontent is felt. The discontent hardens, and at some point intuitively a new image is conceived. This image is not an isolated thing, concerned purely with the plastic arts, but a sort of socio-plastic entity; that is, it conceived a new way of life, a new sort of technology, and a new image all in one, but in rather a vague sort of way.[36]

Debate over the "Modulor" and systems of proportion came to a lively crescendo on June 18, 1957, during yet another discussion at the RIBA. A motion to accept as foundational a statement concerning Le Corbusier's "Modulor" system and attributed to Albert Einstein—"that Systems of Proportion make good design easier and bad design more difficult"—was defeated by a 60 to 48 vote. Reporting on the defeated motion, Peter Smithson proclaimed that "proportion was important to architects, as a matter of tooth and claw debate, in 1948 and 1949. ... The right time for the Palladian Revival was 1948."[37] Then, architects had been looking for something to believe in and it had been important to get back to some simple principles, before moving forward to a new sort of control that arose naturally from a building's organizational patterns. Architects looked at Palladian buildings to find "something to believe in ... something that stood above what they were doing themselves." But this concern was passé by 1957: "In conclusion, I think it reasonable to suggest that 'systems of proportion' only touch the fringe of the problem of values in architecture, and, if anything, confuse the issue both of the creative process and the environment as received."[38]

Rudolf Wittkower, present at the RIBA debate, reiterated his position that no universal system of proportion, implying a system of general values, had ever existed. Since proportional systems were relative, not universal, they were a matter of subjective and personal choice. It was therefore senseless for the younger generation to try to forge a pragmatic tool out of scale, proportion, or unity.[39] A few years later, recalling this vote of rejection, Wittkower remarked that Le Corbusier's "Modulor" "is amateurish, dynamic, personal, paradoxical, and often obscure. When you think you have it all sorted out, you wonder how practical the Modulor really is."[40]

In "Talks to 5th Year Students" (1959), the Smithsons sought closure on the matter of "systems of proportion" or appropriate techniques for mass production by questioning not only AR's Townscape advocacy but also the Classical turn in the early postwar years. The purpose of these talks was to refocus attention on the fundamentals of architecture and the pragmatics of reality.

> Innovation—or change of style—now enters society horizontally from mass-production industry and its ad-men, with back feeds through the old fine arts and through pure technology. In this situation it is impossible to *induce* society to "improve the taste" of its natural predilections. (The technique proposed in "Outrage Counter Attack"). It is necessary to change the whole focus of their desires, produce new cultural objectives.[41]

As far as learning from history went, however, Wittkower could still be a guide:

> Every generation recreates the past to satisfy its own needs. ... They do not CHOOSE to take from the past—they feel an inner compulsion—which compulsion is born of the forces of the present, and this compulsion is felt to a greater or lesser extent, according to their degree of awareness by all artists in the field of those forces; by us.[42]

The Smithsons gave two examples of this inner compulsion shared by others: the neo-Palladian movement after World War II and the Peasant revival of Mediterranean forms from North Africa, the Greek islands, and southern Italy. These latter forms, which the Smithsons had first become familiar with at the CIAM 9 meeting at Aix-en-Provence in 1953, became influential not by mimicking their shapes or styles of living but by taking them as "spark-points" for action. It was essential to understand the unity of past ways of building and "the lyrical discipline" of great historical periods: "Without this, a mastery of building techniques or draughting [sic] is meaningless."[43]

The Postwar CIAM: A Generational Divide[44]

The words of Alison and Peter Smithson, quoted above, hint at an alternative direction that some members of the younger generation were pursuing, a movement in which the "process" of architectural design became the focus. This path was further developed in discussions that led forward from CIAM 9 (Aix-en-Provence, 1953), where the younger generation of the Smithsons, William Howell, John Voelcker, Jaap Bakema, Aldo van Eyck, Sandy van Ginkel, Shadrach Woods, and Georges Candilis first met each other, an event which sparked their coming together as Team 10.

The editors of *AD* were diligent in covering CIAM events and following the interests of younger architects present at those meetings. CIAM 6 was the first such occasion on which a younger attending generation (including two members of the Dutch CIAM Group of 8—Jaap Bakema and Aldo van Eyck—a group soon labeled "Les Jeunes") could express its interest in the ideals of the older modernists.[45] This manifestation of interest convinced the five leaders—Le Corbusier, Walter Gropius, Sigfried Giedion, Josep Lluís Sert (President), and Jaqueline Tyrwhitt (Secretary), following suit as "Les Anciens"—that the continuation of CIAM was after all justified. These younger architects were struggling to find a voice and mode of expression in the presence of an older generation whom they obviously admired and whose advice they continued to seek. As the young gained strength, the generations began to diverge over what architectural forms would be appropriate for the times—a debate also strenuously waged within the ranks of the younger architects themselves. But before this internal dispute, we examine the conflict between the older and younger generations of modern architects and over whether CIAM should continue to exist.

The postwar meetings at CIAM 6 (Bridgwater) and CIAM 7 (Bergamo) were influenced, if not actually dominated, by Giedion's interest in "new monumentality." Monuments, he argued, were translations of the people's collective force into symbols, and expressed recognition that society was required to pass on something worthwhile to a future generation.[46] Yet this call for "new monumentality" was out of sync with ideas held by many younger architects. In particular, younger members of the Dutch Group of 8 opined that the arts and architectural expression were not the most pressing topics for postwar debate: Jaap Bakema dispatched a report to CIRPAC,[47] the organizing agency of CIAM, underscoring their belief that the most vital and central architectural problem in postwar Western Europe was "the housing situation."[48]

AD's report on CIAM 8 (Hoddesdon) openly criticized the path CIAM was taking.[49] Leading figures of the older generation had stated publicly that it was time for younger architects to take over leadership of CIAM, but *AD* questioned whether there was anything left to be taken over. The congresses had devolved into showcases for a few exhibitionists, and if the pioneers of modern architecture who had created CIAM in 1928 withdrew from the scene, CIAM would surely collapse. *AD* complained about the town planning surveys displayed at CIAM 7.[50] "Some were puerile, many were simply long-winded, few could show anything new in technique of aspects to study or methods of presentation," while the British examples at CIAM 8 "exhibited only uncertainty and a plunge into meandering romanticism to avoid the terror of decision." Yet *AD* had to admit there was still a need to toe the modernist line, for England had yet to forge a formal solution—a coherent form—to its aesthetic ideals.[51]

These generational disagreements moved CIRPAC, at a May 1952 meeting in Paris, in preparation for CIAM 9, to pose the much larger question of the future of CIAM itself. Younger members of established groups wanted to take a more active role in the congresses. Could the older CIAM evolve into a new-style CIAM by incorporating additional groups and members while pruning dead branches that no longer served any purpose?[52] For example, in May 1953, William Howell, John Voelcker, and the Smithsons were formally elected to membership in MARS, and thus the doors were opened to their attendance at CIAM 9 (Aix-en-Provence, 1953) and other such congresses.[53] But this would only create more tension between CIAM generations.

CIAM 9 met in Aix-en-Provence at the end of July 1953, marking the twenty-fifth anniversary of the Congress. "Man and His Dwelling" was the theme intended to materialize a *Charte de l'Habitat* (Charter of Habitat) modeled on the remarkable and resilient boilerplate *Charte d'Athènes* of 1933. *AD*'s report claimed sympathetically: "The provision of millions of homes is a world priority second only to food."[54] Even so, *AD* asked:

> Can we yet claim, in our post-war planning, to have achieved that sense of neighbourliness which is still to be found in what is arrogantly described as the slum? Do our new towns and housing schemes provide that sense of belonging and that quality of human identity which are fundamental to man's well-being? The answers, still unknown, will only be found through an ever closer response by planners to the challenge of man's requirements and by a closer collaboration between architect and planner. This is the food for thought which CIAM provides.[55]

The last day of the Congress was spent at Le Corbusier's just-completed Unité d'Habitation in Marseille. This was of course a thrill to the younger generation, and *AD* captured this emotion:

> This building is an expression of that vast creative upsurge and hopefulness which characterizes this generation, whether the critics recognize it or not. Cynics were seduced and the spoken and written word rendered empty. We were in the presence of the stuff of which architecture is made.[56]

In preparatory meetings for CIAM 10, discussions continued about the merits of turning over the organizational work of CIAM to the younger generation. CIAM, *AD* reported, had changed since World War II; its founders were now in power in the profession and the university, many were living and working in the United States, and most were too busy to discuss utopian schemes. Here was an opening for the younger generation, who claimed they had something to say.[57]

The older leadership eventually, in June 1954, entrusted the organization of CIAM 10 to Jaap Bakema, Georges Candilis, Peter Smithson, and Rolf Gutmann, who would end by reorganizing the working method of CIAM to better reflect their own interests. This eventual course of events was not looked upon kindly by the older generation, who had given the younger members a mandate to prepare the tenth Congress, as it were, "intellectually and spiritually" but were far from having yielded authority to change CIAM's structural organization. The youngsters soon added more members to their group.[58] This enlarged group of CIAM 10 organizers—later known as Team 10 for its organizational role in this congress[59]—no longer wished CIAM's work to be based on the study and analysis of the "four functions" of living, working, recreation and circulation, each goal in isolation from the others. Instead they proposed to examine all functions in light of different scales of association: dwelling, village, town, and city.

There were further concerns to be addressed: town and countryside were disintegrating before one's eyes, being swallowed up in sprawl without any architectural solution. The younger generation sought formal expressions of an integrated community that could counteract uncontrolled growth. Wanting also to assuage the disruption of community life in housing estates, they were looking for a method to build "true" villages, towns, and cities that demonstrated both architectural unity and formal concentration, while allowing for growth and change.[60]

AD doubted that a "Charter of Habitat" would result from CIAM 10, but thought the Congress a valuable meeting place for architects from all over the world, and hailed it with a cheer: "Let the conversation continue!"[61] And so it did: whether at CIAM 10, held at Dubrovnik in 1956 (the last official CIAM), the first Team 10 meeting in Otterlo, in the Netherlands, in 1959, or subsequent Team 10 meetings through 1981.

To return to the generational conflict, the young organizers of CIAM 10 were brutally honest: senility, mediocrity, and exhaustion had turned CIAM into a mutual admiration society. There had been too many attendees (3,000 members and a hundred observers) at CIAM 9 to achieve anything substantial.

CIAM had begun as a spontaneous grouping of like-minded architects seeking to place modern architecture on national agendas, but it had lost its common cause.[62]

> We, the young, received a shock at Aix-en-Provence, in seeing how the wonder of the Ville Radieuse had completely disappeared from CIAM. CIAM 10 ought to be a congress of participants. Today each of us recognizes the existence of a new spirit … this is manifested in our revolt against the mechanical concepts of order and in our passionate awareness that order lies in the complex ties between life and the realities of the world. CIAM 10 ought to show that as architects we accept responsibility for the creation of form. We accept the responsibility for each act of creation albeit very small. We ought to find the means of realizing in architecture the idea of a world constantly in evolution, inconceivably complicated, although at each moment absolutely finished.[63]

The older generation, irritated by the younger generation's constant criticism and continual quest for a greater role and more meaningful participation in the Congress's organizational meetings, fussed over the trivial but emotive issue of whether the name "CIAM" should be conferred upon the younger generation or not. Were the "youngers" trustworthy acolytes to bear the torch of CIAM forward? Were they ready to act on their own, or would they merely reduce its message to vague and mystical thought?[64] The elders had offered the younger generation at CIAM 10 a choice: continue as CIAM II (Le Corbusier's proposal), or eliminate the name altogether (Giedion's more radical one). But the Congress, under the sway of the organizing group, had rejected both choices, believing they themselves were able to decide on their own whether to continue with CIAM or drop the name.[65]

The English members of Team 10 were particularly adamant, however, that CIAM had collapsed. William Howell claimed in 1956 that CIAM 10 committed a ritual suicide in the manner of old religions so that it could be reborn: "CIAM is dead ... long live CIAM."[66] And the following year, Peter Smithson and others proclaimed in *AD* that CIAM had collapsed.[67] The founders' "functional city" which divided a city into four separate and independent functions—living, working, recreation, and circulation—produced schemes resembling "filing cabinets."[68] British Team 10, by contrast, was interested in a new set of conditions: growth and change in cities, technological innovations such as mass communication, complex networks of cars and motorways, and the rise of a consumer society driven by new desires.

Peter reiterated this position in a 1960 piece in *AD*.[69] The real change in postwar architecture had, he said, instigated a new focus on "process." The "process" idea began with the British government's sponsorship of Hertfordshire Schools in the late 1940s. The design of each was regarded as a "systems" building, with each part replaceable as the need arose, amounting to a "transient architecture" based on a thirty-year cycle. The second instance of "process" involved community-level systems planning: it began with discussions in Holland and devolved from four concepts. The first was that communities were not mere abstractions but, rather, "associations" of individuals; second, that people needed to be able to "identify" with a given place or risk alienation. Thirdly, a new social and physical "mobility" had come into being; while fourthly, the three foregoing concepts, or forces, themselves amounted to nothing less than a "pattern of growth and change" in a particular community. These four "processes"—association, identity, mobility, and pattern of growth and change—were important to Team 10 and diverged widely from the static forms of the "functional city" as championed and implemented by the older generation of CIAM.

With such divergent generational interests, could CIAM continue, then, or not? Various statements made to the press after Team 10's 1959 Otterlo meeting to the effect that CIAM was dead, so that Team 10 would no longer deploy that name, shocked the elders. In January 1961, *AD* published an open letter signed by Sert, Gropius, Le Corbusier, and Giedion.[70] It was a defense against attacks and misconceptions leveled against the *ancien régime* by the younger generation over the past five years. The elders proclaimed in their defense:

> CIAM has fulfilled its initial task as far as Europe is concerned. To create a positive workable platform, ... [for] the vast areas coming only now into the orbit of the contemporary evolution, would be a true continuation of the mission of CIAM.[71]

A reply by Bakema, who had attended the congresses since 1947, was published in *AD* as well.[72] He tried to pacify the elders by setting the record straight and correcting misunderstandings. But he seemed to have muddied the waters: he wrote that Team 10 had not dissolved CIAM.[73] Yet it remains the case that Bakema's "Concluding Statement" at Otterlo had rejected the name of CIAM: "To intensify the attempts for finding a new architectural language, individuals and groups must work in their own way. It is therefore they concluded that the name of CIAM will be used no more in relation to future activities of the participants."[74]

What was clear at Otterlo, Bakema explained in responding to the elders' outrage, had already been set forth in the writing on the wall at Bridgwater, Bergamo, Hoddesdon, Aix-en-Provence, and Dubrovnik—namely, that the architectural issues of "around-1920," when new techniques had to be introduced, were different from those of "around-1960." Now "the moral function of architectural expression" must be reintroduced—but this dispensation is no longer covered by the term "Modern Architecture," as included in the acronym "CIAM." Most attendees at Otterlo agreed on this point, though they stopped short of wanting to give up completely on CIAM, it being after all their rightful inheritance; so Bakema begged the elders to continue to supply "help and encouragement" without wasting time on trivial issues such as naming rights.

> The name will come of its own accord the moment that the around-1960 problems have been defined.
> In Otterlo we made "Post Box," so as to have a means of communication about our methods of defining the architectural problems around-1960. It is available for those who want to exchange views on the subject of the development of Habitat.[75]

Yet tensions had been revealed within Team 10: the British group was more strident, claiming CIAM was dead, while the Dutch were more respectful of their CIAM inheritance.

II. Coming Together as Team 10—An Uneasy Proposition[76]

Histories of groups often iron over internal differences, portraying the group's ideology as unified and consistent when in fact its discourse was marked by numerous points of disagreement, competitions among individual members over who should have the last word, and misunderstandings of each other's statements. This smoothing tendency is on display in the accounts of Team 10 by Alison Smithson commissioned by *AD* from 1960 to 1975. *AD* offered Alison Smithson guest editorship of the debates of Team 10 in "CIAM Team 10" and "The Work of Team 10," both published in May 1960. These were followed in December 1962 by her edited edition of "Team 10 Primer" and supplemented in May 1975 by her "Team 10 at Royaumont 1962."[77] The legacy apparent in Alison Smithson's accounts appears smooth and non-confrontational. All members appear zealous about maintaining limited entrée to group meetings; this exclusivity seems to reinforce a sense of allegiance to each other and an acceptance of the general direction the group was moving in. The reality of this unity is, however, questionable.

More than most other architects in the postwar decades, Alison and Peter Smithson developed their ideas about architecture by testing them in both writing and practice. They drew inspiration from their Team 10 associates as well as from their architectural colleagues, artists and critics at the London Institute of Contemporary Arts (ICA), where the so-called Independent Group (IG) met from 1952 to 1955. Alison Smithson's retelling of Team 10 history will be analyzed in later chapters; below, I examine the actual development of ideas in the give-and-take of Team 10 preparatory meetings and epistolary debates, so far as we can know this from the records.

Aftermath of CIAM 9 (Aix-en-Provence, June 1953)

The earliest fragment of this multi-sided back-and-forth begins with the English members of the younger generation who had attended CIAM 9—William and Jill Howell, John Voelcker, and the Smithsons—and their reflections on CIAM 9 (not published until 1982).[78] They claimed that CIAM was no longer facing up to contemporary problems, which necessitated the redefinition and reformulation of the role of the architect/urbanist and all the techniques involved. They suggested the use of geographical units drawn from images contained in Patrick Geddes's "Valley Section" regional planning model, first developed in 1909; i.e., detached house (isolate) village, town, city. If this geographical arrangement were used, then the continuity of social scale and the basic arrangement between man and his physical environment could be maintained, and his identity enhanced. Also, there was need for a direct method of communication. "We should attempt to investigate the nature of the 'Significant Image': the ability to select such images, both visually and verbally, is an essential technique to the architecture/urbanist."[79] And, "Note: Few of us have seen more than 4 drawings of the St. Dié Reconstruction Project by Le Corbusier, yet these 4 drawings express visually a total and fully differentiated image of a township."[80]

The theme of imagery, brought up so prominently in this statement from the Howells-Smithsons-Voelcker group, was of particular interest to the Smithsons. Indeed, images were essential for the Smithsons' developing ideas during the 1950s. "Image was the favourite word of the period," Peter Smithson recalled in 1993. "A 'good image' was the highest possible praise, for a newspaper photograph, for an advertisement … in fact for anything."[81]

Nigel Henderson taught them, Peter later recalled, to look carefully at street life in his early 1950s photographs of Bethnal Green. The "as found" aesthetic first came to them in viewing his photographs: children's play-graphics, hoardings on the sides of buildings, detritus of bomb sites, the street life of a community. The Smithsons inserted these photographs of play-graphics into their CIAM 9 grille along with plans from their 1952 Golden Lane Competition. Thenceforth the "as found" aesthetic fueled their "Cluster" ideograms, diagrams, and theories, which they continued to develop in concert with the preparations for CIAM 10.[82]

Between CIAM 9 and CIAM 10, the Smithsons began to meet at the ICA with that loose assembly of artists and art historians eventually labeled the Independent Group. As early as April 2, 1952, Eduardo Paolozzi, Nigel Henderson, and the Smithsons submitted a proposal to the ICA Management Committee for an exhibition to be entitled "Sources" (eventually relabeled "Parallel of Life and Art"). The original title referred to the exhibition's images being drawn from life, nature, industry, building, and the new landscape revealed by scientific instruments, now understood to be antecedent sources of modernist abstractions. The exhibition's creators believed that such material formed a background for anyone trying to look closely at the modern world, a background so taken for granted that it sank beneath the threshold of conscious perception.[83]

In the Smithsons' personal archive are notes proclaiming important intentions behind this exhibition on "Sources" and outlining their position on different generations of architects. The starting point was a manifesto, "Document 53," written by them and presented to the ICA in 1952.[84] In it they claimed that the first great creative period of modern architecture had ended in 1929, and that after a long period of exploratory work, a second period was beginning: "Both periods are characterized by simultaneous parallel development in architecture—engineering—painting and sculpture; the attitudes, theorems, and images of each finding unsought consonance in the others."[85] In the 1920s, art and architecture presented a finite composition of simple elements, of which none was autonomous: each existed only in relationship to the whole. In the 1950s, the problem was how to retain the clarity and finiteness of the whole while giving each part its own internal discipline and complexity. This second great period of creativity was to

> be proclaimed by an exhibition in which the juxtaposition of phenomenon from our various fields [of the exhibitors] would make obvious the existence of a new attitude.[86]

> By representing phenomena from our various fields we can demonstrate the existence of a new movement—classical—complex—human—a fundamental outlook from common sources (outlook) to future synthesis.[87]

2.2
Alison and Peter Smithson, Urban Re-Identification Grid, CIAM 9, Aix-en-Provence, 1953. Smithson Family Collection.

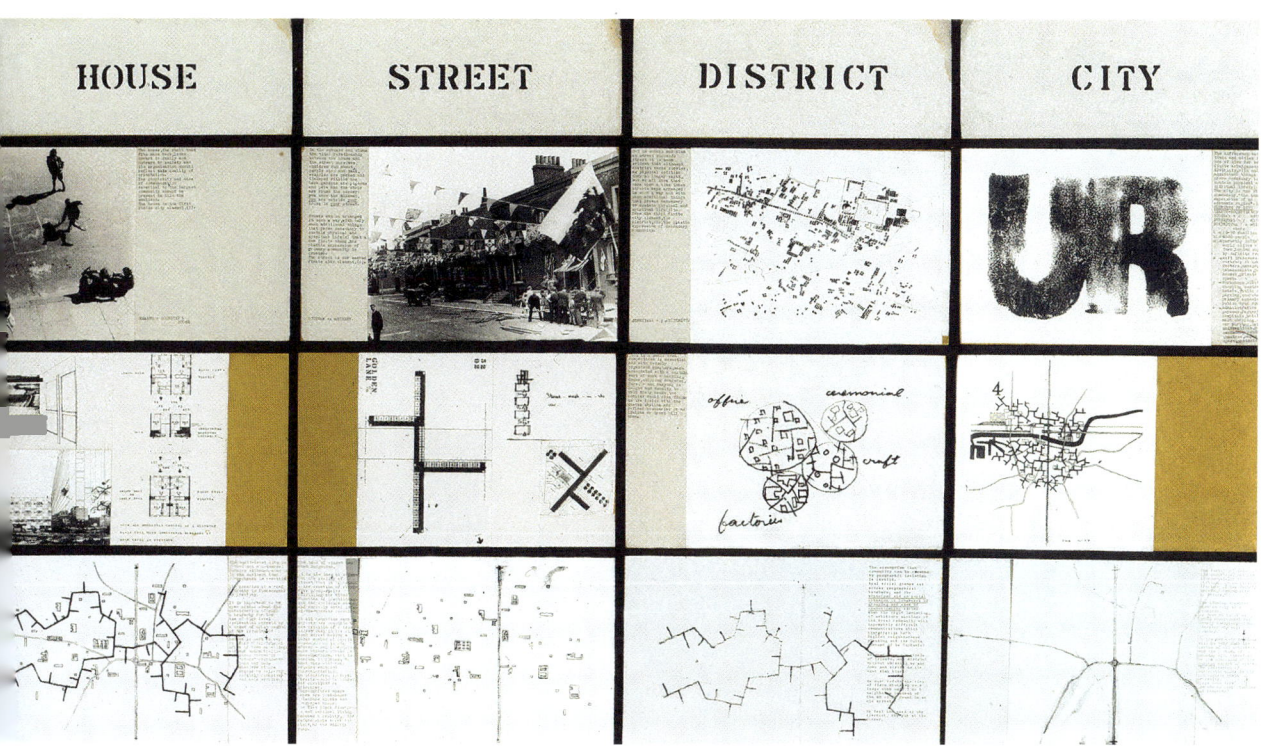

"HABITAT"   SMITHSONS

1) It is useless to consider the house except as a part of a community owing to the inter-action of these on each other.

2) We should not waste our time codifying the elements of the house untill the other relationship has been crystalised.

3) "Habitat" is concerned with the particular house in the particular type of community.

4) Communities are the same everywhere.
   1) detached house - farm.
   2) Village.
   3) Towns of various sorts (Industrial
                             (Admin.
                             (Special.
   4) Cities (multi functional.

5) They can be shewn in relationship to their environment (Habitat) in the Geddes valley section.

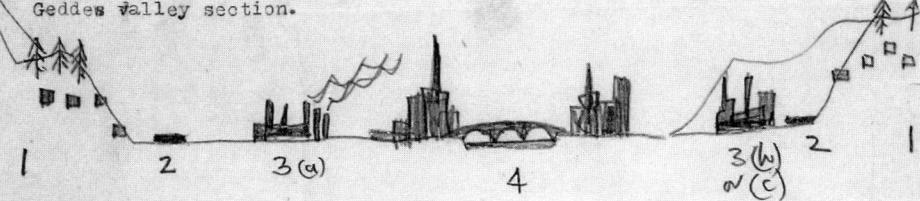

6) Any community must be internally convenient - have ease of circulation, in consequence whatever type of transport are available, density must increase as population increases, i.e. (I) is least dense (4) is most dense.

7) We must therefore study the dwelling and the groupings that are necessary to produce convenient communities at various points on the valley section.

8) The appropriateness of any solution may lie in the field of architectural invention rather than social anthropology.

2.3
Alison and Peter Smithson, draft of "Habitat" declaration in preparation for meeting at Doorn, 1954, with Patrick Geddes Valley Section ideogram, 1954. Smithson Family Collection.

When the exhibition took place (September and October 1953) it was a few months after the Smithsons participated in their first CIAM meeting (CIAM 9) and met a group of like-minded colleagues.[88] They would meet again with these new acquaintances in Doorn, Netherlands (January 1954). There would be subsequent organizational meetings with Team 10 members preparing for CIAM 10 (1956) and lively correspondence debating organizational differences for this Congress.[89] Their back-and-forth movements between IG activities and meetings with members of "Team 10" obviously influenced their evolving concepts and theories as expressed in their writings and bracketed by their architectural competitions and constructions,

Their search for the "Significant Image" continued with preparations for CIAM 10, including the 1954 meeting at Doorn, which produced the closest thing to a Team 10 manifesto that would ever appear. This was fundamental to the Smithsons' way of thinking and communicating—text and image integrations produce an "as found aesthetic," imply a continuum of different types of communication via significant images, ideas, and words. A continuum of messages was no doubt a gloss on lessons learned at IG meetings where the continuum between high and popular art, between different modes of communication, were avidly discussed. But their quest for a "significant image" was also part of the search for a method capable of communicating directly new patterns of association in contemporary society.

Doorn, January 1954

The organizing committee for CIAM 10 (Jaap Bakema, Aldo van Eyck, Sandy van Ginkel, Hans Hovens Greve, Peter Smithson, John Voelcker) decided to meet independently at Doorn (January 29–31, 1954) to discuss how best to proceed.[90]

Peter Smithson reiterated to the Doorn group that six "commissions of atmospheres" should be set up at CIAM 10 based on the images supplied by Geddes's Valley Section. It was impossible at Aix, he noted, to look at the grilles from the point of view of relationships, there being many different scales between house and city.

Bakema agreed and, in rather poor English, described the new focus to be placed on visual relationships:

> New term of architecture is: *relationships.* Many architects with great capacities come to decorational architecture because of lack of [being] connoisseurs of *relationship* and *identity*. ... To know that visual relationships are of great influence of man, whether in traffic or in their chair. By situating one type of building (dwelling) in a certain position we put this influence.[91]

The Doorn meeting produced a "Statement on Habitat," which Alison Smithson would later relabel the "Doorn Manifesto." It read in part as follows:

> As a direct result of the 9th congress at Aix, we have come to the conclusion that if we are to create a Charte de l'Habitat, we must redefine the aims of urbanism, and at the same time create a new tool to make this aim possible.
>
> Urbanism considered and developed in terms of the Charte d'Athènes tends to produce "towns" in which vital human associations are inadequately expressed.
>
> To comprehend these human associations we must consider every community on its particular *total* complexity. In order to make this *comprehension* possible we propose to study urbanism as communities of varying degrees of complexity.[92]

In later days, the Smithsons were adamant that a new and shared way of thinking had arisen out of Doorn. Henceforth the group accepted "an ecological approach" that entailed studying different "scales of association" based on Geddes's Valley Section. This "shared way of thinking" was really an imposition that smoothed over differences always ready to burst through to the surface. But "particularity" did become part of the Smithsons' extended vocabulary. "'Habitat' [they wrote] is concerned with a particular house in a particular community."[93]

Peter reflected in the 1990s on the "Doorn Manifesto's" stress on "particularity":

> A long-after-afterthought on this Manifesto reveals what I now believe to be the main direction of Team 10's effort, in a word towards *particularity*.[94]
>
> It is in *particularity* that the ambition of the Manifesto reveals itself; for the norm of architecture "after the books" has been to accept a formal model and to use that model more or less without regard to location (or indeed to use).[95]
>
> The Manifesto's bid for *particularity* at this most common practical level seems a natural thing. For if the house format takes account of the presence of the access land it enjoys a sense of *bonding*, a strengthened territoriality, consequent of individual actions guided by the *particularity* of place.[96]

Debate over "Instructions for CIAM 10"

The English Group, led by Peter Smithson, wanted a "revolutionary" break with CIAM and were uncompromising about any changes to the position advocated in their proposed Framework for CIAM 10, which they maintained was a direct descendant of the Doorn Manifesto.[97] Consequently there was a good deal of debate among the Team10 members concerning various drafts of "Instructions for CIAM 10" (to specify the mandatory Framework for CIAM 10 discussions).

Team 10 met in London (August 28–29, 1954) to discuss Peter Smithson's Framework, which specified that each presentation should be classed under one of the four settlement types identified in the Doorn Manifesto's Valley Section. Under this scheme, all CIAM 10 attendees should present their concept in a grille composed of four different panels: (1) Identification Image, i.e., a poetic photograph or drawing depicting the environment and the concept; (2) Development Pattern (program); (3) Development Type (plans, sections, elevations); and (4) Contribution to the Aims of CIAM.[98]

Bakema wanted to make changes to Peter Smithson's "Instructions." He felt that the framework ignored various suggestions made by the Dutch. Aldo van Eyck took it upon himself to develop a new text that attempted to realize "interrelationships."[99]

Van Eyck agreed with the Smithsons that CIAM 10 should adopt an "ecological approach" by studying each habitat in its particular environment, but wished to extend that position:

> The traditional association hierarchy is expressed in the words City, Town, Village, Isolate which are symbols—image entities—that stand for a much more complex series of relationships. ... Although they may be mutating it is important to retain them as starting points as they are whole things and particular things and it is as whole things in a *network of relative whole things* that we wish to consider the problems of Habitat.[100]
>
> The words, the entities, may change. At CIAM 10 we may put our finger on this change and find new patterns of association.[101]

However, as a framework for discussion, the "Instructions," in addition to the stress on "totality," should incorporate three additional problems or questions:[102] (1) "The Greater Reality of the Doorstep," how habitat can reflect and stimulate contact between man and man, between man and thing, and overcome the dualities of the inside-outside, part-whole, permanence-change relationships; (2) "The Aesthetics of Number," how standardized elements can be repeated or combined in groupings, setting up a rhythm that gives rise to an aesthetic solution; and (3) "Growth and Change," how time can be given plastic form, how habitat can lose its finite and static character and become flexibly open-ended, allowing for spontaneous development by those it serves.[103]

The English Group (Howells, the Smithsons, Voelcker) were confused over the Dutch interpretation of "Instructions for CIAM 10." Writing to Bakema, Peter Smithson was direct:

> I question validity of isolating any aspects of our problem and codifying them in this way. We empirical radicals (the bloody English!) feel terribly, & I hope, creatively, against analysis which may not be relevant to the nature of the enquiry, or of pre-supposing that say the disciplines of "number" or "growth" are the *most important* things at this time or if they are essential to the discipline of built-form *at all*.
>
> I have good & rational (natural?) doubts.[104]

Van Eyck's document had inserted changes that had never been discussed by the group as a whole; new ideas such as the "doorstep," "aesthetics of number," or "growth and change," were not acceptable to the English Group. They sought absolute loyalty to a "common factor" and feared that any unilateral alteration would cause a breakdown of group action.[105]

Bakema wrote a personal response to Peter Smithson: "Dear Peter, We are in the period in which laws of society and art are confrontated [*sic*] by the wonder of totality (interrelationship). / This is *our* period."[106] He proposed that yet another draft Framework be written to clarify this totality, and that the additional three problems for working groups (proposed by the Dutch part of Team 10) remain as a supplementary proposition until all agreed on an acceptable approach.

In early December, Howell wrote to Bakema to explain the new framework of the English Group's draft, with a rewritten Preamble by Alison and Peter Smithson. They had redrawn the image of Geddes's Valley Section on flat ground.

> This at once removes any suggestion of a reversion to Geddes, which some people have criticized, and also the removal of the "Valley" means that the higher forms of organization [no longer] tower above the humbler ones, suggesting that they are qualitatively more complex, more highly organized.[107]

This new draft eliminated all "jargon," keeping only "Human Association" because that was the key to the whole reorientation the younger group was proposing.[108]

> The [Doorn] meeting therefore attempted to formulate a new way of thinking about urbanism that would consider each problem as an entity, as a unique example of Human Association at a particular time and in a particular place. It was felt that only within such a concept of urbanism could Habitat be studied.[109]
>
> To comprehend the human associations we must consider every community as a particular *total* complex.[110]

Bakema accepted this draft of "Instructions to Groups," sending it out to all CIAM groups along with a sample grille created by Voelcker. But he still felt a need for greater precision, and wrote to the English Group reiterating the Dutch position and requesting inclusion:

> I think that we are right by telling that each problem of habitat must be studied as part of a field of human associations. But the tools we use to recognise the background of human association are in our time—interrelationship (doorstep)/growth and change/aesthetics of number/and I think we have to underline these aspects for the commission[s].[111]

Although he accepted the English Group's determination to control the wording and method of research sent as instructions to would-be attendees of CIAM 10, he wanted to add the Dutch supplements. Bakema wrote an explanation of this position to the Harvard "professors" (Giedion, Gropius, and Sert):

> More precise directives were proposed by the Dutch part of the CIAM 10 committee but refused by the English part.

> It is therefore that van Eyck and me took the responsibility for a Dutch supplement by which groups are invited to give their own more precise ideas about the work of proposed working parties.
>
> ...
>
> CIAM 10 has to define the existence of new fields of human associations, expressed by new patterns in architectural planning.
>
> This is by recognizing the Key problems, indicated by the words: interrelationship (of inner and outer space f.e.) [for example]./aesthetics of number (repetition, rhythm, f.e.)/growth and change (flexibility f.e.).
>
> You find this in the document I hope you received already.[112]

The English Group was quick to write to Giedion to protest the idea of circulating Bakema's document and other Dutch Group corrections as supplements to the Instructions:

> This [final draft] represents Team 10's agreed basis. The English Group is firm in their belief that the important thing is to produce projects which contribute some small thing to our understanding of the problems of Human Association. ... Our aim is simple, to discover archetypal groupings of dwellings which are as vital for our society as were squares, streets, kraals, etc., in other societies.[113]

The "elders" were not pleased with the internal disputes that Bakema reported. Giedion wrote: "we are not well satisfied with the program of Team 10, but we agreed to pay and so we will go forward."[114] He worried that CIAM 10 would not be well organized, would not present precise ideas, that "human association" was too vague a term to produce concrete results. Alison and Peter Smithson responded:

> Perhaps we should not find it surprising that the "old guard" are worried about the "spiritual and material organization of the Congress" for it was just for that reason—to change *their* organization—that we took on our task.[115]

CIAM's old guard had been sufficiently worried over these skirmishes and imprecise terminology to suggest CIAM 10 be postponed at least until 1956 while the younger organizers prepared.[116] This suggestion to change the date annoyed the Smithsons. They believed it suited only the "professors" at Harvard, not the needs of the Congress.[117] There had already been a flurry of letters over the designated meeting place (Algiers). It seemed to many members a dubious spot for a meeting, and after the War of Independence broke out in late 1954 it became impossible. The Congress was postponed indefinitely, until the Yugoslavian Group suggested they host CIAM 10. They were ready to organize a boat from Venice to Dubrovnik and back again.[118] The organizers accepted this invitation.

Yet the elders continued to be worried. A few months before CIAM 10 was convened, on June 12, 1956, Sert wrote a letter to Le Corbusier and other members of the Advisory Council, as well as to a few Team 10 members.[119] He felt that CIAM 10 would be an important meeting, but he placed CIAM under "a moral obligation" to see that its historical record be accurately relayed, since past actions were coming under increasing criticism by the youngers. It was also important to discuss the proposed changes in the organization of CIAM. Thus Sert proposed that the elders meet beforehand at the Storione Hotel, Padua, on August 2–3, to plan for their involvement in CIAM 10 and develop a carefully organized final program of work.

CIAM 10 met in Dubrovnik, August 5–11, 1956. Le Corbusier did not attend this Congress, but he sent Sert a letter on July 23 reiterating his opinion that CIAM ought to dissolve the organizational Commissions set up at Bergamo, allowing the distinction between real workers and hangers-on to become apparent.[120] Le Corbusier believed the new generation (i.e., those no more than 40 years old in 1956) ought to be responsible for the "metamorphosis" of CIAM 10, for they were the only representatives qualified as actors on this new stage of CIAM who were dedicated to solving the problems of the times. And so he passed the baton to the younger generation, hoping that they would keep the language of modern architecture alive and worth inheriting by a future generation of architects.

Things at CIAM 10 did not go as well as Le Corbusier or the Organizing Committee hoped. In fact, the atmosphere was poisonous. The elders decided at Padua that the focus of CIAM 10 be limited to one issue only: the preparation of a *Charte de l'Habitat* based on a prolegomenon written by Giedion. They also decided that the Congress would proceed with two different groups operating in tandem. The older CIAM members would form one group, drawing together materials from CIAM congresses 1928–1955 (the historical record), while another group, comprising Team 10 members and like-minded persons, would study the grilles submitted to CIAM 10 and extract from them "new material about relations." This second group would have four subcommittees, each focusing on a type of "interrelation" already suggested by Bakema: (1) organic unity, or Van Eyck's concept of "doorstep," (2) the problem of mobility, of interest to the Smithsons, (3) the problem of "growth and change" or the "aesthetics of number," a particular Dutch concern, and (4) urbanism as related to habitat, which Candilis had proposed.[121]

The older generation thus effectively split CIAM into two factions: those (mostly younger) who focused on analyzing grilles, mainly submitted by Team 10 members; and those (mostly older) who debated with greater intensity whether CIAM should continue or not, and if not, how to make certain its legacy was clear.[122]

The younger members of CIAM 10 set about analyzing the 39 grilles or grids submitted under their laboriously worked-out "Instructions." The grilles were hung in groups of association (isolate, village, town, and city) and supposedly studied by the four groups called for in Padua, although it is difficult to discern how this system actually operated.

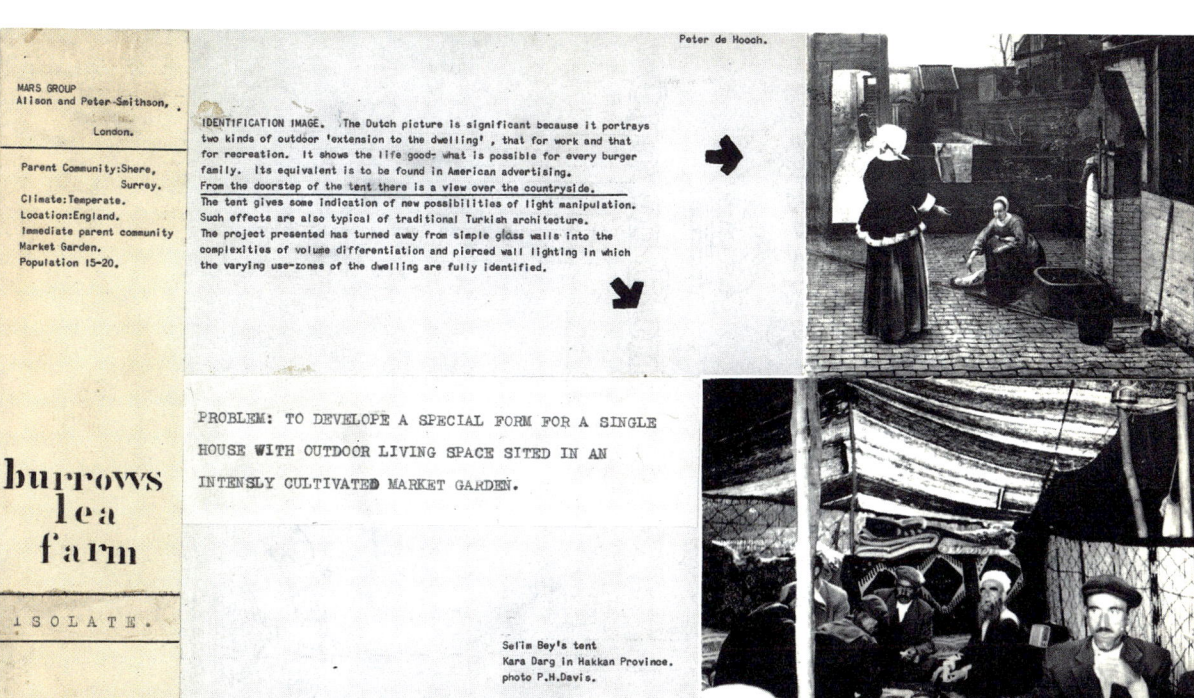

2.4–2.8 (above and following pages)

Themes related to Valley Section of the Doorn manifesto that appear in Alison and Peter Smithson, CIAM grille for CIAM 10 (1956): figure 2.4, Isolate and extensions to dwelling: Bates House (known as Burrows Lea Farm), Yorkshire Dales Hamlets; figure 2.5, Galleon Cottages, Yorkshire Dales Village and OUTRAGE; figure 2.6, Village: Fold houses infill for Village; figure 2.7, Town: Close Houses riding the landscape; figure 2.8, City: South Facing Terraced Houses). Smithson Family Collection.

MARS GROUP
Alison and Peter Smithson.
London.

Parent Community:
Bainbridge,
North Riding,
Yorkshire.
Location: England.
Climate: temperate upland.
Population: 150.

galleon
cottages

1

Typical standard housing which is universally applied without reference to location or type of community.

Staithes: North Riding of Yorkshire shewing 19th century additions on cliff top.

OUTRAGE

IDENTIFICATION IMAGE. These images are symbols of the collapse of a village building tradition and the total failure of architects to find specific solutions.
In England the concentration on the 'planning' of the dwelling has prevented the recognition that the standard Council House units were:-
1/. not things in themselves.
2/. cannot be considered in vacuo (outside specific environment.)
3/. incapable of addition into any significant pattern.

the tradition

MARS GROUP
Alison and Peter Smithson.
London.

Parent Community:
West Burton,
North Riding,
Yorkshire.
Location: England
Climate: temperate upland.
Population: 350

fold
houses

VILLAGE.

1

TIREE: croft community. 1/Preservation of the terrain and herbage.
2/. a family of dwellings.

PROBLEM: TO INVENT A "TYPE HOUSE" FOR USE IN INFIL DEVELOPMENT IN A VILLAGE.

POROS: Identical unit 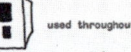 used throughout (other island villages have their own unit) give an identity of coherence - like red apples on a tree.

MARS GROUP
Alison and Peter Smithson
London.
Parent Community: New Town
Location: England.
Climate: Temperate.
Population: 40-60,000.

close houses

TOWN.

1

Tents at Crimean War.
Water holes - Sahara. 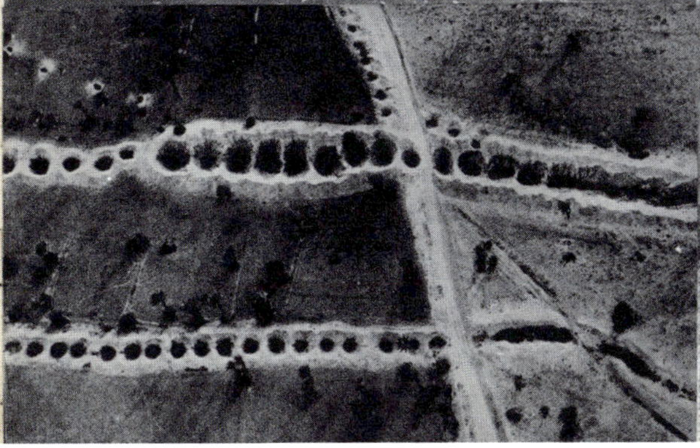
Yard pattern - Holland.

IDENTIFICATION IMAGE.
These shew the possibilities of free-moving linear arrangement of elements and the aptness of the yard idea to the human habitat.

PROBLEM: TO DEVELOPE A NEW TYPE OF COVERED STREET SUITABLE FOR A NEW TOWN.

MARS GROUP
Alison and Peter Smithson
London.
Parent Community: London.
Location: England.
Climate: Temperate.
Population: 8 million.

south facing terraced houses

CITY.

1

The two servicing vehicles are symbolic of the traditional "street" way of living in a city. Our problem is to make a new system of "streets" to the standards of our new means of transport.

Servicing London Streets.
(Bethnal Green 1952)

THE PROBLEM: TO CREATE A TYPE OF COMMUNITY SUB-DIVISION SUITABLE FOR INFILL DELEOPMENT IN A LARGE CITY. A TYPE WHICH CAN BE PUT INTO AN EXISTING RECTANGULAR TOWN PATTERN WITHOUT EITHER LOOSING.

By now Alison and Peter Smithson were expressing their opinions vociferously: they submitted five grilles in order to fully explain their advocated patterns of association, each with its "appreciated unit," now referred to as a visually identifiable group or "cluster."

The Dutch accused the Smithsons of revealing a "sentimental Regionalism" at CIAM 10; a close examination of their five four-panel grilles shows why.[123] The first panel of each grille comprises an "identification image" or two, and a stated problem to solve. For example, the first panel, "Burrows Lea Farm" (the "isolate" grille), had two images: first, a Pieter de Hooch (1629–1684) image of two Dutch women in an exterior patio extending the house for work and recreation, the equivalent of images found, the Smithsons contended, in American advertisements; and second, an image of a typical Turkish tent structure, modulating sunlight and piercing the wall with extended views over the countryside. The "problem" to be solved: what visual form should a single-family house with outdoor living space take if sited in an intensively cultivated market garden? Its "development pattern" is explained in the second panel: being located within such a garden, this "type" had no need for a private garden, and the car could move inside the ground level of the house "like a yacht in its mooring," allowing views over the countryside from the second floor. There was a "historical parallel," as evidenced in the accompanying photograph of a dwelling (Castle Rising) surrounded by a raised earthwork in Norfolk, England. The third panel presents a plan and section of the house, while the fourth panel, "Contribution to the Aim of the Congress," read as follows: "SIGNIFICANT IMAGE: Earth moving is one of the most effective ways of moulding the land to make the immediate environment suit the human habitat. It provides a point of contact with pre-history."[124]

Alison and Peter would later admit: "Of all the isolated houses we designed in the 1950s and 1960s, this [the Burrows Lea Farm] is the house we should most like to have built."[125] By sitting lightly on the land, this

> "floating form" … "possesses" this everyday landscape, compound of every age, in its own, new spirit—by a single bold act—extending its aesthetic of structuring of spaces into that landscape.
>
> Appreciation of the English landscape requires any house's windows to have "eyebrows" against the glare of our overcast skies—in the way that the Regency verandah came into being as soon as the house extended out into the garden as foreground to the greater landscape. Lattice screens appear for the first time in our work in the antiglare clerestory lights.[126]

The other four Smithson grilles examine Fold Houses, an infill type house for a small village; Galleon Cottages, an infill type for a larger village; Close Houses, a new type suitable for a new town; and South Facing Terrace Houses, a type of community subdivision for infill development in a large city. Images of regional architecture accompany each grille: for example, houses on the Greek island of Poros offer an image of coherence likened to "apples on a tree," an image labeled "Outrage" points to a typical council housing site incapable of addition to any significant pattern, and images of tents in the Crimean War, water holes in the Sahara, and a repeat of the Pieter de Hooch image all reveal "possibilities of free-moving linear arrangement of elements and the nature of the yard idea in human habitat."[127] Finally, Henderson's photographs of servicing vehicles in Bethnal Green (1952) "are symbols of the traditional 'street' ways of living in the city."[128] The Smithsons' stated aim was to establish a new approach to urbanism in all five grilles through historical, even primitive precedents, revealing "clarity of organization, that is comprehensibility."[129] Yet quixotic text-image juxtapositions—houses surrounded by earthworks, clusters of Greek island habitats, nomadic tents as "Significant Images"—appear to reflect English Picturesque and regional values far from being "radical" and "new" sources of art.

Working Together as Team 10

No matter how much the members of Team 10 may have disagreed about the "Instructions," or how seriously they took their debates, all appeared intent on capturing their developing thoughts in meaningful language, pursuing a back-and-forth between tentative image and words until both became precise. The process was interactive: they learned from each other as one introduced a term and another challenged it, ricocheting off each other, adopting or rejecting, transforming and distilling.

Thus, the Smithsons utilized the word "cluster" in Dubrovnik to express the idea that each pattern of development was free yet systematized, that each habitat responded to a specific environment or particular situation.[130] They had discovered "the complete image system, for an order with a structure and a certain tension, where every piece was correspondingly new in a new system of relationship" in the works of both Jackson Pollock and Eduardo Paolozzi.[131] They extended this discovery to their architectural projects, believing that every form of association had to have a correlated settlement pattern.

The Dutch, for their part, offered the concepts "growth and change," "the aesthetics of number," and "doorstep," which reverberated across the Team 10 discussions. These corresponded to what Giedion would later call the four options broached by Team 10 in the revision of CIAM doctrines: "the twin notions of individual liberty and communal order" combined with the desire for "frenzied change" and the "wish for constancy."[132]

Uncertainty over the future of CIAM, and the fact that members of the younger generation were responding to and learning from each other, prompted the Smithsons at the end of August 1956 to send a note to their colleagues in which they referred to themselves as "Team 10 England."[133] They expressed delight that an alternative was being developed within CIAM by the new generation, taking the ecological approach: "Doing the right thing—if necessary destructive—in the particular, Human, Physical and Built situation (Growth and Change)."[134] This generation sought control over development in a much freer, collaborative way: imposing an attitude, not a plan, and developing a "briefing technique" (Cluster) and a technique of social prognosis focused on communications and power (Mobility).[135]

Despite this optimism, worries over CIAM's future pressed on Alison and Peter as they continued to circulate their opinions of what to do next. "At Dubrovnik one had the feeling that the 'Team 10 Idea' was being compromised, but it was never quite clear in what way."[136] A few months' time allowed their reflections to be more objective. First: "We must make a complete break with the name CIAM. In CIAM 'Architecture Moderne' has a specific meaning, the aesthetic of 1920's. This aesthetic is dead."[137] Second, they could agree with the aims of the old CIAM but not the means, not its "diagrammatic thinking" (i.e., "Cartesian layouts for cities," "public ownership of the land"). The Smithsons' way of thinking had, they said, changed; they now thought it far better to make CIAM part of history, and start a new group with new aims and a new name reflecting a new attitude.

> The words we commonly use,
> radical
> pragmatic
> non-diagrammatic
> non-geometric
> reflect our desire to create an architecture which is the image of a new ideal in society, a society of free, dynamic, change and growth.[138]

Maybe it would be sufficient to call the new organization simply "TEAM." TEAM XI (Structure of Communities) TEAM XII (Domestic Equipment) A.S.O., [and so on] each title reflecting a change of composition of the team to suit changing objectives, which reflects our general attitude.[139]

Thinking ahead to the next meeting (the Otterlo meeting, 1959), they argued that a "new CIAM of 30 [participants]" was wrong. Each TEAM meeting should be constructed specially for that meeting and should not consist of architects only, but be divided into two parts, an ideological one and a practical one. Thus engineers, historians, critics, and specialists in all sorts of fields could participate in part one, allowing only architects and associated technicians to meet in part two.[140]

By March 1957, the Smithsons were ready to declare the end of CIAM publicly, in a self-styled "manifesto" titled "CIAM Reorganization or Dissolution?"[141] Yet the new group of younger architects had yet to define its aims, so its members needed to work together with greater intensity. This was not possible within a CIAM-type formal organization, with its dispersal of energy. An informal contact group would be better, and there would be plenty of time to develop such an organization once the group (i.e., Team 10) decided what they wanted to do.[142] Within a few days, Team 10 England was circulating the Smithsons' "manifesto" over the signatures of Howell, Lasdun, the Smithsons, and Voelcker.[143]

Meanwhile (mid-April 1957) the "professors" at Harvard (Sert, Gropius, Giedion, and Tyrwhitt) sent a letter to Bakema, the liaison with Team 10. They suggested that an "Exchange Information Center" could be set up by the younger generation employing the same *initials* as CIAM. Thus, the younger members could begin to explore their research ideas on the visual problems of the human habitat without deploying the *full name* of CIAM. During this period of reorganization all official Congresses would be suspended.[144]

The "professors" soon sent a more strident letter to the Smithsons (May 1957). Why did the English Group think they could publish or circulate discussions about the dissolution of CIAM?

> The majority of the members of the Reorganization Committee, elected at Dubrovnik, were drawn from this Team 10, but it seems that some of them have forgotten that attitudes suitable to members of the opposition cannot always be maintained when they have taken over the responsibilities of government.[145]
>
> Everybody knows that during the last thirty years something like a modern tradition in architecture has come into being, and that now—to quote a recurrent phrase of J. Robert Oppenheimer in his present lecture series discussing the effects of recent discoveries in physics—"it is not a question of abandoning the old, but of supplementing and transcending it."[146]

Though reprimanded, the Smithson continued their opposition, sending a letter to their Team 10 colleagues expressing regret that they would be absent from the organization meeting at La Sarraz in September 1957: "Since CIAM 10 at Dubrovnik we have felt many times about CIAM that 'one can only recreate what one loves by repudiating it'; this is why we felt it necessary to be fiercely polemic about a new sort of international organization."[147] A few days later they wrote out their proposition for naming the new formation of architects, suggesting it be called "CICON": "The word CICON is derived from CIAM Continuity/Continuità/Contuit."[148] This proposal was followed by two typewritten pages, unsigned but written by Peter, explaining that the driving force behind the CIAM idea of 1928 had been the machine. Now, however, it was necessary to make the word "function" include so-called "irrational" and "symbolic" values, and to allow architecture to give meaning to the space around buildings—this in the context of the whole community.

> This is what Bakema calls "urbanism through architecture" and what I call "socio-plastics."
>
> This idea *is* the new driving-force. And this is why the old CIAM—created as a tool to serve a different idea—must be changed.[149]

Aldo van Eyck sent a long, acerbic, undated letter to the Smithsons explaining that he found "the whole thing 'sickening like muddy water'." He had

> no desire to continue Team 10 activity if we can't get over this kind of shoddiness (action shoddiness) I thought all was clear—hard-sharpened-clean after London. How I abhor this kind of soft—arbitrary—sloppy-licking every arse that budges its fat at you attitude.[150]

He was referring to the question of whom they should invite to the next meeting [at Otterlo] and whom they should say no to. He noted that Bakema's habit of writing "pink epistles" (referring to the color of paper he used) was very compromising. Van Eyck had already suggested to Bakema that they should use the letters B.T.C. ("Building and Town Construction") as a label in place of "CIAM" or "Team 10."

> I used the letters B.T.C. = Building and Town Construction as stop gap symbol. …
> I said: look Jaap. Here's a B.T.C. team called Team 10. There are from time to time B.T.C. team gatherings such as we had in London. Then at longer intervals B.T.C. Team 10 feels that it would be good to discuss B.T.C. problems among a larger group of *carefully selected* B.T.C. participants (ca 30).[151]

Van Eyck had also suggested creating a B.T.C. postbox for those who wanted to communicate with each other but he warned that they must, however, be careful about whom they allowed to use the postbox and not send pink letters to those "who should go to hell," since the letters might become spy sheets.[152] It is unclear who he thought were spies, but clear how he meant to apply the initials he proposed: B.T.C. participants; B.T.C. ideas, problems and plans; B.T.C. meetings, discussion, activity; B.T.C. publications; B.T.C. postbox: "*it's all one thing, our thing* and not another thing each time or anybody's thing. It's *US* and *building and town construction.* God it's as simple as that what is less simple doesn't belong to it."[153]

Otterlo (September 1959)

Had Team 10 been so split at Dubrovnik that it could no longer exist under the umbrella of CIAM, or was it possible to find a way of continuing? It appears that members both wanted to continue and wanted to change. The name "Team 10," whether one liked it or not, remained in everyone's mind. While proclaiming that its roots lay in CIAM, the group was trying to produce a new theory and imagery of town building. Sometime in 1958, an unsigned proclamation was sent out about the group's name and a plan for working together. It said, in part:

> This field of forces is now represented by the work of: Costa, Scharoun, Kahn, Smithson, Bakema, Johansen, Erskine, Utzon. Therefore these constitute the new Team 10.

Only they can hold together a movement. They will take over the Reorganisation Committee to call the Congress in their own name.[154]

By May 3, 1958, Bakema had sent out forty-three invitations to the next working congress of CIAM, to be held at Kröller-Müller Museum in Otterlo, in September 1959.[155] The Smithsons, however, were still obstinate. They wrote to Bakema to explain again their feeling that a smaller number of people should meet very quietly, and that the effort to make the list mimic an "international representation system" was arbitrary, with too many unknown people. They would like, of course, to join the meeting in September 1959, but only if relatively few people accepted Bakema's invitation. They suggested that the group fall back on the "old" Team 10, more or less, with a few select people—Louis Kahn, Paul Rudolph, Hans Scharoun, Ralph Erskine, Lúcio Costa, John Johansen, John Vitsur, and so on.[156]

By September a separate problem arose: the Smithsons did not want to invite the Italian Group to the meeting, because it had opposed the reclassification into patterns of association for CIAM 10 and its leader, Ernesto Rogers, believed the new CIAM should not break with the old. Peter Smithson announced that he was now willing to accept, albeit reluctantly, that a list of 40 be invited to Otterlo—but he also explained: "You know I am *not* willing to go on unless some way can be found of getting rid of Uncle Ernesto & other corrupted or 'consumer' type people. I think it can be done!!"[157]

The Smithsons sent a letter to Lúcio Costa, Ray and Charles Eames, Ralph Erskine, Philip Johnson, John Johansen, Louis Kahn, Paul Rudolph, and Hans Scharoun, whom they hoped might be interested in the "new CIAM," expressing their wish to communicate with like minds working on similar problems. The letter asked its readers if they were interested in a more formal or organized exchange of ideas.[158]

Philip Johnson replied: "We could have a grand time and naturally I will join in anything that is around since I would rather join things than be a spoil sport."[159] Paul Rudolph was also sympathetic to the idea of communicating more directly, but unsympathetic to the idea that any of these activities be called the "new CIAM."[160] Ralph Erskine was more

2.9
Max Risselada at opening of the exhibition "Team 10 1953–1981: In Search of a Utopia of the Present," NAi, Rotterdam, 2005. Photograph by M. C. Boyer.

sympathetic to the "new CIAM,"[161] and Johansen was even more interested in the stress on urbanism. The prize invitee, Louis Kahn, sent a Western Union Cablegram: "Agree Heartily with New Group ... Agree to Attend Otterlo I will find Funds to come ... = Louis I Kahn."[162]

And so Team 10 met in Otterlo in 1959, with Bakema as coordinator of a loosely organized group of 43 attendees. The resulting discussions were too diverse to be coherent, and some attendees decided it was time to resign from CIAM—indeed, to end the organization. As we have seen, Giedion's open letter the next year reiterated that Team 10 could not abolish CIAM, only the general assembly of CIAM could do so, but Aldo van Eyck's reply carried the day:

> I think it's true that we learnt how to fly from you people. Stop shouting this around all the time. We can fly ourselves now, with you perhaps. Now that we can fly we don't want to do so in quite the same way (we're men not birds) as you taught us, but we're thankful for what you did. Yet we're not sure you taught us to fly in the right way nor are we sure that you taught us to fly in the right direction. I for my part know that both the method and the route were wrong. Not only in the light of to-day but also in the light of yesterday. The story of modern architecture—let alone urbanism— is terrifyingly weak, hollow, rational and abstract if you compare it to avant-gardism in other creative fields of art and science—it follows the 20th-century political story more than the spiritual-creative one. Architecture and urbanism especially have simply sidetracked the main issue of constituent contemporary thinking.[163]

III. Conclusion

In an archival box of the Smithsons' writings, records of evolving thoughts not yet fully developed, lie a few pages by Alison on the 1950s, marked as a "50s field of enquiry" but not specified as when written. The 1950s was, she writes, a time of ferment:

> Our thoughts tended to touch on everything, because everything seemed worth looking at seriously. ... Our enquiring as to its worth, its necessity, its role in society, was not in any sense political but through wanting to know what our society really wanted ... to be able to foresee how these aspirations would affect patterns of associations, patterns of mobility, the look of places, and so on.[164]

New sensibilities were rooted in the 1950s, and Alison admits that "Team 10 quietly— perhaps too privately—attended to the growth of the new sensibilities."[165]

By the Smithsons' own account, they began their architectural careers "in an unbelievably arid period ... there was nothing, anywhere."[166] That is, the period was arid because they had nothing to build and little inspiration to draw on from older architects. The Smithsons therefore used writing and publication as a way to create.

Also as a way of finding out what it is we have ... this—as far as Team 10 [members] were concerned—meant discovering the nature of what it was we had together as distinct from what we were apart. Our own graphics are always generated by what we are saying and how we want to say it; each "document" is an invention of communication. We were incredibly fortunate with the openness to ideas shown by Monica Pidgeon who created the Heroic Days of *Architectural Design*. ... Not least in choosing to assist her first Theo Crosby, next Kenneth Frampton, then Robin Middleton. Again I must touch on the scene before the Heroic Days of *AD*.[167]

Thus, running parallel to the intramural Team 10 discourse of the 1950s is another, contained in the pages of *AD* and written by Alison and Peter Smithson, to which we turn in the next chapter. The Smithsons' voice had dominated at Dubrovnik, sharpened by their search for the "Significant Image" and for what Peter described as "socio-plastics," but the problem remained: could they achieve a new architecture of "associated ideas" that melded image and ethics?

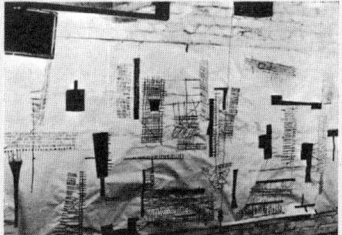

It was necessary in the early '50's to look to the works of painter Pollock and sculptor Paolozzi for a complete image system, for an order with a structure and a certain tension, where every piece was correspondingly new in a new system of relationship.

It is our thesis that for every form of association there is an inherent pattern of building.

The first study was at the relatively simple level of association—the village. It concerned itself with 'infill'—the placing of new dwellings in and around the old village in such a way as to revalidate the existing pattern.

Above: West Burton, Yorkshire
Below: village infilling all round the fringe, at the ends of the secondary access system. The new is placed over the old like a new plant growing through old branches—or new fruit on old twigs. The fold is a wind break. Each house has its back thus to the prevailing wind. This instead of the 'housing Manual' type house, sent down from the suburbs—a barrow boy on the fells.

Typical addition to a village irrespective of location

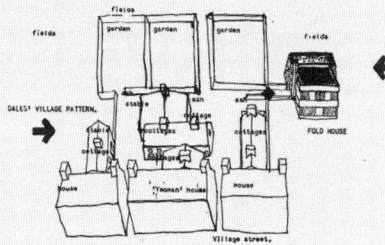
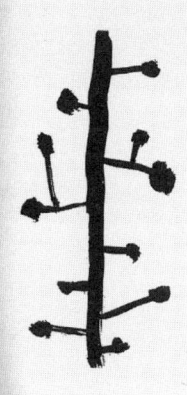
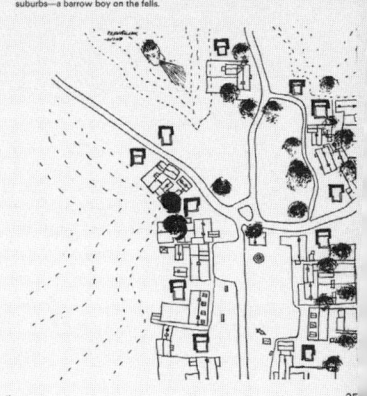

3.1

Alison Smithson, "Ideogram of infill to a village—completing and making clear an old structure so it can serve today's needs. A.M.S. 1959."
Alison and Peter Smithson, *Urban Structuring* (London: Studio Vista; New York: Reinhold, 1967), 34–35. Smithson Family Collection.

3
Thoughts Touching Everything

Leaf through a dictionary or try to make one, and you will find that every word covers and masks a well so bottomless that the questions you toss into it arouse no more than an echo.
Paul Valéry[1]

Prologue

In the 1950s, Alison and Peter Smithson were critical of the shortcomings of modern architects who lived off worn-out beliefs vested in rational diagrams and the geometry of the right angle. They examined and interpreted with fresh eyes the situation "as found," formulated a new "aesthetics of change," and offered a new set of keywords. This chapter studies the conceptual language of Alison and Peter Smithson as expressed in articles published in *Architectural Design* (*AD*) (1950s–1960s). It examines their associative modes of thought, how they deployed a special graphics of communication, utilized multievocative images, and argued over the meaning and sources of New Brutalism. They learned from sociologists and anthropologists how people lived and dwelled, then turned back to the language of architecture, hoping to modernize it intellectually, bringing it up to date with concerns drawn from London slums and Algerian *bidonvilles*.

I. Associative Modes of Thought

The postwar, younger generation of European architects—Peter Smithson claimed in 1958—wanted an "active socio-plastics ... rather than old style rational":

> As to its imagery, the magic having flown from the rectangle it is much freer in its use of form, more rough and ready, and less complete and classical.[2] ...
>
> Its key words are: *cluster, growth, change* and *mobility.* Around which stones you can roll your own snowballs.[3]

Where did this penchant for coining keywords come from, this desire to replace the modernists' diagrams of measurement and functionality with more natural, open-ended forms based on new relationships and processes? This was a quest made manifest in their "as found aesthetic" and their focus on process in Team 10 discussions. In response to this need they conceived an "open" aesthetic, a "living extension" of the "closed aesthetic" of functionalism in which form follows function as a glove fits the hand. Rejecting closure and any mechanical concept of order, the Smithsons passionately believed that right architectural order would reflect complex ties with the realities of the world, though not in the "closed," mechanical manner of pure functionalism. Theirs would be an experience-oriented theory, allowing everyday conditions to counter modernist abstraction and rationalization and taking projects back to first principles, sensitive to the contexts in which they were placed.

Seeking a new imagery, the Smithsons drew inspiration from images of Jackson Pollock's spatter paintings, first seen by Peter in Peggy Guggenheim's Palazzo Venier dei Leoni, Venice, in 1949: "It was revelatory."[4] They may also have viewed Pollock's work at the 1953 exhibition "Opposing Forces" at the Institute of Contemporary Arts, where one of his unstretched canvases hung limply over an entire end wall. In any case, Pollock soon became a new hero, praised by the Smithsons for subverting formalistic artistic conventions, for replacing the universalizing grid of the picture plane with an all-over open-ended painting of huge scale and expanse, and for adding "gesture" to the notion of design.[5]

The sculptor Eduardo Paolozzi, a fellow member of the Independent Group, also influenced the Smithsons in their search for images of the time (see chapter 2). Paolozzi gave autonomy to each image, allowing the spectator to draw spontaneous parallels from image to image, as in a scrapbook.[6] In the Smithsons' view, not only had scientists and artists revealed a new landscape that could inspire architectural expressions and reenergize urbanistic ideals, they had enabled an aesthetic based on open-ended associations between images, allowing analogical leaps via novel juxtapositions and parallels. "It was necessary in the early '50's," they claimed, "to look to the work of painter Pollock and sculptor Paolozzi for a complete image system, for an order with a structure and a certain tension, where every piece was correspondingly new in a new system of relationship. … It is our thesis that for every form of association there is an inherent pattern of building."[7]

Graphics of Communication

The Smithsons also drew lessons from Paul Klee (1879–1940).[8] His *Pedagogical Sketchbook* (translated into English in 1953 by Sibyl Moholy-Nagy) taught them how shapes worked together, making possible a new ordering of image making.[9] Klee took hold of a void and charged it with potency: the line took a walk, an arrow became a trace of energy, condensing, displacing, and elaborating. Openly indebted to Klee, the Smithsons developed "ideograms" in the 1950s; their "streets-in-the-air," "cluster of street-twigs," and "cluster diagrams" showed how the coming-together of images generates new forms, indicates new patterns of association, of use, of identity, and of movement, making a building's ordering comprehensible yet open to change.[10]

David Sylvester, an art critic and friend of Nigel Henderson and Eduardo Paolozzi, had reviewed Klee's use of ideograms in 1951 in Sartre's monthly *Les Temps Modernes*. (Given his connections, it is likely, though not certain, that the Smithsons read his review.) He noted that Klee abandoned a single focal point in preference for an all-over treatment of signs and symbols which held multiple significations.

> No other artist has used the multievocative sign … to establish associations so unconventional and unexpected or to make his associations appear so inevitable.[11]
>
> … The function in this system of the multievocative signs is to draw attention to resemblances between diverse objects, just as in life one kind of object frequently reminds us of another, seen some time beforehand …[12]

Though Klee had been dead for over a decade, his influence was strong in London in the early 1950s. An exhibition of Klee's drawings at the ICA in the fall of 1953 was accompanied by a symposium on his *Pedagogical Sketchbook*. Victor Pasmore, an abstract artist, IG member, and symposium attendee, assessed Klee's influence as follows:

> The study of nature which Klee proposes … is not of the kind which tradition expects of the artist. If anatomy and perspective are considered it is not in relation to external effects as in traditional textbooks, but as analogies of internal processes. … This implies that the representation of things seen was not his concern. It is what the painting becomes that matters. If the *Sketchbook* can be described as an anatomy, therefore, it is not the anatomy of Nature's effects, but of its processes. As such its teaching centres around how to think, rather than how to see.[13]

Klee's teachings, Pasmore said, focused on the act of marking a pictured surface, and his marks were inherently dynamic. Form was the result of "growth and change." Klee was interested in processes of becoming, and this interest—Pasmore said, and Reyner Banham reiterated—had turned him into the most quoted source in recent seminars at the ICA.

The Smithsons, in their turn, claimed that Paul Klee invented an "intellectually indicative graphics,"

> not as a notation of people and vehicle movement, useful to urbanists, but a teaching graphic to convey the ability of shapes to work together—as if the rasping legs of a grasshopper—to put over a message that a new ordering was possible and moreover, that this new ordering had been invented. … The personal graphs of Klee taught our generation to sense the self-ordaining power that resides within ideas at the moment of their inception, when they are returned from the as-yet-invented into the fabric of the new vision.[14]

In developing their graphics of movement the Smithsons borrowed more directly from Louis Kahn's vehicular movement patterns, especially his "stop-go" system and the deck and bridge infrastructure he designed for the center of Philadelphia. They deployed these notations in their Berlin Hauptstadt road system project (1958)[15] and invited Kahn to the Otterlo meeting of the nascent Team 10 the next year, wanting to learn more about his notational system. And when Alison Smithson assembled the "Team 10 Primer" in 1962, she inserted some of Kahn's staccato vehicular-movement graphics to illustrate the text. Kahn, she said,

> managed a graphic trick of illustrating new ways of thinking about character patterns in traffic movement: this graphic was teacher.[16]
>
> Kahn saw further: that rhythms of vehicular movement offer a programme for a formal ordering of the city as indicatively obvious as his favourite Carcassonne, among other medieval orderings of city walls and entrances defensible against assault by bows and arrows, slings and swords. And that an ordering of traffic has a potential for places of particular space within the city fabric; as in his much drawn Siena. Essential that slower paced places could but enhance and preserve those quality enclaves a city possesses.[17]

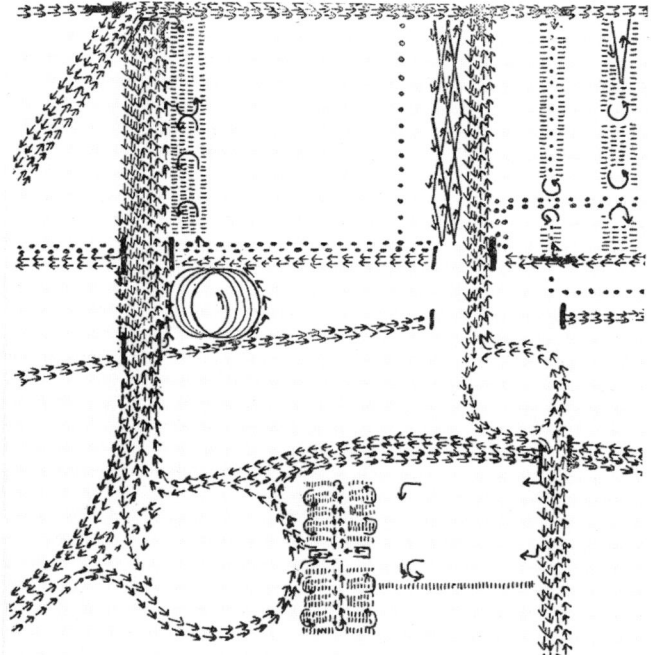

3.2
Louis Kahn, Philadelphia city traffic movement pattern. In Alison and Peter Smithson, *Urban Structuring* (London: Studio Vista; New York: Reinhold, 1967), 79. Smithson Family Collection.

The Smithsons also found inspiration in the visually fresh wallpaper of Arne Jacobsen, with its movement between date twig and round-leaf creeper, "a graphic that seemed to suggest pause-walk-pause."[18] These notations helped the Smithsons develop an "angular graphic of pedestrian linkage between associations of dwellings at a high density," places where pedestrians reigned supreme: close houses (i.e., houses accessed by pedestrian ways only) and covered way routes, with incident blobs expressing enter-walk into the dry-center.[19]

They were still discussing the impact of Kahn's graphics at a Team 10 meeting in 1962. Alison asked rhetorically:

> What is it that we see in Kahn? We trust Kahn's shape[s] because he has done diagrams of Philadelphia, which we feel have a message for us, and we trust Kahn rather blindly, I think. Because his buildings no more fulfil what he says, really, —I'm thinking particularly of this [Salk] laboratory which he is now doing, with the community house, which is just like Hadrian's Villa.[20]

Despite the Salk Laboratory, Kahn's graphics had been an informative teacher and enabled the Smithsons to make their own ideas manifest. Graphic notational systems and written texts, Alison said, went hand in hand.

> Writing—and the making of the graphics of communication—is used by us to identify and define and to pre-digest ideas, so that by the time we come to make a building some distance has been put between ourselves and the original impulses for change. In architecture, distance is essential if any building is to become more than one idea thick and become sufficiently dense to serve more than one generation.
>
> The graphics we apply to our writing—and to our communication in general—is to help ourselves have ready in our hands a skill of putting into an order that transmutes into shape.[21]

As a gift to each Team 10 member at CIAM 10 (Dubrovnik, 1956), the Smithsons offered a copy of a meter-long scroll illustrated with their indicative graphics. They organized the scroll around the stenciled keywords "identity," "association," "cluster," and "mobility." At the top of the scroll they placed a diagram of "urban structuring plan for a small city," identified as taken from their Urban Re-Identification Document (1952). This was followed by Alison Smithson's 1951 "Cluster Diagram of involuntary/voluntary Association," then by her 1951 "Cluster Diagram of Association" and by a diagram of linear close houses arranged in a freely moving pattern that responded to topography and landscape features, e.g., mature trees and rolling ground.[22] The "cluster arrow" diagram, which indicated that a cluster contained the house, hamlet, village, and city housing types, toward the fulfillment of which their work was moving, was the closest thing to a direct borrow from Klee in the scroll. Next came diagrams for "Terraced Crescent Housing" (1955) and finally a diagram explaining how a new town could keep

ASSOCIATION: AIX JUNE '53. GRILLE BY A. AND P.S.
TOWN STRUCTURE.
THIS GRILLE IS CONCERNED WITH THE PROBLEM OF IDENTITY. IT PROPOSES THAT
A COMMUNITY SHOULD BE BUILT UP FROM A HIERARCHY OF ASSOCIATIONAL
ELEMENTS AND TRIES TO EXPRESS THE VARIOUS LEVELS OF ASSOCIATION:—
THE HOUSE, THE STREET,
THE DISTRICT, THE CITY.

IT IS IMPORTANT TO REALISE THAT THE TERMS USED, STREET, DISTRICT, ETC.,
ARE NOT TO BE TAKEN AS THE REALITY BUT AS THE IDEA, AND THAT IT IS
OUR TASK TO FIND NEW EQUIVALENTS FOR THESE FORMS OF ASSOCIATION FOR
OUR NEW NON-DEMONSTRATIVE SOCIETY.

THE PROBLEM OF RE-IDENTIFYING MAN WITH HIS ENVIRONMENT CANNOT BE ACHIEVED
BY USING HISTORICAL FORMS OF HOUSE-GROUPINGS, STREETS, SQUARES, GREENS,
ETC., AS THE SOCIAL REALITY THEY REPRESENT NO LONGER EXISTS.

WE ARE OF THE OPINION THAT WE SHOULD CONSTRUCT A HIERARCHY OF HUMAN
ASSOCIATIONS WHICH SHOULD REPLACE THE FUNCTIONAL HIERARCHY OF THE
CHARTE D'ATHENES.

AIX COMMISSION 6. REPORT BY SMITHSONS AND HOWELLS.

1/THERE SHOULD BE A BASIC PROGRAMME FOR THE DWELLING IN TERMS OF THE
ACTIVITIES OF THE FAMILY, CONSIDERING THEM INDIVIDUALLY AND IN
ASSOCIATION WITH EACH OTHER. (THE HOUSE).

2/OUTSIDE THE HOUSE IS THE FIRST POINT OF CONTACT, WHERE CHILDREN LEARN FOR
THE FIRST TIME OF THE WORLD. HERE ARE CARRIED ON THOSE ADULT ACTIVITIES
WHICH ARE ESSENTIAL TO EVERYDAY LIFE — SHOPPING, CAR CLEANING, BICYCLE
REPAIRS, LETTER POSTING, EXERCISING THE DOG. (THE STREET).

3/OUTSIDE THE STREET PEOPLE ARE IN DIRECT CONTACT WITH THE LARGER RANGE OF
ACTIVITIES WHICH GIVE IDENTITY TO THE COMMUNITY. (THE DISTRICT).

4/DISTRICTS IN ASSOCIATION GENERATE THE NEED FOR A RICHER SCALE OF
ACTIVITIES WHICH IN THEIR TURN GIVE IDENTITY TO THE ULTIMATE COMMUNITY.
(THE CITY).

ASSOCIATION: THE DWELLING THOUGHT OF IN TERMS OF HUMAN ASSOCIATION SHOULD TAKE ACCOUNT
HOUSE. NOT ONLY OF THE FAMILY BUT ALSO THOSE ADDITIONAL RESPONSIBILITIES WHICH
VARY IN ALL COUNTRIES AND WITH ALL FAMILIES — THIS ADDITIONAL ACTIVITY
GIVES IDENTITY TO THE DWELLING.

ASSOCIATION: ALTHOUGH IT IS EXTREMELY DIFFICULT TO DEFINE THE HIGHER LEVELS OF
PATTERN. ASSOCIATION, THE "STREET" IMPLIES A PHYSICAL CONTACT COMMUNITY, THE
"DISTRICT" AN ACQUAINTANCE COMMUNITY, THE "CITY" AN INTELLECTUAL
CONTACT COMMUNITY.

DOORN JAN '54. P.S.

URBANISM CONSIDERED AND DEVELOPED IN TERMS OF THE CHARTE D'ATHENES
TENDS TO PRODUCE COMMUNITIES IN WHICH VITAL HUMAN ASSOCIATIONS ARE
INADEQUATELY EXPRESSED. TO COMPREHEND THE PATTERN OF HUMAN
ASSOCIATIONS WE MUST CONSIDER EVERY COMMUNITY IN ITS PARTICULAR
TOTAL COMPLEXITY, IN ITS PARTICULAR ENVIRONMENT. (THE ECOLOGY OF
THE SITUATION.)

CLUSTER. LA SARRAZ. SEPT. '55. A. AND P.S.

THE AIM OF URBANISM IS COMPREHENSIBILITY, 1e. CLARITY OF ORGAN-
ISATION. THE COMMUNITY IS BY DEFINITION A COMPREHENSIBLE THING,
AND COMPREHENSIBILITY SHOULD ALSO THEREFORE BE A CHARACTERISTIC OF
THE PARTS. THE COMMUNITY SUB-DIVISIONS MIGHT BE THOUGHT OF AS
"APPRECIATED UNITS". AN APPRECIATED UNIT IS NOT A "VISUAL GROUP"
OR A "NEIGHBOURHOOD" BUT A PART OF A HUMAN AGGLOMERATION WHICH CAN
BE "FELT". THE APPRECIATED UNIT MUST BE DIFFERENT FOR EACH TYPE OF
COMMUNITY. ITS SCALE MUST INCREASE WITH THE SCALE OF THE COMMUNITY...
A LARGE COMMUNITY CANNOT BE BUILT UP FROM APPRECIATED UNITS
EVOLVED FOR A SMALL COMMUNITY UNDER DIFFERENT CONDITIONS (eg HOUSES
ROUND A SQUARE.) FOR EACH PARTICULAR COMMUNITY ONE MUST INVENT THE
STRUCTURE OF ITS SUB-DIVISION. THIS IS THE KEY PROBLEM OF HABITAT.
ARCHITECTS YEAR BOOK 7 '56. A. AND P.S.

TEAM X ARE NOT BLIND TO THE FACT THAT THE PATTERN OF HUMAN

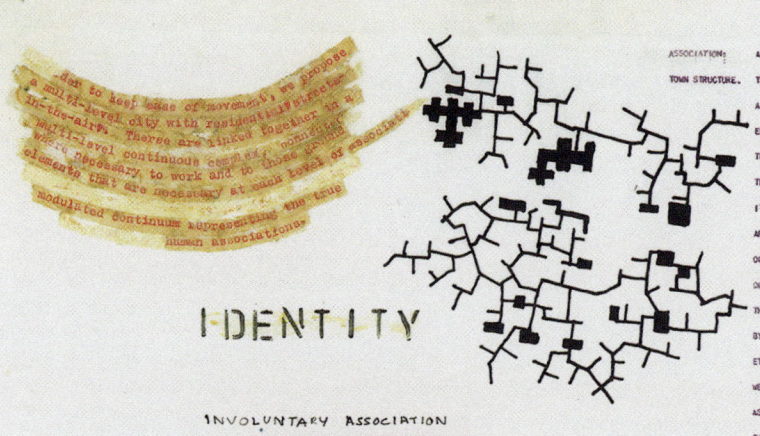

IDENTITY

So as to keep ideas of movement, we propose a multi-level city with residential districts in the air. These are linked together in a multi-level continuous complex connected where necessary to work and to those elements that are necessary at each level to form a modulated continuum representing the true human associations.

INVOLUNTARY ASSOCIATION

VERY LITTLE IN COMMON	house	NEIGHBOURS
ONE CONFIDANT	street	NODDING ACQUAINTANCE
WORK ASSOCIATES	district	RECOGNITION
VERY MANY LIKE MINDS	city	NATIONALITY

VOLUNTARY ASSOCIATION

ASSOCIATION

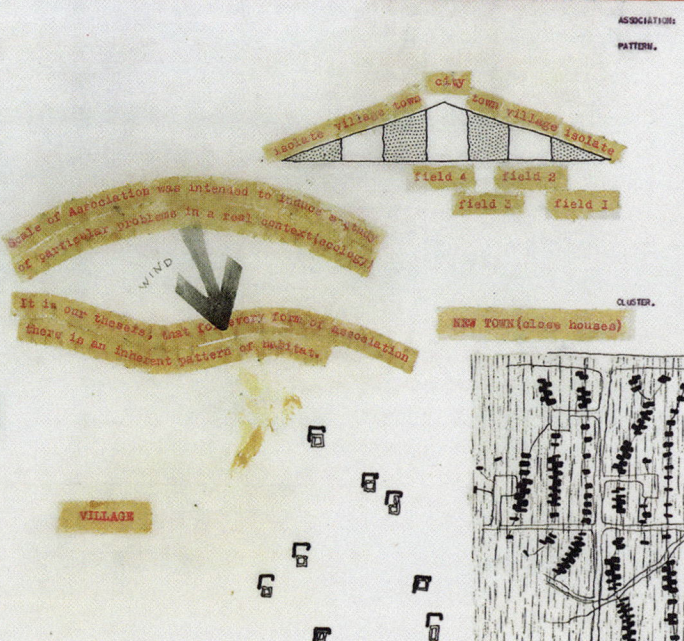

Scale of Association was intended to suggest a way of particular problems in a real context (ecology).

It is our thesis, that for every form of association there is an inherent pattern of habitat.

WIND

NEW TOWN (close houses)

VILLAGE

isolate village town city town village isolate
field 4 field 2
field 3 field 1

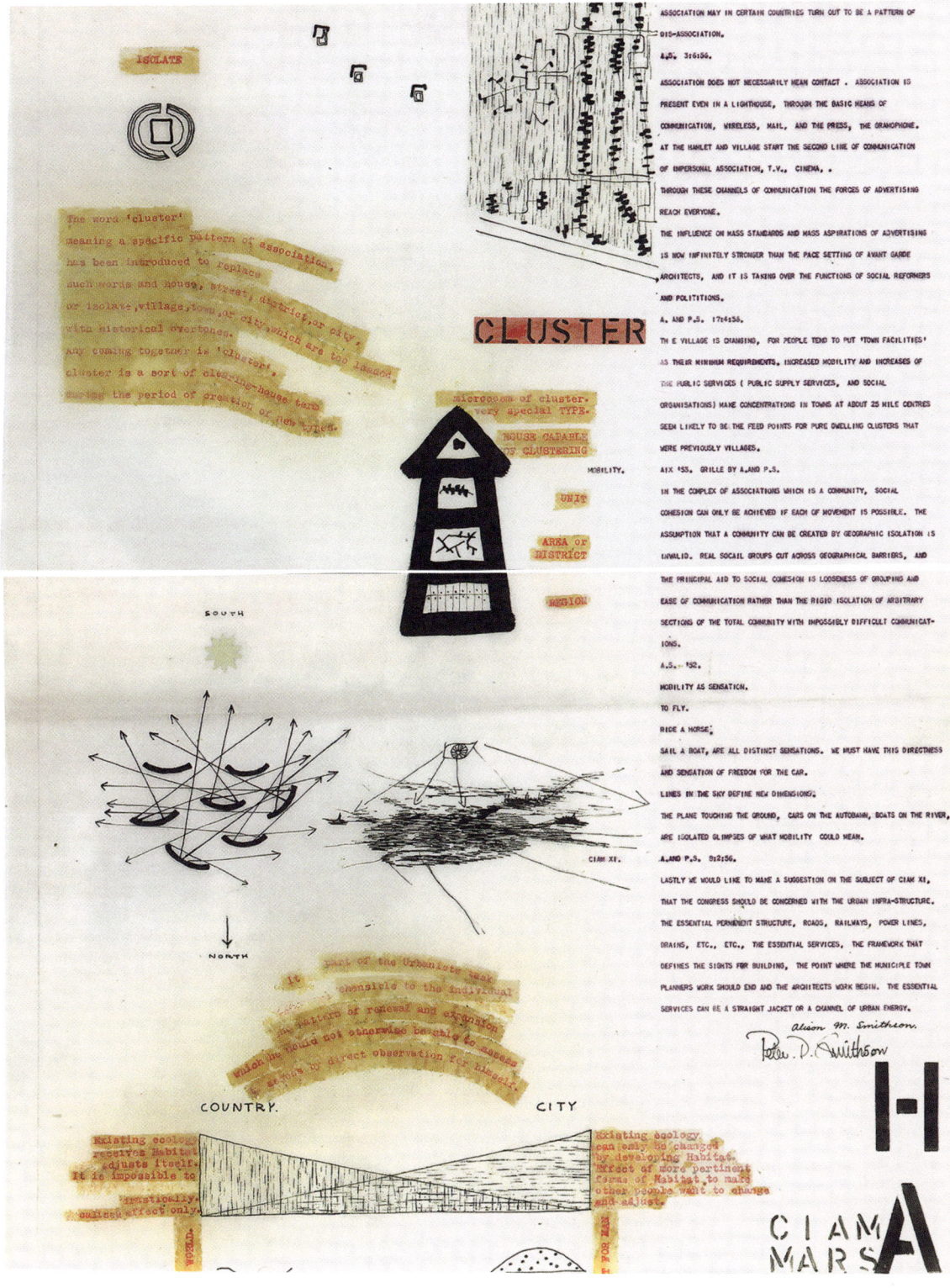

3.3 (above and preceding pages)
CIAM 10 scroll ideograms (1956). The Alison and Peter Smithson Archive, Special Collections, Frances Loeb Library, Graduate School of Design, Harvard University.

its identity through each phase of development. The scroll then returned to its beginning by repeating the four stenciled words "identity," "association," "cluster," and "mobility." The Smithsons would claim at a future date that it was not the words but the graphics of their Re-Identification scroll that would influence later generations of architects, their "random aesthetic reaching-out to town-patterns not based on rectangular geometries, but founded in another visual world."[23]

In spite of earlier attempts at ideograms and scrolls, Alison claimed that the first "graphics of communication" the Smithsons developed was "Urban Structuring" (in *Uppercase 3*, 1960, edited by Theo Crosby).[24] Here they used two colors, red and black, which Alison Smithson later claimed came closer to fulfilling their ideal of communication of ideas than either *Ordinariness and Light* (1970) or *Without Rhetoric* (1973).[25] Alison thought her best known "graphics of communication" outlining a new way of thinking was the "Team 10 Primer" of 1962, intended to allow each student to find their own, most congenial route through a mix of individual voices. It could be turned on its side and read in a vertical strip manner or horizontally across the page; one might follow a zigzag course or indulge in spot reading; a reader might select a different path each time. "The Primer" offered a new kind of freedom in "education-communication" (the primer's own phrase for itself), as had its predecessors, the Bauhaus books, which Alison consciously intended "The Primer" to match both in power of message and in correspondence of message to graphics.[26]

In 1983 she reflected back over this work:

> Part of my task was to evolve this graphics of a communication-of-ideas, in a manner that discouraged lifting the surface veneer, but required some work of mental digestion on the part of the recipient …
> so that the reader is helped in making himself,
> his own language as an architect.
>   There is some logic in the graphics' being not unlike an annotated Primitive Methodist Bible …[27]

In using graphics to make ideas manifest, Alison claimed, "The Primer" had an immediate descendant: *The Euston Arch and the Growth of the London, Midland & Scottish Railway* (1968)[28] (or *The Euston Arch*, as it is known in Europe). This book was an illustrated text of the building of the Arch and a protest against its wanton destruction. It was also a reminder of the importance of monuments in everyday life, and the responsibility of an architect to acknowledge such when they build. She described the book as being

> A collage, part words
> Part anthology of images,
> Part use of the "voice" of the witness, and in this the "verbal illustration" entered our graphics. The writing and the images dovetailed, one into the other, jointed like a good bit of traditional furniture, so they are one.[29]

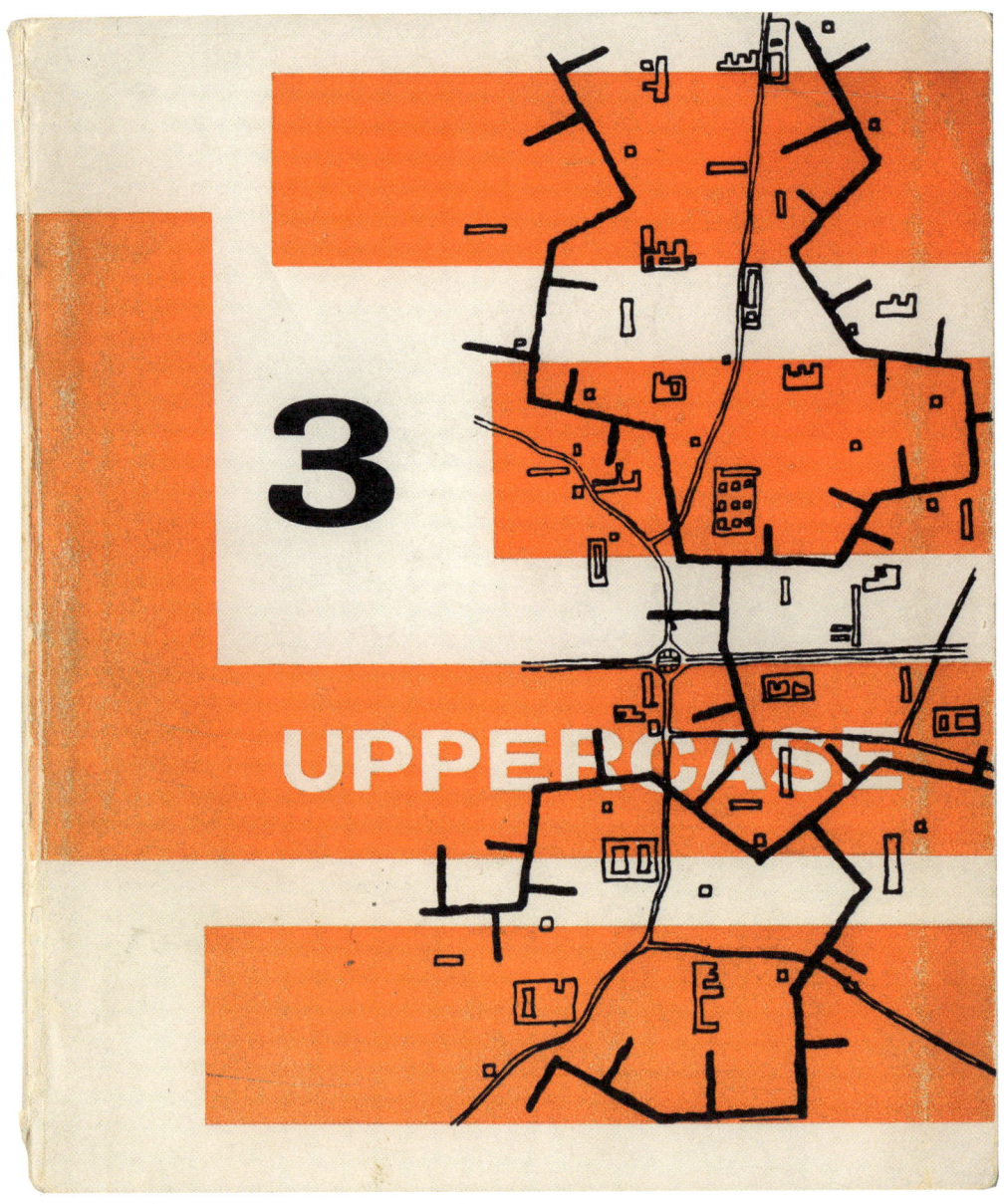

3.4
Alison and Peter Smithson, "Patterns of Association,"
Uppercase 3 (1960). Cover designed by Theo Crosby.
Smithson Family Collection.

> In this turning over ideas seemingly outside architecture, yet in parallel with the business of buildings, we are following a tradition, because architecture carries a responsibility. ... Instinctively, we, in Europe, hold dear a kind of moral responsibility whose roots turn back to the battles for beliefs and ideas that form part of an inherited memory. A working architect's turning things, ideas, over in the mind and the hand has always to do with making, for our expertise is in our hands. ... We can think through our hands. ... Allow form to gradually emerge in our minds. ... Or put things together in our minds.[30]

> The ability to deal with ideas, or discern patterns, is rare in architecture—as it is in other disciplines: most are straightforward practitioners like perfectly adequate doctors. ... The things that will change men's minds, and feed future generations, are not always clear to those contemporary to their manifestation ... potential remains mysterious ... because it is not clear how it can be consumed (that is its immediacy aspect) ... where it is leading or how it can be followed (the inheritance aspect) so that it can become a discipline that is a second nature; an ordering-of-approach that allows both an upholding of the general language in an individual's own language and, through the input of his buildings, an extension of the language of architecture.[31]

> Even to its creator, a thing's true nature is not always clear until a passage of time. A pattern is not discernable until a sufficiency of things and distance.[32]

Another document in this loose series of "graphics of communication," *AS in DS: An Eye on the Road*, which Alison Smithson called a "sensibility primer," was worked on by her in the 1970s and published in 1983. It contains a chapter on the "Graphics of Movement."[33] Interested in the official graphics of road signs, the graphics of road alignment in the landscape and the visual character of the road itself, she notes that

> the graphics that would instruct movement include triangles that could be Klee's ... the prongs of tuning forks illuminated on a background of reflective glass grains ... two-way arrows ... soon followed by discs, blue, with arrows, all aslant: these indications, heraldry of the roads.[34]

A road lined with signs is likened to an abstract painting: a horizontal bar pointing left, more discs and bars and lines, strings of tiny white cat's eyes running into the distance.[35] Amid the plethora of roadside communication symbols is a riot of color on signs passing so fast they can hardly be grasped: orange letters, green frames, red triangles, black arrows, red frames, gold letters, green signs, green frames, black lettering, red triangles. They speak in tongues quicker than they can be written down.[36]

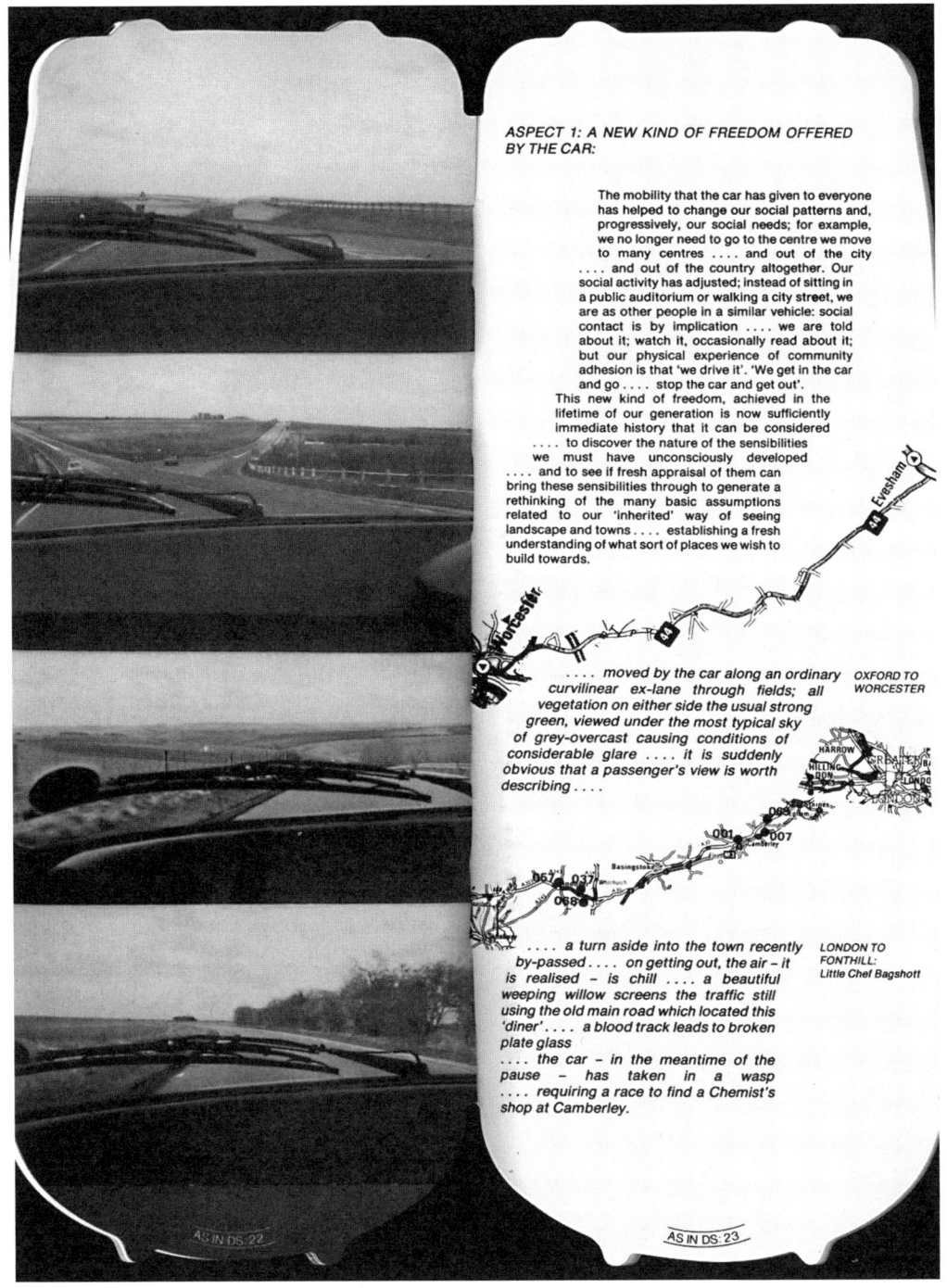

ASPECT 1: A NEW KIND OF FREEDOM OFFERED BY THE CAR:

The mobility that the car has given to everyone has helped to change our social patterns and, progressively, our social needs; for example, we no longer need to go to the centre we move to many centres .... and out of the city .... and out of the country altogether. Our social activity has adjusted; instead of sitting in a public auditorium or walking a city street, we are as other people in a similar vehicle: social contact is by implication .... we are told about it; watch it, occasionally read about it; but our physical experience of community adhesion is that 'we drive it'. 'We get in the car and go .... stop the car and get out'.

This new kind of freedom, achieved in the lifetime of our generation is now sufficiently immediate history that it can be considered .... to discover the nature of the sensibilities we must have unconsciously developed .... and to see if fresh appraisal of them can bring these sensibilities through to generate a rethinking of the many basic assumptions related to our 'inherited' way of seeing landscape and towns .... establishing a fresh understanding of what sort of places we wish to build towards.

.... moved by the car along an ordinary curvilinear ex-lane through fields; all vegetation on either side the usual strong green, viewed under the most typical sky of grey-overcast causing conditions of considerable glare .... it is suddenly obvious that a passenger's view is worth describing ....

OXFORD TO WORCESTER

.... a turn aside into the town recently by-passed .... on getting out, the air – it is realised – is chill .... a beautiful weeping willow screens the traffic still using the old main road which located this 'diner' .... a blood track leads to broken plate glass

.... the car – in the meantime of the pause – has taken in a wasp .... requiring a race to find a Chemist's shop at Camberley.

LONDON TO FONTHILL: Little Chef Bagshott

The As Found and the Charged Void

Despite the loving efforts they lavished on such projects as the CIAM scroll, *Team 10 Primer*, and *AS in DS*, the Smithsons did not think images and graphic notation systems sufficient to convey the new aesthetic they were reaching for in the 1950s. Believing that "life falls through the net of the four functions [of CIAM],"[37] they turned a sensitive eye toward a new set of relationships and processes that they saw in their environment. The "as found" was more than an object or an image but also an attitude where art was created in the process of selection rather than design. It was a new way of seeing found poetics in the simple and the ordinary: objects and materials that were honest without compromise, images that were never extreme or even original but prosaic, unthought-of things that could reenergize inventive activity. It was to think of design as a process of finding, selecting and comparing, and it was also a matter of making do with the few materials and things that postwar scarcity allowed. This new sensitivity of the eye, this new visual awareness of ordinary things, must be elevated to the "status of ideas" to make their architectural language speak to the specifics of time and place. They took accepted ideas "as found" and reorganized them, added to them, and reformulated them, hoping to bring about a redefinition of the processes through which a language of architecture relevant to the contemporary postwar world might be approached.

Peter Smithson would remark decades later that they were "always trying to make the space communicate rather than communicating intellectual ideas through words."[38] Nevertheless, words could not be entirely dispensed with. Expressing, questioning, and grasping experience through images generated affective concepts that required verbal embodiment. The Smithsons wanted to see, feel, and sense what their images, projects, *and* words could do, how these various modes of expression created rather than represented thinking, enabled orientation toward a multi-vocal rather than linear mode of expression. Through words, in particular, they aimed to organize and articulate the problems of architecture and urbanism in the 1950s and 1960s. How different were the problems their generation confronted from those faced by the founding heroes of modern architecture? Was it possible to rethink inherited terms and what they presupposed, to make them explosively evocative of contemporary issues and project them toward the future?

3.5
Double-page spread from Alison Smithson, *AS in DS: An Eye on the Road* (Delft: Delft University Press, 1983), 22–23. Smithson Family Collection.

In any language system, however, there is a gap between the word and the thing. This gap the Smithsons called "the charged void": a space full of tension that seeks, to use one of Alison Smithson's neologisms, a "releasant." To provide the necessary releasants, they coined new words, trying to trigger flashes of provocative insight that would bridge the gap between word and thing. These coinages accompanied a lateral, scanning mode of vision which they endorsed and which, they thought, the geometry of linear perspective denied. The words they created tended to contain both connectivity and distancing, e.g., a space or hyphen in "yard-gardens" or "street-decks"; a space was left open for interpretation between the words they wrote and the projects they made, as in such titles as "The Fine and the Folk" and *Ordinariness and Light*, or in the equivocating "but" of "But Today we collect Ads," or in Peter Smithson's most-quoted *mot*, "Mies is great, but Corb communicates."[39] Sensible affects, shimmering thoughts, language-stretching associative metaphors take the reader beyond recognizable meanings into a future possibility of architecture/urbanism as well as into areas that are not quite architecture.

No matter what imaginative affinities the Smithsons posited between language and architecture, an unbearable tension persisted between their aspirations and reality, an inevitable gap between the words they used to express their thoughts and the projects they wished to build or the future they hoped to construct. They had identified a gap, the "charged void," but could not bridge it to their own satisfaction: indeed, it became a widening abyss. The releasants had failed, and this failure would lead to disillusionment and bitterness in the 1970s and 1980s. Perhaps it was due to the Smithsons' inability to develop a critical position on the language they were inventing; perhaps, had they constructed a dictionary of their own terminology, it might have illuminated that abyss in which so many unfulfilled dreams were ricocheting about.

The Verbal-Visual Amalgam of "New Brutalism"

Alison and Peter Smithson, having become instant architectural celebrities when their design competition entry for Hunstanton Secondary Modern School won first prize in 1949, tried throughout the 1950s and 1960s to gather a movement around their concept of a New Brutalism. The expression has been attributed to Alison Smithson, who apparently first used "brutalism" to describe the exposed structure and unadorned interiors of a small house project proposed by the Smithsons for London's Soho district in 1953.[40] However, starting in 1955, Reyner Banham intervened in the process of defining New Brutalism, and for most historians he has had the last word.[41] He claimed that "Brutalism" was an amalgam derived from "Brutus"—a schoolboy nickname for Peter Smithson because his head looked like that of a Roman emperor—plus the first two letters of "Alison," finished off with the obligatory "-ism."[42] Banham noted that Peter Smithson was also interested in the French word *brut*, derived either from the phrase *art brut* (which Peter learned in the early 1950s from Paolozzi, who in turn had it from French artist Jean

Dubuffet) or from Le Corbusier's *béton brut* ("raw concrete"), which the older architect exposed in his postwar projects.[43]

Whatever "New Brutalism" meant or would come to mean, most accepted as its first British exemplar the Smithsons' Hunstanton School (1949–1952).[44] While the building achieved brilliance in the mathematical perfection of its proportions in plan and section, as Colin Boyne said in 1954, "[t]here is not one single soft material anywhere in the building," from its gaunt brick walls, exposed, rough, precast concrete floor units painted white, and exposed pipes, to its industrial lightshades. All this rough treatment was evidence of New Brutalism.[45]

The Smithsons fought a battle on two fronts throughout the 1950s, both of which shaped their concept of New Brutalism: first, they sought to restore the strength of the Modern Movement. This entailed learning as much as possible from the precedents created by the masters of the Heroic Period. Second, they wished to infuse this renewed aesthetic with desires, needs, and aspirations that arose from consumer society and its "aesthetics of plenty" during the progressive expansion of the postwar economy. They were supported on both fronts by their involvement with CIAM, beginning in 1953 at Aix-en-Provence, and by the artists, architects, and critics of the Independent Group (IG), 1952–1955.

From these two, seemingly disparate sources—restoration and consumerization—they formed a new amalgam, an association of ideas that allowed them to leap quickly from one to the another, much as Le Corbusier and Amédée Ozenfant juxtaposed an image of the Delage sports car and the Parthenon in their 1923 masterpiece *Vers une Architecture*. The eternal and the progressive, the universal and the particular, growth and form—all were combined in an affinity of ideas and images. Perhaps it is in the forging of this new language of architecture out of words and images that the essential meaning of New Brutalism is to be found (see figure 2.1).

The editors of *AD* asked the Smithsons, as the prophets of the new movement, to supply a definition of "New Brutalism." This was published in an unsigned editorial (widely understood to be by the Smithsons) in January 1955.[46] The editorial claimed that New Brutalism is a development of the modern movement. Its main practitioner had been Le Corbusier, beginning with the *béton brut* of the Unité. Le Corbusier utilized the yardstick of Japanese architecture, its underlying ideas, principles, and spirit: they mentioned Le Corbusier's purist aesthetic, and his use of sliding screens, continuous space, and the power of white and earth colors. "It is," they said, "this reverence for materials—a realizing of the affinity which can be established between building and man—which is at the root of the so-called New Brutalism."[47]

What is new about the movement, they said, is that its closest affinities are not with past architectural styles but with peasant dwelling forms: "It has nothing to do with craft. We see architecture as the direct result of a way of life."[48] New architecture should be aformal in the sense that it is shaped, literally, not by a commitment to any rules of form but by a new understanding of how people dwell and build. And it was an auspicious, culturally ripe time for such a movement:

> 1954 has been a key year. It has seen American advertising equal Dada in its impact of overlaid imagery; that automotive masterpiece, the Cadillac convertible, parallel-with-the-ground (four elevations) classic box on wheels; the start of a new way of thinking by CIAM; revaluation of the work of Gropius; the repainting of the Villa at Garches.[49]

In December 1955 Reyner Banham added his voice to those trying to clarify the meaning of New Brutalism.[50] If the Smithsons were proposing a lateral scanning across a range of cultural values, then Banham completely misunderstood their intention. He did not address their efforts to forge an associative relation between the "significant image" and their architectural projects. Instead he opens and closes his *AR* article with Le Corbusier's proclamation, *L'Architecture, c'est, avec des Matières Brutes, établir des rapports émouvants* ("Architecture is the establishing of moving relationships with raw materials"). The paternity of the Smithsons' movement and its terminology is clear: there is nothing in New Brutalism that Le Corbusier has not fathered. Banham had other self-serving intentions: he wanted to ask what has the influence of contemporary architectural historians been on the field of architecture?[51] (Thinking, perhaps, as much about his own contribution as those of his mentor Nikolaus Pevsner, the CIAM secretary Sigfried Giedion, and even the Smithsons, with their desire to revive the Heroic Period of modernism.) Had these historians, Banham wonders, introduced as much confusion and distortion into architecture as Marx had into capitalism or Freud into psychology? They have done two things: invented the Modern Movement and produced "-ism" terms falling into two categories. Terms in the first category are descriptors applied by critics and historians to specific bodies of work, while those in the second are used by movements as banners or slogans. The trouble is that "New Brutalism" tries to be both at once—both a description of built work and the slogan of a cause. (Banham does not spell out why such simultaneous use must be innately confusing, or name anyone who has in fact been confused by it.)

Nevertheless, he continued with his critique: the trouble was compounded because the Smithsons, as bellwethers of the movement, had for a long time really been talking only to themselves, deploying the term long before any architect had seen anything of its practice. Not until September 1954, when *AR* first published photographs and plans of the Smithsons' Hunstanton School, did anyone have visual evidence of what New Brutalism might be.[52]

There was trouble indeed within wider architectural circles about Brutalist ideas, which had to be taken seriously because they were on every young architect's mind. To offer clarification, *AD* reentered the field in 1957 with an opinion piece on New Brutalism in April (based on a dialogue between editorial critic Denys Lasdun and anonymous commentator architectural historian J. H. V. Davies, but rephrased as one voice for publication) and three additional pieces recounting the dialogue of a panel of anonymous commentators in October, November, and December. Letters in response to previous articles appeared at the end of each "Opinion" piece, and thus set up a dialogue of sorts with outside views.[53]

It was difficult to determine the precise meaning of the term "New Brutalism," the April "Opinion" piece claimed, for the movement was not standing still. At first it appeared to be a revolt against postwar British architecture's lack of rigor and clear thinking. It was a call to order, to a basic classical organization of the parts of a building assembled, as Le Corbusier had shown, into an apprehensible image to which nothing could be added and from which nothing could be taken away. "The Brutalist method of achieving this classic wholeness was by a close concern with the qualities of materials 'as found' and by a passionate moral earnestness about the clear exhibition of structure."[54] New Brutalism might have begun with a building, the glass, brick and steel Hunstanton School—which the Smithsons derived from Mies van der Rohe—but that specific approach did not lend itself to an extended development. The master himself had taken it as far as it could go, so the Smithsons clearly had to move on.[55] But where to? And how to do so using only drawings and words?

That was a crucial problem! New Brutalism could be assessed only through a literary screen, an architectural lecture, or written words: its spatial effects remained obscure. The Smithsons' words might have lent a sense of profundity and mystification to the definition, but what had they actually meant? How could they "create an architecture of reality" without explaining what was "reality"? What did they mean to imply by stating that "the affinity which can be established between building and man is at the root of Brutalism"? Does this reduce New Brutalism to a watered-down version of Humanism? And what does a peasant style of life have to say to the way of life in a complex industrialized society? The Smithsons' vagueness of terminology creates "verbal indigestion," and this, the critic opined, neither helped to clarify their cause nor provided an ordered methodology.[56] To return to first principles is a fine gesture, but overly simplistic, and should not have motivated an architectural movement. It leaves the crucial problem of design methodology unsolved. Thus the critics summed up the situation in 1957: New Brutalism was an immature and ill-defined movement. Like most closed "-isms" it was rigidifying and might already have reached a dead end.

The Smithsons were allowed a "Counter Opinion." The critics had missed the point. The Smithsons were after something different: to show that architecture was still possible in the postwar period, to move away from the design of individual buildings to examine "the *whole* problem of human associations and the relationship that building and community has to them. From this study has grown a completely new attitude and a non-classical aesthetic."[57] In using the word "reality" they referred to all of the cultural objectives of society, its urges, its techniques, and so on. Brutalism tries to face up to a mass-production society, and drag a rough poetry out of the confused and powerful forces which are at work. Up to now Brutalism has been discussed stylistically, whereas its essence is ethical.[58]

The November "Opinion" piece raised the following questions: Did New Brutalism give architects a method to bridge the gap between individual artistic expression and technological determinants?[59] What did vernacular architecture, which the Smithsons cited as part of their Brutalist inspiration, have to say about buildings articulated by industrial processes? An architect, the critics believed, requires "a bulwark of certainty, of unarguable authority, on which the architect's understanding can lean while his conception of a building as a whole, as a unity, takes shape."[60] The certainties that *AD* was calling for would not come from indiscriminately accepting "as found" the most outrageous products and manifestations of industrial society.

To clarify their position, the *AD* critics began in their next "Opinion" piece to specify design principles they could support. Giving a clear nod of recognition to the Smithsons, they nevertheless sought greater clarity to the principles defining New Brutalism. They offered in its place the "objects found" philosophy only as a beginning, perhaps the lowest of philosophies, and not applicable beyond architecture. But this philosophy must not substitute for creative activity.[61]

> Every building has at its heart an image, a generating idea, which must express itself through every part and every detail. Though "Truth to Structure" may be a limiting fallacy, it can illuminate the basic architectural task if structure is taken to include all the laws of a specific building, derived from all the facts about site, materials, functions, cost, and environment.[62]

Other arts can survive in a void, but architecture cannot; architecture constantly affects people's lives, so the architect is obliged to reveal how he fuses disparate objects into a whole, into a work of architecture. "He must penetrate through the communicating elements of a building to its motivating ideas."[63]

The Smithsons tried again in 1959 to clarify their position in a conversation between themselves and Jane Drew and Maxwell Fry, two early advocates of English Modernism. An edited version of the conversation was printed as "Conversations on Brutalism" in the Italian magazine *Zodiac*.[64] By now the original list of New Brutalist criteria was shifting to include more historical material and a more specific interest in town planning—one that bordered on Townscape Analysis. It appears that if *AD*'s "Opinion" pieces were shaped by and responding to the terminology of New Brutalism, the Smithsons in turn were transformed by those opinions, arriving at a more compromised modernism of their own. Now, "New Brutalism" was referred to simply as "brutalism," a "brutal approach," "brutally direct," or "acting brutally."

For example, Peter Smithson noted that a reaction took hold in the 1950s, a time when machine technology itself demanded "a brutal approach," the utilization of machine-made materials such as precast elements and concrete blocks, and this fueled the Smithsons' desire to build poetically through machines. Alison picked up the thread: in the 1940s they were reacting to architects who were using "process materials like Kraft Cheese." That was why the Smithsons had turned to materials they could really get hold of, like wood and concrete and glass and steel—materials some called "brutal." Peter suggested: "the essential ethic of *brutalism is* in town building."[65] What is important is the way buildings fit together and interact on the ground, how they create places in which you move, can feel identity or lack of identity, and overcome the alienation of post-war society. This "way of thinking" inevitably produces buildings that are less complete; one reads the building for what it is, which is at times even "brutally" direct, but it must be read as an extension of itself into a "cluster" of associated types.[66] Alison added a counterpoint: the reason their work on "brutalism" lines up with the masters of modernism is their shared idea of "responsibility"—meaning that a building is relating not just to some intellectual law but to the whole process of town building. (The concept of "responsibility" would also reverberate in the Smithsons' later writings.)

The simple fact that we no longer live in self-contained villages, but are connected to a wider world through press, television, radio, and advertising, an entire net of communication, means that architects have to look outside the merely visual patterning of the town and express architecturally this entire net. Their subsequent architectural expressions might in some situations be "brutal" acts, but are executed in hope that others might change how they relate to these acts.

> The word "expression" is a key one, but one tends to fight shy of it. We are interested in expressing not ourselves, but what is going on and building which denies what is going on is just the opposite of brutalism—it is chi-chi, which is sort of an evasion, in that chi-chi is not just a matter of fashion (because fashion can be a direct communicant), it is the sort of person that cannot be bothered to think out what the situation is, and how to work it out properly, and drops back into a formula of doing it which is a sort of lie—in a way it is a sort of ethical question, a thing being either plastic truth or this sort of evasion or lie.[67]

Clearly Alison and Peter Smithson were having difficulty explaining to the reading public how their open-ended net of communication, a system built on words and ideas, found expression in architectural form. Yet their stress on "ethics" was pertinent: they were not seeking the imposition of set percepts and fixed images, determined solutions and accepted rules to be followed as moral instructions. Instead, their ethics of pluralism was grounded in attitudes, sensibilities, and affects revealing new processes of thought from which actions and judgments would emerge.

Their old foe, Banham, would have none of this open-ended "ethics." He reentered the fray over the confusions fomented by New Brutalism with a sharp "assessment" of the Smithsons' architectural career in 1961 and a book-length reiteration of his critique *The New Brutalism* in 1966. There is thus something of the straw man about the New Brutalism that he pummeled in these later writings; for instance, he ignored the Smithsons' more modest position on "brutalism" as linked to town building, expressed in *Zodiac* (1959). Yet repetition would, in the end, guarantee that his position won out over what he complained was the muddled thinking of the Smithsons. The real reason they could no longer lead the younger iconoclasts or drive forward the entire profession of architecture was, he said, "their lack of a consistent style. Though the rationalization and elaboration of their position over the years has been a fairly straight-line argument, their stylistic development has been marked by complete and spectacular discontinuity."[68] The Smithsons' insistence on taking each design problem on its own merits, on going back to first principles without formalistic preconceptions, offered the profession no standards, no design principles, no methodological procedures to follow.

It is clear that Banham never understood the Smithsons' use of associative modes of thought and imagery, both of which were central to their advocated position of New Brutalism, or just plain "brutalism." The Smithsons were of course hurt by his attack, and responded within a few months of his book's publication. Their wounds, they said, were only half-healed, but their minds were fresh and their archives intact.[69] They called Banham's truncated and expressionistic definition "Myopic's Brutalism," and likened him to a "war correspondent" who got the emotions of the battle right but relied on "gossip" and secondhand information for details of the actual engagement. Only real combatants could relay what the exact positions had been and what the battle was all about. Banham was right about one thing: the Smithsons were pursuing an architectural language of social dialogue (what he called their "ethics"). But he was wrong on everything else, especially the details: "For writing and printing somehow turn the haphazard brute facts into a sequential and meaningful flow of events, and can cause typesetting errors to grow to manhood as fully authenticated myth."[70]

In a second response, a manuscript written for *The New Statesman* in 1966–1967 but never published, the Smithsons wondered what Banham's playfully provocative book was all about: "a laugh, a bloomer, a bang (in the eye), a whiz, a guffaw, a howler, a near miss, per page—P. R. B. carries all before him."[71] Whatever his comic intent, the Smithsons were indignant, for

> the situation still hurtful if too closely, meticulously picked over …[72]
>
> Our generation—Brutalist against Blockage—can be made afraid by Blockage. We have a syndrome that takes effect either the fourth time through Checkpoint Charlie or our fourth aesthetic control.[73]

Obviously, Banham was the hateful regulator, the one laying down law and order, the arbitrary gatekeeper. He was thus aligned with the worst of the British Blockage morality against which Brutalism had struggled. The Smithsons reiterated their warning to all art historians: "you have to have been there to know the terrors and the commitments this jocularity covers."[74]

Best British Blockage (Wilson as Winner)
Self Blockage (Connolly as King)
Blockage or queue mentality of the age groups hit by the two war/slump sandwich
Chips on shoulder Blockage
Bureaucratic got-your-gas-mask blockage.

Almost Banham's last words "but the lingering tradition of its ethnical stand ..." This, for me [Peter Smithson], is the continuing validity of the New Brutalism.[75]

Bold New Brut, after shower, after anything: now has to bash at Blockage.[76]

The book "The New Brutalism" itself might be an example of Blockage. Passing over the Self Blockage, there is a dearth in this country of positions sufficiently endowed for those Art Historians who might be prepared to be as careful as once Warburg Wittkower, Penguin Pevsner, or Save-our-Scrap Simmons.[77]

In their introduction to a 1973 collection of reprinted essays, *Without Rhetoric: An Architectural Aesthetic, 1955–1972*, the Smithsons fired a late shot in the skirmish over the conceptual meaning of New Brutalism.[78] Here they repeated the array of characteristics which they had deployed when they first defined New Brutalism in January 1955, but added points of clarification. With hindsight they could acknowledge that at first they had not understood the hidden implications of this new aesthetic and were merely responding to advertisements they saw in glossy magazines; such a response was intended to be a surrealistic gesture.[79] This fascination seemed anachronistic to New Brutalism "unless you read the advertising images as visual telegrams with a specially loaded message about possibilities for the immediate future"[80]—and their open-ended conception of New Brutalism welcomed the creation of future possibilities. They focused on advertisements as a deeper communication system because they also wanted to respond to people's aspirations as quickly as people discovered they had them, which was what a good advertisement could do.

The reason for coining new words was simple: "the English only think in terms of words."[81] In spite of the many other inquiries into the derivation of the term "New Brutalism," they repeated, once again, their own source.

Coined on sight of a newspaper paragraph heading which called ... the Marseilles Unité "Brutalism in architecture"—that was for us: "New," both because we came after Le Corbusier, and in response to the going literary style of the *Architectural*

Review which—at the start of the 'fifties—was running articles on the New Monumentality, the New Empiricism, the New Sentimentality, and so on.[82]

Le Corbusier's Unité in Marseille, which they first visited during CIAM 9 (1953), was an obvious model to work with. So were Japanese houses, which they first viewed in the film *Gate of Hell* (1953), as these houses represented a way of life and reverence for nature and for materials.[83] This respect for materials was basic to their way of seeing and thinking about New Brutalism.[84] No one seemed to understand that what was also "new" was New Brutalism's affinity with peasant dwellings, because such dwellings were statements about ordinary, prosaic life, "a poetry without rhetoric."[85]

The Smithsons never gave up on specifying their overlapping images of New Brutalism or deploying their associative modes of thought. Always "shifting sideways," the series of images became a generative device. Houses and cities were designed with the art of inhabitation in mind (the ethics); the array offered a pictorial image correlating each item with the next in a series that extended in an open-ended manner toward the future (the aesthetic). As they explained in *Without Rhetoric*,

> We have to *know-instinctively* to be at peace, to sense rather than to see: and this means that we have to raise the individual items or elements above themselves, shifting sideways the emphasis of their bare selves, to the level that they recess together and subtly serve as *signs* to help us know how to *behave* in our buildings, guide how we want to live as a society in our cities.[86]

Toward the end of the 1980s, Peter Smithson looked back over the contributions their generation of architects had made in the 1950s:

> Two compulsions held together the generation building in the "fifties": to make ordinary buildings—factories, schools, houses—with the maximum of intelligence in their ideas and construction ... a richness that could reach everyone ... [and] to get the most out of a material or a process ... for to build with the minimum, for engineers and architects alike, was then an adventure.[87]

And so new materials were "sacred" to "brutalism": concrete blocks; reinforced concrete, stainless steel, galvanized mild steel, enameled metals, common plywood and blockboard.

In all their attempts to explain New Brutalism, emphasizing the nuances and shifts entailed and the problems of design engendered, the Smithsons were taking a stand against compromised modernism as seen in the pages of *AR* and the architectural norms of the 1950s. They were seeking to insert into architectural debate the same ethics of integrity that had once guided the Heroic Period of modern architecture. Fighting back to first principles in structure, materials, and plan, section, and site, then extending outward from there to consider functions, needs, and users' desires was intended as only the start of New Brutalism's attention to the affinity between man and building. This affinity had to be thought of in a free-falling manner—not a geometrically imposed formalism, but an arrangement "capable of recognizing unfolding orders."[88]

In an unpublished text first written in 1966 and revised in 1999, "From the Astringency of Necessity to the Astringency of Choice,"[89] Peter Smithson reflects on the importance of Jackson Pollock's drip paintings and Dubuffet's materiality to the Smithsons' developing sensibilities in the early 1950s:

> [I]t was the capacity to hold together a great complexity of joined-together linear imagery that was astounding … "the first manifestation of a new ordering."
>
> In both Pollock and Dubuffet the image is manifestly material. In Dubuffet especially, materiality seems sometimes all.
>
> In our own work in the 'fifties, an astringency of necessity manifested itself. … From lines drawn with dilutions of Chinese ink to the "as found" of the wash-basin, or Braithwaite Tank.[90]

II. Coining Keywords for Aesthetics of Change

We now turn to the Smithsons' mixed language of architecture and associative ideas, their open-ended approach to architectural thinking that allowed one thought to emerge from another, one sign to point to an encounter with another, and one idea to loop back and jump forward as it was smoothed and extended over time.

The Status of Ideas

Alison and Peter Smithson were interested, as they put it, in "the status of ideas" and the extended formal pattern of living and dwelling. They therefore took accepted ideas and reorganized them, added to them, even reformulated them. They never let an idea sit still, but worked on it and transformed it over time. No doubt this got them into trouble with critics who would have preferred precise methods, tight definitions, and normative rules rather than shifting and sifting through idioms of life. Yet obscurity was never the Smithsons' goal: they thought that the architect should be an intellectual "without rhetoric," that is, plain-spoken, direct, earnest, and brutally honest if necessary.

Their dictionary of ideas began in the early 1950s with two "keywords," namely "association" and "identity." Peter wrote down a list of concerns about contemporary life: first, communities were not estranged abstractions but "associations" of people. Second, people needed to "identify" with a sense of place in order not to be alienated in mass society. Third, a new physical and social "mobility" had been promised by the Conservative government, which came into power in 1951 on the slogan "You've never had it so good." Together, "association," "identity," and "mobility" influenced the pattern of "growth and change," which is what the process of town planning was all about.[91]

"Growth and change" also entailed an ecological approach as a response to site, place, and building—a spatial response (growth) susceptible to the variance of time (change).[92]

The Smithsons introduced the word "cluster" at CIAM 10 in 1956 in Dubrovnik.[93] They meant by the term a specific pattern of open-ended association, any coming-together of architects and ideas in an attitude of collaboration. On reflection, Alison thought it was in the mid-1950s, about the time they designed the "House of the Future" for the Ideal Home Exhibition (1955–1956), that she and Peter started to think about grouping houses within the framework of a community or "cluster city." Here again was an "extended" idea: they took the idea of "a house" and put it in contact with the realities of the postwar situation, not allowing it to signify a stand-alone mechanical container—a "machine for living," in Le Corbusier's 1923 phrase—but "the house within a community."

3.6
Alison and Peter Smithson, "Looking Up and Looking Down," Hauptstadt Berlin (1960). Drawing signed by Sigmond '58. Smithson Family Collection.

And so they conceived the "cluster": "a close knit, complicated, often moving aggregation, but an aggregation with a distinct structure."[94] The architect's role was to provide a "sign" or "significant image" for this new idea that would capture all the functions, aspirations, and beliefs of the community and accumulate them into a comprehensible whole. The "cluster" concept thus generated a new "image of the city" that combined new and old elements, and provided not one center but several. It offered a solution for a mass-production society, including the engineering of roads and communication systems as its backbone and offering a structure that could grow while remaining clearly legible at each stage.

"Mobility" was another keyword, not only because contemporary society was a mobile society, the car a new symbol of freedom, but because the automobile engendered the need for a new road system on a colossal topographical scale, which in turn affected the structure and pattern of new urban forms. To lay down any road meant that an entire geographical and social structure might be transformed in its wake, thus the road system must be designed as a unifying system.[95]

Even more broadly, the Smithsons were interested in a multifaceted definition of the *poetics* of movement: how it generated a new sensibility to human patterns and collectively built forms. Like Jackson Pollock's drip paintings of 1949, "motion and change" called for an *n*-dimensional and multievocative ordering, entailed "a writing-in of vehicles, mechanisms and services into the idea of the city."[96] They developed their concept of "mobility" in competition plans for Hauptstadt Berlin (1957–1958). Providing separate systems for pedestrians and for cars—straight streets, free and irregular pedestrian platforms—results in a variety of viewing experiences. From a pedestrian platform, people look down to the roads: the movement of cars becomes a new spectacle, and from cars, people look up to pedestrians moving on escalators and terraces. People and objects in motion and change became the stuff and the decoration of the new urban scene.[97]

Peter Smithson explained that "cluster" was a collective concept entailing all the other keywords. It thus included ideas expressed in their manuscript entitled *Urban Re-identification*. The book had been written during the Korean War, when a pause (1954–1962) in building activity throughout England began due to a worldwide shortage of steel. "This pause seems the right moment to try to establish a basis for a new beginning,"[98] they wrote. *Urban Re-identification* outlined the major themes the Smithsons had been working on and was "intended originally for publication as a popular general statement of an idea (its format based on Le Corbusier's classic work 'Propos d'Urbanisme')—[yet] was in fact never published as a whole and has lain unread over the intervening years."[99] Its themes remained valid, however:

> the restoration of the feel of the land; the invention of an architecture structured by notions of association—of place; the re-direction of our cities and towns towards safe-movement, openness, and light by the insertion into the old structure of urban "events" at the scale of our new patterns of communication.[100]

On the back of the book was placed a series of definitions of the sign "U.R.," standing primarily for Urban Re-identification.

> Ur the archetype
> UR the city that renewed itself
> Urbanism
> Urgent.[101]

People seemed, in practice, to form their own "idea" of association: at the level of the house, the street, the district, the city. And it was this "idea"—not merely the empirical reality of these vital new relationships—that endowed a mobile society with a renewed sense of "identity." The task for the Smithsons was to find forms expressing these levels of association in order to forge the reidentification of man with a house that looked inward to the family yet outward to society.

3.7
The original manuscript binder for *Urban Structuring*. Smithson Family Collection.

> The approach to a house is the occupants' link with society as a whole—
> a lengthy climb up a rickety stair or down into a basement
> up an avenue
> up an estate road
> along an air-conditioned artificially lit corridor.
>
> These are man's links with society, the vistas down which he looks at his world; they frame his perspective view.[102]

Thinking along the lines that Le Corbusier advocated and his house/city analogy, the "house" became the Smithsons' first definable city element. The second was arranging houses to create a street, stressing the idea of enclosure and identification to overcome alienation.[103] When the house and the street reentered the city they formed the third city element, a district, and the fourth, a city. This was the missing quality in contemporary cities: man needed to identify with his street and his community if he was to avoid being alienated. Thus a community based on a hierarchy of "associational elements"—house, street, district, city—all expressed algebraically, one added to the other, compounding the associations.[104] As Le Corbusier had taught, a city of districts, living and working together in harmony, began with the house as the center of all activities and extended outward to the entire city.

The kernel of this extended idea can be found in the Smithsons' 1951–1952 Urban Re-identification Project. This was a competition entry for Golden Lane Housing, intended to be built in Bunhill Fields, an area of London razed during the Blitz, used as a rubble dump after the war, and finally chartered for redevelopment by the London County Council. Although their entry failed to win, the project became a pivotal axis of "ideas" expressing the direction in which they were working.

The Smithsons believed that "life-in-the-streets" was a survivor from former times, now invalidated by the automobile and a shift toward middle-class values. No substitute had yet been developed for such an evolving, mobile society. To simply revive the street would have been historicism, yet there was something about its life that offered a valid pattern, a freer sort of organization.[105] Thus they proposed for their Golden Lane housing project three levels of "streets-in-the-air," or decks, as places for gathering, shops, telephones, and postboxes, as opposed to corridors or thoroughfares. The crossings of these decks formed points for communal activities for the 90 families who lived along the length of each. Every house had a "yard-garden" connecting up with the deck, allowing ever-changing vignettes of life and sky and providing room for gardening, bicycle cleaning, joinery, pigeon-fancying, children's play, or any other activity that identified man with his street.

To ease movement across the city, the Smithsons extended their idea of residential "streets-in-the-air" to provide a multilevel decked-in city. Everything connected up with this continuous complex; extending outward to link hospitals, hotels, and workshops, greens, market gardens, grocery shops, places of work and leisure, to its system. The

3.8
Alison Smithson, photomontage of Golden Lane Study showing the planned construction process, a tower-crane not used in England at the time, c. 1952. Smithson Family Collection.

Smithsons would later write in *Ordinariness and Light* about the ideal of "an opened-up, pedestrian-decked lived-in city":

> The idea can be simply stated.
>
> It is an idea capable of extension. Its deployment is not dependent on geometric rigour, and sections can be built as sites become available, and linked up later.[106]
>
> Every city would be able to feel its form; see the land roll about it.
>
> The man in the street would see the city landmarks that at every move spear him into exact relationship with his surroundings.
>
> No longer would city contours go unnoticed and famous buildings be tucked away: like Istanbul we should see our city swing about us in ever changing meaningful patterns.[107]

(The Smithsons were so deeply influenced by the work and writings of Le Corbusier that they often selected his favorite images, such as Istanbul, to illustrate their own thoughts.)

With time, the concept of Urban Re-identification gave way to the "cluster city," a new image with which to think about mobile society that took into consideration how roads and communication nets change the pattern of cities, and suggesting instead an open-ended network of multiple centers. This, too, would shift, and by the 1970s the Smithsons noted that planners "in practice completely missed the golden rule of satisfaction: a good road goes somewhere, a bad road does not. This is the holy hierarchy that has been so often terraced under into oblivion."[108] Housing estates imposed their pattern of living on occupants, assuming all inhabitants aspired to middle-class values. "Behind the geometric façade our washing, our china dogs and aspidistras look out of place. Life in action cannot be forced behind the netting of imposed pattern."[109] The problem, as they saw it, was how to link man with his street and his community in structures that borrowed from avant-garde solutions yet allowed him to identify with his values and traditions from the past.

> The architect or planner will be fortunate if he can add one genuine thing to a city. Let this thing be large or small it must be big in its solution, its idea immediately apparent to the ordinary man so that each and everyone can re-orientate himself in relation to it.[110]

Coining "Socio-plastics" in the 1950s

It is difficult to compile an etymological dictionary of the Smithsons' shifting terms. The precise meaning and origin of "association," "identity," "cluster," "growth and change," and "mobility" must remain uncertain, as these terms were constantly reworked and their meanings extended over time. In fact, compiling any dictionary, much less an etymological one, would run counter to the Smithsons' open-ended approach to the language of architecture, for dictionaries explain words and things, attempt to fix meanings and significations. Used prescriptively, they hold the power to determine universal reference and proper use. That is why, in the Smithsons' view, every language of reform must invent its own terms, destroy old meanings, and liberate discourse. It is also why, wherever bureaucracy seizes control of all aspects of social life, it attacks language and reduces the poetry of life to the vulgar prose of information and orders to be followed.[111]

To the contrary, the Smithsons focused on how language could be freshly deployed to capture transformative processes in the built environment, and how these terms reflected the pragmatics of architectural practice. Although they sought rooted novelty, the Smithsons were, however, open about their borrowings: the "status of ideas" depended on sources that could be modified and extended. This is why they objected to any insistence that their words be precisely defined, their ideas made explicit, their method expressed in rules and regulations. It was their intention to do better than Mies's formalisms, and Le Corbusier's Unité was merely a point at which to start. In a talk given to fifth-year architectural students in 1959, they underscored the importance of having an inherited language of architecture with which to speak:

> To work within an existing formal vocabulary gives us confidence—it has been done before, therefore we know it works, and the difficulties of visualizing it are decreased. Furthermore, it makes communication of our idea simpler, for others are familiar with the vocabulary and can see the aptness of the practical and technical solution without any strain on their power of imagination. (I speak here perhaps a little bitterly, for we have found in our own works that the further we have got in evolving a personal, a formal language, the more difficulty one has with communicating the idea. In terms of speech, that which one wants to say no one can understand and that which can be understood one no longer wishes to say.)[112]

One of the difficult terms that requires explanation is "socio-plastics," their quest to transform their experience as social beings into plastic form, in which they borrowed and extended ideas received from sociologists studying working-class communities after the war, and anthropologists interested in how other societies lived and dwelled in the new world order. Bethnal Green, for example, had long been of interest to British architects, and would remain a source of influence for the Smithsons immediately after World War II.[113]

When the London County Council took up the challenge of Bethnal Green in 1943, planners argued that obsolescence, overcrowding, unsanitary conditions, lack of open space, inadequate road systems, and extensive bomb damage made this borough eligible for reconstruction.[114] They set about demolishing its buildings and rehousing its residents until a borough that had had a population of 108,000 in 1931 was reduced to 54,000 in 1955.[115] Two sociologists from the Institute of Community Studies, Peter Willmott and Michael Young, studied Bethnal Green between 1953 and 1955. Their report, *Family and Kinship in East London*, was published in 1957, selling over a million copies.[116]

When these two participant-observers stepped into Bethnal Green they discovered a tightly knit working-class district, a village in the middle of London, suffused with the warmth and friendliness of intimate family groups.[117] Theirs was a startling finding, for up to that point English observers of slum areas had seen only poverty and isolation, lack of social ties, and failure to achieve collective representation.

In the early 1950s, Alison and Peter Smithson were actively studying the writings of sociologists, from which they concluded that communities were the places where social rejuvenation should begin. Although they referred pejoratively to Willmott and Young as "academic" sociologists and preferred to acknowledge the influence of articles such as Rattray Taylor's "The Social Basis of Town Planning" (1951), nevertheless, it was from works such as *Family and Kinship in East London* that the Smithsons learned that humankind throughout the ages reveals an urge to associate, or form into groups.[118] They coined the word "socio-plastics" in an attempt to change the design language of architecture to include such patterns of association, which they now witnessed firsthand in Bethnal Green.[119]

Their friends Nigel and Judith Henderson had moved to Bethnal Green in 1945, when Judith became the anthropologist in charge of a course entitled "Discover your Neighbour," offered to professionals delivering services to the community.[120]

While Judith studied the anthropological profiles of their neighbors, Nigel attended art classes at the Slade. Though untrained in photography, he got hold of a camera and began to peruse the streets of the East End, hoping "to create images that could expose the collage-like nature of everyday life."[121] He became a poignant documenter of the everyday life of the working class: its leisure activities, its consumption patterns, its daily habits, its celebrations. Photographing the uninhibited street play of children, he stressed a freer sort of social organization, an informal and loosely connected system of relationships with an ease of communication between the parts.

These photographs, plus numerous visits to the Hendersons and Paolozzis in Bethnal Green, began in the early 1950s to influence the Smithsons' design thinking, inspiring them to design with "human associations" in mind and to consider the street as the place where a *physical contact community* resided, the district as an *acquaintance community*, and the city as an *intellectual contact community*.

> In the suburbs and slums the vital relationship between the house and the street survives, children run about (the street is comparatively quiet), people stop and talk, dismantled vehicles are parked: in the back gardens are pigeons and ferrets and the shops are around the corner: you know the milkman, *you* are outside *your* street in *your* house in *your* street.[122]

Each community subdivision the Smithsons termed an "appreciated unit," its structure to be invented anew for each type of community. Their selection of common words to name different groupings, from private space to common ground, always stressed

HOW OTHER PEOPLES DWELL AND BUILD

by E. A. Gutkind

5
Mohammedan houses

THE type of the Mohammedan private house varies considerably within the large region which is inhabited by the adherents of Islam. But they all have in common a strict separation of the living- and reception-rooms from the women's apartments. In general the latter are, in the Mediterranean region, on the upper floors, often with oriels or windows covered with *musharabiya*, behind which is arranged in many cases a wide and comfortable divan with rugs and cushions. In the East the women's quarters are mostly in a separate second court.

The great variety of dwellings may be reduced to two basic types, though this should be taken with a grain of salt because all generalising classifications are open to a justified criticism. The most primitive form is the bee-hive hut built of clay and mud. This type can be found in many parts of the Mohammedan world where the poorer classes have to make the best of the locally available building materials or where a semi-nomadic population has settled in its first stage of transformation from an itinerant to a sedentary way of life. Bee-hive huts are, therefore, often erected in the outlying quarters of the cities and towns by people who have only recently, and not yet completely, given up their agricultural or pastoral activities, and who are slowly absorbed into urban life. The second type prevails where timber is available for the building of flat roofs. The ground plan in this case rectangular or square and often a second storey is added the size of which is frequently smaller than that of the ground floor so that the remaining part can be used as a terrace. Both types can be combined: the lower part of the bee-hive hut becomes a cube while the cupola of the roof is preserved and stands out above the flat roof as a hemi-

sphere. The dome of the mosques may have developed from this primitive combination of the flat and spherical roofs. Another combination of the circular and rectangular forms results in a barrel-vaulted roof: the house is a long rectangle and the cupola is, as it were, stretched out in the shape of a barrel-roof. This latter type can be found especially in the South of Tunisia and neighbouring parts of the country, while the former, the square cupola-house, has spread over the whole Islamic world and even to Southern Europe.

As already said, the reduction of the great variety of dwellings to two basic types is an over-simplification, but it may help to understand some of the fundamental principles which have given shape and character to many Mohammedan buildings.

Mohammedan towns developed mainly either through the influence of agriculture or as nodal points of lines of communication. In the former case they have all the principal characteristics of an oasis town; in the latter they are in the first instance market towns. However, there are many examples where both factors coincide. The towns are not communities in our sense, nor is there anything like an influential guild system as an administrative nucleus which would create a corporate unity. The plan of a

(continued overleaf)

Above: an Algerian street. Note the women's balconies supported on brackets. Below: a covered market in Fez. (Photos: Exclusive News Agency.)

159

3.9

AD published a series of articles by E. A. Gutkind in 1953, "How Other Peoples Dwell and Build," ranging from the houses of the South Seas, Japan, and China to Africa, Arab nations, and native Americans. This page on "How Other Peoples Dwell and Build: 5 Mohammedan Houses" appeared in *AD* 23 (June 1953), 159.

the public space of sociability: words such as the "life-of-the-street," "the doorstep," "yard-garden," and "street-deck."

How people dwell and live, how architecture provides the framework for ways of life, were crucial components in the Smithsons' "status of ideas," as evidenced in their extended idea of "socio-plastics." They drew lessons from criticism expressed by the MARS group about CIAM's postwar concentration on "habitat" as the main focus for its activities, the word being difficult to translate into English. The group asked, instead, that "habitat" be interpreted as "the dwelling and its immediate environment" with emphasis placed on environment—the extras—rather than on the dwelling itself.[123]

> MARS feels it is now vitally necessary to study the immediate environment of the dwelling unit: the matrix in which it is set; the space—covered and open—required for communal activities and communal services, affecting and affected by the way of life of the community.[124]

Another influence came from MARS member Erwin Anton Gutkind's writings, although the Smithsons never acknowledged Gutkind's effect on their conceptual formations. Yet similarities must be recognized between concepts in Gutkind's *Revolution of Environment* (1946) and his *Community and Environment: A Discourse on Social Ecology* (1953) and those in the Smithsons' "Urban Re-identification" document (1952), and subsequent writings. Gutkind was the first to utilize terms such as "patterns of association," "patterns of mobility," and "cluster" to discuss the relationship between house, street, and district and "how people dwell and live." He introduced a different mode of thought into architectural discourse: instead of thinking that architectural forms were simply solid lumps of stuff, he suggested a process view, an emphasis on dynamic aspects such as production, marketing, communication, and human associations. This was exactly what the Smithsons were aiming at as well—an architectural process that considered a new set of relationships between man and his environment, an "ecological approach." Thinking in processes meant seeing relations between things and understanding how these processes interacted with internalized feelings. Gutkind wrote:

> The goal is "wholeness" and not a mere adding together of details collected at random. How to work out a relationship with the external environment and see it as an ever-changing pattern of phenomena and events?[125]

In 1953, Gutkind wrote a series of six articles for *AD* on "How Other Peoples Dwell and Build." These range over the houses of the South Seas, Japan, China, Africa, the Arab nations, and native Americans.[126] All appeared in the winter and spring, before CIAM 9 (Aix-en-Provence) at the end of July. Gutkind explained that his intent in this series of articles was to examine the interplay of ideas that moved people in different parts of the world to build their homes as they did, and to formulate the language of forms in which these ideas were expressed. There were two serious reasons for his series: first was the lack of awareness about and subsequent neglect of the need of millions around the world for adequate homes. The second reason for the series of articles was to aid architects when they did consider the provision for housing, to help them take into account the varying needs, customs, and aspirations of the recipients of their aid. A standard universal solution, such as modern architects had promoted before the war, was no longer applicable. The West had lost the values which bind people together in a spirit of community, but in past Western societies, and still in various non-Western and "primitive" ones, housing forms a part of the social and spiritual life of a people, of the local group and the whole community—and this, Gutkind warned, must be respected and understood by architects hoping to build as well for the West.

So it was with Gutkind's words fresh in their minds that many of the young architects went to CIAM 9 at Aix-en-Provence.

The Impact of Aix-en-Provence on "Socio-plastics"

At Aix-en-Provence, Alison and Peter Smithson saw for the first time, displayed in some of the grilles, a "housing of hope": structures designed not for universal man, but for the man of the slums, of the *bidonvilles*, taking into consideration his local needs, his everyday life. For example, CIAM-Alger's grille of the Mahieddine *bidonville* in Algiers was a huge display of forty-nine vertical stripes spread longitudinally across dividing screens and stretching around one and a half sides of the presentation hall. They were amazed as well by GAMMA Maroc's grille, with its golden suns on wands and new language of architecture generated by patterns of inhabitation.[127] Never before had the Smithsons been exposed to the world of *bidonvilles*, or learned how to approach other civilizations from a humble point of view, but these experiences must have resonated with their own recent encounters in Bethnal Green, and perhaps with their readings of Gutkind.[128]

The GAMMA grille, *Habitat du plus grand nombre* ("Housing for the greatest number"), was presented by Georges Candilis and Shadrach Woods. It displayed a range of photographs, including aerial views of North African *bidonvilles*, and provided information on the demographic forces that gave rise to these congested settlements: "We tried to show that the bidonville negotiates between a tradition and a modern way of life. It stands halfway between the two."[129] Their text maintained that it was impossible to distinguish between an individual habitat and a group habitat, for habitat always involves the entire environment and mediates between the artificial and natural, the social and technical.

> The original habitat: the "Casbahs" of the Sahara, the ksours, fortified villages in the Atlas, the collective fortified towers reflect this aptitude of people to live next to each other in respecting domestic intimacy, while directing, with common agreement, the affairs of community interest.[130]

Absorbing these new lessons, the work of the architect "in cultures-in-change," Alison and Peter Smithson would stress, is to make visible the community to itself, to give it identity.

> The way he does this is to create building types which by themselves read "house" or "church" or "shop," and which in combination read "particular community."
>
> The typal-images for the various functions within the culture give general legibility, and the variations and systems of combinations give the exact identity to a particular group.[131]

Here the Smithsons were thinking of Le Corbusier's structures at Chandigarh; though the buildings were "Europe 1950," this preformed order had been extended to meet local environmental requirements. And they mentioned the ATBAT-Afrique housing project in Casablanca (1953), where courtyard housing was laid out on a regular grid yet was reminiscent of housing in villages beyond the Atlas. The architects' solution was to provide a multistory, modern, hygienic casbah arranged around open space.

> Now what is good about these buildings is that they manage to be African, and yet not be simply an academic restatement of traditional African forms, and they do not try to ignore the existence of the dynamic technology and aesthetic of European architecture of the immediate past, especially Le Corbusier's in the 1920s. Yet they do not copy that either.[132]

The most an architect can do in cultures-in-change is

> to constitute themselves as "image-making" ginger-groups who try to face up to the problems of the present.
>
> They must try to find out, for example, how to group houses together so that the group has identity and meaning within the community.[133]

III. Conclusion

From sociological and anthropological sources the Smithsons turned back to the language of architecture, hoping to modernize it intellectually, bring it up to date with the new set of concerns they had witnessed in Aix-en-Provence. Yet misgivings over the success of their modernizing reforms began to trouble them in the mid-1960s, and culminated in outright skepticism by the 1970s. This was a period in which they had few building projects, which may have led them to question their "ideational" stance as well. Had they reached the end of the line, a place where their words doubled back on themselves? The practice of hyphenating words, blocking out a space for open-ended meanings to emerge, now strung out into longer and longer lists such as "motorway-and-public-transport-nets-design-thinking" or "freely-arrived-at-group-form."[134] The inevitable gap between word and thing was getting larger, not smaller, and in that expanding void a sense of insecurity, even pessimism, began to creep into their thoughts.

They had called for architecture on the scale of the new times—big enough to dominate the topography of the landscape. Yet this gave rise to the "sky-blue thinking" [*sic*] of megastructures in the mid-1960s, which forced the Smithsons to develop a "counter-thesis" against the built-in inflexibility of such structures, which locked together in one unalterable embrace both circulation systems and occupied parts.[135] "Put crudely, self-assertive buildings full of rhetoric and gesture seem to occupy more space and use up that space's absorbency leaving less room for people."[136]

They were compelled to evaluate retrospectively their own serviced and served buildings as antidotes. Thus, in their Economist Building (1959–1962) they had separated out each element, giving systems of occupancy and of servicing enough room to develop, before coming together to build outward toward the collective group. "The 'space-between' is the collective of all spaces that each building carries within it."[137] This was the important relationship, a kind of "anti-space space," if you will. Three separate, nearly symmetrical elements were then "hooked onto, or bedded into, a much freer circulation system."[138]

3.10
Alison and Peter Smithson, architects, Economist Building (1959–1962), three men on the plaza, looking towards Brook's Club in St. James's Street, photograph by Michael Carapetian, 1964. Smithson Family Collection.

Peter Smithson explained in gentle tones: "In a garden one thinks and builds outwards from the house into the surrounding space, looking for limits, looking for uses, giving sense to random places. So also should the city grow."[139] A city should have a poetry of movement and yet a sense of quietude too. Spaces should be ordinary, "to be enjoyed with the same directness and deeply felt contentment we can still feel in the fishing harbour, the market place, the quayside, where older technologies and ways of doing things still hold."[140]

The question was how to continue the tradition of the city as a collective work of art, how to unfold the present yet allow for new technologies and change. Peter Smithson offers an extended answer:

> By discovering the routes which would give a sense of release, and from which one could feel the structure of the city.
> By building buildings which quietly indicate what one might do there.
> By personal commitment to place. To one's own place, to the city as an extension of oneself, comprehended bodily and extended as one extends one's arm or builds a garden.
> What do we know about how to do these things?
> We know that roads can be used as a way of controlling intensity of use, and that through them we can loosen-up the texture of the city.
> We know that buildings can have capacity-to-make-places built into them, for example:
> By systems of linkage.
> By form compatibility.
> By style compatibility—a capacity to live with one another by the use of neutrality.
> ...
> You may say that we do not know very much. But the whole notion of "building-towards-the-community-structure" has been lost. What was once the natural way of building has become too metaphysical to be grasped even by my own students.
> So it will mean a great deal of effort before what we do know becomes language accessible to all.[141]

And thus we cycle back to the need to create a *language of architecture.* "Appropriateness" of building forms and building groups depends, the Smithsons explained, on "radical organizational thinking ... *but it is also a question of language.*" If the language of architecture does not meet the needs of people, then undefined, unarticulated longings will cause trouble in the end.[142]

A SPECIAL NUMBER OF THE ARCHITECTURAL REVIEW FOR DECEMBER 1950 VOLUME CVIII NUMBER 648 THREE SHILLINGS AND SIXPENCE

man made
AMERICA

4

Messages from America

[N]o other country in the world has publicized itself, by one or other of the visual techniques which are available to contemporary societies, more than the United States of America. Through the motion picture, fictional and documentary, through magazines and books, the world's millions have received a two-dimensional picture of a vast landscape which, so far as such things go, is amazingly complete. ... Not until he [the visitor] is able to move about in the landscape can he understand it as a living work of art, and assess what we have called the "form-will" of the nation that fashioned it.

Editors of *Architectural Review*[1]

Prologue

AR published two surveys of American architecture, "Man Made America" (1950) and "Machine Made America" (1957). They found little worthy of praise across the wasteland of the United States. In articles in *AD* in the 1950s, architectural critic Lawrence Alloway countered *AR*'s scurrilous attack (as he saw it) on America as the land of the culturally deprived. To the contrary, Alloway found American culture—brash, noisy, popular, pragmatic, and assertive—an antidote to the arrogant, claustrophobic, postwar culture of English fine art. The generational difference expressed by the editorial policies of *AR* and of *AD* in the 1950s could not be more evident. Moreover, "Pop Art," as Alloway defined it, was an urban art, the art of the crowd, fashion, and automobile styling. It was an art of representation concerning signs and media images visualized in the streets of American cities or gleaned from American magazines, comic books, pulp fiction, and Hollywood. This chapter analyzes the influence of ideas and images coming from America on the younger generation of postwar British architects, artists and designers; the awareness of the city as defined by games, by crowds, by fashion; Norbert Wiener's technical ideas about communication; Claude Shannon's theory of the relationship between coder, channel, and decoder; and Charles and Ray Eames's reverence for pretty objects, toys, photographs, tackboard displays, and their film *Communications Primer*. It examines Alloway's *AD* writings as an unacknowledged influence on the Smithsons' Pop sensibilities.

4.1
"Man Made America," *AR* 108 (December 1950), cover.

I. Learning from America

Land of the Culturally Deprived

In addition to its conservative consensus notion that English architects must learn from the nation's traditional towns and vernacular forms, *AR* feared there was something going on in postwar America that might infect English character and good taste. Its editors and some of its writers spoke disparagingly about American brashness and immature design habits. Pevsner, for example, believed that the postwar American automobile symbolized riches and power: "That sort of noisy show comes off in the United States where it is at least in accordance with its people."[2] Thus the popularity of American designs, which *AR* decried, was blamed on the common man, even though this was the same common man—or at least an American counterpart of the same English common man—that *AR* was trying to listen to and educate. Setting the tone for the high art/popular art debate, its editors explained that "the common man feels and only the uncommon man thinks."[3]

In 1950, *AR* turned its pictorial eye upon the American landscape, devoting an issue to "Man Made America."[4] Looking for the "form-will" of American society, the editors, assisted by city planner and landscape architect Christopher Tunnard, considered the American landscape of "townships, roads, railways, electricity grids, clearings, afforestation schemes, backyards, real estate ventures, wastes, wilds, ornamental parkways, ribbon developments"—whatever shaped the three-dimensional picture of the society.[5] The editors believed that "the picture a nation creates of itself out of, and upon, its landscape is a more realistic self-portrait than many of us like to admit."[6] And they were repelled by the self-portrait they beheld. Five characteristic features stood out in America: standardized gridiron city plans, garden suburbs, agglomerations of cubist objects in the centers of towns, skyscraper districts, and vast urban projects of unprecedented scale, such as the colossal highway system.

AR was shocked by the untrammeled visual chaos reigning supreme throughout America. The youngest, wealthiest and most powerful nation in the world had not been able to produce a culture that amounted to anything other than a "symbol of promise, the question mark,"[7] and Americans, the journal opined, were alarmingly complacent about the symptoms of this disease, exhibiting a failure of will to control the spread of materialism. Europeans were stunned by this vulgarity because "inside every European is an American" who in some way not only identifies with the American adventure but feels responsible for it and implicated in it—no matter how condescending this might sound.[8]

America, *AR* continued, instead of creating a new paradise and experimenting with a new way of life, is concerned merely with "thinking bigger, going faster, rising higher, than the Old World; with improving on the Old World, that is to say merely quantitatively … it has merely raised to the power of 'n' the potential of the old."[9] The unfortunate ultimate effect of this crass materialism and gigantism is to destroy the dream every European holds of America and to dash any hope that America would establish a life purged of materialism. Instead, American laissez-faire capitalism had produced a "visually scrofulous waste-land" spreading across an entire continent, "a combination of automobile graveyard, industrial no-man's land and Usonian Idiot's Delight" (a reference to Frank Lloyd Wright, who coined the word "Usonia" for his vision of a redeveloped American landscape).[10] *AR*'s survey revealed, the editors believed, that the American landscape exhibits the same symptoms of infantilism and arrested development as does the baby-talk language that the Americans speak. In the end, America may have nothing to offer Europeans other than Marshall Plan dollars and crooners of popular songs.

Nor was that the worst of it. America's naive belief in technological progress as the path toward salvation, its unshakable faith that technology would solve every problem, "is the pistol the U. S. holds to the stomach of western civilization."[11] This naiveté and childishness are deadly dangerous to democracy as it struggles to survive in the Cold War era. *AR*, with tongue in cheek, praised American popular art—given that "comics were a less lethal form of escape than gin"—but drew a sharp distinction between the popular and fine arts, the latter being the world of the "spirit," for which America showed little indication of concern. Americans were big children who should be reminded that their frontier days were over and they "no longer galloped in ten-gallon hats after Redskins."[12] *AR* scolded them for not applying themselves to the development of sedentary values, and attending to their chaotic and disreputable visual environment.

As if *AR*'s attachment to the English Picturesque had not poured enough petrol on the younger generation's sense of outrage, its dismissive treatment of American-built forms and disdain of its popular culture threw on more. England in the early 1950s was still climbing out of the debris of World War II; food rationing did not cease completely until 1954, and household appliances and products remained in short supply. Living in cold-water flats and confined by the art academies' strictures on visual design, the younger generation of artists and architects looked to America in this period as a land of luxury, as revealed by the images of consumer products pouring out of the glossy pages of every American magazine. America was the future! The younger generation basked in Hollywood glamour; Detroit styling; bulbous, streamlined, or borax designs; and science fiction, comics, and Wild West stories. Reyner Banham would later recall:

> One of the great trainings for the public's eye was reading American magazines. We goggled at the graphics and the colour-work in adverts for appliances that were almost inconceivable in power-short Britain, and food ads so luscious you wanted to eat them. Remember we had spent our teenage years surviving the horrors and deprivations of a six-year war. For us, the fruits of peace had to be tangible, preferably edible. Those ads may look yucky now, to the overfed eyes of today, but to us they looked like Paradise Regained—or at least a paper promise of it.[13]

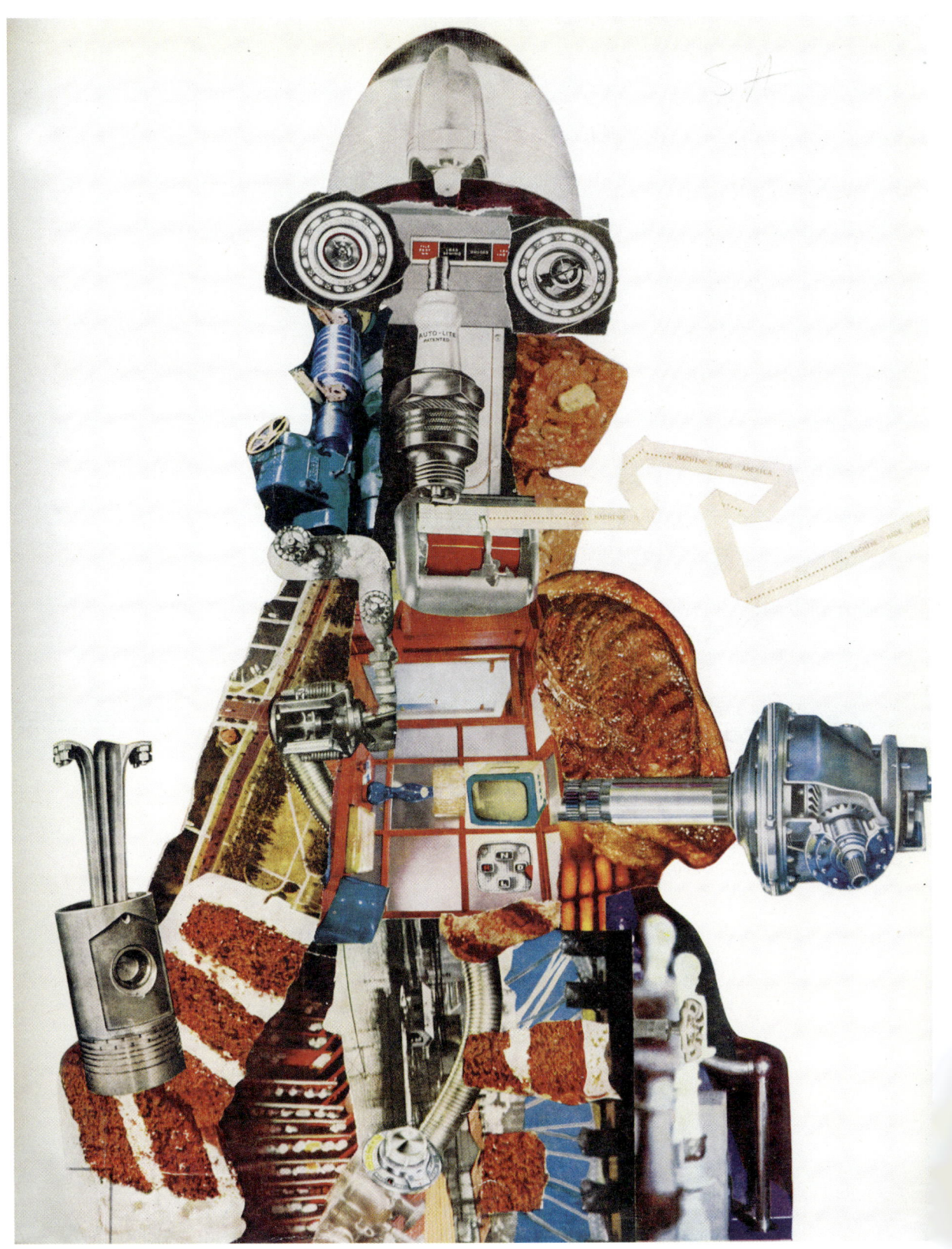

4.2

"Machine Made America," cover designed by John McHale, *AR* 121 (May 1957). "The Cover personage, by John McHale with the tetragram of power—Neutral, Drive, Low, Reverse—graven on his heart, was assembled from typical fragments of the cultural complex that he also symbolizes; Machine Made America. The source of material was one of America's favourite flattering mirrors, coloured magazine illustrations, and reflects a world of infra-grilled steak, pre-mixed cake, dream-kitchens, dream-cars, machine-tools, power-mixers, parkways, harbours, ticker-tape, spark-plugs and electronics."

In 1957 the editors of *AR* came to believe that back in 1950 they may have focused too strongly on the failure of America to control its "malignant growth of unplanned sprawl" and visual squalor. They therefore returned for a second look, devoting another special issue, "Machine Made America," edited by Ian McCallum, to what they now termed a "success story."[14] *AR* contended that American self-confidence and conviction had not only constructed an impressive quantity of buildings since World War II, but had promoted the industrialization of the curtain wall as "the syntax" of design for a new vernacular architecture. Many architects, from East Coast schools to the grass roots, displaying considerable creative ability, had deployed this syntax to generate noteworthy structures. But, *AR* equivocated, this success had to be seen against the double background of both the Modern Movement, whose great masters had moved to America at the beginning of the Holocaust in the 1930s, and the fact of American engineering know-how, the country's technological culture. "Machine Made America" was *AR*'s attempt to teach the American architect that

> the task of discovering "an entire universe and—a complete language" is a task he has shared with trail-blazers of the modern movement everywhere; it was just this that the new architecture demanded of its practitioners whether in the old world or the new. The collective achievement in roughly fifty years is a partial universe and an incomplete language, but it is no mean one in face of the task.[15]

Yet in America, architects were clearly not fulfilling all the functions demanded of them. Many of their buildings were too cold or too hot, too noisy, too leaky, too inflexible, and much too expensive. No wonder architects were actually responsible for only a minor proportion of constructed buildings. People were aware that something did not add up.

> What doesn't add up are the kind of things they are beginning to take for granted like cars, television sets, refrigerators and washing machines, when set beside their buildings. They have heard, because architects, among others, never stopped telling them, of the great advantages to be gained, from prefabrication, standardization, modular planning, and so on; but architecture, it seems, still fails to benefit. All the arguments of the architects and builders as to why architecture cannot compete don't quite avail against such standing comparisons as the refrigerator and the washing machine.[16]

It may be an unfair comparison, *AR* opined, between industrial prefabrication of building components and consumer goods, but people expect glitter and efficiency, good design and good performance in both

Steering toward its preferred Townscape frame of mind, *AR* complained that abundant paraphernalia like refrigerators and cars had proliferated over the urban scene, making a mess. The marks Americans are leaving behind on the ground, the signs of their existence, are so disorderly that it is "often impossible to see the building for the advertisement, the advertisement for the sign, the sign for the traffic, the traffic for the speed. The curtain wall will not solve all of this, but it can help."[17]

AR noted a growing phenomenon: the American grand tour was becoming almost obligatory for the young European architect because "the development of American architecture has been so rapid in recent years, and the idiom [of the curtain wall] is becoming so consistent that the picture seen from a distance spreads itself thin and takes on a distressingly two-dimensional appearance."[18] The young architect has to see for herself or himself what the past fifty years has produced in the way of three-dimensional American architecture, and to understand that only a "gargantuan struggle and nothing less, as prizes, than a new-made world and a new language of vision could have fired it."[19]

What America taught, *AR*'s editors said, was an all too apparent fact:

Mechanization is part of almost every detail of our lives from the mechanical brain to the "untouched-by-hand cake mix" ... : already it has its poets and its painters; an architect like Mies, a painter like the late Jackson Pollock (action painting has a very direct relationship), the new kind of artist-technician like Charles Eames, all give witness to the credit side of the balance (putting material benefits on the debit side as, I suppose, in the light of the highest ideals you should). It has its popular art, no less fascinating and instructive, perhaps, for being on the debit side (in light of the highest ideals). The cover of this issue [by Independent Group member John McHale] is an example of an artist using a popular aspect of mechanization (coloured advertising) as the raw material of his art. It is easy to decry the strange, and often suggestive, shapes of the latest American cars, it is harder to laugh off, except in pure snobbery, the genuine enthusiasm and excitement they generate. We are fond of explaining that modern architecture is still in its infancy, that the maturing process is always a long one; is it not possible that this may also apply to popular art, however different the methods by which it is produced?[20]

If Britain remained inhibited before mechanization's inevitable onslaught, *AR* warned, then the nation would soon be "engulfed by its monstrous aspects. ... [W]e don't laugh at it or with it enough and we haven't house trained it."[21] America's excess of enthusiasm over its engineering devices and other achievements, *AR* continued, drives out all reason, and "is no doubt evidence of immaturity and hard to tolerate for long, but it often signifies a healthy adolescence—a period of rapid growth."[22]

This criticism appended *AR*'s visual concerns, its editors said, to what Le Corbusier had said in the 1930s. Only when America began to think in visual terms, planning new buildings in intimate relationship with older ones and taking into concern regional differentiations, would the country display signs of maturity. Meanwhile, "industrialized building, with its origins in Europe and its adolescence in America, may finally become truly international; for when it is efficiently exploited and when, and if, tariff barriers come down, buildings will come through as well as motor cars and refrigerators."[23]

Drawing sharp dichotomies between architecture and consumer products, English townscapes and American urban sprawl, and European mature intelligence and American adolescence was not likely to win over the younger generation of British artists and architects, who wanted to learn everything they could from American culture. That culture seemed to be able to transform massive amounts of material spewing from multiple communication channels into forms of art. They dreamed of visiting America to see firsthand its cornucopia of delights; they were fascinated with the very junk that pervaded the urban scene. But from what source did such diffusion of information, with its plurality of messages and its fantastic lifestyles, spring? And who might teach them what it all meant?

Gung-Ho for America

Members of the younger generation of artists and architects forming the so-called Independent Group (IG) at the Institute of Contemporary Arts (ICA) in 1952–1955 gushed enthusiasm over almost everything emanating from postwar America.[24] They saw there the convergence of commerce with art, and sought inspiration from its iconography of ordinary visual environments. Steeped in the nonmathematical aspects of Norbert Wiener's ideas about feedback and Claude Shannon's theory of information, they searched for patterns in the signs and codes they perceived in America's newspapers, television, glossy magazine advertisements, pulp fiction, comics, and movies.

Lawrence Alloway, an art critic associated with the IG whose views will be discussed extensively in this chapter, believed that he could discern a pattern of culture spanning a continuum of high art and popular art, a continuum that blurred and eradicated boundaries. He was interested in mass-media communications, topical material, and transformative situations. He apparently coined the phrase "Pop Art" in 1954, but meant something different by the term from what it has come to mean since:[25] he was referring to technologically reproduced products of the mass media, a mechanized public art aimed to deliver a message. This kind of art, he said, joined him at breakfast on a Kellogg's cereal box, followed him to work via street signs and shop windows, infiltrated his leisure hours while reading a comic book, and inevitably seeped into his dreams and desires.[26]

Theo Crosby, as technical editor of *AD* from 1953 to 1962, editor of the five issues of *Uppercase* magazine (1958–1960), and organizer of the "This Is Tomorrow" exhibition (1956), saw to it that *AD* published work by IG members Lawrence Alloway, Richard Hamilton, John McHale, and Alison and Peter Smithson, offering them opportunities to explain their enthusiasm for American popular culture, consumer products, and advertisements, as well as the communications and cybernetics revolution—the very same street clutter and mechanized culture that *AR* despaired of as evidence of American adolescence and immaturity.[27] The younger generation of postwar architects were not frivolously interested in popular imagery; they were directly involved with what Crosby called the "great communal projects of the 1950s," including designing thirteen New Towns, planning the National Parks system, providing social housing, and teaching in the new and expanded university system.[28]

Yet in all these realms there was generational conflict over assumed architectural and artistic styles. *AR* was ambivalent not only about America but about European modernism, seeking an English way out through an art drawn directly from nature, seaside vernacular forms, and the English townscape. The IG architects and like-minded colleagues, in contrast, who tended to give tongue in the pages of *AD*, were enamored by the Heroic Period of modern architecture of the 1920s and 1930s, focused their architectural discussions on "history" and "precedent," and traveled to see heroic modern buildings in Europe as well as the masterpieces of past centuries.[29] And one of the countries they traveled to most—via imagery and imagination, at least, if not always in person—was the United States.

World War II had disrupted the education of many members of the IG, as some were in the military and others worked in factories. All benefited, however, from the postwar Labor government's financial support program, which allowed them to continue their education as mature students. In the early 1950s, images of war and destruction were still fresh in their minds, and no wonder, with piles of rubble and vacant lots still strewn about British towns. Magda Cordell McHale claims that this led them to search for new images to replace the old, especially images from America—a place they knew, at first, only from magazines, books, and movies.[30] Richard Hamilton believes the IG was held together by skepticism and a desire to know what had been happening during the lost war years—hence their interest in pure, not applied, research.[31] What seemed to bind them together more than anything else was enthusiasm for the internally powered, brash energy of the iconography pouring out of the US.

The IG—at first called the Young Group by its members—held its first meetings at the ICA in the spring and fall of 1952.[32] It would hold sessions again in 1953–1954, these involving a larger group, and continue to meet sporadically until July 1955. The first meeting, of *Bunk!* fame, was memorable.[33] Paolozzi gave an informal lecture, bombarding those present with images: "the first time images had been shown—Blam, blam, blam—with no order or link," Colin St. John Wilson recalled.[34] He used an early form of overhead projector called an epidiascope to project pieces in rapid succession. Although no definitive list of images from this presentation exists, judging by his extant collages they probably included covers from *Amazing Stories*, advertisements for Cadillac and Chevrolet, a drawing from the Disney film *Mother Goose Goes to Hollywood* (1938), sheets of US Army aircraft insignia, and fictional robots.

But Paolozzi's enthusiasms were not congenial to all. Herbert Read, one of the ICA's directors, was intent on preserving the divide between high art/high culture and popular art/popular culture. He, like many English intellectuals, disdained the low-brow culture coming from America. To bolster his criticism he cited a review of Eric Gill's *Beauty Looks After Itself*, warning that the fine arts

> will wither in the new social atmosphere that has come into existence with the increasing mechanisation of life and industry. A people whose occupations are mechanical, whose leisure is spent in motor cars and cinemas, whose ideal is speed and whose god is money cannot discover points of contact with the arts whose existence presupposed life lived in a more leisurely and contemplative fashion. They belong to different worlds and no communication is finally possible between them.[35]

But the more hostile the reception given to the messages from America, whether in the *AR* or from trustees of modernism such as Herbert Read, the more the younger postwar generation exaggerated their emphasis on passion, play, eroticism, fun, flux, change, and open-ended systems and processes. Signs coming from America, and fresh ideas about the rules that operated upon these signs, inspired the members of the IG. They eagerly shared the latest books and magazines, quickly adopted neologisms from American slang and technological lingo, and wrung new meanings from odd juxtapositions. Forget the modernists' boring classifications and hierarchies, by which they would impose their schemes of order on the city! That approach had to be discarded so that the latent design of city streets could become something worth exploring: one must appropriate, not disparage, the streets' messages and signs, learn from their fashions and their ambiance, and so in time develop a new language of design. This reaction was in some ways a return to the Surrealists' cult of the *objet trouvé* (found object), a new cherishing of all sorts of items "as found," including advertisements and publicity images, the detritus of consumer society, even the junk in the streets. All this flotsam and jetsam could be salvaged and recycled as art.

In "The Development of British Pop" (1966), Alloway recalled the interest that members of the IG had in the city as seen from a new perspective: "as a symbol-thick scene, criss-crossed with tracks of human activity. The feeling is not an easy one to set down, but it was a kind of subjective sense of the city, as a known place, defined by games, by crowds, by fashion."[36] Alloway was the most prolific writer on American culture in the IG, his voice the strongest in relaying a concept that Pop Art was urban art, forged in the streets and to be grasped via the imagery flowing from America. I will explore his intriguing work on this subject shortly.

Most of IG's members, as already indicated, shared Alloway's pro-Americanism. It was a useful stance to fling against European esthetes who turned up their noses at the pathologies of American capitalism. Each, as the IG member Toni del Renzio later claimed, wanted to be a "knowing consumer," a skill that could be learned only from the cornucopia of American consumer goods. The tone was of all-or-nothing commitment to America: no timidity, no compromise, a brash devotion that could override the deterrents of American politics, McCarthy witch hunts, and the atom bomb—because

American capitalism delivered the goods. Yet, del Renzio complained in 1976, IG's playful opinions of the early 1950s hardened and became uncritical as the years passed, "especially in a blind acceptance of everything American as therefore good; and if there was a choice between an American and a European product, the American was automatically superior."[37] To begin with, in any case, "America" was a place of refuge, the major source and form of an information and communication explosion inundating the young designers' world.

The Information Revolution

IG member Geoffrey Holroyd recalled the American influences he received while attending graduate school at Harvard in 1952, and taking trips to Chicago and California in the spring and summer of 1953. There he "learned a way of seeing architecture as part of a general cultural situation focused on daily life and experience."[38] Art could be approached from a psychological and sociological viewpoint; design theory could be based on assemblages of signs and symbols. This moved the image away from static fixity toward a constantly changing model of popular life. When he returned to England in 1954, he brought with him a clutch of books that included Norbert Wiener's *The Human Use of Human Beings* (1950) and Suzanne Langer's *Philosophy in a New Key* (1942), the latter being one of the first cheap paperbacks printed in the US.

It was not just the phraseology of cybernetics, systems analysis, and information theory that the younger generation borrowed, but their working assumptions. Norbert Wiener, for example, urged that "society can only be understood through a study of the messages and the communications facilities which belong to it,"[39] and it was in this spirit that IG surfed the wave of popular culture. Wiener, a professor of mathematics at MIT, defined cybernetics broadly as "a chapter in the theory of messages,"[40] and stated that "the fundamental idea of communication is that of the transmission of messages."[41] The ability to adjust to the contingencies of the outer environment and to live effectively within that environment depends on a process of receiving and utilizing information: "To live effectively is to live with adequate information."[42] Wiener noted that every pattern can be considered as a message: a radio, for example, produces patterns of sound, a television patterns of light, neither being different in principle from a "message" consisting of a sequence of symbols. Recent advances portended the coming of a second industrial age based not on mechanical processes but on the transformation and transmission of information and messages.[43]

In *Cybernetics* (1948), Wiener outlined how a dynamic system can be controlled or regulated by feeding back into its operations inputs or information gathered from its environment.[44] Such dynamic monitoring and control, or "cybernetics," is used to direct the system toward a stated goal and can be applied not only to machines such as guided missiles but to chemical, biological, and societal processes. All purposive behavior is

COPPER CLOTHING COMPANY SALVAGE LTD.

Laundry bowlers were out played

22.I.68.

Dear Mr Smithson,

We were very lucky to be able to re-call our Mr Henderson (late Area Manager Macclesfield Malt Hose and Sphagnum Moss Marketing Developments) from a Goodwill Sporting Tour where he is currently fully committed as captain of our outstandingly successful Team of Laundry Bowlers (who have in fact only lost one match this season as the caption in our Mourning Newspaper testifies.)

Whilst awaiting his return to the Depot we have taken the liberty of opening your esteemed communication and note your suggestion that he should contact the Manager of the London firm of Moulded Garments & Extruded Gaiters, in which we understand you have an interest, with a view to taking over the Experimental Department concerned with developments in the Fancy Frog Fronts and Tattooed Toecap lines.

Should nothing come of this approach we should like you to know that we have a number of other Sporting & other Avenues we wish to explore.

EXPERIENCED ARCHITECTURAL YOUNG LADY

BONUS SURVEYOR & PERSONAL MILK MINDER

Cricketers lose at football

Increases in N-E Essex population

TOC H MINIBUS APPEAL

4.3
Nigel Henderson's newspaper cut-ups in an amusing letter sent to Peter Smithson (January 22, 1968). Smithson Family Collection.

a matter of negative feedback—dampening oscillations, mitigating loss of information, controlling a trajectory toward a stated goal.

Systems analysis, a theory outlined by Ludwig von Bertalanffy in works first published in German in the 1930s and translated into English shortly after World War II, also influenced members of IG.[45] Bertalanffy believed that narrow scientific specializations prohibited the exchange of information across disciplines, hampering innovation. The functioning of a whole system could not be understood by studying its separate parts, for there was always an exchange going on between the system and its environment. Systems theory formulated the principles needed to study a set of elements in interaction—to see "things in relationships."

IG members absorbed such influences, most flowing from America, and concluded that change emanated not from things but from processes, from the way things are done. They were seized by the insight that systems of variables, whether in a mechanical device, computer, society, or urban environment, can keep up constant communication across registers of diverse elements, images, and signs. Full of admiration for new technologies and new machines, they thrilled over the fantasy and wonder of images while theories of consumer control and spectator feedback swirled in their heads. Their mood presaged a "systems aesthetic" based on cybernetics, communication theory, and systems analysis.[46]

Information has the interesting property that it can be not only transmitted and copied, but altered and recombined. Texts and images could be cut up, rearranged, and turned into an assortment of collages and messages bearing fresh meanings. John McHale had been experimenting with cut-ups and strips of language in his collages, what Alloway called "constructions as viewer-participative."[47] McHale's "Transistor" collages of 1953 were visual metaphors for the processing of information, and Nigel Henderson also investigated how bits of paper torn from newspapers and magazines could be organized into humorous messages.[48]

Such visual-verbal amalgams meant getting rid of absolutes—doing away with either/or logic and adopting instead a both/and approach, as John McHale put it, celebrating

> the swift transference of cultural forms across and through multicommunication channels. All are associated with varying degrees of accelerated stylistic change and with the coexistence of a huge number of available and unconditional choices open to the participant or consumer, i.e. there is no inherent value of contradiction implied in enjoying Bach *and* the Beatles. The situation is characteristically *"both/and"* rather than *"either/or."*[49]

"Both/and" liberated members of IG to compose heterogeneous lists of items, drawing on the vast flow of images and signs that the mass media offered up with ever-increasing speed. For example, juxtaposing seemingly disparate culture phenomena in a heterogeneous tabular list enabled Richard Hamilton to compose his poster "Just what

4.4
Page from the catalog of the exhibition "This Is Tomorrow," Whitechapel Gallery, 1956. "Collage of the Senses" contribution from Group 2 (Richard Hamilton, John Voelcker, John McHale).

is it that makes today's homes so different, so appealing?" for the multimedia exhibition "This Is Tomorrow"(1956). Both/and logic enabled the Smithsons, Eduardo Paolozzi, and Nigel Henderson to create an environment called "Patio and Pavilion" for the same exhibition.

The Smithsons designed a crude wooden shedlike structure before departing for CIAM 10 and leaving Paolozzi and Henderson to fill it with "as found" objects and contrasting images. The intended product was a symbolic habitat responding to fundamental human needs: a view of the sky, privacy (with the patio for leisure time), protection (the pavilion), a piece of ground, the presence of nature and animals.[50] The walls of the structure were built of reflecting materials to give an impression of spatial extension, the ground was covered with sand, and various items strewn about—a wheel, a huge rock—suggest that here was an archaeological site recently uncovered, or the detritus of a post-apocalyptic landscape. To this array, Henderson added a brutish photo-collage of the "Head of Man."[51]

One year later (1957), Richard Hamilton wrote a letter to Alison and Peter Smithson, in which he suggested a follow-up exhibition.[52] We can only surmise why he wrote this letter. Presumably he saw in the Smithsons' collaborative contribution something worthy of deeper analysis. He was, he said, still interested in the role that art played in the domestic environment, but thought the "tabular image" of his poster could be expanded and made more coherent. He had tried to build an image of the contemporary domestic environment by making a careful selection of bits and pieces of mass-media imagery, snipping them from their context and putting them together in a new pastiche that never lost sight of their individual meanings or coalesced into an overall composition. Did Hamilton know that the Smithsons' "as found" aesthetics was a matter of making strategic choices before grouping these selected items in distinct arrangements and figures within a system of multiple open-ended relationships? Hamilton's "tabular image" reflected a similar attempt to allow a multiplicity of statements about modern life to be arranged together in a distinct formation.

He began by writing down a list of images that he wanted: "man, woman, humanity, history, food, newspapers, cinema, TV, telephone, comics (picture information), word (verbal information), tape recording (aural information), cars, domestic appliances, space." Beneath this list he wrote: "The image should, therefore, be thought of as tabular as well as pictorial."[53] Hamilton was clearly making a statement that sexual relationships were now mediated by all kinds of communication devices and consumer items, but his juxtapositions may not have projected a shift in cultural values or a new mode of domestic existence as clearly as he desired.

Hamilton thought another exhibition might be more disciplined in its approach, productive of a better "table" of images. He explained to the Smithsons: "The disadvantage (as well as the great virtue) of TiT ["This Is Tomorrow"] show was its incoherence and obscurity of language." A new show might be based on collective adherence to specific requirements:

4.5
Alison and Peter Smithson's collage of the
Patio and Pavilion for "This Is Tomorrow" (1956).
Smithson Family Collection.

a domestic environment e.g. some kind of shelter, some kind of equipment, some kind of art. This solution could then be formulated and rated on the basis of compliance with a table of characteristics of Pop Art. ... [He set forth a tentative list.] This is just a beginning. Perhaps the first part of our task is the analysis of Pop Art and the production of a table. I find I am not yet sure about the "sincerity" of Pop Art.[54]

Survival of cultural values despite the shift toward an affluent society was a concern generally shared by the members of the Independent Group; this may have been another reason for Hamilton to write to the Smithsons, as he was not really sure about "Pop Art" and wondered if it was worthy of his attention. Perhaps the Smithsons, so convinced of the value of what they called "the significant image," could persuade him. Or, Hamilton may simply have written to the Smithsons because they were leaders of the younger British generation of architects and would be strong allies in exploring the domestic environment. In addition to "Patio and Pavilion" they had recently exhibited an amusing "House of the Future" for the Ideal Home Exhibition of 1956. In this design they looked at how appliances have revolutionized the pattern of life. Ad-men sell innovations, changes of style, and these feed back into the fine arts: the architect is forced to design a house with mass-produced components, an expendable throwaway structure.

Communication, as English telecommunications engineer Colin Cherry said in 1957, is a social affair. That is, it involves the act of imparting information, sending messages to one another, and sharing news, experiences, and modes of life according to rules that govern the usage of certain signs.[55] Theo Crosby, as convener of the "This Is Tomorrow" exhibition (1956), hoped that communication in this social sense would thrive in collaborative efforts between architects, painters, and sculptors. The exhibition was a beginning, he proclaimed:

> Our environment is a mess because most people have eyes that do not see, they do not feel the need for visual organization. The exhibition is evidence of attempts towards a new sort of order, a way towards the integration of the arts that must come if our culture is not merely to survive, but come truly to life.[56]

Alloway thought a better notion for the "This Is Tomorrow" exhibition would have been "antagonistic co-operation," as the ideal of symbiotic feelings shared by artists and architects had yet to be achieved—hence "tomorrow," when communicative collaboration might become possible. But what was most important, he argued in the catalog's introduction, is that each of the twelve groups experimented with "several channels of communication" while avoiding any totalizing idea of a synthetic unity. Different channels would thus compete with as well as complement each other, exposing the viewer in an open-ended manner to messages comprising "space effects, a play with signs, a wide range of materials and structures, which, taken together, make of art and architecture a many-channelled activity, as factual and far from ideal standards as the street outside."[57]

the artist and architect has limited their efficiency to narrow mutually exclusive areas. It is this that has made collaboration difficult. Seeing art and architecture in the general framework of communications, however, can reduce these difficulties by a new sense of what is important.

GEOFFREY HOLROYD, TONI DEL RENZIO, LAWRENCE ALLOWAY.

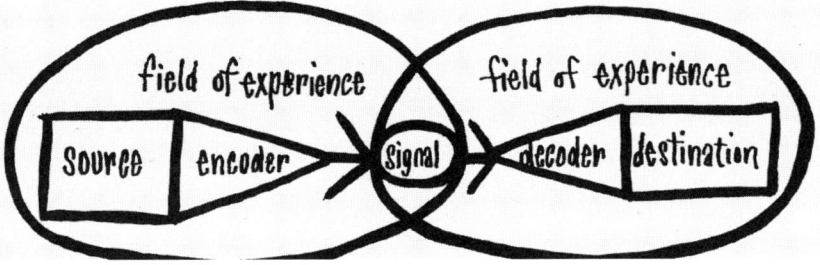

4.6 and 4.7

Two pages from the catalog "This Is Tomorrow," Whitechapel Gallery, 1956. Figure 4.6, the contribution from Group 12 (Lawrence Alloway, Geoffrey Holroyd, Toni del Renzio), is based on the communication diagram of Claude Shannon; figure 4.7 reviews the type of "tackboard" mounted in the exhibition.

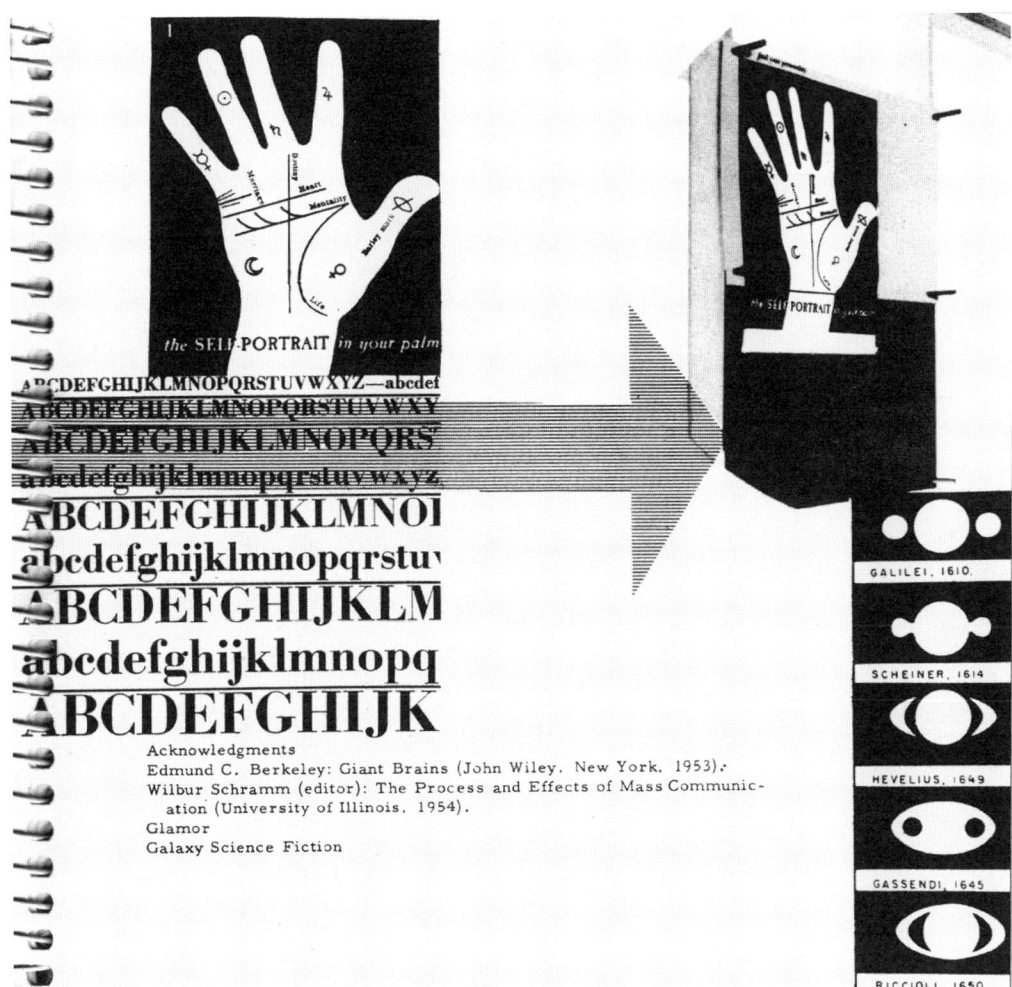

Acknowledgments
Edmund C. Berkeley: Giant Brains (John Wiley, New York, 1953);
Wilbur Schramm (editor): The Process and Effects of Mass Communication (University of Illinois, 1954).
Glamor
Galaxy Science Fiction

It was up to the spectator to become a "knowing consumer" of the urban environment, able to read and understand the symbols that came at them from every street and city wall, assembling meaning from individual perspectives and eventually rejecting all inherited, stereotypical modes of thought. "The freedom of the artists and architects concerned is communicated to the spectator who cannot rely on the learned responses called up by a picture in a frame, a house in a street, words on a page."[58]

The Group 12 exhibit at "This Is Tomorrow," in which Alloway participated with Geoffrey Holroyd and Toni del Renzio, continued this discussion of "communications research which offers a means of talking about human activities (including art and architecture) without dividing them into compartments," as their statement in the catalog put it.[59] Perhaps they were drawing on Colin Cherry's theory of communication, Cherry being a frequenter of ICA talks and exhibitions. They were aware of Norbert Wiener's cybernetics and Claude Shannon's encoder-channel-decoder diagram, but were most strongly influenced by their interpretation of the pinboard work of Charles and Ray Eames, which Holroyd would have seen on his 1953 visit to their Santa Monica office.

One of Group 12's figures in the catalog is a facsimile of Claude Shannon's graph of a generalized communication channel divided into source, channel, receiver — here deployed as an approximation of, or metaphor for, how messages are sent between any two fields of experience. Unlike Shannon, who was interested primarily in the physical apparatus of communication and who explicitly excluded "meaning" from his definition of "information," Group 12 was concerned with how meanings enable communication to occur, noting that at the human level both sender and receiver must have some overlap in their fields of experience in order to be mutually intelligible. Modern technology had increased the variety of communications channels, so mass audiences, as receivers of this diversity of messages, needed new ways to organize them. Group 12 offered, as a pointer to how the new multiplicity of messages might be engaged, a table with columns labeled "physical objects," "arranged in or on," "operated or produced by," and so on, with each row filled with elements such as "marks," "pen pencil," or "fingers." They hoped to thus suggest new ways of thinking about well-known objects and subjects.

Their installation linked information to the aesthetics of the tackboard, with objects and images pinned up as a continuum (in the IG sense) of visual materials, aiming again to upset conventional modes of perception and open new channels of communication.[60] On one side of a board was a system of gridded panels of photo-images of various communication devices, showing, as Holroyd put it, "how to organize and think with imagery."[61] On the other was a tackboard displaying images that changed daily. The intent was to enable spectators to understand how they participated in communication, how they individually read and brought meaning to the images they saw.[62] The entire ensemble thus became "a channel to facilitate the use of more channels."[63]

A few other examples will clarify how widespread was the excitement in this period, and in these circles, around the tropes of message, channel, and network as radical expanders and intensifiers of the cultural milieu. In 1960, recent Cambridge graduate Robert Freeman, recruited by Alloway to work on exhibitions at the ICA, edited issue 17 of *Cambridge Opinion*. He dedicated the issue to looking back through the 1950s

> at certain aspects of our cultural SITUATION in terms of COMMUNICATION. Man's whole relationship to machines has changed through the studies of cybernetics, and through automation. Machines are now an extension of his personality whether he is driving a car, programming an electronic brain, controlling the direction of a missile through radar, or putting a piece of toast under the grill. With complex urban communications his social mobility has increased enormously and as a result his whole horizon of choice and experience has been widened. Television has provided him with home entertainment and a world picture that is heightened by its topicality, its range, and its personalization.[64]

Peter Smithson, writing about cars, mobility, and transportation nets in 1959, often slipped into a broader discussion of communications. In a conversation about Brutalism, he remarked that

> the space in towns has to indicate that it is a net of communication.
> People know about things more—therefore [there] is more feeling of connectedness rather than the feeling of being in villages which is self-contained, and which you know perfectly well, ideas are communicated by press, television, radio and so on, advertising, which knits practically the whole world into a net of relationship where people understand each other … [and] this net of communications we know exists must find expression in architecture.[65]

The suggestive categories of communications theory had opened up a new concept of mass cultural exchange, with viewers not merely passive receivers but active participants in decoding messages and translating them into actions. All art and architecture could now be viewed as set within this net of communication. Norbert Wiener had written about the "human use" of information and a "theory of messages"; Alloway and other IG members adopted and extended these ideas, being concerned more with viewer participation than with information channels as such. Alloway closed his introduction to the *This Is Tomorrow* catalog with the following sentence: "This is a reminder of the responsibility of the spectator in the reception and interpretation of the many messages in the communications network of the whole exhibition."[66]

A Gift from America

As already noted, another influence on the younger generation, this one from the west coast of America, was that of Charles and Ray Eames. The impact of the Eameses' magical ideas was received not only by looking at magazine spreads (e.g., of their amazing Case Study House No. 8, 1947–1949) but also by visiting their Santa Monica studio in

Just a few chairs and a house: an essay on the Eames-aesthetic

Peter Smithson

In the 1950s the whole design climate was permanently changed by the work of Charles and Ray Eames. By a few chairs and a house.

Now chairs have always been the forward-runners of design-change. They have for some mysterious reason the capacity of establishing a new sense of style almost overnight.

Rietveld established a whole new design mode with a chair. So did Macintosh with his.

In the 1950s the Eames' moved design away from the machine aesthetic and bicycle technology, on which it had lived since the 1920s, into the world of the cinema-eye and the technology of the production aircraft; from the world of the painters into the world of the layout-men.

In a sense both the machine-aesthetic and the Eames-aesthetic are art-forms of ordinary life and ordinary objects seen with an eye that sees the ordinary as also magical.[1]

The machine-aesthetic selected with care those objects from ordinary life that were based on simple geometries—on cones, on spheres, on 'engineers' profiles' **1**; objects whose commonality was 'composable', ie pictures could be made from their arrangement, and out of which and art-discipline could be erected[2] **2, 3, 4**.

The Eames-aesthetic, made definitive in the House at Santa Monica Canyon, California, 1949 (as the machine-aesthetic was given canonical form in the 'dwelling unit' in the Esprit Nouveau Pavilion, Decorative Arts Exposition, in Paris, 1925), is based on an equally careful selection, but with extra-cultural surprise, rather than harmony of profile, as its criteria. A kind of wide-eyed wonder of seeing the culturally disparate together and so happy with each other **5**. This sounds like whimsy, but the basic vehicle—the steel lattice frame and in the case of the house, the colour film and colour processing in the graphics work, the pressings and mouldings in the case of the furniture—are ordinary to the culture **6, 7**.

And this is what separates the Eames' 'selection and juxtaposition' technique from neo-victorian screen-making and pop art forms of either the Barbara Jones or Peter Blake sorts.

Charles Eames is a natural Californian Man, using his native resources and know-how—of the film-making, the aircraft and the advertising industries—as others drink water; that is almost
▷445

[1] This sounds like a description of the role of Hollywood film as myth-maker to America.
[2] See Ozenfant's *The Foundations of Modern Art*.

1
Geometric solids. From *Vers une architecture*, by Le Corbusier
2
Bottles and glasses in the L'Esprit Nouveau Pavilion, Paris 1925. From *New World of Space*, by Le Corbusier
3
Bottles and glasses. Painting by Jeanneret, 1919. From Le Corbusier Palazzo Strozzi catalogue 1963
4
Advertisement for yellow-cake mix
5
A group of Eames cards. (See also pages 443, 448, 462)
6
Santa Monica house with reflection of the slope of the hill
7
Santa Monica house, wall detail. (See also overleaf and pages 444, 446, 450–52, 463–67)

443 Architectural Design September 1966

person and viewing their films on toys and ordinary objects, especially *A Communications Primer* (1953), projected at the ICA in 1955. The intention of the film, as an advertising pamphlet (1954) by the Eameses stated, was to "open some doors to the many and various aspects of the subject of communication which is becoming increasingly important to all of us."[67] Their ability to explain the technical concepts of communication in simple terms enabled them to influence the IG members' thoughts about spectator reaction to mass-media flows. Charles Eames would later write that *Primer* was "based on a feeling the processes based on information technology must be essential to city planning," a feeling that would have resonated with the "urban" ideals of the IG.[68]

Interest in the Eameses was also sparked by several other events: for example, Lawrence Alloway chaired a discussion at the ICA (April 1956) entitled "The Toys and Films of Charles Eames," and Charles Eames visited London in 1959, lecturing at the Royal College of Art (he would become a fellow in 1960) and at the Royal Institute of British Architects. In his lecture Eames claimed that

> [o]ne of the most penetrating of the changes is that change which makes our society almost completely dependent on current information, that is, information current, and as contrasted to information that is accumulated. ... Ours is a world so threaded with high frequency, interdependence, that it acts as one great nervous system. It requires all the feed-back controls man has devised to keep from oscillating itself out of existence.[69]

4.8
Peter Smithson, "With Just a Few Chairs and a House: An Essay on the Eames-Aesthetic," in Alison and Peter Smithson, eds., special issue "The Eames Celebration," *AD* 36 (September 1966), 443. Smithson Family Collection.

Theme of N.M.A. Exhibition

The open aesthetic

a/ "open" opposite of 'closed' i.e. can develope

~~[struck out text]~~

~~[struck out text]~~

b/ Casual, 'informal art'
net of human relations
or we on see them
the NON-OBVIOUS STRUCTURE — play *BRUBECK*

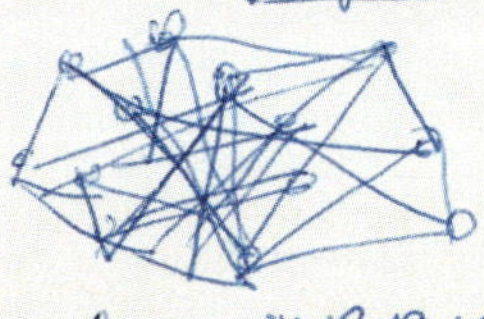

c/ Closed City implies
Coherent of region, New Sorts of
I, V, T, C.

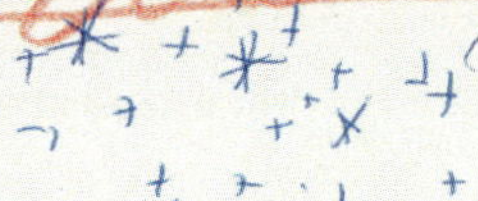

[scribbled text]

(masked part only)

The Smithsons' aesthetic sensibilities were influenced by the Eameses' "aesthetics of collage," their approach to "functioning decoration," and the contrasting images displayed in their tackboard displays and "House of Cards" toy (1952). The latter consisted of two decks of notched cards, a "picture deck" and a "pattern deck," that allowed the player to build various three-dimensional structures. The picture deck cards featured photographs by Charles Eames of such everyday items as buttons, measurements, spools of thread, watch hands, toy locomotives, and garden vegetables. Constantly viewing such ordinary images, turning the cards over this way and that, allowed players to extend their ideas and imaginations—to become accustomed to disparate images cohabiting happily together. The Smithsons also greatly admired the Eames House (1947–1949), calling it a "cultural gift parcel" that sustained an inner dialogue with their ideas for years to come.[70] With Californian casualness the Eameses imbued their carefully selected and juxtaposed objects, clean and pretty, with "extra-cultural surprise." For Peter Smithson this set off a

> kind of wide-eyed wonder of seeing the culturally disparate together and so happy with each other. This sounds like whimsy, but the basic vehicle—the steel lattice frame in the case of the house, the colour film and colour processing in the graphics work, the pressings and mouldings in the case of the furniture—are ordinary to the culture.[71]

Geoffrey Holroyd was the first member of the IG to visit their studio, in 1953:

> Through these and other American influences, I learned a way of seeing architecture as part of a general cultural situation focused on daily life and experience. ... I returned to London in the summer of 1954, impressed by Charles Eames's visual intuitions of a design theory based on assemblages of signs and symbols.[72]

4.9
Peter Smithson's diagram of "Play Brubeck, a casual, informal net of human relations."
Page containing this diagram is titled "Theme of NMA [Extension of Man] Exhibition]. PS 23:10:62 BB041—GSD Archive." The Alison and Peter Smithson Archive, Special Collections, Frances Loeb Library, Graduate School of Design, Harvard University.

The fine and the folk
An essay on McKim, Mead and White and the American tradition
Peter Smithson

The strongest architectural tradition in the United States is the tradition of careful detailing in expensive materials—granite, travertine, bronze, plate glass and lately in stainless steel.

This tradition can safely be said to have been founded by McKim, Mead, and White. The monograph on their work* covers the period 1879-1915, and this may be assumed to be their high period, although one's own feeling is, that what one always assumed to be export McKim, Mead, and White, such buildings as Selfridges, Bush House and the Rootes Group building in Piccadilly, were still being finished in the late 1920s.

The present-day architecture of this tradition, that of Skidmore, Owings and Merrill, is the only architecture in the United States that foreign architects regard as really American. And, as with Detroit cars, they admire it without the restraints that would operate against the admiration of such architecture were it a product of their own culture. It is admired for its unmatched technological competence.

They are, of course, perfectly aware that its underlying planning models are those of the late Beaux Arts: banal, overblown, official 6.

But the expertise that has been brought to bear can lift the product into the category of the new —and this is what fascinates, the hint of 'another architecture' outside the traditions of Europe and Japan.

This, of course, one has been able to see only recently and is apparent in very few buildings, and only a breath of it can be felt in the works of the founders of the tradition—McKim, Mead, and White.

But there is no doubt that Skidmore, Owings, and Merrill's Union Carbide 5 and Chase Manhattan Bank buildings 1, 2, 3 & 4 in New York are so well made and of such expensive materials that one cannot imagine who could have made them. They arouse the strongest cargo-cult feelings in foreigners, and are truly hints of *une architecture autre*. Yet the same architects' Connecticut General Building is a load of nothing (in some way one senses really life-diminishing for its occupants); and the same tradition's Lincoln Centre a load of near-wicked nothing (actually kind of morally corrosive).†

*Paul Wenzel, Maurice Krakow *A monograph on the work of McKim, Mead and White*, 1879-1915. Architectural Book Publishing Co. N.Y. (There seems to be no biography of this firm. This would make a good subject for a European's Ph.D. Thesis.)

†One can be definite in one's judgments of this latter sort of building for the architectural language fumbled after is a known one, the cribs obvious, the intentions too familiar.

394 Architectural Design August 1965

Holroyd brought the films and ideas of Charles and Ray Eames to the ICA, drawing attention to their "multi-image involvement" as an attempt to "drive through the audience's habitual responses by the sheer quantity and rapidity of change of images in order to rearrange the responses."[73] Holroyd commented on a 1953 Eames film about bread-making from rye to tacos, at the original screening of which Charles orchestrated smells through the ventilation system to complement sound and image so that the viewer was confronted with a complete experience, even raising their hunger level. The Eameses believed that "art is a chair, a test tube, a loaf of bread ... art is a mathematician's formula, a philosopher's way of life, any man's dreams."[74] By breaking down barriers between fields of learning, the Eameses sought a collage of opposing images that acted together and so made thought a little more intuitive.

Peter Smithson would also visit the Eameses in California, staying in their house on his second visit to America (1958). The Eameses had sent him a ticket for the California Zephyr from Chicago to Los Angeles and added $50 cash, which Peter described as a "spontaneous act of friendship."[75]

> They were friends with Billy Wilder, the film director, then making *Some Like it Hot* — and I've been in love with Marilyn Monroe ever since. I was on the set when they were making that marvellous scene where the two boys are in the sleeper and Jack Lemmon has ice put down his neck. Everyone on the set was in hysterics.[76]

He celebrated the Eameses' influence, noting that with only a few chairs and one house the Eameses had changed the entire design climate in the 1950s. They "moved design away from machine aesthetic and bicycle technology into the world of the cinema-eye and the technology of the producers of aircraft; from the world of the painters into the world of the layout-men."[77]

The Eameses revealed with apparent casualness a new balance between rational thought as background and a language of images up front. Alison Smithson reflected on the great debt the younger generation in England owed the Eames aesthetic and the "available-around-the -corner technology of America. ... Our generation were as children reborn from post-war Britain to love objects of a particular international flavour. The Eames gave us courage to make sense of anything that attracted."[78]

4.10
Referring to the continuum of the Fine Arts and the Folk Arts, which Alloway stressed, this image is taken from the first page of an article by Peter Smithson, "The Fine and the Folk: An Essay on McKim, Mead and White and the American Tradition," *AD* 35 (August 1965), 394. Smithson Family Collection.

4.11
Max Risselada opening Alison Smithson's "magic" scrapbook, photograph by M. C. Boyer (May 2011). Smithson Family Collection.

The Eames aesthetic revered an object's integrity, making it respectable to like pretty things. Peter Smithson acknowledged this debt:

> [I]t is the California Man's real originality to accept the clean and pretty as normal, it is not surprising that it is the Eames' who have made it respectable to like pretty things. This seems extraordinary, but in our old world, pretty things are usually equated with social irresponsibility. That we can be persuaded to accept the pretty is because their work is by no means without a sense of law. When we say "that's a very Eames photograph" we all know what it means. It is a special way of looking at things, a special sort of composition. It communicates a love of the object photographed, a kind of reverence of the object's integrity. The Eames aesthetic is to do with object-integrity. This is what gives their whole output cohesion.[79]

Alison wrote:

> Ourselves and Eduardo Paolozzi know where it ["the prettiness of our lives"] came from. It is possible Nigel Henderson alone could have led us to steam engines and the ephemera of life via old boots, bits of sacking, ancient postcards magicked over by photography, but I like to think it is to Ray and Charles Eames we owe the debt of the extravagance of the new purchase. The penny whistle, the Woolworth's plastic Christmas decoration and toy, on to the German pressed metal toy and the walking robots: fresh, pretty, colourful ephemera.[80]

The Eames reverence for objects, toys, and images fit perfectly with the collage mentality members of the IG were developing. Henderson, Paolozzi, and Alison Smithson were avid scrapbook-makers; Alison, in particular, extended her childhood habit of collecting scrapbooks full of Christmas stickers to a large private collection. She pasted cut-out images from contemporary events at random into a *Pictorial History of Old England* until its seams were bursting and only a few pages left unadorned. Collage in writing and imagery would remain prominent in many of her later works, as exemplified in her manuscripts for children's books. Similar collage work can be found in the pages of Henderson's sketchbooks, where cutouts from magazines are arranged in artful layouts. Paolozzi's famous scrapbooks were part of his working method as well: an archive of pasted images utilized as influences for subsequent collages, sculptures, and writings.

Decades later, Peter Smithson talked about the enduring influence of Charles and Ray Eames: "What we are talking about is an inheritance. … It's a game in a way, like a children's party game: identifying the moods that people like. But essentially it is ideological, insofar as the intention of our thought was not to be eclectic."[81] The Smithsons, he said, had used "the select and arrange technique" in the designing and equipping of their houses, "a design method close to 'flower-arrangements,' and to 'good taste' in the furnishing of rooms. It uses things for what they are, each object being enhanced and speaking more clearly of itself by virtue of the 'arrangement.'" It was a technique they had learned from the Eames aesthetic of "functioning decoration."[82]

II. Continuum and Topicality in the Writings of Lawrence Alloway

Impact on the Smithsons

Two expressions Alloway frequently used in his criticism of art and culture were "the fine art/popular art continuum" and "topicality."[83] His writings exemplified the fine-popular continuum by ranging from monster movies to fine art exhibitions, from advertising and graphics to product design and fashion. Art belonged to the world; making it required understanding of how the mass media feed back to mass audiences, and how they in turn react to these messages. Alloway was searching for an iconographical art full of meaning and immediate sensation, and was dismissive of what he saw as English snobbishness, pastoral Picturesque yearnings, or academic theorizing. In popular or market-driven American culture—brash, noisy, pragmatic, assertive, and topical—he found his antidote to arrogant, claustrophobic, postwar England.[84]

Alison and Peter Smithson seem not to have acknowledged the contribution Alloway made to their own aesthetic sensibilities during the years they shared IG and ICA activities and events. Alison referred to Alloway, Banham, and del Renzio as the "grey men" (theoreticians) of the IG, and stated that they and their friends Eduardo Paolozzi and Nigel Henderson formed merely a "splinter group" of IG. Perhaps Alloway was exaggerating his own importance as group leader when he claimed that the IG members possessed

> a common "vernacular urban culture" ... limited to mass-produced and largely exotic elements, imports from America, movies, science fiction in the form of pulp magazines, pop music, advertising largely as it appeared in American magazines, Detroit car designs, office equipment by IBM, *Time* and *Newsweek*.[85]

Still, his authority over IG activities and his discussions of Pop Art as an "urban art" were substantial, and topics discussed at the ICA with Alloway and the others inspired the Smithsons' own writing.[86] An archival box containing the Smithsons' writings for lectures to be given in the 1950s and 1960s contains a list of "13 Topics" prepared by Peter Smithson in 1957. The list gives us a snapshot view of how the IG discussions, and in particular Alloway's concerns about the "continuum" of the arts and the issue of "topicality," blended with Peter Smithson's thinking on the plastic arts generally, and some specialized topics on architecture and city planning:

> The first: "But today we collect ads. Advertising the new popular art, the influence of mass production and the Ad man in changing the focus of the desires of society. Contrast with historic European aristocracies/artists taste set-up."
>
> The second: "And What about Action Painting? Is the traditional relationship between the plastic arts still valid? Discussion on the function of the fine arts in a mechanized culture."

The third: "Styling in Automobile Design. Contrasts between American and European automotive trends and their social and economic and cultural basis."

The fourth: "The Patterns of European Cities. Questions answered on the growth of specific types of city e.g. Leiden, Florence, Mykonos.

The fifth: "Are Present Methods of Education Adequate? Education for a more complex sort of life than ever before."

The sixth: "Outstanding Buildings of Europe and what they Stand For."

The seventh: "The House of the Future. How the needs of a new way of life and a new technology may change the shape of our homes, the new town structures." a.s.o [and so on].[87]

The Smithsons were always concerned with how their ideas translated into built form—that is, how elements that constituted the "common urban vernacular," to use Alloway's phrase, affected their design sensibilities. Alison would comment several years later on what the "Pop Artists" were seeking in the 1950s. That decade, she noted, witnessed expanded mass aspirations for heating, mobility, casualness, leisure. No one foresaw the negatives—the importation of verbal "Americanisms," the extremes of junk food, the Dallas fabric of no-place—so many influences she resisted now (in the 1970s), but not back in the 1950s. "The American artifacts which Pop artists were looking at in the 1950's had a sort of internally powered, energy … but [fortunately] Pop has passed."[88]

The Ordinary and Excluded Middle

Even in the 1950s, however, the IG's enthusiasm for mass media was of course not universally shared. Toni del Renzio recalled that IG members rejected Herbert Read's emphasis on geometry as the route to higher aesthetics, wishing to replace these absolutes with expertise based on understanding subject matter on its own terms. Alloway recalled that Read "was committed to the idealistic aesthetic in which high tasks were assumed to be proper for art and so much got neglected and so, on that basis the mass production methods were a way of opposing Sir Herbert. There was nobody much else to attack."[89] IG's members, he noted, grew up with mass media: they never experienced the arrival shock of radio, movies, and illustrated magazines, as their parents had. Old-hat art historians such as Roger Fry and Herbert Read had dominated cultural opinion since the 1930s but gave no indication of how to read, see, and use the new mass media. Glossy magazines showed Alloway's generation images of what a home could be, revealing new fashions, while the pulps described patterns of behavior not yet common in England (or on planet Earth, for that matter). Alloway's generation wanted to explore the excluded middle where most of the symbols that people lived by resided, symbols that formed part of the field of general communication. They wanted art to belong to the same field as advertising—or at least within a definitive continuum shared by both forms.[90]

Another favored term of Alloway's, "topicality," referred to his search for new information in artistic expressions, new topics previously overlooked, and artists who had been marginalized or were not yet discovered. Making connections between art and society meant helping the spectator—or consumer of art, as Alloway preferred—to examine unfamiliar environmental spaces and unknown objects and images. To be inside art—art as it now must be—demanded that one consider the shifting conventions and patterns of thought, how fantasy and wonder were fed by technology, how the communication system, a product of technology, created expandable information: i.e., shifts in topicality, the new and the current. Fine-art standards were inflexible, elitist—incorrect and useless for the inhabitant of the mid-twentieth century; the mass arts were a new standard of validity, driven by economic necessity and dynamic technological novelty.

To Alloway, the new media environment offered what a later age would call empowerment. In 1958 he quoted the editor of *Astounding* as saying, "A man learns a pattern of behavior—and in five years it doesn't work." But "[p]opular art, as a whole," Alloway responded, "offers imagery and plots to control the changes in the world; everything in our culture that changes is the material of the popular arts."[91] Those arts excel, in other words, in "topicality." They project culture horizontally until it includes the entire complex of human activities. This tendency to encroach on everyone's ground is what the fine arts fear most. As one fine-art critic explained: "Shelter, which began as a necessity, has become an industry and now, with its refinements, is a popular art."[92] Far from being a disaster, Alloway concurred, this is evidence of the democratization of taste, a shift of authority over manners and morals from the few to the many. The popularization of "shelter" is a good example of how effective the mass media have become. American magazines for women and young marrieds link West Coast domestic architecture and stylish interiors with leisure activities, promising readers that they too can attain this good life. They expect desire to be unstoppable.

The challenge today, Alloway maintained, is for fine art to understand that it is merely one of several channels of communication in a framework that also includes the mass arts. To reject the popular arts because they are mass-produced is not a defense of culture but an attack upon it.

In his essay "The Long Front of Culture" (1959), Alloway wrote that modern communication systems arrange knowledge in nonhierarchical form. Their illustrations, and junk mail, are all guides to our possessions. The advertiser intentionally juxtaposes the story of a heroic woman with the goods she possesses. American movies offer lessons in the "drama of possessions": models for luxury houses, diagrams for bedroom arrangements. One could discover lessons of consumption without getting bogged down in matters of morality.[93]

> When the movies or TV create a world, it is of necessity a *designed* set in which people act and move, and the *style* in which they inhabit the scene is an index of the atmosphere of opinion of the audiences, as complex as a weather map.[94]

Humanists and fine-art purists, Alloway believed, missed the point: they refused to handle, via the media, the technology that was transforming the environment, ideas about the world and ourselves.

The media, however, whether dealing with war or the home, Mars or the suburbs, are an inventory of pop technology. The missile and the toaster, the push-button and the repeating revolver, military and kitchen technologies, are the natural possession of the media—a treasury of orientation, a manual of one's occupancy of the twentieth century.[95]

Alloway excelled in listing disparate items, a form of collage thinking that linked missiles to toasters, Mars to suburbs. Such thinking was desirable, in his view, because in everyday experience visual material was coming at viewers as they crossed Leicester Square or Piccadilly Circus, thumbed through the pages of an illustrated magazine, ventured into a CinemaScope movie, or watched the telly.

British Pop Art as an Urban Art

Often credited with coining the term "Pop Art" in 1954—though whether John McHale should actually be credited is a matter of dispute—Alloway used it to refer not to fine-art products referencing popular culture but to the raw popular imagery that Eduardo Paolozzi and Richard Hamilton were exploiting as material in their art. He attributed their love of such imagery to a deep interest in the symbol-thick scenes of activity that busy city streets provide. "Pop Art" was above all urban art—the art of the crowd, fashion, automobile styling. It was an art of representation, of signs and media images. (Later, in 1961, he would similarly insist on characterizing "junk culture"—assemblage art—as "city art.")[96] For Alloway, Pop Art was "about signs and sign systems" and was intended to confuse expectations. It must, he would claim, include at least one of the following: syntactic complexity, diverse media, familiar subjects, and connections to technology.[97]

In the early days of English "pop," Alloway made his debut in *AD* with an article on Paolozzi, who, he claimed, more than any other artist in England, "integrates the modern flood of visual symbols, a primary fact of urban culture, with his art."[98] Paolozzi's vision projects a photographic eye, and like anyone who has grown up with movies, newspapers, and advertisements, he combines this material in visually striking new ways. The very quantity of these ephemeral images enables Paolozzi to make connections between unlikes, producing multievocative composite images that he extends serially toward a new set of limits. Thus, in Paolozzi's art, "the head is a head, a planet, an asteroid, a stone, a blob under a microscope; it is big and small, one and many."[99]

4.12 (following pages)
Lawrence Alloway, "The Arts and the Mass Media," *AD* 28 (February 1958), 84–85.

The arts and the mass media

Lawrence Alloway

The immaculate pre-war gentleman private detective (The Thin Man, M.G.M.)

The Man in the Gray Flannel Suit: day wear replaces evening dress and its wearer is haunted by war memories (20th Century-Fox)

James Stewart in The Man From Laramie (Columbia): the battered hero

The new space of CinemaScope has increased spectator participation: To Hell and Back (Universal-International)

Academic pop art: the destruction of the temple in Samson and Delilah (Paramount)

In *Architectural Design* last December there was a discussion of ' the problem that faces the architect to-day – democracy face to face with hugeness – mass society, mass housing, universal mobility '. The architect is not the only kind of person in this position; everybody who works for the public in a creative capacity is face to face with the many-headed monster. There are heads and to spare.

Before 1800 the population of Europe was an estimated 180 million; by 1900 this figure had risen to 460 million. The increase of population and the industrial revolution that paced it has, as everybody knows, changed the world. In the arts, however, traditional ideas have persisted, to limit the definition of later developments. As Ortega pointed out in *The Revolt of the Masses*: ' the masses are to-day exercising functions in social life which coincide with those which hitherto seemed reserved to minorities '. As a result the élite, accustomed to set æsthetic standards, has found that it no longer possesses the power to dominate all aspects of art. It is in this situation that we need to consider the arts of the mass media. It is impossible to see them clearly within a code of æsthetics associated with minorities with pastoral and upper-class ideas because mass art is urban and democratic.

It is no good giving a literary critic modern science fiction to review, no good sending the theatre critic to the movies, and no good asking the music critic for an opinion on Elvis Presley. Here is an example of what happens to critics who approach mass art with minority assumptions. John Wain, after listing some of the spectacular characters in P. C. Wren's *Beau Geste* observes: ' It sounds rich. But in fact – as the practised reader could easily foresee . . . it is not rich. Books with this kind of subject matter seldom are. They are lifeless, petrified by the inert conventions of the adventure yarn '. In fact, the practised reader is the one who understands the conventions of the work he is reading. From outside all Wain can see are inert conventions; from inside the view is better and from inside the conventions appear as the containers of constantly shifting values and interests.

The Western movie, for example, often quoted as timeless and ritualistic, has since the end of World War II been highly flexible. There have been cycles of psychological Westerns (complicated characters, both the heroes and the villains), anthropological Westerns (attentive to Indian rights and rites), weapon Westerns (colt revolvers and repeating Winchesters as analogues of the present armament race). The protagonist has changed greatly, too: the typical hero of the American depression who married the boss's daughter and so entered the bright archaic world of the gentleman has vanished. The ideal of the gentleman has expired, too, and with it evening dress which is no longer part of the typical hero-garb.

If justice is to be done to the mass arts which are, after all, one of the most remarkable and characteristic achievements of industrial society, some of the common objections to it need to be faced. A summary of the opposition to mass popular art is in *Avant Garde and Kitsch* (*Partisan Review*, 1939, *Horizon*, 1940), by Clement Greenberg, an art critic and a good one, but fatally prejudiced when he leaves modern fine art. By kitsch he means ' popular, commercial art and literature, with their chromotypes, magazine covers, illustrations, advertisements, slick and pulp fiction, comics, Tin Pan Alley music, tap dancing, Hollywood movies, etc.'. All these activities to Greenberg and the minority he speaks for are 'ersatz culture . . . destined for those who are insensible to the value of *genuine* culture . . . Kitsch, using for raw material the debased and academic simulacra of *genuine* culture welcomes and cultivates this insensibility ' (my italics). Greenberg insists that ' all kitsch is academic ', but only some of it is, such as Cecil B. De Mille-type historical epics which use nineteenth-century history-picture material. In fact, stylistically, technically, and iconographically the mass arts are anti-academic. Topicality and a rapid rate of change are not academic in any usual sense of the word, which means a system that is static, rigid, self-perpetuating. Sensitiveness to the variables of our life and economy enable the mass arts to accompany the changes in our life far more closely than the fine arts which are a repository of time-binding values.

The popular arts of our industrial civilization are geared to technical changes which occur, not gradually, but violently and experimentally. The rise of the electronics era in communications challenged the cinema. In reaction to the small TV screen, movie makers spread sideways (CinemaScope) and back into space

Architectural Design February 1958

The dream of flesh: in pop art (*Flirt* magazine)

Nightmares in pop art: spectacle of decay on a horror comic cover

The romanticism of the control board in cybernetics (*Galaxy SF*)

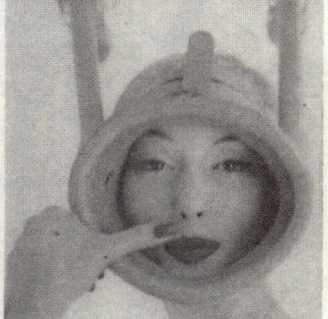

The ghost of flesh: a fashion model converts diving apparatus into a new hat (*Charm*)

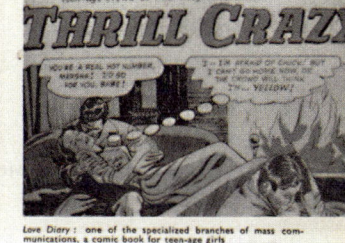

Love Diary: one of the specialized branches of mass communications, a comic book for teen-age girls

Pop art dada: Hermione Gingold does the Mona Lisa

West Coast Architecture extrapolated as a setting for leisure on the planet Altair 4 (*Forbidden Planet*, M.G.M.)

There is in popular art a continuum from data to fantasy. Fantasy resides in, to sample a few examples, film stars, perfume ads, beauty and the beast situations, terrible deaths, sexy women. This is the aspect of popular art which is most easily accepted by art minorities who see it as a vital substratum of the folk, as something primitive. This notion has a history since Herder in the eighteenth century, who emphasized national folk arts in opposition to international classicism. Now, however, mass-produced folk art is international: Kim Novak, *Galaxy Science Fiction*, Mickey Spillane, are available wherever you go in the West. However, fantasy is always given a keen topical edge; the sexy model is shaped by datable fashion as well as by timeless lust. Thus, the mass arts orient the consumer in current styles, even when they seem purely, timelessly erotic and fantastic. The mass media give perpetual lessons in assimilation, instruction in role-taking, the use of new objects, the definition of changing relationships, as David Riesman has pointed out. A clear example of this may be taken from science fiction. Cybernetics, a new word to many people until 1956, was made the basis of stories in *Astounding Science Fiction* in 1950*. SF aids the assimilation of the mounting technical facts of this century in which, as John W. Campbell, the editor of *Astounding*, put it, 'A man learns a pattern of behaviour – and in five years it doesn't work'. Popular art, as a whole, offers imagery and plots to control the changes in our culture; everything in our culture that changes is the material of the popular arts.

Critics of the mass media often complain of the hostility towards intellectuals and the lack of respect for art expressed there, but, as I have tried to show, the feeling is mutual. Why should the mass media turn the other cheek? What worries intellectuals is the fact that the mass arts spread; they encroach on the high ground. For example, into architecture itself as Edmund Burke Feldman wrote in *Arts and Architecture* last October: 'Shelter, which began as a necessity, has become an industry and now, with its refinements, is a popular art'. This, as Feldman points out, has been brought about by 'a democratization of taste, a spread of knowledge about non-material developments, and a shift of authority about manners and morals from the few to the many'. West Coast domestic architecture has become a symbol of a style of living as well as an example of architecture pure and simple;

(VistaVision). All the regular film critics opposed the new array of shapes, but all have been accepted by the audiences. Technical change as dramatized novelty (usually spurred by economic necessity) is characteristic not only of the cinema but of all the mass arts. Colour TV, the improvements in colour printing (particularly in American magazines), the new range of paper back books; all are part of the constant technical improvements in the channels of mass communication.

An important factor in communication in the mass arts is high redudancy. TV plays, radio serials, entertainers, tend to resemble each other (though there are important and clearly visible differences for the expert consumer). You can go into the movies at any point, leave your seat, eat an ice-cream, neck, parade; (2) it satisfies, for the absorbed spectator, the desire for intense participation which leads to a careful discrimination of nuances in the action.

*Although for purposes of this general article I have treated the mass arts as one thing, it is in fact highly specialized. *ASF* is for scientifically and technically minded readers, whereas *Galaxy SF* leans towards mainstream stories. SF editorials tend to stress the unlikeness of the field to the rest of the mass media. There are, in fact, a multitude of audiences within the great audience (*Mademoiselle*, for example, is aimed at female readers from eighteen to thirty), but here I just want to separate the popular from the fine arts.

this has occurred not through the agency of architects but through the association of stylish interiors with leisure and the good life, mainly in mass circulation magazines for women and young marrieds.

The definition of culture is changing as a result of the pressure of the great audience, which is no longer new but experienced in the consumption of its arts. Therefore, it is no longer sufficient to define culture solely as something that a minority guards for the few and the future (though such art is uniquely valuable and as precious as ever). Our definition of culture is being stretched beyond the fine art limits imposed on it by Renaissance theory, and refers now, increasingly, to the whole complex of human activities. Within this definition, rejection of the mass produced arts is not, as critics think, a defence of culture but an attack on it. The new role for the academic is keeper of the flame; the new role for the fine arts is to be one of the possible forms of communication in an expanding framework that also includes the mass arts.

Robert Adams

An exhibition of recent works by Robert Adams, the abstract sculptor, opened at Gimpel Fils Gallery on February 4th. All his new work is in welded iron and steel and deals with space, either forms or lines moving through space, or space caught by curved planes and then sent shooting outwards. This is not an art of Becoming, of organic growth, but an art of Being, of actuality. He is also showing some interesting drawings that are plans of what happens to the space within his sculpture.

Alloway and America

A few months before his first visit to America in 1958, Alloway published the *AD* article "The Arts and the Mass Media." This included further evidence of Alloway's pro-American sensibility: all but one of its examples and images were drawn from US mass media (the lone exception being P. C. Wren, a British writer of adventure fiction).[100] Alloway was concerned in this revealing piece with the impact that large size—or hugeness—had on democracy, be it mass society, mass housing, mass media, explosive population growth, or universal mobility, and how this "mass society" concerned every artist who worked in a public capacity. In an overt attack on the editorial policies of *AR* as well as the bastions of English fine art in the postwar environment, Alloway claimed that it was no longer possible within "mass society" to sustain "a code of aesthetics associated with minorities with pastoral and upper-class ideas because mass art is urban and democratic."[101]

In this essay, which appears to have been a late reaction to Clement Greenberg's 1939 "Avant-Garde and Kitsch," Alloway expresses his dissent from the aesthetic conventions of fine art, which called the mass arts "kitsch," "ersatz," and "commercial" while maintaining a contemplative or external point of view on the world. Alloway favored the mass media because they required an internal view, one taken from inside the conventions, from whence they could be seen as "containers of constantly shifting values and interests."[102]

Fantasy, Alloway emphasized in "The Arts and the Mass Media," was a realm in which the mass arts excelled—the glamour of film stars, perfume ads, terrible deaths, sexy women. These could be tolerated by fine art, at times, if conceived as a substratum of the folk and the primitive. But this view entailed a misunderstanding, because "mass-produced folk art is international" and so does not constitute evidence of a national or folk vernacular: "Kim Novak, *Galaxy Science Fiction*, Mickey Spillane, are available wherever you go in the West."[103] Moreover, fantasy, such as is found in the iconography of science fiction, always takes a topical edge:

> the sexy model is shaped by datable fashion as well as by timeless lust. Thus, the mass arts orient the consumer in current styles, even when they seem purely, timelessly erotic and fantastic. The mass media give perpetual lessons in assimilation, instruction in role-taking, the use of new objects, the definition of changing relationships, as [sociologist] David Riesman has pointed out.[104]

Alloway finally embarked for the United States in the spring of 1958, visiting Washington, Philadelphia, New York, Boston, Detroit, Chicago, and Los Angeles (perhaps even more cities) in the land of wishful fantasies. This trip revealed to him another side of America—the architect is only one of many specialists who shape cities—and brought home the fact that American cities offered something different from what stuffy British architects allowed. The trip gave him new ammunition with which to respond directly to

AR's attacks in "Man Made America," and excerpts from his travel journal appeared in a double-page spread in *AD* in January 1959, under the title "City Notes."[105]

He began his offense by singling out the architect, who was misled by architectural theory into thinking that he had control over most of the built environment. He was mistaken, for in reality he controlled no more than a single building, or occasionally a block. Second, the architect was arrogant, calling the user of his buildings interference, noise in a perfect communication system that was destroyed when the occupant's paraphernalia was spread about. These "obstinate human features" may soon change, however, because the sociologists in their urban studies have reintroduced the idea of "the people" into the city—something architects appear to believe is irrelevant.

Alloway could admire architect-controlled places such as Rockefeller Center and Mies van der Rohe's Lake Shore Drive apartments, but the real American city lay elsewhere. This was the important lesson that the exponent of "Pop Art" drew from his travels: "the American city is the model of maximized industrialization, towards which most of the world is heading, its lessons may be bigger than that of unique individual buildings."[106]

America taught Alloway that cities are the piling up of people's constantly changing activities, a messy overlapping of developing forms (e.g., buildings being destroyed, under construction, empty lots waiting to be built on). In such a state, architects' formal principles are unlikely to survive intact or achieve the role of unifier. "Architects can never get and keep control of all the factors in a city which exist in the dimensions of patched-up, expendable, and developing forms."[107] Architecture, consequently, had a limited role in what makes the urban scene the source of inspiration for the popular arts. Images of the city were far more important than architecture; they were the major contributors to the "real urban environment." Alloway drew up a tabular list of his favorite American communication-saturated environments shaping public opinion via "transmitter-audience feedback": do-it-yourself advice from women's magazines, a cycle of crime movies stressing the complexity of urban morality, neon lights, traffic signals, drugstore windows, the environments of airports, restaurants, bars, and hotel lounges, the sound surround of light and pop music, the panoramic view from inside a luxurious car echoing the horizontal screen of CinemaScope, "Operation Airwatch" in Los Angeles broadcasting information about traffic conditions during peak hours from helicopters.[108]

4.13 (following pages)
Lawrence Alloway, "City Notes," *AD* 29 (January 1959), 34–35.

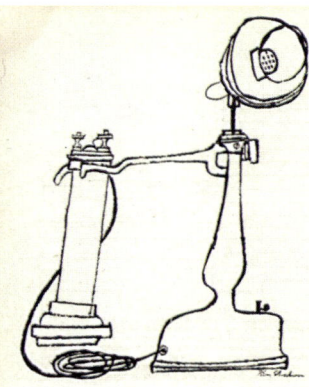

City notes

Lawrence Alloway

'Any consideration of the arts in the life of a modern people which neglects the movies, illustrated newspapers and magazines, cartoons, posters, other pictorial advertising, commercial design, as represented, for example, in the automobile, would simply miss nearly the whole picture so far as the art of the masses is concerned.'*

The architect is only one of many specialists who shape cities. Geographers, demographers, historians, politicians, sociologists, the military, all make basic contributions. The architect, accustomed to think of himself as the potential creator of environments, and encouraged to do so by much architectural theory, has exaggerated the significance of his contribution to the city. In fact, the area over which he has control is rarely more than the unit of the single building, occasionally the block. As a result architecture is usually related in a highly competitive way to both its neighbours and its users. For many architects the users of their buildings seem to be simply interference, noise in a system which was perfect until it was inhabited; then, partitions go up, the 'wrong' furniture is brought in, and bicycles are left in the hall. Coinciding with a wane in the prestige of geometric ideals, however, is a new awareness of the obstinate human factor as defined in urban studies, which may signal a change of architectural outlook.

A recent visit to the United States, during which I went to a dozen cities, brought home to me the fact that what cities offered was different from what architects offered. I admired the architect-controlled places, such as Rockefeller Centre and GMTC, and single structures from the Flat Iron Building to Mies' Lake Shore Drive Apartments. The cities contained these monuments, just as they contained jewellery stores, but the real city is more than this. As the American city is the model of maximized industrialization, towards which most of the world may be heading, its lesson may be bigger than that of unique individual buildings.

Cities are, to quote John Rannells,† 'the piling up of people's activities' and these change quicker than buildings or architects' ideas. To describe architecture as 'the creation of pure forms of an uncompromising technical perfection and aesthetic integrity,' as Colin Glennie did, leaves you alone on an island with Mies. Louis Sullivan had a better idea when he said that it is 'the drama of created things' to go 'into oblivion'. This is nowhere more visible than in the crowded, solid city and nowhere are 'permanent' formal principles less likely to survive intact. The past, the present, and the future (symbolized by buildings being demolished for new developments, work in progress, and vacant lots waiting to be built on) overlap in a messy configuration. Architects can never get and keep control of all the factors in a city which exist in the dimensions of patched-up, expendable, and developing forms.

The city as an environment has room for a multiplicity of roles, among which the architect's may not be that of unifier (except in off-beat cases, such as Karlsruhe). Consider, for example, images of the city in the popular arts which reflect and form public opinions in that transmitter-audience feedback which is the secret of the mass media. *Charm*, 'the magazine for women who work' gives a bachelor-girl's eye-view of the city, in terms not only of serviceable clothes and crisp make-up tips, but also in terms of the theatre, restaurants, good books, office equipment and work schedule ('alive after five . . . thanks to her Remington Electric Typewriter'). The centenary number surveyed the technology that has changed female status (the sewing machine, the typewriter and the telephone), especially as they affected the careers open to women in the big city.

Another aspect of city imagery was seen in American crime films of the late 1940s, the titles of which were, for once, an apt guide to content: *Naked City, Cry of the City, The Street with No Name, Dark Corner, Knock on Any Door, Dark City*. There is a clear link between this imagery and the anti-urbanism of nineteenth century

reformers, typified by John Silk Buckingham, designer of the model city Victoria. His avenues had 'no secret or obscure haunts for the retirement of the filthy and immoral from the public eye'. The film cycle dwelt on the secret haunts, which are the negative side of the privacy that is, in fact, one of the city's great amenities. Lately the secret lives of Taste Makers and Opinion Leaders have been exposed in such urban-valued stories (made into successful films) as *Sweet Smell of Success* and *The Great Man*. These expose urban evils without being anti-urban. In fact, the city-dweller who consumes this fare, like the native Chicagoan who opposes the values of Park Forest, sees a city's violence as, within limits, an index of intensity and responds to the complexity of urban morality. A Chicago taxi-driver told me, with pride and knowingness: 'You got something you want to try out. If it won't work in Chicago, it won't work anywhere.'

The mass arts contribute to the real environment of cities in an important way. It is absurd, to print a photograph of Piccadilly Circus and caption it 'ARCHITECTURAL SQUALOR' as Ernö Goldfinger and E. J. Carter did in an old Penguin book on the County of London Plan. In fact, the lights of the Circus are the best night-sight in London, though inferior to American displays. Related to the neon spectacle are other aspects of the popular environment. The drug stores, with dense displays of small bright packages, arrayed in systems to throw the categorist. The LP environment at airports, restaurants, bars, and hotel lounges, of light and long-lived pop music that extends radio and TV sound outside the house into a larger environment. The CinemaScope screen, with its expanded visibility also has connections with the 'real' environment. The American cars, which match the scale of American streets with a visual ease unimaginable in England, link with the movies. This is not only a matter of design symbolism (rocket outside, theatre within), but also of spatial experience. The panoramic view from inside the luxurious car (comfortable as a first-run cinema) echoes the horizontal screen. Thus the windscreen is both a communications device itself and the analogue of another communications device. Linkages of this kind abound in the communications-saturated environment of the U.S.

The American city, more than most European cities at present, is geared to the communications systems of modern technology. In Los Angeles advice about avoiding traffic jams is given from a helicopter and picked up on car radios. Broadcast at peak hours 'Operation Airwatch' is one of the most listened-to programmes in the area and includes commercials between traffic news. This compound of traffic signals and ads is characteristic of the symbol-

Above: knowing commentary on urbanity, Steinberg's murals at EXPO 58 emphasized human occupancy of the city, formerly neglected by architects. The presence of human activity, in forms that specialists often see as illogical and fantastic, is at the heart of modern urban studies, which are re-introducing people to the city.

Below: GM Tech Centre seen through wide windscreen, an echo of cinema techniques

* *Leisure. A Suburban Study* by George A. Lundberg, Mirra Komarovsky, Mary Alice McInerny (Columbia University Press, 1934)

† *The Core of the city* by John Rannells (Columbia University Press, 1956)

Above: Chicago with numbered buildings, No. 1 being the Allerton Hotel, which gives away this postcard. One of the possible ways of organizing the data of a city without reference to a hierarchy of architectural value

34 Architectural Design January 1959

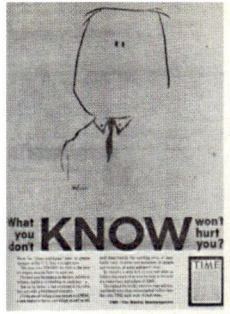 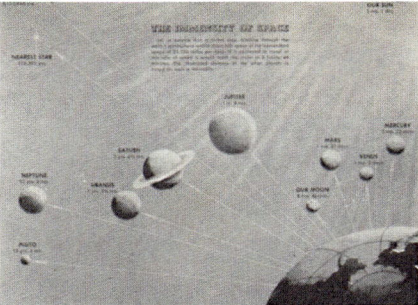 

Above left and centre: popular art is part of a big communications system. The American pre-occupation with communication shows in much throwaway material, such as the drawing by Osbourne (a full page ad for *Time*) and the chart of the solar system in relation to Terra (a paper napkin from a drug store in Washington)
Above right: the Hilton City of Hotels is a brilliant image not only of the number of hotels in the chain, but also of their homogeneity, the way in which they form one predictable environment despite the urban and regional differentiation of the places in which they occur.

thick environment of American cities and highways.

Consider the function of one set of symbols for a visitor arriving in a strange city. The city is a complex of communications (postman's route, housewife's route, motorist's route, etc.) which the stranger is not tuned in to. The anonymous and recognizable displays of the entertainment section, however, act as instant signals. (Almost every city in the U.S. that I went to was showing *The Bridge on the River Kwai* and *Teacher's Pet*.) The services symbolized by the lights and the posters are an extension of the channels of easy communication of trains and planes. The ride from Chicago's O'Hare Airport into the Loop at night is a journey along a noisy, narrow corridor of neon. To the compilers of the *Architectural Review*'s 'Man Made America' this would be 'unintended squalor', intolerable to people living the architectural way. In fact, it is one stretch of the lighted street which runs across America. It starts in New York, runs with only marginal regional differentiation across the continent for 3,000 miles, and ends

in San Francisco's Market Street. A traditional postcard of Times Square at night, with wet streets to double the blaze, is captioned: 'Night time comes to the rest of the world, but not to "The Great White Way".' The Great White Way, in a sense, belongs to all urban America, just as the hotels, to an extent unknown in Europe, provide a predictable, standardized service from coast to coast.

Los Angeles is for many liberal intellectuals, including architects, the end of the (designed) world. Satirizing this body of opinion, S. J. Perelman dubbed it 'the crucible that men call Hollywood'. A typical rejection of the crucible is Dwight Macdonald's 'I have just returned (Sept. 15) from my first visit to Los Angeles, which is to New York, so far as attractiveness, sense of the past and human scale are concerned as New York is to London'. However, Los Angeles, the flat city, is built for cars and it is the only city in the world that is. In London and New York ('the cross town traffic', murmurs Clark Gable as an acceptable excuse for lateness in *Teacher's Pet*) the past and the technological present conflict. Los Angeles, on the other hand, unlike the East Coast of the U.S., has no past to get in the way of the cars.

In Los Angeles close friends can live twenty or thirty miles apart, which gives a kind of privacy, but they are easily accessible by car on the freeways, which restores intimacy. The houses are mostly low, never far from plentiful vegetation, the roads wide, with concentrations here and there, but not very dense, as at Hollywood and Vine. It is diffuse suburban space with metropolitan occupants. It works and works well for the Los Angeles resident who uses his car like a cowboy used his horse, as a natural adaptive extension of his legs. (Despite the closing down of Hollywood film studios, Los Angeles is still a mass communications centre. Low, open houses, with a nature-admitting patio, is the symbol of the leisure environment to-day that has replaced the high-

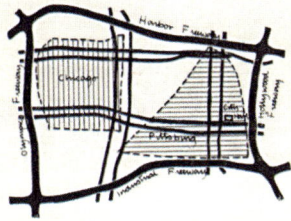

Above: created originally without 'architectural' pretensions, Times Square is beginning to exert its lure on architects
Right and below: Los Angeles, with its alternation of multi-level freeways and intimate suburban spaces, is 'the city of the future' extrapolated on the basis of automobiles. The future of LA, in a map from a West Coast newspaper, includes KING SIZE PARKING LOTS, bigger than Pittsburg's Golden Triangle and Chicago's Loop put together

up penthouse of popular taste in the 1930s.)

Attempts are now being made to bring within architectural reach much of the pop art that has thrived without being architecture in the qualitative sense of the word. *Forum*, in August last year, discussed an upcoming reciprocal interchange between architecture and popular taste. This was presented as a programme for *schmaltze*, symbolism, and *shariwaggi*. Stone's success is a symptom, Yamasaki's Memorial Conference Hall at Wayne University an auger, of the new mood. (The presence of *shariwaggi* in the list is ominous to the British reader with a bitter knowledge of the sweet taste of the Festival of Britain whimsy, the crown of the British picturesque revival.)

It appears that the architects' professional desire to shape the world may lead them to feed off the public gingerbread. In fact, however, the city seems to be unplanable in popular terms, precisely because of its extension in time and the way people keep moving. At Eastland Shopping Centre, for example, carefully tailored spaces and interior colour schemes, intended to match the products in Hudson's central block, have been lost as the store's departments switched. When I was there last spring garden furniture occupied the original baby clothes section. Usage is always outpacing planning.

Architecture has its own popular art, without incorporating (and, of course, 'improving' in the process) the complex, untidy, fantastic, quick-paced environment. Pop architecture now would include the West Coast domestic leisure style and the Mies' vernacular office towers and slabs, spread by Skidmore, Owens and Merrill. Popular art in the city is a function of the whole city and not only of its architects. If the architect learns more about subjective and 'illogical' human values from the study of popular art, then architecture will have gained, and so will future users; but to adopt playful and odd forms, without their spirit, without their precise functions, will make a solemn travesty of the environment in which pop art naturally thrives.

Messages from America

Alloway was full of praise for Los Angeles in particular, calling it the archetypal "American City": to elderly snobs repugnant but to the young "the symbol" of the leisure-time environment with its low, open houses and nature-admitting patios, its diffuse suburban spaces with easy automobile accessibility provided by a system of freeways. To architects who claimed that Los Angeles was the end of the line as far as design was concerned, Alloway replied: "It works and works well for the Los Angeles resident who uses the car like a cowboy used his horse, as a natural adaptive extension of his legs."[109]

Why then, Alloway asked, did modern architects like Ernö Goldfinger and E. J. Carter write "Architectural Squalor" beneath a photograph of Piccadilly Circus in *AR* when it was well known that the lights of Piccadilly are the best "night-sight" in London? In American cities, the narrow corridor of neon stretching along every street was an amazing sight. The strip allowed a stranger to find his way about, and was an excellent communication device.

> To the compilers of *Architectural Review*'s "Man-Made America" this would be "unintended squalor," intolerable to people living the architectural way. In fact it is one stretch of lighted street which runs across America. It starts in New York, runs with only marginal regional differentiation across the continent of 3,000 miles, and ends in San Francisco's Market Street. ... The Great White Way, in a sense, belongs to all urban America, just as the hotels ... provide a predictable, standardized service from coast to coast.[110]

No matter what *AR* might think, Alloway contended, and in spite of the fact that its editors had made several attempts to extend their program of Sharawaggi or Picturesque Townscape to the American city, the latter "seems to be unplanable in popular terms, precisely because of its extension in time and the way people keep moving."[111] It is important for architects to remember that

> [p]opular art in the city is a function of the whole city, and not only of its architects. If the architect learns more about subjective and "illogical" human values from the study of popular art, then architecture will have gained, and so will future users; but to adopt playful and odd forms, without their spirit, without their precise functions, will make a solemn travesty of the environment in which pop art naturally thrives.[112]

But Not All Agreed

Democratic, anti-intellectual, technologically sensitive, attuned to feedback from users and the environment, Pop Art came at the viewer as messages from American cities and their real-life environments. But despite Alloway's advocacy, many in England did not want to listen to what America had to say: it was not an example to emulate but one to fear and ward off. This view was ably represented by *AR*: American culture pandered to the amorphous classless masses, its architecture might be technologically perfect but was aesthetically banal, its cities were childish expressions of individuality and free will, its consumer society was stimulated and controlled by an external and autonomous system of capitalism.

To the contrary, members of the IG believed that the spectator-turned-consumer needed to be taught how to decode the new values of culture across multiple levels of meaning. As the Smithsons wittily claimed in "But Today we collect Ads" (1956),

> To understand the advertisements which appear in *The New Yorker* or *Gentry* one must have taken a course in Dublin literature, read a *Time* popularizing article on Cybernetics, and have majored in Higher Chinese Philosophy and Cosmetics. Such ads are packed with information—data of a way of life and a standard of living which they are simultaneously inventing and documenting. Ads which do not try to sell you the product except as an accessory of a way of life. They are good "images" and their technical virtuosity is almost magical. Many have involved as much effort for one page as goes into the building of a Coffee-bar. And this transient thing is making a bigger contribution to our visual climate than any of the traditional fine arts.[113]
>
> ...
>
> Mass production advertising is establishing our whole pattern of life—principles, morals, aims, aspirations, and standard of living. We must somehow get the measure of this intervention if we are to match its powerful and exciting impulses with our own.[114]

As this passage indicates, the Smithsons accepted the affluent, market-driven society, believing that consumer choice led to greater equality, greater freedom, and greater democracy, all on display in increased social and physical mobility. Following Alloway, they believed it was the role of the artist/architect to teach the new spectator/consumer how to make discriminating choices, how to move knowledgeably and confidently within this expanded field of cultural values.[115] Alison and Peter were for years enamored, on these terms, with the society of affluence and its economy of consumption; they offered no principled resistance to the market economy, no alternative to determination of the future by the profit motives of industrial society. Only their equivocal "But" in "But Today we collect Ads" hints at a future reassessment.

For now, members of the IG had had quite enough of what they perceived as stifling morality and elite attitudes in the arts. Alloway, in particular, was too enamored with "the drama of possessions" that advertisements and American movies narrated to develop a critical message about the "consumer." The lessons of consumption lay inside the pattern of entertainment, not entangled with morality! He, with other IG members, was thus affirming the capitalist aesthetics of plenty—while failing to apply a critical perspective to the outpoured images and their sources. He simply ignored the negative aspects of consumption and the fetishistic adoration of consumer goods. Even though the continuous flow of commodities from automated factories required—problematically—that the designer manipulate and amplify the consumer's subconscious desire for consumption, that is, induce them to project their fantasies onto a given product in order to motivate their purchase.[116]

III. Conclusion

Alloway and his fellow IG members constructed "America" as an "anti-British" template that they could evoke against the grain, a fantasyland peddling dreams that fueled their elders' disdain. This America excelled in technological marvels, exuberant mass media, figurative advertisements, energetic ephemera—"here with a bang today, gone without a whimper tomorrow."[117] America was in fact an emerging superpower after World War II: its role in the Cold War, as its British admirers saw it, was to guarantee progress through evolution and reform. It would do so by ensuring social mobility, keeping democratic channels of communication open, making sure that technological advances fed back to society and enhanced the consumer paradise of plenty.

The US, strengthened rather than pummeled by World War II, was the first nation to experience the rise of consumerism in the long postwar period of economic recovery. And it delivered the goods! In the still-hungry United Kingdom, Alloway and his fellow IG members became acutely attuned to these channels and their flood of multievocative symbols and signs. They sought an expanded field for the arts, true believers in the boisterous, all-embracing continuum that Alloway described: where the timeless and enduring crisscross with the expendable, topical, and accessible. Signs and symbols could be stripped out whole from the culturally complex and ambiguous consequences of abundance, capitalism, and the Cold War.

And among the many messages from America, the influence of the Eameses cannot be overestimated: Peter Smithson acknowledged that the "Eames Aesthetic," like "Pop styling is specific to its situation."[118] Additive juxtapositions of objects and images from a continuum of sources that included the popular and commercial was part of the Eames philosophy, as of that of Alloway and the IG, all of whom took a deliberate stance against the exclusivist masters of fine art. The Eameses were the first to assess the impact of excessive information that caught the postwar design professions unawares, making overload inevitable. They were also the first to warn that the designer must learn to convey the essence of their ideas in clear terms. They believed that designers and architects had a responsibility to utilize the latest tools of communication to transmit signs, signals, and thoughts across multiple channels, breaking down the barriers between each. It is the web of communication that holds a society together—"communication," the voiceover of *A Communications Primer* explained, "means the responsibility of decision all the way down the line."

When Alison Smithson wrote her tribute to the Eames aesthetic, she wondered whether Peter Blake's generation of Pop artists

> knew the people who made so much of the ephemera acceptable.[119]
>
> …

> The Eames gave us courage to make sense of anything that attracted. ... The Eames support the West Coast world for us and help support our European Dream of America as a great free place to be in.[120]

The Eameses taught the Smithsons to keep an eye out for a "fresh family of things"[121] and to see beauty in the ordinary. "The Eames' [House of Cards toy] gave us the courage to collect whatever pleases us. Hardly anyone has escaped the influence. Ephemera and its consideration becomes part of an intellectual activity."[122] The toy's juxtapositions were like those on the message space of the tackboard—another gift from the Eameses—allowing disparate materials drawn from eclectic sources to stand side by side in odd arrangements, reassembled and rearranged, giving rise to fresh linkages. This was the core of the communication revolution of the mid-1950s, based in mass-media technology and its layers of signifying potential. Such were the messages coming from America.

5.1
Max Risselada opening Alison Smithson's "Magic" Scrapbook. Photograph by M. C. Boyer (May 2011). Smithson Family Collection.

5

Fashionable Modernity

None of the other nations of Europe has so abject an inferiority complex about its own aesthetic capacities as England.

Nikolaus Pevsner (1956)[1]

Prologue

The Smithsons excelled in collage writing or associative modes of thought, which was also exploited in advertisements of the 1950s and photo essays of *Life* magazine. Students at the Royal College of Art (RCA) followed these trends in their magazine *Ark*, extending the methods of the older generation of Pop artists and architects (Alloway, Banham, John McHale, and the Smithsons). Reviewing the pages of *Ark* in its heyday (1956–1962), this chapter follows the revolution in the graphic arts at the RCA that helped make Pop Art in England a graphic affair, and turned these student designers toward an expanded field of background scenes in fashion photo shoots, television, cinema, and all the signs and symbols that media communication brought to bear. Interspersed with discussion of *Ark*'s influential commentary are remarks on Alison Smithson's writings on fashion, advertising, and Italian design, the creation of a fashionable "House of the Future," and her unpublished novelette about a woman correspondent working in the advertising industry. The chapter concludes by examining the rise of environmental design and the responsibility of designers—as Peter Smithson advised—to consider the total pattern of living.

I. Collage Thinking

Le Corbusier's Clothing

While in Chandigarh in June 1953, Le Corbusier wrote on the question of modern habitation to those who would meet for CIAM 9 in Aix-en-Provence.[2] He wondered whether this art truly existed—the joy and not the despair of living—and hoped the conferees would look at the roof of his Marseille Unité, which they would visit, and learn a new point of view about bringing up children. Education should not be looked on as implying suffering, control, reprobation, or punishment; a more lenient approach was associated in his mind with modern clothing and, from there, with modern housing:

> The body, either naked or clothed, at its ease in both cold and hot seasons … having at its command the necessary accouterments for the care of the animal. In our present reality it consists only of a cage for a stripped and scraggy wolf, a lion worried by fleas. … One must leap over the bars of the cage.
>
> I am writing these notes at Chandigarh, in the tropics in summer; I am completely naked. No one asks for anything more in any climate here. Yet one cannot help reflecting on the question of clothing as a utility and as a diverting pleasure.
>
> A mutation of clothing has been accomplished little by little during 50 years under our eyes without us noticing it.
>
> Modern clothing did make an appearance—certain clothing that is to say and the reaction of the native was: "I have the right to remain naked or semi-naked or even a quarter naked. I have the right to have no crease in my trousers or alternatively to crease my trousers to excess if I go to see my lady friend in the evening. This crease is an homage to other people."
>
> And on another level I could place:
> Men,
> Women
> Their children, sons and daughters
> each with their rights their tastes and their ambitions—all to be satisfied in their materialistic natures …[3]

How to associate the various levels of utility with pleasure, and education with new sensibilities? Such is the problem of clothing and habitation: how to please men, women, children, all with their own tastes, desires, and needs. Le Corbusier ends:

> I should like to finish by making an avowal. This is it: To lie down under the sun,—to sleep under the sun (on a Dunlopillo, of course), is often pleasant. To be seated on one's behind and not on a chair will bring you a reasonable happiness and a healthy economy.[4]

Le Corbusier here demonstrates what might be termed *collage thinking*, an association of apparently disparate items and levels of inference that allows the reader to draw suggestive meanings from juxtapositions of clothing, nakedness, taste, education, and architecture. This associative approach, in which meanings are boldly cross-linked, was much in favor among artists in the 1950s, as we saw in chapter 4. It was apparent, for example, in the Eames aesthetic and was fully exploited by the Independent Group. It was manifest in the Smithsons' thoughts touching on everything reviewed in chapter 3.

A shortage of paper continued in England well into the 1950s, encouraging the Smithsons' habit of writing on small scraps. This practice of reusing bits and pieces may also have encouraged their collage thinking.[5] Alice Smithson remarked in hindsight (late 1980s) that sometime in 1954 or 1955, Paolozzi, Henderson, and the Smithsons made an agreement to "collect snippets out of newspapers or magazines of lines and phrases striking us as demonstrating the sort of nonsensical 'explosion' in use of images and words that was happening."[6] The collection never added up to much, but "this interest in groups of words was perhaps connected to watching us collage typescripts in Doughty Street while editing our *Urban Re-identification—UR—*manuscript, with its proposed covers in Neapolitan ice stripes. The text was finally published as part of *Ordinariness and Light*."[7]

Collage thinking was also exploited as a structural method of advertisement in the 1950s and beyond, constructing suggestive and imaginative meanings via juxtapositions of text and image.[8] With its prevalence came enhanced abilities to scan a magazine layout, quickly peruse photographic or drawn imagery rather than subjecting it to in-depth scrutiny, and view striking and paradoxical montage sequences telling stories of new social tendencies, deployments of technology, and diversions associated with everyday life. Le Corbusier's riff on clothes, housing, and education can be likened to an advertising collage that places a naked man into his habitation, enjoying his comfortable seating arrangements and all his modern accouterments. The architect's intended meaning evolves out of the interrelationship between disparate images; like an advertiser, he uses images and figurative descriptions to sell a message to the members of a younger generation, to change their style.

The "New Realism" of the Market

The debate in 1950s England over commercial art was as intense as that surrounding Picturesque townscape. The contest between two aesthetic modes—roughly, nostalgic and consumeristic "realisms"—was only one level of the dispute: struggle was also engendered over values and ideologies. "Realism" in British art of the 1950s was, as cultural historian Juliet Steyn puts it, "precariously balanced between two concerns: truth to visual experience and the imaginative transformation of reality via the media—hence its incongruities, prevarications and discrepancies."[9] As pursued by *AR* in its Townscape Analysis casebooks, "realism" was interested in the concrete world as subject matter for an art of ordinary life, documenting landscapes of urban and industrial culture that might strengthen a sense of national identity. But there was also a "realism" of the free-market economy, fully on display in America and linked to freedom of choice in purchasing, to individual autonomy and mobility, to living over that range of variety and abundance which advertising promoted. Popular "realistic" images from American commercial art were (as IG members saw them) aggressive, not sentimental or picturesque; they cleverly deployed photographs and text in striking assemblages; they could be used to formulate new ideas, to think with. Even so commercial art implicitly markets a particular system of thought or political order, thus could not be said to faithfully depict the real world.

Photography, featured in many American advertisements, was the preferred medium for advertising food and other necessaries, where perceptions of photographic truth

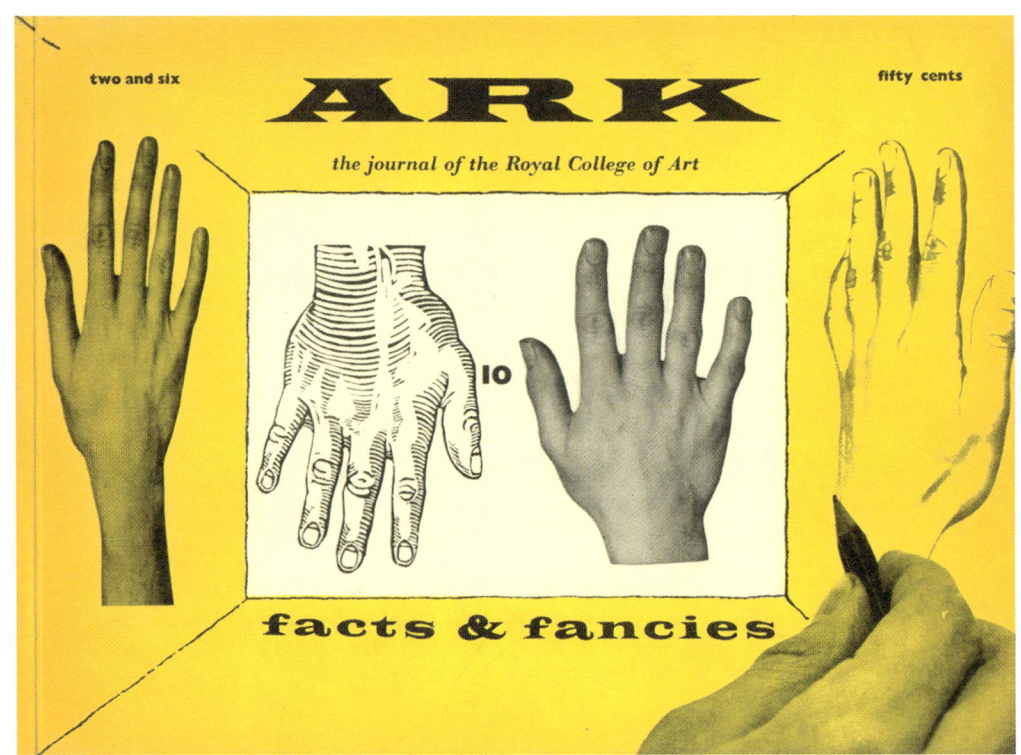

5.2
Cover of *Ark* 10 (Spring 1954). Photograph of a hand drawing a hand—an early use of photography by RCA students. If the hand is one of the marks of humanness, and handwriting the master of identity, then what does a photograph of a hand drawing imply? Royal College of Art.

were indispensable.¹⁰ Nothing could be more "realistic" than a photograph, a 1950s American primer on advertising suggested: "The more realistic the picture, the broader is the appeal to the masses."¹¹ In Britain, however, photography remained a contested medium, especially among older British illustrators. Paper shortages and equipment expenses also tended to keep its professional profile low. A few illustrators of AR's Townscape issues were avid photographers, such as Paul Nash, John Piper, and Eric de Maré, but their work focused on images depicting the "functional tradition," not on commercial art or avant-garde representations.¹² Even the bastion of "modern" art, the ICA, gave little support to creative photographers in the 1950s. It sponsored only a few photographic exhibitions: one was an exhibition of photographs from *Life* magazine (1952), and another was "Photo-Images," by Nigel Henderson (1954).¹³

Denigration of photography as not "art" and frowning upon its deployment even in commercial illustrations did not stop IG members from drawing on American visual primers that included photographic work, such as László Moholy-Nagy's *Vision in Motion* (1947) or György Kepes's *Language of Vision* (1944). These were inspiring sources for the IG's own innovative exhibitions, mostly photographic displays such as "Growth and Form" (1951), "Parallel of Life and Art" (1953), and "This is Tomorrow" (1956).¹⁴ Nor did such disapproval stop students of design at the Royal College of Art (RCA) from being interested in American photojournalism and photographic realism, or in British fashion photography, which achieved some renown in the 1950s.¹⁵

The art historian Ernst Gombrich, however, would be sufficiently concerned by the mid-1960s to warn about this version of photographic "realism." Its apparently absolute evidence was anything but direct.

> The word "evidence," of course, derives from *video* and implies that what lies in front of our eyes cannot and need not be questioned any further. But the point is here, as always, that visual evidence never comes neat, as it were, unmixed with imagination. The processing of visual information is impossible without this ingredient. Whether we are students of man-made images, of tracks left in the sand, or of intelligence photographs, we must scan the configuration for the message, for its meaning. In doing so we make ready to construct the answer from the elements of possible solutions we have stored. We are always trying for a fit, and this process can never be completely halted so long as our mind remains active.¹⁶

"Trying for a fit" of an image in a specific pigeonhole was not the IG's conscious objective, of course: its members sought to keep the process of associations actively open-ended. They were trying to rewrite the place and space of Britain in the postwar climate of retrenchment; in their own way, they were no less attentive than the Townscape advocates to shifts in the nation's geopolitical position. The art world was relocating; France no longer held the dominant position, and new possibilities were flowing from America. The intent of the younger generation was to open up British visual sensibilities to new fields of consumer culture, especially the products of the mass media, heretofore considered frivolous or not in good taste: photographic illustrations, the fashion industry, commercial design, the movies. This brassy, aggressively intrusive, primarily American material might infuse the battered and bruised British national ego with new vigor, wit, and aspiration.

Writing about these postwar trends in commercial art took place largely within a "contact zone" between two sets of designers and architects, one at the ICA (mainly in the IG) and the other at the RCA, where in the late 1950s students revived interest in the former and exchanged influence with it.[17] The IG innovators of the early 1950s had left little in the way of a paper trail, being swept up in discussions, exhibitions, teaching, and practice; they did not begin to *write* extensively about "pop" and mass media until after RCA students began to discuss these subjects in a student publication, *Ark*, around 1956. The RCA students and their guest writers revived interest in the lessons of the IG's innovators, giving their ideas a second lease on life and prompting them to write their own history of these expressions.

5.3
Another form of scrapbook is this page spread of Alison Smithson's collage manuscript entitled "Paradis Eloigne." Photograph by M. C. Boyer. Smithson Family Collection.

The RCA people tended to be younger, but the distinction was not exactly a generational one. The initial push had come from the innovators of "pop" who formed the IG; their exhibitions and discussions produced a reaction from the RCA people, and this reaction in turn exerted a pull on the IG members' interpretations and special interests. The two groups' concerns overlapped and extended each other. Influence flowed both ways. It is certain, in any case, that affluence was not sufficiently widespread in the early 1950s to support a leisured perpetual-student minority in the editing of lush magazines and printing of manifestos. Publishing writings and printing photographs were therefore kept to a minimum. But there was plenty else to do. Alison Smithson commented: "[t]he Independent Group produced no broadsheets, nor seemingly had any energy in that direction; everyone was too busy working."[18]

If the first generation of Pop artists, from the IG, dreamed of being educated consumers in a time of plenty and experimented with the blurring of fine art/mass art distinctions, smoothing them into a continuum, the RCA students of the mid-1950s were directly involved in illustrating, designing, and consuming all the dreams that money could buy. A million or more people between the ages of 15 and 24 were added to the British population in the 1950s. This group was the biggest purchaser of some commodities, and it felt an intense urgency to learn from its forebears and to record the "hypnotic impact of a popular iconography," as Robert Freeman put it in 1959: "We have moved from the treasuring of fine arts fetishes to the age of expendable iconography—At least—some of us have."[19] Its members were, like the IG, passing along, walking across, thumbing through public spaces and illustrated magazines, allowing their "eyes [to] feed upon a smothering selection of visual material," all of which informed their attitudes toward the living environments of the everyday.[20]

Writing about Fashion

Dress is particularly sensitive to shifts in generational desires. For British youth in the 1950s, fashion quickly became an image for an aestheticized relationship to the urban world. It was uppermost in the minds of both the IG and its successors at the RCA. The witty, decorative effects of fashion—American, Italian, and British influences amassed in collage arrangements—became ammunition to fling against those who still maintained the standards of "good taste," denying wider cultural currency to images outside the realm of high art. With an eye for youth and awareness of the new consumer market, British *Vogue* began a "Young Idea" section in January 1953, noting that it would cover what youth were wearing, doing, thinking. Illustrations for the new section included drawings by RCA design students, making a tight connection between fashion, commerce, and the academy of arts.[21]

Tied to the trivial and often thought of as feminized terrain, fashion writing has in general been undervalued. Yet clothes and magazine articles about clothes reveal much about the cherished beliefs of popular culture, its oppositional posturings against high culture, and the slow movement—real or dreamed-of—toward a classless society in which creativity, not birthright, would be the defining feature of each life. Clothing makes a statement: cool detachment, subversive transgression, individualized choice; or conformity, officialdom, power. It entails the pleasure of seeing as much as being seen, of both refusal and acceptance in the marking out of personal space and identity.

Alison Smithson was well known for her clothing—which she experimented with not because Le Corbusier spoke about clothing, but because it was important to her for its own sake. "Fashionable" was never quite the word for her attire, which was sometimes outlandish, sometimes utilitarian, and always individualistic. She once recalled a Team 10 meeting in La Sarraz, Switzerland, in September 1955. She and Peter had traveled there with William Howell in their Jeep, and found all the Dutch members sitting round the table like good burghers.

> Wholly unsmiling because I was wearing black woollen tights, top, balaclava helmet and jeeper boots against the cold of an open vehicle in a wet autumn. Aldo [van Eyck] afterwards had one of his emotional storms—said it was disrespectful—when I said Merkelbach, van Tijen, and so on [Dutch architects], had looked "prune faced."[22]

During her wartime asylum in Edinburgh, Alison avidly read the *Ladies' Home Journal* every month, sent as a gift from America throughout the war: "I read about Birds Eye, miniature Singers, Dating Problems; Green Man Monster Peas ..."[23]

> This proved to become my foundation reading for our theories to do with "aspirations," which we spoke about in the Independent Group meetings at the ICA, London, 1952–55; "fed back" to America by an exhibition touring in the 1990–92 and who's [sic] catalogue refers to our writings of the early 1950s when we illustrated our texts with the full page advertisements of the "Ladies Home Journal" and the "Ladies Home Companion."[24]

Thinking back to the formative period of the IG, she recalled that

> the artists who made up the Independent Group were talking about another way of seeing, thinking of the images as collage material, as we ourselves had done so, 1949 to 1953, in making up the sheets of coloured images of food that would paper our kitchen in Limerston Street, September, 1953 ... you have to realize it was still largely an era of black and white images ... the kitchen was a place of spectacle for visitors.[25]

Perhaps Alison sharpened her interest in fashion and magazines from attendance at the second series of IG meetings, organized by Lawrence Alloway and John McHale in the spring and summer of 1955.[26] There were discussions on "borax" designs and American advertising. Toni del Renzio, as assistant to the director of the ICA beginning in 1951, played a major role in the ICA lecture series throughout the 1950s, lecturing himself on

"Fashion and Fashion Magazines." Gillo Dorfles and Reyner Banham led a conversation on "Aesthetics and Italian Product Design." Frank Cordell lectured on the impact of technology and mass communications on popular music under the heading "Gold Pan Alley." There were conversations on "Children's Books and Periodicals" with John Nicholson Low, editor of *The Dandy*, Geoffrey Trease, author of *Tales out of School*, and G. Harry McLaughlin, who worked on a children's magazine. In the fall of 1956, Toni del Renzio began planning an exhibition of fashion photography, which never materialized (perhaps due to the Suez crisis). Nevertheless he continued to pursue this interest, lecturing to a general ICA audience on "The Strategy of Fashion" in March 1957.[27] Particularly for Alison Smithson and the students at the RCA, all of this was primary material, to be stirred into an associative soup from which innumerable ruminations would spring.

In 1956, the Smithsons expounded their theory of advertisement in a personal statement published in *Ark*, "But Today we collect Ads."[28] With only slight hesitation—signaled by the "but"—they embraced the art of advertisement, with its powerful myth of progress and promise of material wealth. The "goods" in advertisements represented this wealth; the ads contained "good" images, and represented not a lowering of artistic standards but essential ammunition in the campaign against the tastemakers of "good" form. The Smithsons went even further:

> Advertising has become respectable in its own right and is beating the fine arts at their own game. ... The traditional function of the fine arts, the definition of what is fine and desirable for the ruling class and therefore ultimately that which is desired by all society, has now been taken over by the ad-man.[29] ... Ads which do not try to sell you the product except as a natural accessory of a way of life. They are good "images" and their technical virtuosity is almost magical. ... And this transient thing is making a bigger contribution to our visual climate than any of the traditional fine arts.[30]

The ad-man was edging the architect and the artist out of their traditional roles, while advertising itself, a democratic blurring of provocative images, was creating "our whole pattern of life—principles, morals, aims, aspirations, and standards of living. We must somehow get the measure of this intervention if we are to match its powerful and exciting impulses with our own."[31] As the Eameses had taught, architects had a "responsibility" to understand and utilize communications invading their visual sensibilities.

The Smithsons' argument was exactly what the students at the RCA were longing for: a reversal of "good taste," a tempering of high art with graphic design, an intent to be serious without solemnity—hence the invitation to publish the Smithsons' article in *Ark*.[32] Like the Smithsons, the student editors hoped the advertising industry might shake up the art establishment and lighten the drabness of the London scene. The Smithsons did indeed "collect ads"—from the *New Yorker*, *Ladies' Home Journal*, *Gentry*, *Time*, and other magazines that formed their visual climate. Such advertisements supplied data about a new way of life that was being invented and documented simultaneously. They believed that the objects illustrated in these magazines, in the "good image," offered fresh impulses and could help to "re-identify" an old society such as England and instill within it an "inventive energy" a "technical, historical, indigenous energy."[33] American popular culture and its commercial art were necessary correctives to British conservative habits and alienating ways of life, *but* were to be absorbed in an "indigenous" manner.

In an unpublished novelette, "Madame Representative—Woman Correspondent," begun in 1959 and worked on over several decades, Alison Smithson reveals more of her relationship to magazines and other cultural currencies. Madame, the story goes, as the representative of the Associated World News Organization, covered committee meetings of the World Social Organization (WSO), where she attracted many "strong and competent men" to her side. Her associates were no doubt the generating force that gave Madame's reports their humane quality. The 1940s and 1950s having seen the rise of the acronymic organization, Alison Smithson depicts the conversation of delegates to UNUN, UNILEP, UNITAP, and so on (she marked her fictitious list on a scrap of paper). These international meetings were "a world within the world. Geared to run like clockwork. Unforeseen forces are excluded."[34] Madame, having to report on so many different decisions coming out of so many commissions, was one of the few persons to change the way newspapers looked: "re-thinking of layout, typography, classification of the news presented."[35]

> Madame always acted not as an inventive-creative but as a manipulative-creative. She created mechanisms of communication. She transmitted the presence and character, the soundness or unsoundness, the responsible or irresponsible, the sincerity or hidden aims (and these could be ugly). Telling can add nothing to Madame. But it can add to these men, to their well-springs and to the morality with which they handled a multiplicity of loyalties.[36]
>
> She was always trying to "move" the problem. … She never once accepted an idea without knowing also what should change.[37]

"Madame Representative" is a thinly disguised autobiographical account of Alison's own experience as stirrer and recorder of Team 10 and as an expert in collage writing. She would be guest editor for *AD* of "CIAM Team 10" and "The Work of Team 10" in May 1960, followed in December 1962 with her edition of "Team 10 Primer." The latter allowed her to experiment with layout and typography. In her fictional account, she is setting the record straight: as recorder of Team 10's positions, she neither added nor subtracted from events. All the group's members discussed their problems in detail and arrived together at practical solutions. To the "Madame Representative" mélange she adds fashion and interests shared with IG members (e.g., advertising and film as reflectors of mass desires) and stirs in aspects of New Brutalism, and of reading the signs of the countryside from the passenger's seat in a moving automobile.

Speaking in the voice of a male reporter who has worked side by side with Madame, Alison introduces the reader to her heroine by noting that in her early years of studying and commuting she was too busy to take care of herself; only later did she have the money and time to have her hair done regularly. Amid commentary on Madame's associates (many of whom are based on CIAM participants) and their involvement with various international organizations, the reporter inserts comments on Madame's appearance, which improved in tandem with her status. For parties she was often outlandish, her makeup capturing the mood in the most startling fashion, for she always had the sense of what the evening might be. Her appearance would change to match the seasons, the mood of a city, or the type of work. She began to resemble—but not mimic—film stars of the day: the really glamorous ones, such as Dietrich, Garbo, Hepburn, or Hayward. Films in which she saw competent people, especially women, moving about were "signs" to her. By keeping track of the experts, she was prepared for aspirations of the average. She remarked: "'I like to watch their pleased looks because they *know* they are good'."[38]

This was her method. By means of her News Letters in the 50's and 60's, and her Press Conferences she tried to remedy the deficiencies of the individual's ordinary experience by revealing the underlying continuity as she saw it, and preparing Mr Ordinary for what would be effecting [sic] him. With a confidence bordering on the Kennedies she prepared the man in the street for his reaction. By elimination of "shock" she enabled people to give proper consideration to events.

Our period of work together in the World Advertising and Press Liaison and Investigation Bureau was—looking back—a vital link in Madame's training.[39]

Her only light reading matter while commuting were fashion magazines, and she would leaf though the same one for days as if sunning herself in it. She never bought a paper. She never took an early copy. Instead she would persist in the most annoying habit of reading your galleys over your shoulder, or wander round and read the paragraphs in the typeset or on the machines.[40]

Madame Representative liked cars and cigarettes. She liked army vehicles of the 40's, Cadillac's of the 50's, Camel cigarettes. It was always a pleasure to me [the reporter inserts] to see her accept a Camel cigarette and smoke it dangerously. That <u>was</u> Deitrich [sic]. No one else could do it. Maybe no one else dared. ... To watch an army vehicle moving at speed along a road, to spot a Cadillac in the traffic: was sufficient pleasure of the moment.[41]

Though Madame Representative was a newspaper reporter, the reader is informed that newspapers distort immediate problems, detailing intentions rather than progress toward results or the effects of those results: "The reporting of what people said was just too easy to be really true. In this sense it was not reality. The reality lay in the ultimate effect—results, which would in turn become the problems someone would be examining a decade later."[42] Thus, newspapers stuck to reporting "transient trivia."

This while advertising at its best—and there was some in the 50's and 60's—did a multitude of tasks. It not only catered specifically for a specialized society: the tight groups where meanings taken for granted in one circle were almost incomprehensible to another, but it acted as a link in the form of "desire creation" that passed from one group to another. It gave cohesion to leisure pattern groups, taking over from the old "class" structure. It provided humour for the initiated. The Newspaper was at best a sort of narrow front "dirt" sheet outside the international picture language popular magazine (typified best by the two French publications *Match* and *Elle*). Everyday a jumble of ill-assorted facts was cast to a group of generations who were as unable as the newspaper men to utilize them. The information the newspapers dished out was undigested and undigestible [sic]. Universal literacy was not being made to function. The idea that the newspapers could repeat to you any more than the loud noises of life was unthought of in the 50's. Basically because there was no universally believed ideological framework into which anyone might fit knowledge. An unplumbed fund of information went unused and unwanted. It engendered sluggish minds which affected the whole mental attitude.[43]

… Madame was caught with the way in which the advertising man was presumably expressing as well as forming societies morals. For example certain high standard women's magazines censored drink and later smoking nevertheless took it as a matter of course that unless you cleaned your teeth—washed—did your hair—watched your smell—you would not be prepared for kissing and so on. She made the famous report on Advertising's creative power with regard to "desired illigitiacy" [sic] which appeared in the 60's. She never left such an investigation unlegislated although it often had a way of becoming something else.[44]

"Desired" illegitimacy—a tweaking of fashion, which most would say did not count as a subject of serious study—provided fodder for other concerns and expressions. From time to time in the late 1950s and early 1960s, Alison wrote under the name Margaret Gill, her middle and maiden names, in the *Architects' Journal*.[45] Her column, "Not Quite Architecture," covered subjects such as fashion and clothes. English youth culture and street fashion were just beginning their assault on mainstream publishing and high-tone couture, and were about to come under serious consideration in the 1960s. In 1959 she noted that the greatest thing to come out of the RCA was its King's Road boutique, "Bazaar." This had just opened a Terence Conran-designed Knightsbridge branch, and its prêt-à-porter was hard to beat. "Clothes [mostly designed by Mary Quant] are so dramatic that a Monkey (as near Russian Black Bear as you can now get) busby [military head-gear made of fur] and trim to a high-waisted black leather coat can turn the heads of a whole top deck," i.e., on a London bus.[46]

Girls' short skirts, she said, were brave statements, even more outlandish if they wore colored stockings as well, while their mothers' were a good foot longer and very passé. Clothes were *supposed* to mark a degree of rebelliousness! In one column she recalled getting out of the car in Edinburgh and taking off the fur hat she wore because their car was cold due to so many openings and closings of doors. (Mobility and fashion seem quirkily associated in Alison Smithson's mind.) Of course, her friends commented, "you're not going to wear that thing and expect to go in with us." She returned with a hairy white Scotch wool hat, and what did she see walking past her but pale blue trousers and pale blue boots! She could, she said, have kicked herself for conforming and not contributing to the scene with green suede boots going up into pale pink knitted leggings.

Clothing, for Alison as for Le Corbusier, was associated with architecture. If only one were supplied with greater choices for both! The "regulator" and the "conformer" were both her enemies! "Supply and demand; the right client and the right article and aesthetic control would be a thing of the past."[47]

An affluent society on the rise offered more leisure and more travel, all to be duly reported by Alison. Saint-Tropez was her model for a leisure society's seaside town: the shops terrific, the clothes cheap, Brigitte Bardot still in, and seventeen the age for trim buttocks. Gold sandals were also in, bare feet even more so because cheaper. The look was "inexpensive" but clean: grooming, washing, and sun all being inexpensive. "It makes me think magazines are useless. For all those on the grape vine *know*; those on are not telling … and those off it cannot recognize it even when they see it at the organized fashion shows and attempt to report it."[48] She was no doubt reporting on her own fashion instincts, off the page and generally not recognized by her associates except as outlandish and questionable. She was also writing about group mentality and insider knowledge, as she had in "Madame Representative."

The Italian Allure

Magazines, as the foregoing has already made clear, always held a stylish attraction for Alison Smithson.

> In the heyday of magazines [she wrote in 1984], when *AD* was a magazine in the old sense, with Monica Pidgeon as editor, Dutch Forum [to the contrary] was not seen around all that much in people's houses, and so on (for example we once saw *AD* being carried in a Bombay street), fashionable among foreign magazines were the Italian, not least because of it being a good place to go, fashionable to sport their dark glasses, their posters, Olivetti showrooms, typewriters, Gaggia coffee machines a.s.o. [and so on] the whole culture was "food" and the magazine was an appurtenance announcing a person's affiliation with that culture's energy (and the sun).[49]

Reyner Banham claimed that the trend for everything Italian had burst upon the London scene in 1950 but passed away by the middle of the decade. Before that point, however, a team of middle-essayists, lady film-critics and Establishment art-pundits wagged their heads gravely over the influence of *espresso*, scooters and Italian films on the English way of life. It was this kind of discussion that … left a question uppermost in one's mind—what made the Italian influence tick?[50]

That influence, Banham claimed, was short-lived because Jayne Mansfield soon replaced Gina Lollobrigida, Plymouth substituted for Ferrari, and Mies van der Rohe stood where Ernesto Rogers had been. "Italy, in fact, had been a 'clean' substitute for America in the panic years when the onset of the Cold War had forced puzzled pinks, tweedsmen and do-gooders generally to face the fact that FDR was dead, and that you couldn't incline to the gusto and busto of the American Way of Life while leaning to the Left."[51] Reflecting back over the 1950s from the vantage point of 1961, however, Banham revised this view of the Italian craze, shifting it slightly to 1953–1960 and claiming that it had little to do with the notions of "good" design that every Italian product expressed and more to do with the rise of teenage affluence and the vast quantity of inexpensive, fashionable Italian clothes.[52]

For Alison Smithson, however, the Italian influence was not to be so summarily dismissed; Italy had supplied generations of architects with an "intellectual food package."[53] Many years later, she ruminated on what she called a larder stocked with Italian images: the simple ordering of an urbanism viewed in paintings and ideal cities from the Renaissance; color, especially the striped white and green buildings; the power of photographs taken in early-morning light, as well of those of architecture and towns taken in the nineteenth century by the Alinari brothers of Florence. These photographs and others enabled the extension of the Roman language of architecture at least up to her father's generation and enhanced explorations into the classical orders of Brunelleschi, Bramante, and of course Palladio. This collage of associative ideas allows the reader to grasp the meaning of her "intellectual food package," which she had first sensed through books and photographs:

> I started architecture school at 16, in wartime: travel was impossible until later in the 1940s, learning was from books although book production was minimal: in the late 1940s the first book on architecture I was able to buy was a monograph on Bramante, on wartime paper that is now tan coloured: it gave the scope of works although photographic reproduction was even worse than my inherited Anderson. … I did not travel to Italy until August, 1948, when we entered by train to start with Terragni in Como, we found the apartment block of Sant Elia a curiosity. Our reactions, faced with the actual works, were to the current state of both the fabric as found and the patterns of use of Italy. … For we had to replace the images acquired, by osmosis, of Italy … with Italy as discovered to be.[54]

In Venice she saw how the city was dressed by banners and carpets hung over balconies, how the edge of canals was marked with posts. San Marco was revelatory: her first experience of Mogul spatial organization, with paths raised on plinths above tanks of water and flowerbeds. A person walking in these gardens is thought to be in Paradise, suspended between heaven and earth. In the cathedral, too, one passes through the golden light of Paradise. But of equal influence was the language of architecture from the Middle East. The Doge's Palace is all about horizontal layers, its paved plane raised up in space among pilotis, above the level for walking by ordinary citizens, and its brick walls rich screenings of patterned fabric. She remembered on this same trip her first visit to Palladio's Villa Capra and her amazement at the suburbanization of rural Italy—not the picturesque English countryside, but a green lawn for someone's rabbit. It was astonishing to realize that Palladio's work was merely a casing on a medieval building that remained inside: "If Greece in 1951, was our discovery of light: Italy, 1948 was the discovery of shadow. We were taught Sciagraphy ..."[55]

Toni del Renzio was perhaps the IG member closest to Alison's interest in fashion, magazines, and popular consumer culture. He was particularly apt at reporting cultural events, moving between London, Paris, Rome, Milan, and Zurich, maneuvering between art worlds and the zone of sub-Fleet Street mass-circulation magazines. Often he was deployed on a Saturday night, at good pay, to provide copy for the picture pages of *Sunday Pictorial*, covering show-biz folks on their foreign trips; this work, he claimed, put him in a different relationship to "pop culture" than that of most members of the IG.[56] While remaining active in ICA events, he worked part-time for various fashion magazines and finally joined *Harper's Bazaar* in 1958 as art director.

Critical of the naiveté of other IG members, del Renzio recalled that in the early 1950s they "had still to learn that 'pop culture' was pluralist and to draw the lessons from Riesmann's [sic] peer-group sociology."[57] Most IG members held only Marilyn Monroe worthy of eulogy; otherwise they kept to their Hampstead middle-class "good taste." Audrey Hepburn was cast "as the girl most of the architects would like to have photographed in one of their buildings. She was remote from urgent rock and roll culture."[58] He called the dominant ideology of the IG "contradictory": many esteemed Sigfried Giedion's *Mechanization Takes Command*, and to a lesser degree his *Space, Time and Architecture*. They were enamored of Marshall McLuhan's *Mechanical Bride*, Norbert Wiener's *Human Use of Human Beings*, Harold Rosenberg's notorious action-painting essay (1952), and Parker Tyler's writings on cinema. But these different ideas could hardly be spun into a coherent ideology. If there was a unifying principle of IG, it resided in an apparent but not real contradiction: "a rejection of the very institutionalization of modernism it most admired in New York."

In an article entitled "Shoes Hair and Coffee" in *Ark* 20 (1957), del Renzio noted that any attentive reader of American women's magazines could understand the success fashion photographers had had in taking the well-tried formula of "sleek car and chic

Fashionable Modernity

mannequin"—both items described as "models"—and substituting for the car a fresh image of "glabrous architecture." This has been achieved not only in pages of *Woman's Home Companion* and in *Vogue* but in material describing GM's Technical Center (designed by Eero Saarinen). This new conflation, del Renzio claimed, cast serious doubt on the separation of architectural aesthetics from the expendable aesthetics of automobile design.[59] Automobiles, with a high rate of obsolescence, and buildings, with a supposedly lower rate, both function symbolically—both are items in the continuum of popular culture—and their symbolism is a timely corrective to pure, formal design and highbrow "good taste." "The sex appeal of the Technical Centre is no less than that of the 1957 Cadillac."[60]

Many fearful conservative men have been led by their women to accept popular design—"fashion," appealing primarily to women, thus being one of the major means of discovery by men of an expendable aesthetics. Nor were "fashion" and "expendable aesthetics" confined to the advertising pages. Del Renzio pointed out that lively design trends had also infiltrated hairdressers' salons, shoe shops, boutiques specializing in sportswear and casual attire, and coffee bars. These places were successful because they appealed specifically to women. The Italians were the first to create this feminine appeal via powerful suggestions in product design, and the Italian influence had been spread through espresso, the motor scooter, and movie heroines:

> Design operates in a communication network where new responses are casually and easily learned. This process inserts itself into the continuum of popular culture as a new but acceptable expression. This is clearly demonstrated by the association of many coffee bars with "skiffle," "rock 'n roll" and other new but esoteric jazz forms. Both these popular arts permit improvisation within closely understood limits, according to a pattern, conventional but newly established, a set of permutations of untarnished figures. Both have a certain cosmopolitanism, narrow, restrained, unmistakably British, the Palladianism of Twentieth century folkways, brass and neon missions in the asphalt jungle.[61]

5.4
Toni del Renzio, "Shoes Hair and Coffee," *Ark* 20 (Autumn 1957), 17. Royal College of Art.

A collage of chance associations—the Italians, their clothing, scooters, coffee machines—was held up as the epitome of trend-setting design, the pinnacle of Continental "good taste," which *Ark* put forth with vigor and conviction to enliven dull English sensibilities. Scooter boys in proper uniform stopping to drink an espresso were flaunting important identity markers. Take a glimpse at the London street scene and one readily finds a young person walking hand in hand with an Olivetti typewriter! The pages of *Ark* praised Olivetti's high-quality publicity materials, able to draw attention via elegant detachment. Joseph Rykwert claimed that the virtues of an Olivetti typewriter "are the same as those of the publicity—an elegance dependent on economy of means, choice of colours, and limitation of all embellishments to essentials."[62]

A Fashionable House

All this fashionable discourse, moving back and forth between innovators and followers of "pop," fed back as inspiration into architectural design. In a 1957 issue of *Ark*, John McHale discussed not only how technology had transformed the home but how all of its extensions, such as the automobile, the espresso café bar, the movies, and even the pub, had influenced its form.[63] He cited the designs of Alison and Peter Smithson for the *Daily Mail* Ideal Home Exhibition (1956). Their "House of the Future" represented for McHale a pragmatic attempt to extrapolate from now to 25 years hence—a house designed for a working couple with no children, costing about £20,000. It was constructed from repetitive moldings of resin-bonded plaster, which turned the domicile into a single enclosure with only one opening for a door. This opaque envelope—an all-over smooth surface, ceiling, walls, and floor with clearly defined joints—created an elegant sense of containment, with views out to an interior garden patio. Alison Smithson described the building as follows:

> The rooms flow into one another freely like the compartments of a cave, and as in a cave, the skewed passage that joins one compartment to another effectively maintains privacy.
>
> Each compartment is a different size—a different area and a different height—a totally differentiated shape to suit its purpose.[64]

Production methods were borrowed from the car industry—the parts replaceable, hence expendable. Alison explained: "The floor, walls, ceiling, being considered as a single unit, the lighting is integrated into this surface and is designed to give a different character to each part of the home."[65] Furniture was part of the architecture, with four types of chairs—the pogo, the egg, the tulip, and the saddle—the only mobile pieces allowed:

> The house in 25 years' time will be different, not only in itself but also in the way in which it is arranged within the framework of the community.

> This particular house has been thought of as a town house; it is not set in its own garden, but contains the garden within it. Such a house can be grouped together to form a compact community. The tiny garden is obviously inadequate for the play of bigger children so you must imagine this the home of the couple young or old perhaps with baby or toddler.[66]

McHale highlighted technological details that revealed the designers' sensibility to marketing trends: a fridge whose small size was offset by ample storage containers, a drip-dry cupboard rather than laundry equipment. Retrograde divisions separating kitchen/living space were bridged over by equipment such as a trolley cart supplied with an infrared grill, toaster, and hot storage plugged in at a variety of outlets located about the house. The same was true of most of the kitchen appliances, which contained built-in electrical elements. Waste disposal, electrostatic dust collector, and curved moldings were intended as labor-savers. In the bathroom were other conveniences: floor-flush bathtub molded to human form, separate shower with warm-air drying, and freestanding pedestal washbasin. In the dining/living room, a hexagonal table moved from floor level to dining- or coffee-table height as the inhabitants might desire.

Sportswear designer Teddy Tinling based the actors' clothes for "The House of the Future," captured for posterity in well-known photographs, on the advice of a costume historian predicting future trends in fashion design.[67] The clothes for the man, Tinling said, were "plain and unembellished. This in keeping with the times, a kind of Superman trend to fit in with the Space Age. ... Especially in the house, men will revert to the bright colors which they wore before the Industrial Revolution." While men changed to leisurewear in bright colors when they returned home, women dressed up as super-feminine beings:

> Out-of-doors their clothes will have to be almost as severe as men's. ... As a reaction to this, I feel sure she will want light, pretty clothes to wear in her well-heated home. Through history women have emphasized their femininity by décolleté necklines, and our women of the future will be no exception.[68]

Tinling's conception of clothing may or may not have been shared by Alison Smithson, for the latter's remarks on the project do not mention clothes.[69] But she does note that the couple who were to occupy this house acted as if they were both friends and sexual partners, revealing a certain ambiguity over postwar gender roles.

5.5 (following pages)
Teddy Tinling clothing designs for Alison and Peter Smithson, "House of the Future" (1956). The Alison and Peter Smithson Archive, Special Collections, Frances Loeb Library, Graduate School of Design, Harvard University.

The wartime "masculine woman" was redomesticated and refeminized, and the family was once again becoming the central institution in society; consequently, the man and woman in "The House of the Future" were a "team," working and playing together.

Peter Smithson would note: "[t]he art of making territory starts with our clothes, with their style and with our gestures and postures when we wear them."[70] And nearly 50 years later, when asked about "The House of the Future" and its relationship to new technology and materials, he replied that it actually had nothing to do with technology but everything to do with urban form.

> We said that you don't get a new house without a new urban fabric. We did a house that was inward looking, and the garden was placed inside the house. This was a different formulation—a new piece of urbanism. It was a specific-modern for couples, old people, and small children. It was not the typical family house with a garden. Most cities contain a multitude of house types. You have an enormous choice available, disregarding the money problem (there are all of these houses that you might like but can't afford). There are hundreds and hundreds of types. The idea of a new type for a new situation was not very realistic. You could say it was idealistic.[71]

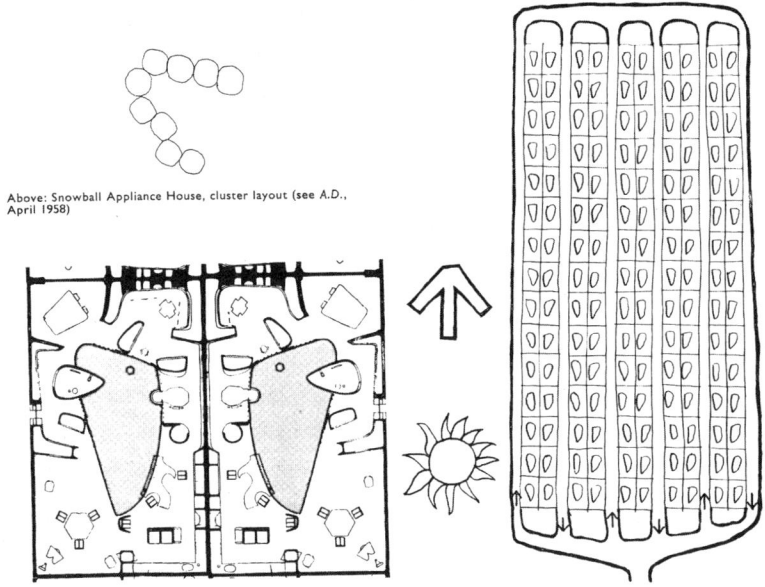

Above: Snowball Appliance House, cluster layout (see A.D., April 1958)

5.6
Left: House of the Future, exhibited at the Ideal Home Exhibition, 1956; right: Fougasse layout, showing a group of these houses clustered together. Alison and Peter Smithson, "Scatter," *AD* 29 (1959), 150. Smithson Family Collection.

II. *Ark* Magazine and Graphic Design

Visual Uproar

"Pop Art" in 1950s Britain was by and large a creation of the graphic arts. Lawrence Alloway felt that this influence was too strong. Banham believed, to the contrary, that the "Pop-graphics alliance" was there from the start: "Pop-Art was created largely out of graphics like corn-flake packs, adverts, comic strips, record sleeves and stuff—but the connection is very real and precise. The point of connection is the Royal College of Art's [RCA's] pseudo-student magazine *Ark*, the time of connection the first of the issues edited by Roger Coleman in 1955."[72] The brilliant designs issuing from this Pop-graphics alliance were giving the impression that the entire RCA was obsessed with being "with it" and attuned to the latest fashion, whereas a perusal of back issues of *Ark* would quickly reveal that its School of Graphic Design nearly missed the revolution in visual communication, confining itself instead to art drawing and art lithography.[73]

If the student designers of the RCA had by the 1960s become facile manipulators of fantasy's iconography, their irony and visual wit having run out of steam, nevertheless this visual uproar of signs and symbols was the outcome of a real revolution in the graphic arts in postwar England. Even the term "graphic design" was new, used first in Britain by Richard Guyatt after he was appointed Professor of Publicity Design at the RCA in 1948. An irate article in *The Times* had complained about the phrase "publicity design," so a new title was sought. Guyatt explained: "With a certain sense of relief, but not much conviction, the name graphic design was chosen. No one was quite sure what it meant, but it had a purposeful ring."[74] This "ring" enabled Guyatt to free graphic art from any connotation of commercial art, and to reconnect it with the fine arts. He held artists who "could not draw" in some disdain and would eventually open the School to photography, modern typography, and graphic information, but not until the mid-1960s.

Discontent over the parochialism and drabness of the British art and design scene began to creep into the pages of *Ark*. This slow student rebellion came to fruition when Roger Coleman edited *Ark* issues 18 through 20 (1956–1957).[75] Coleman recognized that even in England, graphic artists were now designing for a new culture: in addition to the old methods of illustration, typography, and exhibition design, they were creating schemes for the marvelous new culture of television and fashion design, and expressing new interest in collage and ideograms. He therefore intended to change not only the contents of *Ark* but also its layout. RCA students had been exposed to avant-garde European and American graphic designers through firsthand experience, while studying at Yale with amazing teachers such as Paul Rand, Leo Lionni, Saul Bass, Lou Dorfsman, and via European and American magazine layouts, far more modern and elegant than anything available in England at the time. Exposure to this imagery inevitably influenced their own approaches.

5.7
Cover of *Ark* 4 (Spring 1952) by David Gentleman. Royal College of Art.

5.8
Men's Fashion, design by David Collins for Richard Smith, "Man and He-Man," *Ark* 20 (Autumn 1957), 13. Royal College of Art.

the journal of the Royal College of Art price 2s 6d or 50 cents

Ark 19

Roger Coleman and his art editors—Angela Rimmer, Gordon Moore, Alan Bartram, and David Collins—tried to produce an English equivalent of the foreign magazines they admired.[76] The covers they produced for *Ark* 19 (a red-green comic-style Mona Lisa) and *Ark* 20 (a blurred Coca-Cola logo) are among their most striking achievements.[77] The entirety of *Ark* 20 is a masterpiece produced on a shoestring: Toni del Renzio designed the spread for his own essay, "Shoes Hair and Coffee," printed in red on a transparent yellow sheet which facilitated transforming juxtapositions when read backward or forward. The issue included a crude black-on-white photo essay by A. J. Bisley on professional wrestling, "On the Mat at Lime Grove," followed by a minimal layout of Richard Smith's "Man and He-Man," which placed a man in formal dress against Superman in mid-flight and the singing cowboy Gene Autry against an overlay of actor Glenn Ford as a gunfighter.

Students at the School of Graphic Design regarded the word "beauty" with great suspicion, and were eager to be offensive. They turned common visuals into protest art, hoping to stand for the complete opposite of "good taste," able to achieve a faster effect than the slow burn of provocation that the IG Pop generation had perfected. In spite of Banham's insistence that all manifestations of Pop sensibilities were indebted to the IG, the link between ICA and RCA had actually begun to form in the early 1950s, when the art historian Basil Taylor was appointed RCA's first librarian and founder of the School of General Studies.[78] Many articles included in *Ark* during the 1950s were the result of Taylor's invitations to artists and scholars he knew to speak at RCA lunchtime meetings. This is how Reyner Banham, the Smithsons, Lawrence Alloway, even Herbert Read, found their way into the pages of *Ark*.[79]

Even if revolutions were restricted at the RCA to the graphic arts, Pop belonged to wider changes in visual communication: an entirely new environment was arising, one in which "good taste" and high art were no longer uniquely pertinent. It was this shift in the graphic arts of the mid-1950s to early 1960s that kept the innovations of the IG alive and their attitude worth inheriting by students at the RCA. Forget the "standard frames of reference" in fine arts, Roger Coleman advised in 1957, "for the majority these frames are non-existent, and they think, as it were, in a different visual language."[80]

5.9
Cover of *Ark* 19 (Spring 1957), design by Gordon Moore. Royal College of Art.

If a new consciousness of design in our surroundings is to be, then it must come from within society itself, it must grow naturally out of social necessity. … Mass communication networks have changed society in this century to a degree that would have been difficult to foretell, that is, in character not extent, and in the sphere of the arts has not only changed the shape of the existing forms but introduced new ones like the cinema and television. The mass-media of visual communications are today's background to the arts.[81]

Background Environments

The first issue of Ark edited by Roger Coleman (Autumn 1956) came to the attention of Lawrence Alloway. It was a fortuitous encounter, for although Coleman was still a student, he was asked to join the Exhibition subcommittee at the ICA in 1957. In exchange, Ark provided Alloway with a means to spread his ideas about art and the IG's legacy to a younger generation at the RCA, long after IG had ceased to meet but during a time when the ICA continued to be a center for lectures, discussions, and meetings. In 1989, Coleman explained: "I think Alloway saw ARK as an opportunity and a platform to promote abstraction and there weren't any others. … The College supplied an audience. When I was involved with the ICA later it was often terribly difficult to get people along to fill up a programme. So here were another group of people who could be tapped to keep the programme going."[82] The editor of Ark 24 and 25 (1959–1960), Ruddy Maude-Roxby, said: "Alloway helped us greatly in our attempt to make ARK more international and be aware of what was happening elsewhere. What we wanted most of all was to be in tune with what was happening on the Continent and particularly in America."[83]

Alloway made six contributions to Ark in 1956–1959, all reflecting his nonhierarchical, all-inclusive approach to cultural values. His articles were divided evenly between the iconography of Pop culture and that of continental avant-garde painting.[84] Alloway was intensely interested in the "communication background of movies," meaning by "background" not only the actual setting for a film but also the environment of the city or the home, and the background of ideas and ideologies implicitly or explicitly stated.[85] He explained in "Communications Comedy and the Small World" that a physical setting expresses an ideological scene. The American frontier, for example, was not only a physical setting for Western movies but reflected a state of mind about and belief in the destiny of the nation. A communication background always offered information about itself, playing with the channels of communication by which a program reached its audience. Hence, Alloway argued, the communication background of films may serve to orient the public in a world that is growing smaller and more complex with each improvement in communication.

Alloway's interest in the background of mass-media communications greatly influenced the designers of Arks 18 through 20. Roger Coleman, for example, in "Dream Worlds, Assorted" (1957), reiterated Alloway's advice almost word for word. One of the characteristics of living in an urban world is to become saturated with a plethora of images pregnant with meaning and bursting with information, all obtained from magazines, pictorial newspapers, advertisements, cinema, and television.[86] But rather than focusing on the shock appeal that Alloway introduced and members of the IG exploited, Coleman saw these images as being accepted in a nonchalant manner, as they have by now become commonplace background environments. Such images, he noted, have a directness that is denied to words; they are instantly perceivable upon flipping through the pages of a magazine or glimpsing its ads while traveling on an escalator. Absorbed in a passing, blasé manner, not with conscious concentration, such images lay dormant in the mind until an association brought them to the surface. Coleman was interested in how information itself was processed as mere background, on the fly—how the message imprinted subconsciously on the mind was nevertheless embedded in associative networks, waiting to be decoded at a later date.

Thumbing through *Vogue* or *Harper's*, for example, the viewer accumulates exciting images of worlds other than one's own. These image worlds create an "after-atmosphere" that affects reality, influencing both the desirability of standards of living and the reception of fine art. But rather than stress the continuum of images, as Alloway did during many IG discussions, Coleman focused on what del Renzio called "glabrous" (literally, smooth or hairless) views—an image from *Vogue* in which a model poses in front of a de Staël canvas, the photograph shot during de Staël's recent exhibition at the ICA. The painting is reduced in this image to a textured contrast for the folds and fall of a tweed outfit worn by the model. Coleman praised this reduction of fine art to mere background because in his view it offered the viewer a whiff of the contemporary art world, making its strangeness and distance more palatable and thus more popular. The glamour factor of fashion, with all its artifice, is the desired aftereffect of the image, which conflates art gallery, art work, and model.

In the late 1950s, for the first time, photography dominated the production of English fashion imagery and became the trendsetter for visual dream worlds.[87] Coleman openly acknowledged that the most important image for contemporary times was now the photographic image, its frequent appearance in newspapers and magazines making it obvious that the camera determined the reader's conception of everyday events. Members of the public feed on such images, which extend their views into worlds they ordinarily would not know: celebrities are introduced to adoring audiences, fabulously strange technological objects such as computers and space capsules become familiar, and modern architecture forms a background for fashion shoots.

During IG's era, drawn comic books and painted pulp fiction covers had explained the postwar world to pop-eyed viewers; now it was the camera lens, a technical device that both fit in with and popularized an increasingly technical world. Fashion photography captured elegant, composed young ladies gliding and posing among technological wonders, Coleman wrote, thus shattering these objects' mysterious aura with the calm assurance of people at home with this new world of gadgets and machines.

Fashion by its very nature must be up to the minute, so naturally finds any world that is similarly wised up, fairly companionable. Tweeds at Farnborough [a yearly air show] are every bit as reasonable as evening dresses at the Villa Rotunda. The fashionable girl of the fifties finds life on any level, exciting. The FD2 [a British supersonic aircraft that broke the World Air Speed Record in 1956] as well as Palladio are her oyster.[88]

Vogue, true to type, scenting new developments goes stepping in where all but science fiction writers and tech-men fear to tread, creating in their wispy steps another kind of tech-mythology to take its place alongside of automation, heat-barrier problems, earth satellites and so on.[89]

And why not? Photography was a scientific invention that could proudly stand beside the latest technological gizmos. *Vogue* recognized this and executed a splendid series of fashion shoots at the Saarinen-designed GMC Technical Center—a smart outing among the mysteries of automobile styling and architecture: "such familiarity can only be attained by the girl who treats her car, and we assume her refrigerator, air conditioner, Hot Point press button cooker rather like a dress, as an item that could enable her to look and feel her best on any occasion."[90] The frequent appearance of cars in American ads and fashion photographs underscores the dreams these automobiles embodied and the consumer market that enabled many Americans to own a new dream car every few years. Coleman echoes del Renzio's position: these images have a double reference point. Photographs turn architecture or a technical component into a background and into forms that bear resemblance to images in art galleries. Art, fashion and technology share a common space of performance in modern society.

Steel frame windows silhouetted from inside recall Mondrian's grid obsession. … [I]t is the camera that clinches the Mondrian analogy and materializes it on a popular level.[91]

The same idea-climate affects the painter, the fashion photographer, and technologist alike, but it is often left to the more popular arts like the cinema and fashion to register the changes of, and even within, that climate. The public can be up-to-date just by looking.[92]

5.10
Smithson Family Cut-outs. Attributed to Peter Smithson, c. 1996. Smithson Family Collection.

A Turn toward Environmental Design

The new interest in communication backgrounds or the medium that carries the message foreshadowed Marshall McLuhan's famous dictum that "the medium is the message" (1964). McLuhan's ideas, spread by such books as *The Mechanical Bride* (1951), influenced both Alloway and Coleman in their attempts of the late 1950s to achieve a synthesis of the arts and technology. This attention to the background of mediation was an advance beyond the IG's interest in the expanded field of vision. As evinced in Coleman's essay on fashion photography (1957), technical miracles of the late 1950s were influencing the expanded sensibilities of the students at the RCA. The Sputnik launch of October 4, 1957, had opened the world's eyes to startling new visions.

Critical inquiry into the background environment, the support structure disseminating technical images, albeit rather blurry at first, was coming very slowly into focus. The editorial in *Ark* 30 (Winter 1961), an issue dedicated to "Art, Fashion and the Spirit of the Age," drew attention to the fact that "Basic Design," an innovative course for first-year students in the Department of Industrial Design (Engineering), had recently been added to the RCA curriculum. In the opinion of editor Stephen Cohn, this challenged traditional methods for training painters and sculptors.[93] He invited Denis Bowen, who taught the course, to debate the artist's role with Ken Baynes, a former editor of *Ark* whose opinions were at odds with Pop Art. The issue ostensibly was a dialogue between "abstract art" and "realist art," but the dispute reverberated across multiple channels of background environments.

Bowen opened the sally in his article "A Reply to 'What is it?'" A British aesthetic reaction to the impact and meaning of the "now" in the age of technical achievement and technological threats—he believed—has been totally inadequate. He quoted Louis Armstrong's definition of jazz: "Man, when you got to ask what it is, you'll never know!" So with abstract art: if you have to ask "What is it?"[94]

Teaching of both the fine arts and industrial design now focuses, Bowen continued, on "problem-solving" situations: contemporary art must thread its marvelous path through a maze of continuously expanding technology, confronting the spectator with new images of direction, warning, and control. Via electronic spectacles and vision "apparati," art gives mood and structure to the surrounding environment, and it is amid this environment that we now evaluate ourselves and find our aims and identity.

> Electronic seeing has given a new meaning of image and object and direct action techniques, automatic structurising, and programmed constructivism, are now normal means of creating aesthetic realities—art and technology are combined. Hot rod tachism, drip dry action, pop optics and space constructions are all operative art forms and commentaries with long abstract tentacles which reach into the technological arena. They are above all means of mind, eye and body control which man uses to visually determine the spatial characteristics of matter and materials.[95]

The communication revolution had arrived with full force in the realm of artistic expression; if vision and reality were to be integrated, and man were to remain in control of such spontaneous autonomous combinations, then both intuitive thinking and rational planning were required. It was no longer merely the visual intrigue of images never before conceived, which had entranced and amazed the IG members, but something far more influential—the entire background and all its technological supports. As far as Bowen was concerned, since "abstract art" was now mediated by electronic and technical "apparati," artists must cease to be elitist and oriented to gallery viewing, and instead learn to control various technical instruments and produce with them their intended forms.

Ken Baynes confronted Bowen's position head on in "Better and Worse Dreams (some ideas about design)," deploring both the contemporary trend toward abstraction and the greater integration of technology with art.[96] He drew a line between the designer and the artist: the former shapes the "environment" while the latter reflects upon it and the relationships between individuals. Most abstract artists, he said, have rejected the act of storytelling expressive of humanistic ideas in favor of being manipulators of color, texture, and form. They have become nothing more than designers and decorators of mood—or background artists.

Baynes was interested in the tradition of English "realism," and how good and bad dreams worked themselves out in art and design. Modernist Puritanism, he opined, was an intolerable point of view: it made men miserable and forced them to live without hope. On the contrary, there was nothing wrong in seeking the joy of living in more humanistic terms—"in grass, birds, the tottering of children, the sun, the moon, and the stars, the hum and buzz of large cities, the making of things, love and affection."[97] The nostalgic, picturesque qualities of English art were resurfacing, and once again the opposition would be hard put to make a defense. Reaction was growing within *Ark* circles to Pop's too-easy acceptance of everything "new" and marketable, also to the belief that technical innovation is inevitably progressive. As Baynes explained, humanistic values were superior to any technological claim.

> Believing we have a UNIQUE rendezvous with history to become scientists, aviators, saviours of mankind, motor-car builders, action painters, computer operators, technologists, or super-rationalists, we could quite easily be led to forget other things that are the essential and moving elements of life.[98]

The artist, Baynes believed, has an obligation to be tempered by the needs of mankind. He cited Peter Smithson's comments at the World Design Conference in Tokyo (1960):

> [F]or it is highly possible the objects we are so painfully devising may be the wrong ones and it is a good thing every now and then to let other specialists into our private world to see if their specialization makes our own irrelevant or, what is more

probable, produces a mutual modification of concepts. It is particularly obvious in the case of cars and signs and roads and buildings that the underlying concepts are wrong, and it is quite mad to think of styling and not in terms of change in the total living pattern, not in any philosophical sense, but pragmatically as things affect the use of other things.[99]

Thus, Baynes continued, the designer had to work for an environment that is not merely "an expression of technology," not only "an expression of communication society," but "an expression of man's essential humanity" across the media he employs. As Peter Smithson suggested, the entire living pattern might have to be adjusted to ensure that man controls technology, not technology man. Technology may be able to give substance to man's dreams, but these are always dreams of a better and more humane life. The role of the designer is then to maintain "a human conscience, jogging a technologist's elbow whenever he does anything intolerable, gently but firmly eschewing jargon in styling or cliché in design; not making a myth but getting as near to economy, beauty, delight and richness as he can."[100]

Soon, *Ark* would turn its ironical eye upon the world of the beloved ad-man and the scandalously affluent society that progress and technology had engendered. Bill James, editor of *Ark* 32 (Summer 1962), dedicated the issue to "NOW Find your way amongst *ARK*'s crowd," for "the 20th century is fast becoming the era of the crowd."[101] The language deployed in this issue of *Ark*, filled to the brim with Pop images, is full of ironic satire: nothing stops the "Motivation Man," armed with computer surveys and his hands on the controls to manipulate and subjugate what can only be labeled a "group mentality." There is an insidious side to advertising, market research, and the Welfare State: they have destroyed the need to think, or take care of oneself. A terrifying new language has erupted over the last 20 years to describe the mindless, directionless staggering of the crowd—"status seekers," "organization men," "hidden persuaders," minions of the "affluent society." "When the hustings roar of the telly has faded, when the supermarket has closed for the night, when for a moment the twentieth century goes quiet, we must still learn to live with ourselves."[102]

Ironical, hilarious, and outrageous statements meant to poke fun at somber self-righteous criticism nevertheless suggest that something was going wrong with the world of appearances and communication so lavishly praised over the past ten years in the pages of *Ark*. The new problem, which the writings of *Ark* unearth, is the "environment," whether simulated or natural, technological or humanistic, or at the scale of outer space, the city, or the domestic interior. At issue is the role of the "designer" as the shaper of this environment. James called on Misha Black, one of the exhibition designers for the Festival of Britain (1951), to fire the issue's last shots in an article entitled "A Thing for a Crowd."[103] Black took aim:

> The pop art protagonists are the weepy sentimentalists of our decade, they are the Pre-Raphaelites of the 1960's. They have recoiled with too delicate a sensibility from the reality of existence and they find their peace only in the fag-end of a dying epoch. Desperately writhing to avoid being sucked into involvement with the emergent present, they cling to what is left of the past, the sediment of the cafe and violence in the back street, the cinema poster and the tangle of local shops battling for a miserable individuality.
>
> ... this self-destroying sentimentality will not do. We must look in the dung heap of our civilization for the new germinating seed and ally ourselves with that, even if its raw unsophisticated newness and its brash wide-eyed belief in the future is not to our liking.[104]

James too had his doubts about the era of the crowd, not the individual. He believed the true leaders of the age were the Motivation Men controlling the dials of hidden persuasion, depriving man of the capacity to make judgments for himself about what to wear, eat, or drink, as well as the "all-benign glow of the Welfare state" destroying the *need* to look after oneself.[105] Yet amid all of this detritus of liberalism, Black saw a new seed germinating, developing into a "wide-eyed belief in the future":

> This new seed is social awareness, the children in their new schools in which architecture has been demoted to the playing with a meccano set of prefabricated parts, the new housing estates and the Health Service, Penguin books, the New Scientist and the New Statesman, diesel locomotives and works canteens, nice clean pubs and coffee bars. The dreary boring beginnings of a social revolution with which we must come to terms, which we must clothe with the living flesh of art if we are not to dissipate our energies in nostalgic nihilism. For the industrial designer there is no escape from this decision. By his choice of discipline he has jumped positively into the present. An action painting solution will not serve for an aeroplane, it is impossible to design a nihilist gas cooker. The industrial designer can only operate if he is prepared to work half a step ahead of the present so that what he has designed will be acceptable to sufficient people, to have justified its tooling-up, when on sale twelve or eighteen months after its original conception. If you work in the market place an esoteric demeanour is as unprofitable as a white collar in a coal mine.[106]

Black believed that industrial designers and engineers were also artists and so, by definition, moralists: they feel a missionary zeal to convert the world to their images and therefore must constantly be in tune with the crowd, which is far from homogeneous. Within the triangle of forces formed by materials, manufacturing processes, and use, they search for the elegant solution to carry "[his] vision of the proper shape of a motor-car, the right disposition of controls on a ship's bridge, the ideal coffee percolator, and the most delectable keyboard for a typewriter."[107] The painter works for a small audience, the designer for the crowd—but the crowd is now so split and divided itself that there is a market for the Tudor settee and for the Eames chair, for the sleekly polished television set and for the Braun transistor radio, for the whale of a Rolls and the Mini-Motor. Into the crowd's confused contradiction the industrial designer carefully insinuates himself, he chooses his own ground for his moral affray.[108]

There is no alternative: the designer has to confront the crowd, edging himself slowly, step by step, toward his objective, the transformation of the surrounding environment. He needs to compromise and prevaricate, give false explanations for his essential purpose, wheedle and coerce. "But he will take private pleasure in a line straightened, a control more reasonably placed, a thing slightly better made."[109] To be an industrial designer in the age of the crowd is to be the microscopic grit in the oyster, hoping and believing that one day he/she will be the catalyst for a beautiful pearl.

Black was no doubt drawing aim at Reyner Banham, to whose "Design by Choice" (1961) the editors of *AR* had affixed a clarification: section "ID" now referred to Industrial Design, not Interior Design. This piece appeared in a split-page format typical for Banham, in which the text columns were offset by an alphabetical listing of important events and influences during 1951–1961.[110] It was a decade, Banham noted, in which "design theory" had crumbled, stripping the architect of his mantle of universal designer of the interior and exterior environment. The architect's primary role had been ceded to the industrial designer. Therefore it was necessary to question what role architects now had, what field they surveyed. He assumed that it was natural for architects to be concerned with the design of things like automobiles, lampposts, refrigerators, and crockery because these objects inhabited the same space as or supplemented the functions of their buildings. But even if they are no longer responsible for the "whole human environment," architects cannot simply retreat, providing "background architecture" of studied neutrality. They must offer some guidelines to an inhabitant on where to put things, must "exercise choice and background control over the choice of others, to advise, suggest and demand on the basis of knowledge and understanding."[111]

How much braver than Banham's controlling or advisory ideal was Black's optimistic view of the designer, the grit in the oyster! Banham offered a restricted view: the designer could influence a list of beloved appliances and brand images, Citroën and Volkswagen automobiles, Detroit styling, bits of the Italian craze and Pop Art. In Black's view, the designer is a provocateur, a challenger, even while he introduces a more pragmatic realism.

III Conclusion

Alongside the expanded vision of fashion, graphic arts, and Pop Art, a growing awareness of the "surrounding environment," of a larger, more responsible commitment to the design world—yet another form of "realism"—had its start in the 1950s. Alison Smithson wrote: "My writing evoking fresh sensibilities dates from 1956 although it was some appreciable time before I distilled and discovered what it was I had been writing towards; that is, before the true nature of the sensibilities emerged."[112] What happened in 1956, the year *Ark* published "But Today we collect Ads," the year the Smithsons designed the "House of the Future" and "Patio and Pavilion," and attended CIAM 10 in Dubrovnik? As Alison explained it, 1956 saw the start of two new sensibilities: the first keyed to the automobile, mobility, and change, the second to "ecological thinking," what we might now call "thinking green" in architecture (although "green" was not yet used as a synecdoche for environmentalism). "Ecological thinking" meant a range of things to be developed over time, but it began with the House of the Future, which dissolved the barrier between inside and out, making a connection of interior to patio, to nature, to birds perched on a dipper resting on the basin of a rainwater spout. This mingling of inside and out was picked up and examined in "the Patio within the Pavilion" (Smithson's words), respect for the ground on which they built (sand), and a wish to look upward to include the sky (giving an expanded sense of territory).[113]

It is to this expanded view of the environment that developed after 1956 and through the 1960s, as lensed through the writings of Alison and Peter Smithson, that we turn next.

6.1
Alison Smithson sitting in Jeep, Peter Smithson standing right. It is assumed this photograph was taken near Hunstanton School, Norfolk, c. 1954. Photograph by Nigel Henderson. Smithson Family Collection.

6
Vehicles of Desire

> The car rivals the house as an alternative zone of everyday life; the car, too, is an abode, but an exceptional one; it is a closed realm of intimacy, but one released from the constraints that usually apply to the intimacy of the home, once endowed with a formal freedom of great intensity …
> Robin Boyd[1]

Prologue

This chapter explores different ideas about automobiles and mobility that the Smithsons and Reyner Banham expressed in their different writings (1955–1983). Banham held the American car to be the symbol of accelerating change, a product of the live culture of the twentieth century. He wanted architects to listen to industrial designers, who, he said, knew how to deploy an aesthetic of expendability. The Smithsons drove in a different direction. For them the automobile was a home on wheels, and "mobility" in all its extended meanings generated new building types and urban patterns. For Alison, the view from the front seat of a moving automobile engendered a quickened sensibility to the picturesqueness of the English landscape.

Part I. Mythology of the American Car

Competing Views

In America the car was, from an early period, not a luxury item but an everyday need. The automobile industry became an iconic image of modernity, a triumph of twentieth-century capitalism, the standard by which economies have been designated "Fordist" (i.e., based on mass production by capital-intensive industry) and "post-Fordist" (i.e., based on information and service industries). In its heyday in the 1950s, the American automobile industry could design and produce a new fleet of car models every six months. This meant, however, that automobile sales soon reached market saturation. Built-in obsolescence, exaggerated styling, and "glabrous" advertising thus became essential marketing tools, necessary to entice buyers into replacing their cars every few years. "Tail fins" were an obvious example of "styling": in 1948, a finned "look" based on the twin-fuselage P-38 bomber designed by Lockheed during World War II was transferred to the Cadillac. From about 1950 to 1959, tail fins—which their inventor, Harley Earl, maintained, meant "prestige"—fed the American consumer's desire to keep up with the Joneses by buying a new car every few years.[2]

Once the automobile became part of the normalized background for capitalist enterprise and technological progress, its very ordinariness worked against critical assessment.[3] Yet there is no doubt that the automobile was one of the primary images and objects through which postwar modernity was viewed. It was imbued with ideals of freedom, privacy, autonomy, mobility, efficiency, convenience, communication, and progress. It entailed an entirely new complex of objects, from the car itself to highways, parking arrangements, garages, suburban sprawl, and more. It offered a sense of freedom to explore the open road whenever one desired, to move and dwell in semiprivate isolation, to be embraced in a powerful, comfortable metallic cocoon. And it opened a new sensibility to the mobile view. Let no one trammel this icon of free enterprise: neither the government nor cultural critics!

For all its individualistic mystique, automobile culture rose on the back of massive government subsidies, with the development of a vast physical, social, and regulatory infrastructure, and was accompanied by the proliferation of suburbs and sprawl. Yet none of this could defeat the mythology of the automobile as a source of pure freedom that extended where people could go and what they could do. Nor did it interfere with the promise of a new way of inhabiting space in a mobile living room, with the guaranteed freedom of democratic choice.

It is difficult to assess who loved automobiles more, Banham or the Smithsons. Who invested more psychic energy in describing and extolling their presence and the impact of "mobility" on everyday life? Did their interests in these quotidian objects influence each other? How did they differ in approach? Both Banham and the Smithsons, in their individual appraisals of the automobile, deflected critical thought, accepting the car as a normal consumer item like clothing and housing. The mythology of the car enshrined it as a goddess or *déesse*, as the initials of the Smithsons' own Citroën "DS" were pronounced in French. It was, as Banham was eager to elaborate, a status symbol achieved via its sign system, used and consumed through its iconography. And as the Smithsons understood, it was linked to a complex of industries from car parts to roadside service stations, urban design, and leisure time planning.

Banham was convinced that American automobile designers could (in essence) see into the future, while Europeans were blind to the impact of automobiles on space, society, imagination, and desire. In the immediate postwar years the English, according to Banham, had to look to America to imagine what the colonization of everyday life by this metallic machine actually entailed, what the conquering of space and time by mobilization implied. (The first sections of England's first divided highway or "motorway," the M1, did not open until 1959.)

In the mid-1950s, Banham believed that European architects and designers, with their machine aesthetic, were once again at war with "technology."

> The defence of this filleted aesthetic—bones kept, flesh throwaway—has always been its alleged appropriateness to a machine situation ... the resulting Machine Aesthetic worked wonders in the hands of Bauhaus masters and the Purists in the twenties, it was left dead on its feet when technology grew out of the Bleriot/Bentley phase and passed through into the non-filleted world of streamlining and Borax bulges.[4]

It was time to give the consumer a machine aesthetic reflecting an "emotional-engineering-by-public-consent" that produced "vehicles of palpably fulfilled desire." Banham doubted whether architecture or any other twentieth-century art could achieve this goal, as implicitly set by American designers of automobiles![5]

Banham claimed that the automobile itself was consumed as image, and the Smithsons agreed: in their 1955 definition of New Brutalism, they singled out 1954 as the year that American advertising struck them with its overlaid imagery, when the Cadillac convertible captured their imagination—"parallel with the ground, four elevations—classic box on wheels."[6]

Banham, for his part, writing "Vehicles of Desire" in the same year as the Smithsons' New Brutalism article, held the American car to be the symbol of accelerating change, its technology coming from a live culture of the twentieth century.[7] The car, especially the Cadillac, is a cult object of Pop admiration: viewed mainly in two-dimensional imagery, it is anti-monumental, anti-big, anti-architectural, and moreover replaceable, expendable, and not in good form. Yet in Banham's opinion it is as worthy of iconographical analysis as any fine-art object.[8]

He acknowledged that Peter and Alison Smithson were the

> New Brutalists, pace-makers and phrase-makers of the anti-academic line-up, having delivered a smart KO to the Land Rover some months back, [and] have now followed it with a pop-eyed OK for the Cadillac convertible, and automobile aesthetics are back on the table for the first time since the Twenties. The next time an open Caddy wambles past you, its front chrome-hung like a pearl-roped dowager, its long top level with the ground at a steady thirty inches save where the two tailfins cock up to carry the rear lights, reflect what a change has been wrought since the last time any architect expressed himself forcibly on the subject of the automobile.[9]

For Banham, the motorcar was a "hollow rolling sculpture":

> If the form of contemporary automobiles reflects jet-plane, rocket-ship, and other streamlined forms, it is because the motor-car is the average citizen's toe-hold on a technological culture that he admires, but can possess only in a dream or symbol.[10]

However, there was much that architecture needed to learn from industrial designers who knew how to handle the rich stream of loaded symbols the automobile contained. Reviewing the progress made during the 1950s by industrial designers, Banham noted that architecture was no longer the universal analogy of design, because architects were no longer steeped in technical knowledge. They were unable to relate their designs to human needs and desires. They had abdicated this role to the new breed of industrial designers, communication theorists, Pop artists, even sociologists. They might be sensitive to the design of objects "like automobiles, lamp-posts, refrigerators and crockery, since these are objects that commonly, inhabit the same view, occupy the same space, supplement the functions of their buildings,"[11] but had lost ground in their combat with technology.

The basic reason, Banham claimed, could be found in the "aesthetics of expendability," which automobile design typifies but architects reject. Architects think in terms of a fifty-year timescale, while industrial designers work on a range of timescales because they must respond to opposing forces of stabilized investment and technical improvement that differ from the equilibrium governing the design of buildings. Imagine a sixty-year-old car: it might work mechanically, but if allowed on the streets with more nimble models would create traffic jams and cause accidents.[12] To regain lost ground, the architect must become a knowledgeable consumer of industrial designs: "His choice [of interior equipment—chairs, tables, lamps, radios, etc.] must be disciplined by a clear idea of what the building has to do, and … his choice must be adventurous."[13] He must learn to appreciate technology and the "aesthetics of expendability," or fail to match ever-shifting desires.

Banham thus saw the automobile as an aesthetic acme, a nexus of brilliant design, subject to no excellence but its own, sui generis. The Smithsons, in contrast, wished to subordinate it to architecture's wise plans for the city as such. Writing about the 1959 Le Corbusier exhibition in London, Peter maintained:

> Now it will be held that the definition of a machine environment as an aim was the work of the Futurists, but for me their environment was one *dominated* by machines. Le Corbusier's dream of a Ville Radieuse has the machine firmly under control, and even though some of his aesthetic techniques may have been carry-over ones, he was never confused about his all-over objectives. His city was to be one of shining towers in a sea of trees, with the automobile used at the scale at which it is a moving poetic thing and not a stinking object—an essentially controlled, *quiet* environment with the energies of transit and communication channelled and not randomly and wastefully *displayed*.[14]

Banham and the Smithsons also expressed different views of the automobile-serviced society: Banham favored exotic images of sex-injected automobiles as dream car prototypes, vehicles of desire, while the Smithsons envisioned cities serviced naturally by automobiles, their routes channeled and mastered. In *The New Brutalism* (1966), Banham repeated his praise of the Smithsons' 1955 Cadillac reference, which he saw as affronting "good taste" by praising "bad designs" from America. He took this opportunity to expand on his admiration for Detroit's aesthetic inventiveness, which he believed still could not be matched.[15] For Banham it was always American engineering techniques that captured the imagination, throwing down time and again a gauntlet to which no European designer could react.

When Banham coined the expression *une architecture autre* in his own New Brutalist manifesto of December 1955, he was looking for a rebellious trend, something the traditions of architecture could not or did not represent.[16] In contrast to his praise of the Smithsons' views on the Cadillac, he thought their architecture and urban proposals represented a compromised position. Their acceptance of "the realities of the situation" and their quest for an ideal solution for "a particular place at the present time" were no different from the Picturesque injunction "to consult the genius of the place in all." Their many attempts to bring the automobile under control were normalizing gestures, far from revolutionary or subversive. Eventually, "Brutalism in Britain was tamed from a violent revolutionary outburst to a fashionable vernacular."[17]

Peter Smithson was moved to retaliate: "Those who still cannot see what Brutalism is about should consider this: The E type Jaguar, the Jeep, the Deux Chevaux *and* the DS19 are all Brutalist cars."[18] Instead of standards of practicality, or fixed points in a world of rapidly changing car design, which these "little brute cars" represented for the Smithsons, Banham praised Detroit's motorcar revolution for its unconventionality, boldness, and aesthetic inventiveness. He claimed that "Detroit was a symbol also for the War of the Generations, and the language of American automobile advertising became the language of revolt among the young."[19] Banham would add that outside the advertisements, the occasional American-made cars to be seen on London streets in the 1950s belonged to embassy officials or NATO dignitaries. Private citizens could not import them; hence any reference to these American icons by anyone of Banham's generation was evidence of "Detroit Machiavellismus"—a term coined in Germany to describe everything felt to be hateful about American design.[20]

II. The Automobile as a Home on Wheels

A Love Affair with Cars

As the 1960s passed, car styling went off its jet kick, unable to retain its top rank as status symbol. Mini-automobiles and compact cars smothered it to death. Banham's tone became more realistic as he covered this shift: "And just when architects were despairing of ever making much visual and spatial sense of domestic exteriors lumbered with *two* status-boasting, jet-styled Detroitniks, suddenly there were compacts and Mini-minors."[21]

6.2
Alison and Simon Smithson in the Smithsons' Jeep on a hot day, Regent's Park Circle, July 1955. Photograph by Peter Smithson. Smithson Family Collection.

The Smithsons had never been particularly inspired anyway by Banham's paeans to the jet-styled American car. Their writings sought rather to capture the dual aspect of automobility, conceiving the car both as a vehicle of freedom and as offering a mobile spectator's view (the latter developed at length by Alison in *AS in DS*, 1983). They liked their automobiles to be ordinary and fit for purpose. Peter Smithson had learned to admire the functional machinery of World War II, such as the Bailey bridge and the Jeep. The Smithsons purchased a surplus Jeep near the end of the 1940s (Eduardo Paolozzi remembered going down in this open-topped car on cold days to view the progress of Hunstanton School).[22] This would eventually be replaced by a VW Beetle, then a Citroën ID, then a Citroën DS.

The Smithsons' Beetle was a beloved car, lamented when superseded.[23] But it had to be superseded, for the model's design was evolving. Alison Smithson, looking back from the 1980s, claimed to have foreseen the whole sad process: first there were two ovals for back windows, then these transformed into one oval, then a big oval, and finally a wraparound VistaVision window. The designers could go no further than that; they had killed the Bug! But in its time it had been a perfect machine, no bugs in the Bug, always starting:

> After a late fifties snowy winter I remember us driving off leaving all the street standing. … And even if you did let the battery go, or run out after you'd switched the emergency tank it could be pushed. Not so the Jeep …[24]
>
> You wore your Volks.
>
> I remember thinking you were so close together in the Volks and so far apart in the DS your relationship as a married couple was bound to subtly change …
>
> Then it was love in a box.
>
> After it a big car was a kind of physical divorce. If ever one got the chance to repeat the space experience we must all have had in a pram, it was the Volks. It was a well-made quality job, clean, cleanable, went without trouble, took you there and brought you back, comfortable, warm. And you were in return right up against it, looking out at the world.[25]

There were anecdotes of life in the dark green Beetle. When their two oldest children were small, Peter Smithson recalled, they were driving "Lou" Kahn (to Roehampton, he thinks), and as they passed a Lyons ice cream factory, which always gave off the smell of burnt fat, their youngest child, who would not be prevented from leaning forward from the middle rear seat, regarded Lou and said, "There's a smell of burning, is it his face?" Kahn took no offense, for evidently he was an excellent car entertainer, keeping passengers in fits of laughter. Another: while being totally lost on suburban roads of North London, Kahn amused them with his repertoire of nun stories. One ended with the caution, "It's OK. As long as you don't get into the habit."[26]

6.3
Citroën Traction Avant and Citroën ID Safari, in Priory Walk, Kensington, January 1975. Photographer unknown. Smithson Family Collection.

Despite his love for Detroit's behemoths, by 1961 even Banham acknowledged that the standard against which most designs were judged had become the VW, not the Cadillac. The VW's simple spare parts and service requirements set a new standard.

But the overwhelming virtue in the eyes of men of liberal conscience was that in a world of automotive flux its appearance remained constant and that in a period when cars grew larger year by year, it remained the same size. In other words, it was a symbol of protest against standards of Detroit, the mass media and the "pop" arts.[27]

The Citroën, too, was a fixed point in a world of rapidly changing car design—until 1957.[28] In that year the familiar 1934 Citroën Traction Avant (French for front-wheel drive) design was replaced by the DS 19. Its shape was criticized, but Banham reports that

brand-loyalty coupled with something like awe at its technical specification served to establish the DS, almost at once, in the same position of esteem as was enjoyed by the preceding model, and by the end of the decade its radical appearance no longer excited the same alarm as before.[29]

The Smithsons used images of their various automobiles to recall adventurous travels.[30] For example, after ferrying across the Channel, they traveled by Jeep to the CIAM 9 meeting at Aix-en-Provence in 1953, and recalled Jeep rides down to the Mediterranean to swim.[31] While in Austria, en route to CIAM 10 in Dubrovnik in 1956, loaded with precious projects of their own as well as those of the Howells, their car was bumped off an embanked road by a passing veterinary surgeon and overturned.[32] Austria's roads were, apparently, brutal at the time: every car arriving by road had body damage and was caked with dust like icicles around the bottom. "I believe the Bakema's [family] got a new car on return to Holland. All the way up the coast we kept lending our meths-stove to Dutch men to vulcanize their inner tubes."[33] And at the Dubrovnik Quay, Bakema drove his old black Citroën 5 Traction Avant off a boat and down a shaky makeshift ramp: "Only he would have dared."[34] The story was rich enough to repeat on another occasion: Bakema and the Citroën with a camping trailer, crosswise to the quay, had to back up repeatedly in order to even get the rear wheels of the car off the ramp while the sailors restrained the trailer. "Only a Dutchman unafraid of canals, who had lived on a boat as a child, would have dared take that car off. … Bakema shrugged it off, saying he had to, or have the car return to Venice."[35]

Mobility—a Keyword

The Smithsons were less interested than Banham in styling or fashioning *une architecture autre.* They were earnest about architecture and the necessity to create a design language responsive to the times—an ethical duty they never shirked. Most of their automobile references, therefore, were either fond and quirky, more about intimacy than space-age power fantasy, or else embedded within extended discussion of design issues relating to adaptation of architectural and urban forms to the increasing use of automobiles, interlocked with an amalgam of social practices and styles of inhabitation.

By the end of the 1950s, the Smithsons evaluated the situation "as found." They understood that the motorcar had changed the patterns of life, but this fact had yet to find a visible expression in the house or in community planning. Alison was particularly critical of the English New Town planners, who lived in a dream located somewhere between William Morris and Camillo Sitte. They were "unwilling to come out into the bright reality and the hard world of these fast motor cars and the styling changes, and how people are really living now with their television, and their appliances."[36] And Peter, while he would not praise American architects, did look positively on the American civil engineer, as Le Corbusier had taught. The road maker was

> a sort of king, capable of majestic feats, mass earth moving and so on, because the programme is well set it is simple. They make a road from A to B and it is not complicated by much high level thought as to what is happening in the city or the region. But when they do the road they do it beautifully and it has this heroic scale, but with a sort of irrelevance about it when it connects to other things. At Detroit, for instance, communication has become an end in itself.[37]

And after his first visit to the United States in 1957, Peter Smithson thought that the European, looking at America, must examine the situation "as found" and interpret it anew, for preconceptions formed by images in magazines could hardly be matched to its reality. American cars were evidence of the nation's deep-seated "folk-need" for "squareness and symmetry"—something the industrial designer Raymond Loewy had successfully imposed on automobiles after World War II. Americans, he judged, were nearer to design truth in their cars than in their buildings—for with automobiles, at least, they did not rely on worn-out European models.[38] American cars offered proof that Americans desired square, rational forms uncomplicated by doubt, uncorrupted by concept—an attitude that they applied more weakly to architecture and city plans.

> [A]ll successful American cars are rectangular on plan and on all four elevations, and are roughly bi-axially symmetrical (projection of the bonnet and boot are more or less equal). From the top of buildings car-lots and streets are a mosaic of coloured rectangles—the origin of "Broadway Boogie Woogie" [by Piet Mondrian] is, for sure, the view from the top of the Empire State looking down into the streets and parking lots below.[39]
>
> American values are communicated through an imagery created without self-consciousness.[40]

Peter Smithson was even able to wax lyrical about the American industrial landscape and "God's own junkyard." He thought the New Jersey Meadowlands the typical American landscape:

a dream world of refineries and factories and marshlands, criss-crossed with Skyways. This is the supra-image of the American urban landscape—the urban excreta squeezed out from the old city over the last fifty years—and something like this is the industrial landscape norm.[41]

There was much to admire in America and to wield against the "good taste" of Europe, but there were also anomalies in the American suburban expanse. Its transient background of movement and flux required, Peter Smithson opined, some sort of "fix" or system of permanent reference points. It demanded a *big* fix: a controlled background of forests, agricultural lands, unused space, or freeways against which the throwaway immediate environment and its transient aesthetic could be set. This background permanency had to be controlled by a supra-authority so that the throwaway environment—not built architecture, but things that get tossed out, like cars and washing machines—could be discarded with less offense. If the house-plot-road relationship is not changed in America then, Peter Smithson believed, the architect would evade his responsibility to give the social pattern both form and meaning.[42] This concept of "fixes" against "transient backgrounds" would be worked on by the Smithsons over the years, and reappear in various writings.

But first, there was much to praise about postwar "mobility"! Within a few years of the abolition of wartime rationing in England by the mid-1950s, a new feeling of genuine egalitarianism had developed; people now had more leisure time and more education, and wanted to travel.[43] They sought via their motorways to have "somewhere to go—both inside and outside the city."[44] Thus the network of motorways, with all its "fixes," served those who wanted to get away from the entrapment of their home places. Alison believed that "this feeling of being trapped-in-a-jungle-of-irresponsibilities has made the car and its corollary, the urban motorway, into necessities for mental quietude in the metropolis—they represent escape and freedom."[45] "Fixes" such as huge motorways, giant intersections, and built landscapes kept mechanization under control; channeled noise and excitement to appropriate, no-harm areas; created pools of calm where they would not otherwise exist.[46] Automobiles afforded people access to a country retreat, a more disorganized way of life, closer to nature. People could now attain an isolated shack in the middle of nowhere or a pocket of shacks crowded together, such as at caravan sites, groups of holiday bungalows, extended villages surrounded by countryside.[47]

The Smithsons were obsessed with "mobility" in all of its meanings. Alison would, however, object to my repetition of the word "obsessed," maintaining that their interest in movement systems and how they influenced perception was simply part of their business as architects, the automobile, after all, being now a normal part of everyday life.[48] They simply sought to draw out the implications of motorization, of the entire concept of a mobile, fragmented community, and the life of the street. Mobility, for the Smithsons, was the new key to town planning; roads were fixed things, architecturally important because they were big and because their cycle of change was slow. They wielded the same power as any topographical feature, modifying geographical and therefore social divisions, generating the pattern of urban existence.[49]

Snippets of this interest in urban infrastructure and mobility found their way into "CIAM Team 10 Meetings" (1960, edited by Alison) and into the "Team 10 Primer" (1962).[50] The lack of comprehensibility and identity in big cities, she wrote, was due to an unclear road system which should instead be a unifying visual and symbolic system that makes the whole thing work.[51] In their 1959 "London Roads Study," the Smithsons explained how town structure interlocked with architectural form to create a fine-grained network. This "net," an image they found more useful than through routes or ring routes, would allow traffic to flow freely from point to point. Such "a comprehensive system of urban motorways is the only thing capable of providing the structure for a scattered city."[52]

This net would not be a Cartesian grid but a loosely interconnected cluster of high-density points representing an aesthetic of change. As roads entered a built-up area they would divide into interlocking "tangential" routes, becoming a net thrown over the area. Each pattern adjusted itself to the existing structure of a city, extending south or west, for example, to create new areas of intense use, developing communication where none existed, without any hierarchy of importance, an open system that allowed points where use is the greatest to become the densest. Such a net was already exemplified in the pedestrian and automobile platforms of the Smithsons' Hauptstadt Berlin project (1957–1958).

A motion picture was the obvious format for displaying the Smithsons' notions about mobility and urban restructuring. Born at the same time, motorcars and the cinema had (the Smithsons thought) a natural affinity. When automobiles began to parade across the city, the motion camera was there to capture them. Thomas Edison's *Automobile Parade* (1900), a hundred-second film showing the police escorting a stream of horseless carriages on a city street, exemplifies this relationship, as does the film *Hauptstadt Berlin* (1959), which illustrates the Smithsons' and Peter Sigmonde-Wonke's "Hauptstadt" submission for the redesign of Berlin (1957–1958). The film was a collaboration between two IG members, John McHale and Frank Cordell, with the Smithsons.[53] McHale and Cordell wrote the script and did the filming and editing; Cordell also provided a musical score.

Hauptstadt Berlin demonstrates patterns of association and patterns of movement, explaining the Berlin project with live material using such techniques as partial animation, detailed scanning of big drawings, stop-motion, and cross-cutting in the drawing sequences to selected shots of reality. Since the filmmakers did not have enough money to travel to Berlin, London serves as the real-world environment. These sequences are shot with a handheld camera, mostly from a moving car (Frank Cordell's Ford convertible). The introductory musical theme (played by a small jazz group) and what the Smithsons termed the central "musique concret" [sic] section, are constructed from Cordell's collection of sounds. Voice-over commentary is by Peter Smithson. The plan of the Hauptstadt project was, according to the Smithsons' explanation, simple:

6.4
Alison and Peter Smithson and Peter Sigmond-Wonke, 1957 competition drawing for Hauptstadt Berlin. Photographer unknown. Smithson Family Collection.

The main idea is to give the motorist and the pedestrian *equal* rights to freedom of movement and freedom of access discriminating against neither. This is an old idea, but what is new in this plan is that the concept is communicated by the buildings themselves. For example, in the main shopping zone there are two interrelated systems of movement and two interrelated aesthetics. The motorist-pedestrian shopper uses the street net at ground level, and the public-transport-pedestrian shopper uses the platform net (on top of the shops) at the ten meter level, the aesthetic of cars being straight streets and right angular intersections, and that of pedestrians non-parallel narrowing and widening routes and angled junctions. The platform net crosses the street net once between every street intersection, and at this point the two systems are connected by continuous running public (free) *escalators*. This escalator system makes the high level platform net really practicable—for no one will use a fly-over or sub-way to cross a road if it involves extra effort.[54]

In his 1966 book on New Brutalism, Banham was critical of the Hauptstadt competition design. In this latest stage of Brutalist town planning, he detected a reappearance of Picturesque visual composition. "Accepting the realities of the situation" as the Smithsons advocated it was no different, for Banham, than *AR*'s Townscape casebook. The Smithsons' concepts of cluster, association of people and activities, and irregular nets of vehicles and pedestrian ways were, in fact, absolutely reprehensible Picturesque tactics. It was obvious to Banham that the gap between Brutalist and Picturesque town planning principles had narrowed by 1957 and would be closed by 1962.[55]

The Smithsons were seeking a place for the car in the structure of city and countryside and, simultaneously, a way to identify the individual with a sense of place. They wanted to design for a complex city of many parts, with clusters of varying densities and different landscape views and places of retreat. They juxtaposed their "Cluster City" idea to Los Angeles, which for them lacked legibility and therefore did not allow the city to be seen as an extension of oneself—a place that gave one a sense of identity. The layout of Los Angeles, a form constructed entirely by its movement pattern, had produced a colossal scattering of places and people, but could "not indicate places-to-stop-and-do-things-in."[56]

"Fixes" needed to be spatially fixed, while "transients" were ephemeral and locatable. The two types of item had different cycles of change. The road system itself was a fixed, inviolate thing lasting about 75 years, whereas housing, drug stores, advertising, sky signs, and shops were more transient, and people and their personal extensions (clothing, cars, posters, shop windows, magazines) changed on the shortest cycle of all, reflecting moods and needs. The shorter the cycle, the less control was required.[57] "An aesthetic of change, paradoxically generates a feeling of security and stability because of our ability to recognize the pattern of related cycles."[58]

The road was for the Smithsons a liberator, offering the possibility of "release."[59] The outlook through a windshield revealed a new and exciting set of picturesque views;

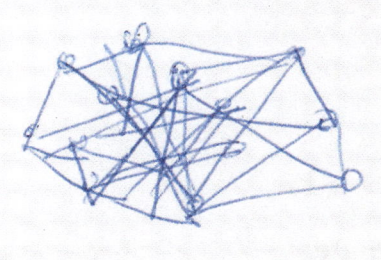

6.5

Ideogram of Play Brubeck, detail from figure 4.9.
"Ideogram of net of human relations, P.D.S.
a constellation with different values of different
parts in an immensely complicated web
crossing and recrossing. Brubeck/a pattern
can emerge." Alison Smithson, guest editor,
"Team 10 Primer," *AD* 32 (December 1962), 589.
Smithson Family Collection

the route established a series of "identifying fixes" as it crossed rivers and passed parks, historic districts, and landmarks; these became places where the relationship to the structure of the city could be observed from the road, such as along the South Bank of the Thames in London, where a fix was had on Westminster and the City.[60] The road system itself was a "fix for movement" running through the entire community; its big intersections, such as the Los Angeles Mixmaster or San Francisco Skyway, congealed into sculptural features, the images of which struck the Smithsons' attention.

Styles of Inhabitation

In the meantime, other influences related to automobiles and movement systems inspired the Smithsons. They simulated the design and advertising process of automobiles when they developed their prototype "House of the Future" (1956) for the Ideal Home Exhibition. This was composed of specially formed pieces designed for a limited role, like the parts of their Citroën car, each component a different size, height, and shape to suit its purpose. Recalling automobile obsolescence, the house components were expected to change every year.

Reyner Banham mockingly praised their design, a powerful image expected to sell by itself,

> smart, slick, styled-up, mechanically advanced, gimmicky and expendable, like a car. This was done without a trace of cynicism (no half-timbering): an honest *andare al popolo*, made possible by their involvement in the ICA's investigations into Pop culture.[61]

Banham felt that the Smithsons, by sticking to a derivative "image," no matter how brilliant, had compromised their modernism. The House of the Future was not an example of *une architecture autre*, something one would expect from their manifesto on New Brutalism, because the design did not establish a radical break with conventional concepts of house building. In the end it was a false promise—not like a portable object at all but stuck in a stylized image, speaking of a compromised aesthetic.

The automobile had, in any case, become a fixture in the Smithsons' writings and projects. It demanded spatial accommodation and rearrangement of the urban scene; it was a habitat that moved as well as a symbol of freedom and consumer choice. Any mention of the automobile, however, was always intermixed with reference to other needs, including problems of parking, access, and play space. In "Scatter" (1959), they wrote: "If the car is to be a convenience and a pleasure, it must be easy to use it."[62] In other words, there must be a new relationship of the car to the house as a function of family needs, and new forms of inhabitation related to those needs. It was nice to use the car for family excursions, but it was no picnic if there were fifteen floors to negotiate with two elevators carrying babies, baskets, buckets, and spades. The car was linked invariably to recreational needs: a bit of sheltered outdoor space as an extension of the house

6.6
The Smithsons' Citroën 93 DLT. Packing up from picnic at Garesdale Head. Spring half-term, 1965. Photograph by Peter Smithson. Smithson Family Collection.

is good for babies up to age two; then a space to play safely close to the house up to the age of seven; spaces for wild running and little excursions are essential up to age eleven, and from then on there is need of places to go to and things to do in shiny new cars.

What the Smithsons called the "hotel-type of housing," generally built after World War II, offered a maximum of privacy, anonymity, and simplicity of service. It was fine for single people, students, childless couples, and the elderly, who were all well served by (for example) Mies van der Rohe's Lake Shore Drive apartments or Swedish point block housing, where access was swift, secret, and completely enclosed, and windows looked out onto anonymous space. But the hotel-type of housing was no good for families. Family living required low-density housing, although most low-density models were "culturally obsolete," failing to provide an adequate living pattern for present-day life, or to offer equipment necessary to service that life.[63] The automobile provided access to low-density living. As for services and noisy cumbersome appliances, the Smithsons tried to address these problems in their design for "Appliance House" (1958).

An appliance way of life, they argued, must be a put-away type of life, like life in a Japanese house, in which storage goes unnoticed. Storage units must determine the entire spatial organization of the house.[64] They looked back over the past thirty years of house storage design with art-historical curiosity. First were Le Corbusier's and Charlotte Perriand's bank of storage units for the Salon d'Automne Exhibition House of 1929, which looked like "fittings in an expensive lingerie shop." Then, in 1935, came Le Corbusier's storage cabinets in the Brussels Exhibition, styled like office furniture, designed for the room of a young man. Anonymous equipment hardly existed in those early years of modernism; the appliances chosen, such as cookers with plain functional shapes, were industrial accidents more than planned.[65]

Today, the architect has only to look at American appliance advertisements to find revolutionary equipment that changes the pattern of living. Yet these items do so as mere adjuncts to the spatial organization of the house. Consequently, houses in the 1950s are cluttered, and the American kitchen and garage take up more than half the house. But advertisements reveal that appliances are getting smaller and more mobile; they can be distributed about the house. Thus in the Appliance House each item is given a "cubicle" in which to operate, and it is assumed that each appliance will change over time. Only the shell of the house is a permanent structure. And so it was that ad-men, with their constant innovation and sensitivities to changing styles, fed back into the old fine arts and forward into new designs for inhabitation.[66]

The Smithsons also believed that their Appliance House offered a potent symbol to satisfy cultural aspirations. For housing to become a community, its densities must be regrouped according to the patterns of life of the people. When this happens the pattern of the community becomes a cluster of varying densities with many different parts, like a bunch of grapes. This in turn creates a new road/green-space system and new city centers for common meetings for business, government, and administration

Peter Smithson
Parallel Inventions

Parallel Inventions pursues a small speculative discovery from my 1980 ILAUD lecture in Urbino. With it, I believe, the cycle of lectures on the idea of the 'Three Generations' closes.

Let me now read the two paragraphs where this thought began. "One final thought concerning an aspect of our inheritance the existence of which has only risen into consciousness during the months of the preparation of this reflective genealogy: that much of our inheritance reaches us through the female line ....
Lily Reich
Charlotte Perriand
Ray Eames.
For the invention of a new spacial container needs the separate invention of the objects and decoration of the play of life within it. It needs the invention of those ways of walking and holding the head, of dressing, and of setting the table, and of putting down one's book – and all that these involve; and that has come from the female line."

. . . .

In the late 'nineteen fifties Alison made a number of exploratory designs for houses around the idea of storage and appliance 'cubicles' .... the 'put-away' aesthetic. She said then about one of them (Snowball House, 1 bis, 1957) "The 'put-away' aesthetic involves a change of location of the storage spaces or appliance cubicles, so that the enclosing shells punctuate the house area. Insulating each effectively from the others. Cubicles contain all connection points for services and mechanisms while the outside of the shell, in its folds, carries the lighting for the house-space proper as in the House of the Future."
And about another ..... (Appliance House 2, 1957-58) "The general aim is to regain as much as possible of the house as usable space by continuing to assume that appliances do away with the need for the work space in the old sense."

These designs like that for the earlier House of the Future (1956) were based on the assumption, that ownership of domestic machines-appliances and the increase of possessions in Europe would follow North America. It has: and nowhere is this more obvious than with young people. Yet the dwellings made specially for them in the Universities and the hostels for young workers do not reflect this now-very-obvious change of possession-style .... obvious that is to our generation, whose spartan aesthetic – 'brutalism' – was a direct continuation of the possession-style of an army in the field and of those on ship-board.

White walls, bare-boards, four bricks, one plank and six books .... was, we are told, the possession-style of the young Marcel Breuer and of Mondrian in the earlier generation .... of Bertoldt Brecht in the post-war period. Certainly it was ours.

. . . .

It is in the last fifteen years that possession-style has changed so dramatically. Living spaces now seem so easily overwhelmed by the objects which are regarded as the bare essentials – even of student life. Cupboards get crammed tight. Things spill out, lie about, get fallen over.

One asks therefore if 'storage' is now 40% of the living volume what step forward is needed from the 'cubicle' organised space idea of the late 50's?.
That cubicles be made like air-craft holds, with container racks that hold fibrous boxes that one could load direct into a trailer when one moves? That appliance

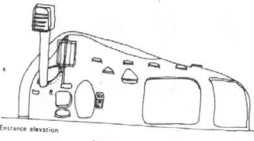

Entrance elevation

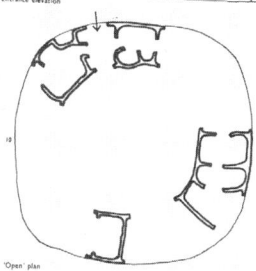

'Open' plan

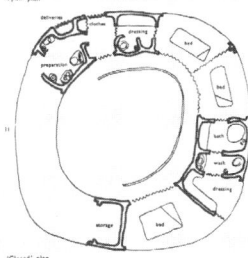

'Closed' plan

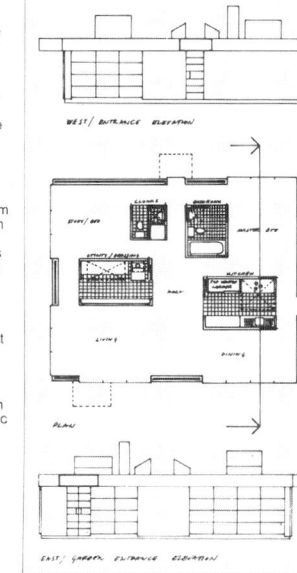

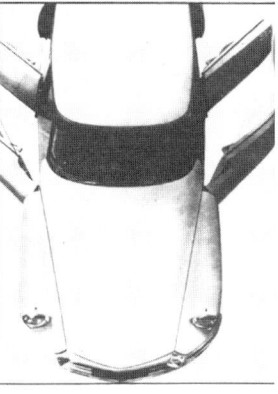

6.7
Peter Smithson, "Parallel Inventions":
Appliance House and Citroën,
from 1980 ILAUD lecture in Urbino.
Smithson Family Collection.

as well as restaurants, clubs, theaters, parks and shops. In all these centers, shopping will increase, "for going to town is essentially a social *gesture* of voluntary association with one's fellows, an act of communion."[67] It is also an act of identification with a group and means giving something up for a greater self, which can happen only in the center of a town. This is where the appropriate symbol must be provided: a "cathedral of the mind." This "cathedral" image lies beyond religion, and is evoked instead "as a symbol of a feeling of community, of cohesion, of unity of aims, that the cathedrals of Northern Europe were first built (often by ridiculously small communities), more or less as an act of crystallization."[68]

No wonder Banham lamented the reemergence of a freely grouped picturesque cluster as an image of "a close-knit complication, often-moving aggregation, but an aggregation with a distinct structure."[69] He may also have been annoyed at the notion of individual rights being subsumed by those of the community. But most of all he did not believe that the Appliance House put the power of its gadgets to work in creating an environment for living in a radically new way.[70] In Banham's lament, the Smithsons' vocabulary merely reduced itself to a set of Picturesque visual compositions.

For the Smithsons, however, "mobility" in all its meanings involved conceiving of building types and urban patterns as demanded by motorization. In 1959, Alison claimed that "caravans"—travel trailers, in American English—were the embryo of or a close approximation to their Appliance House.[71] Though these were generally thought to be an eyesore, she decided to take up Paolozzi's position: seek out the positive forces in a given situation and try to make something worthwhile out of them. The caravan provides a couple with "a 'home' at the right time, at the right price; with little or no outlay on furnishings and which is technological, twentieth century, new or very nearly so."[72] The causes for the popularity of caravans were several, but a major one boiled down to the fact that the standardized version of the Garden City is a medieval throwback in terms of the amenities it provides, and no solution for a "home of one's own." On the other hand, a caravan is neat—really a big piece of equipment with a place for everything, like the Appliance House. It plays with scale by miniaturizing appliances and space, yet is comfortable and answers a need.

Both the car and the caravan represent a new freedom: they are "a sort of symbol as well as a sign of 'population flux'."[73] The caravan offers a cheerful, safe, transient feeling like the feeling one gets driving along in a car. Alison believed that the young people who live in caravans are generally newly educated craftsmen, far from the craftsmen for whom the 1917 Garden City was originally intended. This new generation likes to watch television and utilize leisure equipment, and has all kinds of gear for outdoor activities; it participates in the affluent society and is more educated than its forebears. Its women are more independent, its couples express a new set of aims and desires. Consequently, their choice of a caravan is the best the market offers for their needs, though inadequate as a total solution for housing or for congregation in a camp environment.

Yet in its very primitiveness it can make us re-examine the premises for all the expensive miles of estate roads, the street lighting along these attenuated miles, acres of tiny "gardens" all requiring fencing of some sort; whether the brick permanent house[s] which we are perpetuating at great expense in initial cost and subsidies are what the new class of technologists (to take only one section of the community) really want.[74]

Reyner Banham agreed that the automobile was a "cell of perfected technology," but disparaged "the revenge of the picturesque" which he saw in Alison Smithson's sense of mobility. He celebrated the American automobile from a different point of view: he was an architectural historian, at times a historian of industrial design, not an architect obliged to construct buildings or to develop a set of design rules for a style of life in accordance with the mid-twentieth century. The American automobile of the 1950s symbolized for Banham the extreme glamour of technology and the infrastructure on which an affluent society would rise. He agreed with the Smithsons that the car promised a revolution in mobility, but insisted that it was a technical revolution as well. This was Banham's basic belief: technological innovation and industrialization held the key to tomorrow, and his role as historian was to flush out where science and technology were going.

Banham edited a series of five articles on "Stocktaking," all published in AR in 1960.[75] Pevsner referred to this discussion of the intellectual climate of the profession as "the full Banham treatment. The great curiosity is that the authentic claims of the architect, i.e. the architectural side of architecture, come in through a back door at a nowhere stressed moment."[76] From the start, in the first article of the series, with its columns setting tradition on the left against technology on the right, Banham used his witty pen to mount a full-scale attack against the compromised Townscape policy of AR and the conventions maintained by architectural historians—which led him eventually to be against the Smithsons, for having compromised their Brutalist modernity with "as found" doses of Picturesque theory. "Tradition," Banham lamented, is the stock of general knowledge that has been assigned to the discipline of architecture by previous generations. Architects seek to maintain their professional identity and integrity by refusing to deviate from the narrow line that tradition (classical, picturesque, functional, or formalist) provides. So they operate by passing on its conventions from master to pupil as a succession of slightly mutating attitudes and preconceptions. Conversely, "technology" was "the method of exploring, by means of the instruments of science, a potential."[77]

Following closely the Smithsons' approach to the house as meeting the needs of a family, as well as the impact of the automobile and the caravan on architectural thinking, Banham placed on the side of technology the architect who does society a service by providing fit environments that support human activities. For Banham, however, measurable performance standards are the test of "fitness" or a "style for the job":

> Yet the Functionalist slogan "a house is a machine for living in" gives nothing away because it begins by presupposing a house. Far more seditious to the established attitude of architects is the proposition that, far from caravans being sub-standard housing, housing is, for many functions, sub-standard caravans.[78]

Automobiles, the supreme symbolic objects of technological culture,

> are the irritant that causes constant revision of a number of cherished concepts. These revisions are not always radical, but, nevertheless, it is no longer possible for architects to think of cities as collections of buildings with spaces between them, but as collections of buildings with streams of metallic objects flowing round them—a revision that requires them to think differently about the way the buildings touch the ground, differently about the relationship of building to street, differently about the relationship of building to those who look at it, since the viewers may now be passing it at sixty-plus mph on a gently rising curve or in an underpass whose sides may effectively blank off the whole of the lower storey when the viewer is on the axis of the main façade.[79]

Banham agreed with the Smithsons that automobiles as discrete objects provide environments for human activities, and therefore offer a standard of comparison for the activities of the architectural profession. He also agreed with Peter's view that American automobile designs surpass American architectural forms. And he, too, had more praise for the design methodology that produces automobiles than for that which produces architecture. Just look at the scale of automobile production—the close link between product design and consumer desires—how styling is tailored to fit clients' social status! Then compare all these achievements to the aesthetic ideals, the formalistic designs, of architecture! Banham asks the reader to think about built-in obsolescence in automobiles, and how this might influence the design of "expendabilia" in housing. Except for the Smithsons' House of the Future—and even here Banham has qualms—no architect had ventured into this field.

III. Emerging Landscape Sensibilities

The Smithsons' Own Stocktaking

Pop Art elevated the American automobile to the heights of adoration in the 1950s, but by the mid-1960s the Smithsons evaluated the scenery with a bit more skepticism. Peter noted in 1965 that the architecture of Skidmore, Owings and Merrill might be the only sort that Europeans regarded as "really American." "And, as with Detroit cars, they admire it without the restraints that would operate against the admiration of such architecture were it a product of their own culture. It is admired for its unmatched technological competence."[80] A few more years of affluence, and things had changed:

The present possession availability/desirability level of domestic equipment and personal transportation in industrialized Europe has stabilized. Most people have—or are encouraged to expect by advertising—hot water and some heating, a washing machine, refrigerator, and one and a bit motor-cars per family.[81]

Any territory, rural or urban, has now to share with "larger metal animals, i.e. cars and delivery, service, disposal vehicles and they travel larger distances ... territory is over-occupied ... bigger animals are a great deal noisier and more violent."[82]

High density propagandists rightly say that only when there are densities of upwards of 300 persons per acre can certain desirable things—play decks, local shops, fully segregated movement, etc.—be supported: but the human animal knows when it is surrounded by layers of a thousand snoring heads—the air is somehow used up, the circulation spaces over-used and under-cared-for, plants renew themselves less actively. The environment gets exhausted. The human animal cannot be kidded by clever arrangement that it has enough space when it has not.[83]

It was time, in *Team 10 Primer* (1968), to reflect back to 1953. In the interim Europe had experienced a change of "life style" symbolized by the motorcar. Now almost the entire society was serviced by the serial production of Pop-styled fashion and "gear." Only the Smithsons' major concern, the house, remained a shameful example of how the architect was forbidden any notion of serial production. If fashion designers could utilize serial production with respect to clothing, if industrial designers could produce serial models of automobiles, why could not architects so design homes? They must face the situation "as found" and accept what now has become the norm for society: motor ownership, the proliferation of radios and other sound-producing equipment and appliances, higher living standards, and higher purchasing power. Unless these needs are met, we are not sure "where we want to walk and where to ride in our bouncy new clothes and in our shiny new cars."[84]

By the early 1970s, the Smithson reevaluated once again the scene of vehicles and their ordering system: "That we can think vehicles is because almost twenty years ago Louis Kahn, the Philadelphian architect, brought vehicle movement systems to an idea level."[85] In the USA, motor vehicles in large numbers dated from the mid-1930s, so Kahn grew up with these machines and knew how to design for them. But an overall sensibility to a machine-served city was a slow-growing concept in Europe, and only in the last 20 years has a delicacy emerged that considers the city as a "humans-related-to-place mix."

We have been taught to see the big city Ghetto as a rich setting for making a special sort of people as any Polynesian Island, and they say we have tampered with its delicate balance of human patterns too confidently in the recent past.

In general, those town-building techniques that can make the community more comprehensible are:

(1) To develop the road and communication systems as the urban infra-structure. (Motorways as a unifying force.) And to realize the implication of flow and movement in the architecture itself.

(2) To accept the dispersal implied in the concept of mobility and to re-think accepted density patterns and location of functions in relation to the new means of communication.

(3) To understand and use the possibilities offered by a 'throw-away' technology, to create a new sort of environment with different cycles of change for different functions.

(4) To develop an æsthetic appropriate to mechanized building techniques and scales of operation.

(5) To overcome the 'cultural obsolescence' of most mass housing by finding solutions which project a genuinely twentieth-century technological image of the dwelling—comfortable, safe and not feudal.

(6) To establish conditions not detrimental to mental health and well-being. Past legislation and layout were geared to increasing standards of hygiene; in countries of higher standards of living this is no longer a problem. Criteria* have to be found to define under-mining environment. These might be: noise level, polluting and polluted environment, overcrowding, pressing and pushing, no space for the social gesture, all those demands made on the individual in societies inhabiting accumulated built forms.

'Forum' (Holland), 7, 1959. A. & P.S.

The studies of association and identity led to the development of systems of linked building complexes which were intended to correspond more closely to the network of social relationships, as they now exist, than the existing closed patterns of finite spaces and self-contained buildings. These freer systems are more capable of change, and particularly in new communities of mutating in scale and intention as they go along.

It was realized that the essential error of the English New Towns was that they were too rigidly conceived, and in 1956 we put forward an alternative system in which the 'infra-structure' (roads and services) was the only fixed thing. The road system was devised to be simple and to give equal ease of access to all parts.

This theme of the road system as the basis of the community structure was further explored in the Cluster City idea between 1957 and 1959, in the Haupstadt Berlin Plan 1958, and in the London Roads Study 1959.

'Uppercase'. A./P.S.

Roads can be deliberately routed and the land beside them neutra-lized so that they become obviously fixed things (that is changing on a long cycle). The routing of individual sections over rivers, through parks, or in relation to historic buildings or zones, provides a series of 'fixes' or local identity points. The road net itself de-fining the zones identified by these 'fixes'.

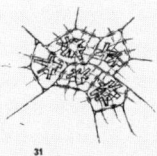

The form of the city must correspond to the net of human relations as we now see them.

The changing arrangements of this net are effected by changing systems of communication and changes of social aims.

The architect can act directly in this situation. He can control systems of physical communication and he can offer new con-cepts.

And in fact the two things are wrapped up with each other, for putting increased emphasis on physical communications in-volves throwing over traditional æsthetic values which were mostly concerned with fixed relationships; and on the other hand rejection of Cartesian æsthetics, because they are incapable of carrying the cultural loading of our time, inevitably leads to an 'æsthetic of change' the plastic resolution of the problems of mobility.

31 'Down-town', diagram, P.O.S.

32 'The architect can control systems of physical com-munication and offer new concepts', diagram, Kahn

* Criteria for Mass Housing, etc.

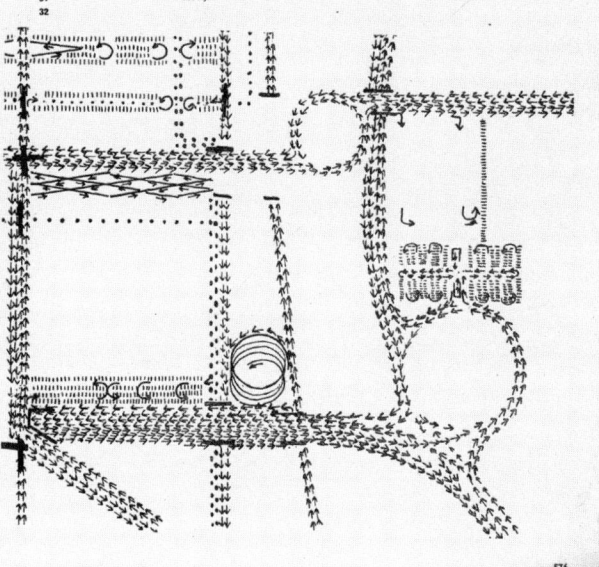

6.8
Detail of Louis Kahn's Philadelphia movement systems from "Team 10 Primer," AD 32 (December 1962), 593. Smithson Family Collection.

But we have come a long way from Marinetti. We know we are involved in new levels of sadness and destruction and we have a view of things unimaginable fifty years ago.[86]

That the city as a mechanism is very delicate we each have learned from our own experience of its breakdowns during the recent past—the New York power blackout, the dislocation of air-communications across all Europe caused by the strike of air-controllers in France ... , the sense of chaos caused by the dustmen's strike in London. The mechanism-served city, again to repeat, is very delicate and demanding of its citizens—they need to be more disciplined, and more thoughtfully involved than ever before.[87]

For an English architect to be aware of "*the mix*" should be easy—fed from earliest years with sociology and with the theory of the picturesque. But, there is all the difference in the world between "melting-in" and the discovery of an ordering which suddenly makes the whole mix make sense. That ordering, if we can invent it, will mean a writing-in of vehicles, mechanisms and services into the idea of the city.[88]

The Smithsons knew that the automobile symbolized a new kind of equality and freedom of movement, a knowledge they shared with Jaap Bakema, who spent his life celebrating and helping others to celebrate this new freedom. At the time of Jaap's death in 1981, Alison recalled his ability to *move*—to turn up in his car and to be of use, to work, to make contact.[89] At the crematorium where his funeral took place, she reported, noise of passing traffic sprayed into the "garden of rest" and offended those gathered, who wanted instead to peacefully celebrate the many things they had shared with Bakema, especially a European sensibility in reading landscape and building. The role of memory, times, patterns, uses, attitudes: these connections formed a shared community in which they had lived together as a group. Now it was time to ask: "How do we view the town and the landscape through the veil of this inherited memory ... ?"[90] What do we do with this landscape as moved through, what inventions of landscaping, settlement patterns help to protect us from the noise of movement?

She still admired the automobile as a private room on wheels:

a piece of technology in the landscape for all seasons of the European year, day or night.

To be within one's own surfaces, with one's things, perhaps enjoying a picnic seated in armchair comfort, looking at a view we choose, when we choose—this is the freedom given by technology, satisfying the delicate balance between togetherness/apartness.

Our sensibilities have been affected by our use of our "room on wheels" but also, there comes a new awareness of the responsibilities inherent in our comfortable view of just anywhere. Our idea of quality of place, our will to bring through quality

AS IN DS

AN EYE ON THE ROAD

ALISON SMITHSON

DELFT UNIVERSITY PRESS

In this diary – a passenger's eye on english roads in the 1970's – a sensibility to car movement has its beginnings.

in all things, these should also be affected by our position of a cell of perfected technology.[91]

[But what] is the legacy of Bakema's generation? ... What conclusion can we draw from a stock-taking ... ten years after the making of the Diary [*AS in DS*] in the early 'seventies? What do we want to contribute to extension of the possibilities we have inherited? How do we want to mutate places by which we wish to build towards; that we may rather enjoy freedoms and yet nurture new sensibilities?[92]

The view of the landscape from a moving vehicle prompted the growth of a new sensibility, with new ways of seeing and new patterns of contact engendering a new identity between individual and place. Alison claimed that 1955 was the "start point" for taking an "ecological approach to the problem of habitat"—being sensitive to how a house was placed on a particular site, and how it formed part of an existing community.[93] Additional influences also touched on this developing sensibility, such as the type of space that orders of movement engendered. Peter Smithson explained in 1984:

> We have long been engaged with the common places of vehicular movement; we know our sensibilities have been changed; so can now look where we might expect to find the "natural" physical change in our cities and landscape ... in their geometric format; in the mediators between machine and men, between machines and building-fabric and between machines and grown-fabric. And we can also reflect on how we now "see things differently."[94]

It was this new sensibility that led Alison to write a diary from the passenger seat in a moving vehicle. Peter Smithson clarified:

> It is the intention of "AS in DS" to record fragments of the process which has led us to see things differently (and to make things differently) without conscious thought. ... For there has been, to repeat, a change in our sensibilities.
>
> In this diary—a passenger's eye on the English roads in the 1970s—a sensibility to car movement has its beginnings.[95]

6.9
Cover of Alison Smithson, *AS in DS: An Eye on the Road* (Delft: Delft University Press, 1983). Smithson Family Collection.

AS in DS: NEW FREEDOMS: 1:1

ASPECT 1: A NEW KIND OF FREEDOM OFFERED BY THE CAR

The mobility that the car has given to everyone has helped to change our social patterns and, progressively, our social needs; for example, we no longer need to go to the centre we move to many centres.... and out of the city .... and out of the country altogether. Our social activity has adjusted; instead of sitting in a public auditorium or walking a city street, we are as other people in a similar vehicle: social contact is by implication........ we are told about it; watch it, occasionally read about it; but our physical experience of community adhesion is that 'we drive it'. 'We get in the car and go ...... stop the car and get out'.

This new kind of freedom, achieved in the lifetime of our generation is now sufficiently immediate history that it can be considered..... to discover the nature of the sensibilities we must have unconsciously developed........ and to see if fresh appraisal of them can bring these sensibilities through to generate a rethinking of the many basic assumptions related to our 'inherited' way of seeing landscape and towns.... establishing a fresh understanding of what sort of places we wish to build towards.

moved by the car along an ordinary curvilinear ex-lane through fields; all vegetation on either side the usual strong green, viewed under the most typical sky of grey-overcast causing conditions of considerable glare.... it is suddenly obvious that a passenger' is worth describing....

a turn aside into the town recently by-passed.... on the air - it is realised - is chill.... a beautiful wee screens the traffic still using the old main road which 'diner' .... a blood track leads to broken plate glass.... the car - in the meantime of the pause - has taken in a wasp.... requiring a race to find a Chemist's shop at Camberley.

DIAGRAM OF DIARY INTERVALS ON A TYPICAL JOURNEY PATTERN

AS in DS (1983)

AS in DS was the first pedagogical and picturesque essay of Alison Smithson's series of "sensibility primers" to see print.[96] These primers will be examined in chapter 10; here it suffices to note how *AS in DS* presents her sensibility to car movement and a new kind of landscape immediacy. She recalled from the vantage point of 1983, when *AS in DS* was published, that writing on the project began in 1970 because

> it suddenly seemed worthwhile to describe in words the passenger's view from a moving car.[97]
>
> That is, my instinct told me that car movement had reached an apogee. At the time, I thought this apogee was in car design and in the manners and obvious pleasures of car users in England. But looking back we can now see several other aspects of this apogee of 1970:
> — there was not yet a ground swell of environmental concerns
> — the worry about lead in petrol could only occasionally be found in a scientific or medical journal (Britain came out against lead only on April 19th, 1983)
> — the oil crisis was unthought of (it occurred in 1973)
> — a few road improvements were beginning in England, sufficient to offer other alignments in the landscape than for the horse and cart.[98]

Thus *AS in DS: An Eye on the Road* was the story of an ordinary passenger's view — an innocent account before things were inverted, and the violence that road building and automobiles enacted became evident.

> AS in DS has to do with the recognition, that from a car — a forward moving vantage point if we are a front passenger — we must see landscape, places differently from our predecessors.
>
> This must seem obvious; there is already a beginning of a literature and an art of the roads, but nothing of the run-in, sensibility-definition, that would parallel the recognition-of-sensibility literature by Alexander Pope, Oliver Goldsmith, and so on, that provided the ground for the English Landscape Garden style.[99]
>
> Yet, as nearly everyone is in cars, we are all experiencing, exploring, a new sensibility, in the way the makers of the English Landscape Garden first experienced the Grand Tour in their coaches, explored it in literature, responded to an art being made and being bought by contemporaries.

6.10
Mock-up page design for *AS in DS* (1983).
Smithson Family Collection.

> Eighteenth century Englishmen made use of their awareness of their new sensibility when they came to make gardens, utilized it in order to discover what it was a garden was to serve, what was its function—as an art of the garden, what it should express—its spirit, what sensibilities it should engender in its users.
>
> A person in the garden was expected to want to have the garden induce certain types of thoughts while breathing the dank smells of the evergreen or the perfume of the box hedge after it has been raining. In certain characters of place, to want to react to the solemnity of ivy on wall or on the ground or have rocks allude to terror and the awfulness, awesomness [sic] of remoteness; or for sheet water to cause contemplation, and distant views bring tranquillity.
>
> The garden was to make real the connection to:
> Memories held in common
> Things read
> Pictures admired places visited (often on the Great Tour)
> Scenes appreciated (the Campagna often in the Alps)
> (The appreciation of other places is perhaps one of the arts of the English!) The garden embodied a certain disembodied ethos* held in common by the English.
> *(ethos: characteristic spirit of community or people)
>
> Expression of affection towards the landscape is acceptable, the pastorale was an acceptable part of the classical education. The subjugation of self to the "as found," the genius loci, the spirit of the place, supported the sensibility that energized the English Landscape Garden.[100]

Thus we find Alison Smithson—never driving, always in the passenger seat—scribbling down thoughts as the Smithsons' Citroën DS 19 travels from London to their retreat in Fonthill, with other travel notes interjected here and there. She kept and renewed her driver's license, though after some criticism of her driving technique from Peter Smithson, she never again took the wheel in her hands.[101] Nevertheless she kept her eye on (and off) the road, offering a diary of a passenger's view of movement in a car as a "cultural food package"—"to put impressions, ideas, into words—because sometimes we think in words."[102] The book is cut in the actual outline of their beloved Citroën—soon to be replaced—making the primer as much a nostalgic memoir as a pedagogical treatise.

Sketchbooks were carried on the back floor of the Citroën, with a bunch of color pencils in the ashtray. They were necessary: "An ingredient of previous identifications of emergent sensibilities as to landscape has always included the 'sketch'."[103] A notebook was also in the automobile. For safety reasons, family conversations were kept to a minimum while the Citroën was moving, allowing the front-seat passenger time to think, look, write, and sketch.[104] In this manner the text of *AS in DS* was written in 1972–1973, though its illustrative approach evolved later under the influence of sketches of English gardens by the Picturesque "sensibility-formers."

AS in DS was a teaching document, but it had to be admitted up front that this "sensibility primer" might reach a reader only obliquely, and over a long period of time. Such long gestation was not abnormal or objectionable; Peter gave the example of traveling in their Jeep to view the progress of their first project, the Hunstanton School (1949–1953). It was remarkable to view from their open tray on wheels the field boundary lines formed by Scotch pines, layer crossing behind layer. They intended to record the experience in a film; the film never materialized, "but the notion of layers, of the mysterious occlusions that occur in layers passed, entered the form-language of our architecture in the late 'sixties. The time-elapse is twenty years from observation to invention."[105] And so might be the slow-motion effect of *AS in DS*. Alison would add: "First: the insight: record is made for some reason, some use, some need; as yet unformulated at the time of its inception."[106]

In *AS in DS*, free associations flow along with the route: service stations, overpasses, trees overhanging and framing the way, hedgerows lining the road, mists in hollows, water-washed clouds of gray, rain on pavement, climbing hills, night stars twinkling, lorries with tarpaulined loads, roadside poppies, fine drizzle, birds singing overhead, soot-brown woods, cloud-muted moon, beech leaf drifts, swooping down a lane in armchair comfort, chasing tail lights—these are among the hundreds of moments captured on paper as the car moves into and across the landscape. The DS's movements are full of routes that repeat, seasons that return, recurrent exits from and entries into cities. Each journey is a turn of the kaleidoscope, a figure that implies both permutation and continuum.

Pleasure gives rise to responsibility, the greater awareness that sensibility brings.

> The achievement of movement, the release, is possible because others make it so … any mechanical movement implies a support network that is a phenomenon of collective responsibility more impressive than that of any previous system—the railways, the canals—partly because it seemed in the early 'seventies virtually open-ended. Compared with the horse-drawn carriages—repaintable, repairable on a one-off basis, drawn by horses whose by-products in the proper place only improved the earth—car travel is supported by great collective effort and mutual responsibility.[107]

We take for granted the miraculous, encapsulated privacy of the family car.

> [I]n all forms other than the private car, you are with people … immediacy is lost: except when you open the door of the personal car on a new place. … All to do with a sensibility of the magic wrought by the withdrawal of noise, vibration, disequilibrium … the getting away from the sense of others.[108]

> Sealed in a car, the urban scene is glassy, even fume-free; clean in that your surface is between you and surfaces others have had access to, relatively silent beyond the immediate engine noise: but car-joy—becomes increasingly dearly bought: the period

documented had to be a transitory, *raw* period; the next *sensibility* will have to be about others—a *sensibility* about people caring one for another.[109]

Would thinking through the inherited way of viewing landscape and towns shift sensibilities toward fresh understanding of the kinds of places the Smithsons were building toward? If the experience of encapsulation was one that reinforced distance and detachment, how could a new way of thinking about the quality of place be thus generated?

> The mobility that the car has given to everyone has helped to change our social patterns and progressively, our social needs; … [in an automobile] social contact is by implication … we are told about it; watch it, occasionally read about it; but our physical experience of community adhesion is that "we drive it," "We get in the car and go—stop the car and get out."[110]

But would automobile movement be sufficient to transform sensibilities? There was an inherited manner of viewing that had to be changed.

> With landscape, we are most encumbered by established English sensibilities; and so deeply involved we have in front of our eyes almost a pre-formed vision, the where-with-all to relive the whole spirit of the English picturesque. To surmount this fixed-vision, the passenger has behaved towards scenes passing the windows almost as mechanically as the needle of a seismograph.[111]

> It is through this largely "static veil" that we view our inheritance of landscape.[112]

Alison wanted to have the roads, the services, the vehicles, the suburbs, the landscapes impress themselves anew without being embedded in a past way-of-seeing, only in the past of fleeting memory: "the result desired being an unmisted record of the countryside of the 'seventies passed through by the car on the road: however, where past aesthetic references came into the mind, these have not been suppressed."[113]

Alison is convinced that perceptual shifts must be reaped from and triggered by the automobile: first, the ability to distinguish between an inherited view and a fresh view of the landscape; second, the invention of a new style of landscape gardening, a new way to protect nature and dwellings from pollution and noise. Both shifted perceptions and landscape innovations should be discernible from the road, bringing "a fresh recognition of the nature of what we see."[114]

As much as the Smithsons loved their car and their travels, there is an intriguing ambivalence in Alison's writings about the automobile. Not all is well, perhaps, on the Road of the Future. Landscapes are threatened as well as revealed and reseen; numbing and indifference beckon. There are even moments of despair about the impact of motorization on the English landscape: would it ever return to "park-like-perfection"? Would human voices once again become the greatest noise? Would sky clouds be purified and no longer polluted?

Her hoped-for sensibility failed to emerge even within the Smithsons' family: "the smallest passenger beginning to notice the scenery: the others never really aware—no amount of hopefully-connective-patter made the others conscious of much beyond selected cars, brands of services to car and obtrusive passengers."[115] And England's expanding motorway (divided highway) network gave early hints that its sensibility tunings might be discordant. The distant look from the motorway revealed problems: "the city gets more confining, the discerning pedestrian need-be myopic, as views are pierced by obtruding blocks and skylines become studded with vile profiles—it has come so that to raise the eyes is to risk seeing another developer's monstrosity breaking the homogeneity."[116]

It is therefore necessary, by the time of *AS in DS*'s publication in 1983, to assess whether a shift in sensibility has developed during the ten years since the initial jottings for the book. It is now accepted that "we need to mutate places by building towards an image of towns-in-the-landscape that will satisfy the new sensibilities and allow freedom from pressures of all kinds."[117] Such late stocktaking enables Alison to assert an insight: the targeted topography of the new motorways, their embankment profile risen well above the level of the passenger's view, was in fact first created with the railways. The builders of motorways fail, for all they have added is breadth to route-taking to the magnificent memory of travel by train. In comparison,

> the targeted topography of railway-make is viewed rising right-up-against the windows of the carriage compartments; or falling away immediately below and even more exaggerated, passing the passenger on tight-rope rails across girder-bridges—for the car's passengers, no standing up and pressing forehead to the glass, squeezing the most out of scarifying spanning—route-works for motor transport provide greater spaciousness; rarely dramatic excitement or minimal-width pioneering—these swathe-spaces are especial to car movement, therefore the motorway shows passengers a new aspect of England; relatively unreminiscent—.[118]

Before Alison's eyes appears a silver-shiny train paused on a bridge, the stone arches of the viaduct spanning a canal; from thence she turns to consider a bridge over the motorway and bluntly asks, "will any future generation feel sentiment for what it does?"[119] The automobile on the improved motorway is so steady, one can read a newspaper on one's lap or do one's makeup or nails, and if one should "glance up" one remains unaware that one's sensibility to movement has changed, but not for the better: one has become so accustomed to not looking at views directly, one fails to read the landscape as before.[120] There is remorse: "Cobbett's was the last 'sensibility of travel' but one, before the railways intervened—"[121] and now his way has become the A34 road. Cobbett wrote of the England he saw; he followed the ups and downs of the road, viewed the curvaceous boundary of fields—but not so the automobile that flies over a downward depression on a ridge of fill, whooshes past sliced-off mounds and grass embankments.

Nothing of automotive travel by motorway can be likened to the heroic tales of travel by horseback, then by carriage, and next by steam train! Being encapsulated in moving-arm-chair-comfort, where motion appears to be magically effortless, is the reason why the hoped-for sensibilities to the moving view, the ever-opening landscape, never arrived.

On the new motorway there is plenty to annoy her: the little dodgem cars, the crash barriers separating opposing lanes, old familiar places bypassed never to be seen again, junctions that confuse drivers, and never knowing what place this is. To her dismay the exposed motorway rolls on, cars and trucks competitively pass without letup, and the buildup of traffic increases as the motorways extend their reach. Trips in the DS are over. Alison comes to an abrupt halt with a guilty aside: there was the old car, so dearly beloved, weather-tight, and comfortable, "shaming us in our knowing we sell it—."[122]

IV. Conclusion

Automobiles—their production, consumption, proliferation, symbolic meanings, and urban consequences—were much discussed in the works of both Banham and the Smithsons. Indeed, the automobile, with its links to patterns of inhabitation, whether in Britain or the USA, was the discursive foundation around which their ideals of modernity revolved. Autonomy and mobility, automobile and habitat, were conjoined: each expressed and produced the other. The automobile offered freedom of movement; it was linked to a range of images determining its meaning and marketing; it was part of a larger industry of resource utilization and environmental management; it required a complex of investments in road building, services, maintenance, and regulations. Yet they saw the entire systemic structure of "automobility" as evolving naturally, spontaneously, without human agency or responsibility—or at least, this was their attitude until the mid-1970s.

As Banham and the Smithsons entered the 1970s, their paths begin to diverge even further. Banham was outraged at the Smithsons' kowtowing to the Picturesque and retreat from *une architecture autre*. They must rearticulate architecture's relationship to temporality—the fast-moving present and the immediate future of technology and science. The Smithsons, on the other hand, looked at the mounting environmental crisis and turned away from wastefully dumping buildings on a site, searching instead for a right fit in the landscape. They began to ruminate on the past, shifting their gaze backward to evaluate anew their responsibilities as inheritors and successors of the Modern Movement—to develop new sensibilities toward the land and its traditions, a lighter, more human touch. We turn to their written ruminations in chapter 8; but first, in chapter 7, we turn back to examine the crucial role of Team 10 in forming the Smithsons' discourse.

7.1

Alison Margaret Smithson, 1956 at CIAM 10 Dubrovnik (background left Jill and Bill Howell). Photograph by John Voelcker. Smithson Family Collection.

7
Team 10: Keeping the Language of Modern Architecture Alive

Prologue

Alison was the editor of several Team 10 documents published in *AD*: "CIAM Team 10" and "The Work of Team 10" (both May 1960) and "Team 10 Primer" (December 1962). These documents form the basis for an exploration into Team 10 discourse, and can be supplemented by three other documents edited by Alison Smithson: the book form of *Team 10 Primer* (1968), "Team 10 at Royaumont 1962" *AD* (1975), and *Team 10 Meetings: 1953–1984* (1991). This chapter also examines the myth and making of Team 10. In the early 1980s, Alison Smithson was asked to give three graduate seminars at the Architectural Association in London on the history of Team 10. To form the basis of her discussions, she used an assembly of CIAM- and Team 10-related documents published in facsimile form as *The Emergence of Team 10 out of CIAM* (1982). Her outlines for these seminars are essentially a personal recall of Team 10 meetings dealing with people and places.

I. Team 10 Discourse[1]

Team 10 as it existed in CIAM was broken at Dubrovnik but
whether we want it or not the name Team 10 represents
in everyone's mind that field of forces with its roots in CIAM
which is producing the new theory and imagery.
Team 10, undated[2]

Passing the Baton

Le Corbusier did not attend CIAM 10 (Dubrovnik, 1956), sending instead a letter from Cap Martin in southern France, where he was vacationing.[3] The evolution of CIAM was, he believed, a generational issue between the founders of 1928 and the new members of 1956 (now over forty years of age). Before passing the baton to the younger generation, he felt it necessary to repeat the principles on which CIAM had been founded: foremost, solidarity among those who prepared the Athens Charter and obtained worldwide recognition of its principles. This first CIAM, Le Corbusier wrote, held housing (that is, equipping the new machine civilization) to be its major concern, and toward this end had formulated a program, detailed and prioritized all the necessary chapters of the so-called "book." Now the job of "conquering" the world, persuading it to accept this new modern architecture, was finished, and many of the founders had become so rigid in their ways that it was impossible for the first CIAM to continue.[4]

He understood that the younger generation of 1956 was committed to practical action based on global needs expressed through empirical facts. This action, Le Corbusier thought, carries into fruition the ideas of the first CIAM, yet it was still necessary for this second CIAM to create a new, coherent program so that in thirty years' time it, too, could pass the baton on to a still younger generation. And in 1956, the second CIAM had indeed picked up the relay of the first CIAM—therefore Le Corbusier felt there was no need for him to be present at Dubrovnik.[5]

Just what did "picking up the baton" and continuing the relay mean to members of Team 10? And how did this issue of continuity bear on the invention of a new language of modern architecture? To answer these questions, Team 10 embarked on a journey of its own (1956–1981), during which its members would debate the meaning of images, the use of words and aesthetic expressions, and the invention of new concepts, ideas, and architectural forms. From the start, words, projects, ideas, and designs were the "baton" of the new CIAM.

Keeping alive the inheritance of modern architecture also meant constituting a new expressive language; at least, that is what Alison and Peter Smithson thought Le Corbusier was asking of the members of Team 10. But what this act of constitution entailed would be open to debate, as discussed in chapter 2. Here we want to discuss Alison Smithson's role as editor of Team 10 discussions published in various editions of *AD* and supplemented by additional materials. As editor for Team 10, Alison was in a position to shape the recorded flow of discourse to establish points in the argument that she was constructing. The texts she selected play off each other, spin into associative links, even contradict, yet set up a platform on which the language of architecture and the philosophy of Team 10 could be reworked and extended—as she wanted it to be, to some extent. Her task was one of re-mediation, her role to be (in her phrase) "Stimulator and Stirrer" of Team 10 ideas. The goal, as she saw it, was to keep the language of modern architecture alive.[6]

"CIAM Team 10" and "The Work of Team 10"[7]

The aim of the first Team 10 Meeting in Otterlo (1959), Alison explained in this *AD* publication of 1960, had been to discover "if a true affinity of thought exists between participants, not only in spoken and written words, but more profoundly on the level of plastic invention, through the communication of direct building ideas."[8] Alison might argue that Team 10 sought an architecture that was open, inclusive, and interactive, but Otterlo revealed that their meetings would henceforth be closed. An open society did not necessarily entail an open group structure; not everyone was allowed to join this new research group. She admitted the issue was emotionally charged and far from nonpartisan. Incompatible approaches had been expressed by some of the invitees at Otterlo, and this impeded a united stance. Three groups were represented, only one subscribing to Team 10's advocated position. Henceforth, the other two would be excluded: those who still followed the Athens Charter of CIAM and those Italians, led by Ernesto Rogers, who were interested in expressionistic monuments such as the Torre Velasca. These two excluded groups stood for a "closed aesthetic" imposing formal and static solutions on users. Instead, Team 10 advocated an "open aesthetic," which Alison called "the living extension of Functionalism." This definition enabled Team 10 to pick up the foundational statements of CIAM and project them into the future. Alison repeats the consensus first pronounced by John Voelcker: "CIAM is finally dead," replaced by a fluid membership with no formal organization but marching together under the moral banner of "what needs to be done."[9]

Team 10, however, did not want to break with the tradition of CIAM; indeed, it needed to draw upon its authority for a foundational text or set of ideals, one their own discourse could endlessly comment upon and bring up to date. The approach of Team 10 was, according to Alison Smithson, clear: continuity maintained yet change allowed. (This enabled the selected texts to weave back and forth between foundational principles and new applications.)

"The Work of Team 10" consisted of description of and commentary upon a series of buildings from the Arctic to the Mediterranean, from Spain to Hungary, followed by two position statements, one by Jerzy Sołtan and another by Kenzō Tange, and a summary by Giancarlo De Carlo.[10] All three pieces were used by Alison to position Team 10 within the older CIAM discourse.

Sołtan, who expressed the clearest link to the past, as a former member of Le Corbusier's atelier, suggested the new CIAM's task was simple: it must develop ideas built on the base provided by CIAM. Yet this required great moral strength for unmasking and fighting the new enemy of "superficial bourgeois modernism" from Beirut to Boston. This internal enemy, the false "brother-modernists," must be guarded against, for they no longer supported CIAM's philosophical ideals but manipulated aesthetics in an autonomous manner.[11]

Kenzō Tange was more critical of CIAM's heritage. It was wrong, he said, to assume, as CIAM had done, that urban and environmental dilemmas were curable within the existing technological society: internal conflicts cannot be eliminated, nor can society revitalize its own order. "Aestheticism" is caused by this escapism, establishing abstract beauty that spreads a "fairy story over chaotic reality."[12] The alternative was "vitality," a form of energy arising wherever criticism and opposition to Western culture and pattern of life occurred. Tange advised Team 10 to dig out the "vitality of masses underneath society"—to make "the suppressed voices and hidden energies" of Africa-Asia resound throughout their work: "Vitalism is always destructive to our reality, but is constructive for our future."[13]

In his closing summary, De Carlo criticized CIAM for its conviction that the aim and language of modern architecture needed only small improvements. This put a brake on criticism and therefore on progress, and had paralyzed the discourse of CIAM since 1947.[14] While recognizing the genius of Le Corbusier and noting that CIAM slept beneath this giant oak, he nevertheless contended that Le Corbusier's architectural concept was subjective and renounced all obligations to find discipline through method. Thus Team 10, to renew the language of architecture, must accept that Le Corbusier's focus on man, society, and nature was based on "worn out prototypes" and "inanimate diagrams."[15] Le Corbusier's contribution had been immense, opening a path toward the radical renewal of architecture, a path that Team 10 wanted to follow, but the group must be careful how it extended the language of modern architecture, and how it deployed the inheritance Le Corbusier had bequeathed.

Through constant commentary on foundational ideals, De Carlo said, Team 10 expressed its gratitude for, yet divergence from, the heroic gestures of the older generation. They would work opposing research methods into a new synthesis. They would prune and exclude from discourse "brother-modernists" who deviated toward aesthetic formalism. They would enliven their architectural expressions with new energies and voices from outside the West. But Team 10 would extend the discourse of CIAM by comparing different examples of built work, grounding their discussions on "factual data" derived from investigations into basic principles and means-end analyses embedded within practical works. This would take their discussions beyond the "generic" quality that had paralyzed postwar CIAM meetings.

"Team 10 Primer"

When *AD* published the "Team 10 Primer" in 1962, Alison explained that most of the members of Team 10 were teachers in need of materials expressing not only their individual positions but the reasons they had come together in mutual support, and how they had extended the language of architecture as they went about the business of architecture. Alison took their "root ideas in their original naïve form," juxtaposed commentary in an associative counterpoint, and presented this mixture as a schoolbook primer. Various "voices" allowed different readers to pursue different trains of thought. She gave their aim a new title: "Utopia of the present," or building for a more humane existence.

The Primer format was elaborate (unprimerlike) and required reading instructions.[16] Each pair of copiously illustrated pages should be read together by turning the magazine sideways. The largest typeface carried the main message on the left side of the page, with supplementary texts in a smaller face and "verbal illustrations" in a third, smallest face. The primer's running commentary on the foundational texts of the Moderns serves Team 10 in two ways: such commentary allows criticism to be directed outside the group, enfolding its differences and oppositions safely within acceptable bounds; and provides pedagogical material, with an explanation of how they had spent their intellectual family inheritance.

It was Alison's intention to stress the language of architecture as she rearranged the elements of Team 10's back-and-forth discussions. To bolster her position, she inserted a quotation from a 1959 RIBA lecture given by Reyner Banham on "Futurism" (though he did not participate in Team 10's conversations). Banham claimed that no one teaches style any longer, or a plastic system pertaining to architecture:

> This escape from style is reflected, quite naturally, in the buildings that are going up around us. It would be wrong to say that the builders are using the language of building badly, because they do not realize there is such a thing as a language of building: they do not know the words from which to construct sentences in my opinion, an architecture which is incoherent is useless. … One finds more and more that one is talking in a stylistic void. Such a stylistic void makes any teaching, any writing, any talking, almost a waste of time.[17]

Peter's interest in concepts and their meaning, in how a language of architecture might communicate, was persistent. As if in reply to the Babel of styles that annoyed Banham, Alison quoted Peter:

> As far as architecture is concerned, the question of appropriateness is a matter for radical organizational thinking; but it is also a question of language. What are the appropriate organization forms of buildings and building groups which respond to today's needs?
>
> How is the response to this need to be communicated? If no forms are discovered and no suitable language is evolved, the needs are not met and there remain unfulfilled, undefined longings in society as a whole.[18]

The purpose of coming together as Team 10, according to Peter Smithson, was to pick up, reiterate, and record a series of attempts to revitalize this language of architecture, to make it communicate society's unfulfilled needs and undefined longings.[19] Textual reiterations state and restate this position: Bakema, who claimed the entire alphabet of spatial forms must be deployed to explain the man–total universe relationship;[20] Van Eyck, who added the in-between realm and the imponderable to the expressions of architecture;[21] and again Peter Smithson, that one had only to make a comparison between the Barcelona Pavilion and Villa Savoye to see that "MIES IS GREAT BUT CORB COMMUNICATES." While both architects were deep sources from which the Smithsons drew sustenance, Peter held Le Corbusier to be the greater visionary—one who could "make a man leave home and start a new life."[22]

Alison draws her interweavings to a conclusion giving the last word to Georges Candilis, Alexis Josic, and Shadrach Woods:

12 ARCHITECTURAL DESIGN
December 1962 Price 4/-

TEAM 10 PRIMER 1953-62

TEAM 10 PRIMER

Edited by Alison Smithson for TEAM 10

J. B. Bakema	Holland
Aldo van Eyck	
G. Candillis	France
S. Woods	
A. & P. Smithson	England
John Voelcker	
J. Soltan	Poland
Gier Grung	Norway
Ralph Erskine	Sweden
J. Coderch	Spain

There was a time not so long ago when the minds of men moved along a deterministic groove; let's call it a Euclidian groove. It coloured their behaviour and vision, what they made and did and what they felt. Then—it had to happen sooner or later—some very keen men, with delicate antennæ—painters, poets, philosophers and scientists most of them—jumped out of this groove and rubbed the deterministic patina off the surface of reality. They saw wonderful things and did not fail to tell us about them. Our unbounded gratitude is due to them: to Picasso, Klee, Mondrian and Brancusi; to Joyce, Le Corbusier, Schönberg, Bergson and Einstein; to the whole wonderful gang. They set the great top spinning again and expanded the universe—the outside and the inside universe. It was a wonderful riot—the cage was again opened. But society still moves along in the old groove, in bad air, making only sly use of what these men discovered; worse still, applying on a purely technological, mechanical, and decorative level, not the essence but what can be gleaned from it in order to give pretence of moving more effectively. Moving securely and lucratively along the old circumscribed groove. We know this, it can't be helped. But do we know that architecture has been doing the same for the last thirty years or so? No need to mention the few marvellous exceptions. A damnable truth this. When are architects going to stop fondling technology for its own sake—stop stumbling after progress? When are they really going to join the riot and stop gnawing at the edges of a great idea? Surely we cannot permit them to continue selling the diluted essence of what others spent a lifetime finding. They have betrayed society in betraying the essence of contemporary thought. Nobody can really live in what they concoct, although they may think so.

Now what is wonderful about this non-Euclidian idea—this other vision—is that it is contemporary; contemporary to all our difficulties, social and political, economic and spiritual. What is tragic is that we have failed to see that it alone can solve them.

Each period requires a constituent language—an instrument with which to tackle the human problems posed by the period, as well as those which, from period to period, remain the same, i.e. those posed by man—by all of us as a primordial being. The time has

Its getting cold again over here—and always when it does I start thinking about how to warm up architecture, how to make it lodge round us. After all, people buy clothes and shoes the right size and know when the fit feels good! It's time we invent the built thing that fits them—us.
Van Eyck, 1959.

How to read the Primer:
The object of this Primer is to put into one document those articles, essays and diagrams which TEAM 10 regard as being central to their individual positions.

In a way it is a history of how the ideas of the people involved have grown or changed as a result of contact with the others, and it is hoped that the publication of these root ideas, in their original often naive form, will enable them to continue life.

The first part of the document—the role of the architect—is concerned with the attitudes which the subsequent project material speaks about in another way. The project material has been roughly grouped into three sections—'Urban infra-structure', 'Grouping of dwellings', and 'Doorstep'. Each of these sections tends to be dominated by one person or group—he or they, whoever developed the root idea—and the complementary or commentary material by others is printed alongside making a kind of counterpoint.

The 'carrying text'—that which is intended to carry the main message from page to page—is laid out in the largest face on the left hand side of each page. On the right hand side of the page in a smaller face is the supplementary text. Between them, in italics, are the 'verbal illustrations', and in the right hand margin, in the smallest faces of all, are the footnotes, and, in italics, the captions.

Note: The following abbreviations are used throughout.
AD. Architectural Design.
AR. Architectural Review.
AAJ. Architectural Association Journal.
AJ. Architect's Journal.
J.V. John Voelcker.
A.P.S. Alison & Peter Smithson.
P.D.S. Peter Smithson.
A.M.S. Alison Smithson.

559

7.2
Cover of "Team 10 Primer," *AD* 32 (December 1962), Alison Smithson, guest editor. Smithson Family Collection.

7.3
"How to read the Primer," page from "Team 10 Primer," *AD* 32 (December 1962), 559. Smithson Family Collection.

The important question is not "how?" but "why?" or "what for?" Town planning, like architecture, has to help society to achieve its ends, to make life in a community as rich as possible, to aspire to a present utopia.

There is no quarrel with the past; the past is a guide unless it is used to compromise the future; only the techniques and means have changed, and these "must be used to open as many doors to the future as possible."[23]

Team 10 Primer

When the *Primer* was republished in book form in 1968, Alison referred to those quoted therein as the "family of Team 10": those who had attended three or four "family meetings," were compatible, understood the "real quality of being together." These family members shared a common link, seeking each other out in order to exchange and develop ideas through built form. Their meetings displayed a "working-together-technique" whereby each paid attention to the individual and to the whole, as in any respectful family.[24] Given the emotional sensitivity of such dialogue, the family membership had to be restricted to a few. A larger organization might be good for creating manifestos, "but ideas can't be developed, can't be kept alive that way. Just as a fire always goes out if a small number of people are not on fire themselves. Team 10 is needed to keep the Primer alive."[25]

A new preface composed of "reinstated convictions" is inserted before the original Primer, which remains essentially unchanged except for a new format which no longer has the look of a catechistic bible.[26] The new prefatory text, which calls the Primer "a widely used dictionary" by clients, scientists, students, even family members, opens with a statement by Ralph Erskine explaining the purpose behind the team's continued meetings.[27] Through continued interchange of ideas, he explained, it was hoped that each architect would achieve "a certain excellence in our own work, — in architecture and community building, in speech and writing."[28]

Charles Pologni felt that *AD*'s Primer was a dictionary that need not be revised, only updated here and there to conform to Team 10's way of thinking: "Dialogues provoked in that way and the continuous contact between members will help in the evolution of the ideas, enabling them to continue their life." ... "But a good dictionary doesn't make the poet. Not even everyone using the same dictionary arrives at the same meaning for a given word."[29] De Carlo was convinced that if

7.4
Cover of Alison Smithson, ed., *Team 10 Primer* (Cambridge, MA: MIT Press, 1968).

forms appear expressive, unexpressive, unrhetorical, ambiguous, unambiguous, open, closed, elemental, complex, and so on, each of these reflects a difference on the theoretical lines and on the ideological background. ... To assess the reason of our being together implies now a confrontation of the whole system of our personal behaviour from ideology, to theoretical lines, to forms.[30]

New additions must, however, be made to the architect's dictionary. It is a matter of housing the greatest number, Shadrach Woods explained, not as the poor relations of architecture, but grouping their dwellings so they influenced the form of the city. Bureaucrats never understand that it is in everyone's interest that each should have a decent dwelling. Yet the two greatest industries, war and automobiles, both diminish the demand for, as well as the supply of, dwellings to a desperate extent: "We have to think otherwise, to image *une architecture autre* (and other politics); as we began to do together ... and, with all the best will in the world, I believe, that we owe it to ourselves to go a good bit further along this road together."[31]

"Team 10 at Royaumont 1962"

This document, first lost then partially retrieved, was published in abbreviated form in *AD* in November 1975.[32] Alison explained in her introduction to this piece that it was "quite a different 'animal' from the Team 10 Primer." It was a "chase after ideas," edited to show members of a family talking to each other. The Primer had culled ideas from their formative period "as a young family within CIAM," while the Royaumont document showed "the family in full bloom talking amongst itself, with certain guests."[33]

The need in 1975 to restate Team 10's convictions was obvious. It was important to admit and keep open the discrepancy between the loud noises of "unpoetic utopians" and the quiet voices "without rhetoric" that acted as a bond. At the time of its publication, Peter Smithson claimed: "this text is a rare and historic document. ... It is the only firm link between Team X emotions and manifestos of the fifties and the seventies when their ideas began to come to fruition ... at Toulouse le Mirail, at Terni, in the Berlin Free University, in Nakagin steel capsule bachelor apartment tower in Tokyo, in the Catholic Church at the Hague, and in Robin Hood Gardens."[34] Most of these projects were in preliminary design phases at the time of Royaumont (1962), but formed part of the backdrop to the group's discussions on urban infrastructure.

The Royaumont meeting had been disharmonious, revealing a good deal of anxiety and misunderstanding about how the "family" should proceed together. The Smithsons objected to the presence of James Stirling, and Alison would suppress his contribution in her written accounts.[35] Invited guests such as Christopher Alexander and Kisho Kurokawa introduced new topics. The influential force of Louis Kahn after his Salk Institute design (1959+) was openly questioned, as were the configurative designs of Kenzō Tange's Tokyo Plan (1961)—not to mention Van Eyck's promotion of the "casbah organisé" and his advocacy of his student Piet Blom's Noah's Ark (1962). Configurative design, collective forms, individualistic expressions, the responsibility of the architect—all were debated. As Jaap Bakema asked, "Is it true that everybody can understand what we are saying? We are always speaking English here. Well, if it is true that everybody can understand what we are saying, then that is fine, but that's the first time." Peter Smithson quickly replied: "I don't understand."[36]

One of the topics at Royaumont (1962)—discussed between "family" members and invited outsiders—was the distinction between archetypes and prototypes with respect to solving architectural problems. This discussion reveals not only how ideas were worked out together, but also whose ideas were allowed to stand in the debate and what method the accepted ideas engendered. By now, however, it was clear that the only thing keeping the family together was the commitment of its members to work together on contemporary problems, to support an open-ended approach to both architecture and dialogue. At Royaumont they struggled with the moral responsibility of the architect *not* to impose compositional solutions on "anonymous clients ... we don't see";[37] *not* to create "stiff (formalist) architecture,"[38] but to develop a system allowing for "change and growth."[39]

The Royaumont discussion opened with James Stirling's designs for Leicester University. This prompted newly introduced family member Amancio Guedes to discuss the difference between "prototype," and "archetype," asking how a building such as Leicester University can be very formal yet at the same time immensely personal, and cannot then be used as a prototype, cannot be copied around the world?[40] Stiff, formal prototypes operate at the level of ideas—yet what they were seeking was an *archetype*, capable of infinite development and flexibility. If an architect designs a prototype, "people will copy it, irrespective of what his intentions were."[41]

Here Alison Smithson inserts Peter's remarks:

> What one is looking for in a problem is its essence, its roots, as it were; and these inevitably, as human problems, stem from the same thought, is that we are men in a situation; search out the deepest roots in a situation you come up with an archetypal solution ... capable of infinite development and flexibility.[42]

Invited guest Christopher Alexander noted since there were three billion people in the world but only a few designers, something more than intuition was needed. He believed the architect's "purpose is to develop prototypes, organizational prototypes," not plastic prototypes.[43] Prototype problems are the only ones that an architect is fit to discuss.[44] Alison's immediate response is curt: "This sounds completely ridiculous. ... With the power of communication nowadays, maybe all we need is one good designer to so live with his work that he can be an example to us all."[45] Peter clarifies: if something is well done the designer does not have to generalize intellectually, because with good communication, everyone knows the solution and the person needing the information receives it immediately. Alison persists: "I think we are certainly not concerned with prototypes." And Peter says simply: "Archetype."

Van Eyck interjects: "A prototype is a fixed thing which is authorized and forced on you to do whereas an archetype of a thing is an inspiring, grand form which somehow is basic; it seems to be so valid that you can evolve your own thought from it." He considers the Marseille Unité to be an "archtype."[46] Peter continues: "so that the attitude towards producing the system produces a proliferation of archetypes: you push the problem back so that it is the general approach to urbanism and architecture which produces solutions." Alexander disagrees; this deep-rooted attitude toward archetypes is an old problem, one that Gropius tried to solve but could not. Because there are not enough architects to go around, an architect can only latch onto prototypes and repeat them.[47]

It seems apparent in this disagreement that the family discourse remained open-ended, not forced into accepted patterns of thought, allowing thought to evolve individually while remaining within the framework of an accepted position—in this case, affirmation of an archetype which other people could follow, prototypes being banished from discussion and analysis.[48]

Team 10 Meetings: 1953–1984

The idea of inheritors and successors—working together to keep the language of modern architecture alive, pushing Team 10 further along the road, so that this language would be worthy of being inherited by a still younger generation—had taken on definitive shape during the 1980s, when Alison Smithson edited another volume of Team 10 discussions, *Team 10 Meetings: 1953–1984*.[49]

Team 10 had come together, Alison thought, as a "family"—somehow sacred and inviolable, yet part of everyone's life. They were a "family of equals," a family of different individuals who talked openly in confidence the way a real family did; who followed the "lead energy as found," developing verbal shorthand and odd reference points, sensing where their discussions were going and keeping them running.[50] Alison was full of praise for how the entire "family" came together to present its members' individual ideas, debating or defending them in a state of wonder amid the fresh smell of newly worked material.[51]

The family was intentionally small, so that dialogue could fill their minds with creative activity. It was also a "private family," so "only a certain amount of agreed communication" of their thinking was published without the Team's consent. The work of Team 10 was "inward facing, but outward looking."[52] There was also a confession to be made: Alison and Peter Smithson needed Team 10 the most, and "personally nurtured Team 10 as an 'extended family'" so they could further their own thoughts.[53]

7.5
Cover of Alison Smithson, ed., *Team 10 Meetings: 1953–1984* (New York: Rizzoli, 1991).

team 10 meetings

edited by alison smithson

Rizzoli
NEW YORK

Aldo van Eyck insisted that group discussions had to be open to new members if Team 10 wanted to keep alive the language of modern architecture. In a 1969 essay, "A Miracle of Moderation," he clarified his position: to "force conception and perception (concept and the data found to support it) to coincide completely is to contract rather than to extend the meaning of either. The poetry lies in the persistence of scope—scope for undefined and latent multi-meaning."[54] In spite of Van Eyck's concern, throughout the 1970s the Team 10 "family" continued to meet and to discuss its built work—and stayed small.

The 1970s were troubling times for the language of modern architecture. The muteness of its forms was under attack by a generation of postmodern architects who longed for an architecture that communicated directly and openly with the street through symbols and signs. If architecture was to speak, then, some believed, it must be decorated with visual signs that could be read, or must at least relate visually to the city through materials and icons. These efforts to attain an *architecture parlante* ("speaking architecture") were not what some of the members of Team 10 had meant by the morality of built forms, or a democratic way of living, or even form as visual communication.

Added to this troubled environment were protests over urban renewal in city centers, calls for citizen participation in community redevelopment projects, and challenges against the Welfare State for tampering with free-market ideology. All these factors began to politicize group discussions in ways that could not be contained. "Family" members were being pulled in different directions. Probably also disruptive of Team 10 was the pessimism increasingly expressed by many architects in the 1970s—the future was lost, the time for utopian thoughts over. These pessimists believed that attempts to foresee the future or plan for its betterment were ill-fated, naive at best. Team 10's commitment to *think* together about the future as a way of *making* the future was a utopian ideal, now considered by many to be as moribund as Team 10's members once thought CIAM's original language of modern architecture to be. Ad hoc architectural expressions and short-term social adjustments, the pessimists argued, were all that should be allowed. The rise of contextual architecture, the study of urban morphology such as the street, the square and the block as the literal forms that any new architectural insertion into the city must address, completely overturned the open aesthetics and informal structures of growth and change advocated by Team 10. The search for a utopia of the present was drawing to an end.

The End of Team 10

As the 1970s progressed, Team 10's meetings began inevitably to lose momentum, and postwar modernism began to be a thing of the past. In 1974, two Finnish architects, Reima Pietilä and Raili Paatelainen, wrote to the Smithsons about an upcoming Team 10 meeting in Rotterdam.[55] They were worried about the future of modern architecture as it became a historical subject. It was no longer acceptable, they believed, that a visionary generation of architectural pioneers, the intellectual nobility in society, an intimate circle of the avant-garde, should decide on a shared message before spreading it throughout society. Was the work of a minority group still needed to keep alive the language of modern architecture? If not, then what should be the mission of Team 10 in the 1970s? "Consensus" had made a small group like Team 10, with its morality and social commitment, irrelevant as an avant-garde model. Was it possible, Pietilä and Paatelainen asked, that architecture now belonged to a postarchitectural culture?

A shift in Team 10 thinking was indeed taking place as architecture moved toward historical retrospection and postmodern pastiche. The Smithsons thought by 1977 that the collaborative meaning of Team 10 needed to be reemphasized, as individual expressions seemed to thwart their ideal of collective effort. Peter Smithson attempted to draw up "A Proposition at Bonnieux," hoping to summarize their working method. The essence of Team 10, he claimed, was

> its design morality: this long-shared morality surely ought by now to make us capable of designing reciprocally one with another as we have individually already shown that we can design reciprocally with architecture of the past.[56]
>
> I believe we are under an obligation to try and do something separately together, to do with altering the feel of the emptying cities. This would present a method for an alternative urbanism: a method which, I believe, would correspond to the next period of European social idealism. After all, why not try, most of our other dreams we have in some way realised.[57]

In spite of hopes for renewal, however, the end of Team 10 was in sight. Frequent gatherings, formal and informal, became infrequent and eventually stopped after the death of Jaap Bakema in 1981. Team 10's meetings henceforth would be a matter of memory and recall.[58] It was time to reflect on what they had inherited. Peter believed that the members of Team 10 instinctively knew that the language of modern architecture they were inheriting in 1956 needed new words, the old "tools" no longer being useful:

> New words of changed meaning enabling us to talk together about ideas born of the thirty years of achievement of the modern movement.
>
> New words for the bits we were about to invent.[59]
>
> We were reaching for the old dream that in the 1920s lived alongside conservatism, anarchy, communism, fascism, commercial democracy because of democracy turning into bureaucratic socialism (Sweden) we were believing in the individual coming into his own, moving freely through society, an educated man thinking freely (objectively, rationally, functionally) freed of fear of want, therefore of selfishness and envy, freed of ill-health, therefore energetic, creative, freed from oppression therefore making his life in his own image; choosing his pattern (his life-style) to his own mind not another's.[60]

> They were not concerned—none of us were concerned with facades but structure of the renewal, the insertion, the patterns of movement, … the housing group as place, what it looked like then their least concern.[61]

In notes for working meetings to be held in London and in Portugal to prepare for a Team 10 get-together in Rabat, Morocco (1982), Alison wrote:

> The feeling being that the mood was ripe for these two, close together, well-prepared, linked, working meetings; both to help us in the next stage of the development of our personal languages, and to reaffirm the sense of the Team X family; to touch again its supportive nature and to further tap a meeting's power of extending our minds; not least to celebrate our individual and collective confidence in the continuity of modern architecture … the modern movement.[62]
>
> It would seem that the change in the societies in which we work, for example, the change in their attitudes to nature, to conservation, to resources, should bring out from the younger of the two generations with whom we work, parallel new architecture/idea/structures such as we brought to architecture at Aix-en-Provence.[63]

Over time, Team 10 developed a long list of new concepts that had extended the language of modern architecture: "choice; identity; possibilities for change; connection (both actual and the sense of); protection from violation (by noise; of one's sense of privacy; and so on); release from pressures of all kinds."[64] That was the challenge held up to a future generation, the point of so much discussion—the study of words and concepts as moves in a game of controversies. Others might want to know: "What was Team 10?" But Team 10 might reply: "Why? What will you do with the knowledge?" Will the record of this discourse "help you regenerate the language of Modern Architecture so that it would again be worth inheriting?"[65]

II. The Myth and the Making of Team 10

In retrospect the story of Team X is one of children in a playground:
at a certain moment they need each other. Then a certain child
does not come, the season changes … the play stops.
Peter Smithson, 1989[66]

In any field of endeavor, famous groups typically go through a primary, productive period followed by a period of mythmaking and narrative-forging, a process in which members of the group may or may not participate. For decades thereafter, popular and scholarly beliefs about the group can depend crucially on who does the narrative-forging. Team 10's productive period, during which actual meetings were held, ran from 1953 to 1977; the retrospective narrative-making period, overseen primarily by Alison Smithson, ran approximately from 1982 to 1993. Through a series of seminars and publications,

Alison organized and reorganized anecdotes and archival records to produce the image of Team 10 that she desired. That image, as we have seen, centered on a notion of a multigenerational "family" preserving and handing on an intellectual heritage, was neither false nor complete.

In the early 1980s, a few years after Team 10 ceased to meet, Alison was asked by Royston Landau to offer three graduate seminars on the group's history at the Architectural Association in London in conjunction with an exhibition of Team 10 materials. As the basis of her discussions, Alison used an assembly of CIAM- and Team 10-related documents published in facsimile form: *The Emergence of Team 10 out of CIAM* (1982).[67] The time of activity was over; the time of retrospectives, revivals, and narrativizing had begun.[68]

Her outlines for the seminars are essentially a personal recall of Team 10 meetings, dealing with people and places, plus marginal asides about what was presented at these meetings. The first seminar, labeled "A Calendar of Remembrances," covered CIAM meetings from CIAM 9 (Aix-en-Provence, 1953) to the Otterlo Meeting of Team 10 (Holland, 1959).[69] The second covered what Alison referred to as "Team 10 in CIAM," how and why they were committed as a group to extending the language of modern architecture. She focused the third seminar on why students in the early 1980s were interested in Team 10.

"A Calendar of Remembrances"

The Smithsons traveled to Aix in their Jeep, parked it under the trees, entered the porch, and moved toward the trestle tables for the reception of delegates manned by students. So began (Alison wrote) a momentous journey soon to be shared with a newly found group of modern architects![70] The younger generation stayed in a hall off this main courtyard:

> The older generation were elsewhere, in one or more hotels; quite aloof for they were the old family ... we never thought to enquire where they were. The aloofness engulfed certain members of the middle generation also: BBPR [Banfi, Belgiojoso, Peressutti, Rogers], for example; although the Voelckers had worked in their Milan office during 1950 and had, with the Howells, been taught by Ernesto Rogers, BBPR were only persuaded to eat one evening meal with the young English ... more along side us, not very communicative and offering less camaraderie than complete strangers ... this lack of connective will was to provide the rotten core of CIAM.[71]

The Smithsons were pressing at Aix to introduce a new terminology, to extend the language of modern architecture over the constant resistance and blockage of the older generation.[72] They believed, at that time, that a word like "neighborhood" was debased, its imagery too powerful—consequently it was necessary to substitute a new term such as "cluster." With meager means to put their ideas into built form, the Smithsons pursued their ideas with "an intensity and an urgency that was sometimes hard to bear; for ourselves or for others."[73]

All of the Smithsons' projects in 1952–1953, she continued, had tried to present a more dynamic relationship of built work to site. On one hand they investigated the potential of earth-shifting equipment, and on the other extended the lesson of Mies van der Rohe: that one's built world could form a whole pattern. They deliberately spurned the idea of any "prima donna" building which did not want to and never could speak about a totally ordered environment.[74]

There were memories to recount from Aix as well. André Wogenscky (an assistant to Le Corbusier), accompanied by a heavy-shouldered Alsatian dog, seemed to patrol the Congress; occasionally he had to be approached in the courtyard to "clear" any use of the secretariat, set up on trestle tables under a tree and manned by students (valuable allies).[75] Jaqueline Tyrwhitt wanted all of the grilles from Aix for publication; they were stacked up on one of the hall entrances and never seen again.[76] There were other remembrances: glimpses of Léger walking with Le Corbusier; how intelligent Josep Lluís Sert appeared; Cornelis van Eesteren spoke the only understandable French; amazement over Pierre-André Emery's colonial starched cotton suits and Vladimir Bodiansky's white Russian flying suit with black boots up to the knee.[77] The phrase "Le Plus Grande Nombre"—attributed by Alison to André Wogenscky—which Aldo van Eyck knew by heart: "À chacun le droit de l'habitat—le plus grande nombre—"[78]

The Smithsons had gone to Aix as innocents, merely to address the theme of the ninth Congress, but found the Congress struggling with the malaise of a withdrawal of energy by the middle (second) generation:[79] "We felt this middle generation had let the language of architecture slip; become devalued in their hands."[80] Inspiration came from elsewhere:

> The Algerians were the most sure sub-middle generation; most of whom we knew nothing about. Their natural leader was Emery, ex-Corb office,—the architect's equivalent of de Gaulle—and by far the most striking person at the Congress, like most of the North Africans, dressed in light khaki safari clothes with shoulder tabs.[81]

At Aix, the official language of CIAM was French, and cries of *en français* (say it in French) would crescendo during general debates. On the last night, Alison remembers, the cry was rudely aimed at the Dutch, especially Van Eesteren, who plaintively replied: "But I am speaking in French."[82] The hot arguments were like wind in the treetops, beneath which the younger generation went on feverishly discovering each other.[83]

During the Aix Congress, a day visit to Le Corbusier's Unité at Marseille was arranged, where attendees heard a concert of *musique concrète* and viewed a Jacques Cousteau diving film.[84] The group of newly formed friends then drove off to Marseille's Old Port to eat camel meat ham in a Moroccan bar, led by

> Candilis in his old Dodge, [which] as we were leaving snapped off a young tree in Unité's car park. Shad leapt out and popped it in the back of a lorry … elated with the marvellous idea of the driver finding it somewhere else in France.[85]

In the Moroccan bar, around a table, in the middle of the night, the first Team 10 meeting was held: Georges Candilis, Shadrach Woods, John Voelcker, Sandy van Ginkel, Aldo van Eyck, William and Gillian Howell, and the Smithsons.

The preparatory meetings for CIAM 10 at UNESCO in June 1954, as Alison wrote—though she was not in attendance—already revealed two different strains of thought in the younger generation. Voelcker, Howell, and Peter Smithson were included in a field trip to the newly restored Villa at Garches. This group took a "binding interest in the 'inventions' of the past that served as cross-reference material to many; Bakema, Candilis, Shad [Woods], Erskine, held no inner dialogue with history; they were the children of the modern movement."[86] The tug of history and outmoded objects held no interest for them as it did for other Team 10 members, yet everyone kept their individualized interests within agreed-upon bounds.

The following September, in Paris, the group met again to prepare a statement of intent for circulation to the National Groups of CIAM 10, in hopes of regenerating the Congress.[87] They visited Le Corbusier in his rue Nungesser et Coli apartment, because he wanted personally to hand over the organization to the younger generation in an orderly manner. Supposedly, he said: "If you want to continue, continue in your own way."[88] The visit to Le Corbusier was a surprise, not only because they found Giedion there but because there was a sense of déjà vu:

> It was a more peculiar sensation to step into the studio, so wholly known from the "Oeuvre Complète," ... yet with its paintings in different positions; without the man with lamb on shoulder; with the two industrial-style racks for books; a tea trolley on which were arranged neat piles of small sketch books (publication beginning October 1981) ... the dining room with the marble table no longer shiny but well worn ... in all, a shock of beholding "instant" aging.[89]

The tenth Congress was to have been in Algiers or Casablanca in September 1955, but was postponed a year and moved to Dubrovnik because the Dutch members of the CIAM groups "Opbouw" (literally, "on construction") and "de 8" felt that "whilst our brothers are fighting for their freedom" in North Africa, CIAM should not occur there even if it meant losing momentum.[90] Despite an automobile accident while crossing Austria, the Smithsons caught the boat from Venice to Dubrovnik for CIAM 10 (July/August 1956). On board, CIAM attendees debated how to continue CIAM,

> with the result Tyrwhitt was quite bossy: being sent to argue, for the middle generation, every bit of terminology: they [the younger generation] kept sending her back to argue "cluster" (not wanting neighbourhood) until we were quite rough with her over the accepted term: "cluster of grapes."[91]

The "girls" of the secretariat responsible for documenting the Congress, including Alison Smithson, were short-tempered "after van Eyck put our first set of Team 10 documents down a lavatory—after only reading the first paragraph. I had to borrow Voelcker's portable Olivetti typewriter and re-type master copies from memory in a lunch time."[92] Alison had made a Team 10 stamp for this meeting by taking an old office stamp and resurfacing it with a linocut. Bakema was not amused by this early display of "team" identity, since his loyalties were in support of the middle generation, and even Voelcker was nervous. Alison admitted in an aside that

> Voelcker's bad nerves [were] possibly a result of discussions on the boat; possibly because he had stayed in England with his "This is Tomorrow" group and had witnessed the blazing row between Magda Cordell, John McHale and Richard Hamilton, as to the quality of "Pop" and where "Pop" became snigger.[93]

In 1956 Team 10 was not yet a family in spirit, and debates at Dubrovnik could hardly be called calm.

> It was in one of these explanatory meetings, triggered by someone—perhaps [Margarete] Schütte [Lihotzky] of Austria—speaking from the floor in German, that there was nearly a riot; Bakema leapt to his feet and said he would answer in his concentration camp German as to why he still strongly felt morality of modern architecture had to be maintained by CIAM. We understood little—as I said the official language was French and this was pushed hard; perhaps by the middle generation knowing we could not partake.[94]

The Smithsons sat beside Shadrach Woods, whose translations were cryptic, though he was fluent in French. After two minutes of somebody speaking in French, he would translate: "He doesn't agree." Another minute and a half of someone else's screamed French, and again: "He doesn't like it either." Half a minute of impassioned French … and so on. (The gist of the argument in question was that UIA [International Union of Architects] members were political "fellow travelers," i.e., Communists, and should be expelled from CIAM.)[95]

Team 10 in CIAM

It is unclear at what date Team 10 began to meet independently of CIAM, as a supportive group. Alison Smithson claims that it was in Paris, 1959: "This was the meeting when visiting as a group became established practice."[96] When there was a lull between meetings, it "was partly one of confidence in the family's being there, a sense maintained by casual contacts … [and] also due to our travelling further to seek fresh intellectual fodder, a kind of retrenchment after the blow of Brasília" (1968).[97] (The blow of Brasília was that the Smithsons' 1964 contract to design and build the British Embassy was first postponed a year by government authorities, then placed under review, and finally terminated in April 1968. Terribly disappointed, the Smithsons refused to publish their designs or to discuss the matter for years to come.)

The second seminar focused on how Team 10 grew out of CIAM yet developed a distinct set of concerns. The members of the nascent group were young and boisterous, yet deadly serious. All had survived World War II and felt in tune with the masters of the Modern Movement because they shared the principles over which the war had been fought: freedom, choice. They had grown out of the same earth as had the Modern Movement, born at its formation, so eagerly accepted the rightness of its aims and principles, the clarity of its hope.[98] Their memories were long enough to know what had gone on in the 1930s, and why a battle had been fought in Europe for *espace, soleil, verdure*. As an aside, Alison notes that it took years to understand the nature of the contribution of the 1930s and only now, in the early 1980s, could she discern the strength that surrounded the principal action of CIAM. One day there might be a sequel to the Heroic Period.[99]

> The adhesion amongst Team 10 was the acceptance of responsibility for the continuance of the main stream of architecture passing through the Modern Movement. We all ... readily accepted the task of taking up the responsibility for extending the language of architecture because to varying degrees we considered our "uncles" of the middle generation were so singularly failing to take up CIAM's hopes and—as should already be clear—all of Team 10 had a certain moral attitude towards responsibility to our societies (real or adopted).[100]

"Growth and change" was Bakema's favorite phrase: belief in change was indeed central to Team 10's thinking, and was its second bonding element (after the evolution of the language of modern architecture).[101] Other cohesive beliefs were the complexity of society and the richness of human patterns to inherit (although Alison crosses out "to inherit").[102]

An interweaving of different Team 10 thoughts began, organized toward "change"—"an evolving ever forward-looking concern."[103] As part of their responsibility as architects, they accepted that their function was to invent a language for the evolving present; an extension of the language of modern architecture that was equal in weight to that of their masters, if not equal in power because the world had changed: "Samurai gestures are just not the answers that have been needed in our working life time. So much for principles."[104] They would utilize similar means—the interchange of ideas that Le Corbusier and others had engaged in when they created the reservoir of energy that was CIAM. The elders had set up CIAM in an "academic" period, in the pejorative sense of that term; the youngsters formed Team 10 in order to end this period.[105]

Why Be Interested in Team 10?

In the final seminar, Alison Smithson wonders out loud why she is now breaking the trust made with family members not to communicate outside the group. Why is she telling the students about what had been exclusively family matters? Two reasons.

The first reason is purely functional: to get my mind round the exposure that will result from the agreed exhibition [of Team 10 materials at the AA].

A second reason has to do with the situation that half of Team 10 are now dead. ... Therefore, already, there is a sense of loss; of loss of energy; of momentum passing behind us; a quizzical sense of distance travelled; a persuasion of entering into some other phase of life.[106]

What were the effects of the Team 10 meetings? Had they made any difference? Why were students currently interested in the history of Team 10? And what did the students intend to do with this knowledge? Perhaps this rediscovery of Team 10, Alison mused in her early preparatory notes, might shed some light on the cultural turmoil of the 1980s and allow the students to "work with history" as their inheritance, in some new way.[107] Why say more than had been said in already established Team 10 publications? What had these publications intended to express that now needed further clarification? Their graphics were generated by what they were saying and how they wanted to say it; thus each document is an invention of communication.[108] "*The Primer*, the handbook for those who taught, is in the grand tradition of Vitruvius, Frontinus, Serlio, etc., in the need to make clear to oneself—in this case a family—'to see what we had got'."[109] Team 10 members were under no illusions as to what they were trying to escape from: from platitudinous generalities into fresh thinking, from poor copies of copies into invention of appropriate forms.[110] Alison believed that although CIAM's teachings had been significant, they risked becoming "academic," partly due to its twenty-five-year effort to produce a *Charte de l'Habitation*. She had warned the nascent Team 10 as early as 1956 that they should be careful about publishing "documents out of architects' drawers"—at a time when people were looking to CIAM for a lead, a new set of aims, not a catalog of old ideas.[111]

The Myth and Message of Team 10

Evidently these seminars, in addition to others given by Alison to students in America in 1983, raised more questions than answers, so she continued to ponder: *Why* were people interested in Team 10? What message was implied by the myth of the family, what by the reality? What was the inheritance that Team 10 passed on to a younger fourth generation; and what example did this group of individuals set, each in their own different way?[112]

She had written to Bakema in 1978:

Who is Team 10 is very difficult, and as in many families, at any time there are as many opinions as members; some withdraw for a number of years, perhaps due to workload, then reappear. And I think we have had rather a high proportion of deaths. ... For this reason, if there is any publication under a Team 10 name, it has been our policy that one of the members takes the responsibility of editorship.[113]

Criticism was tough within the family, helping each member sharpen their ideas, accepted in unvoiced loyalty to the Modern Movement, a moral attitude to their mutual inheritance of responsibility for extending the language of modern architecture.[114] Alison reiterated that Team 10 was kept small, a few family members to think with openly in confidence, to concentrate intensely in a hothouse atmosphere where ideas could be nurtured, flourish, and take root. As in every working family, there were different roles: Bakema and Candilis took turns in organizing the larger meetings, but otherwise all met by mutual agreement whenever the time seemed ripe, without a secretariat, the way a family does, without jealousy or worry as to who was responsible for what. People who insisted on being guests never understood this family concept and the need for confidentiality.[115]

In 1983, Alison pondered "the myth and the message" of Team 10 once again, this time in a poetic style, a frequent turn in her writing.[116] She opened her musings in the following manner:

> Team 10 was alone, a family unto itself,
> and yet it played, almost from the beginning, a star role.
> It is the exact nature of this role,
>   its influence,
>   that I would like to address
> But why now?
>   Every so often,
>   it is our personal habit,
> to stand back and see
>   what it is we have got
>   in this case, what it was we had.[117]

The dialogues of Team 10 had continued over twenty-five years, sometimes casually, sometimes in assembled meetings, without administration, without a secretariat:

> To receive some nourishment for the mind
>   you have to give something special
>   to those others with minds of an ideated form,
> and the giving
>   and the receiving,
> works most sweetly when a dialogue is established over a period;
> then communication is by verbal "short hand" …
> by establishing the odd reference point;
> the half sentence finished by a wave of the hand;
> using the easily triggered recall of shared observation
> during visits to each other's buildings …
>   for these were the locative impulses.[118]

…

Like CIAM, Team 10's magic was in the nicely balanced
sum of its members;
to the individuals, different myths attached.
Team 10 worked as it were, inward facing but outward
thinking, with a sense of reaching out towards new needs.
Because we were interested in each architect making himself
    giving his own answers.
We cannot look for the ordinary answer (to the question what did you do with the knowledge).
We are used to looking for a style
    emanating from one man
        taken up by others
listening for one theory
    which developed can become a school.
We cannot expect to find these things resulting from
the individual teachers among Team 10.
We are obviously looking straight past what its inheritors
are making of their direct contacts with their teachers,
not hearing the evidence build-up;
the spirit of hope seems to have returned to the soil
—not unlike the teeth of Cadmus—[119]
    But, no doubt, distance,
given by time, will allow us to see, recognize, the harvest
as it sprouts up,
    hear the messages;
        those will be true
attributes that will accrue to the myth.[120]

"CIAM 9, 10 … Still Counting"

To these personal ruminations of Alison Smithson on the story of Team 10, Peter Smithson would add his counterpoints from time to time, claiming in 1984: "My Story—from the edge of memory—is to be a witness of stirring times told in the old way (with heroes and gods given names)."[121] He offered his list of heroes: within CIAM were Le Corbusier, Gropius, Rogers, Emery, Sert; outside were Mies, Rietveld, the Eameses, Kahn, and Prouvé (Peter had met Louis Kahn in 1957 and Mies van der Rohe, the Eameses, and Frank Lloyd Wright in 1958). At CIAM 8 (Hoddesdon, 1951)—"There we saw Le Corbusier for the first time, instantly recognized from just the back of his head. It was an incredible moment to see a hero made flesh."[122] Aix-en-Provence (1953) was different, even better. All the old heroes were present: Le Corbusier, Léger, Gropius, Van Eesteren, and Bodiansky (a second-generation fellow in a dirty white flying suit). The younger generation was for the first time face to face with their idols.

For these children, the period of out-of-contact architect with architect (lasting ten years, from 1938–48, the Greek Civil War ending only in 1949) made the first generation of the modern movement mythical ... (The Achaeans were ten years before Troy).[123]

The old ones were heroic figures to be lived-up to ... that feeling later made necessary the ritual death of the old CIAM (Howell wrote something like this at the time); (we were all for anthropology then).

We could only live-up to them if we were faithful to our own generation's insight that the social fabric is the generating source for urban-form.[124]

He added later: "For us it was an electric time. I was thirty. Alison was twenty five."[125] The mood the English brought to Aix, Peter reflected in unpublished notes, was a consequence of the war, after which all things seemed possible. We were "confident children," believing "that Europe belonged to us," and that we had "by extension a right also to shift Europe towards a greater social equity, not through political action but by an architecture of social engagement."[126]

Historians of art like to argue that culture is enriched and deepened by clashes between older and younger generations—that a constant alternation between poles of acceptance and rejection pushes the argument along.[127] But as the Team 10 discourse shows, the third generation of architects accepted the task of keeping the language spoken by the first generation of modern architects alive, of making it worthy of being inherited by a younger fourth generation. Peter noted that both the first and third generations spread over 28 years: "1928–1956 = 28 years /1956–1984 = 28 years."[128]

But now, in the 1980s, it was time to pass on the baton again. Peter addressed the fourth generation (in an unpublished 1983 text) in the following manner:

In periods of catastrophe "what seems necessary" has to be faced ... thought out from its very roots.

What evolves from this process is, in the beginning, imageless, raw.

In the post-second-world-war period those who had lived with rhetoric for forty years were more than ready "for what seemed necessary" thought out in this way— new social institutions, new towns, new sources of electrical power, new methods of construction, new universities—all accepted raw and in the anticipation of a kindlier more just society which was believed to be evolving.[129]

For the fourth generation, however, society appeared more venal and complex than the one their parents had known:

For them, maybe, things needed to be raw again and the un-anticipated consequences of the effects of welcoming the machine faced with the radical energies of the 'twenties and the 'fifties.

> For this [fourth] generation something materialized after the first moonshot—literally a new view … the feeling that the world is both beautiful and fragile; that it is a gift we have to take care of. But it is not an absolutely new feeling and there has been time enough for something to be emerging from this change in our sensibilities.[130]

Peter believed the technology that produced the miracle of the moon shot would eventually produce technical and social innovations, although in the beginning all appears imageless and raw. But given time, this new technology would develop its form.[131]

> As architects we are energized by the new. And what is the new if it is not "what seems now necessary"; a question of one's "own voice"; of Billy Holiday or John Lennon literally; or Courrèges, or Boeing Aircraft Corporation; each of the makers of unmistakable things; each special to the culture which grows them; each true to its time; each an effort seemingly newly born.[132]

Yet the interest of the fourth generation in the history of Team 10 was worrisome, too, and Peter expressed hesitation

> to "the going-back" in 1982.
> It is from the need for authenticity that the instinctive "one must never go back" stems: to prevent the original memory being replaced by a seeming original.[133]

Yet he could not contain his own reminiscences. In 1989, Peter prepared a few comments on the work of Team 10 for a seminar in Ankara.[134] Each Team 10 meeting had a theme: a short statement about this theme written by Alison was sent out in parallel with an invitation to meet. These themes now reside in the history books: Identity, Patterns of Association, Cluster, Mobility, and so on. For the early meetings, family members brought projects; for later meetings, members went to see a participant's built work. No outsiders were allowed; mutual trust was complete in an atmosphere of true interdependence. "Commitment [to one's work] means giving a bit of oneself."[135] The Smithsons tended to present "ideas in formation"—not what they had done, but what they would try to do. The essential Team 10 ethic emerged later: "that the building's first duty is to the fabric of which it forms part. Team X's work, our work, is about fabrics; interventions into old fabrics, the making of new fabrics; repairs, patches, the weaving of extensions onto old and new fabrics."[136]

Peter Smithson would comment on what these meetings engendered at the book party in Delft for *Team 10 Meetings* (1991):

> Ideas are not bred there, they are brought towards hatching
> it is the host's duty to provide the correct conditions
> if you arrive with no eggs you come away with no chickens. (it may take a lifetime to see some of them fly).

> At Aix ('53), Dubrovnik ('56), Alison and Peter Smithson had a strong sense of mission,
> at Doorn ('54) there was a sense of mutual support, of shared feelings,
> at Otterlo ('59) of determinism.[137]

Submitting one's project to the private scrutiny of one's peers without outsiders, journalists, or historians present encouraged each to exhibit the pursuit of the perfection of their idea; this tested one's determination, one's doggedness in the pursuit of getting things right. Nobody in Team 10 tried to influence anybody (in spite of sharp criticism). "This is the thing that is hard for others to understand."[138]

Peter commented upon the central role that Jaap Bakema had played in Team 10.[139] At all meetings, Bakema's underlying idea was to substitute for the machine-like repetitions of Ludwig Hilberseimer or Amsterdam South, which was his inheritance, a more family-like arrangement of buildings. "His words varied, 'the visual group', the 'family holding hands', 'possibilities for growth', but underneath was a single idea. He never faltered pursuing this objective." Peter explained that to write down one's ideas after an event acts as a kind of fixative for ideas in development at the time, ideas held just below the level of consciousness. Thus, after an eventful meeting in Rotterdam (1974), Alison and Peter began to write their "Collective Design" essays, including one called "How to Recognise and Read the Mat-Building"—these essays "were incubated in Holland."[140]

Then, in 1993, Peter Smithson reviewed Team 10s activities one last time.[141] First the principal actors of Team 10 had to be put in place: those who came together in Aix out of a spontaneous recognition of there being others whose ideas were parallel to their own. "For the group originating then, Alison Smithson was the necessary primitive force to its existence; for she has said 'We [Alison and Peter Smithson] needed Team 10 most'."[142]

Peter called the Doorn Manifesto (1954) the founding statement of Team 10: it shifted emphasis away from the four functions to "human associations." It attempted to understand community as a "total complex."

> A long-after-afterthought on this Manifesto reveals what I now believe to be the main direction of Team X's effort, in a word towards *particularity*.[143]
>
> It is in *particularity* that the ambition of the Manifesto reveals itself; for the norm of architecture "after the books" has been to accept a formal model and to use that model more or less without regard to location (or indeed to use).[144]
>
> The Manifesto's bid for *particularity* at this most common practical level seems a natural thing. For if the house format takes account of the presence of the access land it enjoys a sense of *bonding*, a strengthened territoriality, consequent of individual actions guided by the *particularity* of place.[145]

It is the journey toward this *particularity* of place in the writings of Alison and Peter Smithson that the following chapters address.

8.1
Assortment of "right touch" tissue-paper ephemera for seasonal festivities, from Alison and Peter Smithson, *The Shift* (London: Architectural Monographs and Academy Editions, 1982), 58. Smithson Family Collection.

8

Retrospective Ruminations

[T]he subtle nature of the change in the aesthetic of our architecture during the 1970s amounted to a "stepping back" to a more recessive architecture that hands responsibility for its quality of use to its inhabitants; a "backing away" to beckon people on to creative inhabitation; a lighter touch, gently signalling to those who inhabit, to do so in a way that maintains the urban fabric and hands it on, capable of regeneration, to the next generation.

Alison Smithson (c. 1978)[1]

Prologue

A slow shift took place in the writings of Alison and Peter Smithson throughout the 1970s and 1980s. During a period of little built work, they began to look back over the development of their ideas and projects, and to reposition them within a more sensitive and contextual understanding. They developed a cyclical manner of narration based on a retrospective, rather than evolutionary, development. In writings, exhibitions, and projects, themes were envisioned as layered, flowing like underground streams that would feed their architectural projects many years later. Or, to shift metaphors: ephemeral ideas in the air drifting by were caught, looked at, and then released to find their way into other work.[2] Thus hindsight—retrospective ruminations—enabled them to navigate in the built world, partly well known to them, partly hidden from their consciousness as water might be hidden from a fish, the field of force that engenders form.[3] Collages, exhibitions, and lattices became part of their art of layering. They became self-consciously more sensitive to the determinants of place, topographies, memories, preconditions and preconceptions as inheritors of the language of modern architecture.

The responsibility of the architect-urbanist to inherited sites and buildings triggered a new series of writings on "Initiators and Successors," a manuscript sometimes considered one of the "sensibility primers," a group that includes articles published in *AD* in the 1970s under the general title "Collective Design." Long after an architectural invention, they argued, come elaborators on the theme set down in advance. Each elaborative act acknowledges the originator. Those who follow have an individual and collective responsibility for the condition of the fabric of the city they inherit; if not renewed, reenergized, it will die. Architects must be conscious of what they are doing to the balance between inhabitation and environment; they must let the natural live. This shift to a greater awareness of people, places, and nature became for the Smithsons, by the late 1980s, "the wider role of the architect."

I. The Art of Layering

The History of Layering

No doubt it was Richard Hamilton who drew attention to how lattice displays could create exhibition places of temporary pleasure. He conceived and curated the "Growth and Form" exhibition at the ICA (July–August 1951) with initial help from Nigel Henderson.[4] In a one-room walk-through installation, Hamilton's exhibition presented blown-up photographs, electro-micrographs, radiographs, and photograms of sea urchin eggs, bull chromosomes, a jellyfish, a goat pelvis, and so forth.[5] He used mirrors to relay images, flashing strobe lights, and cinematic projections above and below to decenter the viewing environment.[6] In one section of the room, an open frame-and-panel lattice structure allowing a glimpse of the wall behind added a sense of transparency to this multilayered view, enhancing a shifting of scales intended to draw the spectator's attention to his or her own role in interpreting this strange and exciting environment.

If we turn to the work of Alison and Peter Smithson, who increasingly reflected back over their work in the 1970s and 1980s, we find them drawing many lessons learned from Hamilton's display lattice and exhibition. Above all, there is a further opening to the sensibility that visual imagery bestows on perception as a major vector of architectural experience. During their long retrospective period, a duality arises in their work: they are interested in collages, exhibitions, and lattices similar to those developed by Hamilton, but also increasingly aware of places, topographies, memories, preconditions, and preconceptions as inheritors of that language of modern architecture which they sought to extend. Their examination of the situation "as found" produced an "aesthetics of change" and an "imagery created without self-consciousness"; both recall Hamilton's open-ended processes at work.[7] As Alison mused in a 1981 manuscript, "A History of Three Natures of Layering," layering of planes and posts in series and in depth entered into the Smithsons' exhibitions as well, to which color was added, building up "into a magical abstracted lattice … so many games with layers and reflection used to extend to others the 'thinking about architecture'; trying to inculcate a conscious patronage of thoughtful, considerate buildings."[8]

"A History of Three Natures of Layering" gives insight into not only the influence of the Hamilton exhibit but the convoluted linkages within the Smithsons' own thinking at this time. In their layers of rumination, ideas associate in a stream of consciousness, becoming reflective images linked one to another. These, in turn, shift the concept of architecture and its relationship to place.[9] "Layering," Alison Smithson explains, is the history of their "exhibitions in lieu of buildings; another way of learning to be an architect. … A not un-English, nor unglentlemanly [sic] activity ... Inigo Jones virtually created Renaissance Patronage in England through his Masques."[10]

If an exhibition stands in for the reality of unbuilt projects, she argues, it does so by creating a reflective place offered to the public in an easily assimilated art form.[11]

> To project the impression of layers of possibilities ...
> Of frameworks in depth
> Of perspective
> By inviting people to pass between the layers of
> Translucent screens that carry imprints of the essence of structures. They transmit the sense of inhabiting possible spaces.
>
> > Substituting for the substance of a building the very insubstantial impression of reflections playing with layering in depth. Traces of the coloured frames ... [make one] dream of another sort of place.[12]

Alison begins this layering of retrospections by reminding the reader that

> [e]very now and then it seems possible to decipher a new pattern in work already accomplished; a pattern thrown into relief by present concerns. These fresh insights lance through the body of work, showing, as it were, another grain; enabling us to not only take fresh pleasure in what we have done—but more importantly—to draw the necessary energy from our corpus of work in order to proceed. This re-consideration of a body of work is not unlike turning a prism, this way and that, so that catching the light differently, we see fresh colours.[13]

When the Smithsons are not building, they "tend to do rather a lot of thinking—in an English sort of way."[14] This state of pondering, Alison continues, is all too familiar when one is groping toward an extension of one's language of architecture, and this is why reference to the route already covered helps: retrospective ruminations are meant to extend current architectural thought. Ruminations continue the style of collage writing she has deployed before, a scanning technique gliding horizontally from theme to theme in search of parallels and similar patterns. They also accommodate the process of "layering": one idea or form selected from the past is given new meaning as it rises to the surface through layers of rewriting and repositioning.

The Smithsons were, in fact, developing a cyclical approach to writing history—the spinning of a retrospective narrative rather than the telling of a linear evolutionary tale. Past events and projects were repositioned through selective recollections that clustered around new stories and memories but were given a gloss of working all the while toward a stated goal: namely "socio-plastics," now relabeled the "responsibility of an architect."

Alison admits that the concept of "layering" may have resided in their earliest work, but only in the late 1970s, she says, did they begin to consciously talk of layers and layering and the magical change that thereby took place.[15] She reaches back to earlier

THE SHIFT

The ideas and images of these exhibitions gradually found their way into real life: as walled garden at Upper Lawn, 1959; as the seemingly private Plaza at the Economist Building, 1964; as the protected central green space and street-decks of Robin Hood Gardens. In all these designs there were territories that could be taken over emotionally, places that were intended to be dressed and decorated, and a fabric of gentle proportions that supports the interpretation of successive occupiers. To say more is to anticipate, for in the early 'fifties we were still engrossed in rounding out our vocabulary of forms.

What was the garden, the landscape with the right fit of the buildings? What were the signs of occupancy of territory, so that the building would seem naturally rooted? What to draw that was not inappropriately in the language of intersecting, winding footpaths and assorted freestanding trees of Le Corbusier's Ville Verte?

This is Tomorrow Exhibition, 1956.
Patio and pavilion line drawing by P.S.
Signs of occupation, E. Paolozzi

Patio and pavilion. (Photo: Nigel Henderson)

Opposite
This is Tomorrow Exhibition, 1956. Interior of pavilion showing translucent roof.
(Photo: Nigel Henderson)

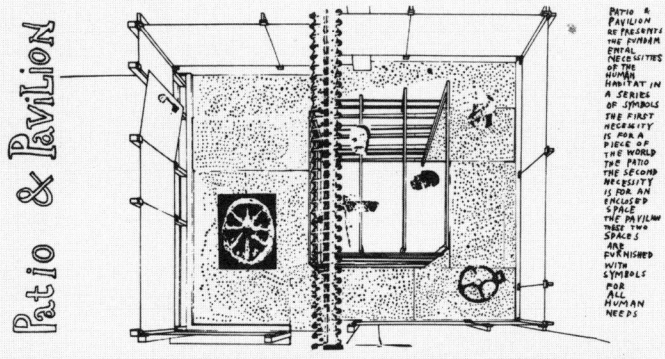

projects by outlining three types of layering and the places they created: reflection of images on transparent screens, lattices both large-structure and close-grained, and brightly colored, energizing places. Color interrupts her thoughts, she says, and calls to mind their first experience of layering color—at their Hunstanton School (1949–1954), surfaced in brick and black-finished steel. She recounts

> watching the structure go up, the colours of its various coats applied … the steel came red
> Was welded, painted silver
> Finished black.[16]

Then she picks up the thread of reflections as "layering," beginning with the private patio world of "This Is Tomorrow" (1956). There the

> compound screens of this "could-be, might-be" language were aluminium faced ply (then relatively new on the market) to produce slightly blurred, friendly—that is, not disconcerting—reflections. If you faced the reflections you saw yourself, and what was behind and beside you; you became drawn into the misty realm; engaged in make-believe as surely as if, in passing through the reflective gate, you had been transposed from the drab outside.
>
> At your feet, clean, sharp sand … Suggesting to us then, a solar-energy served society, in which an easy, Gîtane [holiday rental-home] style of existance [sic] was possible; a society in which a family would perhaps have several secure Gîtes in places where they wished to take their leisure/pleasure. The hut of random sawn planks—as if as found on the beach was roofed by clear corrugated Perspex (then also new). On this were laid relics of the world you left outside. By being arranged by Nigel Henderson these relics were presented for fresh appraisal … like a prism turning.[17]

8.2
Patio and Pavilion page from Alison and Peter Smithson, *The Shift* (London: Architectural Monographs and Academy Editions, 1982), 32.
Patio and pavilion line drawing by Peter Smithson.
Photograph by Nigel Henderson. Smithson Family Collection.

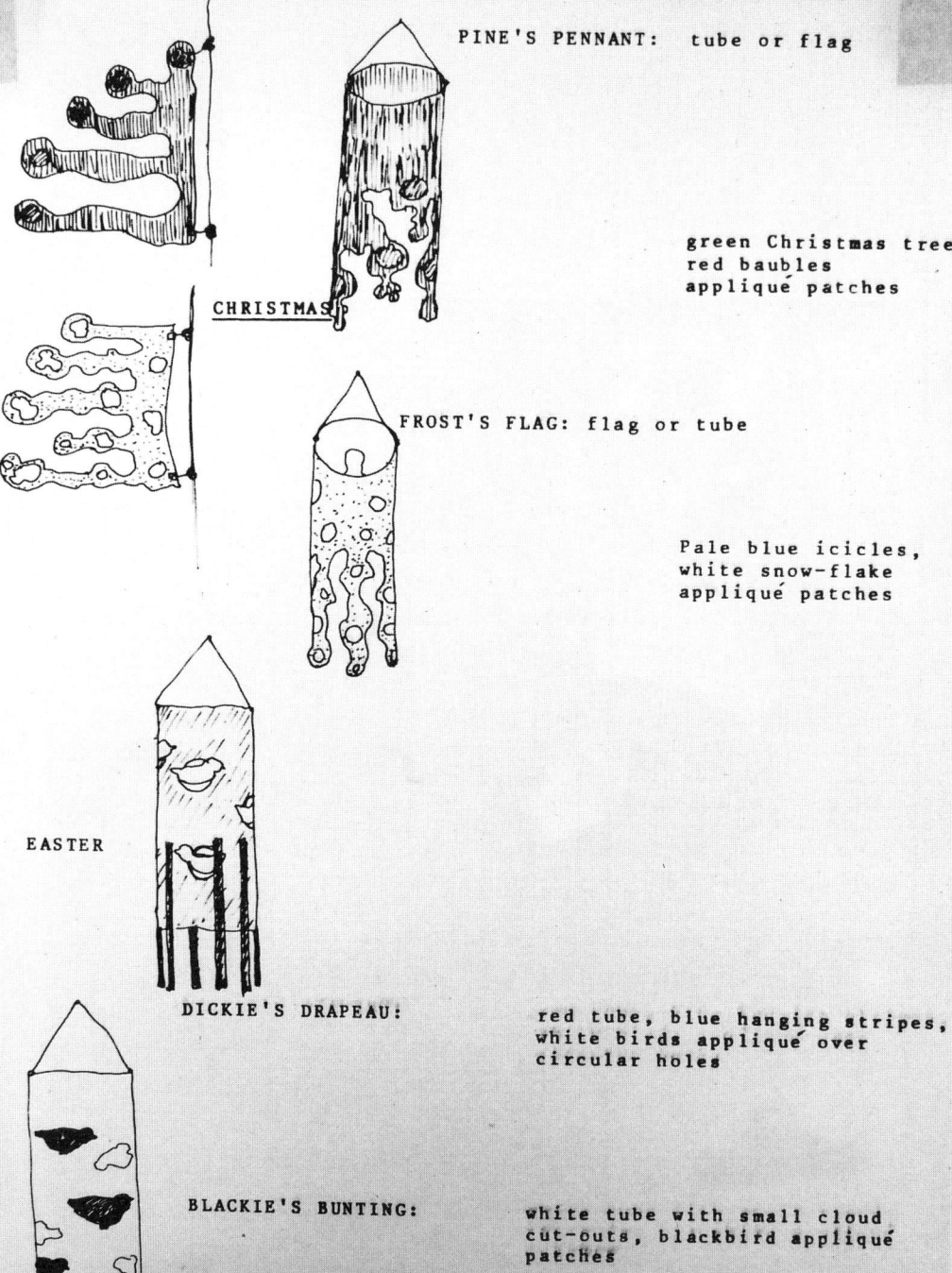

PINE'S PENNANT: tube or flag

green Christmas tree
red baubles
appliqué patches

CHRISTMAS

FROST'S FLAG: flag or tube

Pale blue icicles,
white snow-flake
appliqué patches

EASTER

DICKIE'S DRAPEAU: red tube, blue hanging stripes,
white birds appliqué over
circular holes

BLACKIE'S BUNTING: white tube with small cloud
cut-outs, blackbird appliqué
patches

All tubes cotton poplin; to be hung as wind decorations in windows,
in passageways, nurseries or outside.

The Smithsons used lattice screens in many exhibitions: for example in Edinburgh, 1975, for their Christmas Hogmanay exhibition. There, subterranean lights reflected off the red lattice structures through which spectators passed, and layers of reflections—the "'now you have it, now you don't' of silver reflections, as if the 'This is Tomorrow' was a background"[18]—began to appear in their built projects as well. "Again reflections used to settle the new into a tender group, Magdalen College, 1975 … Reflections as a way to gently add to the historic buildings; realize architecture of the barely perceptible intervention. / Reflective covers to the routes through Pahlavi Library, 1978; … streams of reflections over rills of water."[19]

Almost without realizing it, the Smithsons became interested in the "architecture of a lighter touch." This was found in gardens, where lattices create a layering of space through which the eye penetrates, allowing people beyond to become part of the celebration, enabling discovery of another, more elusive sort of place.[20] Layers happen with creepers grown on a wall, dappling the view, enhancing the play of light and shade.[21] The Smithsons discovered this ephemeral layering

> in the creepers successively grown on walls: Limerston Street, Chelsea, 1953–67 [the Smithsons' own house]. The seasonal clothing of a surface; decorating, transforming. The creeper offers a series of layers in itself, its stalks, its leaves, its flowers: Priory Walk, 1967–1971 [another Smithsons' house]. Together, cover for another layer of habitation … birds, mosquitoes.
>
> …
>
> Against a building, as a second skin, the growing layer can be thought of as an intermediate element belonging to the outside and to the inside … A bridge … a layer of pause before the building enters the air.[22]

The third story, about layers of color, begins, Alison says, with the red steel of the Hunstanton School, which had started these ruminations to begin with; this layering had to wait some time further for another colored kind of place to present itself, which it did in 1973 with the red Lucas headquarters, a colored structure that worked its way around existing lines of green trees, a landscape that was also a fringe to the city. The layers of the structure take up this theme of bridging between country and city and play with it, creating a place that invites its inhabitants to decorate its framework as they inhabit the structure. So the Smithsons came to speak of "layers of occupation" as described below.[23]

8.3
Ephemera: tubes of cotton poplin; to be hung as wind decorations in windows, in passageways, nurseries or outside. Page of drawings by Alison Smithson. Smithson Family Collection.

Shifting Ruminations

In *The Shift* (1982) and then again eleven years later in *Italian Thoughts* (1993), Alison and Peter Smithson recount a transformation that took place in both their language and aesthetics of architecture in the 1970s.[24] They had been looking most of their careers, they said, for "inter-relatedness, [a] state of change training an architect's mind in a kind of free-fall ordering" in which infinite variations and unfolding orders could and should occur.[25] To this open-ended turns of the architectural prism they now added new sensibilities, in part to deflect ill use of the built fabric, in part to invite an occupant to take on the responsibilities of inhabitation, in part to include a consciousness of layers of meaning in historical depth.

These two books continue the Smithsons' attempts to reread and reposition earlier projects within an enabling framework or "mood lattice" that marks a shift toward a greater sensitivity to ephemera, events, atmospheres and celebrations. They were looking back over their past exhibitions and projects, reflecting on how they first staged ideas as theatrical scenes in exhibitions full of ephemeral stuff before extending these into built form.[26] There were also ideas in their ephemeral writings, unconscious musings first given unclear form and then sharpened in outline over time. Some would argue strongly that this shift to ephemera was an outrage when set against their Brutalist stance; others would call it the result of reflections on a lighter-touch architecture; yet others, as proposed here, see it as a gradual unveiling of a sensitivity to the English Picturesque that had been there all along.

Never forsaking their concern for the renewal of modern architecture, however, they likened their maneuvers to embroidery of the canvas provided by the Heroic Period of modern architecture, their needle moving away from then returning to that canvas, each time tracing in the air considerations from two generations' inheritance.[27] In this to-and-fro or circular manner they developed the habit of writing down their insights and the theoretical underpinnings of what they would try to do next. Allowing an "idea-so-far" to be reflected upon was equivalent, they believed, to their "place-response" urbanism, in which what already exists on-site is reassessed in the "coming-into-being" of the work in hand. Writing and drawing alternated, the ephemeral and the permanent intertwined, graphic work and built work intermixed—always extending the associated ideas outward toward built form. Essays resulted from insights gained in construction work—more essays as construction dropped off, fewer when design and construction picked up. They were continuing a tradition set by Le Corbusier, for whom reflection and construction went hand in hand.[28] Reflection thus marks a subtle shift that questioning the road so far engendered:

> We were people picking up and quizzically turning things over in our hands, reconsidering everything ... from the shard of the antique site, 1951, picked up as a connective talisman of the most ordinary artifact, evidence preserved across time of the love put into clay by a man's fingers ... to the exotic fallen leaves of the Royal

Botanical Gardens, Rio de Janeiro, 1964 (on the advice of Charlotte Perriand, then living in Rio), picked up as evidence of another place on earth.

Things found, things cast away. The story of rejection in a society identifies strange, even remote resentments. In written ephemera we have tried to identify these blind moves—that are sometimes rages—within a society where they coincide with periods of inventive activity: the heroic period of modern architecture and graphics in Germany; the heroic period of the railways; the British in India; etc. etc.[29]

Thus ephemera of the period gave just the right atmosphere to Alison's "sensibility primers"; the stuff and decoration of the urban scene set the theatrical tone. But rage and blockages also brought awareness "that a very great shift of mind was required if a formal language was to be found that could activate, not merely support, the dressings and interpretation of things and places."[30]

"With each of these successive and overlapping concerns, with objects as found, with collage, with planes and with layers, we tried to extend the spirit of the Modern Movement beyond its heroic (and wonderfully head-clearing) exclusive Puritanism, towards an invitation to the arts of inhabitation."[31] Collage techniques, "materials as found," throwaway objects, city jetsam—the Smithsons looked at it all avidly as they struggled toward a new ordinariness.[32] They sought—their ruminations continue—"the upturning and retuning of existing space" via collages on the ceiling of the room of Ronald Jenkins (1952), decorating a box for Arup and Partners' slide projector (c. 1952), or Greek newspapers cut into polygonal strips and stuck on the basement stairwell in Limerston Street (winter c. 1953?).[33]

Reflective layering in exhibitions extended the inherited language of architecture from that of the first generation to that of the second generation as seen in many Eames exhibitions and in the Smithsons' own—i.e., "Parallel of Life and Art" (1953), "Patio and Pavilion" (1956), "House of the Future" (1956), "Painting and Sculpture of a Decade" (1954–1964), and "Wedding in the City Milan Triennale" (1968). Banners and flags became means of spatial organization,[34] allowing "constant renewal of the permanent fabric of city by transient events and decorations"[35] and offering an in-between room for illusion and change.[36]

Experiments with exhibitional lattice arrangements extended into design projects: Golden Lane's streets-in-the-air (1952–1953) and Hauptstadt Berlin (1957), for example, were read (in hindsight) as fabrics in the form of overlaid nets making interconnected spaces. Hauptstadt Berlin was

> a "platform net" of variable mesh, weaving and diminishing to respond to irregular movements and attractions for persons walking, superimposed on the largely straight-line rectangle grid of existing vehicular streets: this can now be read as one lattice overlying another[37] … the spatial form was the counterpart of an imagined social form of tangible freedom and mobility.[38]

More rereadings occur in the Upper Lawn Pavilion (1959–1980), where the new lattice frame is dropped "partly over and partly within the fabric of the accrued farm-yard walls, themselves layered on the landscape, that in England is itself all man-made layers over the land form: such is the permanent fabric."[39]

Seeing through layers, lattices, and meshes, reflections or ruminations in circular time move from exhibitions into built projects and then forward to understanding the built fabric as a layering of different uses living together in a state of equipoise. Alison wrote:

> We learn to see things as found, whose reality includes a consciousness of layers of meaning in historical depth. To be sensitive to the genius of the place it is necessary for the observer to be somewhat at peace, contemplative. To be considerate of places, things, people, is to be in some state of repose, of inner balance, of receptiveness.[40]

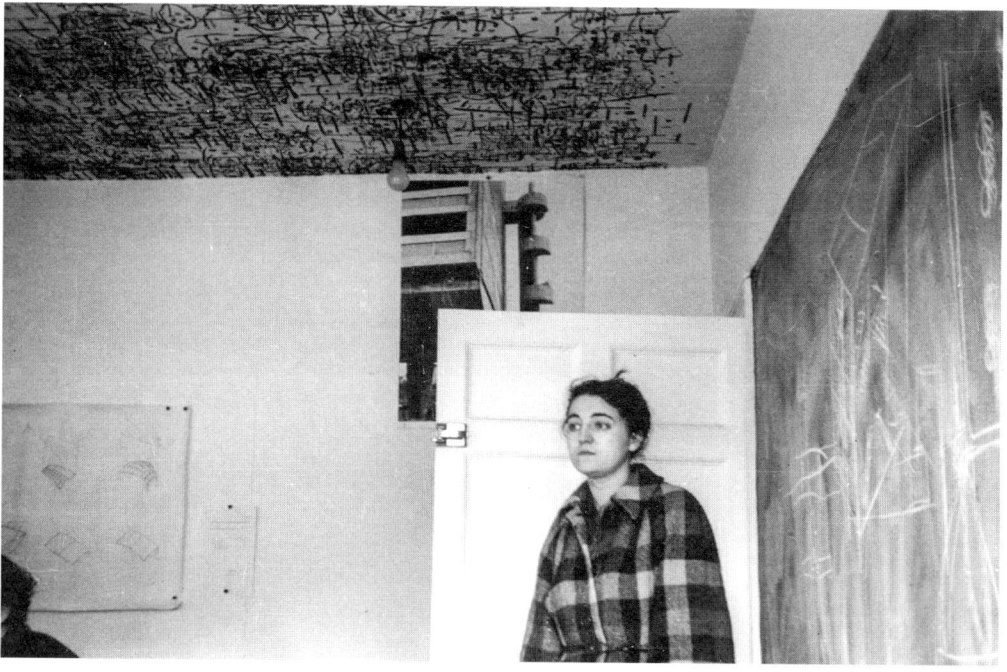

8.4
"The upturning and re-tuning of existing space" in the room for Ronald Jenkins, Charlotte Street, London, 1952. Alison Smithson in Jenkins's room; wallpaper ceiling by Eduardo Paolozzi. Photograph by Peter Smithson. Smithson Family Collection.

Peter had added his thoughts on "The Slow Growth of Another Sensibility," in 1965:

> I now think that it is *reflection*—thought, re-thought, lessons re-learned, experiences re-experienced and action taken in the light of reflection—that plays a paramount part in the growth of a sensibility. ... All the practical arts from engineering and rocketry to medicine are reflective, concerned with the inner workings of their own discipline: they're difficult, available only to a few, absolutely not instant.[41]

Buildings display a rich layering in the city by extending responsibility beyond their form, their materials, and their placement on the site to the furnishing of the city: "These extensions of responsibility—steps, railings, signs, lamps, and so on—held out a hand as it were to the next owner to act likewise by the city."[42] These layers of history express how a community wishes to behave toward itself; how it transmits order

> by making a surface to be walked on, of materials that elevate the citizen in his walking to the state of a civilized being; the size of the units of paving, their finish, the way they are laid, the appropriateness of the pattern, the style of the ordering. ... The sum of all the urban decisions as to furnishing and surfacing signal to the passer-by, citizen or stranger, the current sense of urbanity ...[43]

It is the responsibility of the architect-urbanist to understand this sense of urbanity and to respect the layers of history.

II. Collective Design

> The American artifacts which Pop artists were looking at in the 1950's had a sort of internally powered, brash, energy ... but Pop has passed: in its place, a sort of common denominator, now pressed upon us. ... American life-style threat ... to use and move on ... to me this bland, American, common denominator is the capitalist equivalent to the previous common denominator of the Welfare State.
> Alison Smithson, 1984[44]

New Keywords

Looking back from the late 1970s and early 1980s, Alison and Peter Smithson thought that their writing, polemical in the 1950s, had begun to turn inward by the late 1960s. It was then, they thought, that they began to see the pattern of what they were about. The years of writing manifestos in the 1950s—of being the bellwether of New Brutalism, stirring the formative ideas of Team 10—were over, but their ethic of responsibility was sharpening and new sensibilities were coming to the surface. They were critical of the Welfare State and its regulatory reforms, even though their own built projects of earlier years, such as their housing projects of the 1950s, were intended for London County Council estates; their Economist Building (1959–1962) benefited from the redevelopment of St. James's Street that was led by the London County Council; and the Smithsons celebrated the government-driven expansion of motorways, writing the motorways' pattern of movement into their city plans. None of these projects would have occurred without substantial state involvement. By the 1970s, however, England was in the midst of a cultural and political backlash against national development policies. There was a growing awareness that mass society and mass consumerism had brought an inevitable watering-down, even Americanization, of English culture. The writings of the Smithsons register this shift.

In 1965, they said that the Heroic Period of modern architecture (1910–1937) is "the rock on which we stand. Through it we feel the continuity of history and the necessity of achieving our own idea of order."[45] The responsibility of their inheritance from the Modern Movement remained a strengthening force into the 1970s, but one that now received fine-tuning and constant renewal. In retrospect, they identified a particular Team 10 meeting in Rotterdam during Easter 1974 as the origin of their shift in attitude toward a new humanism that brought with it a renewal of the modern tradition, a commitment to connection (of architecture to place) through repetitions, and fresh observations on the use of historic places such as Delft.[46]

At the 1974 Rotterdam meeting, Shadrach Woods's legacy was discussed (Woods had died on July 31, 1973). The Smithsons outlined a potential book or an issue of *Carré Bleu* about Woods's life's work and discussed the responsibility, now left to all the remaining Team 10 members, to absorb and deploy the ideas, spirit of hope, and morality they had developed so far.[47] "Responsibility" became a stressed word in the Smithsons' subsequent writings. They were increasingly aware, as "inheritors" of the fabric of place, that that fabric needed to be continually renewed and reenergized, or it would die. Their responsibility as inheritors was to make sure, in turn, that there was something worthwhile to pass on to their own successors. Alison would later write about the "Architect as Witness":

> Architects and urbanists address not only their own generation but the generations they knew and to which they therefore bear witness, as each architectural grandfather dies, each time the head of the inheritor is more exposed, their flanks unprotected, as their few like-thinkers are lost! The process of bearing witness opens for our generation the possibility of extending old dialogues left ravelled at a death.[48]

Peter was receptive to renewal of the modern tradition, for he intended during this 1974 trip to give a lecture at the Delft University of Technology entitled "The Free University and the Language of Modern Architecture."[49] He had sent an outline of his talk to Bakema a few months earlier, noting that

> Modern Architecture is a language: at its beginning as fresh and direct as that of Brunelleschi, and, as it continues, as capable of adaptation to changing circumstances and new sensibilities as the language of the architecture of the Renaissance.

As that beginning of Modern Architecture recedes in time we can determine something of the pattern of development of its language.[50]

With his interest in examining the contributions of different generations to modern architecture, Alison believed "it was her husband's realization that the strongest, purest inheritors of the modern movement, both in the second and third generation, worked under the strongest impulses of the first period."[51] He outlined the different extensions of this language. It began with the Heroic Period (now limited to 1922–1932), which reached the level of an architectural language with Purism and de Stijl, and served the object-building. Next it embraced the machine (1932–1939) and was adapted to mass needs, repetitive standards, and engineered constructions, yet still served the object-building. In 1952 the language accepted the city as a continuum; it was bent to existing patterns, allowing for connectivity and interactive processes. A building was now seen as a modification of a pattern in a much greater fabric. Then came the planned crescendo of his speech: "It is here the F. U. [Free University of Berlin] finds its place as one of the few really innovative buildings of its period. For those with eyes to see it opens a difficult door another 200 mm … enough to let others through." Its great achievement, in his view, was "to serve a new sort of town-fabric and a new sensibility."[52] He would later expound on this idea of fabric, calling it "the essential Team X ethic … that the building's first duty is to the fabric of which it forms part. Team X's work and our work is about fabrics, interventions into old fabric, the making of new fabrics, repairs, patches, the weaving of extensions onto old and new fabrics."[53]

With the turn to fresh keywords such as "responsibility," "sensibility," and "fabric," a new series of overlapping concerns began to inform the Smithsons' thinking and architecture: inheritors of the Modern Movement, yet interested in developing a new urban fabric and a new architectural sensibility; seeking to elevate their inheritance into a higher level of language for a changed and changing society.[54] There was also something new being expressed: a bitterness, a melancholy awareness that a threshold had been crossed and a different end game was about to be played. The Smithsons' absolute allegiance to the utopian intentions of the Modern Movement, including their ethical commitment to the development of an architecture of progressive improvement promising better living conditions for the greater number, was beginning to crack. Though this commitment had been generally shared by members of Team 10, something had gone wrong with the delivery of housing to the poorer classes; something unexpected had been generated by the inept bureaucracy of the Welfare State. This they painfully acknowledged in reference to their council housing project Robin Hood Gardens (1966–1972), which had been trashed by its "unworthy" inhabitants. Perhaps this is why the generational theme became so recurrent in the Smithsons' writings of this period, as they tried to understand how to recover the wealth of the heroic moderns, whose original intentions had somehow gone so wrong in the present.

Only if the government would get out of the picture, allowing them to relate directly to their clients, would collective responsibility for place become possible. As they expressed in a 1975 letter to Bakema,

> protest on the grounds of imbalance and inequality seems an attitude left from the turn of the century. ... It might also be for the moment in England that we have seen the best balance that can possibly be directed by burocracy [sic] and only the gradual elimination of the administration of "government" as "middle man"—for example as the present organizer-administrator between the anonymous client and ourselves—can make for the next step (and make me breathe more freely). A return to action, a turn away from paper-work: true contact.[55]

The Mix that Makes Sense

From Alison's admiration of Peter Rabbit's cupboards to Peter's discussion of heroic relics such as arcane trams or antique locomotives, to the titles of their two books of republished essays—*Ordinariness and Light* (1970) and *Without Rhetoric* (1973)—unstated assumptions about what it means to be English in times of retrenchment abounded. The Smithsons were nonconformist yet traditionalist, aware that things need to be both ordinary and heroic. They wanted it both ways: an England of traditional villages and bucolic landscapes with the aesthetics of the automobile somehow written in; a city that services the needs of a technological society yet reminds one of Camelot. They write of this ambiguity in *Without Rhetoric*:

> For an English architect—fed from earliest years with sociology and with the theory of the picturesque—awareness of the mix should be easy. But, there is all the difference in the world between "melting-in" and the deploying of an ordering which can make the whole mix makes sense.[56]

The mix that made sense entailed, for them, a sensibility to human patterns of inhabitation and to the collective—not an individualistic language expressed by object-buildings that spoke of repetition or ordered sameness, but an alertness to how people read signs of the city and instinctively know what they are to do and where they are to go.[57] This mix, with its unspoken assumptions about how the English read the words of their culture, is particularly evidenced in their writings on "Collective Design" in the 1970s as well as in the unpublished essays (1980s) that extended their thoughts on responsibility to the fabric of cities, which I discuss below.[58]

To the Smithsons, seeing the city as a collective work of art meant that they must find the right words to constitute a form language for contemporary times.[59] In an unpublished "Introduction to Places Worth Inheriting" (1983), Alison wrote that we most often associate "structural" changes in society with the violence of war, in which the state has the power to disrupt and destroy. But now individuals take up this attitude of "war" against places,

> disrupting the fabric of towns and cities for quick gain; mean-building replaced well-building. Faced with this physical evidence of disregard for society, this disparagement of civic pride that had been expressive of "togetherness" bred internal enemies until the threat to security has become a disease.[60]

If all the costs to Britain alone were added together—those of

> the magistracy, the judiciary, the prison system, the probation system, the police, the Diplomatic Protection Group, the army-in-defence-of-the Civil-Power, the Staff Colleges' work on anti-terrorism/anti-subversion activities, the secret State internal security services, the private security companies, the railway police, and so on and on …

—the amount would probably equal the total defense budget added together of every country in Western Europe. "That is the effort of protecting against the internal enemy is greater than against the external enemy."[61] Obviously, this money would be better spent on curing such wanton diseases as spatial destruction. We must, Alison continues, remember the lesson of the nineteenth century:

> that wide streets, the clean-water, the sewers, the public wash-houses were municipal adventures with private money: the continuation of a much older impulse to civic well-being and civic pride. … Acts of conscience, the arts of the middle-class.[62]

Social change in the nineteenth century was a product of peace and an idealistic hope of defeating human miseries: sanitary improvements, cheap transportation, the Arts and Crafts movement, the Garden City movement. "Each took place when their parent community was largely at peace with its external enemies and friends outnumbered internal enemies."[63] Internal and external forces worked together to produce the shape of things to come:

> Structural changes came about through a multiplicity of small interventions organized from a multiplicity of wills-to-change and their differing sources of investment. The small, precise, accurately directed intervention—the so-called homeopathic intervention—then caused a major shift in the direction of our culture. … The shift now must have to do with an enlargement of choice.[64]

Recognizing the failures of the Welfare State in the provision of housing, acknowledging that civic interventions of the nineteenth century were often the acts of private citizens, holding the recipients of government largess accountable for not understanding the laws of the collective, were indicators of the Smithsons' shift toward the conservative politics of the 1970s.

Initiators and Successors/Inventors and Inheritors

Alison Smithson, always interested in the "quality of place," wrote Bakema in 1976 to summarize her current position on collective responsibility. She included her unpublished essay on "The Quality of Place," explaining that the English were always concerned with this issue, and she believed that the "continual renewal of this quality is a collective responsibility of maintenance and should be the result of a meaningful, if instinctive, dialogue between the love bestowed by the occupier and the sensitivity of the form giver."[65] Applied to the built environment, "quality" had now to be extended to include the spectrum of meanings concerning a satisfactory life in various kinds of places, as well as the idea of restoring a creative interaction between individual and collective responsibility.

Quality of place, Alison argued, had two aspects: the tangible built form and the intangible, appreciated form.[66] The latter had to do with human connection, attitude, and accepted patterns of use. It is the "stuff and decoration of the urban scene."[67] But since the 1940s, ordinary people have seen a loss in the quality of place. "The idea is to restore creative interaction between individual and collective responsibility as to quality of place: a fragmenting to this end of the growing bureaucracy whose unproductive control the collective can ill afford to support and no wish to live with the results."[68] Confrontation results when changes are administered or planned for instead of resulting from direct contact and "finger on the pulse" of those who live in specific places.

A great concern for the Smithsons in the 1970s was the nature of collective responsibility for the quality of place. They believed that long after an architectural invention is made, others elaborate on the theme. Each act is made in acknowledgment of the originator. Those who follow have an individual and collective responsibility for the condition of the fabric of the city, which they inherit.[69] The earliest impulse to mark out time and place (season and territory, measure and pattern) is followed by the desire to elaborate, to enhance, to decorate. Take the Greek temple, for example, the result of a long-lasting embodiment of an idea generated by a set of men, but able to receive extension of meaning or tokens of renewal from other men long after the initiators were gone. These changes, ephemeral or not, might last a day or an age, but each was made in acknowledgment of those who had come before.[70]

Because of the British loss of "urban nerve," Alison reported, there was a need to regain sensibilities as to the quality of place, and to engage the individuals in the renewal of their responsibilities. Toward this aim, they had directed a major writing and design effort reawakening sensibilities and forming buildings that responded to climate, movement, times of day and season, rituals of cohesion and expectancy.[71]

Hence the Smithsons drew together a never-published collection of writings under the original working title *Initiators and Successors: Rebuilding the Meaning of Cities*, a manuscript sometimes referred to as one of the "sensibility primers." This combined the "Collective Design" article series published in *AD* from 1973 to 1975 with various rearrangements and additions made in subsequent years.[72] Peter's particular intent in

8.5

Peter Smithson, "Collective Design: Initiators and Successors," *AD* 43 (October 1973), 621. Smithson Family Collection.

this collection of writings is to further the form language of architecture, while Alison directs her comments toward the social context in which this language is spoken. They construct a discourse that tries to strengthen the connection between an ideal base on which modern architecture stands and the contemporary concerns of a machine-serviced city, which this language must also address. Historical examples are particularly prominent in this series of articles, for they are the rock on which the form language of modern architecture could be stably based while being brought up to date.

Concepts worked out in earlier CIAM and Team 10 meetings, such as "identity," "association," "cluster," "mobility," now find corollaries in interlocking meshes between past architectural forms and present uses and sites. The rhetoric of their written statements, the aesthetic clarity of their vocabulary, the examples they reflect on, and the visual images they deploy intermingle as perfect counterpoints or working meshes. They are concerned with the inner workings of the language of architecture with lessons learned and relearned in different contexts, and seek to apply these design principles in an open-ended, nonauthoritarian fashion that allows for "growth and change." The wish is to keep the delicate elements of the urban fabric quietly and calmly talking to each other.

The Smithsons begin their discussion that will lead to the "Collective Design" series with a 1972 essay subtitled "Signs of Occupancy." This opens with a statement about an ideal house being "that which one can make one's own without altering anything. Make one's own in the usual way, that is within the limits of the fashion of the time, and without feeling any pressure either to communicate one's trivial uniqueness or to absurdly conform."[73] The search for a style to match this ideal is "the floating centre of our design effort." They are looking for the gentlest of styles, one that gives a notion of structure within but leaves itself open, even suggests interpretation without itself being changed. "Style" is important because it

> is a special flavour of form-language that is fundamental to architecture. A word which is solidly established in form-language can help one to recognise self; and, at a practical level, it can tell what a thing is and how it is to be used. ... The words of a form-language ... are inventions; the evolution of the language not the work of a particular person but of a whole period.
>
> In our period we can recognize certain needs, that have been with us for years and can reasonably be assumed to be a permanent aspect of our life, for which no appropriate forms have been invented.[74]

Based on this idea of collectivity, older form languages were "instant communicators," but today, the Smithsons argue, there are many usages without form, such as the journeys from a car park to a supermarket, garage to house, car silo to terminal building, underground to office. And many contemporary places, such as "Disneyland, and lately Port Grimaud, which are so unashamedly pleasure indicating forms that one suddenly begins to think of the language of present day architecture as a pretty inarticulate affair."[75]

"Standardization," once committed to solving the problems of the many, now communicates merely "indifference," even a kind of "indolence."

A form language makes a clear statement about how one dwells in mutual social support. Indicating clearly how a place is to be used, it never leaves occupants in doubt yet refrains from telling them where to walk or to play. A form language, the Smithsons declare, indicates and enhances the use of places; it sets up a dialogue between architectural objects and users. If it is used well the object improves, and if it is used badly the object degrades and the dialogue ceases. The task of the contemporary architect-urbanist is to develop a form language for the contemporary stage of industrialized society based on the pleasures of common usage.

Peter Smithson opens the "Collective Design" series with an essay subtitled "Initiators and Successors."[76] The message becomes clearer: a dialogue between user and object depends on collective action. The base form is first initiated, then perfected, before being invested with deeper levels of meaning by successors. To explain how this form language is elaborated over time from initiators to successors is Peter's charge. He uses as examples Greek temples, town squares, and high streets. Each, he claims, is an embodiment of a long-lasting idea that can give rise to elaborations over time that acknowledge the generating form. Thus the architect contributes to collective design: the addition of a single building to an existing group ensures that its space locks onto existing ways and geometries, and is itself "dressable." He again likens style to a "flavour" in a form language and draws another analogy from his bag of historic examples: the architect is "anticipating the occupier's and future occupiers' design activity as a ship is designed in anticipation of its three-yearly re-paint, designed in a way that knows what change and re-generation a re-paint can bring."[77] A collective design for an entire building group therefore requires general agreement on its "common generative intention" and awareness of its ability to *respond.*[78] The aim is to develop "an urbanism with a sense of unfolding":[79]

> Reciprocity—the response to what is already there, the mechanism of unfolding—seems generally to be a difficult idea ... that a new building, or an open space, or a new means of access, or a new wall, or a change of level can sustain an already established collective notion and at the same time give it a new inflection, runs against the norm of architects' perception of their activity.
>
> It means submission, yet demands real invention, something absolutely specific to place.[80]

The Smithsons would measure a building's effectiveness in two ways: how far it communicates "the dream" of its originator, and its day-to-day "livability." The dream requires "lightness of touch," which in turns allows a building to be "interpretable" by its occupiers in novel ways. This makes a building what Peter calls "dressable," that is, capable of responding to seasonal or festival decorations, or to temporary ephemeral changes made by the occupant, without any need to shift the underlying structural form or destroy its meaning.[81] Thus, for example, the Smithsons' exhibition for the 1968 Milan Triennale was a dressable tableau called "Wedding in the City." The nineteenth-century city had been full of these dressable assets:

> *The space between* being constantly transformed by tram-wires, lamp posts, change of paving pattern; by the horse-manure that Ruskin hated, by carts, cars, tourist buses; by rain and floods; by weddings, funerals, seasons and ceremonies; by street sellers, shop-fronts, sky signs, graffiti, posters; by people's ways of walking and dressing and by what they are carrying. All these things are the city's invisible decoration, invisible because they change so slowly, because they are so normal.[82]

8.6
View of one end of the exhibition "Wedding in the City": traditional decoration of the city by use. Milan Triennale, 1968. Alison and Peter Smithson, *The Shift* (London: Architectural Monographs and Academy Editions, 1982), 15. Smithson Family Collection.

The Violent Consumers

By the 1970s, as we have seen, Alison and Peter Smithson were disillusioned with the Welfare State's policies and programs. It was time, they felt, to get rid of the intrusive State that dictates moral rules for ordinary citizens. Disrespectful inhabitants had trashed their Robin Hood Gardens apartment block (1966–1972), presenting them with a new dilemma. This architectural project had been willed to society; it was a collective design, not meant to be devoured or destroyed by its occupants, yet: "The week it opened," Peter exclaimed, "people would shit in the lifts, which is an act of social aggression."[83] The causes of such consumer violence were historical: since 1947, Alison lamented, the State had encouraged locally inspired destruction of the urban built fabric, leaving holes in the center of cities. "This destruction effectively killed the idea of city as a consistent civilized inheritable place and contributed to the loss of whatever urban nerve the British ever had."[84] She listed the effects of such destruction: loss of pride of place; blight feeding vandalism; swings of recession in the construction industry; and "lack of choice due to a high proportion of the bravest proposals being obstructed."[85] The Welfare State had promised but not delivered "some rationalisation as to placement, some clear order signalling the greater equality of the collective. … [T]he planning legislation has also not done what it stated was its reason for being, avoidance of land waste, sprawl."[86]

> Fashion in lifestyles and social ethics play over the face of cities: we see built fabric used over generations. And to sustain this long-term use, individual buildings need to have a quality of fabric; provision of quality being an affirmation of respect for, and belief in society, a visible confirmation of subscription to that society, a willingness to further ideals. Lack of quality speaks clearly to everyone of the converse.[87]

Thus the next "Collective Design" article, by Alison, is subtitled "The Violent Consumer, or Waiting for the Goodies," and is a full-throttled outrage against the failures of the Welfare State and the trashing of Robin Hood Gardens.[88] Alison opens with the following disclaimer: Words such as "jealousy," "greed," and "avarice" were used in the first consumer society of the nineteenth century to express "revulsion" at the disintegration of character witnessed in those less fortunate workers who produced but could not consume "the multifarious supply of *goodies*." The same words, she notes, have been resurrected in the present age of resentment but are now used to characterize almost the whole population, whose members feel they have been marked down by the affluent society because they are not frontrunners in the race to consume.

Acerbic words describe the destroyers of the "goodies," whom Alison now feels bitter about. Not only do these persons feel marked down, but they resent the handouts and many-layered social services provided. They even become vandals and destroy their subsidized homes and places. With no sense of accountability or any kind of collective tenant control, the welfare system grinds on relentlessly: "But the lack of reciprocal obligation is there for all to see, encouraging to the *baddies* to continue their destruction, immensely discouraging to the creators and providers of the *goodies*."[89]

Though with good intentions, architect-urbanists unaware of this widespread discontent keep designing forms ill-matched to the needs of contemporary society. This is paradoxical:

> By tradition, modern buildings are releasant, not at all overpowering or threatening. Yet it could be that this very quality does not provide the necessary *protective* framework for lost human animals: the apparent lack of discipline, the light touch, the lack of rigid, strict, imposing rules might be actually bewildering to wild human animals requiring basic rules for decent life.[90]

The media have not helped to alleviate the situation. First in films, then on television over the last four decades, the media give the impression that "baddies" are subdued by a "goodie" who sweeps in, sometimes subverting the rules of the Welfare State, to do a little philanthropic service before vanishing into thin air. The "baddies" learn from these examples just how far they can go in their wanton ways:

> Mass communications tend to be an iceberg: the bit most of us never see—baser films, banal magazines or comics, baser instant paper-backs, blatant advertising—is that to which the ship of state is most vulnerable. The hidden bulk of the iceberg out-balances all the visible face civilized society judges as acceptable—that is, free education, the family, the creative minority in the community, the myriad balancing *good* works of government, state, municipality, and institutions.[91]

The Welfare State, the architect-urbanist, the media—all deliver corrosive messages! What is required is a "precise meshing" between resources available and collective ideals shared by the makers of society over what they want society to be. This meshing would entail an honest understanding that care of possessions does not result from an increased supply of "goodies." It is a matter of establishing a dialogue: to reveal the desired patterns of association and identity and to remove the hidden costs imposed by the Welfare State. Through dialogue, disgruntled tenants might realize that their resentment derives from feeling trapped in the city, immersed in an anonymity they find alien and frightening. They must be brave enough to leave their detested council flats and target more realistic dreams cut to their size. They might even decide to leave the city behind, moving to easier-going places with a less competitive pace.

Even the British education system is part of the problem. Why, she asks, should everyone be given the same level of book learning, while the training of students for the interdependence that community life requires is neglected?

> Some syllabus must be capable of transmitting the nature of civilized community; in all its aspects, self and possession maintenance, self and budget management, the where-with-all to make value judgments in the face of the mass media geared to selling, responsibility for self and others.[92]

Welfare recipients, she opines, do not understand what it means to be English: "We assume we are English with English standards, and that all-comers see these standards clearly and will go along with them and contribute to their furtherance."[93]

She decries the fact that society since the nineteenth century has failed to find a method to diffuse accepted English standards, ethics, and unspoken codes of behavior to all of its members. The result of this failure is, she says, obvious:

> de-Anglicizing ... effectively swept away the incestuous control mechanism of our Englishness. The glue of a particular society became less and less adhesive. Gradually, the visible result, a hundred years after such emancipation we see the loss of the particular English milieu: today an indigenous cultural mix that permits the last break-up of towns and cities, and these somehow get rebuilt in a life style more alien to many of us than ever were Victorian Italian Romanesque or Victorian Venetian Gothic. In many buildings, added even to cultural institutions, instinctive sense of English scale seems lost.[94]

Veering between the moral decline of welfare tenants and the visual disarray of the urban fabric, Alison is caught up in the twists and turns of her own critique. For many users of the city, she complains, the mix is becoming incomprehensively strange, even though we continue to assume "our communal Englishness." This is now patently impossible, when migrants are so many strangers in the land. She repeats her basic argument: the provision of welfare services without prior thought gives cause for the beneficiaries to smash and foul in blind violence the sections of the city so provided. Large urban building complexes are the reason why the "them" and "us" of nationalism, patriotism, and religion have been transformed into "mass-resentment movements of the haves and have-nots."[95]

Alison suggests fragmenting mass movements into smaller, more manageable groups as a potential solution.

> Fragmentation, so that the pieces each become the size that mends minds, responding to those demands in society that are poles apart at the moment: the wish for anonymity—or identity; the desire for pattern of association—or dissociation; a turn away from the solution to be universally consumed toward solutions personally made or chosen; a return to different quality of life to be enjoyed in built places.[96]

She turns back to the architect-urbanist, and to places overrun by tourism and distorted by the consumer ethic. The moral responsibility of the architect-urbanist, she argues, requires him or her to provide different places that are "work-based, ethnic-based, mind-reasoned ... whatever real motivation can be brought together, so that each maintain their chosen characters and become more themselves."[97] This will inevitably lead to the rediscovery of patterns of association where like-minded people, "in unison with mood and quality of life," will find a place. Alison Smithson has made a full retreat from the utopia of the present and ideals of "identity," "association" or "cluster."

COLLECTIVE DESIGN: REAPPRAISAL OF CONCEPTS IN URBANISM

Alison Smithson

The Garden City . . . think about it . . . what does it suggest? . . . simply houses set out in a garden; no sounds louder than the birds, no pollution to disturb the calm of the garden; all the looser-knit pleasures houses take in an expansive garden: no roads! no cars!

To make this thing, the *Garden City*, that has been talked about for seventy years or more, we still need a special order of a looser kind of thinking. The horror of the actuality of Letchworth, or Welwyn, is of a laid-out amorphous suburb, where one immediately gets lost looking at awful houses, barely screened by handsome planting, bordering meandering roads of equal value that lead goodness knows where.

We still need a way of thinking *garden city*; not in terms of a density – such as a town is wonderfully dense within its fortifications – but loosely, without roads and regular putting-down of units, municipal impedimenta, all the clobber of urban-man.

A change to garden-thinking . . . one does not get lost in a proper garden. The term *garden city* should refer to all that is the reverse of the layered strata of historical meaning and consciously urban disciplines, without falling over into historical-agricultural analogy. The garden city must show no signs of bureaucracy, nor the same self-control necessary for an urban area.

Being unclear about what *garden city* should be, means we have also become sloppy at all levels of thinking about the converse, the true nature of city . . . without which we cannot be lucid about the way any urban-form is acting on the urban fabric: nor can we know how to care about lack of clarity. A garden city might need a wall . . . the majority of gardens have some kind of boundary.

Wall-building . . . Lou Kahn, at Otterlo, took umbrage at any idea of people as gates, yet played the Carcassonne game the rest of his life, and – in the face of economic circumstance, one supposes – made people-cabinets for state housing. A wall with people inside, a sheltering wall . . . Beginhof, Antwerp; in its inside, a surface of windows set discreetly back behind yards and out-buildings which might be wash-house, entrance hall or chapel. In its narrow street, the wall, giving seclusion to out-buildings and yards, is softened for the Servitors of those in the seclusion of these almhouses, made thought-worthy by the language of architecture.

The use of walls to the outside world, to the inside world, here demonstrates clearly there are a number of ways of protecting others while protecting self . . . provided the language of architecture is rich enough. We know the device of the acoustic wall, which can even be in series whose gradual stepping-up provides greater and greater acoustic-shadow and protection to levels behind. Higher walls returning to the language of architecture of low-wall-beside-people, high wall above people, higher wall way above people.

'Courtyard of the almshouses'. Painting by Johannes Jelgerhuis, 1821.

Begenhof, Antwerp.

Begenhof, Antwerp.

The Kaiser Wilhelm period, Berlin apartment-house-façades extended the language of the *palazzo* as far as it would reach. With the time of the introduction of lifts, came other kinds of equality as well as the mechanical, parting people from the traditional stacking common to European cities; a layered arrangement whereby the noble in spirit could find their economic level *sous les toits*, over the noble in birth: comprehensible form made obsolete with accessibility, undesirable with resentment, eliminated by political/bureaucratic systems of administering equality. What language finger-holds do we have left on big wall, bigger wall, if the most pervasive pressures have been all kinds of equating, levelling ones? What anchors are there in the protective-urban-living-wall for any language of architecture rooted in traditional ways of communicating about people to people? What is the nature of such private-life-protective walls, where the end wall of the last unit of a standard row is actually doing a different job, whether it is the quiet end to the inside of a group, or the end to the external, noisy world?

Naturally enough, as places where families are to live have got higher off the ground, we have become aware that needs become differentiated in so far as security in space is concerned. When high wall is façade to many levels of dwellings, each level ideally requires:
different balcony heights;
different window conditions;
different openings for looking out at different sky/ground relationships;
different width to cill and balcony top;
a change in the nature of balusters;
different types of *open space* available to each dwelling;
different protections to collective-use space.

But in the interests of economics, standardisation, democracy as politically/bureaucratically operated, simplicity of thought/instruction/action, none of these qualities of difference have been explored since the beginning of this century.

Berlin apartment-house facades

Berlin apartment-house facades

Smithson sketch (from *Uppercase* 5) . . . 'When high wall is facade to many levels . . .'

COLLECTIVE DESIGN: COLLECTIVE QUALITY

Alison Smithson

The time of the feast without thought for the quality is hopefully over. The period of collectivity begins with collective thinking, and that requires a quite different mental framework. Take as an example how an action purely for more pleasurable circumstances taken by an individual inside his house can affect the collective . . . a neighbour can build a chimney for a newly positioned fireplace in an opened-up house; the collective might have designated the outside envelope of the house as part of a place worth preserving; yet, like-as-not, the man will, where obvious ignorance and modern insensibility are the best armour against control, manage to remove the old characteristic chimney from its traditional crest position, and slap up a new chimney in a very untraditional relationship to roof and outside walls: of course perhaps re-using the bricks or other minimal-cloak-device. Only the man of trained sensitivity for the old quality knows exactly what is wrong, and mayhap, as one of the neighbours, is the only one of the many daily observers who is actively hurt by the action. The man in the house sees nothing, feels nothing, knows nothing but the warmth of his fun-fire. The bureaucracy of the collective can control, but control is often pushed only so far as it is sensed the controlled can comprehend.[1] The collective neighbours are for the most part, unknowing of what is the deep nature of that being preserved in their name and sometimes with their participation.

Protection of the fabric of our possessions is tempered by our consumption from the market . . . we may ourselves not directly get full qualitative benefit for our actions in the collective except in the mind . . . when a man paints a house – the outside of a house – only from certain positions near his windows can he see that his cill, his reveals, his window-bars, are so and so. All passers-by see; all his neighbours live with his house in their windows: chimney and house painting are true acts of the urban collective. No amount of guided participation by sociologists will guarantee the quality of the act; it is by chance if a specialist in a relevant field is one of the collective and articulate and forceful enough to communicate his expertise to the others.

Then where is the freedom of the individual to remember quality, have a quality insight, make the instinctive, unpremeditated contribution that might enrich the depth of quality of place?

What is the collective nature of the civilising choice? Keeping to this problem of the house, how do we play the Pieter de Hooch game? . . . match the inside to the outside face, and both to daily life? . . . the acts of placing, caring, renewing, cleaning, enjoying . . . so that they mesh together to become the fabric of a culture? . . . every item of life contributing to a unison whose nature joins the poetry of the collective?

A feast . . . or a culture?

Collective thinking – to achieve the Pieter de Hooch plane of consistency – has to become a supportive, all pervading feeling for quality . . . perhaps we now want it many-streamed in response to wide-band world-culture. If we like to think in terms of severality – the co-existence in parallel of a variety of quality collectives – it would appear that each quality-group has to be large enough not to have idefensible raw edges vulnerable to unacceptable pressures from the next different group.

Existing achievements of collective life: building control against collapse, for fire-protection and escape, health control against disease spread, are sorts of collective control we are barely perfecting; most would think it quite stupid to hazard a break-down of such measures designed to protect the collective. In speaking of severality of choice of quality-difference we are all assuming that the other quality-group's freedom will not threaten or endanger personal or collective freedom in any way proven unpleasant in the past. That is, society tends to think of the Arab Quarter in Marseilles, the no-go area of Belfast, Harlem or Watts, as quality-differences of barely tolerable sorts because threats pop out of them in various guises, they can be used as hide-outs; and it is occasionally clear that all is not well inside these self-declared areas . . . the people inside are dissatisfied with the collective they themselves have made and do in fact suffer for the way they have framed their outlook on the world outside. We extend pity to these people because they seem to insist on a self-afflicted way-of-life, on old-life-style in the sense that the Irish have been classified as seventeen[illegible] centurists . . . . everything brought to a confrontation of force: in Paine's mind, a Burke[illegible] world, outdated, invalidated, by the message of the French Revolution. Man makes the slum, the slum cannot induce slumminess where none existe[illegible] in man : although it may brea[illegible] hearts. Yet it is suggested th[illegible] the difficulties of these old-lif[illegible] style people, full of force a[illegible] antagonism when stirred, ca[illegible] become solved through partici[illegible]pation.

What is the nature of par[illegible]cipation? How achieve particip[illegible]tion among an odd collection [illegible] people whose only collecti[illegible] ideology may be their followi[illegible] of football: for their being sta[illegible] housed is not in their opin[illegible]

Pieter de Hooch consistency

Baucis and Philemon

. . . Their poverty was no burden to them, because they admitted it and bore it with contented minds . . . When the two gods reached this humble house, and, stooping down, went in through a low door, the old man Philemon pulled forward a bench and invited them to rest their limbs. Baucis hurried up and busily threw a rough covering over the bench . . . and Baucis, with her skirts tucked up and with trembling hands, began to lay the table. One of its three legs was too short, so she put a piece of pottery under it to make it level. . . . She wiped it with green mint, and put on it, all in earthenware dishes, some green olives – the fruit sacred to Minerva – some autumn cornel fruit that had been pickled in wine, endives, radishes, and eggs lightly done in the warm ashes . . . and around the table there were cheerful faces, friendliness and ungrudging kindness . . .

From *Men and Gods* by Rex Warner.

Reappraising Urbanism[98]

Alison's next attack, in "Reappraisal of Concepts of Urbanism," is waged against the worn-out policies of the Garden City ideal once expected to stop a flow of population from across the former Empire crushing into the core of London. Even though the State-mandated creation of green belts and new towns had been severely curtailed for decades, the policy was still worthy of criticism because it was based on mistaken assumptions. Such regulations imposed too much control and surveillance, placed too much concern on keeping those inside separate from those outside—even though she had just advocated fragmenting society into like-minded enclaves. Garden cities, Alison believed, require a looser kind of thinking, an order without signs of bureaucracy or the self-control necessary for urban areas. Society as a whole was never clear as to what it meant by a "garden city," and its thinking about the meaning of a city was sloppy as well. Therefore "we cannot be lucid about the way any urban-form is acting on the urban fabric: nor can we know how to care about lack of clarity."[99] A garden city may require a sheltering wall; it is a thought-worthy element in the language of architecture.

She draws an example from the wall-buildings along a narrow street of almshouses in Antwerp, calling them a clear demonstration that if the language of architecture is rich enough, there are ways to protect others while protecting oneself. Another example is Edinburgh's Old Town tenements, which are clustered together yet raise their sheer wall to extend the city's famous rock. This is a kind of collective design that current regulatory controls cannot tolerate, denying the aspect-prospect that such places achieve.

> What language finger-holds do we have left on big wall, bigger wall, if the most pervasive pressures have been all kinds of equating, leveling ones? What anchors are there in the protective-urban-living-wall for any language of architecture rooted in traditional ways of communicating about people to people?[100]

8.7
Alison Smithson, "Collective Design: Reappraisal of Concepts in Urbanism," *AD* 44 (July 1974), 403. Smithson Family Collection.

8.8
Alison Smithson, "Collective Design: Collective Quality," *AD* 44 (November 1974), 719. Smithson Family Collection.

8.9

Alison Smithson, "Collective Design: The Good Tempered Gas Man," *AD* 45 (March 1975), 163. Smithson Family Collection.

We need, Alison reiterates, a suitable language of the wall for both garden cities and the city—an understanding that an enclosing space is a place to look out from, not just a wall-skin. We have allowed the vandalizing and brutalizing of sensitivities to historical places, housing blocks, garden cities, and protecting walls, instead of developing bridging devices that can stitch the new into the as-found in a meaningful way.[101] It is upon such acts that a reappraisal of urban concepts depends.

Alison continues her examination of how a wall or a roof generates a need to think collectively about the quality of built form in the next article, "Collective Quality";[102] it makes one understand that an individual's actions inside his home affect the community outside. She tells the story of a man who built a new chimney for a fireplace in a new place within an opened-up interior. The collective had designated the exterior of his house worthy of preservation. Unwittingly, by slapping up a new chimney without any awareness of the damage he would do, this man was destroying the characteristic chimney in its traditional crest position. "Only the man of trained sensitivity for the old quality knows exactly what is wrong, and mayhap, as one of the neighbours, is the only one of the daily observers who is actively hurt by the action."[103] Yet the bureaucracy, charged with protecting the fabric of our collective possessions and supposed to regulate such hurtful actions, believed it could control only as far as the controlled can comprehend. Therefore it did not condemn this chimney-slapping behavior.

To the contrary, it is a matter of playing what she calls the Pieter de Hooch game, learning how to match the inside to the outside face, and both to acts of daily life. Can one understand

> the acts of placing, caring, renewing, cleaning, enjoying—so that they mesh together to become the fabric of culture?—every item of life contributing to a unison whose nature joins the poetry of the collective?
>
> ...
>
> Collective thinking—to achieve the Pieter de Hooch plane of consistency—has to become a supportive, all pervading feeling for quality—.[104]

The extreme fragility of our society requires greater social discipline: notions of freedom in a highly specialized industrial society where many pieces interlock have themselves to interlock: ... Interlocking-freedoms might pertain to the material world, what we do with things, and individual freedoms within a gentle form of collective will have much to do with those things touching the poetic qualities of natural things.
... If we can capture a vision of a quality of nature, this ... could become both bases and measure of quality of life of man-made things.[105]

Next in the series of "Collective Design" is a story Alison tells about "The Good Tempered Gas Man."[106] She is quite annoyed by the way in which city spaces have been cleared to make way for the automobile, cleared of the unseemly and the vagrant.

"The collective gesture has withered to vandalism."[107] Is there any space left for the collective to take place? Can the space between buildings be used for collective activities, some even decorative?

> There used to be so many places to get away from others—docklands, warehouse areas, empty market places: now can anyone be courting or frolicking by night among city office blocks? By day how can one walk undisturbed by cars, thoughts not wiped out by window displays, speech not blasted in holes by discothèques;?— Must the hard-surface urban walk-land always be an old street rescued—by concrete tubs and spindly birch made urban garden-simulation? Are these enough of an invention, these transpositions?[108]

Looking for collective spaces in the contemporary city not ruled by the automobile, and finding none, she turns to the nineteenth century to reflect on the great servicing-surfacing upheaval wrought by the laying down of pipelines and underground subways, and the hard surfacing of roads for vehicular use. In a curious aside, she avers that although this upheaval was no doubt great, there were side benefits: it provided many places for waifs and beggars to get water, food, warmth, and shelter. After vehicles took over the public right of way, such multiuse collective places were eliminated, transforming the city into a place of people passing, faceless masses in transit, ebb and flow. She laments the failure to provide spaces for the collective in the contemporary city, and ponders whether we can invent spaces to idle in, spaces for short-term activities, spaces for viewing spectacles—in short, "the provision of realistic places for the individual to enjoy greater freedom."[109]

Peter Smithson finishes the "Collective Design" series with a discussion of "Making the Connection"—"meshings" between buildings and nature—reiterating also many of his concerns about the proper form language of modern architecture.[110] He turns to his favorite city, Bath with its Royal Crescent, where the meshing of building and nature has been worked out to perfection. Mindful of the prospect, the structures along the half-crescent (built 1774) are sited to face the sun; the ground slopes to the south, giving each inhabitant a wonderful view.

> Its *order is ideal*—grand, classical, regular—but at the *real* level those columns carry also the irregularities of construction, and of first inhabitants' special requirements, as easily as they now carry the *dressings* of the successor inhabitants.[111]

> Bath is an *ideal* city, theorized-about in advance by its architects, and realized sequentially at the high tide of the landscape movement.[112]

Bath is a fine example of English Palladianism, and of how a consciously generalized architectural language can be the agent of a direct connection between structure and land. Most architect-urbanists, to the contrary, believed that the classical tradition was cerebral and uncommunicative, and so replaced it with the deliberate simplicity and directness of the Arts and Crafts movement. Peter disagrees:

> From its isolated temple beginning, the language of classical architecture had become the language of cities, not absolutely specific to particular folk or place, seemingly not invented by actual individual men—even attributable innovations, such as the baluster or the tabernacle window, seem as if they had always been part of the language. Each generation extended, enriched, re-worked an accepted base.[113]

For contemporary cities, he continues, a cool, rather impersonal architectural language is required to deepen the base connection, to give it meaning and a sense of meshing with modern structures: "For modern architecture was intended as both an affirmation of an older dream of a machine-civilisation, and a cry of joy at an actual arrival."[114] This modern language connected the *ideal* and *real* levels, and is the language that Peter's generation inherited and which they had the responsibility to modernize and to extend, endowing it with new moods while resonating with its generalized theoretical base and its language.

> To trigger the impulse to collective design, it is connection at the *real* level that seems critical: for the inhabitants to know without conscious thought where to offer their abilities—
> to dress,
> to plant,
> to play,
> to drive,
> to clean,
> to innovate
> to manage for themselves
> and their group.[115]

Favorite Walks

Topping off this look at the Smithsons' articles on "Collective Design," and various comments on "Initiators and Successors," I turn to Peter Smithson's walks around his favorite cities: Bath, Oxford, and Cambridge. He published remarks on these in *AD* (1969, 1976) and reworked them as chapters for an unpublished manuscript, "The Space Between."[116] Bath, he tells the reader, appears inside the shell of a previous culture, allowing the force of the past to dwell in the present "like a city turned over to other uses: with, at its edges, overgrown terracing and mounds, disused waterways and bridges, springs, ex-farmhouses, cows, pigs and horses, allotments, all *within the walls*."[117] The surviving built form still offers the rambler the feeling of what it was like once upon a time. Bath exemplifies the form language of collective design: a language consciously known by all and consciously adhered to by all over the intervening years.

Oxford, on the other hand, is "a lexicon of mediators in the language of architecture ... enclosing wall, turreted gateway, snicket, cloister, passage, screens passage, stair, set-door … all devices of mediation."[118] These "words," invented for the English manor house yet appearing in the colleges of Oxford as well, are evocative of multiple-field architectural space. One large "establishing-act-of-building" sets up a general field in which later insertions overlap, field upon field, until they culminate in a strong visual clamor. The irregular arrangement of streets, the closeness and jostling of buildings, allows smaller buildings to set up and hold their own field. Such is the formulation of the English "space between," mediated by such architectural devices.

Cambridge, on the other hand, "is miraculous, as university and as town."[119] It arouses English emotions and recalls to the architect "our duties—to make ordinary places beautiful, so people want to live in them and to visit them for pleasure."[120] It, too, comprises layer upon layer of invention and inventive management, so that place and ways become part of the body and the mind.

In the early 1990s, Alison Smithson wrote a preface to the unpublished "Space Between" collection entitled "The Architect as Witness."[121]

> Each inventive architect refuels his energy by connections he sees, doing so at an almost incommunicable level, and addresses these recognition-insights in order to develop his own language of architecture. A working architect, in the presence of a building sometimes has insights into how its architect was moving in the territory of his mind at the time of its inception. Strange things can trigger this; sometimes even a building's restoration presenting again a building site—from the insights can be surmised attitudes, involving instinctive reactions, that the architect of the building perhaps did not know at a conscious, verbally communicable level, he possessed … from these and from known or admitted patterns of influence, either particular to individual or more general, we can undoubtedly recognize transmutations, twists, re-energizings.[122]

The Wider Role of the Architect

"Responsibility," a word that appears with great frequency during the 1970s in the Smithsons' "Collective Design" articles, continues to be stressed in the 1980s. As they use it, the term refers to an architect's obligation, as successor and inheritor of the Modern Movement, to extend the direct line of this inheritance. This entails a responsibility to change the language of architecture, to record thought processes, and to comment on how each architect manages their art.[123] It demands above all that an architect engage each building in a genuine dialogue with place, climate, and intentions "by way of taking responsibility for the irrefutable identity of place."[124] This, at least, is how Alison Smithson discusses the "wider role of the architect" in the mid-1980s, "in the hope that words, then images, will strengthen the resolve of some of you and will help others to hold course to their convictions."[125]

She renews her criticism of the British Welfare State, laying on it the blame for the way public housing is occupied, for the buildings are not inhabited in such a way that they can be inherited by future generations; the occupants waste the community's investment and treat society meanly![126] She criticizes as well the spiritual and cultural impoverishment of America and asks, in a world of mobile people, why the inevitable result has to be Americanization:

> Or can difference be reasserted?
> To my taste, if difference is only a tourist attraction,
>   A Reserve,
> The world will have lost a whole quality
>   A whole sense of freedom.[127]

After a decade of pondering the wider role of architects, keywords had been added to the Smithsons' vocabulary, and these words are still being deployed by them in the 1980s: "appropriateness," "response," "needs," "undefined longings"—all expressions that conveyed a sense of "growth and change," but also "responsibility."[128] It is, Alison argues, the architect's *responsibility* to respect the integrity of different cultures, while as inheritors remaining aware of the irrefutable identity of place. The architect also has the responsibility to reveal the wider role of a building:

> What it gives to the place.
> What, in receiving from place, it re-energizes
> How it plays its role, the while easing, renewing, the functioning of place.[129]

This new awareness of place must be shared:

> In the matter of language of architecture, what is it we inherit?
> What language of architecture are we extending?
> The way we were taught the art of architecture, it was assumed
> That the British inheritance included the Greek and Roman world,
> Because these had led through Italy and the Netherlands and France
> To our own Renaissance.[130]
> So where is the provenance of our respective inheritances?
> Is it now the world?—
> When I travel to look at other cultures,
>   I am looking at how Doric or Sinan managed their business
> And I consume their buildings as intellectual food
> See them as demonstrations of the thought process
> Of which an architect is capable[131]
> I am interested in difference.
> At home, I work at an extension of an English language of architecture—

Whose most striking characteristic is, for me, its English scale.
However I believe there is a collective inheritance and it is in the air around us: the vegetation / the climate / the topography / there for all of us to respond to /
For in the last years of this century, least of all must our inheritance be in life-style so transient and
Most easily and fashionably, influenced
Or corrupted—depending on
The shade of one's dissenting inheritance.
The stress needs to be on an allowance for nature to do its own thing.
In other terms, to recognize we are all transients in this world.[132]

And again, architects have the *responsibility* to be conscious of what they are doing to the balance between inhabitation and the natural. It is this new awareness of people, places, and nature that come to signify by the late 1980s, in the language of the Smithsons, the wider role of the architect. Architecture is a dialogue with nature and with the national characteristics of the land and the people.

III. Conclusion

The shifts in the Smithsons' thought throughout the 1970s had to do with the responsibility of the architect as inheritor of an urban fabric, a responsibility to build in recognition of architectural precedents and the spirit of place. In subsequent years they would continue to write about "place-response" urbanism, developing the gestures formulated in their "Collective Design" articles on the general assumption that every place has a general, directive, permanent impulse—the land or the river and its crossings, the sea and the land's defenses against it, the airport and its noise, major road and vehicle flows, the periodicities of markets and festivals, the quiet of parks and Virgilian retreats. The architect-urbanist has the responsibility to recognize these impulses: "the comprehension of these 'big systems' is the basic understanding of urbanism: place-response—'the ephemeral'—is architecture."[133]

Collective activities, first invented then perfected, have to do with placating and subduing reality, and subsequently with investing that reality with deeper levels of meaning and joy. It comes naturally to people to mark out territory, seasons, measures, and patterns, and to elaborate these by dwelling on the land, enhancing it, decorating it.[134] The best example of an inherited form, for the Smithsons, was the Greek temple, a long-lasting embodiment of ideas, its meanings extended by others long after its initiators were dead. So too, inheritors of the urban fabric must know how to mark it with gently changing objectives while allowing the layering of time to remain exposed.

We turn now to investigate the wider responsibility of the architect to establish a dialogue with nature.

9.1
The western end of the main block of Hunstanton School, view from ha-ha, c. 1954. Photograph by John Maltby. Smithson Family Collection.

9

Landscapes of Lyrical Appropriateness

The historian's job ... is to go backwards, the architect's to go forwards.
Nikolaus Pevsner[1]

Prologue

In writing about the English landscape, time becomes mobile for the Smithsons, even reversible. They draw on their stock of memories, some from childhood, others from travels, and still more from architectural images and visited sites. They write of idyllic enclosures and restorative enclaves placed in nature—Noah's Ark on the sea, St. Jerome's study in the desert. Alison writes a fairytale collage, "Paradis Eloigne," to announce a tentative "green" romanticism, employing a style of lyrical appropriateness that began in the 1970s. Now they turned wholeheartedly to Picturesque theory, even deploying many of its original terms as they begin to build up their own forms of connective landscapes.

The Smithsons designed several projects in the Middle East, developing a sensitivity to the way in which "Islamic" architecture registers climate, light, water, noise, and color. They were searching for an "other" architecture, extending the "mat building" into a "conglomerate ordering." They put these ideas into action in their idealized garden design for Parc de la Villette, and their idea of climbing ground was exemplified in their entry for the Acropolis Museum. They call their "Speaking to the Sky" manuscript a "reminder-aid" to the rediscovery of the genius of place.

I. Did You Know There Is a Ha-Ha at Hunstanton?

I head these ruminations on the landscape of "Englishness" in the Smithsons' life work with a statement of their own: "We always considered ourselves very English. ... We have always been oriented towards Europe and never deviated, reacting to aspirations beamed out of America that we saw as irresistible, but also, recognizing these as part of a wider threat to Europe's cultural identity."[2] An acute feeling of "Englishness" and deviations from this norm thus called the architects to both its correction and its defense! Looking back over four decades of architecture and writing, Alison, in circular reflection, stressed the "English" identity of their projects and ideas as much as Pevsner had spelled out the "Englishness of English Art" in the 1940s and 1950s.[3] They saw themselves as the inheritors of the European language of modern architecture, domesticating its modernity by making it compatible with their sense of Englishness. By the 1970s, their stress lay on continuity of ideas, traditions, and ways of life, not on oppositional stances, with the exceptional need to say "No" as an ethical position. Compromise, democracy, responsibility, and collective spirit became the "English" characteristics of their writings, as Pevsner had defined them. To respond to the threatened landscape required a shift to a more humane, lighter-touch or ecologically minded architecture of inhabitation. Place, climate, the topography—these were the earth in which the Smithsons' projects and writings were rooted. Even their most Brutalist structures or modernist renditions, such as the Hunstanton School and the Economist Building, were reedited and inserted into an English continuum of time and place.

Reyner Banham denigrated such topographical considerations as the "revenge of the picturesque." He denounced the Smithsons for capitulating to the side of the Picturesque forces and abandoning their defense of New Brutalism. They had been seized by the Picturesque as early as their "Cluster City" article (*AR*, November 1957), but the site plans for the Economist Building were unabashed.[4] Ignoring Banham's accusation, the Smithsons were happy in their shift toward a landscape of lyrical appropriateness.

Thus, for example, they described the outdoor spaces of Hunstanton (1949–1954) in the following manner in 1982, stressing a "language of connective landscape," of "thoughtful, considerate buildings":

> The school's approach side had the indented verge to the ha-ha, by which the school territory was separated from the road (as at Vanbrugh's Seaton Delaval [1718]); making clear which was public ground and which was the school. The walking surfaces were gravel, as befitted a country school, but slightly formal, echoing the walks of nearby Sandringham [the Royal estate with its house set in 60 acres of gardens in the heart of 20,000-acre estate]. By being raised up, the gravel walk on the playing field's side mastered the field's surface; its grassed fore-slope took up the difference in the crossfall, forming a softer edge to the podium on which the school stood. At the sides were hard playing pitches, contained by the kitchen-garden-type walls.[5]

Reflecting on the Economist Building's possession of space and its place-creating dynamic, Peter Smithson wrote:

> Architectural Space [*sic*] is difficult to describe, record, comprehend. So when one has an insight about *the space between* one writes it down with a real sense of an offering—we have said that The Economist Building makes a new sort of space—and that although certain special qualities were consciously sought what is there on the ground is more than that sought for.

> It would seem that the spaces and sub-spaces have the *charge* to engage with the surrounding existing buildings and spaces drawing them into its system. To do this needed a match of spatial energies.[6]

He goes further, and

> classifies The Economist Building under the heading "Education for Town Building." It is this aspect, its pedagogic intentions, its teaching towards a built-fabric that can activate a collective sense which ties the building to its moral stature. In this "collectivising" intention all our projects, buildings, ephemera, could be said to be "pedagogic."[7]

This "pedagogic" intent involved developing a landscape language. In "Growing a Landscape of Lyrical Appropriateness" (1984), Alison Smithson reports:

> In 1976, we identified our landscape language as Lyrical Appropriateness. … Our current work is directed towards a new sensibility: our instinct is that we are on the threshold of a new romantic period. … A time when people begin to look about, to see how their acts could become one with an idealized land. A time of a new growth of humanism in the spirit-stirring, all pervading, European sense.[8]
>
> We have always been concerned with a landscape that would extend outwards the language of our buildings … support their meaning and complete their connection to place.[9]

Making meaningful connections requires that an architect be both a "remembrancer" and a "continuer" of a given culture, both going back to the past and moving forward to the future. Things seen and inquired about form facets of the mind, which later give off previously unimagined illuminations: "that is, connections to pre-language are not all direct, obvious; indeed must not be literal if they are to have generative life beyond passing fashion and develop to seed a style."[10]

> Obviously, any beginnings of a language are personal and bound up with certain predilections—you do not suck ideas out of one's thumb. In my case, the power of the undulating surfaces in the Dales (waking up at Easter time to see the ankles of cows in their first let out of spring, skipping across the green field rising to fill a rear bedroom window), overlaid by a familiarity with Durham pit spoil, most economically heaped up in cones, together might be considered the pre-language of the mound family at Robin Hood Gardens: conical depite [*sic*] the G. L.C.'s [Greater London Council's] landscape section explaining spoil is spread about English Landscape Garden style. But shapes without meaning, without a cultural cohesiveness, do not make a new language of landscape … whereas an "as found" volume of spoil piled into a cone with sides of a slope at which a 3-gang cutter can operate gives a diameter plus cutter run-around that can only go in one position on the R. H. G. [Robin Hood Gardens] site.[11]

9.2
Children playing on the mounds of Robin Hood
Gardens, c. 1972. Photograph by Sandra Lousada.
Smithson Family Collection.

Landscapes of Lyrical Appropriateness

In writing about topographical effects, the Smithsons are searching for a priori ideas and images, a wellspring on which to draw, to bring forward into consciousness what was already there, below the level of consciousness. The before comes afterward—knowable only when the memory affects the present. Going back in order to move forward, re-viewing images already past, yet drawing them out as inspirations already present—thus the Smithsons mobilize time; time coming forth from a pre-language of images and crystallized in discontinuous moments and discrete perceptions, some imaginary, some after the fact.

An art of topography is one of these pre-languages of form, not always literal but filled with emotional meanings and perceptions that resonate with and move the viewer. Meaning has to do with how the land is used: slopes invite climbing, running down, rolling, calling from, tops for kings-of-castles, jubilee bonfires. Topographical meaning is a language of composition, still handed down, albeit not as rich as yesteryear.

> That is, our language—both built and grown—faces a situation where people bring less to spaces by way of patterns of association; the giver of form is therefore under a greater obligation than ever to deploy his language meaningfully, moreover, to found meaning in function[12]

Meaning also has to do with ordinary language use: "Park" means green place, "Walk" means graveled, shaded or sheltered place for strolling, "Mall" means sheltered route but with an elaborate pattern of associations, for strollers, horsemen, carriages. The careful deployment of language with an acute sensitivity to the meaning of words reaches back to Picturesque theories of the eighteenth century and extends them into the present.

In searching for lyrical appropriateness, which is another pre-language of form, two sides of the problem had to be considered at once: a negative one, which required the rejection prior to creation of certain notions based on knowing what the accepted language will not do; and a positive one, which enabled the acceptance of the as-yet-undefined forms of the language generated by new aspirations responding to changed patterns of use.[13] Therefore, knowing that 25 years and World War II separated them from the Heroic Period of modern architecture, the Smithsons rejected, in their Golden Lane project of 1952, the "Green Park … end-of-the-roads Jardin-Anglais" thinking of Le Corbusier.[14] The accepting side came forth suddenly in the winter of 1949–1950. As they waited each morning for the tram in Theobalds Road, realization came that the calm green center of Gray's Inn continued its life because the containing buildings protected it not only from the traffic inside the walls but from the exterior city traffic as well: "It was the content, not the language, that engaged our attention, to become an integral part of the new 'containing' architectural language of Sheffield University, 1953."[15] And in subsequent projects they tried to extend this language—first protecting, then settling their buildings into the ground, in Bates House (1953) and Churchill College (1959): "Churchill's hedges against the Cambridgeshire winds mutate to be barriers against dust-bearing hot winds in the Brasilia Embassy compound, 1964; a containing language in the Parc de La Villette, 1982."[16]

II. Of Idylls and Enclaves[17]

For the Smithsons, lyrical appropriateness extends to how pavilions in the landscape are positioned as "idylls" and "enclaves." "The Dictionary definition of 'idyll'," Alison Smithson wrote in 1987, "is as follows: 'a description of a picturesque scene or incident, especially in rustic life; an episode suitable for such treatment'."[18] She grouped three pavilions that embodied for her the meaning of "idyll": Farnsworth House (Mies van der Rohe), the Santa Monica House (the Eameses), and the Upper Lawn (the Smithsons). Each one of these pavilions was a place where one's energies could be restored. Each of the three pavilions was

> A place made "Idyll"; where one could experience the dream of
> a stress-free way of life.
> A domain—often a garden—controlled and selected—
> Often in the pretend "wild"
> That is in nature.[19]

All three pavilions were effective "form-inventions" for a fragment of a would-be enclave placed in nature, whose integrity depended on the decent behavior of others. They are, in "the St Jerome sense"—a term to be explored below—"a 'study' from which to appraise, contemplate, consider, re-assess, the city."[20]

> What we have really been looking at, is the territory necessary
> To support the pavilion as "Idyll"
> To allow the illusion of idyllic life.
> That is important in this story
> Not the formal solutions
> Which are very personal
> And already history.[21]

9.3 (following pages)
Front and back covers of Alison Smithson, *Hieronymus Die Wüste Das Studierzimmer / St. Jerome: The Desert and the Study* (Lauenforde, Germany: TECTA, 1990). Left back cover: Antonello da Messina, *Saint Jerome in His Study*, 1456–1460: "Possibly the most famous Study, meticulously and mysteriously formed and spanning between the Gothic mind and that of the Renaissance." Right front cover: Rembrandt Harmenszoon van Rijn, pollard willow. "The Study is in nature; sheltered, quiet, refreshed and cooled by the stream … surely the European's dream of Paradise." Smithson Family Collection.

LEFT BACK COVER   GERMAN MISSING.   TOP

(German)   (English)

"THE ENERGISING CELL"

SAINT JEROME the Desert ✧✧✧✧✧✧ the Study

210

NOTE: WIDTH OF SPINE FOR BINDING OR FOOD FOR TYING TO BE ALLOWED FOR THESE OR FOR RIBBON

210

BACK (LEFT OUTSIDE)

TYPEFACE = BERLING BOLD
(ie BOLD ROMAN WITH CURVED LEG TO R)

please have printer send sample

IF TIE
(AS OUR

RIBBON
CARDINA

(OR CHUR

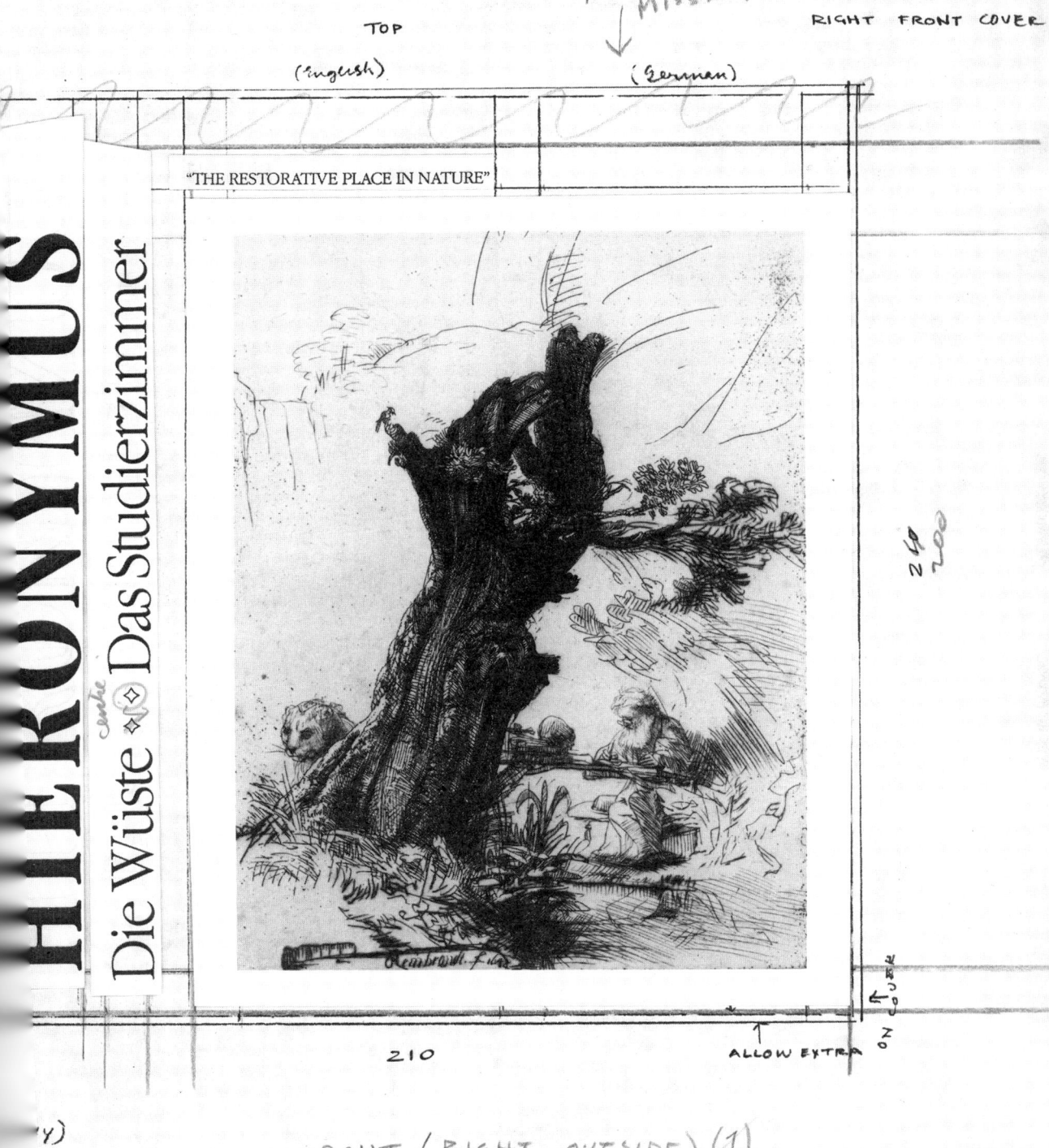

These three pavilions offered the possibility for a new kind of "light touch inhabitation."[22] All three accepted the sun; all three had stable surfaces immediately outside their interiors into which the pattern of inhabitation could be extended; all three took position in their territory, which became the "right" inhabitation of "field"; and all three had a sense of vertical territorial depth.

> Inside the territory the eye looks down on the stable surfaces or the grass immediately outside
> looks through glass at the window trees
> looks out at the middle ground
> looks towards the territories' fringe trees;
> that is, the eye has a sense of possession of a particular aspect of nature in each field of vision, all within the territory.[23]

Each pavilion unobtrusively possessed its territory, both visually and as a necessary "idyll support." The Farnsworth held in its view the Fox River nature reserve on the farther bank, the Eameses' house the Pacific Ocean, and the Smithsons' Solar Pavilion 360 degrees of the Wiltshire horizon. Within their protecting walls, seasonal weather and moods at different times of day were appreciated. Birds and animals became part of the territory "as found." The pleasures of place extended into the night as outside lights allowed the territory to be seen in different ways. All three pavilions achieved a sense of modern man being in nature.[24]

Unfortunately, the "idyll of the pavilion in the territory" was a fragile concept, and hard to maintain. Invasions of noise caused two pavilion owners to leave. Only the Eameses' territory appeared to be protected by the topography of its ledge, placing it high above the coastal road and secluding it from the noise of "modern cowboys" and their mechanical toys. The pavilion in the landscape calls for emptiness, for light-touch inhabitation. In this sense all idylls are delicate, easily destroyed by noise, by intruders, by the automobile, and by stuff. Peter Smithson would note a few years later:

> The imprinting of territory is the fundamental act which establishes the style of a period. It is to the performance of this act that all our efforts—of investigation, of scientific enquiry, of testing, of language invention—must attend—that act through which the territory begins to be made into a conscious work of art.[25]

These territorial acts Peter learned by studying the many black-and-white photographs he had taken of Le Corbusier's houses in the 1950s, and comparing them to photographs in Le Corbusier's *Oeuvre Complète*. He suddenly discovered

> the overwhelming characteristic of the house from the 'twenties is that for Le Corbusier the space outside the confines of house and garden was part of the house. The space "beyond" was imagined into the composition of the house.

> Everywhere in his sketches, the garden and the distant landscape is seen outside the windows and the building as a volume is set into that landscape. This setting is always pastoral, never suburban or industrial.[26]

And he looked at drawings Mies van der Rohe made in the 1930s for court houses where

> "the space beyond" was included in the composition of the house *but* it was indicated as being controlled by walls, trees, bushes, and so on. Mies accepted that "the space beyond" could not be assumed to remain "pastoral" or "empty."
>
> It is probable that our own instinct to try to think into the composition of a building a fragment of a supporting territory; to think in "the beyond," dissolving the generalized public domain; derives from the instincts of the "old ones" differently observed.[27]

"Paradis Eloigne"

A retreat, an enclosed and enclosing world, dreams of a future of "lyrical appropriateness"—these recurred again and again in the writings of the Smithsons during the 1980s. Since every part of England had been marked by some period of inhabitation, imprinting layer upon layer of occupation, throwing a mesh of earthworks over the countryside, the Smithsons reflected on their "changed sense of territory" both in England and elsewhere.[28] Thus "lyrical appropriateness" gave rise to poetic devices, as Alison's writings show. Lyrical appropriateness allowed for spaces of imaginative exploration, like children's fairytales of secret gardens, places where real-world problems could be reworked in safety. Thus "lyrical appropriateness" offered the chance to present "once upon a time" narrations: to discover an Arcadian future of idyllic landscapes.

Fairytales or stories to think with form the narrative basis of the short fictional work "Paradis Eloigne," written by Alison Smithson over 1975–1986.[29] As her handwritten aside implies, the style is like that of "a child talking to an invisible companion."[30] Alison claims that this

> short writing was begun during a lovely autumn, when our DS Safari was parked in the garden and could be used as a "summer house" to write in. This was in a seemingly unreal period in the early 1970's, whose character of disconnection from external happenings, coming together with the unreal setting, suggested a fantasy where a "green peace" was more fully realized than its protagonists could hope for.
>
> The writing describes the enjoyment of the seasons but does not forget enjoyment of the built fabric in a future, sparsely inhabited, cleansed world.[31]

Her French dictionary defined *éloigné* as "removed, distant, remote, even foreign,"[32] and she avers: "Fantasies have always created an affectionate framework to sustain something in us; otherwise we would not have in Europe Baroque or Rococo churches; nor flamboyant Gothic and so on … we would run out of energy for our renewal."[33]

She writes of stones that normally are inanimate, and how the land is transformed by many generations of human action. But in her fantasy stones will reassert themselves, the landscape will manage its own growing, and man will begin to appreciate a self-renewing world. "Paradis Eloigne, is, in many of its vignettes, a tribute to Charles and Ray Eames, their Eames House, their exemplary way of living appreciatively on this planet."[34] It was, after all, the Eameses who taught Alison and Peter Smithson to love "pretty things."[35]

The folder of the first manuscript of "Paradis Eloigne" is compiled as a scrapbook, with small illustrations taken from tear sheets then pasted in a loose-leaf arrangement. The scrapbook is accompanied by a series of annotated and illustrated notecards for both future editing and insertion into the evolving manuscript. Alison always retained traces of the scrapbook arrangement, however, for she expected the reader to rearrange the narrative bits in many fanciful, colorful juxtapositions. "The only person to see the manuscript—of spring 1984—considered it over-edited," Alison confessed, "but that is how I work—however—the editing of 1986 bore this in mind."[36]

The vignettes in this fictional narrative were grouped under twelve separate themes: (1) Scene, (2) Tracks, (3) Persons, (4) The Sense of the Year, (5) Occupations, (6) Walls, (7) Timber: Zimmer: Domus, (8) The Inhabited Landscape, (9) Polis, (10) Dwellers, (11) Pairi-daeza in the Landscape, and (12) Terma.[37] Alison opens her story by setting the scene for the "self-healing earth":

> The time had come and was now past when all that had been founded on base impulse and all that had been displeasing to the eye had gradually and cleanly disappeared.
>
> Poor quality buildings fell into a disuse that was more organic than dilapidation … and so decayed into soil. Things badly begun never came to fruition. … Everywhere this process resembled Penelope's weaving, there remaining nothing of a day's unwanted work.[38]

The "fabric of this world" having been destroyed, a great cleansing took place; the entire world was refreshed until it created "places of happy memories, kindly nature, its decoration and scene according to the season."[39] Fewer inhabitants remained, but those who did took pleasure in their work, finding life on earth peaceful, attractive, enjoyable: "The balance re-achieved is such that it seems as if the idyll might free-wheel on forever."[40]

9.4 and 9.5
Manuscript pages from Alison Smithson, "Paradis Eloigne," c. 1974, unpaginated. Smithson Family Collection.

Inhabitants wander over the self-repairing land. Dwellers in tents enjoy seasonal migrations, characters move their houses each month of the year, inhabitants in balloon homes float above the level of the earth's mists in order to experience the season's sunlight from different perspectives. "Sites of polis" are reinhabited; new cores of islands rise out of the sea; coastal plains create extensive shoreline habitats, protected by sea-breaking chains of offshore rocks. Sands retreat, creatures return; where self-restoration is well established, buildings become stacked in layers, the favorite "haunts of colonies of returned baroque and rococo Angels."[41] Magic mountains supplement the earth's own, while nature's mists are interspersed with additional vapors from machines extruding clouds tinted in many colors, creating unexpected spectacles at sunrise and sunset.[42] "These artificial clouds are the final caress to resedimented landscapes that were once eroded plains."[43]

There are people to meet: ghosts of Greek heroes, pigeon fanciers, a crusader, a minotaur, a child, a white unicorn, a picnic party, the observer, the spectator, the watcher, the pilgrim, the walker, the monk, the bard, the curator, the balloonist.[44] Some characters are taken from the writer's imagination, others from life. The reader becomes adept at following the rotating images as if turning a kaleidoscope—a familiar Smithson motif. Alison Smithson explains:

> By holding to the forehead, the small imageability box, by moving it in a tender, circular motion, a Seurat-like image can be obtained of a scene remembered. … Depending on the state of mind of the rememberer: an irresolute image might contain precise details, as if by Carpaccio; another remembrance might produce a faded image with almost indecipherable blotches similar to those on a found Daguerreotype. However, as the first image obtained can be aide-memoire, a series of remembrances might develop.[45]

Alison's cyclical reverie unfolds with the months of the year, the seasons, every turn of the earth. The reader discovers different aspects of sunlight and shade, unique smells, flowers and foliage, insects and birds, the silence of snowflakes that move over the landscape, and light rain that falls on a dampened ground.[46] Scenes of remembrance intermingle with scenes of inhabitation caught by an odor as it passes by on some breath of air. Times of day, kinds of days, meanderings, and adventures prompt the immateriality of memory, becoming collector's items in this scrapbook of associated imagery.[47]

> … to move belongings, to mend a roof, are no greater than the passing of the winds.[48]

> Where memories are good, yet it is possible to come across an oasis of sound, where no buildings of worth ever were. … In such places sounds murmur among lovingly tended trees whose fruit or shade the inhabitants enjoyed. Among their flowers, vegetables, sing their song-birds; while the beloved cat or dog somewhere dozes, twitches, runs.[49]

There are walks along the tops of walls where one enjoys the prospect over the land and recalls butterflies, birds, and the faces of sheep.[50] Trees overhang every wall in sight: willows, poplars, aspens, oaks. They offer uses: walnuts on branches to be gilded at Christmas, olive leaves to be thrown at marriage feasts, dried leaves to cover beds of rushes.[51]

> The wall; the post; the pot; the step, the cill; all rest where they do for a purpose. An obvious pleasure of use shines in every positioning, permanent or temporary.
>
> To give an example, the stake that supports the plant does so with premeditated artlessness, in a way that both exhibits the plant as unique and enlightens us as to the nature of stake.
>
> Any portion of any place can be contemplated and not found wanting in quality.[52]

By using the old Iranian word "pairidaeza," meaning exceptional gardens often enclosed in walls, Alison's vignettes on "Pairidaeza in Landscape" make overt reference to the Islamic dream of Paradise depicted as a man-made garden where trees fruit, flowers bloom, birds sing, and water runs. One garden stands out above all, a place where scattered pavilions of various complexities can be discovered—

> reached by a network of water, over-sailing pathways, lacing between pools where waterlilies flower. Each tiny pavilion straddles channels of
> water whose flowing—
>
> : divides, doubles-back
> : angles, runs straight
> : slithers or ripples down inclines
> : races, pours over steps
> : converges, falls.
>
> As running water is encountered in each confined space it distinctly sings each inhabitant's song.[53]

> In the pairidiso [sic], the kept and the unkept sublimely interweave. Two opposing natures advance, give way; meet over a concealed rabbit run; step back to pass some fine worn track. Cultivated globe artichokes and tall grown wild parsley are passed over within a trice by dancing butterflies. Along the high terrace walls, the leaves of fruiting branches tremble as the wasps sip the mossed stone tank.[54]

Cows pass from milking parlor to grazing pastures; plough-oxen part unkempt fields, flocks track across a tangle of vines. "So throughout the pairidiso, inhabitants, animals maintain these delicate traceries that apportion and join: orchard to dim stores; garden places to kitchens; outer slopes to their presses; sunflowers, bee hives, herbs, each to their stores."[55]

Not surprisingly, Alison's writing of "Paradis Eloigne" took place during a period of work on a Kuwait Urban Study (1969), the Kuwait Demonstration building (Mat-Building, 1970), the Kuwait Dune Gardens (1975), the Pahlavi Library, Tehran (1977), Damascus Gate, Jerusalem (1979), the mat mosque beside the Gül Baba türbe (tomb) in Budapest (1987–1988), and the Bibliotheca Alexandrina (1989). According to Peter Smithson, she was the lead architect on all of these projects except for the Pahlavi Library.[56] The Smithsons' new understanding of how what they termed "Islamic architecture" responded to climate found its way into Alison's paradise fiction: the light bringing to life or draining surface of color; the garden, an enclave that refreshes and protects a place by excluding noise, where only the rustling of foliage and the trickling of water can be heard. "The 'oasis,' the naturally occurring paradise, is by comparison with its desert surroundings, almost miraculous in its luxuriousness, sustained by water; it suggests that the Islamic mat-garden should offer something of the oasis."[57]

In Search of an "Other" Ordering

The Smithsons began to travel in the Middle East in 1951, though they admitted that as northern Europeans they were unable to react properly to a bright-light climate. Their first architectural attempt in the region was a hospital design in Doha (1953), but this did not yet give evidence of "an other ordering," which they felt—intuitively—must exist in the tradition of "Islamic" architecture and urbanism.[58] Studying how the fabric of Arab cities was woven eventually moved them to extend the language of "mat-buildings" and to apply their concept of "lyrical appropriateness" to subsequent projects. The term "mat-building," coined by Alison in 1974, referred to a conglomerate structure that repeated and varied a modular unit, allowing growth and change in both directions; the interconnectedness of its buildings lay somewhere between architecture and urbanism.

Ideas expressive of new freedoms of movement had been percolating for some time in earlier concepts: interconnections, close-knit patterns of association, and clusters of buildings or collective groupings. All of this earlier work came into focus when they began to track down the antecedents of what Alison called "protective-visual clothing." Intrigued by the neutral dwelling cube found in "Islamic" cities, a calm cell that could change, that could add pieces of fabric over public ways as needs grew, she noted that both man and donkey could gently service the fabric of such loose-fitting cell structures.[59] This was the start of rethinking a "mat-building" and its conglomerate ordering.

No doubt the first mat-building, the casbah-influenced Free University in Berlin (designed by Candilis, Josic, and Woods, 1963–1973), influenced the Smithsons' promotion of "new freedoms of action through shuffled order."[60] In a mat-building, density resulted from weaving together dwellings, streets, and urban elements, knitting different scales of built and social activities into the urban tissue. Peter Smithson thought the defining characteristic of the mat-building was "evenness of attack."

> The language of the mat-building in its pure state is the same-all-over, as it were like a sand-dune.
>
> The other characteristic, one now sees twenty-five years later, is that the architecture maybe finds its beginning in the making of outside enclosures, the language of the holes.[61]

Rethinking the idea of a "mat" guided their proposal for the future urban tissue for Kuwait's urban form (1968–1970). Here they sought to extend "what the world recognizes as the Arab tradition, not a mere modification of what is fashionable in America, Europe, or Europeanized North Africa."[62] They proposed that the emerging financial center of the Old City of Kuwait retain a low profile, in direct contact with the water—a littoral city between desert and sea with the smell and feel of both throughout, a city in which pedestrians walk in shade in every direction, sheltered from the movement of cars and their noise:

> A city of apportioned vehicular movement and parking
> A city with some of its best old features restored and put to use
> A city which rejects overt expression of the individual struggle for power and money characteristic of north American Cities, and which keeps to the patrician tradition of the subdued public face—for the status and wealth being "understood" within a close-knit society do not need to be advertised or proved in any way.[63]

Alison explained that in such a city, a continuous frame or "mat" is layered over existing "patterns of human association: the patterns of use, the patterns of stillness, quiet, noise … and the patterns of form."[64] The mat frame gives identity to the whole system, and keeps disparate elements from chaos that otherwise would be in hopeless competition. The frame is given an overall intensity of activity from the start, so as not to compromise its future. Planning begins with the stem or urban framework, not the houses: its basic structure must include all domestic services, all extensions of housing, commerce, culture, education and leisure activities, roads and walkways. It is conditioned by mobility: speed, not length, is the determining factor. Mats as described by Alison "are not the sum of length, height and largeness but rather a two-dimensional dense fabric, where man walks and lives in."[65]

In their consideration of Arab urbanism, they remarked to themselves that it was time to take another look at the "functions" of modern architecture; those which Team 10 had been dissatisfied with in the 1950s had become by the 1970s an extended concept, an evidence of "an other ordering." "Therefore my use of the term 'function' is expansive: an armature of an architecture/urbanism of response. / The Islamic functional tradition's response to climate …"[66]

In their Kuwait project (1969) they aspired to achieve the "other ordering" found in Islamic cities. They looked for precedents in earlier buildings, starting with accessible

Egyptian architecture. In Dier el Bahari, Egypt, they first recognized "that what we were looking at was a 'mat-building' … the beginnings of an 'even-laying-down'—that was to become common to all Islamic buildings."[67] Next they discovered an early mosque, the Mosque of Amr ibn al-As (also known as the Mosque of Amr), Cairo, built in 642 CE. They found that the penetration of light into the interior, illuminating the floor, invited the correct use of the building: "Amr is at the start of the 'other ordering' by Islam."[68] Every hole in urban space, Alison clarified, must have a lining offering the user a reason for crossing that space. This was illustrated by the interior wall condition in the Mosque of Amr.[69] And they understood from the mat village of Gorfas, Tunisia, that an evenly ordered fabric needed to lie on flat topography to retain its mat characteristics.[70]

Next they turned to understanding the crevices and holes built into the fabric of mat-buildings, a functional response to the bright light and hot climate of the Middle East. These openings offered crevice routes, servicing individual units, or a cul-de-sac of houses, or a school or mosque. The Smithsons made more discoveries: the Al-Azhar district of Cairo contained a capillary network of shaded routes that induced air movement—a cool route in wonderful contrast to an open landscape in the sun's full glare. In the casbah of Algiers, crevices in the fabric were lit by reflected light, providing private open spaces.

In Kuwait's urban form, the only historic markers visible from the air in 1968 were minarets, so the Smithsons took these as fixed nodes for a new mat fabric of the city.[71] The importance of minarets is to function as sight lines orienting pedestrians by lining up several others across the city.[72] And the making of a crevice grid was the start of a language of "an other ordering" for the Kuwait Government offices (1970).[73] Here they extended the mat language into the enhancement of air movement, mediating windows, and control of light. They had witnessed how, "at the touch of a woman's hand, light is modulated, the air movement is controlled: Merchant's Houses, Cairo."[74]

In turning to a project for Damascus Gate, Jerusalem (1979), Alison recognized it as a hole in the fabric of the city.[75] Holes of dereliction were part of life in English cities, where abandoned, industrialized areas left tears in the urban fabric, or motorways cut raw gashes across the city's woven texture. These, she believed, could "form great, secret areas" if mended and given new grain, their connective quality extended; they then could become useable mystical holes.

The Damascus Gate was such a hole, a void full of rubble extending northward, where donkeys and camels once rested, where goods first changed hands and were stored before entering the city. Its function as a service space—a coming-and-going space—had to continue. There was precedent in Jerusalem for dealing with a hole-in-city; the Temple Mount (Haram-esh-Sharif) occupied one fifth of the area within the old city walls.

> On the Damascus Gate site—outside the city—I see the hole being emptied of its fill, the rock exposed to serve a directional function on the expanse that would be paved: as the surface of the central podium in the Haram-esh-Sharif is paved.[76]

She felt that the site must form a "seam" in the divided city, connecting the Arab city to the east and the Jewish city to the west. Buildings could not fill it, because either side would read such acts as aggressive. Therefore it must be the people in their daily use of the paved space who make the sense of connection, form the "seam." To enable this, a lining of administrative offices is created for the hole:

> If the city's social services could be integrated in the occupation-mix, so that the Arabs have to walk over to the west side, and the Jews over to the east side, the lining would be brought to life through use of the space. When you cross the paved area, you pass into the shade of the edge of the lining. To illustrate this sort of tradition of arcaded edge, between open space and columnated interior space, there is the Mosque of Amr, Cairo. … This "openness" and difference of precinct is one of the most important elements of Jerusalem: that is, the walled city is made up of many, different, walled precincts.
>
> You can see we are gathering up the references to the continuing architectural/urban language and bringing them together into a new language.[77]

Arcaded linings are a Mediterranean tradition; they are "climate-ameliorative forms." Thus the hole of the Damascus Gate site will be structured

> so that time will enhance it, change it; just as time has furnished the Haram-esh-Sharif. And to root the language of the space and the lining in the traditions of the Muslim and classical cultures of the Mediterranean in such a way that what is done becomes an "instant fit" and will in no way aggravate either side, but will serve the whole of Jerusalem … making a contribution to thinking about those holes in cities that occur in every culture in change.[78]

Conglomerate Ordering

In these extensions of the mat-building concept the Smithsons were seeking a given naturalness, the feeling of a fabric being well-ordered, a condition they referred to as "conglomerate ordering." This was an order in which one could lose one's way, yet sense a direction from the source of light, the warmth of air on the skin, the density of the entire composition.[79]

> Conglomerate urban space is in essence Islamic; for it is in the countries where Islam has built that one finds a dense building-mat interrupted by the great lumps of separated buildings which were or are its religious and secular seats. These great lumps jostle irregularly together; the spaces between being simply somewhat wider than the cracks in the rest of the building-mat.[80]

In 1991, Alison Smithson added a new introduction to her unpublished notes on the "mat tradition." It was, she said, time once again to reflect on the layers of ideas that went into this concept, because the period that began to "think green" coincided with wars in Lebanon, Afghanistan, Iran, and Iraq, bringing havoc to these countries and devastation to many monuments of Islam. It was

> pertinent to consider again the functional tradition in Islamic Architecture, to deliberately take another tradition to the natural inheritance from Greece, Rome, the Renaissance, so that we may look dispassionately, coolly, at function in Architecture/Urbanism in relation to climate, in relation to the art of inhabitation.[81]

Alison and Peter were hoping to pick up threads of Arab/Islamic influence, providing a bridge to other languages of architecture that in reflexive relationship might renew and extend those rooted in European soil. In Romantic terms, they sought "a bridge back to the white forms in the very special light of North Africa that awakened European artists from Delacroix onwards to colour, and our own modern movement of 'espace, verdure, soleil.'"[82] The inheritance of what they perceived as "Arab/Islamic" architecture interrupted their normal expectations; it offered, in complex territorial and climatic terms, something radically different from the European norm, an "other ordering." What has been aptly termed "orientalism"—a concern with Eastern places of romance, exotic beings, haunting memories and landscapes, secret holes—affected what they saw, perceived, and translated into elements of their design vocabulary.

In the 1980s they began thinking of "conglomerate buildings," turning structures inside out to accept the sun, weaving routes of intricate patterns with space between to absorb intruding noise.[83]

Alison explained:

> By city I mean a conglomerate of activities, patterns of association and patterns of movement ...
>
> Of stuck together buildings
> Of spaces adhering to the buildings
> Pockets of planting where the sun reaches down
>
> ... Everything making city sense, coming together to have an identity of being one particular city ... we have written elsewhere that even looking at a piece of trodden earth in a city you can tell whether it is Pekin or Paris.[84]

Parc de la Villette

The Smithsons thought that the closing years of the twentieth century would begin a new Romantic period, engendering a "search behind the scented scene: a time when people begin to look about, to see how their acts could become one with an idealized land."[85]

In their own spiritual awakening to the sensibilities of land and climate, the Smithsons sought a structuring device, a language of containment for their idealized places. Protective enclaves shutting out pollution and noise "offer a sense of release, of interlude, a safe place for doing nothing in, in between one building and another."[86] Their competition entry for Parc de la Villette, Paris (1982), offered such a noise-free, protected zone. It was accompanied by a patchwork descriptive text, a montage of ideas drawn not only from the fantasies of "Paradis Eloigne" and competition requirements but from the Smithsons' growing sensibility of lyrical appropriateness. Could the transcendental imaginary and idealized narration on display in "Paradis Eloigne" engender an analogical counterpart in material form?

> To achieve a sense of Parc
> We have to create conditions
> Whereby leaf rustle may be heard
> And bird sounds predominate.[87]

Putting the ephemeral ideas of "Paradis Eloigne" into practice, this urban park would be a "sweet balance between 'a city in a garden, and a garden in a city.'"[88] The first gesture was to design a quiet enclosure. Thus the Parc de la Villette vision was laid upon an escarpment, raised up to shut noise out and to allow visitors a dramatic overview of the entire environment and choices presented. A montage of landscape memories engenders a dense mat: an overlaid tracery of colors, sunlight, shadows, sounds, and textures that change with the seasons and enable children to discover the wonders of idealized gardens. The Smithsons' proposal is exhaustive and exhausting in its elaborate detailing of every kind of park adventure that might be found.

Color acted as a structuring device: a "green network" linking together zones of different vegetative colorings. A bold, dark-green ivy hanging on the eastern and northern edges enfolds the Park. The same color appears in the green line drawn by the Porte des Pins they placed to the north, and to the south the Porte des Palmiers. To the west, the green lightens as it passes weeping willows and moves on to Lombardy poplars. To the east, pine green mingles with palm green and these with the blue-green of weeping blue cedars, establishing a "grey-shaded-to-blue-green-matrix." The core of the Park is red, raying purple to the west and orange and yellow to the south and east.

Different textures and types of grass offer a ground cover of various shades. There are green areas for sitting, walking, playing, jogging, and four different pasture playgrounds in remembrance of the pathways traced by the pigs, cows, horses, and sheep that once upon a time crossed La Villette on their way to its abattoir. The Allée des Cochons (Pig Alley) crosses the northwest corner of the site where the Pig Pasture lies, composed of hummocks and tussocks of grass. By contrast, the Cow Pasture is lush-looking, allowing buttercups to grow uncut so they would maintain a sunny color in this zone. So too with the rye grass of the Horse Pasture and the gray-green grass of the Sheep Pasture,

9.6
Alison and Peter Smithson, cover for report on
Parc de la Villette, Paris competition, 1982.
The Alison and Peter Smithson Archive, Special
Collections, Frances Loeb Library, Graduate
School of Design, Harvard University.

the latter simulating striated rocky high-altitude pastures covered with wiry grass. Each pasture is dotted with the appropriate animal statues on which children could play.

Water is a second theme: the still water of the canal axis, colored waters of a medieval garden, clear water running over small pebbles, rippled water flowing round the Islands of the Moon, and active water in a Discovery Garden of Water Sounds. There are thin sheets of falling water scattered about, the water capturing sidelights and moonlight, scintillating against faceted stainless steel. A rotunda lake for swan boats, a channel of water encircling the Grand Hall, and trickles of water wetting the Rocks of France continue the theme. "Kiosks" containing water-handling devices produce all kinds of water sounds: water wheels of various sizes, wells filled with different levels of water, a column of water rising, a chamber of drips, "water rippling, gurgling, chuckling over a variety of 'chadar' or 'washboard' surfaces."[89] Grottoes hidden in half-light behind veils of water form places for ferns, mosses, goldfish, and nymphs.

If that is not enough to entice the visitor, there are mazes, labyrinths, and eleven thematic gardens, most designed as walled enclosures. Each contains an identical gazebo of lattice framework, allowing those who perch atop to look down both into the garden and at the outside space. Some gardens display the histories of French vegetation: roses, soft berry fruits, apples, and pears. Others provide unique experiences: a scent garden for the blind, a dell for woodland butterflies, a medicinal garden, a mixture of children's swings and climbing roses, a grotto full of mosses and ferns.

And of course there are greenhouses: one for maintaining and renewing decorative plants, one to serve as a production laboratory for didactic purposes, another for a range of climates—tropical humid, dry humid, arid, cool—and yet another for conservation of threatened flora. The display from a range of climates has an overlay of mezzanine walkways so the geometric perfection of the plants, particularly of the tropical species, may be fully appreciated from above.

At dizzying speed the text's list of offerings continues—this collection of layered activities leads to a charged space full of energy, anticipations, happenings—each place independent yet ordering the territory around it.

Ark as Idyll

In the mid-1980s, while the Smithsons were concerned with idyllic enclosures and restorative retreats, Alison offered an architectural studio in Munich (1984) and a seminar in Barcelona (1985). She gave students a design problem based on the metaphor of Noah's Ark, which she considered a type of idyll because it was necessary to withdraw in order to survive the Great Flood.[90] "In the context of the [Barcelona] seminar: Noah's Ark … [is] a withdrawal in order to survive, or the idyll in extremis." The idyll's given form is that of a "pavilion in that it is: a place apart, supported by its territory of 'nature in the wild,' a place wherein the inhabitants can re-energize themselves, from where the inhabitants return, able to regenerate life in the real world."[91] The Ark story she compared to that of

9.7
Noah's Ark wooden toy. Photograph by M. C. Boyer. Smithson Family Collection.

9.8
Sketch by Alison Smithson of Noah's Ark toy. Smithson Family Collection.

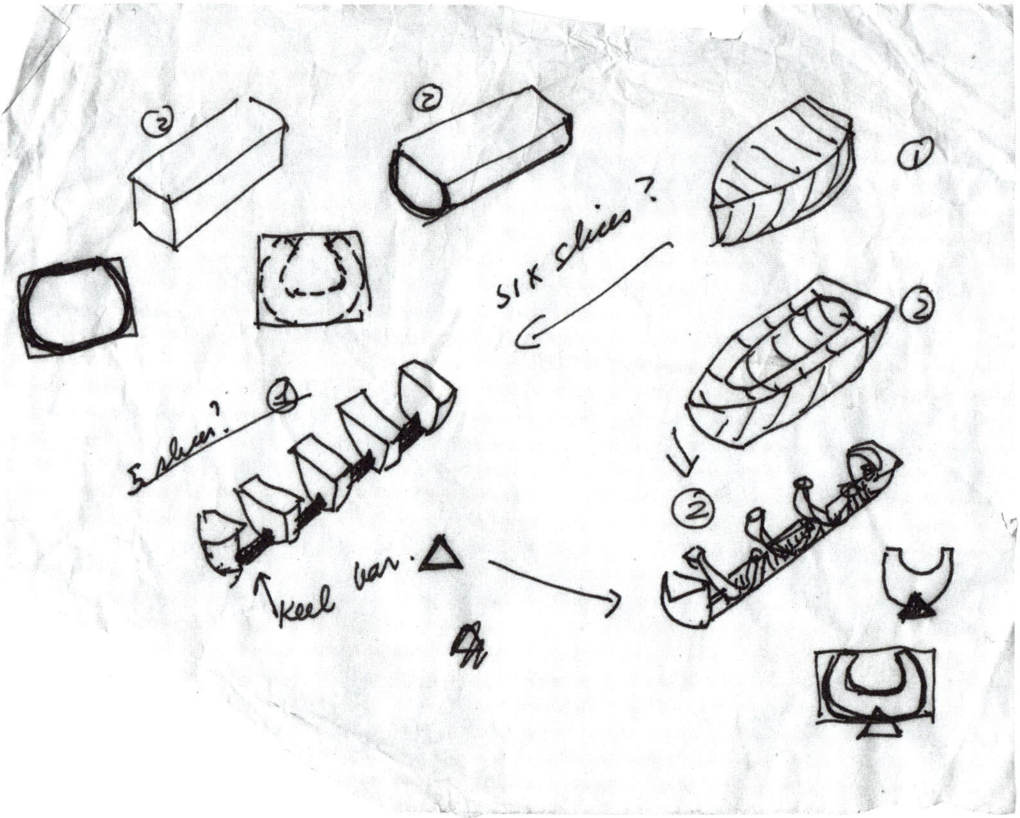

St. Jerome, which offered two alternative idylls: a monastic Study filled with books—an intellectual retreat where one communicated with the world of ideas—and the Desert, where the ascetic retreats into unspoilt nature. The Study and the Desert represented "allegories for (both) a restoration place in nature and an energizing cell supported by urban order."[92] They carried into new territory the theme of buildings rightly fitted to and naturally rooted in the landscape.

The studio brief for Noah's Ark called for an inquiry into fresh impulses that would change a student's response to building in a hostile climate. The student must take a position with respect to acceptable technology, think the situation through inside/outside, and forgo blind acceptances and assumptions.[93] Alison also drew attention to the concept of "futures," a financial trading term for certain kinds of commodity, such as hops for beer, where the price is agreed upon ahead of the year's crop. The word "futures" stressed something Noah practiced: the skill of foresight, which all architects must bring to their work. She asked the students to design and fabricate a small-scale model of Noah's Ark, taking the climate seriously and drawing up specifications for a do-it-yourself survival kit. This was the Ark's function: it must be fail-safe in order to support life on the water. Unlike the biblical Ark, which admitted all animals, the student's Ark must contain animals selected to perform a specific function: such as "to crow for me, to tell me it is morning."

An Ark can be a toy, with a flexible container and contents; a myth with possibly a grain of history in it somewhere; a theme of folk art and fine art, often both at once; and a serious building construction. But what intrigued Alison most about the Ark was its "has-to-work" quality.[94] It is a serious building construction, for the elements surrounding it can turn nasty—water above and below—it has to work! "Noah's Ark can help us think how we should best extend our inherited language of protective shelter into the future."[95]

Alison purchased many toy Arks from antique shops, even though she said they did not attract her imagination. What fascinated her was "intangible," for the Ark remained an "unrealised vehicle."[96] Yet to make an Ark, even as a toy or model, is hands-on architecture. The mythical Ark's shape remained an enigma; one knew only that that it was made of wood. So,

> energized by Holland, why not an Ark like a clog cut out of the solid? The block of wood "as found" on a London skip, dictated the shape: carved it echoed the primitivism of Le Corbusier's sculpture: this is the parallel—as some sort of signal for change—towards a more kindly attitudes [sic] towards the "as found," the Ark has become again a kind of "cult object" for the achievement of green peace in our time.[97]

In such a manner the architect responds to things "in the air," learning to live more sweetly on the ground, with water, with nature and its natural inhabitants, with the sun, wind, and moon. Thus a place like Noah's Ark must be perfectly tuned both inside and out. It must look right, smell right; receive the wind from the right direction or keep it in check; place itself in the right position to receive the sun; allow a sympathetic level of sound—reflected, echoed, absorbed; all so that someone will find pleasurable use of this idyllic place in the future.[98] In this manner landscapes of the mind drawn from many different idylls contributed to the way the Smithsons put things together on the land, seeking a softer, sweeter kind of inhabitation.

Allegorical Idylls

The text *St. Jerome: The Desert and the Study*, written during the period of Alison Smithson's fascination with the Ark, was based on her lecture "Fragment of an Enclave," given in Barcelona in 1985 and revised for Stockholm in 1986.[99] The monk in his monastic cell, the scholar in his idyll, had been a favorite allegory of Le Corbusier's—illustrating a narrative about writing, studying, and developing a secular religion for acolytes to follow and an allegory of the "machine for living," raising the minimal cell to a form of art. For Alison, the humanist ideal in the early Renaissance images of Jerome's Desert and the Study represented an "allegory—about places-apart, first drawing man one way, then attracting towards the other extreme. … Both alternatives are present in a revitalizing role, as the one appears to re-energize the other for man's sense of well being."[100] In these musings, there is constant play with the responsibility of the architect to be aware of the oscillation between inside and outside.

The allegory of St. Jerome in the Desert leaves him outside, alone in nature, standing with no support offered by the surrounding sand or the rocks, between the ground and the infinite sky. It speaks of an asceticism that has few material temptations. Here the "wild" acts as a source of creative energy; the place-apart is energizer of the man-made, affecting his pleasures and pursuits across centuries as he remodels the landscape, both rural and urban, and redesigns his furniture, clothing, and equipment. "Saint Jerome in the Desert expresses a human desire for the freedom that seems to be in nature; the undiminishable freshness in nature's cycle of renewal, of its complex order and balance."[101] Energized by the "wild," he turns back to man-made surrounds:

> St. Jerome in the protective enclosure of his Study stands for different ideas:
> —the desire to enjoy built order
> —the support by civilized services
> —the shutting out of inclement weather, the ability to temper the climate
> —a perfected sufficiency in the functional place of work, with the tools of profession, trade, housekeeping, to hand.[102]

This is an "allegory for perfection of thought; for the creation of the perfected object; for deliberated choice"; "an integral part of a productive academic life."[103] Whether the view from the Study was that of "a fragment encapsulated in nature" or whether the view from the Desert was that of an urban order, both exist within the other, indivisible, reciprocal, equally necessary. Yet Alison asks: What kind of enclave would give us quietude and inviolability at the end of the twentieth century? These idylls of Saint Jerome's—so difficult to achieve in contemporary times—will of necessity bring

> a change in attitudes towards the use of the earth, a use of things without excess, of enjoyment in a less wasteful way. … A merging of the old reciprocity will allow us to begin to think of a new form of restorative habitat for a future *light touch* inhabitation of the earth.[104]

> If in the immediate future we begin to create *fragments of enclaves* that protect our inhabitation, we may come to live closer to the idyll represented in the Renaissance by Saint Jerome's two habitats.[105]

III. Territorial Memories

The architect's need to think topographically remained on Alison Smithson's mind until her last writings in the early 1990s. In unpublished notes for a lecture ("On Climbing Ground: or Not on the Level") given in Stockholm in 1991, she wonders: "Possibly, because we came from the north of England where the ground moves about a bit, we maybe already have had the makings of a mental apparatus to deal with climbing ground. But the reactions of most architects are a 'normal' to our kind; they begin by thinking level!"[106] Why would a city-bred architect give a thought to other than thinking level? Le Corbusier wrote of the right angle, its tyranny if the architect is insensitive to its power. It should be respected, used sparingly, not without thought.[107] The Smithsons felt the need for "thinking-otherwise," taking a nonlevel approach to their designs.

In circulatory reflection, they now understood that the use of falling ground could be found in their own work as early as 1951, in the sloping site of Coventry Cathedral. This was followed by working with the climbing grounds of Sheffield University in 1953. Thinking topographically, allowing their buildings to rest naturally on climbing ground, continued with Llangennith Cluster Housing conglomerate (1977) and the Pahlavi National Library (1977–1978). Different levels dividing secular from religious places would be incorporated into mat-buildings such as the Gül Baba Mat Mosque (1987–1988) and the Acropolis Place (1990). "Hopefully our thinking will continue to develop topographically and our buildings will rest as seeming naturally on climbing ground."[108]

Acropolis Place

One objective of the Smithsons' competition entry for the Acropolis Museum (1990) was to exploit climbing ground.[109] In his unpublished essay on the entry, "On Climbing Ground: Thinking towards the Acropolis Place" (1991), Peter recalls the many times since 1951 they had scrambled over rocky, broken ground to reach Greek archaeological sites, and how on arrival they felt relief at seeing before them the rectangular horizontal of the temple stylobate, an object of wonder. Of course, the most excellent example is "the Parthenon herself approached from the Propylea, sliding uphill to her east end over the rock worn to a high polish by the shoes of this century …"[110]

The brief for the 1990 competition was to create a new museum to house the Elgin Marbles once they are returned to Greece from the British Museum. The Smithsons, however, were unwilling to think of placing these wondrous marbles in yet another museum: the elements were unique and required an exceptional solution. They proposed instead an "Acropolis Place" where the fragments would be placed in their original orientation to the sun and relationship to each other. Fragments of sculpture and buildings were assembled on sloping platforms reached by more steeply sloping ramped ways. In retrospect, the Smithsons admitted, they took the idea of ramps from Le Corbusier, but added:

> We have of course always worked with ups and downs—ramps, ha-ha's, and so on—but never in a very conscious way. Architects like ramps because Le Corbusier liked ramps. But Le Corbusier's ramps were usually of a simple straight-across nature linking horizontal floors. They were not donkey ups and downs but solid geometry ups and downs.[111]

In the Acropolis place, ramps gave rise to lyrical appropriateness:

> the viewing levels play the role of "earth" the alignment maintains the sense of "temple" the light of Attica beams down as remembrance of the gods.[112]

> this is an "architectural family" site—of many temples of many building periods—and each fragment now speaks to the others, achieving a reciprocity unobtainable in their past.[113]

The "roof" of the Acropolis Place looks like an old railway station or market roof held up on masts and sun-protected, controlled by what Peter referred to as "solar clocks." Only the central block of the old hospital—now to be the Center for Acropolis Studies—protruded through this protective covering, which stretched across the top and down the sides, like a *peplos* over a figure.[114] This single transparent cover-all allowed the fragments of the Acropolis to be seen in their original Attic light.[115]

> [T]his light should arrive through the protective skin as directly and with as much as possible of its true spectrum … the "tobacco" colouring by the sunsets of the hot summer of 1951, when we first sat on the Parthenon steps, enlightened us to the span of the quality of ATTIC LIGHT … IT IS TO THIS LIGHT THAT THE EX-PATRIATE FRIEZE, METOPES, PEDIMENT FIGURES, HAVE TO COME HOME.[116]

9.9
Collage cutouts of Alison and Peter Smithson against Acropolis Museum site, Athens (1990). The Alison and Peter Smithson Archive, Special Collections, Frances Loeb Library, Graduate School of Design, Harvard University.

Landscapes of Lyrical Appropriateness

Thinking Green

As if to prove her oft-repeated point that 1951 was the start of their "thinking green," that is, thinking topologically or about landscapes of lyrical appropriateness, Alison circles backward in her thoughts of 1991 to describe seven different layers of their "ecological attitude," reappraising examples drawn mainly from the 1950s.[117] In a lecture still evolving entitled "With Green in Mind," she explains that their "ecological thinking" meant a range of things:

> Thinking about the dissolution of barrier in mind between inside/outside in England's changeable island climate meant to open up buildings as the sun came out, and close down as wind got up or sun went in
> Including the sky in the building's territory, in England meant taking in rare sun from above, guarding eyes of occupants against sky glare
> Response to aspect/prospect and micro-climate, local breezes, not only prevailing winds
> Respect for topography, natural ground, what the surface was and still might want to be
> Always acting as incomers to a place, studying history of occupation, its patterns of use
> Thinking about a sense of territory, remembering all the sense of occupation of place ... sense of privacy, inside/outside possibilities offer
> Broadening basis of art of inhabitation, rethinking the spaces offered to the various age groups of society
> Reappraising the standard disposition and standard allocation of affordable space so that this can cause the reappraisal of everything else.[118]

Climate Register

During the 1970s and 1980s Alison Smithson worked on several published and unpublished manuscripts, her "sensibility primers." She sought to shift architectural sensibilities through anecdote and allegory, as in "Paradis Eloigne" and the Noah's Ark material, stories to help architects see and understand context in a different manner, told from a unique perspective to spark intuition and imagination. She wanted to encourage architects to think about how a building settles into the ground, to be responsive to the air between building and site. And she also hoped that architects would understand how time affects architecture through aging and weathering. Some of these thoughts were published in *Climate Register* (1994).[119]

"Climate Register" was the name of an exhibition at the Architectural Association (AA) in autumn 1994 of four of the Smithsons' buildings: the Economist Building, New Arts Building at Bath University, Kuwait Mat-Building, and Bibliotheca Alexandrina. These buildings reveal a sensibility to wear and weathering, aging and aspects of time, a sense of settling a building into its ground.[120] But the term "climate register" also signifies the putting together of seemingly disparate fragments of observations and ideas. It accommodates the uneasy relationship between the unequivocal physical and technical demands of site and program and the "first thought," the intuitive reading of context.[121] Alison wrote in 1986 that "climate register" means working with climate response devices such as running cornices, breathing gutters and ridges—"devices from the past that have trodden the same ways from urgent necessary response, to practical everyday device, to a seeing their architectural possibilities."[122]

The end of the twentieth century, the Smithsons presumed, would give rise to both an idealization of land and a "spirit-stirring."[123] They were asking older questions with renewed vigor. How to achieve the right fit of a building to its site? How to utilize signs of occupancy of a territory, so that a building appeared naturally rooted to its grounds?[124] They argue retrospectively that their language of connective landscape forms began with Hunstanton (begun in 1949), achieved maturity with Churchill College (begun in 1959), and went on from there. In retrospect, they understand that they had turned wholeheartedly to Picturesque theory, deploying many of its original terms as they began to build up their own forms of connective landscape:

> We have a vocabulary of connective forms that knit the building in with "the roundabout" (Cobbett's term for the sense territory …); the ha-ha and indented slopes; the moat; clean-cut areas of hard surface or grass; graded foreslopes that stitch podium to site; small versions of bigger buildings as out-riders ("the microcosm of the macrocosm"); walls and screens (part of the substance of the building); dense strip-thickets. All these forms were used to define and modulate the territory of the British Embassy, Brasilia, 1964.[125]

They found that the English landscape both sustained and was made "ordinarily enjoyable" by the "inhabitable energy" of those who had worked on it and lived in it. These form-makers overlaid the land with a tracery of cultivation and turned it into an art form: "in the seventeen hundreds paintings became the enabling images in the development of the park within and embracing the farmed estate: a *genre* virile enough to be re-exported."[126] This energy, these devices, turned land into landscape and eventually into the English landscape urbanism of Bath, Edinburgh, and Newcastle.[127] It developed a new sensibility partly communicated through literature, "for generally unmoved by form the English can accept something that can be read about."[128]

Leaving imprints on the land, whether earthworks or buildings, is how men confirmed their control over territory: "imprints shape the *space between* so perform the essential territorializing act."[129] Territory was also where the relationship between man and his environment could be renegotiated, allowing a new sensibility to develop. Retrospective glances into the sources of ideas that helped to develop this sensibility led naturally to reverie upon their childhoods, revisiting territories that renewed their deepest recorded sensations[130] — especially, for Alison, Edinburgh.

Edinburgh, the city of Alison's childhood exile, was her "city-of-the-intellect," the city of which she claimed "ownership" as a resident, and because the city educated her to be an architect/urbanist.[131] Within a "Magic Box" of insights (so labeled by Alison herself) lies a note written in November 1981:

> The city that became a particularly lucid urban landscape in stone ... this final extension of the language of the English Landscape Garden was a particularly Scottish achievement ... culminating with the integration into urbanism of an understanding of the viewpoint of Piranesi.
>
> The English Landscape Garden becomes the urban landscape in Bath; but of a much softer and Roman nature ... Edinburgh is incredibly bold, radical, Greek; Romantic in that fearlessly fragile monument after Lysicrates, an achievement of integration was possible through Edinburgh people's belief in the new.[132]

Edinburgh taught Alison Smithson about the quality of fabric, and about making holes in this fabric. It spoke of urban complexity—no issue isolated, no single answer provided. It showed how urban events are a series of interrelated dots on a program, a field of opportunities and a spin-off of consequences. Edinburgh was a calm city, full of retrospection; it communicated what a city stood for, what it felt like; and knowing this allowed Alison subsequently to visualize other cities, she said, even before visiting them. Edinburgh informed her about landscapes, the feeling of weather, seasons, street lighting, changing city services, and the pleasures of public transport. It preached responsibility for maintenance and the need to address both old and new fabric. From these latter lessons stemmed her "habit of continually putting things in history ... a spin off from observing Edinburgh and by such means, Edinburgh instructed about connections ..."[133]

"Returns" to favorite cities and to childhood territory are a ritual the Smithsons likened to an animal returning to a salt lick: one seeks "the flavor of one's earliest experiences of the territory at its most extreme. One seeks the places where the sensation is sharpest in us."[134]

Of Picturesque Ruins

Another source of lyrical appropriateness lay in the rediscovery of ruins and empty spaces. Now lying about as industrial ruins, which lessened in number every year, such

> disused waterways and walls, induce—for some of us—the same emotion toward that "*heroic period*" which Gibbon felt in Rome ... our enjoyment of ruined places, liberated spaces intended for life but emptied by time, their clean yet evocative stones have, over the years, suggested to us we are on the threshold of a period of lyrical appropriateness.[135]

Fascination with the remnants of industrial England compelled Peter to write a children's book, *The Tram Rats* (late 1960s), and together they lamented the destruction of Euston Arch in a book of the same name (1968).

Classical ruins offered other reminders of how a building conformed to its site, how "the space beyond" entered here as well. Scholars of the seventeenth and eighteenth centuries, educated in the classics, spent time amid ruins, measuring them, absorbing the ethos of their sites, but in the age of the camera this lingering sensibility was unknown. The Smithsons thought a new awareness of classical ruins might generate a fresh sensitivity in the present, and reawaken an "urban nerve."

They therefore proposed an anthology of classical sites composed of passages from classical literature describing the uses of ruins to be found in Greece and throughout the Roman Empire, eyewitness accounts of their most intense periods of use, and descriptive accounts of their earliest excavations. The resulting book manuscript, "Speaking to the Sky," was filled with visual documentation revealing the present condition of ruins and sites. The Smithsons were hopeful that such connective, humanizing methods might enable the present to rediscover and regain an understanding of how a natural, rooted-seeming positioning of a building occurred on a site. It was an enabling document, pushing gently toward a sense of placement and the growth of a fresh sensibility.[136]

Once the classics were common ground, but now it was necessary to offer this anthology (in translation) for architects visiting ruins in the present. Calling their book a "poignancy kit," a set of "reminder-aids" to the rediscovery of the genius of place, the Smithsons hoped it might call forth a few ghosts as nudging but compelling companions, ghosts that would fill the air with their voices, evoking qualities overlooked or not understood. Textual reminders would note where a battle had been fought, how the walls withstood a siege, the use of ramparts, or the location of campsites. Suggesting connections across centuries, the classical ideal stood as a measuring rod for a later period's achievements in urbanism.

IV. Conclusion

The Smithsons felt that over more than four decades of working together they had developed an architecture sensitive to climate and inherited built fabric, an architecture:

> responding to the pursuit of gently changing objectives. Throughout the change—from those objectives inspired by the Heroic period of Modern Architecture, to those affected by our experience of living in a long established industrial society—we have held to a belief that concern could generate invention.[137]
>
> [The] process of allowing the "idea-so-far" to be reflected on seems to be a parallel work process to "place-response" urbanism: an urbanism in which what exists is re-assessed in the "coming-into-being" of the work in hand: every work a new assessment, a new response, to what is already there.[138]

From a period of strident reaction against the tedium of Townscape Analysis in the 1950s to the contextual sensitivity of living in an old industrial country, the Smithsons' writings and projects slipped unassumingly into the pictorial language of the 1970s, mediating between inherited situations and modern architectural insertions, between the weaving and unraveling of the built fabric. They studied and reacted to the "fabric" of place, whether a Greek temple, the rolling hills of northern England, or the holes in Islamic mat-buildings. Their architectural method continued to develop, as it had during their New Brutalism period, in ad hoc reactions to the situation "as found." They did not intend to develop rules and regulations for site planning or to draft typological and morphological studies, as postmodern architects did.

There are as many different ways of being "English" as there are of responding to the art of the English environment; the Smithsons' way was to seek to develop new sensibilities to place, climate, and architectural traditions. In this gesture they were not far from the attributes of Englishness as construed by Pevsner: neither constant nor consistent, but with a predisposition to depict mundane, everyday scenes, treating each place on its own merits (the principle of tolerance in action) with independence in matters of taste, religion, and government.[139] The Smithsons were aware of the "inhabitive energy" of those who had worked the land of England into an overlaid tracery of cultivation—a deep historical sensibility that had turned land into landscape, giving rise to the English landscape garden, extending into all life and eventually to the English landscape urbanism of Bath and Edinburgh.[140] They were aware of the many trees that inhabited the public spaces of England, "the ever-changing perfection of nature that 'settles' an English built place, places it in time, gives it a seasonality, renews it year after year."[141] And they developed a sensibility to "placement," that is, a sensitivity to topographical patterns in the landscape. Open spaces as enclaves offered release or a quiet interlude, landscapes that would survive the passing rush and noise of automobiles. All these awarenesses found their way into the series of "sensibility primers" written by Alison Smithson, to which we now turn.

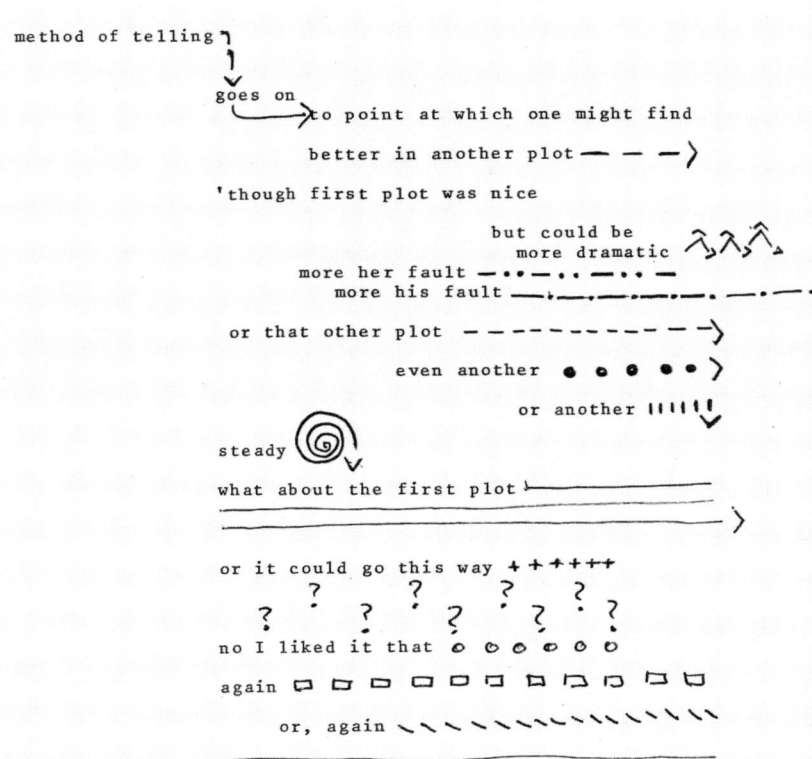

10.1
"Method of Telling," from a manuscript version of
"Quiet Flows the Kamasutra"—sparkling lines of thought
likened to fireworks. Smithson Family Collection.

10

The "Sensibility Primers": Revenge of the Picturesque

In Jane Austen's novels, walks, rain on walks, rides discussed and distances calculated, views of towns from carriages, noises of shod feet and wheels in streets, have all been felt through the eyes and ears tuned to a special English sensibility; for in the idea of the English landscape garden "the English had invented a new environment which was sensible, not only of visual values, but also of the reactions of such an environment on all the states of the human mind in general." By Miss Austen's time the theory of the picturesque had not only been fully realized in the English landscape garden, but it had by natural extension produced that marvel the city of Bath, which she knew well.

Peter Smithson, 1972[1]

Prologue

Starting in the 1960s until the 1990s, Alison Smithson wrote a series of "sensibility primers." She referred to these manuscripts as writings of the "as found" in their detailed documentary quality and documentary graphics. One of the purposes of these primers is to delineate an emergent, but dimly perceived, sensibility as it arose, treating history as relevant to one's discipline and life.

I. The Pedagogic Intent

The writings of Alison Smithson, Peter Smithson said, dealt with states of mind and conditions of movement, but these stories were immersed in machine society:

> [S]he writes of the wider landscapes seen from trains at the beginning of our period of time, of the city's streets and revolutions seen from trams, of the non-communication of closed-cars and peasant-places, of the landscape observed from the air and the idea we now have of the men in that landscape.[2]

> There is already a literature of man and machine as there was man and nature, but there is no equivalent of the eighteenth century's theory of the picturesque which grew to develop that special sensibility which Miss Austen celebrates and which actually changed the relationship of man in nature as well as changing the dream of man in nature.[3]

> Mrs Smithson's life is in the real world of those who try to change the relationship of man and machine; she is qualified by that life to record and to turn into another art-form life lived in the time of the machine.[4]

It is toward this shift in sensibility—a shift in imagery of people, machine, and the environment—that Alison Smithson wrote her pictorial "sensibility primers," beginning in the 1960s. She lists these primers as "Quiet Flows the Kamasutra," on India circa 1880–1900 and the English sensibility of service abroad; *AS in DS*, a diary of car movement in a Citroën DS 19 automobile in the 1970s, examined in chapter 6; "1916 A.S.O." [and so on], about life in Germany 1916–1926 and "the earth of the modern movement," which formed there before and during World War I; and a memory book, "Paris: Maigret's Map." Two of these, Alison explained—those on India and Berlin—explore the attitudes of a girl in a different period from that of the author: respectively, of a girl in India during colonial rule (1863–1898) attempting to find worthwhile activity, and of a girl in Berlin trying to have a professional life but desiring to be married as well. Subtitled "The Earth of the Modern Movement," the Berlin primer covers the period 1916 to 1926 and witnesses the growth of a sensibility that supported the Heroic Period of modern architecture—and the arts in general—and presaged the diaspora of the avant-garde in the 1930s.[5] Alison described these two fictional accounts variously:

> They are also writings of the "As Found" in their detailed documentary accuracy.
>
> One of the purposes of these writings, in which documentary graphics play an integral part in the communication, is to delineate the emergent, but dimly perceived, sensibility. The two writings treat history as relevant to one['s] discipline and life.[6]

> Mine [are] all writings of the "as found"—or you could say the "was found" in the sense of the historically rooted fiction. … The characters are as if they might be found; in that place in their period of supposed existence; the characters do not represent types or attitudes but are themselves—largely unexplainable—as people: that is a person in real life is something in the eye of the beholder, such as we see in Jane Austen's supporting characters and whose "characters" seem to change when the beholder becomes sensible to other qualities in them.[7]

During a 2001 interview, Peter Smithson explained: "What Alison and I write is for oneself. You write about the insights you have. You think, 'well, maybe, if they're useful to me, they might be useful to somebody else'—but never intentionally to influence or instruct."[8] Yet he also averred that all the Smithsons' creative work was pedagogic in intent, and none more so than the "sensibility primers."[9] The purpose of the primers, as this chapter will explore, was to delineate for the reader an emergent but simple sensibility to landscape, climate, and quality of place.[10] Further, Alison chose words to spark different trains of thought in each reader, an associative technique she also developed in her collages. The primers exploit associative, nonlinear language that allows one influence or memory to trigger for each reader the development of a uniquely personal version of the desired sensibility.

II. "Quiet Flows the Kamasutra"[11]

Alison began writing her first "sensibility primer," the novel "Quiet Flows the Kamasutra," in 1966. After many additions, the work was published as *Imprint of India* in 1994. In the earliest version, the manuscript included a working diagram in the form of a firework display to demonstrate that this novel, being pure imagination, had no need to simulate connectivity: any incident could turn and twist and set off vibrations.[12] "There is no one beginning, no single end; just the worrying over this magical happening—if it happens at all—up to an end that could go either way. Maybe this is the kind of novel the Japanese term 'Zuihitsu'; a writing—lacking a cause-and-effect plot—relying for its unity on the personality of the writer."[13]

Any woman's magazine of the day might have offered the plot: girl and boy see each other, speak, go out, eventually get married. But Alison intends the flash points to sparkle up again and again for both pleasure and puzzlement: "The short phrases and essences distilled from possible stories overlap, and flicker like fireworks in a night sky: the fragments interweave and interrelate, repetitions vary slightly: the pieces juxtaposed convey a more extensive theme than any individual theme alone."[14]

As preceding chapters have noted, Alison sought, beginning in the mid-1960s, to conduct an ecological dialogue with place. Such a dialogue full of historical facts would support sensitive responses to differing climates, alter the perspective from which one enjoyed sunlight, rain, snow, wind, clouds, smells, and noises. "Quiet Flows the Kamasutra" reflects these efforts. It would establish ties across cultures "as retrospective histories touch and part and re-touch."[15] An unpublished 1970 preface for the book, then titled "Quiet Flows the Kamasutra: adrift in the years 1863 to 1898," explains that the first experience of a hot place such as India is of being somewhere different, yet "also embodies a whole history of one's own people."[16]

> The simple act of turning a street corner in Bombay might find you facing your own childhood: a Kodak lady in a blue and white striped dress holding a box brownie, figure full size, preserved since the 1930s in the stove enamel on the metal placard. Such an advertisement stood outside every sea-side chemist and post-card shop of any pretension when I was a girl.
>
> Or rounding a corner, you face a building so like the Mechanics Institute, Bradford—you could melt there on the hot pavement, impacted by two entire evocative senses of one's own history.[17]

Today you step into India and instantly there are unexpected and poignant visual contacts: statues, names, signs, objects, buildings—and besides those obvious signs the Indians as well as ourselves know are British-in-India—are a myriad tiny administrative acts of placing, routing, dividing, in the town and landscape, that the trained eye can read more directly and so be more touched: it all upsets; the whole place.[18]

She intended the work, she said in her preface, as a "sense-travel book"[19] designed to tune one's senses in preparation for the experience of a place, just as Cobbett's *Rural Rides*—an eyewitness report of English rural life in the late eighteenth century—"made people look about themselves, or Hare's [Walks in] Rome" was meant to be savored in one's hotel room before venturing out on an excursion.[20] That is to say, it was a "sensibility primer." And the sensibilities thus primed would not be limited to the literal settings of the book, for "such an evocation of service in India—loaded with the putting down of new roots—can then be read equally well in all places the British were fond of—the barren mountain sites of Greece, the incredible spaces of South Africa, the hill towns of Italy."[21] It was to be

> a guide for the imagination; short enough to be read by an air traveller: a means whereby the visitor of a few days might tune their senses to enjoy a fleeting impression of the continent of India.[22]
>
> The traveller is suspended free of routine of time, without responsibility except that of sustaining life to the journey's end: this despite heat, glare, dust, taxing the body's inner supports, nibbling at the mind's resourcefulness, natural cheerfulness, staying power. Being moved can involve a holding operation; become instead an act of self-preservation: equally it can become a test of one's ability to continue to pursue an objective with full mental powers.[23]

Above all, the book was to be colorful: printed in India on India-fabricated paper, gaudy with rainbow stripes, its cover in orange mango and its text ideally in Indian Red, a perceptual shift from standard black. It is not clear from Alison's description if she is writing a travelogue for contemporary readers, a novel about a young girl's travels in India, or both. Each unit of travelogue/novel, bound separately, could be inserted into a folder or an open-ended box and read in whatever order the reader might choose; scenes and events linked together backward or forward. Drawings and collages, grouped to convey and stress the atmosphere of India, would punctuate various streams of the narration.[24]

By the early 1980s, the manuscript had taken on the title "Imprint of India" or sometimes "Breath of India." It now focused on the period from the 1860s to 1900, and "the expansive effect of English sensibility of the experience of another place, another culture in another climate, that make up Service in India, Civil and Military."[25] She allowed an ensemble of short scenes to mutate, exploring a continuum of expatriate experiences. These exasperatingly repetitious scenes, randomly related to each other, are meant to be pleasing, puzzling, and increasingly annoying. She explains that at first the writing was divided into portions by line drawings, in the manner of Indian publications, but as her own sensitivity to architectural climate responses developed, the narrative was apportioned to various sensibilities: "In its layout, swathes of text are thought of as being embedded in monotone collages of textures: trees, water, materials, earth, scripts."[26]

10.2

Cover by Alison Smithson, *Imprint of India* (London: AA Publications, 1994), based on photograph of Alison Smithson by J. S. Lewinski, 1972. Smithson Family Collection.

10.3

Page from Alison Smithson, *Imprint of India* (London: AA Publications, 1994), 14. Smithson Family Collection.

10.4 and 10.5 (following page)

Original collages by Alison Smithson for *Imprint of India*, 1993. Photograph by M. C. Boyer. Smithson Family Collection.

The "Sensibility Primers": Revenge of the Picturesque

Chapter 10

A few pages written in 1981 offer "points of departure" or an outline of chapters to follow. They begin with a question put carefully by a servant while Alison was sitting in a detached suburban house in Chandigarh: "Will you have your eggs hard boiled or soft?" In a city that did not even exist before the British left India, the fact that the servant knows how to ask such a question, even that the question is important to ask, sets off a flood of childhood memories and tears.

The Edinburgh of her youth had been a city to which many professionals returned after their work in the British colonies, bringing back numerous souvenirs. She remembers "the typical box rooms of such people held a curious assortment of ship trunks heavily labelled and business-like picnic baskets; so many who had brought their curios home from bank, army, medical, education or missionary services."[27] A trunk label written with thin strokes—"Miss Urquart, Bombay SS Victoria"—starts another reverie:[28]

> But nothing of its rag store contents can tell us when it was brought back; nor can its bird's-eye marble paper lining inform us what it contained by way of mementos, of merely a journey, or a life spent. If we were to try and pick up suggestions of the trunk's story, the whispers would be drowned by those echoes of expatriate voices that once progressed down the wide and pleasantly exposed wide pavement of Princes' Street.[29]

So overlaid are such voices of experiences of Empire, they muzz each other; we are unable to distinguish the layers. But does it matter? Think of the pulsating crowd of brown individuals outside any main Indian railway station—Victoria Terminus, Cantonment Station, Howrah, Sandhurst Road, Ellis Bridge, Civil lines, City Station, Sabzi Mandi—or before the Sadar or the Evening bazaar, and it is perhaps unimportant that the white memories coincide or even remember the same girl; individual arrivals, five, ten, fifteen years apart might be superimposed. And is it any easier among the only-young-once long service officers?—can any whisper now assure he became Collector, District Commissioner—or was, of course, military, of the Frontier Force?[30]

A traveler to British India could thus arrive in a strange world but be met with signs of home left by myriads of administrators: names of streets, buildings, statues, drinking troughs. "But the placing, routing, dividing, in the town and landscape, a trained eye could also read as a British presence, and by these indications maybe have been more directly moved."[31] The traveler may find it disturbing, unsettling, "when all the strange people, all the strange and familiar memories, rudely crowded the blood stream and jostled for pride of epitome."[32]

There is no order to the memories that rise up: the journeys looping the world, traipsing through climate variations, traveling overland by train, reaching one's destination, departing for home round the Horn.

Heat burns in these experiences so that with the onset of heat the body remembers; whenever the light is right come memories, triggered by hot light.[33]

Travel commits the body to movement; the spirit to departure and loss; often gaily, expectantly, entered into, is it all worth the farewells? Suddenly the wish to hold to those left behind; not leave that which is good for inadequate proof of what is to be gained ahead. The awful commitment of oneself once in movement, however unpleasant the climate, or the economy of the way chosen, or the weather's effect on mid-ocean or mid-air. At times the recognition of the period ahead to be going through strains the inner throat muscles, cauterizes the brain; freezes the person to twigs inside clothes. Then—a magical sense of being no longer going, but returning.[34]

[Into one's time in India] the enjoyment generally spread over large portions of life seems as it were concentrated; among these there are few more than those in which we recognize another climate, the air, soil and vegetation being totally different, and all inspiring new and delicious sensations; when a new page of the endless variety of creation lies open before us.[35]

The narrative points to marks on the land left by the British; the feeling of being squished into a big bus trundling along the Trunk Road, engineered by the Moguls but refurbished by the British; passing irrigation canals built by British administrations over time; the dust of the road blowing over men riding British-style bicycles but dressed in Indian-weave white shirts and turbans, knees spread wide for balance.[36] "Befuddled as we are in mid-century by effortless journeys by car, the sight of human effort only sometimes strikes us with a physical impact. A mode of travel can suddenly call to mind again a whole patch of a journey gone by: or imagined journeys."[37]

Always in this novelistic "sensibility primer" the British presence in India is the central incitement to memory. Whisked along by a crazy motorcycle contraption threatening to turn over at any moment, a familiar sign, "Dalhousie" (originally the name of a Scottish castle), appears—yet the passenger continues past this place name from her own country and history without yelling "stop." Nostalgia ambushes:

Suddenly, in a lane you are walking along, a corner of a wall stands out as a particularly pleasant spot: light is particularly sympathetic. Have others liked this corner? Had anyone had a nice experience here? Sad or glad happenings?—breathless perhaps?—like rain on a soft charcoal night.[38]

There are scents to stumble upon, some as simple as water on dirt, and civic furniture improvised from the oil drums so ubiquitous in India they must be remarked upon. Perforated, a steel drum is used for protection of trees, or filled with earth or other materials to delineate road improvements, mark out roundabouts, support signs, or form roadside seats; flattened, it provides fencing, house siding, roofing, patches for holes in buildings. Its end cap becomes a roof tile or a plaything for a running child.[39]

Imprint of India (formerly "Quiet Flows the Kamasutra") was ultimately published as a companion volume to the catalog *Climate Register*, an exhibition of four Smithson projects held at the Architectural Association (AA) in London in 1994.[40] The primer at last took on definitive form; no longer would loose sheets of writings be rearranged at will. The published work begins with an outline of chapters but develops each chapter as strips of print, sometimes in waving banners, applied over background material drawn from Alison's file of Indian collages. All this is printed in sepia, and nearly impossible to read. Alison retains the idea that her writings are "the analogy of a distantly observed firework display of independent and quickly passing sightings … the encounters flicker like another's fireworks in a night sky whose rapidly spent fragments, in their descent, interweave and interrelate in a variety of patterns."[41] But she delves further and in greater detail than in her earlier drafts into the experience of travel in India, yielding an extended reverie on what it means to be English, to have an English response to an alien place:

> Instead of an easily read, varying landscape [of England] where all items are in their place and distinctive on the line of walk, here [in India] an individual could apparently forever wander every-which-way. … Even if the local people receive their sense of place from qualities of the dust, and far horizons, a passer-by would still have no necessity, because of the great space—no requirement at all seemingly—to be precise as on a path.
> A path! True paths can only be remembered—.[42]

The Indian ground looks as if it has been walked over everywhere by innumerable feet; a pervasive dust cover crisscrossed with tracks, overlapping and interlacing with each other in no discernible pattern, as the pages of this novel were supposed to imitate. Everywhere the air is laden with fine dust. "The noises of the Indian city sigh repeatedly. As if voicing a desire for a let-up in the oppression [of the dust-thick air, of heat, of noise, of smells]."[43] Every place seems to blur into

> similarity of places which add together to so large an expanse of soil-dust that the sum is a vast impression of native journeys. What for?—Where to?—Yesterday, today, sometime last week, a month ago? Time makes no difference on this continent. There is no wind, has been none; there will be no rain for some time.[44]

There are no visible markers on this land to denote ownership.

> No visible connection of pieces of land to inhabited place by a network either of built walls or hedges and ditches to which trees could be bystanders. This immense landscape totally devoid of paths guided by up-heave or significant break of surface.[45]

In comparison, the all-important comparison, England has a varied landscape, easily read, where all items have a place, where walks have distinctive lines. Perhaps it is true that in India the locals are guided by qualities of the dust.[46]

The breath of India is too hot to allow one to think; all faculties dissipate. "Each day burned up means yet another day has passed. A life-span has one less day ahead. This sense of the wastage of the days crawls up the marrow of the bones of her [the young girl's] arms, causing her to stroke her hands, slowly up and down the tight sleeves of her dress."[47] Heat rises up from all surfaces "as if trying to imprint its passing strength on the observer's face."[48] One must learn to walk differently when the air's breath is hot, is oppressive, bakes the earth, burns up each day. The temperature climbs steadily; the clock's ticking keeps time tiptoeing away; the hot season is followed by a humid, even more enervating season, which is followed by another of increasing heat—and so the year relentlessly turns.[49]

The light of India triggers extensive descriptions. That of dawn reveals stages of graining light, layers in different colors printed over each other as in a chromolithograph.[50] It reveals a landscape worn to a powder, empty, absolutely still. "Then come treading animals. These are led out into the landscape of no thickness. Clad in gently flapping linens. Woven of fibres the colour of the dried-out-earth-dust."[51] The bright sunlight of midday is more brazen, it leaches color from rocks, the topography, causes heat to rise from the earth, reducing everything to the same likeness.

[I]s the place begging not to be forgotten amidst so extensive an area of similarity?[52]

The light of sunset placates, even the air's touch is softened by the dusting of earth therein suspended. All the final tints of sunset are appreciable.[53]

Any shade cast in the golden-apricot aura means that specks of gilt are withheld from certain particles of dust. This way, the diffuse shadows cast by the mango trees appear as paler, less luminescent areas. Obliquely striking light is made visible by foliage density; for the trees are huge. Their bulk, on this shadowed side ... is dappled of grey blobs. The brightness of the lowering sun glints through a myriad apertures.[54]

How to work in such an alien climate? It is plainly too hot! India imprints itself on the body, on the mind. Letters from home are passed around, for correspondence helps to keep a sense of national identity, as well as pass the time that keeps flowing away.[55] The imprint of India is about memory that smites, yet as quickly flees—about searching "for that memory which touched a chord a moment or so ago; even to the extent of turning and looking back along the route they have come. Whatever sight acted as prompt is not seen again. Still, she wants to catch the fly of memory on a carefully reconstructed cobweb of her thoughts. What had it been?"[56] And in between these ordinary observations, repetitive as daily life, are interwoven comings, goings, returns, repeating strands of a story about a girl and a man having morning and afternoon tea together, chatting, flirting, meeting, parting, meeting again, continually registering the impact of climate on one's perception of place.

The alien climate of India's heat, dust, smells, and light, the "as found" signs of British rule—verbal commentary was needed to emphasize these peculiarities, to inscribe mental associations with place, and to draw sustenance from written travel guides brought along as companions. Picturesque voyagers had deployed similar operations as they too wrote down what appeared to their eyes as well as their minds.[57] "Imprint of India" represents yet another attempt by Alison to make use of picturesque sense-travel books that tune one's sensibilities before or during a journey. She uses the examples of William Cobbett's *Rural Rides* or Augustus Hare's *Walks in Rome* (1871) and *Walks in London* (1878). This is her attempt to capture the picturesqueness of colonial India, albeit in a rearview mirror.

Inevitably Alison is an outsider, writing about late-nineteenth-century India, in which both the distance in time and the unfamiliarity of place cannot produce a deeper understanding. The boy and girl, the main characters of her novel, remain a mystery to one another, just as the passages of time flare up as surprising sparkles, then disappear amid the quotidian boredom of life on the margins. Alison was learning how to read an alien environment in retrospect: some memories were of visits to India while others were vicarious, drawn from writings about everyday life in colonial India.[58] The result is a strikingly Anglocentric representation: an impression of how the British register and adapt to a colonial space in which the many variations of their presence appear as latent images waiting for the discerning viewer to discover and bring them into focus.

Development by the Smithsons of a sensibility to climate, including the effects on architecture of wear, weathering, and aging, parallels the period of writing "Quiet Flows the Kamasutra" (1966–1978).[59] Alison confesses that she always had "the habit of writing ahead."[60] Peter comments on their slow evolution toward "climate responsiveness" in "Territorial Imprint":

> Our slow step-by-step search for the language of *a sun-acceptant energy-conservant, climate-responsive architecture* is towards the marks which will establish the territory of late 1990s.
>
> What we are after is an architecture which will celebrate the sun—of different organization formats, of different plan forms, of different urban arrangements, of different landscapes. *An architecture of a reaching out*.[61]

III. "1916 A.S.O."

Alison began writing the next of her "sensibility primers," "1916 A.S.O.: The Earth of the Modern Movement," in the spring and summer of 1966, at about the same time she started "Quiet Flows the Kamasutra." This third novel and second "sensibility primer"

ENGINES.
BATTLE AREAS.

TRAMS

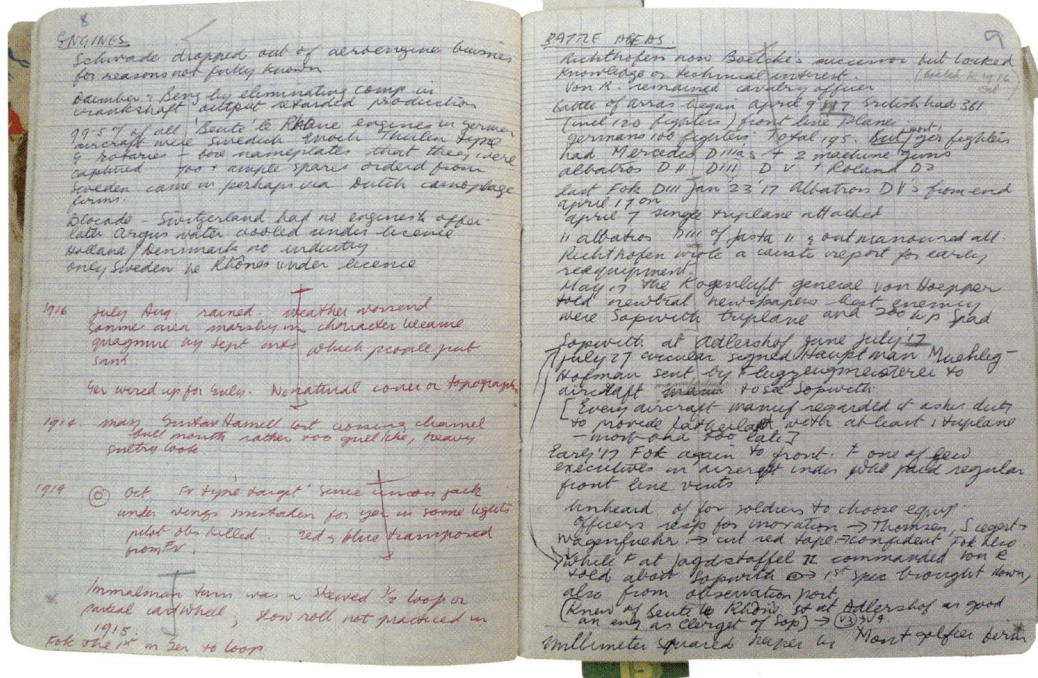

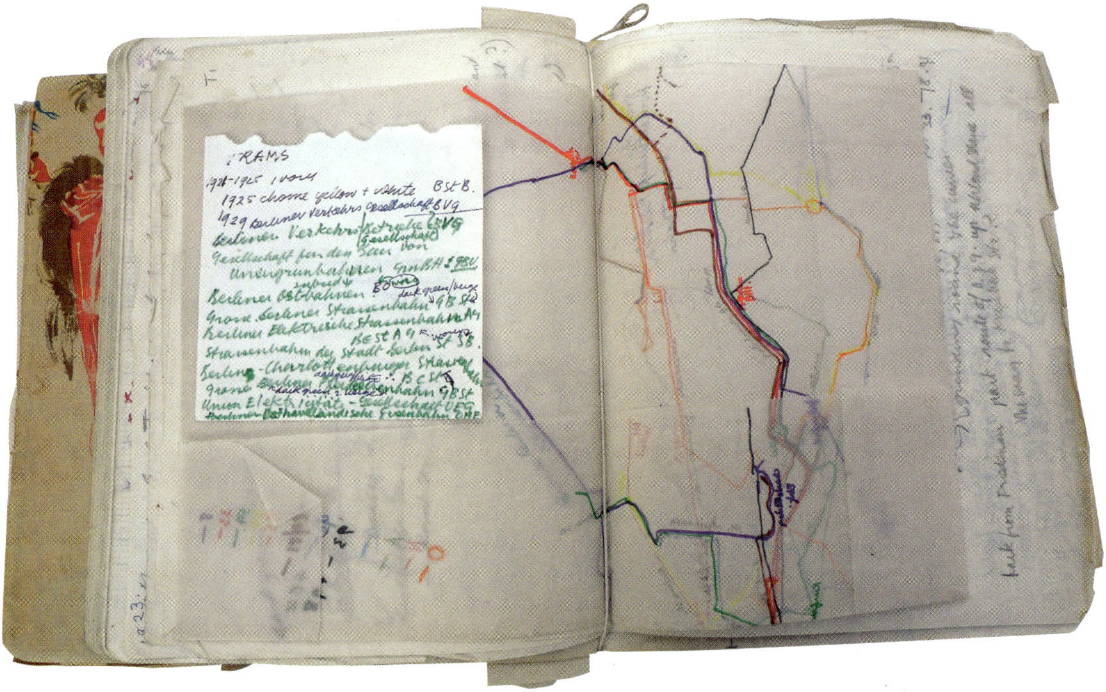

was revised throughout the 1970s, with a final typed manuscript achieved by 1989. It has never been published. A rejection letter from Oxford University Press (1981) said that it had a "boring presentation, not enough recklessness." Alison Smithson referred to the notebook for this "sensibility primer" as a "fact book" covering World War I and its aftermath, and it is full of meticulous details about the novel's historical background. "The War which is still on our conscience (and likely to be for some time) just as the myths of pre-classical Greece were quarried by people in classical times. A kind of Iliad—long ago—place names—lists of boats (now planes)—Heroes."[62] She explains that war is an extreme example of how human freedom can be controlled and ordered about, causing people to live a wholly other-directed life at an incredible intensity. They "adopt manners and skills quite useless if not at complete antipathy to peacable [sic] life."[63] Equally to be feared are "grand designs of an ordered society"; this, she believes, is what Germany taught the world after the experience of World War I.

Peter Smithson adds the following explanation:

> The German novel ("1916 A.S.O."), for example, makes us aware that the shift in sensibility which we associate with the twenties and thirties [Bauhaus period] had already taken place during the war years out of the work situations of the first machine-society. A shift away from the feudal land-and-horse-bound Imperial symbolism towards an imagery of the machine, and that this was not an act of acceptance but the signal of another dream.[64]

Alison draws a "visual spur" for her novel from the colored end sheets of the Profile Publications of the 1960s, which depicted German airplanes of World War I, including camouflage and markings. These graphic designs and engineering feats, she claims, came from the same rich soil from which the Bauhaus had sprung.[65]

10.6
Double page spread of Alison's "Fact Book" on left "Engines" and right "Battle Areas" for manuscript "1916 A.S.O." Photograph by M. C. Boyer. Smithson Family Collection.

10.7
Double page spread of Alison's "Fact Book" on "Trams" for manuscript "1916 A.S.O." Photograph by M. C. Boyer. Smithson Family Collection.

She intended "1916 A.S.O." to speak to those just beginning their professional or artistic careers. Its concerns were, she thought, as relevant to the 1960s as to the era of World War I:

> for most of those aged in their late 'twenties or their 'thirties who sometimes feel a sense of desperation in a lack of personal progress towards what they would prefer to be doing. I mean in this sense: it is as if each were going down a corridor from which they can see out of all the time but not into the incident rooms behind whatever doors are on offer. Other corridors are passing at all angles—all around—rather like Charles de Gaulle airport—each on their own trajectory: some fast, others at all paces. Some spend time working in rooms that appear promising, yet these can turn out to be mere "box" rooms: from these rooms without promise the corridor receives back their person, sometimes in a sense of relief, sometimes with terror at lack of achievement. To mirror this pattern in the narrative "1916 A.S.O." nothing newsworthy seems to happen to the girl or the man: but, in this ordinariness, it has universal relevance.[66]

In hindsight the reader understands that the corridors the girl and the man choose lead toward Fascism. Yet Alison argues that a new style, technique, and discipline can preserve one's loyalties against foul play. (Perhaps she was referring unconsciously to Team 10 meetings, which were taking place during the period of her primers' composition. The Smithsons admitted they needed the support and loyalty of Team 10 members to help ward off the many compromises made by British architects of the time.) Being totally occupied with one's discipline and with its technical and operational problems absorbs the mind, turning day-to-day happenings into trivia. Yet the destructive whims of government flutter on the winds that blow every which way, and from them issue orders, and so the lives of thousands are shattered by bureaucracy. "We must be mad to let a few quite mundane brains of good talkers so control all our separate disciplines and loyalties."[67] Always fearful of orders and regulations that impinge on one's choice of friends, ideas, designs, clothing, Alison warned, in tones reminiscent of earlier complaints about Brutalist blockage:

> [P]ersonal freedom is as fragile now as ever; the operators of any society only just permit each peaceable individual certain freedom of actions: overnight people can find they are expected to drop all, ditch friends, cut up work-networks, prove their intellectual pursuits are not at variance to and do not by some implication threaten, the political establishment. Active malevolence proportions only to how diffuse or tight are the ranks of the operators.[68]

Alison's 1969 rage at mundane Establishment brains must be read in light of the Smithsons' bitterness over their Brasília project. In 1964, they had secured a commission to design the British Embassy in Brazil's capital, on condition that they would meanwhile undertake no work that would compete with the project. This liberated time for pursuits such as creative writing, but ruled out other major architectural projects.

The Smithsons submitted preliminary designs for the embassy by the end of 1964, and working drawings by December 1965. The contract was given in March 1966. Then delays began: they were informed in 1966 that the start date might be as late as April 1968, by February 1967 that the whole project was under review, and in April 1968 that the commission was canceled, as the government did not wish at that time to build a permanent embassy—and that if the government reversed this decision in the future, then who would design the embassy would be once again an open question. This was a bitter disappointment for the Smithsons, who refused to publish any of their designs for Brasília for years.

Writing in "1916 A.S.O." in 1969, Alison represented the pattern of control and opposition as bound to repeat itself unless the lessons of the past are learned:

> In the street scenes of Germany 1919 to 1933 we can see today, and tomorrow: concern as to the working-out of political parties is powerless to stay our fate at these hands.
>
> Some other-directed social ordering will have to be found to ensure that people can follow their chosen discipline—professional or craft—without fear of being messed about by hooligans and governments.[69]

It is within this ideological framework that "1916 A.S.O." focuses on a particular "girl" and "boy" for whom Alison's made-up names are "Berlinerkindl" and "Germanus Preussen," not feasible German names at all (like calling two English characters "Londongirl" and "Britboy"). The action takes place in 1916–1926, years in which the Modern Movement in architecture took root, and a new sensibility grew.[70] It explores the effect political decisions had on its protagonists' lives, breaking them into fragments and disallowing continuity. The man becomes a pilot and sees the Western Front from the air, but his war experience creates anger and frustration that eventually join with other resentments to make him part of the German Diaspora of the 1930s. The new sensibility of the Modern Movement was indeed blighted by such anger.[71] Yet the war also eased many constrictive frameworks, from corsets to religion, and gave the world a new view from the air.[72] Alison's narrative—following the style of other "sensibility primers"—weaves together various layers. Prominent among these is "the earth," from which the Bauhaus grew and flowered into the Modern Movement. Then there are certain residues of the war, including time spent without fruitful work as administrative power grew like a cancer, politicians and nationalism carved up professional loyalties and friendships, and social and political unrest spread. Other layers of the narrative weave together the sense of Berlin in various seasons and descriptions of trams, buildings, and fashion. The novel focuses on the development of airplanes, the fliers' futurist war by machine, the pilots' contact with clouds in open cockpits. It describes how art and technology together produced a new sensibility. The narrative thus becomes a vehicle to express attitudes absorbed and found by creative people, and their weaknesses and frustrations when blocked.

A handwritten notecard in the box of this "sensibility" manuscript quotes from a letter sent by Gustave Flaubert to Louise Colet, January 16, 1852:

> What I mean by beautiful, what I myself would like to create, is a book about nothing, a book lacking all manner of support apart from itself, a book which through the sheer inner force of its style maintains stability, just as the earth hangs in the air without support, a book that would be practically devoid of theme [or in] which at least the theme would remain invisible.[73]

"1916 A.S.O." is an examination of layered events, and how these events affected the lives of plausible individuals. If Alison intended it to be beautiful without visible theme, it does not succeed: it is hugely theme-laden, pedagogic in intent, the exact opposite of Flaubert's themeless mass of pure style. Alison likened her working of these layers to turning over soil, the soil in which the Bauhaus took root. Her story begins nowhere or anywhere and features crowds of details important only to one or two people, who themselves act as stand-ins for everyone who lived through the same period of time—the period of the Bauhaus artifacts we have been living with ever since. Each object described relates to an experience, a remembering, making connections to people, to past events, to emotions.[74] The writing treats history as relevant to all disciplines and lives.[75]

Why did Alison select the year 1916—the midpoint of World War I (1914–1918)—in which to set her novel? Perhaps the date resonated in her mind with a letter Le Corbusier sent to attendees of CIAM 10 (Dubrovnik, 1957), for no better précis of her novel can be found:

> It is those who become 40 years born during 1916, during wars and revolutions, and those then unborn, now 25 years old, born around 1930 during preparation for a new war and amidst a profound economic, social, and political crisis—thus finding themselves in the heart of the present period the only ones capable of feeling actual problems, personally, profoundly, the goals to follow, the means to reach them, the pathetic urgency of the present situation. They are in the know. Their predecessors no longer are, they are out, they are no longer subject to the direct impact of the situation.[76]

Yet Alison was never a writer who worked from merely one, albeit essential, inspiration, and her choice of 1916 also suggests Henry Ford's famous dictum, "History is bunk," a form of which was first pronounced that year.[77] Another thread or layer: at the outset of World War I, airplanes were just coming into military use, mainly for reconnaissance missions. Engineers and pilots learned from experience as they developed the skills to build and fly fighter, bomber, and ground-attack aircraft. Ace fighter pilots were portrayed as modern knights. In particular, 1916 was the year that German flying squadrons were equipped with the Albatros D.I, an airplane that appears and reappears in Alison's novel. It was also the year that aerial photographic surveys began, first to map Mesopotamia (they were in use in Europe by 1918). Alison has her hero fly reconnaissance missions over the Front, his photographic information transferred onto maps back at base. And finally, 1916 was the year German aerial ace and tactician Oswald Boelcke—an instant hero in Germany, regarded as a "gentleman" even in the English press—was killed during a dogfight with DH.2 fighters of the British No. 24 Squadron. Remembrance of this event recurs throughout her novel.

The novel's start point is actually summer 1915, the place the university town of Göttingen.[78] A young man, Germanus, begins to walk home after his courses in the Department of Aeronautics, already late for his family dinner. The rain has stopped. He passes shop windows that fail to seize his attention, though they set the opening scene of the novel.[79] He shuttles past news boards proclaiming in bold red capital letters the victims of war. Something had already changed in his hometown, making his life less reassuring.

> All those school fellows were either at the Front—or beyond. All summer long and into the honied weather, recruiting officers had addressed a sea of attentively tilted boaters, calling for more to join those on the battlefield. No longer beneath 1871 victory flags did wildly cheering crowds sing *to the Rhine*—more often, a sober rendering of *A tower of strength our God shall be*: so the town, despite the University, came to be emptied of young. It was to savour his town further emptied by the weather, to retrieve some feeling of connection, that Germanus walked.[80]

Flash-forward to September 1915, and the fields surrounding the *Armeeflugpark* (air base). World War I would clarify the principles of fighting in the air and supporting ground war from above; gone are the days when generals standing on bluffs directed their troops from morning to dusk. Now war was about aerial combat! Germanus flies toward the Front: "Trench lines ripped the spoilt ground as if it had been puckered by giant tin openers."[81] Turn the layers of events slightly and the reader finds the setting is Berlin during the winter of 1915, where we meet the heroine, Berlinerkindl (Kindl for short) at an unimportant moment:

> Kindl's Papa had arranged for her to be accompanied on Registration Day by a student known through some business connection. Without anything needing to be said, Kindl knew that this young man was not to be considered beyond such a prosaic duty: she looked at the sallow, pockmarked face and the student cap that had seen two summers and saw confirmed there both parental and military judgement.[82]

Apparently this young man was not fit for either the war or Kindl's affection. But turn the layers again, and we find that Kindl will meet and become infatuated with Germanus; their ordinary and inconsequential lives will cross again and again in the pages that follow.

The "Sensibility Primers": Revenge of the Picturesque

Events quickly flash from one point to the next. By June 1916, we find that Germanus is an ensign in the German air service. We do not yet know that his family manufactures airplanes or that he had been a test pilot before the war—that information comes later. Since he had already flown most C, D, and E types of German fighter craft and was familiar with the principles of air fighting, he is commissioned Reserve Class Lieutenant and posted to an *Armeeflugpark*.[83] Here, as elsewhere, Alison pays detailed attention to the notes of her "fact book," trying to be as realistic as possible—utilizing Anglo-German words and drawing attention to historic style of life, clothing, and mentality.

Passages from the tabloid *Jugend* describe the funeral procession of a famous airman, Immelmann, who had accomplished daredevil feats. Exclamations over the size of wreaths carried by two men, a gun carriage followed by a posy on a cushion, perhaps violets from the Kaiser, advertisements as if there was no war—all contribute to a macabre scenario. Meanwhile Kindl is described as she travels across Berlin by various trams (a favorite emblem in the Smithsons' writings), rolls bandages with her grandmother's friends in a church, or makes pillows for the wounded. Despite all this activity, Kindl feels she is a mere observer among the ladies.

Interpolated among these scenes are sights of the battlefield as Germanus flies across the Somme. Huge dark explosions of earth rise up. How, he wonders, can generals continue such an unsavory war? He returns to his airbase with a list of his aircraft's faults. The narrative switches back and forth from the West Front to Berlin and back. After school Kindl goes to a club, the Cafékreis, to work as a transmitter of messages to men on the Front, telling them what they can expect on their next leave if it is in Berlin.

Alison fills her writings with fashion details: the style of uniforms that soldiers wore (Germanus sports a simple Wireless Regiment jacket with Boelcker [*sic*] collar. She comments on the decoration on the small gray Preussen Flugzeugwerke's C airplane that his family manufactured and he had test-flown before the war; it was now painted with a blue and white chevron pattern on its fuselage, pale-blue underwing, small blue and white pattern on wheels and rudder.

> Compared with god-forsaken helots buried in mud, flying fellows were god-like: had Homer ever thought of Zeus in a spluttering, twanging, creaking cradle of spars and cloth? Just as Zeus the child of more ancient gods, so this winger-of-heels, this progeny of archaic box-kites; even now of mythical status to his fellows.[84]

One snippet after another describes the feats of Germanus as he flies through cloud embankments, snowy weather, the fading light of winter, looking down at the enemy's troop maneuvers, the murky, muddy line of trenches on both sides of the Front.

And so the novel weaves in and out of what Alison proclaims are inconsequential layers of detail, the musings of a fighter pilot and the innocent thoughts of a young girl with artistic talent. Kindl, younger than the Berlin Cafékreis crowd, wonders why they allow her to be present, as this is the place where soldiers on leave like to congregate.

She does, however, provide a welcome service: although she does not bake sweets, and is slow to read the most fashionable books, she can draw with pen or brush. So she makes birthday cards, Easter cards, and New Year's greetings to accompany the small packages of cookies and books the Cafékreis women send to soldiers at the Front.[85]

Eventually Kindl and Germanus meet one evening in early February 1917 at the Cafékreis. It is not a fortuitous meeting, for Kindl provokes a nasty incident. Although the reader is not allowed to know the exact words she utters, only the comments of those whom she upsets, we are told in paraphrase that she asks:

> Why us? ... An ordinary generation surely, thus singled out for posterity. Does persecution for a set of ideas, involving food shortages and killing, need to happen every so often as an inescapable wave-pattern of history? But this time, a struggle by proxy: those leaders of nations who had arranged the battle were completely safe at home, without fear the enemy might come close.[86]

Germanus sits in silence for most of the fuss, merely telling her she has the wrong idea about the men at the Front. "Their attitude is that death can be a release—you know—these men at eye level with our earth's surface, existing in clay sweating detritus."[87] Kindl is traumatized by the episode, which reverberates across the novel.

The reader must weave the story together, shuttling back and forth between layers: a pilot and an artist, a fighter and a pacifist, an elite bourgeois and a social reformer, a worldling and an innocent. Germanus and his flying machine up in the skies, or on leave frequenting Berlin cafés where he overhears contentious arguments about strikes, food, and fuel shortages, sees "old women scavenging overturned refuse containers, despite the existence of the stadt-küchewagens that gave out War-bread. ... He pondered rumours that the Franzosen and Britisch still ate their bread white."[88]

Historic details abound: the innovative wrist-worn watch designed in 1904 for Brazilian aviator pioneer Santos-Dumont, because a pocket watch took too long to check in flight; French airplane insignia taken from cheap drawings of lion heads, swallows, or flaming torches; tram-lines knitting together the separate districts of Berlin; hospital trains crammed with the wounded.

Finally, a second, more auspicious meeting of heroine and hero. He is returning on a train with the war wounded, his arm in a sling. She meets the train but averts her eyes from the stretchers, with their broken men. He remarks: "Kindl, we all know how you feel. ... And you were even correct in saying that all those my age would return broken or dead."[89] He and others like him had thought war would cleanse the tensions of an overwrought life: Germanus remembers

> the oppressive sense of too much; too much to eat, too much furniture, ornaments—time after time he had put all the Bulgarische vases of weeping, multi-coloured glass and the painted Bavarian candleholders into his cupboard in order to create space

on the curio shelves for his aviator's trophies—yet the servants had always found them and put them back. ... There had been something of this feeling when people believed the war would be short—a lark—a chance to squander things Franzosen.[90]

[Kindl interjects:] No one in Berlin seems to realise the people filling the cafés are old, so unlovely to look at; really, some of them could be improved by War.[91]

Having recovered from the slight wound to his arm, Germanus returns to the Front. The weather is bitter, the millions of dead—mostly young men—piled up like stiff fallen scarecrows in the fields of autumn. Germanus becomes moody, fighting a war with his own nerves—"he found it unhealthy that he should be ordered to such strenuous exercise in this dangerous situation by politicians, dry in capital cities where nothing trembled the wine in their glasses."[92] He is made a Knight of l'Ordre Pour le Mérite, for shooting down his eleventh victim; celebrations follow, and a much-needed furlough. The whole flying war begins to look insignificant—so many had been killed on the ground. There are flashback thoughts to fliers who had won acclaim, what it was like to become a hero, the many photographs taken, autographs requested, honors bestowed. There are repetitious accounts of the Front, aerial sorties, airplane crashes, deaths of heroes, Allied advances—all in the glorious summer sunlight of 1918. Would this air war continue forever? Then orders given abruptly on November 11 to pack up and retreat within fourteen days.

The war ends. Peace slowly begins, although everyone seems dazed. Germanus and Kindl's meetings become more frequent. Once again Kindl makes a scene at the Cafékreis, speaking against the Army and the government. Must she apologize to Germanus? He replies that her tirade is normal ineffective outrage: "'it is tradition for artists to speak with perennial-student-conceit and so imagine they act; you said nothing extraordinary.'"[93] Marches and protests offer no solution, he says, to the problems Germany faces after defeat; they are merely demeaning to the spirit. Kindl continues her work as a designer of china, glass, posters, furniture, interiors. But what will Germanus do in peacetime? He had gone straight from Gymnasium to flying school, not to Heidelberg nor to the Akademie. "'A driver of an airplane is like the driver of—' Kindl began—discarding tram as too unsophisticated '—an engine.'"[94] Only now does the reader understand that Germanus will continue to fly after the war because his family manufactures the Preussen CII and D1X. Kindl disapproves: they are war profiteers, and she fears airplane manufacturing will be banned with the Armistice.[95]

She is almost right. Germanus can find no work in postwar Germany, and is forced to spend at least two years in exile in the Netherlands, for only there is he able to manufacture and test-fly his company's planes. Germany is forced to destroy all its warplanes by the Allied committees, while the government remains too weak to reinstate the aero-industry's presence. They sell their aircraft, often with men and equipment included, to whatever country is willing to buy. It is awful—so much progress destroyed, hangars dismantled. The prohibition forces men like Germanus into subterfuge; they break these men for the sake of the Allied "peace," but Germanus feels it is the wrong type of punishment for the wrong people. The energy of his generation "has to be turned to action, or contained, or you somehow destroy your fabric; this is another of the destructive forces, knowledge of our inability in the face of life cannot be left out for all to see, like washing in a Moabit tenement."[96]

Germanus's life was unsatisfactory: the Netherlands were fine, the work was good, the food sufficient, but—

> Progress in work, any small success, only nourished a more general discontent that, in part, he recognised as unreasonable guilt in his being alive when others not. He wanted to return to Deutschland, to work to order; this lack of demand for his skills meant he had to keep all his capabilities throttled back. Germanus looked down from his machine, through a depth of wispy fractonimbus, happy in what he was, what he was doing; to a certain extent unconcerned as to where his Field was and—with a mental agony that was also physical—yearned for demands that would use something of his accumulated knowledge, his highly developed ability, these years at the peak of his energies.[97]

Meanwhile, in the summer of 1919, Berlinerkindl is aware of street fighting, strikers and revolutionaries wasting their time in protest, spoiling all the organizations that others had built but not offering anything better in their place. There are disturbing sights of war-damaged men and the poor queuing in long lines. Life seems to be at a standstill, with too much time on everyone's hands.[98] Parties are no longer spontaneous, but aggressive, daring, hard, jangly, full of brittle flashy talk.

> At one party, a man insisted on riding a motorbike up the stairs out of the entrance passage. Only when this had been achieved and the machine was jammed in the bathroom, with the geyser full on and the man revving the motor, did Kindl dare to leave. Since this experience she had decided only to join the Cafékreis if there was a chance to see Germanus, or if her taste in clothes might be exercised.[99]

At last Kindl and Germanus meet again at the Cafékreis. Germanus is dressed in attire less formal than that of a city banker, a suit tailored for him

> in the Russische émigré style; cream silk shirt, collar edges unblemished by any horizontal crease the fashionable pin behind the knitted tie so often caused. She could not greet him as did the others. He stood no less tall, his magnetism undiminished by shedding of the uniform: it had not been the encasing uniform that had distinguished him from all those insipid characters that would show interest in her if she did not find them so devastatingly uninteresting.[100]

Some days, for no reason, she felt hopelessly defeated—like her country's meaningless defeat—and there would arise in her the sensation of being indistinguishably alone among the fluttering papers distributed by people standing tight together in high-sided poster-covered lorries. No longer a student, not a wife, not betrothed or likely to be, unwanted apparently.[101]

Germanus's and Kindl's lives become more intertwined, yet they continue to express opposition and disillusionment. There are passages about Kindl's desire to find work in a man's world, and how she as an artist is emotional and easily excited. Artistic work draws to it many ostracisms—as Kindl experienced—underemployment blighting the talent of those who wanted to work. Had the older generation *wanted* the war, in order to destroy the energy and ideas of the young? Alone and single, she is miserable, while Germanus continues his reveries of war and dead heroes.

Germany as a whole is preoccupied with how to pay 132 billion gold marks in reparations, and protestors march in the streets of Berlin and other cities; there is fear that the Bolsheviks will take over, that the socialists will breed suspicion and jealousy, that Germany will destroy itself. All this Germanus watches from Holland, reminding himself that it is far better to exist there in subterfuge than to be employed in the German administration; such work was unworthy of those who had fought the war: "Administrators, with their pieces of paper are dearly bought devil's lackeys. Everything in which we were taught to believe is under a bad spell. … I need the Allied Commission outed, not outwitted. We waste good years and our energies in activating the inertia of departments of government. These contortions could destroy our culture."[102]

Germanus slowly becomes aware that the entire prewar culture has been swept away; even hats and civilian attire have changed. Once he accepts this reality, he wants even more to return to Germany. There was something important about the tenacity to see an idea to its end. But Kindl wonders: how can one be sure that the idea is correct?

> A dichotomy existed between the life Berlinerkindl wanted—with Germanus across the room so disinterested—and work at the studio where she was wanted and which she would willingly toss away if Germanus would only beckon. Maybe Germanus hated art, fashion; considered her as displaying herself; when to her a dress was something of a victory-flag for acceptance of what was being fought for visually—and always had been fought for! Wearing her own idea was essential to her hopes in a world of rejections: the rudeness of clients when drawings were submitted; when you had bored your eyes out, working late, solving an idea; some did not even pay.
>
> She stands differently—Germanus thought—part of the style of groups that now hang their art in cafés and night spots: the ones who fill the hole in our culture. Simply a new kind of person. Germanus closed his eyes, he felt so isolated these days. … Something had happened to everybody: the old order had failed. Some were ready to throw away all discipline when greater [discipline was] needed.[103]

Time passes; she is anxious, impatience her habit. Was Germanus lost to some Holländerin (Dutchwoman) or aviatrix? But in December 1922 they once again become friends. Her designs for airplane interiors have been manufactured in Holland, and he has some money to offer her. But there are strings attached: she must spend it either on a studio for her art or on a fur coat. The need to spend is imperative, for, he warns, the mark will lose its value very soon. He orders her to be outside the bank in the morning; he won't wait. He helps her spend the money on jewelry, something that suits her taste. Is that all?, she begins to ask, when he interrupts:

> "There is a mystery to you, Kindl. Whether it is the new spirit you found in your Oktober Constructivist Congress in Weimar—that maybe gave you confidence to tell us you condemn Jungendstil, Expessionism, Blaue Reiter, die Brücke, and so on, only you know.—"
>
> "I'm sorry" Kindl interrupted. ...
>
> "There is nothing to be sorry about, Kindl[.] I recognized at Göttingen things were not as flying men intended, should they survive."[104]

Germanus eventually sends her photographs of her work for his airplane company: there are orders for planes with her interiors from South America, maybe more from North America. But eventually the financial crisis arrives, in September 1923. The Berliner Strassenbahn collapses, all the trams stop running, inflation causes a single fare to jump to 15,000 marks or 25,000 for a transfer. Ordinary tram travel is now impossible. The fares keep rising, and Kindl is "frightened in such a society that tried to exclude her by jeopardizing the goal of earning money for her tram fare."[105] Now the wristwatch that Germanus forced her to buy is a godsend; she sells it and uses the money to buy drawing materials for her studio.

As the mark collapses, Berlin parties became even more hilarious, boisterous, splashy, senseless. Such frivolity makes both Germanus and Kindl feel alienated as never before. They meet at such a party and go to his apartment, which evidently she had designed for a friend without knowing the owner was actually Germanus. She had selected the floor linoleum from Holland, designed by Berlage; the rooms reflect ideas culled from photographs of Turkish interiors.

They begin a long affair. Alison, cycling back to the incident that sparked their meeting in the first place, and mirroring her own thoughts about professional life, European culture, war, and peace, writes in Germanus's voice:

> "I was saying you were the irritant in our oyster of the Cafékreis; I was about to explain how I had come to value this—value what you know about because without knowing about beautiful objects we have no culture: we might as well be black Afrika. All this is especially important to me as I have the sense that almost all those with roots in our culture managed to get themselves killed in the first two years of the War. Now,

good design and its appreciation can be an answer to the failure of the money and the Occupation. What I was trying to tell you has been often thought about: that there must be no way back to anything of before: this was not meant to be unkind; it was intended as the highest compliment—."[106]

They continue to talk about compromises, of not following one's own ideals, of being marshaled by other people's commands. Kindl recognizes her own non-success: everyone insists that all creative persons are cheats, fools, or revolutionaries. How might clients learn to accept non-compromise, a "clean solution"?

The minds of those men crouching on street corners must be rotting, for if they do not take to shoe repairing, or wood selling, cart-pushing, they have nothing they can do with their day—the worker's equivalent to a client rejecting a solution. The terrible plunge you take at those moments of repulse; sometimes it takes days to recover, to have faith restored, that your work—therefore life—is worthwhile. The artist or musician can balance things; at other times he recognizes something wonderful. The unemployed can never receive these mind-saving, intuitive, insights. If you are a factory-hand, if you are not wanted, not working for money that is the end.[107]

Life is now difficult in Germany. As costs keep rising, people seek a scapegoat, a way to make an amorphous evil identifiable. If only the street rowdies could be placed under control, thinks Kindl, creative energy would have greater freedom. But even intellectuals might capitulate if driven to despair.

So the novel and the love affair continue, as do the street demonstrations, the long bread lines, the increasing impoverishment, the fiasco of politics. The story comes to an abrupt end: Germanus and Kindl marry in 1924. Airplane travel becomes quick, spontaneous, an accepted way of life. Germanus continues as if writing copy for an advertisement:

"It is therefore imperative to arrive in good order. Otherwise it is not a good story for the idea of a passenger service or our passenger-carrying airplane of our Werke. You [Kindl will] appear in the capacity of a model passenger, an ambassadress for us and our way of travel. It is so. There is no Kaiserene now so it is possible for any woman to hold as fine a position in our culture as she is able. You know it ... and so on."[108]

Alison began to write "1916 A.S.O." in 1966, one year after the publication in *AD* of "The Heroic Period of Modern Architecture."[109] The Smithsons called the latter collection of chronologically arranged images a "work-document," much as Alison refers to notes for "1916 A.S.O." as a "fact book."

They open the "Heroic Period" with an explanation:

In the period just before and just after the first world war a new idea of architecture came into being. In an amazingly short time it mastered its necessary techniques and produced buildings which are as completely realized as any in the previous history of architecture.

The period ended when absolute conviction in the movement died, around 1929.
...
To describe this new "idea" is not easy. Fundamentally, like every Renaissance, it was an upsurge in the confidence of man, in his potentialities and his inherent nobility. This nobility it was felt needed a new way of life in order to find release—a new physical environment; new city structure, new houses, new equipment, new art objects and above all, a new relationship between man and nature. It was to be the Golden Age of the machine.[110]

"1916 A.S.O." was intended to reveal how art and technology produced this new "idea," created a new sensibility capturing "that moment when the dissatisfactions and the rejections [professional blockages] are replaced by a positive all-embracing new conception."[111] It was also the era when the territorial view on the ground was being transformed by aerial photography, and mobility by the replacement of trams and railways with the automobile and the airplane. These would create a new myth and a new style. In an afterthought to "The Heroic Period," they comment:

> The next collection in forty years' time of the architecture of our own period will be quite different for it will not record "buildings," but built-places, and the documents will be mostly air views, sequential photographs and system explanations.[112]

IV. "Paris: Maigret's Map"

Alison Smithson's memory book, "Paris: Maigret's Map," is actually a book-game to be played in leisure time, recalling those of Michel Butor, Georges Perec, and Italo Calvino. By turning the pages of one of Georges Simenon's thirty novels about police detective Maigret, set in Paris, Alison, as the prototypical player, repeatedly selects by chance a street, square, avenue, or quay and allows each name to trigger autobiographic memories accumulated since 1948, the date of her first visit to Paris. Should the same name recur, memories begin to accumulate at that specific location. She lists the memories evoked—a remark, a personal souvenir, a question—without relating anything to Simenon or his characters. The resulting book is based on the assumption that

> each person has an experience and a memory of a city of his own composing [and] implies that this composing both makes and depends upon his attitude to city. To mirror how complex, or distilled, is each individual's thinking about use of city—the personal nature of our pleasures of city—I take the best known city that has accrued a body of fictional history as well as rich changes to its urban fabric ... PARIS.
>
> People think of cities by way of an amalgam of things read, things seen or heard, people met, places visited. ... The built fabric exists around their shoulders in vary-

ing degrees, not as a de Chirico stage set, but as personal compounds remembered, of used rooms, tables sat at, views seen over parapets, incidents, entrances, surfaces, communications, that are all tangibly part of a great amalgam in which there is a sense of there having been a passage of years, not of a quirky—"Disneyland"—reproduction of the "rust" of time.[113]

Memories of "place" cannot be simple in the second half of the twentieth century, Alison believes. Once, such memories were composed of personal experiences and sympathetic acquaintances, contained in accounts by noteworthy authors or given as drawn, painted, engraved, modeled, or stage-set representations; but now the number and types of inputs to memory have increased dramatically and rapidly. Moving cameras amplify stills; aerial views provide new maps; the make-believe of sounds—broadcast or recorded, color television—immediately transmit words, sounds, and images. All of these increase our knowledge and memory of "place."[114]

"Paris: Maigret's Map" was first drafted in 1961 and added to in subsequent years—sometimes with a four- or five-year lapse between bursts of activity—until the final typed manuscript of 1989. Street name memories are interwoven with "read" memories from books as diverse as Proust's *Remembrances* and Orczy's *The Scarlet Pimpernel*. To these are added memories of the Smithsons' own visits, which began in the late 1950s and supported the formation of Alison's way of thinking about cities.[115] "Paris: Maigret's Map" is, we are to understand, a whimsical yet serious instrument for probing the roots of urbanism.

> My document that follows Maigret as he envisages streets and Maigret as he walks, is "urban theory" reflective of the amazing capacity of the thought patterns of the users of cities: offering a mirror to how cities are thought about outside the profession of architecture/urbanism.[116]

> This strange means of proceeding generally demonstrates that kind of fabric-supported, everyday-instinctive-thinking that is vital to the making of satisfactory places that are above all eminently usable, even to the extent of being an anonymous urban structure for our movements and going concerns.[117]

> The quotations from Simenon's Maigret books make the ways through the city for the memories to walk; the words quoted conjure up something of a backdrop of the built fabric that is, in part seasons, in part portions of place … for those with more literary than visual memories.[118]

Alison's method went something like this: She would read simultaneously one of the Maigret books, an unfolded *Plan de Paris*, and a *Liste Alphabétique des Rues de Paris*, the latter two having been bought by her parents on their honeymoon trip to Paris in 1926—and let associativity reign.

I found that Simenon keeps Maigret in Paris within its borders. I used my inherited map for nearly twenty years—so far, half of the period of my use of Paris until it became too brittle: Simenon's copy I imagine as being beautifully framed on a wall near his desk ... when I read a Maigret book I reuse the 1926 map of Paris—to add the pleasures of memory confirmed—so I can be accurately transported into going back to stand again with companions of a visit to Paris.[119]

Each re-pass of each address varied my recall of imagery and whatever visit came to mind perhaps depended as much on what I brought to it that moment as it did on the particularity of the memory amid the inert built fabric of city. ... So that each complete re-read was akin to the many studies of a subject an artist might undertake. Because the self-imposed seriousness required space—the way a pavement artist needs territory—this ritual reading was reserved—as a spread—for Upper Lawn where the half read copy was laid to wait in the shade ... I read in an idyllic setting: each re-read was as much such experience overlaid as Picasso's "re-make" of *"le piquenique sur l'herbe."*[120]

Sometimes this book-game felt like a waste of time—looking up so many of the streets in the list, finding the right spot on the map, over and over, making entries in a long list of narrations.

Champs-Élysées: during our evening strolls, 1948, we used to try to locate on which roof-top Le Corbusier's garden had been made ... twenty years after, a child was taken up: we recognized the description of the fireplace.[121]

Champs-Élysées: every evening, 1948, when nothing else arranged, a determined promenade and at our heels big American cars at snails-pace, purring down the pavement to park between the trees.[122]

Rue de Picpus: Simenon starts us on the northern slope and I see an early morning haze over Paris.[123]

Bois de Boulogne station: the nearest that memory can take me is to look across the Seine at the Blériot factory that July day we went to sit on the "Seurat-bank" (his actual site is downstream, the opposite bank, at Asnières; Seurat's distant factory must be on Isle de la Grande Jatte or Citroën's site). ... *Gare de Lyon:* to which we drove in a taxi through dense traffic one spring evening in 1968, to catch the Sephre to Milan. ... *Boulevard Richard-Lenoir:* Simenon induces us to identify with the inspector who has a good home. ... *Rue de Turenne, Rue Marbeuf, Boulevard Beaumarchais:* Simenon spanning his hand across Paris as if playing chords.[124]

Like the other "sensibility primers," this long list of memory snippets is intended to make the reader think more seriously about mapping the city, more so than prosaically reading an ordinary city map to find one's way. Alison wants each reader to achieve their own autobiography of city usage, convinced that this is actually the manner in which cities are thought about:

> "Paris: Maigret's Map" is, in effect, a new philosophy of urbanism; offering a mirror to how cities are thought about by those who use them; connecting, each way, the people who use cities to the disciplines concerned with changing the look of cities … implying that thinking within the disciplines has to come to match the intricacies entrapped in the commonality of shared myths about cities.[125]

> This strange means of proceeding is an attempt to re-connect professional thinking about place-making to everyday conceptions of places that depend on instinctive reactions and use-remembered-thinking that are necessary to the making of satisfactory—even suitably "anonymous"—usable places; professional education contains no real-life perception of cities.[126]

In 1968, Frances Yates, the author of *The Art of Memory* (1966), published a short article in *AD* describing how the city and its buildings construct a mnemonic metaphor, and thus provide an escape from its natural chaos.[127] Every building, Yates acknowledges, is at first immaterial, having been drawn in the mind of the architect before being built. But buildings also have immaterial existence in the memories of those who have seen them and used them. "Patterns of streets in cities once familiar to us survive indelibly as we traverse them again in dreams."[128] Yet mnemonic visualization is prone to erosion. Artificial memory devices such as books lessen the need to train memory, while memorization of our mobility about the city is inhibited by its very chaos. Pedestrians, users of the city, have to be taught how to read the city as an art of memory in order to envision and help create more lively places.

The classical art of memory as Yates describes it exploited the principle of association: reaching back in memory to a place associated with an icon of recall, building awareness of how the sight of a place or monument calls to mind thoughts of an event that once took place there. Alison, the game-player and writer, agrees. Always the strategist, the instructor, the reformer, Alison believes memory is essential to the renewal of the city. She calls on this topography of remembrance to demonstrate how sites, places, buildings, and intersections anchor and order our memories.

V. Conclusion

With Alison's three "sensibility primers" and one memory book, we come full circle to the "revenge of the Picturesque," the Smithsons' rapprochement with what Reyner Banham saw in 1968 as "the most debased English habits of compromise and sentimentality."[129] Those who cheer for history or steep themselves in tradition are watering down ineluctable directives to progress and development.[130] Picturesque practice is therefore a corrosive influence, manipulating sentimental vernacular elements and offering loose and unrigorous compositions—which the Brutalists' elders had despised.[131]

Finally, the gap between the Picturesque and the Brutal was closed.

This closing of the circle in about one decade re-presents many causes at work—shifts of fashion, loss of polemical urge, idealism making its peace with pragmatism, dreams accommodated to the "realities of the situation," the Englishness of English architects overcoming their interest in exotic influences, the backyard proving a more pressing problem than the patio. ... Somewhere in the process, what the English [Smithsons, William Howell, and John Voelcker] were doing had become separated from Brutalism as the world was coming to understand it. In common international usage, the word was shedding its urbanistic and technological overtones, and becoming narrowed to a stylistic label concerned largely with the treatment of building surfaces.[132]

Make no mistake, the Smithsons urged: throughout the years 1953–1963, they had indeed expressed *"a sense of certainty about what to do,"* while after 1963 "a period of conscious personal retraining" began.[133] What was this shift or retraining (announced here by the Smithsons as starting in 1963, but in other places as taking place in 1968–1978) but the slow growth of a new sensibility toward the land and its traditions, a sense of being at home in a place called "England"? Without compromise, but without rhetoric (in a favored formulation of theirs), they proposed a gentle assembly of associated ideas and materials, a cluster or pattern of associations, of lyrical appropriateness and retrospective ruminations. They admitted a certain inclination toward the Picturesque from the beginning—so it can hardly be called a "revenge"—rather, a working-toward and a "retraining." They used a grab bag of media to express their special interpretation of mid-century "Englishness"—architecture, writings, lectures, exhibitions, drawings, scrapbooks, movies, even outlandish clothing—but in almost every work there was, they averred, a persistent habit of making connections between architecture, the culture, the place, and the climate in which they worked.

Architects and urbanists, Alison concluded, must understand the complexity of many small intricacies,

> entrapped in the commonly shared myths about cities; to provide forms that will be concerned with genuinely regenerative patterns of movement, receptive to patterns of association that will release creative energies in the future.
>
> This is in effect a new philosophy of urbanism.[134]

11.1

Alison and Peter Smithson at Priory Walk, Kensington, 1965; photograph by Jeremy Baker. Smithson Family Collection.

11.2

Alison and Peter Smithson at Cato Lodge, Kensington, 1981; photograph by Otto Daas. Smithson Family Collection.

11.3

Alison and Peter Smithson, Cato Lodge, Kensington, December 10, 1991; photograph by Sandra Lousada. Smithson Family Collection.

11

The Fictional Smithsons: Autobiographical Accounts

So familiar and so pleasurable to us are our post-cards and our books we resent gallery director's arrangements, lighting, interpretations; our familiars give us our own pantheon, our own space.
Peter Smithson[1]

Prologue

Alison and Peter Smithson survived the routine fluctuations of professional life by filling "dead" spots with creative writing and intellectual projects. Alison's only published novel, *A Portrait of the Female Mind as a Young Girl* (1966), is a self-proclaimed New Brutalist book, partially autobiographical. The Smithsons sought to persuade architects to create imaginative books for children as part of a designer's responsibility. They wrote notes on Beatrix Potter's books and children's stories about trams and trains: *The Tram Rats* (1968), *The Euston Arch* (1968), and "Holiday Patterns." Several of their children's books are Christmas stories: "Gouda," "The Crone Calls," "You Meet the Robin." The ephemera of Christmas sparked ideas for studio projects and exhibitions as well. This chapter explores these books and stories.

I. Think of the Smithsons' Home as an Old-Fashioned Family Farm with Everyone Lending a Hand

Alison felt she grew up in a family of outsiders.[2] She confessed: "it's a very odd business, not being able to get on with people, finding yourself culturally different. It was almost like being a black child entering a community of white people."[3] And no doubt this felt marginality, which continued for Alison into adult life, had its roots in her being an only child, evacuated during World War II first to a hill farm in Yorkshire for a summer and then to her grandmother's in Edinburgh for about three years, beginning when she was twelve. And she was indeed an outsider: one of the few outspoken women in the male-dominated arena of architecture in Britain. She never liked giving lectures, and the details of her life never spilled easily from her mouth. But she could, as we have seen, write.

Peter Smithson was also an only child. He believed he was fortunate to "have become famous quite young," although he thought of himself as an "ordinary" person and remained surprised if he was treated as unusual. He was a man of convictions, disciplined yet imbued by a feeling of doom and pessimism, not self-indulgent except for wanting a comfortable automobile.[4]

Another of Alison's self-perceptions—that of being a "northerner"—cast her as staunchly independent, tough, and persistent in the face of adversity, with a "missionary spirit"; she picked a path and stuck to it no matter how rough the going. She felt that she must do so because there were powerful, irrational forces in the world against which she must struggle to create something right and good.[5]

When working, they sat at drawing boards facing each other. They had a complex way of solving problems, Alison said:

> We're both Northerners and I think that Northerners and Scotch people have this fanatical sticking at something, and taking such a rough course for themselves. You read about these people (e.g. Scotsmen in India, or the Industrial Revolution) and you wonder why they make it so tough for themselves rather than just going on and working quietly the simple, rational, non-strain way out of it.[6]

Every minute of their lives was, Alison said, put to good use:

> We are both variously conscious of wasted time. I hate crowds, and we never get into situations you can't get through quickly; for instance we'd never shop in a supermarket on Saturday. We were always easily bored and very easily frustrated; …
>
> We have to keep working … just to keep eating bread. We're just like artists who have to keep painting. And if we succumb to arthritis we'll just have to start cutting up paper, like Matisse.[7]

The Smithsons had three children—Simon, Samantha, and Soraya—and achieved a high interrelatedness between family and professional life.[8] They likened the intermixing of work and family activities to the arrangement of a craftsman's studio in preindustrial times, or to an old-fashioned family farm, with everyone lending a hand.[9] The children were in and out of the office, in and out of other people's offices; they tended to be just around. Peter would later remark about the uniqueness of family:

11.4
Alison Smithson with her children at Upper Lawn,
Tisbury, June 1964; photograph by
Peter Smithson. Smithson Family Collection.

11.5
Alison Smithson on the beach in Brazil,
c. 1964/5; photograph by Peter Smithson.
Smithson Family Collection.

And that leads you to the end where you can see that from the kind of family that Alison and I have, it's got its own rules, separate to society, where the bond is so strong that it makes outside things unreal. ... [I]t was a completely separate world. The politics of the world outside has no meaning whatsoever. It's a kind of conspiracy. Therefore, in a way you're immune to criticism.[10]

The working farm is a good analogy; the animals and the children and the work make a whole occupation.[11]

When the children were young, they made triweekly trips to their "solar Pavilion" in the country, both as relief from work pressures and for the children's health. Foreign travel became a yearly occurrence, but was not always to their children's liking. Alison offers an anecdote:

At one point Samantha was very upset that all the children in her class at school were going on package holidays. I said, "for goodness' sake, one doesn't do that." ...
We took them to Brasilia with us when the embassy seemed a goer, and they looked so happy on the beach we thought, perhaps Samantha is right. So for the next seven years we went on package holidays to Djerba in Tunisia.[12]

It was a major task to manage the ups and downs of their studio work, but Peter claimed that by

keeping our overheads low we are able to survive a slack period. ... We can pay the assistants' salaries but not giant overheads ... this last year [1966] we've turned the heat on to old documents and my wife published a novel which she'd been working on for about ten years. ... But you need the energy to finish it, get a publisher, sit on his chest for three months while he argues you can't do this when you've got to work on buildings because to get them successfully out you've got to keep bashing things out.[13]

Projects like novels often had to drift on their own, because buildings were central. Only in "dead spots"—nonproject periods—could Alison turn to creative writing and Peter to academic or intellectual papers.

A Portrait of the Female Mind as a Young Girl (1966)

A reviewer of Alison's first novel, which she began sometime in the 1950s, wondered at the outset for whom the book was written. It could be interpreted psychologically, or it might be enjoyed for its intimate view of a young girl's imagination, or it might be read for the details of a sense of place that only an architect can offer or even think about with such elaborate care. But herein lay a problem, for it was difficult to judge how a young girl's interest in, for example, the building and development of a Victorian railway viaduct would strike an unspecialized reader, or whether the architectural descriptions would

interest a general public. In any case, the writer should have applied the architectural maxim "less is more," and been more sparing with her few good ideas.[14]

In *A Portrait of the Female Mind as a Young Girl*, Alison reports the conflicting thoughts of a highly sensitive and intelligent young girl from the north of England who is terrified by the prospect opened before her: a future of "suburban café-coffee wife-and-motherdom." She hates the thought of being a kept woman, but does not pretend that being a suburban housewife is creative work, or makes you pleasant or grateful. What kind of man would want a woman who does nothing? She escapes from her frustrations into a bedtime fantasy life where she allows her mind to wander through carefully worked out love stories.

There is no particular order to the sequence of vignettes and commentary in *Portrait*; in many ways the novel mimics, albeit less competently, the streaming of consciousness of its namesake, James Joyce's *A Portrait of the Artist as a Young Man* (1916). Alison's love stories twine around each other and around coincidences from her life. We can read the novel, in which family life and childrearing are interwoven, as a semiautobiographical psychodrama written when the Smithsons' children were infants (Simon was born in 1954, Samantha in 1957, and Soraya in 1964). We can also read it as a monodrama; its singular themes are conflict over marriage and the traditional role assigned to women in society—themes developed in the "sensibility primers" as well. Or we can read it as an architectural drama, expressing its author's frustration over the critical reception of New Brutalism and struggles over unbuilt projects such as Hauptstadt Berlin (1957–1958), Close Houses (1964–1966), the British Embassy, Brasília (1964–1966), and Burleigh Lane Houses (1965–1966).

11.6
"1965 'Young Girl': proposed cover; ochre image red-lead lettering, on silver card and silver paper. 1966 'QFK': proposed cover and pause-indicative illustrations; 1967 'Urban Structuring' (Studio Vista): layout, cover. 1968 'Team 10 Primer' (Studio Vista): layout, cover. 1968 'Euston Arch' (Thames and Hudson): layout (covered marred by colour). ..." Alison and Peter Smithson, *The Shift* (London: Architectural Monographs and Academy Editions, 1982), 62. Smithson Family Collection.

Yet there were pleasures enough during the years of projects unbuilt and competitions unwon. The Smithsons remodeled their weekend retreat, the Upper Lawn Pavilion (1959–1962), driving there over the expanding highway routes of England. Travel in the passenger seat was a preoccupation of Alison's, and she eventually took to journaling the view from the road—an idea which flows into and out of this novel as well. The Smithsons had considerable success in the design and construction of the Economist Building (1959–1964). They traveled extensively during this period: Peter went to the USA in 1957 and 1958, and many trips were taken together during the Easter holidays: Greece (1958), India and Japan (1960), USA (1961), Sicily (1963), Brazil (1965), the Middle East (beginning in late 1952, more frequently in the late 1960s). Meanwhile, Team 10 continued to meet after its inaugural Otterlo session (1959), in Bagnols-sur-Cèze (1960), Royaumont (1962), Berlin (1965), with interim meetings for postmortem accounts or to prepare manuscripts for publication such as *Team 10 Primer* and the Royaumont transcripts. These were also the years when *AD* was open to the Smithsons' publications: "Mobility" (1958), "Scatter" (1959), "The Function of Architecture in Cultures-in-Change" (1960), "The Rocket" (1965), and "The Fine and the Folk" (1965). These articles reveal the Smithsons' fascination with automobiles and the freedom of mobility—ideas that permeate the pages of *Portrait*, as if motion itself might help the "young girl" escape the alienating future that looms behind every love story that she tells herself.

We are introduced to Alison Smithson's method of storytelling in this novel with the following explanation: when something had gone wrong with the day, the girl retreated to her bedroom, to cry into her pillow and to create love stories.[15] If she told the story properly, repeating and embellishing the savory bits, it became more real than the memory of the day. She could go there in her mind, retrieve the feeling of the real place, find herself dressed in all the right clothes. She could also change her point of view: sometimes seeing things as him, sometimes as her.[16]

As a child she felt that she did not fit in, and was often mortified by the thought of what she had done wrong during the day. Only telling stories could restore her.[17] She was hopeful and searching, too, reasoning: "What am I here for if it is not for some use?"[18] She felt she always went in a different direction than others, was never in the right place or at the right time even though her attitudes were of the present. Therefore she imagined societies in which she did fit.[19] When she grows older, the girl ponders her childhood, observing that she must have been an odd child:

> The child that has been alone has a life inside that shows a closed face. She is not afraid of being detached for periods. That does not induce conformity. On the other hand the child that has had few to play with is too excitable, and has not learnt to read a group with wisdom. The group demands constant, recognisably average effort.[20]

Can writer be conflated with character, as James Joyce might be with his Stephen Dedalus? Or would this be misreading both works, assuming that reality is the paradigm of storytelling, that autobiographical accounts act in both cases as entire framework and structure? In Alison's work, the two persons—author, alter ego—seem intertwined yet never quite the same.

> I suppose I would be eleven.
> I used to cry a lot.
> I suppose that is why I cannot bear crying in mine [i.e., in Alison's own children].
> I used to think things that happened to me so terrible. And I suppose crying myself was a way of relaxing. And I squirmed in agony, and still can, over things I could not forget. Things that were not worth remembering. Lost things, and such real rubbish. At these times I do not really want my head or what is in it because it knows things between its bone corners that I do not want to be reminded of. I do not want to go on about it, questioning, examining, worrying, agonising, trying to make it new ways and all right. Yet there is no way of stopping me.
> How desperate are the measures one takes to ward off these disintegrating forces of reminiscences. This part of my mind somehow is over charged, stimulated and throws my whole mind into disorder. Nothing can prevail it. And it is so difficult to think anyway.[21]

Alison was not a precision manipulator of material, an author who could make her words work, express exactly what she meant. While Joyce's word-streaming was deliberate and precise, her style was more like an open vessel into which her words poured. She emptied both social commentary and Joycean verbiage together onto the page.

> Others don't seem to realise citizenship—civilisation—might be foresight. Foresight is a kind of love.[22]

> This book is about love. It may sound crazy to you. But for me it has taken months, years, to get to this point.
> But I knew it when I heard the words down below in the dark. They must have come up from below at an angle. From some point on the street/pavement, across the area, right up, across to me on my bed and in at my ear, and round to the other ear.
> WHY YOU LOVE GET ME MAD? WHY YOU LOVE GET ME MAD?
> Indeed why. Why do THEY do it? In this examination I have had no time to consider as I went along whether what I was writing would make a good story, or indeed, would be at all pleasant to read, for you—or me.[23]

The longest love story is the first to be told. A young girl of 15 lies in bed, daydreaming—wonders if people with fast horses in yesteryear seemed as attractive as *he* is (a neighborhood boy, Chris) with his fast car today. Tears flow because she is too young to be noticed by him. Yet everyone keeps talking about him. She is worried that she will come to nothing in this story; she had better tell another one.[24] Yet she remains enthralled by Chris, who has signed up with an Italian firm to test-drive their cars. He appears at home from time to time and all the girls gather around his car to polish it, fawning over his success. She holds back, for there is nothing unusual about driving Italian cars, it being all the rage. Yet even the neighborhood families find him exciting, not like the usual sons who do things they know about, like collecting taxes or working in banks.[25]

So the elaborate yet repetitive story within the story continues in episodes. She tells herself another story—about a scholar of Greek studying at Oxford—but this is interrupted by the tedious adventures of Chris.[26] She will marry him and travel with him … it is all twisted up with other stories, other loves. She is sitting in a car, she is in the race track pits, she is in Italy, everywhere are signs, "Super Maggiore. Super Maggiore." She tries to make sense of it. In Joycean mimicry she writes:

> only people who had been with you were interested-intensely-funnily. Those who had not been at that track, that race, were not. People who "never left the country" were embarrassed. Super Maggiore. And the sky went on over. The cars round and round.
> She thought.
> Sitting waiting in a car. What it feels like we have no word for. Perhaps if one knew the Japanese word joy/sadness then maybe. But Chris never took a car to Japan. No, it was not at all joy/sadness, it was something else—this sitting in a car simply waiting—part of it was feeling one's ephemeral relationship to outside. There THEY were outside, living at the pace one had also been living at a minute or so ago when the car had been moving. Now inside this stranded box that was shaped and faced forward to go moving in. Yes it was front facing relationship with outside, surely that; because there was no word for it was only savoured dully and no one really realised it. And because there was no word for it no one can develop an appreciation for it in its own right.[27]

If Alison had been Joyce, she might have created a radically new language to think with, but there she sits in a car "waiting," her youthful portrait stuck in paralysis, no matter how much her storytelling alleges itself to be about motion and change. She is attracted to sounds—"Super Maggiore"—or the look of words on the page, yet the power that words have over an expert writer (and vice versa) seems to elude her. She remains stalled in the comforting enclosure of a box on wheels.

There are daydreams about earlier times, peppered with social commentary. One story is about love for a man who is of a lower class, so she has to be careful with her words, for she is the daughter of a Lord and Lady, the owner of the works where his father is foreman. The upper-class girl is disdainful and asks why do the workers grind themselves into such a state of swarming need? Another story, set in Victorian times, is about an engineer, trains, station equipment, and the Victorian achievements of railway construction. It allows Alison to dwell on the promise of mobility and freedom.

> All this new equipment, and so much of it, all being made and brought together into new buildings. It is wonderful to be watching, because it is going to last forever, and I can see it now at the very beginning of its life. I am sure the same is happening all over England. … Also I could come and take a train and leave here. It gives me a sense of freedom.[28]

In the middle of the novel, Alison inserts a long and difficult love story about a brother, Robin, and his younger sister, Ann, who go to Morocco on an archaeological dig. Of course, it will involve automobiles, for the girl always imagines her technique would flower in a box on wheels.[29] This is a more continuous story than most, with few intrusions from the girl in the bed, told in dialogue rather than stream of consciousness. Perhaps its more realistic form is meant to convey the full flavor of an "other" place of hot climate, dust, and exotica.

Alison's storytelling is not really about the education of her young heroine, about seeing her evolve into a mature woman. Her novel is mired in a series of competing teenage romances: it excels in the superposition of times, articulation of places, a disrupted flow of events, but the reader must struggle to put the fragments together. The girl hates wasting time, hates time that passes with no action; she wants to be useful, to make something of herself; but time keeps slipping away and she remains inactive, stuck. In life, Alison never wasted time: there was always something to do. Raising children, going on picnics, traveling, making architectural designs, overseeing school lessons, and writing articles, books, and novels.[30] But her kinetic textual collage of cut-up pieces of time, of gestural features that spill out time, of time endlessly rolling on, never seems to achieve a climax.

> Fill time in. What to do with "one's time"—Oh! the weight of not being able to shed responsibility for time—not even sitting in a car waiting.[31]

Alison loved to write, to play with words, and so toward the end of this novel she explains in Joycean language with a poetic beat how words rushed toward her, how the flow of writing could not be stopped. Writing time was special for her, time her children would never interrupt.[32]

> Catching of ephemeral fingers
> persons in the air around
> chattering love
> catching the words from out of the fire, the lamp, the sunbeams, the curtains, the work that should be in hand, and is;
> but not whole mindedly.

voices from the tap, the brussels sprouts.
song of love from the soap dish.
perfumed words not distilled from chemicals.
amorous advances from the ashtray, the duster, the motes in the air.[33]

What suggested Alison's themes? Clearly some ideas come from travel, others from childhood, and most from dreams: "It just comes on over like the English climate. Sometimes the clouds play with the land. Sometimes they ignore it. Sometimes, like in sunsets, clouds look better than the land. Other-times, the glare bears you down and you wish the sky would just take itself off."[34] Once a situation

> was taken stock of carefully in words and these were the words, or nearly so, for mind words are different from paper words but there was, in the attempt at a report, a recognition of this. The report was carefully listened to and memorised so that the same words should get on to the paper and not carry away from the spirit, carried away by writing-something between the hand and itself. A conspiracy to pay the mind back for all that mental pointing that goes on that you cannot put on paper: nor can you flash the scene on as quick as point to in the mind.[35]

Sometimes she inserts comments on architecture, such as references to CIAM meetings and generational conflicts. She rails against elders unwilling to pass the baton on to a younger generation of racing drivers.

> I have torn myself to pieces on this situation. The old drivers asking where are the up and coming who are to take over, wrest the lead from them: but being continually offended by "mis-understandings" over lack of reverence. Continually stating they wish someone to take over the burden, the changed cars, changed situation, new regulations, wishing "young men" would "storm the barricades": but seeing no faction "responsible enough," cognisant of the code of the circuit, stable enough.[36]

> … Oh! the difference between "against" and "in" in any team world. The "elders" see nothing but disagreement among the "avant garde": not the proper spirit.
> Meanwhile the middle, by-passed generation alternately gives advice to both sides, manoeuvres both sides into position, and tells tales made up out of [thin air]. No doubt they are baffled and hurt by this appeal for young—up—drivers [sic]. And so embittered—alternatively offer to act as go betweens to mediate some settlement—and act as hurt prima donnas all dressed up who sulk in the wings and threaten not to perform—enough to persuade the old stars to lead them on by the hand and present them—just as we had thought we had got rid of them and sighed with relief and about to be feeling sorry.[37]

Inevitably she discusses travel, especially by railway or by automobile. Her childhood was the time of the train and the tram, and memories flow from this site; the future is propelled by the automobile into the unknown.

But that sound of the train whuffing into the sunset may be more part of me than my own voice. Coming out as it did sweet and easy. As if it had always been there in the dale bottom, fully formed. It contained in its sound as much of an aura of space as do Saxon sites, or cave men's sites; the same isolation. It contains a promise that that something would always remain with you, like the rainbow promise only to us now more meaningful.[38]

In the end these love stories are as much about Alison Smithson's childhood, and her love of travel by railway and automobile, as they are about her assumption that every young girl dreams of marriage and children. She ends the book with a paean to the open road and the journey of life. Writing makes language visible: advertising signs appear as if stenciled onto the white page filled with endless writing, playing on words, mimicking a popular tune, setting up a bitter refrain about nothing happening—no projects going forward, time static, immobile, hateful.

> It comes over me. I can feel it coming on.
>   But at unexpected times.
>   It's uncalled for this urge to be somewhere else and go there by road.
>   It does not make sense any longer since everybody's doing it doing it everybody's doing it now [Irving Berlin song lyrics].
>   Near them see them scurrying around.
>   The TOTAL population, a FINA sight was never seen by those who make it their business. Everyone is wanting to SHELL out to satisfy themselves. Give them the POWER and they'll use it to be over the CLEVELAND hills and far away. Shouting I'm ARAL right Jack. ESSO to bed. Only to be up earlier and earlier to try and beat the holiday traffic, get in the JET jam, in among the motley crew—a fine NATIONAL BENZOL MIXTURE we've got ourselves, first the refugees pouring in, then the Commonwealth piling into transport coming here to pile into cars and get on the road: get MOBIL. Once in AGIP of that wheel and it's every B.P. for himself. Every man a king of the road and his front seat passenger a prince REGENT.
>   A bit forced? Maybe but:—
>   If a baby could write "my first year in a box"—from its point of view—it would make us see better our point of view from a box on wheels.
>   …
>   The true mirror of our hardness towards others to our detriment is Council housing—as built and as lived in that mirror of our souls really makes you sweat.
>   What area built up without tree lungs ceases to breathe? The streets with slim dim lamps in the centre where we walked after the pictures. They will do away with them and post their way through some farmer's fields with too wide roads and too bright lights on too tall too ugly concrete posts. A glare in the eye for you at your bedroom window from a crick in the neck, swan neck. Goodbye forever leerie [sic], not a wave

goodnight, no candle to light you to bed. I want a live light, to follow me round the room, not a bulb hanging like a hotel-stare-down-at-me.³⁹

The last word of the book is important: the flow of words must come to a stop, mobility grinding to a halt as she submits to the inevitable:

All motion to the present has been towards life. Now straight ahead is the route towards death.⁴⁰

11.7
Many of the "sensibility primers," *AD* articles, and various book manuscripts were written and rewritten in the yard of the Upper Lawn Pavilion at Fonthill. Alison Smithson working on manuscripts in the open at Upper Lawn (June 1964); photograph by Peter Smithson. Smithson Family Collection.

II. Keeping the Children Innocent

In a 2001 interview with Kester Rattenbury, Peter quotes Alison as saying: "a book is like a small building for us," and "an architect who cannot build is like a man without arms, almost without identity." He remarks: "Those are good quotes. Our model was Le Corbusier, of course. For example, during the seventies really we hadn't any major constructions from finishing Robin Hood Gardens and St Hilda's till the first little building at Bath. We probably did half a dozen competitions, books written, films made, are all preparing yourself in some way."[41] Alberti, he went on to say, wrote books and—no doubt because he was a courtier, a church civil servant—assumed he had the right to write about anything: cooking, composition, perspective.[42] Le Corbusier was also a prolific writer, though he strictly limited himself to architecture and wrote no books on cooking or childcare or childrearing.

In an aside, Peter notes, he and Alison were encouraging architects to write children's stories, books on bringing up children and making well-designed toys, for these too belonged to a designer's responsibility. He had commented on toy towns in the late 1990s.[43] The oldest were made of solid blocks of wood, their edges blurred by sucking and building. These "have an authenticity outside of any qualities normally associated with an art archive—for they have been played with first of all as *things*."[44] To be real, a toy town must make room for activity, must allow children to put things in the arrangements they prefer:

> Children want things to be "in the right place"—the train station to be located in relation to the track, like a real station—signals, buffers all correct. With dolls-houses, kitchen things must be in the kitchen
>
> so also with toy towns—the "institutions"—fire station, town hall, flower shop—each in its appropriate place. A deep sense of wrongness is felt if they are misplaced.
>
> So, taking them all out of the box begins a ritual of getting them correctly located. That is the most anxious, most rewarding, part of the play.[45]

Children's Books

The Tram Rats is a more or less continuous bedtime story written by Peter Smithson "FOR Si. + Sa. + So." The booklet is a collaborative family project: drawings of trams by Simon Smithson, "where the tram went" photomontages by Alison, and the Ratrel verse by Alison and Peter. Notes for a July 1976 ArtNet Lecture, "Keeping on the Right Lines," entailed a reading of the story, with loud tram noises in the background providing emphasis and delight.[46] The depth of England's "embeddedment" in her industrial past, the lecture continued, was profound: both the Causey Arch (1725) and the *Rocket* (1829, an early steam locomotive) were noteworthy examples. The rapid pace of industrialization meant that objects were constantly being set aside to make room for new things: "As a consequence the pace, the style of our thoughts, and the art works that are consequent,

11.8–11.10
Alison Smithson's collages of Trams and Poppies. Smithson Family Collection.

change."⁴⁷ *The Tram Rats* was predicated on an awareness that trams had passed into history. The story opens on the fact that there are town rats, country rats, brown rats, and water rats. "And not so long ago / Tram Rats as well."⁴⁸

Hence the *Tram Rats* story and images are part of the process of digesting what Peter referred to as a "shallower industrial past." Marinetti lived when the Tram was wonderfully new; Futurism and Constructivism could be thought of as the art of the Tram period.

> This shallower past should
> by now have entered our inventive
> blood-stream—for the
> formal inventions—the style—
> of the present must be something quite other.⁴⁹

The displacement of trams by automobiles was a fixture in the Smithsons' writings; they were fascinated with the remnants of England's industrial past, things thrown away and destroyed, such as tramlines uprooted or the Euston Arch demolished. These memories held together three generations of architects, and thus were remarkable icons of the generational shift that the Smithsons so often referenced.

> The change which has had the greatest effect on our senses of possession of territory in this century has surely been that of mechanised movement. If we take "within living memory", the change that all three generations of modern architects "knew about" goes back to horse-trams; the period of excitement over the perfect electric train system—the Futurist Manifesto; the complete acceptance of trams as a normality in the nineteen 'tens; their destruction as these systems were declared misfits in city traffic during the nineteen 'fifties—our "Tram Rats" story written for children in the 'sixties, marked an awareness that trams had passed into mythology.
>   The stages of development of the various movement systems overlap—
>   archaic cars; the excitement of the perfected object in the 'twenties
>   and 'thirties
>   the pleasures of motor-car normality that peaked in the
> nineteen 'seventies …⁵⁰

Trams crisscrossed Berlin in Alison's novel "1916 A.S.O.": the grinding squeal of trams rounding a curve drowned out Kindl's inner twitterings; arriving at the turning-place for trams made her hopeful, because they ended up always going in the right direction, and "something of the rationale of the trams might grind on to her."⁵¹ The sounds of the tram were worth remembering.

> The starting noise and gathering speed of the tram: how could it be adequately described? —With a musical notation? Mechanical sound notation? —Was someone

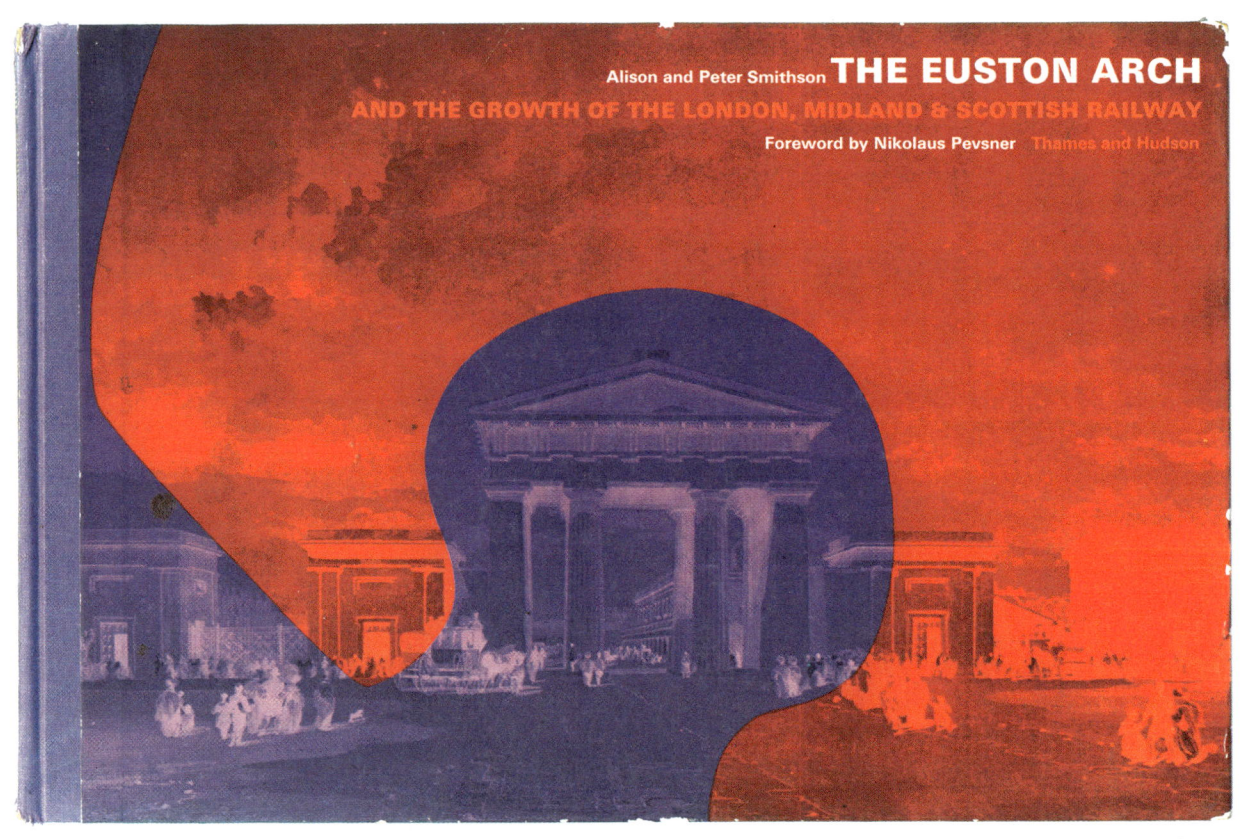

11.11
Cover of Alison and Peter Smithson,
The Euston Arch and the Growth of the London, Midland & Scottish Railway
(London: Thames and Hudson, 1968).
Smithson Family Collection.

working on transcribing, about to make it possible for others to write a symphony for laundry vans and trams? Wheels on rails laid between granite blocks, the man moving the controls making little noises with the brass handle, whirring it round; sounds under the ribbed wood floor with its lift-up panels and flush-sunk brass fitting-rings, the old sing of the pantograph that she could remember from visits to her mother's mother; the skimming along under the wires; the conductor's ticket-punch-percussion dropping little coloured discs: a new world of transporting noises signalling to each other, machines talking about us.[52]

In *The Tram Rats*, the trams have their special destinations spelled out on the Indicator: going to and from Butchers Row, to Highfield Land on Saturdays, to Grandma's on Sundays. "From Comley Bank this tram went To London along the EMBANKMENT." A long list of places flash past, "names as odd as socks."[53] No one sees the little Tram Rats who live in the stuffings, the slattings and under the seats, not even the driver with "the bell pedal under his boot, / Wheels squealing, whining, slowing, TOWN FOOT,"[54] nor the porter who probably wishes he did, not even the Ticket man who clips the tickets or the Sweeper who keeps wondering at the end of each day from whence had come all the crumbs. (The Tram Rats delight in being able to creep into a traveler's bag without notice to munch on the goodies inside.) And so the story runs to the end of the line, and one knows even as night's curtain falls that "Tram Rats will keep the Season's Celebration / Tram grinds on its way to its destination."[55]

The Euston Arch (1968)

Peter Smithson spoke about the range of intentions behind their writings: some ideas are emergent and some reflective, others polemic, still others eclectic and free from narrative form. The Smithsons' writings range from scrapbook to argument to manifesto to poetics.[56] But of all their writings, he claimed, only one was *engaged.*

> It's the book about the Euston Arch. It was absolutely political because it was [Prime Minister] Macmillan in the end who made the decision that the Arch should be destroyed; and that was interpreted as, in a way, an act of vengeance. The power of England which materially fruited in the 1880s and '90s was because of the steam engine. And all that invention was from the North, and the Euston Arch brought symbolically—I'm sure the architect had no intention—the new power of the North. And the traditional power, which Macmillan represented, although he was a working man, you might say, but he married into the traditional power framework. To knock it down destroyed George Stephenson's memory. If it had been a monument to Napier, to a military figure, they wouldn't have done it. That was the arch. It was the one thing which was consciously political in our life.[57]

Other than that book, however, Peter acknowledged, they were not (politically) *engaged*: they did not vote, take part in elections, or join societies. If you join such things you have to be fully engaged, fully participating. "The whole business of Team 10 was like that: it was a life. You'll notice that our children were not born during Team 10 meetings."[58]

Around the time they were writing *The Tram Rats*, Alison and Peter were spending some of the money received from their terminated Brasília project on publishing a limited edition of their "engaged" work, *The Euston Arch and the Growth of the London, Midland & Scottish Railway*, with its poignant subtitle referenced in manuscripts: "The Arch Criminals of the Euston Arch."[59] This was their take on the destruction of architecture in London, also a stand-in for the disaster of government interference with their project for Brasília:

> When a real catastrophe travels round and round in one's bones, it is time to invent the spiralling book—obviously enough spirally bound (limited edition only)—each page an agonising reflection or pang, all continuous, round and round and round.
>
> For to a happening like the annihilation of the Euston Arch there is no beginning—and no end. And each would-be end goes far out of sight, either way.[60]

In a "spiralling book," the writer can speak repetitively in indignation, filled with shaking rage: "A story, running flickering like old books of flick cards—little figures in jerky movement with picks and shovels—such a set of flicks instead of page numbers. A spiral on a stick; to lick at, rather than pore over; rather sickly. / No start or end but spark points."[61] Peter referred to this book as a "wildly signalling assemblage." "It will be easily understood from the content of the book that the ritual destruction of the Euston Arch was felt by us at such a time in a specially painful way."[62]

Euston Station was the first terminus station in London, bringing Robert Stephenson's London & Birmingham Railway from the north into the capital city in 1837. Philip Hardwick designed the station, including its famous entrance arch, a replica of the Doric Propylaea of the Acropolis. Hoping to modernize central London and enable more automobile traffic to flow, the London Transport Commission decided to demolish the Arch in 1960. Its imminent demolition sparked a preservation protest led by none other than John Betjeman and Nikolaus Pevsner and joined vociferously by the *AR*'s editorial gang, who denounced its destruction as "the Euston Murder."[63] Prime Minister Macmillan was deaf to these voices of protest, and so demolition of this monument to the engineering feats of the great railway age began at the end of 1961. The new station opened in 1968 and was quickly denounced as a hideous box.[64]

When the Smithsons' book was published in 1968, it contained a foreword by Nikolaus Pevsner and vignettes at the bottom of each page that reveal as you turn a page how the Arch was erected. *Euston Arch* was a collage, part historical collection of verbal illustrations—the quotations from accounts of the British railway system—part anthology of images of this railway history—and part recollections of a witness to the events.[65] In his foreword, Pevsner proclaimed that "there is a spiritual as well as a material function of architecture and that, whether the architect is aware of it or not, whether he likes it or not, a building has an emotional effect on the beholder. This effect is produced largely by association."[66]

Although the Smithsons were denied the opportunity to construct many of their projects, they still believed that they had a moral responsibility for buildings, for the appearance and quality of places; that they had to battle to preserve the beliefs, ideas, objects, and architecture that formed part of their inherited memory.[67] Thus the "murder of the Euston Arch" was poignantly tied to their own stillborn projects—though the former was worse, because it was utterly final. Alison wrote:

> Incorporating the tragedy which is inherent in creation, together with its never-ending love and devotion; killing effort, care, agony of responsibility.[68]

> The facts are mustered after the indignity of the loss has been suffered. They move me personally and prove my own folk-memory, and after the event confirm the railway-lore tales that one heard as a child. … History is a solace; the facts are part of the story behind some emotions felt—some. Some emotions can only be explained as sensed so strongly by recollection of personal experiences of opposition, blind in-appreciation, unwarranted anti-professional insults cast by persons unknown.[69]

> The death of a great building is not quite like the want of birth of one: an unbuilt project can germinate in the brains of many, send soaring on wings of undefeated ardour future generations of young architects.
> Neither is the death of a landmark—wantonly removed—like the death of a genius who leaves behind something tangible of himself. …
> But the Euston Arch—is just gone—plain gone.[70]

In the preface to the *Team 10 Primer* (1968), Alison had lamented the destruction of "cultural fixes"—England's original railway routes, canals, old turnpikes, land formations—all trampled underfoot.

> Cultural fixes such as Euston Arch, old houses in and around towns, market halls, removed with vengeance = *putsch* = as if represented past culture which if wiped away would miraculously give our country the cultural status of the Riviera. Destruction of cultural reminders which could act as *roots and fixes* is an obviously deep-seated human reaction to stress.[71]

The built environment needed its "anchors," the things the Smithsons had fought for all along: Cultural Roots, Cultural Structuring, Cultural Fixes. They believed we must live with these things, not merely visit them in museums: "Instead it is the time to conserve things, the monuments, the period pieces (St. Pancras as full-dress Victorian Hotel!)—that they may exercise their own power to attract—likely to be more long lasting when all things mechanical have broken or been removed. Each generation can load a load of old stones with its own poetry."[72]

What were the destroyers of the Euston Arch thinking of? Did they not remember

> Stephenson's own battle with the
> anti-railway,
> anti-north,
> anti-industrial wealth,
> anti-liberalism,
> and just anti-.
> Was it the south finally putting in a last dirty anti-north punch?[73]

> The Arch was a monument to the railway age, to an age when for the first time for centuries the power which the court and the south control suddenly came to depend on the industrial energy of the north.[74]

In fact, the Arch had to go *because* it was a nagging reminder that the Empire was based on men working the dirt up north.

Beatrix Potter

Innocent imagination, children's books, and the responsibility of the architect are continuously intermeshed in the Smithsons' writings, particularly in Alison's. The connection is defensible: houses illustrated in children's books, whether factual or fictional, are the normal means through which children are introduced to architectural and social history.[75] They learn from their books about English "ideals of domesticity," making direct connections between the moralities of characters and the qualities of the places in which they live. Alison drew an analogy between the houses to be found in the English nursery classics written by Beatrix Potter in the early twentieth century and the post-World War II houses designed by Le Corbusier. Though superficially dissimilar, both revealed the same detailed and imaginative exposition of a way of life; both strove to become "good container-spaces"; both held the same attitude toward objects and possessions.[76]

> In Beatrix Potter's interiors, objects and utensils in daily use are conveniently located, often on individual hooks and nails, and are all the "decoration" the "simple" spaces need or in fact can take. Those things in secondary use or needing long term storage are in special storage cubicles whose forms define the house space proper—as well as being pleasant spaces in themselves. Here then, we find basic necessities raised to a poetic level: the simple life well done. This is in essence the precept of the whole Modern Movement in architecture.[77]

Beatrix Potter's interiors are tailored to meet the needs of the individual; her rooms perform their functions. All have a cavelike feeling, and in their molded surfaces and their direct handling of materials, her "spaces again touch something of the magic of our masters."[78] In essence, Beatrix Potter expresses the same precept as the whole Modern Movement in architecture. "Where architects failed in their imagination, Beatrix Potter succeeded in making forms of continuing interest in their sympathetic inventiveness for successive generations."[79]

Alison warns the reader not to laugh off the spaces of Beatrix Potter because they are found in nursery stories. They should be seen as manifestations of a new spirit at one with a new attitude to the land, which would become the *l'espace, verdure, soleil* of Le Corbusier and of the Modern Movement:

> Norma Shaw de-classifying, Baillie Scott cottageising, Unwin canonising, bureaucracy standardising. In the face of this final degeneration of values, the spaces drawn by Beatrix Potter might appear a mere dream and the Maison Jaoul an old man's sentimentality. But the strivings of the Modern Movement in architecture cannot be brushed off, however far-fetched it might seem to bring nursery books into the fore to it. Their inclusion might be totally laughed off as fancy were these books not in themselves such "total manifestations."[80]

In an undated article from the 1980s, pondering the process of building for the University of Bath, Peter made the following claim, which can be read profitably in the light of Alison's musings on the spaces of Beatrix Potter.

> For us, an architecture which is palpably built is the most pleasurable of all. An architecture thought-out in terms of its actual materials, its actual processes of fabrication and its actual means of assembly. In such architecture one can sense an ordering from its sticks and stones. From such an architecture one can get many pleasures; from the child's pleasure of feeling a bit to put-together-sticks-and-stones (dolls' houses are most ancient toys); to the grown-up pleasures of consistency of profile, the elegance of fixings ... the re-enjoying of how-a-thing-might-have-been, how lifted up and sweetly come together.[81]

> In Greek and Roman buildings in ruin, the exposure of the neat holes and slots for cramps and dowels adds understanding to the sense of security, of permeating order that we get from the buildings when whole; the seeing of the means of assembly and of the practical reasons for the size of the blocks or beams adds to our enjoyment of an architecture that has been made in the mind first, then carried out with all possible attention.[82]

> A building under assembly is a ruin in reverse. At certain phases of a building's construction the anticipatory pleasures of ruins are made manifest: these pleasures are only enjoyed by those who are part of the process of assembly and even by them, rarely; for building is mostly worry. When the day's work is over or the construction

site closed, under these conditions, the quiet, the semblance of the loneliness of an isolated ancient site takes over: for a moment we do not see worry but silent marvels.[83]

III. Architectural Ephemera and the Marvels of Christmas

There is one time of year, Christmas—a favorite time for Alison, a feeling no doubt shared by her family—when everyone takes responsibility for renewing and energizing the urban scene. "Often a sign will be offered to the world outside that this decorating is taking place—a tree on the balcony—a lighted candle in the window—so that the atmosphere of place is changed,—renewal is being effected."[84] The whole of society, the Smithsons claimed, now could afford to "tune up one's house" to match the mood of the time, to decorate a room for family or seasonal event—"it is to these people that architecture must now offer itself—to their nascent skills in the art of inhabitation."[85]

11.12

Page from Alison Smithson's Christmas card scrapbooks, undated. Smithson Family Collection.

Christmas tales and holiday ephemera lent a "softer touch" for teaching about an architect's responsibility for making linear connections to place: ideas transferred to real life, offering the right touch for celebratory events, making way for the reception of new things, adding to the stuff and decoration of the urban scene. Powerful imagery of inventions, attractive ephemera of a period observed, were turned into material to be manipulated in the hands of architects: "All these [holiday ephemera] can be thought of as exercises towards the right touch for the event, the response that is so exactly pitched to the scale of the problem that it 'triggers' a reciprocity, a wish in others to take a part—to make the place 'as found' receptive to the new thing."[86]

The Smithsons' private archives contain scrapbook upon scrapbook of Christmas stickers; some must have been collected from the period of Alison's childhood in the 1930s. There are scrapbooks of Christmas cards, as well. When they were asked to give a seminar at University College, London just before Christmas 1976, it was a perfect time to display some of this "ephemera" to teach students that decoration of the urban scene is also the responsibility of architects. Alison prepared two booklets for the students: "A Calendar of Christmas" and "Christmas Tree."[87] The latter contained antecedents of the nineteenth-century Christmas tree, carols beginning in 1712, decorations of the tree and ceremonies round it, and so forth. The advent calendar had doors which opened to reveal antique images of Christmas. The research for these documents took place in 1972–1976, beginning even before the seminar invitation, at the point when she recognized that Christmas was the last surviving popular festival. She wanted to reveal how the mythology of Christmas had been sustained over time by continuous invention, adoption, and borrowing of ideas, imagery, and feelings.

Alison also prepared an "Anthology of Christmas" (1979), to be given to architectural students at Bath University.[88] The collected quotations covered the growth and development of British celebrations at Christmas and New Year. As part of the Bath studio, students designed, installed, and lighted an inexpensive framework to display the objects they selected to illustrate something of the history of Christmas decorations. The exhibition, "24 Doors to Christmas," was held at Kettle's Yard, Cambridge, in the month before Christmas 1979. Alison and her students sought to reinforce the sense of expectancy that precedes the festival, so that spectators would leave the exhibition with a renewed will to celebrate through the use of ephemeral decoration, and with the hope that such creative energy would spill over into other seasons and places.

A few years later, the Smithsons staged a series of Hogmanay exhibitions in Edinburgh, which we have already studied in chapter 8. For the Hogmanay exhibition (1980–1981), they utilized the same carrying frame—this time painted red—used previously in "24 Doors to Christmas" (1979).[89] This celebratory feeling of the Smithsons was secular, not religious, but likened to an ode to ephemeral decoration and the many contacts and remembrances that end-of-year celebrations engendered. Among the layers formed by the lattice were items that "dressed" Hogmanay celebrations: greetings sent to absent friends, games affirming local identity, charitable activities. The entire exhibition created a receptive place, calling upon visitors to add their own decoration by being there, passing between the layers, stopping to look. Responsibility is returned to the citizen, for his/her style of occupancy of this new "releasant" sort of place. Alison called this an architecture of a "light touch," with even a romantic flavor.[90]

And so we turn to Alison Smithson's Christmas stories.

"Sensibility Primers" for Children

To keep alive the fantasy of Christmas, to moralize about the art of inhabitation, Alison wrote children's stories. None was dated or published. But Christmas time was opportune to stir the sentiments of goodwill, generosity, altruism, associated with the spirit of the season. We may begin with an undated short story named "Gouda," composed of newsprint cutouts, cartoon caricatures, and yellow and red blotches of color. This concerns the adventures of a round, yellow Dutch cheese who cycles to work and home again every day of the year. We are told that Gouda works at the market carrying bright-red cheeses; then, as if the color red were a signal, the story suddenly shifts to Christmas Eve, with Gouda sitting under one of his favorite trees, resting his feet (which are hurt by the bicycle pedals), thinking about the two bags of presents he has just received from his friends. In particular, a kind cow at the market has given him new yellow clogs. Upon turning the page, a big red man with a small black boy suddenly appear, delivering presents to houses—filling with gifts the Dutch clogs put outside for this purpose. Gouda can see by the street lamp one set of very small clogs the man and the boy had forgotten to fill. Being kindly and selfless, Gouda sets his own two bags of presents and his bright new clogs down beside the unfilled clogs as presents for the forgotten little boy.[91]

"The Crone Calls" (n.d.), another short story, stars animals from classic children's storybooks, namely the three bears from *Goldilocks*; the animal friends from A. A. Milne's Pooh books; Badger, Ratty, and Moley (her names for "the Rat" and "the Mole") from Kenneth Grahame's *The Wind in the Willows*; and a boy and a witch, who is really a Crone, for the difference can be told (a witch wears black and a crone dresses in brown).[92] All are to meet at Badger's for a Christmas Eve celebration, his house being the warmest. The Crone and the child, in his red socks and Christmas mittens, start out across the fields by the light of a candle looking for a small door in the fifth oak inside the forest fence. The Crone's slippers go "flip-scrush, flip-scrush" over the new-fallen snow, after which the child's boots follow, making their noise of "crump-crush, crump-crush." The Christmas moon casts huge shadows over the snow and the forest is dark, without much light. Alison's use of onomatopoeia offers sensory details, which help to engage the listener in what might be a frightening story, and act as prompts to imagining pictures that go with the sound effects.

The Crone begins counting the trees, when suddenly a small brown man, a gnome, pulls at her trailing brown gown and draws her inside an oak, shutting the door behind

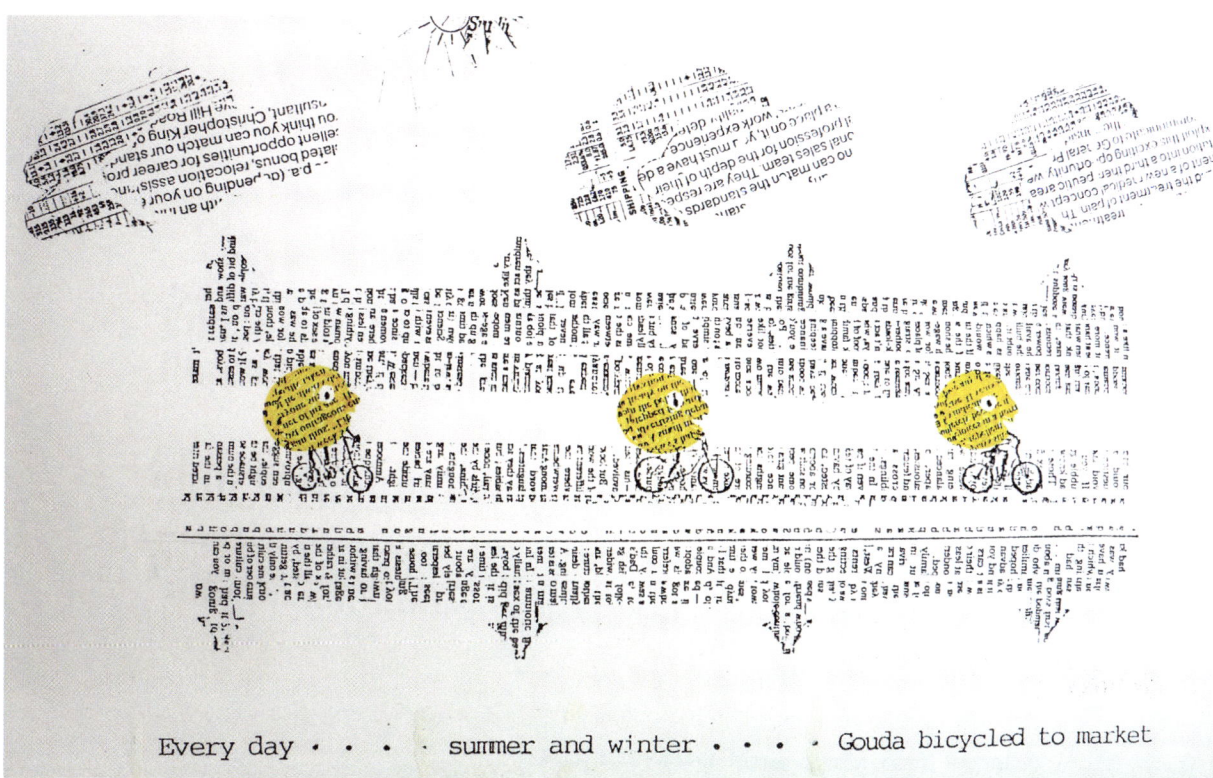

11.13
"Every day … summer and winter … Gouda bicycled to market." Page from Alison Smithson, "Gouda" (unpublished children's story). Smithson Family Collection.

the Crone and the child: "The wooden stair was brightly lit by glow worms, and circled down in an easy wind to a dry, rocky passage, full of warmer air. It smelt of nuts, or fruit, or heather, or was it woodsmoke?"[93] And at the foot of the stair three bears are waiting for them—though this is not Badger's house, which they still have to find. But where is Poo [sic]? They start out along a wide passageway to look for him. Stairs lead off in different directions: signs pointing the way to Spring Flower Store, to the Wishing Well, by Vicarage cellar and lower pond water to the dell. And there is Poo! Now all together, they set off to find Badger's place.

They arrive at Badger's door, knock and ring the bell, but Badger takes a long time to answer; obviously he does not like to be disturbed. Will there be honey? asks Poo. Then "shh"—they stand in an arc around the front door waiting for Badger to open it. First two chains rattle, three bolts are carefully drawn back, a bar is removed, a lock turned and a draft stop slid aside, before they see Badger's striped snout appear. They follow Badger inside: his slippers go flip-flip, the child's boots go tip-tip, and others' feet make staccato-like sounds. "When you had all got thoroughly toasted by the fire, and had time to look round the cavernous kitchen, (of course without Badger seeing you looking—otherwise it would not have been polite), Ratty whispered something in Badger's ear."[94]

It's time to eat the Christmas fare: plates are passed round, there is much laughter, eating, and talking at once. All except Poo, who is deep in thought, wondering if all this honey is to be eaten now or if he has to be polite and wait until asked? Poo knows how to behave at parties, so he murmurs politely that Crone has told him Badger would have honey—and of course there is plenty of honey for Poo to indulge himself. Then there are crackers to draw, hats to wear, whistles and presents inside, and Poo begins to feel a poem well up within him, so happy is he, but before he can begin his recital Badger, who is a terribly kind host, takes them all to the Pantomime. Then it is time to say goodbye, and of course they are polite enough to say "thank you."[95]

So ends this morality tale: teaching children how to be polite at a party, to respect each other, to patiently wait for someone to open the door or give you a present (of honey) no matter how eager one might be to receive such. Politeness or learning the rules of social interaction had to be taught: it allowed communication within a group to move smoothly, harmoniously, avoiding conflicts and confrontations.

Another story, "You Meet the Robin" (n.d.), is about a Robin Redbreast and a cat named Simpkin. Birds adapt readily to anthropomorphic symbolism; they love freedom, yet build homes and rear families, engage in social relations with others of their species, and communicate via structured vocalizations. Robin Redbreast, in particular, has a privileged Christmas symbolism, being both "the bird of December" and "a pious bird."[96] The bird is thus an apt symbol for the Christmas spirit of generosity. While cats are favorite household pets, especially for the Smithsons, and if a family has a cat, no celebration is complete without that cat curled up in its favorite spot, dozing on and off and enjoying the festivities. And yet cat behavior can be devious; a cat must be carefully watched lest it lure a bird to its death. This, then, is a morality tale about mending one's animosity to others by sharing a Christmas meal with a bevy of cats and a kindly, innocent and chirpy bird.

IV. When Architects Write

The Smithsons' writings, graphics of communication, and architectural projects circle around a family of concepts—*patterns of associations, clusters, groups*—each concept flowing into another as an extension of inhabitation. *Mobility, scatter, fixes, identity, freedom*: one word links to another in a deep structure of feelings, inspirations, and aspirations. Another conceptual assemblage is formed by *fabric of cities, holes in the city, mat-buildings*, and *conglomerate order*. The intensity and totality of the Smithsons' word work is consistent with the fact that they used writing and visual imagery to identify and define ideas before they were given form in architectural projects.[97] All their works, including their children's stories, were in essence architectural—and architecture, in turn, was never just about buildings.

They took ideas, seemingly not quite architecture, and placed them in parallel to their business of building. In doing so, they hewed to a sense of moral responsibility whose roots lay in their notion of the Heroic Period of modern architecture. They were, they believed, among the rare breed of architects that deals with ideas, that can discern patterns of association and thus teach others to be clear about their architectural responsibility.[98] They were certain they had been given—handed by Le Corbusier himself—the responsibility to keep alive the language of modern architecture so that it would be worth inheriting by a future generation. The effort was difficult, but necessary; and it required commitment.

> The things that will change men's minds and feed future generations, are not always clear to those contemporary to their manifestation ... potential remains mysterious ... because it is not clear how it can be consumed (that is its immediacy aspect) ... where it is leading or how it can be followed (the inheritance aspect) so that it can become a discipline that is a second nature; an ordering-of-approach that allows both an upholding of the general language in an individual's own language and, through the input of his buildings, an extension of the language of architecture.[99]

> All this, in the hope, that words, then images, will strengthen the resolve of some of you [architects] and will help others to hold course to their convictions.[100]

The Smithsons' interest in words, concept formation, and patterns of association stems from an implicit understanding of how the mind works, how thoughts are formed, how emotions are experienced, how imagination is expressed. They deployed a set of metaphors, both basic and protean: first, that "life is a journey," that is, there are generational inheritances and responsibilities, there are paths leading forward toward a

11.14
Alison and Snuff Smithson (the cat) at breakfast at Upper Lawn on the morning of the great snow, February 1978; photograph by Peter Smithson. Smithson Family Collection.

11.15
Alison Smithson revising manuscripts,
Cato Lodge, Kensington, September 1981;
photograph by Peter Smithson. Smithson
Family Collection.

destination, a choice of directions to be taken, and expectations of changes, shifts and transformations along the route.[101] Then there is the metaphor of family, to which the Smithsons so often resorted:

> [We were] members of the family of architects who give-form-by-thinking-of-the-making, we were attentive watchers of everything the Eames made; we also feel we have a natural right to inherit, as a landscape of the mind, the thoughts concerning the ways of putting things together that stems from Mies van der Rohe. Team 10, once the anguish of making a family was over, a sort of cool acceptance of family, who had not been through the stylistic fire together in the way CIAM had.[102]

> The ideological bond has been the hammering out of the free choice basic for renewal and extension of the modern movement: a tacit acceptance that our kind of intervention, our kind of invention, could not be obvious or dramatic as had been the case of the first period [of modern architecture].[103]

The family metaphor implies a supportive international family, each member offering a helping hand without obligation, free from nationalism, as choice after choice is sought, tested, and savored. The concept of family is extended to other professional concerns: a family of exhibitions, a family of furniture designs, a family of layered concepts, a layering of retrospective ruminations—each project linked to another as family members are bound.[104] And there is a family obligation to the fabric of towns and cities because these form the backdrop for the history of every family, and within any good family each individual has to have respect for and be responsible for the maintenance of the quality of the common fabric.[105]

And finally, there is the overlapping metaphor of the family farm: each member (be it of the Smithsons' personal family or of a family of architectural objects) has to perform many different tasks; members' interactions must interlock, allow for subsequent alterations, remain always sensitive to the need for change. In every family there must be a sense of the arrangement of spaces and provision for the elements of support and service.[106]

Yet when architects write, the following question must be raised. If a word or an object and its associated meanings and metaphors are taken out of context, does this diminish or extend their influence? Peter Smithson's answer would be no, for there are "many meanings, many times."[107]

> If, when we remove a work from its context we lose its meaning … we have lost many meanings, many times.
> from temple to forum to villa to garden
> from church to house
> from villa or garden or house to gallery
> from gallery to photograph

> from photograph to postcard, to book, to poster, to slide.
> We have not killed or plucked the bird when we eat it.
> When we see a painting in the church for which it was intended, it is like seeing a child in a family. ... We feel outsiders.[108]

In the work and writings of Alison and Peter Smithson, words belong to an international family circle, as Aldo van Eyck would draw a circle of words derived from Team 10 meetings. Or, as Bakema would say of an arrangement of buildings, they must be designed to appear more like a family, generating a "family holding hands" possibility.[109] In a similar manner, Peter explained that the "conglomerate order" of architecture is like a farm and all of its enclosures:

> on a farm, a stone wall between fields pens in but also shelters the sheep in the snow time. Each part of a structure needs to perform and encompass many tasks. In our time we thought this way of building should be developed. It is nonformal and does not use classical geometry. If you look out of the window, you can see a certain something that allows you to locate yourself, to look this way and that way. ...
> That's what conglomerate ordering is: to build it like a farmer when he's making a decision—"Well, if I have to do all that work, I also want it to do that and that and that." Everything should have multiple uses.[110]

Building in words, with a family of words, allows each word to reflect off the others into multiple uses. Words can form a pre-architectural conglomerate order, like a farm, like a family farm, like a family, like a family on a journey. Building in words invites one to spin back to childhood memories, to reminisce creatively, bridging past and present to create something new for the future, whether one revisits childhood places to get ideas for children's stories, reutilizes forgotten influences for architectural projects, or stitches a city's fabric so that it spells out a conglomerate order. The Smithsons' work was essentially associative, deliberately nonsystematic, synesthetic, collagistic—language, whimsy, buildings, and daydreams transmute each other and exchange influences in a nexus of sensual play, with results not always either consistent or predictable, not produced by a working out of fixed generative rules. They did not, they said of themselves,

> follow an even ideological track. ... The jumps, the reappearances of earlier ideas often occur for chance reasons: for example, a field boundary on a map, suddenly seen "graphically" as a line; a line with a certain power, which becomes the beginning of an ordering, seemingly without a logic outside its existance [sic] as a line: that line had, maybe, a previous existance in our work of which at the time we were unaware. This pattern of persistence has been clouded by what appears to be a characteristic of the human brain. The brain seems to have a new insight; but frequently this turns out to be an old insight which has been newly arrived at in an entirely new set of circumstances, and through different thought processes.[111]

Memories of childhood territory return, a fresh well of influences, renewing deep sensations. Revisiting Bath, Athens, Cambridge, Milan, Stockholm, Edinburgh, and other favored places becomes a ritual of remembrance set by "the impulse to re-taste the flavour of personal earliest experiences of the territory: at its most extreme a seeking of the places where the sensation is sharpest in us."[112] They are revenants to the stonewalls, fields, hills, and farms of their childhood, reinscribing their northern references in architectural projects, making them reappear as motifs of their children's stories, enclosing themselves in a happy wrapping of remembrance.

Framing the environment mattered to the Smithsons—looking through architecture, beyond walls and hillsides, to the distant landscape. Just as important was to structure their life as a family story, and not only metaphorically: architecture and children fitting together, traveling, telling stories, looking at architecture, remembering and doing in a continuous present, instilling hope for a landscape and an architecture that could survive. Desiring buildings "speaking into the air," registering and responding to climate; moving in a car, tram, or train while perceiving how movement contributes to a new sensibility; observing the many acts of inhabitation and layers of occupation that leave imprints on a house, mark a territory, determine the way a structure sits on the land, draws in the sun; responding to the way that pavilions, idylls, and enclaves take possession of surrounding territory, allowing for quietness and simplicity; recognizing how the barn, farmyard, granary, fort, town wall, gate, and the spaces between charge, energize, and order the land; taking responsibility for creating "places-to-stop-and-do-things-in," for allowing reciprocity and response between the built and the growing. Their list of appreciations grows, continues.[113]

Alison and Peter Smithson belonged to the last notable cohort of twentieth-century architects to be collectively concerned with social issues, owning a complete set of concepts and methods for dealing with the land and creating places worth inheriting, their local character preserved or reclaimed.[114] The Smithsons did indeed love the picturesque English town, the way its buildings fit together and hug the land, every bit as much as AR's authors with their advocacy of Townscape Analysis. If this is "revenge," then the Picturesque had it and the Smithsons are guilty as Banham charged—but so what? In the traditional city, generations of buildings and houses do in fact come together, layers of inhabitation marking each part until they blend into a whole. The Smithsons admitted that their Picturesque sensibility sprung from the literature and landscape of northern England, where such places abounded.

This encounter with architecture as written by Alison and Peter Smithson has explored the way in which they framed their awareness of and responsibility for the architectural field they inherited. In their collage methods of writing and imagery, in scrapbook albums, in clustering concepts and layering projects, in going back to the past in order to go forward into the future, they displayed a passion for words and imagery imbued by both a childlike sense of wonder and an adult sense of responsibility.

Walter Benjamin reminds us that a collector of books, by giving them a rebirth—unpacking them, reading them, bringing them out of literal darkness to metaphoric life—mingles childlike and adult elements: "For children can accomplish the renewal of existence in a hundred unfailing ways. Among children, collecting is only one process of renewal; other processes are the painting of objects, the cutting out of figures, the application of decals—the whole range of childlike modes of acquisition, from touching things to giving them names."[115] For the adult acquirer of books, Benjamin said, writing a book is the "most praiseworthy method" of acquiring one and thereby renewing existence—writing out of dissatisfaction with all the books, pamphlets, treatises, and manifestos that already exist. In this sense, Alison and Peter Smithson were avid collectors of the language of architecture. They believed they had a moral obligation, as inheritors of the language of modern architecture, to renew its world by strengthening that language, by protecting and caring for the assemblage so it could stand, endure, be inherited by future generations. "Thus it is," Benjamin writes—"it" being the collector's sense of responsibility—"in the highest sense, the attitude of an heir, and the most distinguished trait of a collection will always be its transmissibility."[116] This was the very challenge received by the Smithsons from their visionary elder, Le Corbusier: to inherit the language of modern architecture, to keep it alive, to render it transmissible. For the Smithsons this implied protecting the role of the architect as a visionary of a city yet to come.

Notes

Preface

1. They met as architectural students at Durham University, which Peter attended 1939–1942 and 1945–1948, Alison 1944–1949.
2. CIAM stands for Congrès International d'Architecture Moderne (1928–1956).
3. "Not Quite Architecture" is the title of a series of articles appearing in the *Architects' Journal*, to which Alison contributed from time to time.
4. Alison and Peter Smithson, *The Shift*, Architectural Monographs 7 (London: Architectural Monographs and Academy Editions, 1982), 9.
5. Alison and Peter Smithson, *Italian Thoughts* (Stockholm: Alison & Peter Smithson, 1993), 22.
6. Ibid., 101–102.
7. Peter Smithson, "Le Corbusier; First Confrontations with the Work of the Master" (9.1.87), CORB:DLF, 1–5. MAGIC BOX, Folder Le Corbusier. Smithson Family Collection.
8. Peter Smithson, "CIAM-Re-Organisation" (August 28–29, 1957), 1–2, TTEN0002, Folder 17, NAi, Rotterdam; reprinted in Alison Smithson, ed., *The Emergence of Team 10 out of CIAM 1953/1978* (London: Architectural Association, 1982), 82–83.
9. Alison and Peter Smithson, *Without Rhetoric: An Architectural Aesthetic 1955–1972* (Cambridge, MA: MIT Press, 1973), 48–49.
10. Jacques Derrida, *Archive Fever: A Freudian Impression*, trans. Eric Prenowitz (Chicago: University of Chicago Press, 1996), 7.
11. Panayotis Tournikiotis, *The Historiography of Modern Architecture* (Cambridge, MA: MIT Press, 1999), 237.
12. On suggesting that modern architecture exists primarily in the pages of architectural magazines, see Beatriz Colomina, *Privacy and Publicity: Modern Architecture as Mass Media* (Cambridge, MA: MIT Press, 1996).
13. Peter Smithson, "Le Corbusier; First Confrontations," 1.
14. Ibid., 2.
15. Ibid., 3.
16. Soraya Smithson, the Smithsons' youngest daughter, thinks Peter Smithson was responsible for such careful documentation, which stemmed from his training in the Army during World War II. Conversation, May 2011.
17. Kester Rattenbury, "Think of It as a Farm! Exhibitions, Books, Buildings: An Interview with Peter Smithson" (interview before January 12, 2001; text of interview February 28, 2001),

1–11, 1, BOX AS & PS UNPUBLISHED PAPERS + CURRENT LECTURES. Smithson Family Collection. Peter Cook ran the ArtNet Gallery (1972–1979). This interview is also published as "Think of It as a Farm! Exhibitions, Books, Buildings," in Kester Rattenbury, ed., *This Is Not Architecture: Media Constructions* (London: Routledge 2002), 91–98.

Chapter 1

1. The use of terms such as *England* and *Englishness* may be questioned. As in the postwar period, I deploy it as a metonym for the whole UK here and throughout the following text, though latter-day usage would favor either *Britain* or *UK*, inclusive of Wales, Scotland, and Northern Ireland. In particular, I use the term "Englishness" as it was conceptualized in the 1950s—an insular national identity, entailing a series of cultural and racial connotations.
2. Reyner Banham, "Revenge of the Picturesque: English Architectural Polemics 1945–1965," in John Summerson, ed., *Concerning Architecture: Essays on Architectural Writers and Writing Presented to Nikolaus Pevsner* (London: Allen Lane, Penguin Press, 1968), 265.
3. "Banham's Bumper Book on Brutalism, Discussed by Alison and Peter Smithson," *Architects' Journal* 144 (December 28, 1966), 1590.
4. Alison and Peter Smithson, typed manuscript review of "The New Brutalism" by Peter Reyner Banham (intended for *New Statesman*, 1967) (December 1, 1966, revised April 21, 1967), photocopy. Smithson Family Collection.
5. Maureen Waller, *London 1945: Life in the Debris of War* (New York: St. Martin's Griffin, 2004).
6. These ideals were encapsulated in Ebenezer Howard's Garden Cities or Patrick Geddes's regional surveys of local distinctiveness. Peter Mandler, "New Towns for Old: The Fate of the Town Centre," in Becky Conekin, Frank Mort, and Chris Waters, eds., *Moments of Modernity: Reconstructing Britain 1945–1964* (London: Rivers Orman Press, 1999), 208–227.
7. Waller, *London 1945*, 20.
8. John R. Gold, *The Experience of Modernism: Modern Architects and the Future City, 1928–1958* (London: E & F Spon, 1997), 189–190.
9. Nicholas Bullock, *Building the Post-War World* (London: Routledge, 2002), xi.
10. Gold, *The Experience of Modernism*, 89; see also the history of *AR* in "1935–1951: Richards, Pevsner, the War and the Festival of Britain," *AR* 199, special issue "The First 100 Years" (May 1996), 54–69.
11. J. M. Richards was editor of *AR* for more than 30 years. His flat was filled with photographs and other evidence of his interests, which ranged far beyond architecture. He was devoted to the idea that architecture was not about style, but about people and a commitment to social improvement through design and technology. "J. M. Richards 1907–1992: Tributes by Mark Girouard, Sir Denys Lasdun and Myfanwy Piper," *AA Files* 25 (Summer 1993), 30–32.
12. Timothy Mowl, *Stylistic Cold Wars: Betjeman versus Pevsner* (London: John Murray, 2000), 99–101.
13. Nikolaus Pevsner, *The Englishness of English Art* (London: Architectural Press, 1956).

14. The manuscript notes in the Getty archives have recently been assembled and published as Nikolaus Pevsner, *Visual Planning and the Picturesque* (edited by Mathew Aitchison) (Los Angeles: Getty Publications, 2010).
15. J. M. Richards, "Retrospect," *AR* 149 (February 1971), 69.
16. "1935–1951: Richards, Pevsner, the War and the Festival of Britain."
17. Although "collage" is a term commonly used in *AR* articles during the 1940s and 1950s, Alan Powers employs it to illustrate how the English vernacular was revitalized as a modern idiom after the war, as architects made the past palatable with the contemporary through a process of "collage." Alan Powers, "The Reconditioned Eye: Architects and Artists in English Modernism," *AA Files* 25 (Summer 1993), 54–62.
18. For a detailed discussion of the "Townscape" and collage principles, see John Macarthur and Mathew Aitchison, "Pevsner's Townscape," in Pevsner, *Visual Planning and the Picturesque*, 13–19.
19. Editorial, "The First Half Century," *AR* 101 (January 1947), 36.
20. David Watkin (ed. Gavin Stamp), "Architectural Writing in the Thirties," *Britain in the Thirties (Architectural Design Profile 24), AD* 49 (1979), 84–95.
21. John Betjeman, *First and Last Loves* (London: John Murray, 1952), 115; quoted by Andrew Law, "English Townscape as Cultural and Symbolic Capital," in Andrew Ballantyne, ed., *Architectures: Modernism and After* (Oxford: Blackwell Publishing Ltd., 2004), 213.
22. John Betjeman, *English Cities and Small Towns* (London: W. Collins, 1943), 42; quoted by David Matless, *Landscape and Englishness* (London: Reaktion Books, 1998), 193.
23. Matless, *Landscape and Englishness*, 193.
24. "Outrage," *AR* special issue (June 1955), 452.
25. The debate between C. P. Snow and F. R. Leavis exemplifies this discussion between science and art, and the way forward toward modernity. C. P. Snow, *The Two Cultures* (Cambridge: Cambridge University Press, 1998; first published 1959).
26. Mowl, *Stylistic Cold Wars*, 98.
27. The expression "will-to-war" was invoked by government and the press during World War II, generally to imply the maintenance of civilian fortitude and morale. Amy Bell, "Landscapes of Fear: Wartime London 1939–1945," *Journal of British Studies* 48 (January 2009), 153–175.
28. The first use of "Functional Tradition" appears in a 1947 editorial, "The Second Half Century," *AR* 101 (January 1947), 21–26, with a special issue of the magazine appearing in 1950, "The Functional Tradition," *AR* 107(January 1950), 2–57.
29. "J. M. Richards 1907–1992."
30. J. M. Richards, *Castles on the Ground: The Anatomy of Suburbia* (London: Architectural Press, 1946, 2nd edn., London: John Murray, 1973), 14–15, 17.
31. Ibid., 18.
32. Ibid., 19.
33. Ibid., 20.
34. Ibid., 24, 29, 30, 31.

35. Ibid., 32.
36. Ibid., 24.
37. Richards, "Retrospect," 70.
38. Ibid., 71.
39. Ibid., 72.
40. Ibid., 71.
41. Joseph Rykwert, "Review of a Review," *Zodiac* 4 (Fall 1959), 13.
42. Ibid.
43. Ibid., 13, 15.
44. Richards, *Castles on the Ground*, 56; quoted by Rykwert, "Review of a Review," 15.
45. Rykwert, "Review of a Review," 13.
46. Editorial, "The Architecture Review and the War," *AR* 90 (July 1941), 117.
47. Editorial, "The English Planning Tradition in the City," *AR* 97 (June 1945), 170.
48. The *AR* special issue claimed that Banham joined in 1952: "1952–1973: Modernism Triumphs and Begins to Decline," *AR* 199, special issue "The First 100 Years" (May 1996), 70–87. Nigel Whiteley also claims it was 1952: Nigel Whiteley, *Reyner Banham: Historian of the Immediate Future* (Cambridge, MA: MIT Press, 2002), 9, 15. However, Mathew Aitchison states that Banham became assistant literary editor in March 1953 and assistant executive editor in October 1959, holding the latter position until November 1964, somewhat prior to which time he had begun to lecture on an occasional basis at the Courtauld Institute of Art. Mathew Aitchison, "Visual Planning and Exterior Furnishing: A Critical History of the Early Townscape Analysis 1930 to 1949" (PhD dissertation, University of Queensland, 2008), 230.
49. Banham left the *AR* in 1964 to take up a position as Senior Lecturer at the Bartlett School of Architecture, University College, London, where he remained for 12 years. Whiteley, *Reyner Banham*, 26.
50. For a detailed analysis of the development of *AR*'s policy on Townscape, see Aitchison, "Visual Planning and Exterior Furnishing." For a contextual argument on *AR*'s overall postwar editorial policy, see Erdem Erten, "Shaping 'the Second Half Century': *The Architectural Review* 1947–1971" (PhD dissertation, MIT, 2004).
51. "1952–1973: Modernism Triumphs and Begins to Decline." Aitchison notes that Pevsner tried to retire from his editorial position at *AR* in December 1961, but his final letter of resignation is dated June 3, 1970, and accepted by Hastings July 16, 1970. Getty Center: Box 6, Folder: Correspondence: The Architectural Review (1970). Aitchison, "Visual Planning and Exterior Furnishing," 39, footnote 53. Susie Harries writes that Pevsner tried without success to leave the *Review* in 1961; however, his official resignation took effect on January 1, 1971. Susie Harries, *Nikolaus Pevsner: The Life* (London: Pimlico, 2013).
52. *AR* 146, special issue "Manplan 1" (September 1969); special issue "Manplan 2" (October 1969); special issue "Manplan 3" (November 1969).
53. "1952–1973: Modernism Triumphs and Begins to Decline."
54. The pseudonym comes from the eighteenth-century Viennese sculptor Georg Raphael Donner, a favorite artist of Pevsner's. Nikolaus Pevsner, Sacheverell Sitwell, and Anthony

Ayscough co-authored a book entitled *German Baroque Sculpture* (London: Duckworth, 1938); see also "Mr. Donner's little exercises in the London suburbs," in Henry-Russell Hitchcock, "Some Problems in the Interpretation of Modern Architecture," *Journal of the American Association of Architectural Historians* 2, no. 2 (1942), 29–32, 40; Rob Stone, "Privet Theologies of Privacy in Some Modernist Urbanism," in Iain Boyd Whyte, ed., *Modernism and the Spirit of the City* (London: Routledge, 2003), 209–235. For derivation of F. R. Donner, see John Barr, "Select Bibliography of the Publications of Nikolaus Pevsner," in Summerson, *Concerning Architecture*, 278.

55. Aitchison, "Visual Planning and Exterior Furnishing," 45.
56. Peter F. R. Donner [Nikolaus Pevsner], "The End of the Pattern-Books," *AR* 93 (March 1943), 75–79; Peter F. R. Donner [Nikolaus Pevsner], "Edensor or Brown Comes True," *AR* 95 (February 1944), 39–43.
57. Nikolaus Pevsner, "The Genesis of the Picturesque," *AR* 96 (November 1944), 139–146.
58. Ibid., 140.
59. Ibid., 141.
60. Ibid., 142.
61. Ibid., 146.
62. Nikolaus Pevsner, "Price on Picturesque Planning," *AR* 95 (February 1944), 47–50.
63. Uvedale Price, *Essay on the Picturesque* (I, 50); quoted by Pevsner, "Price on Picturesque Planning," 47.
64. Pevsner, "Price on Picturesque Planning," 48.
65. Ibid.
66. Ibid., 49.
67. Ibid.
68. Ibid., 50.
69. Ibid.
70. Gordon Cullen, "Townscape Casebook," *AR* 106 (December 1949), 363–374.
71. Richards, "Retrospect," 70.
72. Ibid.
73. Editorial [Hubert de Cronin Hastings], "Exterior Furnishing or Sharawaggi: The Art of Making Urban Landscape," *AR* 95 (January 1944), 3–8. The editorial is anonymous but has been attributed to Hastings by Erdem Erten, "Shaping 'the Second Half Century,'" 35, footnote 18. Erten reports that an interview with Hastings by Susan Lasdun reveals that Hastings was indeed the author of this article on "Townscape Theory." Aitchison repeats this attribution: Aitchison, "Visual Planning and Exterior Furnishing," 140.
74. Editorial, "Exterior Furnishing or Sharawaggi," 14.
75. Pevsner, *Visual Planning and the Picturesque*, 31.
76. Ibid.
77. Nikolaus Pevsner, "The Picturesque in Architecture," *Journal of the Royal Institute of British Architects* [*RIBA*] 55 (December 1947), 58.

78. Pevsner, *The Englishness of English Art*, 183.
79. Editorial, "The English Planning Tradition," 167.
80. Ibid., 175.
81. For an argument that supports Hastings's dominant influence, see Pevsner, *Visual Planning and the Picturesque*.
82. "Introduction: A Pictorial Anthology of City Life," *AR* 97 (June 1945), 164.
83. Editorial, "The English Planning Tradition," 167.
84. Ibid.
85. Editorial, "The Second Half Century," 23.
86. Ivor de Wolfe [Hastings], "Townscape: A Plea for an English Visual Philosophy Founded on the True Rock of Sir Uvedale Price," *AR* 106 (December 1949), 355.
87. Editorial, "Contents," *AR* 106 (December 1949), 343.
88. De Wolfe, "Townscape," 355.
89. Ibid., 362.
90. Ibid.
91. Editorial, "Exterior Furnishing or Sharawaggi," 8.
92. Ibid., 6–7.
93. Ibid., 8.
94. Cullen, "Townscape Casebook."
95. Ibid., 363.
96. bid.
97. Ibid.
98. Ibid.
99. Editorial, "Contents," 1.
100. Editorial, "The Second Half Century," 23.
101. Ibid., 24.
102. Introduction, "The Functional Tradition," *AR* special issue; J. M. Richards, "The Next Step?," *AR* 107 (March 1950), 165–171.
103. Introduction, "The Functional Tradition," 3.
104. Ibid., 4.
105. Ibid.
106. Editorial, "The Discipline of Functionalism," *AR* 107 (January 1950), 6.
107. Richards, "The Next Step?," 166.
108. Ibid.
109. Ibid., 167.
110. Ibid., 180.
111. Ibid., 181.
112. George H. Gilpin, *The Art of Contemporary English Culture* (London: Macmillan, 1991), 95.

113. Geoffrey Fisher, Archbishop of Canterbury, speech, July 17, 1950, printed in the "Official Book" of the Festival of Britain, n.p. inside of cover. Quoted by Becky Conekin, "The Autobiography of a Nation: The 1951 Festival of Britain, Representing Britain in the Post-War Era" (PhD dissertation, University of Michigan, 1999), 37.

114. Gold, *The Experience of Modernism*, 214.

115. Memo from Gerald Barry, mid-August 1949; quoted by Conekin, "The Autobiography of a Nation," 25.

116. Bevis Hillier, "Introduction," in Mary Banham and Bevis Hillier, eds., *A Tonic to the Nation: The Festival of Britain, 1951* (London: Thames and Hudson, 1976), 10–17.

117. "The Festival of Britain," *AD* 19 (December 1949), 310–311.

118. Becky Conekin, "'Here Is the Modern World Itself': The Festival of Britain's Representations of the Future," in Conekin, Mort, and Waters, *Moments of Modernity*, 228–245.

119. Gold, *The Experience of Modernism*, 210–214.

120. Quoted in "Ninety Years On," *Architects' Journal* 179 (June 27, 1984), 92.

121. Ibid.

122. "J. M. Richards 1907–1992."

123. J. M. Richards, "Old and New Elements of the Core," in Jaqueline Tyrwhitt, ed., *CIAM 8: The Heart of the City* (London: Lund Humphries, 1952), 61.

124. Ibid., 63.

125. Hugh Casson, "Period Piece," in Mary Banham and Hillier, eds., *A Tonic to the Nation*, 81.

126. Johnson-Marshall, quoted by Gold, *The Experience of Modernism*, 220–221.

127. Reyner Banham, "The Style: 'Flimsy … Effeminate'?" in Mary Banham and Hillier, eds., *A Tonic to the Nation*, 194.

128. Both Reyner Banham and Hugh Casson remember *AR* receiving a cobblestone for Christmas, presumably in a reaction to the parochial sentiment expressed in Townscape's campaign during this period. Aitchison, "Visual Planning and Exterior Furnishing," 198.

129. Banham, "Revenge of the Picturesque," 265.

130. Ibid.

131. Alison Smithson, "Identity: Patterns of Association: Cluster" (undated), C1.1–7. BOX AMS LECTURES AS EVOLVED. Smithson Family Collection.

132. Banham, "Revenge of the Picturesque," 273.

Chapter 2

1. Piet Mondrian, quoted in CIAM X ALGER 1955, D2(08), 1. Fondation Le Corbusier (FLC), Paris.

2. J. M. Richards, *Modern Architecture* (Baltimore: Penguin, 1963, original 1940), 9.

3. R. Matthew, quoted in "The Royal Gold Medalist 1953, presentation to M. Le Corbusier at RIBA," *Builder* 184 (April 10, 1953), 566.

4. *AD* began in 1932 as *Architectural Design & Construction*, merging ownership with the free *Architect's Standard Catalogue*. Peter Rawstorne, "Theo Crosby Obituary," *Independent* (September 15, 1994).

5. Elizabeth Darling, "Pidgeon (née Lehmann], Monica Helen Ida (1913–2009)," *Oxford Dictionary of National Biography*, ed. H. C. G. Matthew and Brian Harrison (Oxford: Oxford University Press, 2004), s.v.

6. Barbara Randell, Tony Towndrow's secretary, coedited *AD* with Monica Pidgeon until Randell left the magazine in 1953. Steve Parnell, "Architectural Design, 1954–1972: The Architectural Magazine's Contribution to the Writing of Architectural History" (PhD dissertation, Sheffield, 2011), 93.

7. Monica Pidgeon was born in Chile, educated in England, and trained in interior design at the Bartlett School of Architecture. *AD* was printed by Whitefriars Press, a press owned by the Standard Catalogue Company. The Press subsidized *AD* until 1970, when the Standard Catalogue Company decided to sell the press and *AD* as separate entities. Beginning in October 1970, *AD* became a stand-alone press. Diana Rowntree, "Monica Pidgeon obituary: Editor of Architectural Design for 30 Years," *Guardian.co.uk* (accessed September 20, 2009), http://www.guardian.co.uk/artanddesign/2009/sep/21/monica-pidgeon-obituary; Robin Middleton, "Working with Monica," *AA Files* 60 (January 2010), 26–27.

8. Pidgeon helped to organize CIAM 8. She also drove with Ernö Goldfinger and his wife to CIAM 9 in Aix-en-Provence, where she first met Alison and Peter Smithson. Theo Crosby and Pidgeon went to Expo 58 in Brussels; the same year UIA chose Moscow for its venue, and they went there as well. UIA was held in London in 1961 and *AD* was much involved in this event. Crosby designed the members' pavilion and produced a catalog of contributing delegates' work. Monica Pidgeon, "AD Remembered: 1941–1975," *AD* 71 (2001), 94–99.

9. Theo Crosby, born in South Africa, studied architecture at the University of Witwatersrand, Johannesburg, and arrived in London in 1947. He worked from time to time with Jane Drew and Maxwell Fry on projects such as Harlow New Town, schools for Ghana, and the Festival of Britain. He was friends with Peter Smithson, whom he met in Florence in 1948, and was associated with the Independent Group at the ICA in 1952. In 1953 he became technical director of *Architectural Design* and remained there for eight years, moving back to practice in 1962. He designed most of the magazine's covers. He started a small magazine called *Upper Case*, which ran for five editions (1958–1960). In 1956 he dreamed up the "This Is Tomorrow" exhibition, in which he organized selected artists and architects into working groups. He also mounted a Le Corbusier exhibition at the Building Centre in London. Theo Crosby, "Night Thoughts of a Faded Utopia," in David Robbins, ed., *The Independent Group: Postwar Britain and the Aesthetics of Plenty* (Cambridge, MA: MIT Press, 1992), 197–199. Pidgeon, "AD Remembered," 94–99.

10. The Institute of Contemporary Arts (ICA) was established in 1947 and located in Dover Street, Mayfair. Members of the younger generation of artists and architects gathered there and formed the so-called Independent Group (IG) in 1952–1955. They held discussion groups, lecture series, exhibitions, and many informal meetings in homes and pubs.

11. Nikolaus Pevsner, "C_{20} Picturesque," *AR* 115 (April 1954), 228–229.

12. Ibid.

13. Reyner Banham, "Revenge of the Picturesque: English Architectural Polemics 1945–1965," in John Summerson, ed., *Essays on Architectural Writers and Writing Presented to Nikolaus Pevsner* (London: Allen Lane, Penguin Press, 1968), 266. Nikolaus Pevsner, "Roehampton, LCC Housing and the Picturesque Tradition," *AR* 126 (July 1959), 21, 22, 35; Stephen Kite and Sarah Menin, "Towards a New Cathedral: Mechanolatry and Metaphysics in Colin St John Wilson," *Architectural Research Quarterly* 9, no. 1 (March 2005), 81–90.
14. A. I. T. Colquhoun, "Twentieth Century Picturesque," Correspondence, *AR* 116 (July 1954), 2.
15. Ibid.
16. Ibid.
17. Nikolaus Pevsner, Correspondence, *AR* 116 (July 1954), 2.
18. Reyner Banham, "The New Brutalism," *AR* 118 (December 1955), 355–356.
19. Crosby, "Night Thoughts of a Faded Utopia," 199.
20. Reyner Banham, "The History of the Immediate Future," *RIBA* 68 (May 1961), 255.
21. Peter Smithson, "Le Corbusier: First Confrontations with the Work of the Master," CORB:DLF, 1–5, CORB:DLF, 1–2. P.S. 9.1.87. AS & PS MAGIC BOX, Folder Le CORBUSIER. Smithson Family Collection.
22. Ibid., 4.
23. Parnell, "Architectural Design, 1954–1972," 148.
24. Peter Smithson, "Two Periods of Hope: The Nineteen Fifties & The Nineteen Eighties," HOPE: 1–3, HOPE: 2. P.S. 21.6.88 BOX AS & PS UNPUBLISHED PAPERS + CURRENT LECTURES. Smithson Family Collection.
25. Henry Millon, "Rudolf Wittkower, *Architectural Principles in the Age of Humanism*: Its Influence on the Development and Interpretation of Modern Architecture," *JSAH* 31, no. 2 (May 1972), 83–91; Eva-Marie Neumann, "Architectural Proportion in Britain 1945–1957," *Architectural History* 39 (1991), 197–221.
26. Millon, "Rudolf Wittkower, *Architectural Principles in the Age of Humanism*."
27. Alison and Peter Smithson, "Correspondence," *RIBA* 59 (February 1952), 140.
28. Peter Smithson, "Reflections on Hunstanton," *Architectural Research Quarterly* 2, no. 8 (Summer 1997), 36.
29. Peter Smithson, "The Neatest Parcel," 30.10.78 Notes from various scraps of paper. BOX AS & PS '50s and '60s. Smithson Family Collection.
30. Ibid.
31. Catherine Spellman and Karl Unglaub, eds., *Peter Smithson: Conversations with Students* (New York: Princeton Architectural Press, 2005), 18.
32. Ruth Olitsky and John Voelcker, "Form and Mathematics," *AD* 24 (October 1954), 306.
33. Ibid., 307.
34. John Summerson, "The Case of Modern Architecture," *RIBA* 64 (June 1957), 307–313.
35. Ibid., 307.
36. Peter Smithson's response to John Summerson, "The Case of Modern Architecture," *RIBA* 64 (June 1957), 312.

37. "Report of a Debate on the Motion 'That Systems of Proportion Make Good Design Easier and Bad Design More Difficult'," *RIBA* 64 (September 1957), 456–463. Peter Smithson's response, 460–461.
38. "Report of a Debate on the Motion," 461.
39. Ibid., 463.
40. Rudolf Wittkower, "Le Corbusier's Modulor," in *Four Great Makers of Modern Architecture, Gropius Le Corbusier Mies van der Rohe Wright: The Verbatim Record of a Symposium held at the School of Architecture, Columbia University, March–May 1961* (New York: Da Capo Press, 1970), 203.
41. Alison and Peter Smithson, "Extracts from Talks to 5th Year Students on 'The Shape of Things'," *Architects' Journal* 129 (May 21, 1959), 782.
42. Ibid., 780.
43. Ibid.
44. For comprehensive coverage of CIAM, see Eric Mumford, *The CIAM Discourse on Urbanism 1928–1960* (Cambridge, MA: MIT Press, 2000).
45. Called either "Team 3" or "Junior CIAM" as formulated in Hoddesdon, CIAM 8. Document "CIAM Junior Group—Groupes des Jeunes—Junior Grupen" (undated), BAKE0151 BOX, folder g1. Netherlands Architectural Institute (NAi).
46. Sigfried Giedion, Fernand Léger, and Josep Lluís Sert wrote a manifesto, "Nine Points on Monumentality," in 1943. It remained unpublished until included in Sigfried Giedion, *Architecture, You and Me: The Diary of a Development* (Cambridge, MA: Harvard University Press, 1958), 48; Sigfried Giedion, "The Need for a New Monumentality," in Paul Zucker, ed., *New Architecture and City Planning* (New York: Philosophical Library, 1944), 549–566.
47. CIRPAC, the Comité International pour la Résolution des Problèmes de l'Architecture Contemporaine (International Committee for the Resolution of Problems in Contemporary Architecture), was the executive body of CIAM, meeting between official Congresses.
48. "The Dutch Group of 8," Amsterdam, May 19, 1947, Doc 2, English translation; Doc 3, CIAM VI Bridgwater 7 à 14 Septembre 1949, FLC.
49. "CIAM 8," *AD* 21 (August 1951), 227.
50. The theme of CIAM 7 had been to discuss the Grille/Grid developed by Le Corbusier, a strategy for the visual and critical application of CIAM principles by participants utilizing the four categories of the functional city—living, working, recreation, and circulation—to organize their projects. Evidently it created more confusion than clarity.
51. "CIAM 8," 227.
52. "'Jeunes' and 'Anciens': Conseil extraordinaire et officieux: CIAM-Paris (Mai 1952)," Preparation for CIAM 9 D2 (19) Doc 1 FLC; "On the creation of Junior-Groups," Preparation for CIAM 9 D2 (19) Doc 7 (Sigtuna 26.6.1952) FLC.
53. Denys Lasdun, "MARS Group 1953–1957," *Architects' Year Book 8* (London: Elek Books, 1957), 57–61.
54. "CIAM 9," *AD* 23 (August 1953), 208.
55. Ibid.
56. Ibid.

57. "IUA and CIAM," *AD* 25 (September 1955), 268, 290.
58. "Réunion tenue à l'UNESCO, le 20 Juin 1954" (CIAM 42-JT-13-373–379); quoted in Annie Pedret, "CIAM and the Emergence of Team 10 Thinking" (PhD dissertation, MIT, 2001), 171.
59. The enlarged organizational committee consisted of Jaap Bakema [chairman], Georges Candilis, Shadrach Woods, Aldo van Eyck, Rolf Gutmann, William Howell, Alison and Peter Smithson, and John Voelcker. Pedret adds the names of Brian Richards, André Stud, and E. Neuenschwander, and includes the architect Gill Howell. Pedret, "CIAM and the Emergence of Team 10 Thinking," 172.
60. "IUA and CIAM."
61. Ibid.
62. Francis Strauven, *Aldo Van Eyck: The Shape of Relativity* (Amsterdam: Architectura & Natura, 1998), 271–272.
63. "Instructions aux Groupes: CIAM 10 Draft Framework 3," Team 10 Documents Doc. 1 CIAM 10. FLC.
64. Aldo van Eyck: "In Dubrovnik some people said 'Let us have no more mystical talk, no philosophical talk, no vagueness.' And I remember saying 'Nous avons le droit d'être vague.' It is the people who are always so clear, that always know exactly where clarity is, that are the ones who are always so vague—and the result of all that vagueness is an uninhabitable form of living. I think that is our enemy. Our enemy is the immediate CIAM past." Quoted in Oscar Newman, ed., *CIAM '59 in Otterlo* (Stuttgart: Karl Krämer Verlag, 1961), 197. CIAM 10 was given two charges: to develop a *Charte de l'Habitat* and to make a proposal to CIRPAC for a new organizational arrangement. The plan was for the old CIRPAC members to resign on December 31, 1956, and for authority to be passed to a group of 30 who would become the core of a new CIAM. "Reorganization of CIAM II," August 11, 1956, in "CIAM Report (CIAM 42-X-115), 41–42. Pedret, "CIAM and the Emergence of Team 10 Thinking," 217.
65. At the CIRPAC meeting in Dubrovnik, a vote for continuity with the old CIAM was registered as Peter Smithson for dissolving all ties, sixteen for dissolving the organization but keeping the name, and nine others for dissolving and changing the name. "Minutes of CIRPAC meeting 10 August 1956" (CIAM 42-JY-214); quoted in Pedret, "CIAM and the Emergence of Team 10 Thinking," 216. See also "The Truth about CIAM: Letter from the Four Founders," *AD* 31 (January 1961), 5; reprinted as "What Became of CIAM?," *AR* 129 (April 1961), 154.
66. William Howell, quoted in "CIAM Is Dead … Long Live CIAM," *Architects' Journal* 124 (September 6, 1956), 332.
67. William Holford, Arthur Ling, and Peter Smithson, "Planning Today," *AD* 27 (June 1957), 185–189.
68. Ibid.
69. Peter Smithson, "The Idea of Architecture in the '50s," *Architects' Journal* 131 (January 21, 1960), 121–126.
70. "The Truth about CIAM: Letter from the Four Founders."
71. Ibid.
72. "The Truth about CIAM: A Reply from Bakema," *AD* 31 (January 1961), 53; and "What Became of CIAM?," 226.

73. Ibid.
74. Jaap Bakema, "Concluding Statement"; quoted in Newman, *CIAM '59 in Otterlo*, 10.
75. "The Truth about CIAM: A Reply from Bakema." Monica Pidgeon blamed the entire membership of Team 10, especially the Smithsons, for the role they played in killing off CIAM. She said: "I didn't go to it. I was very fed up with them killing it like they did because I didn't think what resulted was much good either. Team 10, you know. We published Team 10, I shouldn't say this, but it's because of my colleague, Robin Middleton. At the time, we published Team 10 in full, the whole of a December issue. Oh! I thought it was so boring! The Smithsons and Aldo van Eyck and Shad Woods, those 3 and especially Alison, were the progenitors of Team 10. But they threw out CIAM. It was like getting rid of the heritage, chucking the whole thing overboard and starting afresh which I don't think is the way to do things. I think the way to do things is slowly. They felt they couldn't get rid of Giedion, they couldn't get rid of Jackie Tyrwhitt. Maybe they were right. … The only person that linked the two was Denys Lasdun. … I didn't go to Team 10. … It's a lot of blah blah …" Monica Pidgeon, "NLSC: Architects' Lives," F7493 Side A; quoted by Parnell, "Architectural Design, 1954–1972," 277.
76. "CIAM 10 Committee" was the organizing title given to those preparing CIAM 10. But new appellations soon appeared, such as "London Group Team X." Strauven notes that "Team X" was introduced by Candilis in early September 1954, and adopted by Le Corbusier, but spelled most of the time as "Team 10" by the Smithsons (Strauven, *Aldo Van Eyck*, 258, footnote 33). Team Ten files at Netherlands Architectural Institute (NAi) and in the Smithsons' private archive show the Smithsons using "CIAM X" in their letters and unpublished materials, although they may have preferred "CIAM 10."
77. Alison Smithson, ed., "CIAM Team 10," *AD* 30 (May 1960), 175–205; Alison Smithson, ed., "Team 10 Primer," *AD 32* (December 1962), 559–602; Alison Smithson, ed., "Team 10 at Royaumont 1962," *AD* 65 (November 1975), 664–689.
78. Howells, Smithsons, Voelcker, "Reflections on CIAM 9 and proposals for immediate work," December 18, 1953, TTEN0002 BOX TEAM SMITHSON, Folder 3, 1. NAi; reprinted in Alison Smithson, ed., *The Emergence of Team 10 out of CIAM* (London: Architectural Association, 1982), 10–12.
79. Alison Smithson, *The Emergence of Team 10 out of CIAM*, 10–12.
80. Ibid.
81. Peter Smithson, "Team X in Retrospect," ARCH. TEAMX.RET: 1–9, October 2, 1991. Revised March 1994, October 1995, April 1999. BOX AS & PS UNPUBLISHED PAPERS + CURRENT LECTURES. Smithson Family Collection.
82. Alison and Peter Smithson, "The 'as Found' and the 'Found'," in Robbins, *The Independent Group*, 201–202.
83. There are several documents written by Alison and Peter Smithson for the exhibition entitled "Sources," subsequently relabeled "Document 53" and eventually "Parallel of Life and Art." Alison and Peter Smithson, "Document 53," undated, 2 pages, reprinted in Claude Lichtenstein and Thomas Schregenberger, *As Found: The Discovery of the Ordinary* (Baden: Lars Müller Publishers, 2001), 39. Handwritten notes on "Parallel of Life and Art" in BOX AS & PS NIGEL HENDERSON, 3. Smithson Family Collection. Finally, the handwritten notes with additions are reprinted in Alison and Peter Smithson, *The Charged Void: Architecture* (New York: Monacelli Press, 2001), 118.

84. An explanation of the shift of name from "Sources" to "Document 53" to "Parallel of Life and Art" is given in Lichtenstein and Schregenberger, *As Found*, 30.
85. Alison and Peter Smithson, "Document 53," in Lichtenstein and Schregenberger, *As Found*, 38.
86. Ibid.
87. Alison and Peter Smithson, typed manuscript, "Sources," AS & PS BOX EXHIBITIONS. Smithson Family Collection.
88. In addition to their participation in Independent Group meetings (1952–1955), the Smithsons were involved in preparations for the IG's "This Is Tomorrow" exhibition (September 1956).
89. Team 10 members with varied attendance would meet again at a CIRPAC meeting in Paris (June 20, 1954), a Team 10 meeting in London (August 28–29, 1954), a meeting in Le Corbusier's atelier in Paris (September 14, 1954), a Team 10 meeting in Candilis's atelier in Paris (April 12, 1955), another CIRPAC meeting in Paris (July 4, 1955), CIRPAC's meeting in La Sarraz (September 8–11, 1955) and a Team 10 meeting in London (May 28, 1956) in final preparation for CIAM 10 (August 2–3, 1956). List of meetings compiled from Pedret, "CIAM and the Emergence of Team 10 Thinking," 157–204.
90. The Doorn meeting was convened by the Dutch CIAM Group. Invitations were sent to Denys Lasdun, John Voelcker, André Wogenscky, Georges Candilis, Rolf Gutmann, Jaap Bakema, Hovens Greve, Aldo van Eyck, and Mart Stam. Wogenscky, Candilis, and Lasdun could not attend for various reasons; Peter Smithson and Bill Howell came in Lasdun's place. Pedret, "CIAM and the Emergence of Team 10 Thinking," 157–158.
91. Attributed to Peter Smithson, "Notes from 1st meeting Doorn Meeting," January 29, 1954 (morning), 1–4; TTEN0002 BOX TEAM 10 SMITHSON, Folder 6. NAi. A separate set of typewritten "Notes on First Meeting," Doorn (January 29–30, 1954) appears in Alison Smithson, *Emergence of Team 10 out of CIAM*, 17–28. Alison comments: "The minutes of the Doorn Meeting were prepared in Holland most probably by Hovens Greve, although they may have been typed by Mrs van Ginkel."
92. "Statement on Habitat," Doorn Meeting D2(08) CIAM X ALGER 1955 Doc. 1 CIAM Meeting (January 29–31, 1954), FLC; "Doorn Manifesto CIAM Meeting," January 29–31, 1954, Doorn in Alison Smithson, *The Emergence of Team 10 out of CIAM*, 28–32.
93. Alison and Peter Smithson, "Draft of 'Habitat' declaration prepared for Doorn Meeting," in Max Risselada and Dirk van den Heuvel, eds., *Team 10 1953–1981: In Search of a Utopia of the Present* (Rotterdam: NAi Publishers, 2005), 43.
94. Peter Smithson, "TEAM X in Retrospect," ARCH.TEAMX.RET, 5, October 1, 1993, revised March 1994, October 1995, April 1999. BOX AS & PS UNPUBLISHED PAPERS + CURRENT LECTURES. Smithson Family Collection.
95. Ibid., 6.
96. Ibid.
97. Peter Smithson wrote: "We have done quite a lot of work since DOORN, the most of which has been accepted by the MARS group—in fact the Revolution is accomplished. Lasdun is sending an official report from MARS, we are sending a small private report, which will be sent to you this week." Letter from Peter Smithson to Bakema (prior to meeting in Paris, June 20, 1954), BAKE0151 BOX, folder g2. NAi.

98. Strauven, *Aldo Van Eyck*, 259.
99. "Proposition for CIAM from Bakema, CIAM 10 Committee," undated. D2(08) CIAM X ALGER 1955. Doc.4: 1–4. FLC. This draft became known as the "October 24" Draft.
100. Ibid.
101. Ibid.
102. Strauven, *Aldo Van Eyck*, 260–261.
103. "Proposition for CIAM from Bakema," 4.
104. Peter Smithson, letter to Bakema, October 15, 1954. BAKE0151 BOX, folder g2. NAi.
105. Howell, Alison and Peter Smithson, Voelcker typewritten letter to Bakema, October 31, 1954, 2. BAKE0151 BOX, folder g2. NAi.
106. Bakema, letter to Peter Smithson, November 11, 1954. BAKE0151 BOX, folder g2. NAi.
107. Bill Howell, letter to Bakema, December 4, 1954. BAKE0151 BOX, folder g2. NAi.
108. Ibid.
109. "Draft 5: CIAM X … Instructions to Groups," 1. BAKE0151 BOX, folder g2. NAi.
110. Ibid.
111. Bakema, letter to Alison and Peter Smithson, Bill Howell, and John Voelcker, December 27, 1954, 2. BAKE0151 BOX, folder g2. NAi.
112. Bakema letter to Giedion, Gropius, Sert, December 28, 1954. BAKE0151 BOX, folder g2. NAi.
113. Alison Smithson, Peter Smithson, Howell, and Voelcker letter to Giedion, January 4, 1955. Copy sent to Bakema. BAKE0151 BOX, folder g3. NAi.
114. Giedion, letter to Honegger, May 6, 1955. BAKE0151 BOX, folder g3. NAi.
115. Alison and Peter Smithson, letter of response to Candilis's letter of March 25, 1955. Candilis wrote that Giedion was concerned that CIAM 10 would not be well organized, March 28, 1955. TTEN0002 BOX TEAM 10 SMITHSON, Folder 13. NAi.
116. Georges Candilis, letter to Smithson, Bakema & Co., March 25, 1955. TTEN0002 BOX TEAM 10 SMITHSON, Folder 13. NAi.
117. Peter Smithson, letter of response to Candilis's letter of March 25, 1955; in Alison Smithson, *The Emergence of Team 10 out of CIAM*, 42. See also Peter Smithson, letter to Candilis, March 3, 1955, TTEN0002 BOX TEAM 10 SMITHSON, Folder 13. NAi.
118. Alfred Roth, letter to Josep Lluís Sert and copy to Bakema, November 18, 1955, BAKE0151 BOX, folder g3. NAi.
119. Josep Lluís Sert, letter to Le Corbusier on the organization and program of the Congress, June 12, 1956, CIAM Doc. 9 FLC.
120. Le Corbusier, letter to Josep Lluís Sert, July 23, 1956, Roquebrune-Cap Martin. CIAM Doc. 10 FLC.
121. Bakema, letter to Smithsons, Howell, Voelcker (December 27, 1954), BAKE0151 BOX, folder g2. NAi.
122. Strauven, *Aldo Van* Eyck, 265–266.

123. Ibid., 267–271. Dirk van den Heuvel, "Dubrovnik Scroll and Valley Section, 1955–1956," in Risselada and Van den Heuvel, *Team 10 1953–1981*, 50–51. Also Alison and Peter Smithson, "Bates' Burrows Lea Farm, Shere, (1953–1955)," in Alison and Peter Smithson, *The Charged Void:Architecture*, 124–129.
124. For images of the Smithsons' CIAM 10 grille, see Alison and Peter Smithson, *The Charged Void:Architecture*, 132–133, 133.
125. Alison and Peter Smithson, "Bates' Burrows Lea Farm, Shere, (1953–1955)," in ibid., 124.
126. Ibid.
127. "Close House," Grille 1:51, in Risselada and Van den Heuvel, *Team 10 1953–1981*, 51.
128. "South Facing Terraced Houses," Grille 1: 51, ibid., 51.
129. Alison and Peter Smithson, "The Theme of CIAM 10" (March 15, 1955), in Alison Smithson, *The Emergence of Team 10 out of CIAM*, 65.
130. Alison and Peter Smithson, "Cluster," in *Urban Structuring* (London: Studio Vista, 1967), 33–38.
131. Ibid., 34.
132. Jos Bosman, quoting Giedion's 1967 edition of *Space, Time and Architecture*, in which he added a chapter on CIAM: Jos Bosman, "CIAM after the War: A Balance of the Modern Movement," *Rassegna* (December 1992), 19.
133. The Smithsons do not specify what "Berlin Exhibition" they are referencing: Bakema was involved with redevelopment plans for Berlin, and there would be an Interbau Exhibition of competition entries for the "City of Tomorrow" seen by CIAM members meeting in Berlin in September 26–27, 1957, but this letter is dated a year earlier. Alison and Peter Smithson for Team 10 England, "The Berlin Exhibition," August 31, 1956; TTEN0002 BOX TEAM 10 SMITHSON, Folder 1. NAi.
134. Alison and Peter Smithson for Team X England, "The Berlin Exhibition."
135. Ibid.
136. Alison and Peter Smithson, "Future of CIAM to Team X and Old CIAM Council," December 9, 1956, 1; TTEN0002 BOX TEAM 10 SMITHSON, Folder 16. NAi. Reprinted in Alison Smithson, *The Emergence of Team 10 out of CIAM*, 75–76.
137. Ibid.
138. Ibid.
139. Ibid.
140. Ibid.
141. Alison and Peter Smithson, "CIAM Dissolution," March 14, 1957, 1; TTEN0002 BOX TEAM 10 SMITHSON, Folder 1. NAi. Reprinted in Alison Smithson, *The Emergence of Team 10 out of CIAM*, 77.
142. Ibid.
143. Howell, Lasdun, Smithsons, Voelcker, "Manifesto CIAM Reorganization Or Dissolution?," March 22, 1957, 1; TTEN0002 BOX TEAM 10 SMITHSON, Folder 16. NAi. Reprinted in Alison Smithson, *The Emergence of Team 10 out of CIAM*, 78.

144. Sert, Gropius, Giedion, Tyrwhitt, letter to Bakema, April 19, 1957, 1; TTEN0002 BOX TEAM 10 SMITHSON, Folder 16. NAi. Reprinted in Alison Smithson, *The Emergence of Team 10 out of CIAM*, 79.
145. Sert, Gropius, Giedion, Tyrwhitt, letter to Alison and Peter Smithson, May 1957, 1; TTEN0002 BOX TEAM 10 SMITHSON, Folder 16. NAi.
146. Sert, Gropius, Giedion, Tyrwhitt, letter to Alison and Peter Smithson, 2.
147. Alison and Peter Smithson, letter to colleagues about CIAM Meeting La Sarraz (August 23, 1957), 1; TTEN0002 BOX TEAM 10 SMITHSON, Folder 16. NAi. Reprinted in Alison Smithson, *The Emergence of Team 10 out of CIAM*, 80.
148. Alison and Peter Smithson, "Formation of CICON" (August 28, 1957), 1; TTEN0002 BOX TEAM 10 SMITHSON, Folder 16. NAi. Reprinted in Alison Smithson, *The Emergence of Team 10 out of CIAM*, 81.
149. Peter Smithson "CIAM-Re-Organisation" (August 28–29, 1957), 2; TTEN0002 BOX TEAM 10 SMITHSON, Folder 16. NAi. Reprinted in Alison Smithson, *The Emergence of Team 10 out of CIAM*, 80–83.
150. In the NAi archives, Aldo van Eyck's letter appears after letter from Sert, Gropius, Giedion, Tyrwhitt, letter to Alison and Peter Smithson (May 1957, 1–2) and before one cited above, written by Smithsons August 23, 1957. Aldo van Eyck, letter to Peter and Alison Smithson, 1–2, not dated; TTEN0002 BOX TEAM 10 SMITHSON, Folder 16. NAi.
151. Aldo van Eyck, letter to Peter and Alison Smithson, 3–4.
152. Ibid., 4.
153. Ibid., 5.
154. Otterlo Congress and Team 10 Meetings, "THEME Name and Method of WORK," not dated; TTEN0002 BOX TEAM 10 SMITHSON, Folder 19. NAi. See also Newman, *CIAM '59 in Otterlo*, 9–10.
155. "Announcement of next CIAM," BAKE0152 BOX, folder g5. NAi.
156. Alison Smithson, letter to Bakema, with P.S. from Peter Smithson, September 1958; BAKE0152 BOX, folder g5. NAi.
157. Alison Smithson, letter to Bakema, with P.S. Giancarlo De Carlo was introduced to Team 10 by Ernesto Rogers at the Otterlo meeting. In spite of being rejected initially because he was member of the Italian group, De Carlo became a member of Team 10 in subsequent meetings.
158. Alison and Peter Smithson, letter to Costa, Eames, Johnson, Johansen, Kahn, Rudolph, Scharoun, and Whyte, January 6, 1959; TTEN0002 BOX TEAM 10 SMITHSON, Folder 19. NAi.
159. Philip Johnson, letter of reply to Alison and Peter Smithson, January 15, 1959; TTEN0002 BOX TEAM 10 SMITHSON, Folder 19. NAi.
160. Paul Rudolph, letter of reply to Alison and Peter Smithson, February 2, 1959; TTEN0002 BOX TEAM 10 SMITHSON, Folder 19. NAi.
161. Ralph Erskine, letter of reply to Alison and Peter Smithson, April 7, 1959; TTEN0002 BOX TEAM 10 SMITHSON, Folder 19. NAi.
162. Louis Kahn, Western Union Cablegram to Alison and Peter Smithson, June 4, 1959; TTEN0002 BOX TEAM 10 SMITHSON, Folder 19. NAi.

163. Aldo van Eyck, letter to Giedion; quoted by Strauven, *Aldo Van Eyck*, 347–348, footnote 450.
164. Alison Smithson, "50s Field of Enquiry," 50S FOE, 1. AMS BOX EVOLVING. Smithson Family Collection.
165. AMS, Notes on various scraps of paper, August 1984, BOX AS & PS '50s and '60s. Smithson Family Collection.
166. "Team 10 Seminar: Session 3," Graduate School AA (Spring, 1982): TX 3, 3; TTEN0004 BOX TEAM 10 SMITHSON, Folder 37. NAi.
167. "Team 10 Seminar: Session 3," 3.

Chapter 3

1. Paul Valéry, "Man and the Sea Shell" (essay), in *The Collected works of Paul Valéry*, vol. 13, *Aesthetics*, trans. Ralph Mannheim (London: Routledge, 1964), 3–30.
2. Peter Smithson, "Letter to America," *AD* 28 (March 1958), 93; reprinted in Alison and Peter Smithson, *Ordinariness and Light* (London: Faber and Faber, 1970), 136.
3. Ibid.
4. Peter Smithson, "TEAM IN RETROSPECT" ARCH.TEAMX, 1, October 1, 1993, revised March 1994, October 1995, April 1999, and May 2001; BOX AS & PS UNPUBLISHED PAPERS + CURRENT LECTURES. Smithson Family Collection.
5. Alison and Peter Smithson, *Urban Structuring: Studies of A & P Smithson* (New York: Reinhold, 1967), 34.
6. Alison and Peter Smithson, *The Charged Void: Architecture* (New York: Monacelli Press, 2001), 118.
7. Alison and Peter Smithson, *Urban Structuring*, 34.
8. Alison and Peter Smithson, *The Charged Void*, 84.
9. Paul Klee, *Pedagogical Sketchbook*, trans. Sibyl Moholy-Nagy (New York: Praeger, 1953; originally published 1923).
10. Alison and Peter Smithson, *The Charged Void*, 84.
11. David Sylvester, "Klee II" (1950), in David Sylvester, *About Modern Art: Critical Essays 1948–1996* (London: Chatto and Windus, 1996), 44.
12. Sylvester, "Klee II," 46.
13. Victor Pasmore, quoted in Reyner Banham, "Klee's Pedagogical Sketchbook," *Encounter* (April 1954), 57.
14. Alison Smithson, "Louis Kahn: Invitation to Otterlo, Graphics of Movement," 1; TTEN0006 BOX TEAM 10 SMITHSON, Folder 49. NAi.
15. Alison Smithson, "The Wider Role of the Architect," WIDR: 1–30, 6; BOX AMS LECTURES AS EVOLVED. Smithson Family Collection.
16. Alison Smithson, "Louis Kahn: Invitation to Otterlo."
17. Ibid.
18. Ibid.
19. Ibid.

20. Alison Smithson, remark, "Team 10 at Abbaye Royaumont" (September 1962), 14; TTEN0005 BOX TEAM 10 SMITHSON, Folder 43. NAi.
21. Alison Smithson, "Making Ideas Manifest and so Introducing a Sensibility to Car Movement," 1–8, 1; BOX AMS LECTURES AS EVOLVED. Smithson Family Collection.
22. Alison and Peter Smithson, *Urban Structuring*, 36.
23. Alison and Peter Smithson, *Ordinariness and Light*, 11.
24. Alison Smithson, "Team 10 Seminar: session 3," Graduate School AA Spring 1982 TX 3: 1–6; ASIDES 3: 1–2, 2; TTEN0006 BOX TEAM 10 SMITHSON, Folder 37. NAi.
25. Alison Smithson, "Team 10 Seminar: session 3."
26. Alison Smithson, "Making Ideas Manifest," 1.
27. Alison Smithson, "Team 10: The Myth and the Message," March 1983, 7; TTEN0004 BOX TEAM 10 SMITHSON, Folder 35. NAi.
28. Alison Smithson, "Making Ideas Manifest," 1. For more on the Euston Arch book, see chapter 11.
29. Ibid., 2.
30. Ibid.
31. Ibid., 2–3.
32. Ibid., 3.
33. Alison Smithson, *AS in DS: An Eye on the Road* (Delft: Delft University Press, 1983), 91–110.
34. Ibid., 91.
35. Ibid., 93.
36. Ibid., 101.
37. Alison Smithson, "Team 10 Seminar: 2nd Session," Graduate School AA Spring 1982. TX 2: 1–10, 3; ASIDES 3: 1–2, 2; TTEN0006 BOX TEAM 10 SMITHSON, Folder 37. NAi. See also Commission 6, "La Charte de l'Habitation," at CIAM 9 Aix, 1953; Congrès—CIAM X Orientation D2–8, 48. FLC.
38. Hans Ulrich Obrist, ed., *Smithson Time: A Dialogue* (Cologne: Walther König, 2004), 14.
39. Max Risselada, "The Space Between," *Oases* 51 (1995), 53.
40. Alison and Peter Smithson, "House in Soho," *AD* 23 (December 1953); Irénée Scalbert, "Architecture as a Way of Life: The New Brutalism, 1953–1956," in Max Risselada and Dirk van den Heuvel, eds., *CIAM Team 10: The English Context* (Delft: TU Delft, 2002), 57–84.
41. Reyner Banham, "The New Brutalism," *AR* 118 (December 1955), 354–361.
42. Reyner Banham, *The New Brutalism: Ethic or Aesthetic?* (New York: Reinhold, 1966), 10.
43. Scalbert, "Architecture as a Way of Life," 69, 71.
44. Other derivations have been provided. For example, Hans Asplund, the son of Gunnar Asplund, wrote to Eric de Maré stating that he used the word "Neo-Brutalist" in 1950 to describe a house in Uppsala. Eric de Maré, "Correspondence: Et Tu, Brute?," *AR* 120 (August 1956), 72.
45. Colin Boyne, "The New Brutalism," *Architects' Journal* 120 (September 16, 1954), 336.

46. The unsigned editorial is reproduced in Alison and Peter Smithson, *Without Rhetoric: An Architectural Aesthetic, 1955–1972* (Cambridge, MA: MIT Press, 1973), 2. It first appeared in *AD* the page before Alison and Peter Smithson, "Housing in Morocco," *AD* 25 (January 1955), 2–7. Since the original statement was an editorial, most architectural historians have attributed it to Theo Crosby, but the Smithsons repeat it word for word in *Without Rhetoric* without such attribution. In addition, Jeremy Baker lists both "The New Brutalism" and "Collective Housing" in Jeremy Baker, "A Smithson File," *Arena* 81, no. 899 (February 1966), 177–217. In opposition to most architectural historians, whose view it is that Reyner Banham was the first to define "New Brutalism," I contend that the Smithsons' definition came before Banham's in *AR* (December 1955).

47. Editorial [Alison and Peter Smithson], "The New Brutalism," *AD* 25 (January 1955), 1.

48. For commentary on Brutalism and the picturesque, see John Macarthur, "Brutalism, Ugliness and the Picturesque Object," in *Formulation Fabrication: The Architecture of History, Proceedings of the Seventeenth Annual Conference of the Society of Architectural Historians, Australia and New Zealand* (Wellington, New Zealand, 2000), 259–266.

49. Editorial, "The New Brutalism," 1.

50. Reyner Banham, "The New Brutalism."

51. The Smithsons would eventually publish a list of heroic examples. Alison and Peter Smithson, "The Heroic Period of Modern Architecture, 1917–1937," *AD* 35 (December 1965), 580–635. Further commentary on their highly personal list of 1965 was issued as "Heroic Relics," *AD* 37 (December 1967), 542–564.

52. Peter Smithson would call their "Upper Lawn" house "a true Brutalist work. That is, the old walls, the wood, the stainless steel, the aluminum skin, the teak—all the materials—are used so that you feel their quality. ... For example, in the bathroom there were the stone walls of the old house." He goes on to speak of pipes being at first on the surface of the masonry, but condensation becoming a nuisance, so the pipes were buried. "This sort of process is very much like stage design: once you start to run rehearsals and things don't work, you pull them out or change the lighting." Catherine Spellman and Karl Unglaub, eds., *Peter Smithson: Conversations with Students: A Space for Our Generation* (New York: PAP, 2005), 77.

53. The "Opinion" pieces on New Brutalism were "Thoughts in Progress: *New Brutalism*," "Thoughts in Progress: Summing Up I," "Thoughts in Progress: Summing Up II," and "Thoughts in Progress: Summing Up III," *AD* 27 (April, October, November, December 1957), 111–112, 343–344, 395–396, 435–436. Steve Parnell provides clarification of these "Opinion" pieces, which were presented as a series of twelve anonymously authored discussions in dialogue format. The first appeared in December 1956 and compared the Seagram and Shell buildings. They were written by Denys Lasdun, who had just joined *AD* as an editorial consultant. Dialogues on topics such as the curtain wall, Gropius's book *The Scope of Total Architecture*, and New Brutalism (December 1956 through December 1957) were based on taped conversations between Lasdun and the architectural historian J. H. V. Davies which were edited for publication. Parnell draws on "NLSC: Architects' Lives. Monica Pidgeon," interview by Charlotte Benton, mp3 from original tape, July 9, 1999, F7498 Side B, British Library Sound Archive, at http://soundserver.bl.uk:81/C0467X0039XX/021A-C0467X0039XX-1600A0.mp3. Steve Parnell, "Architectural Design, 1954–1972: The Architectural Magazine's Contribution to the Writing of Architectural

History" (PhD dissertation, Sheffield University, 2011), 155–159. The link referenced by Parnell is no longer accessible.

54. "Opinion: Thoughts in Progress: *New Brutalism*," *AD* (April 1957), 111.
55. Ibid.
56. Ibid., 112.
57. Alison and Peter Smithson, "Counter Opinion, the New Brutalism," *AD* 27 (April 1957), 113.
58. Ibid.
59. "Opinion: Thoughts in Progress: Summing Up II," 395–396.
60. Ibid., 395.
61. "Opinion: Thoughts in Progress: Summing Up III," 435–436.
62. Ibid., 435.
63. Ibid., 436.
64. Peter Smithson, Alison Smithson, Jane B. Drew, and E. Maxwell Fry, "Conversations on Brutalism," *Zodiac* 4 (Fall 1959), 73–81.
65. Ibid., 74.
66. Ibid., 75.
67. Ibid.
68. Reyner Banham, "À Propos the Smithsons," *New Statesman* (September 8, 1961), 317.
69. Alison and Peter Smithson, "Banham's Bumper Book on Brutalism, Discussed by Alison and Peter Smithson," *Architects' Journal* 144 (December 28, 1966), 1590–1591. They called Banham's approach to brutalism "Banhamalism" or "Myopic's Brutalism": Alison and Peter Smithson, "The Space Between," *Oppositions* 4 (October 1974), 78.
70. Alison and Peter Smithson, "Banham's Bumper Book on Brutalism," 1590.
71. Alison and Peter Smithson, typed manuscript, "Review of 'The New Brutalism' by Peter Reyner Banham." Commissioned and rejected by the *New Statesman* (1967), 1; AS & P S 1.12.1966 Revised 21.4.1967. Photocopy. Smithson Family Collection.
72. Ibid.
73. Ibid., 3.
74. Ibid., 1.
75. Ibid., 1–2.
76. Ibid., 3.
77. Ibid., 2.
78. Alison and Peter Smithson, *Without Rhetoric*.
79. Ibid., 1.
80. Ibid.
81. Ibid., 4.
82. Ibid., 2, footnote 2.
83. Ibid., 6, footnote 4.

84. Ibid., 6.
85. Ibid.
86. Ibid., 48–49.
87. Peter Smithson, "Compulsions Shared," for Peter Dunican's 70th birthday, re the 1950s, August 1987; FOLDER 1950s BOX '50s and '60s. Smithson Family Collection.
88. Alison Smithson, quoted by Bengt Edman, "Foreword," in Alison and Peter Smithson, *Italian Thoughts* (Stockholm: Alison & Peter Smithson, 1993), 4.
89. Peter Smithson, "From the Astringency of Necessity to the Astringency of Choice," ARCH. ast, 1–2, June 1966, revised April and November 1999; BOX AS & PS UNPUBLISHED PAPERS + CURRENT LECTURES. Smithson Family Collection.
90. Ibid., 1.
91. Peter Smithson, "The Idea of Architecture in the '50s," *Architects' Journal* 131 (January 21, 1960), 121–126.
92. Peter Smithson, "Letter to America," 95; reprinted in Alison and Peter Smithson, *Ordinariness and Light*, 136–137.
93. Alison and Peter Smithson, *Ordinariness and Light*, 33.
94. Alison and Peter Smithson, "Cluster City: A New Shape for the Community," 334, 336; reprinted in *Ordinariness and Light*, 131.
95. Alison Smithson, "Mobility Road System," *AD* 28 (October 1958), 385–389; reprinted as "Mobility" in Alison and Peter Smithson, *Ordinariness and Light*, 144–153.
96. Alison and Peter Smithson, *Without Rhetoric*, 98.
97. Alison Smithson, "Mobility," 148–149.
98. Peter Smithson, "Introduction: *Urban Re-identification*," February 1966; Box unknown. Smithson Family Collection. Part of this unpublished book was included in Alison and Peter Smithson, *Ordinariness and Light*, 17–101.
99. Peter Smithson, "Introduction: *Urban Re-identification*."
100. Ibid.
101. Ibid.
102. Alison and Peter Smithson, *Ordinariness and Light*, 24.
103. Ibid., 44.
104. Alison and Peter Smithson, MARS Group, "Urban Re-identification Grille," CIAM 9 Aix-en-Provence, July 24, 1953; FLC F1-06-60.
105. Alison and Peter Smithson, *Urban Structuring*, 10.
106. Alison and Peter Smithson, *Ordinariness and Light*, 97, 100.
107. Ibid., 100.
108. Ibid., 26.
109. Ibid., 21.
110. Ibid., 23–24.

111. Mustapha Khayati, "Captive Words: Preface to a Situationist Dictionary," in Ken Knabb, ed., *Situationist International Anthology* (Berkeley, CA: Bureau of Public Secrets, 1987), 170–175.

112. Alison and Peter Smithson, "Extract from Talks to Fifth Year Students on 'The Shape of Things'," *Architects' Journal* 129 (May 21, 1959), 779. It is not clear whether Alison or Peter is the "I" here.

113. A MARS (Modern Architecture Research Group) exhibition on "New Architecture" at the Burlington Galleries in 1938 drew attention to Bethnal Green's poverty, crowding, dwelling types, family sizes, and industries. John R. Gold, *The Experience of Modernism: Modern Architects and the Future of the City, 1928–1958* (London: E & F Spon, 1997), 127.

114. *County of London Plan*, prepared for LCC by J. H. Forshaw and Patrick Abercrombie (London: Macmillan, 1943).

115. Christian Topalov, "The Neighborhood of the Social Sciences in the 1950s and 1960s: Three Cross-National Studies" (paper delivered at Max Planck Institute for the History of Science Workshop "Science and the City," Berlin, December 1–3, 2000).

116. Peter Willmott and Michael Young, *Family and Kinship in East London* (London: Routledge and Kegan Paul, 1957).

117. Ibid., vii.

118. For one disclaimer of the influence of Wilmott and Young on the Smithsons' projects, see Alison and Peter Smithson, "Banham's Bumper Book on Brutalism," 1590.

119. Alison and Peter Smithson, *Ordinariness and Light*.

120. Claude Lichtenstein and Thomas Schregenberger, eds., *As Found: The Discovery of the Ordinary* (Zurich: Lars Müller, 2001), 84–85.

121. The Hendersons left London in 1952 and moved to Essex, where Nigel taught at Colchester School of Art, then at the Norwich School of Art. David Robbins, ed., *The Independent Group: Postwar Britain and the Aesthetics of Plenty* (Cambridge, MA: MIT Press, 1992), 76–77.

122. Alison and Peter Smithson, "An Urban Project (Pilot Project Urban Re-identification)," *Architects' Yearbook* 5 (1953), 48.

123. MARS GROUP PROPOSAL FOR CIAM 9 Congress, 1953 Doc. 10: 1; MARS Modern Architectural Research Groups (British Group of C.I.A.M.), June 16, 1952. FLC.

124. Ibid.

125. E. A. Gutkind, *Community and Environment: A Discourse on Social Ecology* (London: Watts, 1953), xii.

126. E. A. Gutkind, "How Other Peoples Dwell and Build: 1 Houses of the South Seas," *AD* 23 (January 1953), 2–4; "How Other Peoples Dwell and Build: 2 Houses of Japan, " *AD* 23 (February 1953), 31–34; "How Other Peoples Dwell and Build: 3 Houses of China," *AD* 23 (March 1953), 59–62; "How Other Peoples Dwell and Build: 4 Indigenous Houses of Africa," *AD* 23 (May 1953), 121–134; "How Other Peoples Dwell and Build: 5 Mohammedan Houses," *AD* 23 (June 1953), 159–162; and "How Other Peoples Dwell and Build: 6 Houses of North American Indians," *AD* 23 (July 1953), 193–197.

127. Alison Smithson, ed., *Team 10 Meetings: 1953–1984* (New York: Rizzoli, 1991), 19–20. ATBAT-Afrique was founded in 1947 by Le Corbusier, Vladimir Bodiansky, André Wogenscky, and Marcel Py and was mainly active in Algeria and Morocco, with its main office in Casablanca. It was considered a research center and intended to forge closer association between architects and engineers, an idea derived from ASCORAL (Assemblée des Constructeurs pour une Rénovation Architecturale), which had been set up by Le Corbusier in 1942 to plan for reconstruction work in postwar France. In 1951, ATBAT-Afrique opened an additional office in Tangiers directed by Georges Candilis, Shadrach Woods, and Henri Piot. Forced to close the office due to political unrest the next year, they joined the Casablanca office. For the three years of its existence, ATBAT-Afrique produced designs ranging from infrastructure to mass housing. Some members were also part of GAMMA, a CIAM group officially accepted at CIAM 8 in 1951. Tom Avermaete, *Another Modern: The Post-War Architecture and Urbanism of Candilis-Josic-Woods* (Rotterdam: NAi Publishers, 2005).

128. Alison Smithson, *Team 10 Meetings*, 19–20. In addition, Committee II for the *Charte de l'Habitation*, "The Role of Aesthetics in Habitat's Report," introduced a new element to enrich Habitat discussions—the architecture of "primitive" peoples: "The attitude with which we approach other civilizations is a humble one. It does not look at primitive civilizations from the point of view of technical development. It manages even in the slums to find traces of a recent balanced civilization. … A low and 'primitive' standard of living is not identical with a primitive aesthetic level. A hut in the Cameroons has more aesthetic value than most prefabricated houses. … What the modern painters have shown us over the last 40 years, namely, that the most direct means of expression are to be found in primitive and prehistoric art, now becomes, with the urgent need of realizing it, a new possibility for deepening contemporary architecture." Doc. 14: Projet de Programme pour le IX Congrès CIAM 1953. FLC.

129. Georges Candilis and Shadrach Woods; quoted in Avermaete, *Another Modern*, 86–87.

130. Avermaete, *Another Modern*, 95.

131. Alison and Peter Smithson, "The Function of Architecture in Cultures-in-Change," *AD* 30 (April 1960), 149.

132. Ibid., 150.

133. Ibid.

134. Alison and Peter Smithson, "Density, Interval and Measure," *AD* 37 (September 1967), 429; Peter Smithson, "Without Rhetoric," *AD* 37 (January 1967), 39.

135. Alison and Peter Smithson, "The Pavilion and the Route," *AD 35* (March 1965), 143–146.

136. Alison and Peter Smithson, "Density, Interval and Measure," 428–429.

137. Alison and Peter Smithson, "The Pavilion and the Route," 144–145.

138. Ibid., 143.

139. Peter Smithson, "Contributions to a Fragmentary Utopia," *AD* 36 (February 1966), 66.

140. Ibid.

141. Ibid., 66–67.

142. "The Architecture of Technology Exhibition," in Jeremy Baker, "A Smithson File," 210. Reprinted in *AD* 31 (July 1961), 289.

Chapter 4

1. "Introduction," *AR* 108, special issue "Man Made America" (December 1950), 342.
2. Nikolaus Pevsner, "Postscript," in Michael Farr, *Design in British Industry* (Cambridge: Cambridge University Press, 1955), 317; quoted in Nigel Whiteley, "Toward a Throw-Away Culture: Consumerism, 'Style Obsolescence' and Cultural Theory in the 1950s and 1960s," *Oxford Art Journal* 10, no. 2 (1987), 9.
3. Alec Davis, "Popular Art Organised," *AR* 110 (November 1951), 326; quoted in Whiteley, "Toward a Throw-Away Culture," 9.
4. Christopher Tunnard, a landscape architect who taught in the city planning program at Yale University, contributed to this issue and eventually published a book of the same title: Christopher Tunnard and Boris Pushkarev, *Man Made America: Chaos or Control? An Inquiry into Selected Problems of Design in the Urbanized Landscape* (New Haven: Yale University Press, 1963). See also *AR* 108, special issue "Man Made America."
5. "Introduction," *AR* 108, special issue "Man Made America," 341.
6. Ibid.
7. Ibid., 339–340.
8. Ibid., 340.
9. Ibid., 340–341.
10. "Conclusion," ibid., 414–415.
11. Ibid., 416.
12. Ibid.
13. Reyner Banham, quoted by Anne Massey, *The Independent Group: Modernism and Mass Culture in Britain, 1945–59* (Manchester: Manchester University Press, 1995), 84.
14. Ian McCallum joined *AR* some time in 1945, became assistant editor in 1947, and was executive editor from 1953 to 1959. Mostly concerned with day-to-day editorial tasks, he was at the *Review* during the time Townscape Analysis was formulated in the 1940s and 1950s. *AR* 121, special issue "Machine Made America" (May 1957), 295–394.
15. "Matrix: American Architecture in World Perspective," ibid., 387.
16. "Syntax: The Contribution of the Curtain Wall to a New Vernacular," ibid., 318.
17. Ibid., 322.
18. "Genetrix: Personal Contributions to American Architecture," ibid., 338.
19. "Matrix," ibid., 387.
20. Ibid., 389.
21. Ibid.
22. Ibid., 391.
23. Ibid., 392.
24. The ICA was founded in 1947 "to promote all that is best and most creative in the arts on a non-commercial basis by means of exhibitions, performances, study groups, competitions and discussions," and offered a diverse, eclectic array of exhibitions. It was viewed by the British press as an experimental laboratory and a museum of modern art. From ICA "Aims

and Activities" pamphlet (1950), Yale Center for British Art, Special Collections Department; quoted by Frank Spicer III in "Just What Is It that Makes U.S. Art so Different, so Appealing? Case Studies of the Critical Reception of American Avant-Garde Painting in London, 1950–1964" (PhD dissertation, Case Western Reserve University, 2009), 56 and footnote 22. As a place of discussion, the ICA spawned the Independent Group. Reyner Banham apparently considered that the members of the IG came from the "Angry Young Men" generation, although they may not have expressed this directly; he called their activities "the revenge of the elementary school boys." David Robbins, ed., *The Independent Group: Postwar Britain and the Aesthetics of Plenty* (Cambridge, MA: MIT Press, 1992), 76. Also, Banham suggested the IG was a class-based challenge to the bourgeois attitudes of the time, claiming that he was a "scholarship boy" and "the working class is where I come from." Reyner Banham, "The Atavism of the Short-Distance Mini-Cyclist," *Living Arts* 3 (1964), 96. The myth of the so-called IG has been deconstructed by Anne Massey and Penny Sparke in "The Myth of the Independent Group," *Block* 10 (1985), 48–56.

25. There is much discussion over whether Alloway coined the term "Pop Art" or not. Anne Massey claims that Alloway's "invention" of the term is flawed because he was really interested in "mass popular art," that is, technologically reproduced products of visual culture. The present chapter explores Alloway's definition of "Pop Art" as an "urban art." Massey, *The Independent Group*, 117. Jasia Reichardt, in reviewing Alloway's meaning of "Pop Art," claims he first utilized the expression in 1954: Jasia Reichardt, "Pop Art and After," *Art International* (February 1963), 42–47.

26. Reichardt, "Pop Art and After."

27. William R. Kaizen, "Richard Hamilton's Tabular Image," *October* 94 (Autumn 2000), 113–128.

28. Theo Crosby, "Night Thoughts of a Faded Utopia," in Robbins, *The Independent Group*, 197–199.

29. Ibid.

30. Magda Cordell McHale, in Robbins, *The Independent Group*, 190.

31. Richard Hamilton, in ibid., 188.

32. Notable members of the IG include the art critic Lawrence Alloway, who was assistant then deputy director of the ICA from mid-1955 to 1960; artist John McHale, who, with Alloway, convened the second series of IG meetings (1954–1955), which focused on mass culture, industrial design cybernetics, and fine arts; artist Richard Hamilton, curator of the "Growth and Form" exhibition at the ICA in 1951; artist and photographer Nigel Henderson, a great friend of Eduardo Paolozzi; artist Eduardo Paolozzi, who contributed lectures on advertising along with Alloway, McHale, and Toni del Renzio; architects Alison and Peter Smithson; artist William Turnbull; critic Reyner Banham; architect Geoffrey Holroyd; and artist Magda Cordell McHale. Toni del Renzio worked as managing consultant for the ICA in 1952, organizing exhibitions and convening the Young Group; he also worked professionally for mass-media publications. The scholarship on the IG is extensive, e.g., Massey, *The Independent Group*; Alastair Grieve, "'This Is Tomorrow': A Remarkable Exhibition Born from Contention," *Burlington Magazine* 136, no. 1093 (April 1994), 225–232; Robbins, *The Independent Group*; Lynne Cooke, "The Independent Group: British and American Pop Art, a 'Palimpcestuous' Legacy," in Kirk Varnedoe and Adam Gopnik, eds., *Modern Art and Popular Culture: Readings in High and Low* (New York: Museum of Modern Art, 1990), 192–216; Brian Wallis, "Tomorrow and Tomorrow and Tomorrow: The Independent

Group and Popular Culture," in Wallis et al., *Modern Dreams: The Rise and Fall of Pop* (Cambridge, MA: MIT Press, 1988), 9–17.

33. This meeting, instigated by Richard Lannoy and Dorothy Morland with help from Toni del Renzio, met at the ICA in April 1952. It has since become a somewhat mythical event. John-Paul Stonard, "The 'Bunk' Collages of Eduardo Paolozzi," *Burlington Magazine* 150 (April 2008), 238–249.

34. Colin St. John (Sandy) Wilson, quoted in Frank Whitford, "Paolozzi and the Independent Group'," in *Eduardo Paolozzi* (London: Tate Gallery, 1971); reprinted in *Eduardo Paolozzi Underground Design*, exh. cat. (London: Architectural Association, 1986), 6.

35. Arthur J. Penty's review of art critic Eric Gill's book *Beauty Looks After Herself*, quoted in Herbert Read, *Art and Industry: The Principles of Industrial Design* (Bloomington: Indiana University Press, 1961; based on 3rd revised version, 1953; original, 1934), 34.

36. Lawrence Alloway, "The Development of British Pop" (1966); quoted in Robbins, *The Independent Group*, 242.

37. Toni del Renzio, "Pioneers and Trendies," *Art & Artists* (February 1984), 26–28, 26.

38. Geoffrey Holroyd, in Robbins, *The Independent Group*, 189.

39. Norbert Wiener, *The Human Use of Human Beings* (New York: Doubleday Anchor Books, 1954; original edition 1950), 16.

40. Ibid., 17.

41. Ibid., 104.

42. Ibid., 18.

43. Ibid., 136.

44. Norbert Wiener, *Cybernetics: or, Control and Communication in the Animal and the Machine* (Cambridge, MA: MIT Press, 1961; original edition 1948).

45. Ludwig von Bertalanffy, "An Outline of General Systems Theory," *British Journal of Philosophy of Science* 1 (1951), 139–164.

46. The interests of Lawrence Alloway (1926–1990) centered on the study of cybernetics, communication theory and mass media, the pluralism of the signs and symbols of the urban street, and science fiction and B-grade Hollywood movies. He moved to the US in 1961 to teach at Bennington College, Vermont. In 1962 he became curator of the Guggenheim Museum. He left that post in 1966 and took up a position at SUNY Stony Brook, where he taught until 1981. Isabelle Moffat, "The Independent Group's Encounter with Logical Positivism and Searches for Unity in the 1951 Growth and Form Exhibition" (PhD dissertation, MIT, 2002).

47. Lawrence Alloway, "L'intervention du spectateur," *Aujourd'hui: art et architecture* 5 (November 1955), 24–26; quoted in Richard Gordon Leslie, "Lawrence Alloway in England: His Criticism in Context" (PhD dissertation, City University of New York, 2003), 172.

48. Eduardo Paolozzi had also been experimenting with cutting magazine covers into strips and rearranging these strips into interchangeable faces. Alex Kitnick, "Eduardo Paolozzi and Others, 1947–1958" (PhD dissertation, Princeton University, 2010), 59–60.

49. John McHale, "The Plastic Parthenon," in Gillo Dorfles, ed., *Kitsch: The World of Bad Taste* (New York: Universe Books, 1969), 99, 101.

50. Alison and Peter Smithson, *Changing the Art of Inhabitation* (London: Artemis, 1994), 106–149.
51. David Mellor, "A 'Glorious Techniculture' in Nineteen-Fifties Britain: The Many Culture Contexts of the Independent Group," in Robbins, *The Independent Group*, 233.
52. Richard Hamilton, "Letter to Alison and Peter Smithson" (1957), in *Richard Hamilton: Collected Words, 1953–1982* (London: Thames and Hudson, 1982), 28.
53. Richard Hamilton, in *Richard Hamilton: Collected Words*, 24; also quoted in Kaizen, "Richard Hamilton's Tabular Image," 116.
54. Hamilton, "Letter to Alison and Peter Smithson," 28.
55. Colin Cherry was a frequenter of ICA meetings in the 1950s. Colin Cherry, *On Human Communication* (Cambridge, MA: MIT Press, 1957).
56. Theo Crosby, "Preview: This Is Tomorrow," *AD* 24 (September 1956), 302–304. Crosby asked Edward Wright to design the catalog for the exhibition. Grieve, "'This Is Tomorrow.'"
57. Lawrence Alloway, "Design as a Human Activity," *AD* 26 (September 1956), 302; Lawrence Alloway, "Introduction," *This Is Tomorrow*, exh. cat. (London: Whitehall, 1956), 1–2.
58. Alloway, "Introduction," 2. Also quoted in Claude Lichtenstein and Thomas Schregenberger, eds., *As Found: The Discovery of the Ordinary* (Zurich: Lars Müller, 2001), 176.
59. Geoffrey Holroyd, Toni del Renzio, and Lawrence Alloway, "Group 12," *This Is Tomorrow*, exh. cat., unpaginated.
60. Holroyd, del Renzio, Alloway, "Group 12," unpaginated; also Toni del Renzio in Robbins, *The Independent Group*, 193–194.
61. Holroyd in Robbins, *The Independent Group*, 239.
62. Ibid.
63. Holroyd, del Renzio, Alloway, "Group 12," unpaginated.
64. In the 1960s Robert Freeman would achieve fame as a photographer and designer of Beatles record covers. In the issue of *Cambridge Opinion* considered here, Freeman included essays by the British communications engineer Colin Cherry and by former IG members Reyner Banham, Lawrence Alloway, and John McHale. Robert Freeman, "Living with the Sixties," *Cambridge Opinion* 17 (1959), 8.
65. Alison and Peter Smithson, Jane Drew, and Maxwell Fry, "Conversation on Brutalism," *Zodiac* 4 (Fall 1959), 76.
66. Alloway, "Introduction," unpaginated.
67. Advertisement for "A Communications Primer," *AD* 36, special issue "The Eames Celebration" (September 1966), 461.
68. Charles Eames, "Language of Vision: Nuts and Bolts," *Bulletin of the American Academy of Arts and Sciences* 28, no. 1 (October 1978), 14.
69. Charles Eames, "Extract from the RIBA Annual Discourse (London, 1959)," *AD* 36, special issue "The Eames Celebration" (September 1966), 461.
70. Alison and Peter Smithson, eds., "Eames Celebration," ibid., 432.
71. Peter Smithson, "With Just a Few Chairs and a House: An Essay on the Eames-Aesthetic," ibid., 443.

72. Geoffrey Holroyd, quoted in John A. Walker, "The ICA, the IG and America during the 1950s," in *Cultural Offensive: America's Impact on British Art Since 1945* (London: Pluto Press, 1998), 23.

73. Geoffrey Holroyd, quoted in David Robbins, "The Independent Group: Forerunners of Postmodernism?," in Robbins, *The Independent Group*, 243. Robbins states that this quote comes from Geoffrey Holroyd, "Architecture Creating Relaxed Intensity," *AD* 36, special issue "The Eames Celebration" (September 1966), 469–470. The quotation does not appear in Holroyd's article, however.

74. Geoffrey Holroyd, quoting from a booklet that accompanied the film, "Architecture Creating Relaxed Intensity," ibid., 458.

75. Peter Smithson's first trip to USA was in 1957, his second was in 1958. On both trips he crossed the Atlantic in a converted Liberty ship run by the Holland-American Line organized by Dutch students which brought European students to the US and American students to Europe. Peter Smithson, "Reflections on Hunstanton," *Architectural Research Quarterly* 2, no. 8 (Summer 1997), 40.

76. Ibid., 41.

77. Peter Smithson, "With Just a Few Chairs and a House," 443.

78. Alison Smithson, "And Now Dhamas are Dying Out in Japan," *AD* 36, special issue "The Eames Celebration" (September 1966), 448.

79. Peter Smithson, "With Just a Few Chairs and a House," 445.

80. Alison Smithson, "And Now Dhamas are Dying Out in Japan," 447.

81. Catherine Spellman and Karl Unglaub, eds., *Peter Smithson: Conversations with Students: A Space for Our Generation* (New York: PAP, 2005), 12.

82. Peter Smithson, "Concealment and Display: Meditations on Braun," *AD* 36 (July 1966), 362.

83. John McHale was the first to quote Alloway's use of the "fine art/popular art continuum" in a 1955 article. John McHale, "Gropius and the Bauhaus" (excerpts), *Art* (London) (March 3, 1955); quoted in Robbins, *The Independent Group*, 182. Lawrence Alloway's writing career began in the mid-1940s: first book reviews for the *London Sunday Times*, then art criticism for the weekly *Art News and Review*. Leslie, "Lawrence Alloway in England." See also Nigel Whiteley, "Lawrence Alloway on Pop since 1949," *Artforum* 10 (October 2004), 57–70.

84. Richard Kalina, "Critical Commentary: Imagining the Present," in Lawrence Alloway, *Imagining the Present: Context, Content, and the Role of the Critic*, ed. Richard Kalina (London: Routledge, 2006), 1–38.

85. For Alloway's claim about shared IG sensibilities, see Toni de Renzio, "Style, Technique and Iconography," *Art & Artists* 11, no. 4 (July 1976), 36.

86. Alison Smithson, interview with Anne Massey (September 16, 1983); quoted in Massey, *The Independent Group*, 79.

87. Peter Smithson, "13 Topics," notes prepared for probable lecture while on *S.S. Zuiderkruis* leaving Rotterdam for New York, September 2, 1957. BOX AS & PS '50s AND '60s. Smithson Family Collection.

88. Alison Smithson, "The Wider Role of the Architect," WIDR: 1–30, WIDR: 6 (undated). BOX AMS LECTURES AS EVOLVED. Smithson Family Collection.

89. Lawrence Alloway, "Interview with Reyner Banham for *Fathers of Pop*," 5; quoted in Massey, *The Independent Group*, 78.
90. Lawrence Alloway, "Personal Statement," *Ark* 19 (Spring 1957), 28.
91. John W. Campbell, quoted by Lawrence Alloway, "The Arts and the Mass Media," *AD* 28 (February 1958), 85.
92. Ibid., 85.
93. Lawrence Alloway, "The Long Front of Culture," *Cambridge Opinion* 17 (1959), 24–26.
94. Ibid., 25.
95. Ibid., 26.
96. Lawrence Alloway, "Junk Culture," *AD* 31 (March 1961), 122.
97. There were linguistic precedents for the term "Pop," of course, which had often (but not always) appeared previously as an abbreviation of "popular": the Boston "Pops" Orchestra (1900), "pop" songs (early 1900s), "populist," referring in the US to the anti-elitist ideals of the People's Party, founded 1891, and the "snap, crackle, pop" of the Rice Krispies slogan (late 1920s onward). Joe A. Thomas, "Eroticism in American Pop Art 1958–1968" (PhD dissertation, University of Texas at Austin, 1992), 15.
98. Lawrence Alloway, "Eduardo Paolozzi," *AD* 26 (April 1956), 133.
99. Ibid.
100. Alloway, "The Arts and the Mass Media."
101. Ibid., 84.
102. Ibid.
103. Ibid., 85.
104. Ibid.
105. Lawrence Alloway, "City Notes," *AD* 29 (January 1959), 34–35.
106. Ibid., 34.
107. Ibid.
108. Ibid., 35.
109. Ibid.
110. Ibid.
111. Ibid.
112. Ibid.
113. Alison and Peter Smithson, "Personal Statement: 1 'But Today we collect Ads'," *Ark* 18 (November 1956), 49; reprinted in Brian Wallis, ed., *This Is Tomorrow Today*, exh. cat. (New York: Institute for Art and Urban Resources, 1987), 54–56; also reprinted in Robbins, *The Independent Group*, 185–186.
114. Alison and Peter Smithson, "Personal Statement: 1 'But Today we collect Ads,'" 50.
115. Cooke, "The Independent Group."
116. Julian Myers, "The Future as Fetish," *October* 94 (Autumn 2000), 6–88.

117. Reyner Banham, "Vehicles of Desire," *Art* 1 (September 1955); reprinted in Wallis, *This Is Tomorrow Today*, 66.
118. Peter Smithson, "Concealment and Display," 362.
119. Alison Smithson, "And Now Dhamas Are Dying Out in Japan," 447.
120. Ibid., 448.
121. Alison and Peter Smithson, "Opening of the Eames Exhibition" (Berlin, September 5, 1979), in Alison and Peter Smithson, "Eames' Dreams," in *Changing the Art of Inhabitation*, 83.
122. Ibid., 84.

Chapter 5

1. Nikolaus Pevsner, *The Englishness of English Art* (Harmondsworth, Middlesex: Penguin, 1984; originally published 1956), 25.
2. Le Corbusier, "Question of Modern Habitation," CIAM 9, Aix-en-Provence, June 1953, written while in Chandigarh. Transcription of "Introduction to Congress," TTEN002 BOX TEAM 10 SMITHSON, Folder 6. NAi.
3. Ibid.
4. Ibid.
5. In an undated essay on the 1950s, written sometime after 1979, Alison Smithson notes that "we still hold the wartime habit of scrap paper," referring to their act of writing on both sides of bits of paper stored in their "Magic Box." Alison Smithson, "50S: Fields of Enquiry" 50S: FOE.1–3, 50S: FOE. 2. Undated. BOX AMS LECTURES EVOLVING. Smithson Family Collection.
6. Alison and Peter Smithson, "The 'as Found' and the 'Found,'" in David Robbins, ed., *The Independent Group: Postwar Britain and the Aesthetics of Plenty* (Cambridge, MA: MIT Press, 1990), 202.
7. Ibid.
8. For an informative dissertation on collage and advertisement as Cold War policies, see John Curley, "The Art that Came In from the Cold: Andy Warhol and Gerhard Richter, 1950–1968" (PhD dissertation, Yale University, 2007), 54–55.
9. Juliet Steyn, "Realism versus Realism in British Art of the 1950s," *Third Text* 22, no. 2 (March 1, 2008), 147.
10. Curley, "The Art that Came In from the Cold," 52.
11. Darrell B. Lucas and Stewart H. Britt, *Advertising Psychology and Research: An Introduction* (New York: McGraw-Hill, 1950), 276; quoted in Curley, "The Art that Came In from the Cold," 52.
12. J. M. Richards, *Functional Tradition in Early Industrial Buildings* (London: Architectural Press, 1958)—illustrated mostly with Eric de Maré's photographs and a few by John Piper.
13. The exhibition of photographs from *Life* magazine was sponsored by Time-Life Incorporated. Already exhibited at MoMA, the exhibition, still mounted, was shipped free of charge. Anne Massey, *The Independent Group: Modernism and Mass Culture in Britain, 1945–59* (Manchester: Manchester University Press, 1995), 65.

14. György Kepes, *Language of Vision* (Chicago: Paul Theobald, 1944); László Moholy-Nagy, *Vision in Motion* (Chicago: Paul Theobald, 1947).
15. Penny Martin, "English-Style Photographs?," in Christopher Breward, Becky Conekin, and Caroline Cox, eds., *The Englishness of English Dress* (Oxford: Berg, 2002), 173–186.
16. Ernst H. Gombrich, "The Evidence of Images," in Charles Singleton, ed., *Interpretation Theory and Practice* (Baltimore: Johns Hopkins University Press, 1967), 56.
17. Interaction, swapping of ideas, interlocking interests and practices across differences and multiple identities occur in the contact zone. The term "contact zone" is used by Mary Louise Pratt in *Imperial Eyes: Travel Writing and Transculturation* (London: Routledge, 1992), 6–7.
18. Alison Smithson, "50s Groups," edited from 1991 U.S. statement, February 1992, for AA Post Graduate, February 19, 1992; revised September 5 for possible use at AA, October 3, 1992, 50S: GRP: 1–3, 50S: GRP: 1. BOX AMS LECTURES EVOLVING. Smithson Family Collection.
19. Robert Freeman, "Living with the Sixties," *Cambridge Opinion* 17 (1959), 7.
20. Ibid.
21. Becky Conekin, "From Haughty to Nice: British Fashion Images Changed from the 1950s to the 1960s," *Photography and Culture* 3, no. 3 (2010), 283–296.
22. Alison Smithson, "A Calendar of Remembrance," Team 10 Seminars Session 1 TX.1: 1–25 (Spring 1982). Quotation from "La Sarraz, Sept 1955" TX.1: 10. TTEN0004 BOX TEAM SMITHSON, Folder 37. NAi.
23. Alison Smithson, quoted in B. S. Johnson, *The Evacuees* (London: Victor Gollancz, 1968), 250.
24. Alison Smithson, "Alison's last thoughts on Team X 1989 + 1991," ARCH.ED: 1–5, ARCH. ED: 1. TTEN0004 BOX TEAM 10 SMITHSON, Folder 35. NAi.
25. Alison Smithson, "50s Groups," GRP: 2.
26. Alloway was appointed to the ICA's Subcommittee on Exhibitions in March 1953, replacing Toni del Renzio. He became Assistant Director of the ICA in September 1955 and would resign in 1960 before leaving for America, where he took up a teaching position at Bennington College, Vermont, until becoming curator at the Guggenheim Museum in New York in 1961. Alex Seago, *Burning the Box of Beautiful Things: The Development of a Postmodern Sensibility* (Oxford: Oxford University Press, 1995), 114.
27. For a partial list of IG activities, see Graham Whitham, "Chronology," in Robbins, *The Independent Group*, 12–48.
28. Alison and Peter Smithson, Personal Statement, "But Today we collect Ads," *Ark* 18 (November 1956), 49–50.
29. Ibid., 49.
30. Ibid.
31. Ibid., 50.
32. *Ark* was established in 1950 by Jack Stafford, who stated in the first editorial: "The elusive but necessary relationships between the arts and the social context are the real objects of our enquiry through the pages of *ARK* and our policy will be to set a subject, give our

answers as students of the arts and ask a selection of those who will see the same subject from other and different viewpoints. We shall serve this mixture up to you with the firm belief that it is best to be serious without being solemn." Jack Stafford, "Editorial," *Ark* 1 (Autumn 1950); quoted in Seago, *Burning the Box of Beautiful Things*, 33. This rather vague definition of aims was typically English, or so Len Deighton, the art editor of *Ark* 10 (Spring 1954), thought in 1989: "No one knew what the hell *ARK* was for. … It was typically English. No one could decide. In England the whole way of living is predicated upon never defining anything because that way no one can get it right or wrong." Interviewed by Alex Seago (January 4, 1989), in Seago, *Burning the Box of Beautiful Things*, 34.

33. Alison and Peter Smithson, *The Shift*, Architectural Monographs 7 (London: Academy Editions, 1982), 9.
34. Alison Smithson, "Madame Representative—Woman Correspondent," January 1959–July 1964, 14. Smithson Family Collection.
35. Ibid., 15.
36. Ibid., 7.
37. Ibid., 9.
38. Ibid., 3.
39. Ibid., 13.
40. Ibid., 3.
41. Ibid., 5.
42. Ibid., 11.
43. Ibid., 11–12.
44. Ibid., 14.
45. Alison's maiden name was Alison Margaret Gill.
46. Margaret Gill, "Not Quite Architecture: If You Want to Get Ahead—Get a Monkey Busby," *Architects' Journal* 129 (February 19, 1959), 283.
47. Ibid.
48. Margaret Gill, "Not Quite Architecture: War-Reporter Looks Back," *Architects' Journal* 133 (January 5, 1961), 62.
49. Alison Smithson, letter to Vincent Theijs, University of Utrecht Art History Department. Theijs was conducting a survey on the history of Dutch FORUM group. Alison Smithson, DUTCH F: 1–4, DUTCH F: 4. (July 20, 1984). TT0002 BOX TEAM 10 SMITHSON, Folder 1. NAi.
50. Reyner Banham, "Not Quite Architecture: Ungrab That Gondola," *Architects' Journal* 126 (August 15, 1957), 233.
51. Ibid., 235.
52. Ibid., 233; "Reyner Banham, "Design by Choice: 1951–1961 An Alphabetical Chronicle of Landmarks and Influences," *AR* 130 (July 1961), 43–48, 46.
53. Alison Smithson, "Italy Consumed as an Intellectual Food Parcel," unpaginated (August 1990). BOX AMS LECTURES AS EVOLVED. Smithson Family Collection.
54. Ibid.

55. Ibid.
56. Toni del Renzio, "Pioneers and Trendies," *Art & Artists* (February 1984), 25–28.
57. Ibid., 26.
58. Alloway, del Renzio averred, would never consider going to a foreign-language film, and always used the term "movie" for film. Ibid.
59. A typical 1957 *General Motors* advertisement for a Cadillac confuses car and classy dame: the copy reads: "it would be difficult to imagine a more wonderful place for a lady to sit in than the passenger seat of a new 1957 Cadillac. To begin with, she is marvelously comfortable. … The seat cushions are soft and restful … the car's interior is wonderfully spacious … and every imaginable motoring convenience is close at hand. And how regal she feels!" (the lady or the car?), *Harper's Bazaar*, March 1957; quoted by Toni del Renzio, "Shoes Hair and Coffee," *Ark* 20 (Autumn 1957), 30, footnote 2.
60. Del Renzio, "Shoes Hair and Coffee," 28.
61. Ibid., 30.
62. Joseph Rykwert, "A Serious Case of Patronage," *Ark* 11 (Summer 1954), 23–30.
63. John McHale, "Technology and the Home," *Ark* 19 (Spring 1957), 25–27.
64. Alison Smithson, handwritten notes, "Home within the Community—H of F 56," 1–4, 2. Smithson Family Collection. Also quoted by Av Helena Mattsson, "House of the Future" (unpublished manuscript), unpaginated. The website has been removed from the Internet. Excerpt of article found in Av Helena Mattsson, "House of the Future: The Sociology of Interior Design in an Age of Consumption," *Site* 5 (2003), 1–2, http://www.sitemagazine.net/issues/5/5.pdf (accessed July 24, 2013).
65. Alison Smithson, "Home within the Community," 2–3.
66. Ibid., 1.
67. Ibid.
68. Teddy Tinling, quoted in Mattsson, "House of the Future" (unpublished manuscript), unpaginated.
69. Mattsson, "House of the Future" (unpublished manuscript), unpaginated.
70. Peter Smithson, "The Chair" (1985), in Alison and Peter Smithson, *Changing the Art of Inhabitation* (London: Artemis, 1994), 144.
71. Catherine Spellman and Karl Unglaub, eds., *Peter Smithson: Conversations with Students: A Space for Our Generation* (New York: PAP, 2005), 43.
72. "Surveying from his new American eminence at the Guggenheim Museum, the present state of the English (or senior) branch of Pop Art, Lawrence Alloway complained that it [Pop Art] was too much under the influence of graphics." Reyner Banham, "Department of Visual Uproar," *New Statesman* (May 3, 1963), 687.
73. Ibid., 687.
74. Obituary for Richard Guyatt, *Guardian*, October 27, 2007, http://www.theguardian.com/news/2007/oct/27/guardianobituaries.artsobituaries(accessed July 25, 2013). Also "Professor Richard Guyatt," obituaries, *Independent* (October 29, 2007), http://www.independent.co.uk/news/obituaries/professor-richard-guyatt-398213.html (accessed July 25, 2013).

75. After Roger Coleman left the RCA he continued to be involved with the ICA's Exhibition Committee, and wrote for *Design* magazine.
76. Seago, *Burning the Box of Beautiful Things*, 112.
77. Thomas Crow, "School of Pop," *Artforum* 10 (October 2004), 43–47.
78. Basil Taylor was unofficial advisor to Paul Mellon when the latter began in earnest to collect British art in the mid-1950s.
79. Seago, *Burning the Box of Beautiful Things*, 158.
80. Roger Coleman, "Comment," *Ark* 19 (Spring 1957), 3.
81. Ibid.
82. Roger Coleman, interviewed by Seago (June 26, 1989); quoted in Seago, *Burning the Box of Beautiful Things*, 115.
83. Seago, *Burning the Box of Beautiful Things*, 116.
84. Lawrence Alloway's articles in *Ark*: "Technology and Sex in Science Fiction: A Note on Cover Art," *Ark* 17 (Summer 1956), 19–23; "Personal Statement," *Ark* 19 (Spring 1957), 28–29; "Communications Comedy and the Small World," *Ark* 20 (Autumn 1957), 41–43; "Marks and Signs," *Ark* 22 (Summer 1958), 37–42; "Laboured Breathing: Technical Manifesto given at the first International Congress of Proportion at the IXth Triennale, Milan, 1947," *Ark* 24 (Spring 1959), 4–7. A final article on Italian avant-garde art appeared in *Ark* 25 (Spring 1960), 21–23, 43.
85. Alloway, "Communications Comedy," 41–43.
86. Roger Coleman, "Dream Worlds, Assorted," *Ark* 19 (Spring 1957), 30–32.
87. Martin, "English-Style Photography?".
88. Coleman, "Dream Worlds, Assorted," 32.
89. Ibid.
90. Ibid.
91. Ibid.
92. Ibid.
93. Stephen Cohn, "Editorial," *Ark* 30 (Winter 1961), 3.
94. Denis Bowen, "A Reply to 'What is it?'," *Ark* 30 (Winter 1961), 25–26.
95. Ibid., 26.
96. Ken Baynes, "Better and Worse Dreams," *Ark* 30 (Winter 1961), 27–30.
97. Ibid., 27.
98. Ibid., 28.
99. Peter Smithson, "Report," *Design* (November 1960); quoted by Baynes, "Better and Worse Dreams," 29.
100. Baynes, "Better and Worse Dreams," 30.
101. Bill James, "Editorial," *Ark* 32 (Summer 1962), 2.
102. Ibid.
103. Misha Black, "A Thing for a Crowd," *Ark* 32 (Summer 1962), 3–6.

104. Ibid., 3.
105. James, "Editorial," 2.
106. Black, "A Thing for a Crowd," 4.
107. Ibid., 5.
108. Ibid., 6.
109. Ibid.
110. Banham, "Design by Choice," 43–48.
111. Ibid., 47.
112. Alison Smithson, "Making Ideas Manifest and So Introducing a Sensibility to Car Movement," 3 (May–September 1983). AMS BOX LECTURES AS EVOLVED. Smithson Family Collection.
113. Alison Smithson, "With Green in Mind," lecture for Syracuse University (October 1991), GREEN.MIIND, 1–9. AMS BOX LECTURES EVOLVING. Smithson Family Collection.

Chapter 6

1. Robin Boyd, quoted by Jean Baudrillard, *The System of Objects* (London: Verso, 1996), 67.
2. "The inventor of tail fins, Harley Earl, oriented his work on the form of an aeroplane and referred to the bodywork as a visible symbol of prestige." Ingrid Loschek, *When Clothes Become Fashions: Design and Innovation Systems* (Oxford: Berg, 2009), 174–175. Cadillac was the "car of cars"; the 1957 Cadillac Eldorado Brougham was "to be a super-prestige car, built in limited quantity." Leo Donovan, "Detroit Listening Post," *Popular Mechanics* (July 1956), 84.
3. Sudhir Chella Rajan, "Automobility and the Liberal Disposition," in Steffen Böhm, Campbell Jones, Chris Land, and Matthew Paterson, eds., *Against Automobility* (Oxford: Blackwell Publishing/Sociological Review Monographs, 2006), 113–129.
4. Reyner Banham, "Match Abandoned," *Art News and Review* 6 (May 29, 1954), 7.
5. Reyner Banham, "Vehicles of Desire," *Art* 1 (September 1, 1955), reprinted in *This Is Tomorrow Today*, ed. Brian Wallis, exh. cat. (New York: Institute for Art and Urban Resources, 1987), 69.
6. Alison and Peter Smithson, *Without Rhetoric: An Architectural Aesthetic 1955–1972* (London: Latimer News Dimensions, 1973), 2.
7. Banham, "Vehicles of Desire," in *This Is Tomorrow Today*, 69.
8. Nigel Whiteley, *Reyner Banham: Historian of the Immediate Future* (Cambridge, MA: MIT Press, 2002), 93.
9. Banham, "Vehicles of Desire," 65.
10. Reyner Banham, "Industrial Design and the Common User," *The Listener* (May 3, 1956), 151.
11. Reyner Banham, "Design by Choice 1951–1961: An Alphabetical Chronicle of Landmarks and Influences," *AR* 130 (July 1961), 44.
12. Ibid., 45.

13. Ibid., 46.
14. Peter Smithson, "Le Corbusier Exhibition February 1959," CC: 1–4, CC: 1. P.S. (February 1959, GSD E-015), AS & PS MAGIC BOX. Smithson Family Collection.
15. Reyner Banham, *The New Brutalism: Ethic or Aesthetic?* (New York: Reinhold, 1966), 63.
16. Reyner Banham first used the term "une architecture autre" in "New Brutalism," *AR* 118 (December 1955). Here the reference is to Banham, *The New Brutalism: Ethic or Aesthetic?*, 67.
17. Banham, *The New Brutalism: Ethic or Aesthetic?*, 89.
18. Alison and Peter Smithson, "Banham's Bumper Book on Brutalism, Discussed by Alison and Peter Smithson," *Architects' Journal* 144 (December 28, 1966), 1591.
19. Banham, "Design by Choice 1951–1961," 45.
20. Banham, *The New Brutalism: Ethic or Aesthetic?*, 62; Banham, "Design by Choice 1951–1961," 45.
21. Banham, "Design by Choice 1951–1961," 47.
22. Eduardo Paolozzi, "Conversation between Eduardo Paolozzi and Alvin Boyarsky" (May 1984), *Underground Design* (London: AA, 1986), 5–13.
23. Alison and Peter Smithson drove a Jeep and then a Volkswagen before driving four different Citroëns: a Citroën ID, Citroën DS, Citroën ID Break, Citroën CX. Alison Smithson, "The Car: Citroën," *AS in DS* (Delft: Delft University Press, 1983), appendix, unpaginated.
24. I. Chippendale [aka Alison Smithson], "Love in a Beetle," *AD* 38 (October 1965), 478.
25. Ibid.
26. Peter Smithson, "Architectural Anecdotes," P.S. (22.5.87), BOX AS & PS UNPUBLISHED PAPERS + CURRENT LECTURES. Smithson Family Collection.
27. Banham, "Design by Choice 1951–1961," 48.
28. According to Wikipedia, the DS 19 was introduced at the 1955 Paris Motor show. However, Banham states the year was 1957. Banham, "Design by Choice 1951–1961," 44.
29. Ibid., 44.
30. The first talk I heard Alison and Peter Smithson give was at Columbia University in the late 1980s, a lunchtime "brownbag chat." The two conversed with each other about wedding trips, vacation adventures, CIAM meetings—all the while only images of their cars appeared on the screen, acting as prompts for recall.
31. Peter Smithson, "CIAM 9, 10—Still Counting," 4. P. S. (November–December 1984, revised from handwritten January–March 1984). TTEN0004 BOX TEAM 10 SMITHSON, Folder 25. NAi. Also, Alison and Peter Smithson, *Italian Thoughts* (Stockholm: Alison & Peter Smithson, 1993), 32.
32. Peter Smithson, "CIAM 9, 10—Still Counting," 5. Smithson Family Collection.
33. Alison Smithson, "Asides to accompany Team 10 Seminars: Session 1," ASIDES: I: 1–12, ASIDES: I: 9. TTEN0004 BOX TEAM 10 SMITHSON, Folder 37. NAi.
34. Peter Smithson, "CIAM 9, 10—Still Counting." Smithson Family Collection.
35. Alison Smithson, "Asides to accompany Team 10 Seminar Session 1," ASIDES: I: 8.

36. Alison Smithson, in Peter Smithson, "Conversations on Brutalism with Jane Drew and Maxwell Fry," *Zodiac* 4 (Fall 1959), 80.
37. Peter Smithson, "Conversations on Brutalism," 80.
38. Peter Smithson, "Letter to America," *AD* 28 (March 1958), 93–102; mentioned in Alison and Peter Smithson, *Ordinariness and Light* (London: Faber and Faber, 1970), 139.
39. Peter Smithson also referred to one American car design that dared not to be square, the Studebaker, which never sold well. Peter Smithson, "Letter to America," 95; mentioned in *Ordinariness and Light*, 135–141.
40. Peter Smithson, "Letter to America," 95.
41. Ibid., 97.
42. Ibid.
43. Alison Smithson pulled together many of their writings on mobility and roadways and published them as a collection of quotations [theirs and others'] under the subtitle "Urban Infra-structure," in Alison Smithson, guest editor, "Team 10 Primer," *AD* 32 (December 1962), 574–586.
44. Alison and Peter Smithson, "Ideal City," ibid., 583.
45. Attributed to Alison and Peter Smithson, "Scatter" *AD* 29 (1959), although quotation does not appear in the original article. Ibid., 582.
46. Ibid., 583.
47. Ibid.
48. Alison Smithson, *AS in DS*, 17.
49. Alison Smithson, "Local Character," *AD* 38 (September 1958), 416–417; reprinted in *Ordinariness and Light*, 144–153.
50. Alison Smithson, guest editor, "CIAM Team 10," *AD* 30 (May 1960), 175–205. Also "Team 10 Primer," *AD* 32 (December 1962), 559–602.
51. Alison and Peter Smithson, *Upper Case 3* (London: Whitefriars, 1959); in Alison Smithson, "Team 10 Primer," 574.
52. Alison and Peter Smithson, "London Roads Study," in Alison Smithson, "CIAM Team 10," 187.
53. Film, *Hauptstadt Berlin: The New Principles of Town-Building* (1958–1959), 16 mm., black and white, sound, running time 13.5 minutes. Master negative held by George Humphreys & Co. Ltd., "The Alison and Peter Smithson Archive," Harvard University, Graduate School of Design, Special Collections, Loeb Library, BB014.
54. Peter and Alison Smithson, "Berlin Hauptstadt" (1957). Originally numbered 180923, later HAUP: 1–9, with collaborator Peter Sigmonde's name added. "The Alison and Peter Smithson Archive," BB014.
55. Banham, *The New Brutalism: Ethic or Aesthetic?*, 73–75.
56. Alison and Peter Smithson, "Scatter," *AD* 29 (April 1959), 149–150. For comparison with Los Angeles, see Alison and Peter Smithson, "Cluster City," *AR* 122 (November 1957), 333–336; reprinted in Alison Smithson, "Team 10 Primer," 583.
57. Alison and Peter Smithson, "Cluster City"; quoted in Alison Smithson, "Team 10 Primer," 585.

58. Alison and Peter Smithson, "Fix," *AR* 128 (December 1960), 436–439; quoted in Alison Smithson, "Team 10 Primer," 585.
59. Alison Smithson, "Team 10 Primer," 583.
60. Ibid., 586.
61. Reyner Banham, "Apropos the Smithsons," *New Statesman* (September 8, 1961), 317.
62. Alison and Peter Smithson, "Scatter."
63. Ibid.
64. Alison Smithson, "The Future of Furniture"; Alison and Peter Smithson, "The Appliance House," *AD* 28 (April 1958), 175–178.
65. Alison Smithson, "The Future of Furniture"; Alison and Peter Smithson, "The Appliance House."
66. Ibid.
67. Alison and Peter Smithson, "Scatter," 150.
68. Ibid.
69. Banham, *The New Brutalism: Ethic or Aesthetic?*, 73.
70. Ibid., 135.
71. Alison Smithson, "Caravan-Embryo 'Appliance House'?," *AD* 29 (August 1959), 348.
72. Ibid.
73. Ibid.
74. Ibid.
75. Reyner Banham, "Stocktaking: Tradition and Technology—1960/1," *AR* 127 (February 1960), 93–100; Reyner Banham, "Stocktaking: The Science Side—1960/2," *AR* 127 (March 1960), 183–190; Reyner Banham, moderator, "Stocktaking: The Future of Universal Man Symposium—1960/3," *AR* 127 (April 1960), 253–260; Reyner Banham "Stocktaking: History under Review—1960/4," *AR* 127 (May 1960), 325–332.
76. Pevsner, in J. M. Richards, Nikolaus Pevsner, Hugh Casson, and H. de C. Hastings, "Stocktaking: Propositions—1960/5," *AR* 127 (June 1960), 388.
77. Banham, "Stocktaking 1960/1," 94.
78. Ibid.
79. Ibid., 95–96.
80. Peter Smithson, "The Fine and the Folk: An Essay on McKim, Mead and White and the American Tradition," *AD* 35 (August 1965), 394.
81. Alison and Peter Smithson, "Density, Interval and Measure," *AD* 37 (September 1967), 428; reprinted from *Landscape* (Spring 1967).
82. Ibid.
83. Ibid.
84. Alison Smithson, ed., *Team 10 Primer* (Cambridge, MA: MIT Press, 1968), 6.
85. Alison and Peter Smithson, "Vehicles, Mechanism, Services: Another Ordering," *AD* 42 (June 1972), 369.

86. Ibid., 370.
87. Ibid.
88. Ibid.
89. Alison Smithson, "AS in DS: Delft," 2–4a, 4b (missing: 1) (n.d.). TT0004 BOX TEAM 10 SMITHSON, Folder 35. NAi.
90. Ibid., 2.
91. Ibid., 3–4a; reprinted and augmented in Alison Smithson, *AS in DS*, 111.
92. Alison Smithson, "AS in DS: Delft," 4a.
93. Alison and Peter Smithson, "The Built World: Urban Re-identification," *AD* (June 1955), 185–188; quoted in Alison Smithson, "Team 10 Primer," 593. 1956 was the starting point for "thinking green"; see Alison Smithson, "With Green in Mind," GREEN.MND: 1–9 (Summer 1991); BOX AMS LECTURES EVOLVING. Smithson Family Collection.
94. Peter Smithson, "Outline for Riverside—Food for Sensibilities, the 50's and the 60's," unpaginated (April 1984); BOX AS & PS '50s and '60s. Smithson Family Collection.
95. Ibid.
96. Alison Smithson, *AS in DS*, 1.
97. Alison Smithson, "Making Ideas Manifest and so Introducing Sensibility to Car Movement," 4. BOX AMS LECTURES AS EVOLVED. Smithson Family Collection.
98. Ibid., 4–5.
99. Ibid., 5.
100. Ibid., 5–6.
101. Conversation with Soraya Smithson (May 2008).
102. Alison Smithson, *AS in DS*, 15.
103. Ibid.
104. Ibid., 16.
105. Peter Smithson, "How to Use 'AS in DS' as a Teaching Document," in Alison Smithson, *AS in DS*, 12.
106. Alison Smithson, *AS in DS*, 15.
107. Alison Smithson, "AS in DS AIM," 14 (February 1972/March 1973 September/October 1974/Summer), 14–15. Smithson Family Collection. These two pages are repeated without italics, as in the original, in Alison Smithson, *AS in DS*, 151–152.
108. Alison Smithson, "AS in DS AIM," 14–15.
109. Ibid., 15.
110. Alison Smithson, *AS in DS*, 23.
111. Ibid., 151.
112. Ibid., 35.
113. Alison Smithson, "AS in DS AIM," 14.
114. Alison Smithson, *AS in DS*, 47.
115. Ibid., 55.

116. Ibid., 73.
117. Alison Smithson, "Aspect 6: Change" (written 1981; edited 1982), in *AS in DS*, 131.
118. Alison Smithson, *AS in DS*, 140.
119. Ibid., 141.
120. Ibid., 141, 143.
121. Ibid., 143.
122. Ibid., 145.

Chapter 7

1. The basic Team 10 documents published in *AD* are: Alison Smithson (guest editor), "CIAM Team 10" and "The Work of Team 10," *AD* 30 (May 1960), 175–205; Alison Smithson (guest editor), "Team 10 Primer," *AD* 32 (December 1962), 559–602. These have been supplemented with Alison Smithson, ed., *Team 10 Primer* (Cambridge, MA: MIT Press, 1968); Alison Smithson, ed., "Team 10 at Royaumont 1962," *AD* 65 (November 1975), 664–689; Alison Smithson, ed., *Team 10 Meetings: 1953–1984* (New York: Rizzoli, 1991). Additional documents are from Team10 archives, NAi, Rotterdam.
2. "Theme Name and Method of Work," Otterlo Congress and Team 10 Meetings (undated, unsigned). TTEN0002 BOX TEAM 10 SMITHSON, Folder 19. NAi.
3. "Message de Le Corbusier addressé au Xème Congrès CIAM à Dubrovnik," FLC Doc 11. Roquebrune-Cap Martin 23-Juillet-1956.
4. In earlier discussions about passing on the leadership of CIAM to a younger generation, Le Corbusier maintained that an "urbanism" implicating many other disciplines could not be accommodated without a body of committed architects, so a new CIAM must be formed. "Preparation of CIAM 9," FLC D2-(19) Doc 1 "Conseil CIAM" (Paris, Mai 1952).
5. "Je tiens pour décisive cette reprise de l'action par la génération *méritante*, c'est pour cela que je ne suis pas à Dubrovnik." "Message de Le Corbusier addressé au Xème Congrès CIAM à Dubrovnik," FLC Doc 11. Roquebrune-Cap Martin 23-Juillet-1956.
6. "Stimulator and Stirrer," quoted from Alison Smithson, "The Wider Role of the Architect," WIDR, 1. BOX AMS LECTURES AS EVOLVED. Smithson Family Collection.
7. Alison Smithson (guest editor), "CIAM Team 10" and "The Work of Team 10," *AD* 30 (May 1960), 175–205.
8. Alison Smithson, "CIAM Team 10," overleaf of 177.
9. Ibid., 178.
10. Ernesto Rogers introduced Giancarlo De Carlo to Team 10 members. De Carlo presented his 1954 Matera project at the Otterlo Meeting (1959) and would soon be considered an active member of Team 10. From http://www.team10online.org/team10/carlo/index.html (accessed July 23, 2013).
11. Alison Smithson, "CIAM Team 10," 191–192.
12. Kenzō Tange, "Statement," in ibid., 201.
13. Ibid.
14. De Carlo, "Summary," in Alison Smithson, "CIAM Team 10," 204–205.

15. Ibid., 205.
16. "I asked Theo Crosby about the Primer and Monica Pidgeon offered us all of December A. D. Printed on its side so that the reprint will bend on the short end and open like an Oeuvre Complète. The reprint would be without advertisements of course and be cheaper than a book. This way we could keep below the 35 shilling price we agreed on in Stockholm." Letter from Alison and Peter Smithson to Jaap Bakema (28.21.1963). BAKE00152 BOX, folder g5. NAi.
17. Peter Smithson's notes from Reyner Banham's lecture "Futurism" at the Royal Institute of British Architects RIBA (1959); quoted in Alison Smithson, "Team 10 Primer," 568–569.
18. Peter Smithson, IAU Catalogue, 1961; quoted in ibid., 564.
19. Ibid.
20. Jaap Bakema, *Carré Bleu* (1951); quoted in Alison Smithson, "Team 10 Primer," 563.
21. Aldo van Eyck, in ibid., 559.
22. Peter Smithson, "Le Corbusier Exhibition (February 1959)"; quoted in ibid., 566–567.
23. Candilis, Josic, Woods, *Carré Bleu* 3 (1961); quoted in ibid., 602.
24. Alison Smithson, *Team 10 Primer*, 1–4.
25. Ibid., 6.
26. "Preface," in ibid., 4–19.
27. Charles Pologni, Ghana (1967); quoted in Alison Smithson, *Team 10 Primer*, 5. Aldo van Eyck wrote that reprinting the *Primer* was a good thing: "As I went from university to university I noticed that it was a cherished document." Letter from Aldo van Eyck to Alison and Peter Smithson (1965—just back from America), 1–4, 5a, 5b, 5b. TTEN0002 BOX TEAM 10 SMITHSON, Folder 1. NAi.
28. Ralph Erskine, Stockholm (February 22, 1967); quoted in Alison Smithson, *Team 10 Primer*, 4.
29. Charles Pologni, Ghana (1967); quoted in ibid., 5.
30. Giancarlo De Carlo, Paris (February 25, 1967); quoted in ibid., 4.
31. Shadrach Woods, letter to Alison Smithson, Berlin (1967); quoted in ibid., 18.
32. Alison Smithson, "Team 10 at Royaumont 1962," 664–689. Before the Royaumont Abbey 1962 report was lost, it was decided in September 1963 that it should be published in paperback form with mainly dialogues and a few descriptions of plans, also limited only to necessary images. Shadrach Woods was charged with asking Washington University, St. Louis, to organize the editing. "Team 10 Meeting Paris, Sept 1963" (TTEN0004 BOX TEAM 10 SMITHSON, Folder 23. NAi). The transcripts of the Royaumont (Paris) meeting—with several pages missing and many pages crossed out—are in the NAi archives. These include "Royaumont Meetings," 26–426. TTEN0003 BOX TEAM 10 SMITHSON, Folder 22; background materials on Royaumont Meeting, TTEN0004 BOX TEAM 10 SMITHSON, Folders 23–40; and "Team 10 at Abbaye Royaumont" (September 1962), 3–53. TTEN0005 BOX TEAM 10 SMITHSON, Folder 43.
33. Alison Smithson, "Team 10 at Royaumont 1962," 664.
34. Peter Smithson (6.3.75), in "Team 10 at Abbaye Royaumont" (September 1962), 1. TTEN0005 BOX TEAM 10 SMITHSON, Folder 43. NAi.

35. Dirk van den Heuvel, "Royaumont (France) 12–16 September 1962—The Issues of Urban Infrastructure," at http://www.team10online.org/team10/meetings/1962-royaumont.htm (accessed July 31, 2013).
36. Bakema and Peter Smithson, in "Royaumont Meetings," TTEN0003 BOX TEAM 10 SMITHSON, Folder 22: 53. NAi.
37. Alison Smithson, "Team 10 at Royaumont 1962," 668.
38. Ibid., 666.
39. Ibid., 668.
40. Guedes, in "Royaumont Meetings," 27. TTEN0003 BOX TEAM 10 SMITHSON, Folder 22. NAi.
41. Ibid., 29.
42. Alison Smithson, "Team 10 at Royaumont 1962," 667.
43. Ibid., 669.
44. Christopher Alexander, in "Team 10 at Abbaye Royaumont," 18.
45. Alison Smithson, in "Royaumont Meetings," 37.
46. Alison Smithson, "Team 10 at Royaumont 1962," 669.
47. Ibid.
48. Ibid.
49. Alison Smithson, *Team 10 Meetings*. The republication of these documents was accomplished by Max Risselada and Alison Smithson.
50. Ibid., 10–11.
51. Ibid., 14–16.
52. Ibid., 14, 24.
53. Ibid., 11, 13.
54. Aldo van Eyck, "A Miracle of Moderation" (1969), in Charles Jencks and George Baird, eds., *Meaning in Architecture* (London: Barrie & Jenkins, 1969), 174; quoted by Jos Bosman, "Team 10 out of CIAM," in Max Risselada and Dirk van den Heuvel, eds., *Team 10 1953–1981: In Search of a Utopia of the Present* (Rotterdam: NAi Publishers, 2005), 249.
55. Letter from Reima Pietilä and Raili Paatelainen to Alison and Peter Smithson about the Rotterdam Meeting of Team 10 (Helsinki 15.2.1974), 1–5. TTEN0004 BOX TEAM 10 SMITHSON, Folder 28. NAi.
56. Peter Smithson, "Team X: A Proposition at Bonnieux—La Croupatière" (June 20, 1977), TTEN0004 BOX TEAM 10 SMITHSON, Folder 31. NAi; quoted in Risselada and van den Heuvel, *Team 10 1953–1981*, 229–230.
57. Peter Smithson, "Team X: A Proposition at Bonnieux—La Croupatière" (June 20, 1977), TTEN0004 BOX TEAM 10 SMITHSON, Folder 31. NAi.
58. Two other members of Team 10 had already died: John Voelcker (September 15 [?], 1972) and Shadrach Woods (July 31, 1973).
59. Alison or Peter Smithson, untitled: two typed pages about Team Life. Written at Tisbury 1970s, typed February 1985. TTEN0004 BOX TEAM 10 SMITHSON, Folder 35. NAi.
60. Ibid.

61. Ibid.
62. Alison Smithson, "Team X Preparation Meeting: London October 25–27, 1980" (26–27.10.80) TTEN0004 BOX TEAM 10 SMITHSON, Folder 33. NAi.
63. Ibid.
64. Alison Smithson, *Team 10 Meetings*, 9.
65. Ibid., 15.
66. Peter Smithson, "Work Presented at Team X; for Ankara, April 1989" (March 1989), ANKARA, 4–5. TTEN0004 BOX TEAM 10 SMITHSON, Folder 35. NAi.
67. Alison Smithson, ed., *The Emergence of Team 10 out of CIAM* (London: Architectural Association, 1982); and Alison Smithson, "Meeting Dec 20th 1981 and Dec 21st 1981 about Team 10 Seminars Feb 1st 1982, Feb 7th a.s.o.," TTEN0004 BOX TEAM 10 SMITHSON, Folder 36. NAi.
68. Peter Smithson, "Some Thoughts for the Team X Book Launch, Delft" (June 25, 1992), ARCH.TEAM X, 1–3 (edited 5.10.93). TTEN0004 BOX TEAM 10 SMITHSON, Folder 35. NAi.
69. Alison Smithson, "A Calendar of Remembrances," Team 10 Seminar Session 1, Graduate School, A.A. (Spring 1982): TX 1: 1–25. TTEN0004 BOX TEAM 10 SMITHSON, Folder 37; Alison Smithson, Asides to accompany Team 10 Seminar Session 1: ASIDES 1: 1–12. TTEN0004 BOX TEAM 10 SMITHSON, Folder 37; Alison Smithson, Team 10 Seminar Session 2 (Spring 1982): TX 2: 1–10. TTEN0004 BOX TEAM 10 SMITHSON, Folder 37; Alison Smithson, Asides to accompany Team 10 Seminar Session 2: ASIDES 2: 1–5. TTEN0004 BOX TEAM 10 SMITHSON, Folder 37; Alison Smithson, Team 10 Seminar Session 3 (Spring 1982): TX 3: 1–6. TTEN0004 BOX TEAM 10 SMITHSON, Folder 37; Alison Smithson, Asides to accompany Team 10 Seminar Session 3: ASIDES 3: 1–3. TTEN0004 BOX TEAM 10 SMITHSON, Folder 37; Alison Smithson, "Team 10: The Myth and Message" (March 1983), 1–13. TTEN0004 BOX TEAM 10 SMITHSON, Folder 35; Peter Smithson, "CIAM 9, 10—Still Counting," for Athens 1984 (revised handwritten notes, January–March 1984; rewritten November–December 1984), 1–6, TTEN0004 BOX TEAM 10 SMITHSON, Folder 35; Alison Smithson, "Otterlo Incident" (July 20, 1984), DUTCHF, 1–4, TTEN0002 BOX TEAM 10 SMITHSON, Folder 1; Alison Smithson, "The Otterlo Incident" (October 21, 1990), OI, 1–7, BOX AMS LECTURES AS EVOLVED. Smithson Family Collection; Peter Smithson, "Team 10 in Retrospect" (October 1, 1993, revised March 1994, October 1995, April 1999), ARCH.TEAM X: 1–9, TTEN0004 BOX TEAM 10 SMITHSON, Folder 35.
All TTEN documents are from NAi.
70. Alison Smithson, "A Calendar of Remembrances," TX 1: 3.
71. Ibid.
72. Ibid., TX 1: 4.
73. Alison Smithson, Team 10 Seminar Session 2 (Spring 1982): TX 2: 6.
74. Alison Smithson, Asides to accompany Team 10 Seminar Session 1: ASIDES 1: 1.
75. Alison Smithson, "A Calendar of Remembrances," TX 1: 3.
76. Alison Smithson, "Asides 1," ASIDES 1: 2.

77. Peter Smithson, "CIAM 9, 10—Still Counting" (for Athens, 1984; revised handwritten January–March 1984), 1. TTEN0004 BOX TEAM 10 SMITHSON, Folder 35. NAi.
78. Alison Smithson, "Asides 1,"ASIDES: 1: 3.
79. Alison Smithson, Team 10 Seminar Session 2 (Spring 1982): TX 2: 4.
80. Alison Smithson, "Asides 1,"ASIDES: 1: 3.
81. Alison Smithson, "A Calendar of Remembrances," TX 1: 6.
82. Ibid., TX 1: 7.
83. Ibid., TX 1: 8.
84. Alison Smithson, Asides to accompany Team 10 Seminar Session 1, ASIDES 1: 4.
85. Alison Smithson, "Asides 1," TX 1: 7.
86. Alison Smithson, "A Calendar of Remembrances," TX 1: 8.
87. Ibid., TX 1: 9.
88. Alison Smithson, "Asides 1," ASIDES 1: 6.
89. Alison Smithson, "A Calendar of Remembrances," TX 1: 9.
90. Ibid., TX 1: 12.
91. Ibid., TX 1: 13.
92. Ibid., TX 1: 14.
93. Alison Smithson, "Asides 1," ASIDES 1: 9.
94. Alison Smithson, "A Calendar of Remembrances," TX 1: 15.
95. Ibid., TX 1: 15–16.
96. Ibid., TX 1: 16.
97. Alison Smithson, Team 10 Seminar Session 2 (Spring 1982), TX 2: 7.
98. Elder members of Team 10—Jaap Bakema, Georges Candilis, Giancarlo De Carlo—had all been in the Resistance. Hence there was "always an undertow of committed responsibility in CIAM and Team 10: an integrity of acting as speaking; so Team 10 felt at home with the masters." Candilis was taken into Le Corbusier's office after he escaped from the prison island Makronisos. Sołtan, who had been a prisoner of war in Germany, finished his education through correspondence with Le Corbusier, then worked in Corb's office in Paris and later taught with Sert and Tyrwhitt at Harvard. "Aldo van Eyck was holed up in Switzerland at Carola Giedion's feet." Alison Smithson, "Session 2," TX 2: 1.
99. Alison Smithson, Asides to accompany Team 10 Seminar Session 1, ASIDES 2: 1.
100. Alison Smithson, "Session 2," TX 2: 2.
101. Ibid., TX 2: 3.
102. Ibid.
103. Ibid.
104. Ibid., TX 2: 4.
105. Ibid., TX 2: 5.
106. Alison Smithson, "Team 10 Seminar Session 3," TX 3: 2.

107. Alison Smithson, "Meeting Dec 20th 1981 and Dec 21st 1981 about Team 10 Seminars Feb 1st 1982, Feb 7th a.s.o.," TTEN0004 BOX TEAM 10 SMITHSON, Folder 36. NAi.
108. Alison Smithson, "Session 3," TX 3: 3.
109. Ibid., TX 3: 6.
110. Ibid., TX 3: 3.
111. "We carried this out to the letter … old correspondence was thrown away unless the signature had a personal association." Alison Smithson, "Asides 1," ASIDES 1: 8.
112. During seminars at MIT questioning the effectiveness of Team 10 thinking, Alison Smithson realized that the greatest concentration of Team members teaching seminars in the US was at Washington University in St. Louis—though MIT, Harvard, and the University of Pennsylvania had all claimed to be the center of Team 10 influence in America. A version of the latter myth was perpetuated by former students from Penn in the early 1950s and 1960s, paradoxically in the teaching of David Crane and Denise Scott Brown. Alison Smithson, "Team Ten: The Myth and the Message" (March 1983), 12. TTEN0004 BOX TEAM 10 SMITHSON, Folder 35. NAi.
113. Alison Smithson, letter to Bakema (June 1, 1978), TTEN0002 BOX TEAM 10 SMITHSON, Folder 1. NAi.
114. Alison Smithson, "Team 10: The Myth and the Message" (March 1983), 3–4.
115. "Sandy Wilson let it out that he was asked to Team 10 and a queue immediately formed on his left of would be Observers. But he understands our policy this time is to try a quiet meeting for thought and study—not argument and excitement." Alison Smithson, "Asides 2," 2: ASIDES 2: 1. See also Alison and Peter Smithson, letter to Bakema (1962), 1–6. BAKE0152 BOX, folder g5. NAi.
116. Here and in other quotations, the format that the Smithsons gave to their writing has been kept, a mixture of prose and poetry, in hopes of enhancing meaning where words have failed. Alison Smithson, "The Myth and the Message," 1–13.
117. Ibid., 1.
118. Ibid., 5.
119. In Greek mythology, Cadmus was a Phoenician prince who was told by Athena to sow dragon's teeth upon the earth. Warriors sprang up from the teeth, some of whom helped Cadmus build the citadel of Thebes.
120. Ibid., 12–13.
121. Peter Smithson divided each page of this essay into three columns of parallel information on the left, carrying theme in the middle, and slides or drawings on the right. Peter Smithson, "CIAM 9, 10—Still Counting," 1.
122. Peter Smithson "Team 10 in Retrospect" (October 1, 1993, revised March 1994, October 1995, April 1999). ARCH.TEAM X: 3. TTEN0004 BOX TEAM 10 SMITHSON, Folder 36. NAi.
123. Peter Smithson, "CIAM 9, 10—Still Counting," 1.
124. Ibid., 2.
125. Peter Smithson, "Team 10 in Retrospect," 3.
126. Peter Smithson, "CIAM 9, 10—Still Counting," 1.

127. "The history of art becomes a constant alternation between the poles of acceptance and rejection." Paul Crossley, "Introduction," in Peter Draper, ed., *Reassessing Nikolaus Pevsner* (London: Ashgate, 2004), 8.
128. Peter Smithson, "CIAM 9, 10—Still Counting," 6.
129. Peter Smithson, "Fourth Generation," notes on a scrap of paper (February 7–9, 1983; revised Bath, April 17, 1983) Folder 1950s. BOX AS & PS '50s & '60s, Folder 1950s. Smithson Family Collection.
130. Ibid.
131. Ibid.
132. Ibid.
133. Peter Smithson apparently offered this warning to Max Risselada. Peter Smithson, "Authenticity," notes on a scrap of paper (June 6, 1987), BOX AS & PS '50s & '60s, Folder 1950s. Smithson Family Collection.
134. Peter Smithson, "A & P S. work presented at Team X" for Ankara, April 1989 (March 1989). ANKARA: 1–5. TTEN0004 BOX TEAM 10 SMITHSON, Folder 35. NAi.
135. Peter Smithson, "A & P S. work presented at Team X," ANKARA: 2.
136. Ibid., ANKARA: 4.
137. Peter Smithson, "Some Thoughts for the Team X Book Launch, Delft" (June 25, 1992), ARCH.TEAM X: 1–3, 1. Smithson Family Collection.
138. Peter Smithson, "Book Launch, Delft," ARCH.TEAM X: 3.
139. Ibid., 1–3.
140. Ibid., 2.
141. Peter Smithson, "Team 10 in Retrospect" (October 1, 1993, revised March 1994, October 1995, April 1999), ARCH.TEAM X: 1–9. TTEN0004 BOX TEAM 10 SMITHSON, Folder 36. NAi.
142. Peter Smithson, "Team 10 in Retrospect," ARCH.TEAM X: 3–4.
143. Ibid., 5.
144. Ibid., 6.
145. Ibid., 7.

Chapter 8

1. Alison Smithson, "An Architecture of Response: An Architecture that by Being a Response Invites a Response" [Cut-up notes stapled on pages], 6 (July 1978, January 1981, January 1988), BOX AMS LECTURES EVOLVING. Smithson Family Collection.
2. Alison and Peter Smithson, *The Shift* (London: Architectural Monographs and Academy Editions, 1982), 10.
3. Alison and Peter Smithson, *Italian Thoughts* (Stockholm: Alison & Peter Smithson, 1993), 1.
4. Nigel Henderson withdrew from collaboration in 1950, but he did photograph the exhibition. See his photograph in *AR* 110 (October 1951), 216. The exhibition was bankrolled by the ICA and sponsored by two corporations, Dunlop Rubber and Pirelli Glass; it was seen by a mere 1,140 visitors and cost £223. For general coverage of the exhibition, see Isabelle Moffat, "The Independent Group's Encounter with Logical Positivism and Search for Unity

in the 1951 Growth and Form Exhibit" (PhD dissertation, MIT, 2002); Anne Massey, *The Independent Group: Modernism and Mass Culture in Britain, 1945–1959* (Manchester: Manchester University Press, 1995), 44; Victoria Walsh, *Nigel Henderson: Parallel of Life and Art* (London: Thames and Hudson), 27.

5. Walsh, *Nigel Henderson*, 27; Catherine Jolivette, "The 'Britishness' of British Art: Landscape, Art and Identity, 1951–1966" (PhD dissertation, Pennsylvania State University, 2003), 180–181.
6. David Thistlewood, "The Independent Group and Art Education in Britain 1950–1965," in David Robbins, ed., *The Independent Group: Postwar Britain and the Aesthetics of Plenty* (Cambridge, MA: MIT Press, 1990), 215.
7. Peter Smithson, "Letter to America," *AD* 28 (March 1958), 93–102.
8. Alison and Peter Smithson, *The Shift*, 22.
9. Alison Smithson, "A History of Three Natures of Layering" (1981), 3NL 1–9. BOX AMS LECTURES AS EVOLVED. Smithson Family Collection.
10. Ibid., 3NL 2.
11. Alison Smithson, "A Family of Exhibitions" (1980s, edited and added to by Peter Smithson, 1994, February, November 1997, February 1999), 1–2. BOX AS & PS UNPUBLISHED PAPERS + CURRENT LECTURES. Smithson Family Collection.

> PARALLEL OF LIFE AND ART: 1953 a space created by and extended by the images hung in varying planes around the observer.
> TURN AGAIN EXHIBITION: 1955 the city street by day, the city street by night, an appeal for quality of fabric in the city of London.
> HOUSE OF THE FUTURE: 1956 new kinds of inhabitable spaces made possible through a then emergent molded technology …
> ART OF THE DECADE: 1964 a flow of spaces generated by the paintings and sculptures: transformation of the gallery space.
> WEDDING IN THE CITY: 1968 the renewal of the city by an event; the event energizes the observer, renews his image of the city.
> A LINE OF TREES … A STEEL STRUCTURE: 1975 the light-touch architecture of response to place … the incoming extends the language of place, sets up a dialogue between the green-fabric and the built-fabric.
> STICKS AND STONES: 1976 "a fabric first made in the mind": from its beginning as element of building to its end as a ruin that can still energize.
> TWENTY FOUR DOORS TO CHRISTMAS: 1979 renewal of place through the energy released by the decorations and events for Christmas: changes of the look of the city.
> CHRISTMAS X HOGMANAY: 1980 the transmutability of city/countryside: how the celebration of the festival reintegrates one in the other.
> TRIANGLE WORKSHOP: 1987 permanent building-transient events (collaborative with invited artists).
> KINDERWAGON: 1992 the interaction of the permanent and the ephemeral.
> TICHLEINDECKDICH: 1993 an effort to move furniture away from "piece" and toward "ensemble."
> CLIMATE REGISTER: 1994 the taking account of the registration of the climate.
> BOOKWORK: 1995 Alison Smithson's building of books with text and illustrations into one artifact.

ON THE FLOOR OFF THE FLOOR: 1998 to explore the effects on use of brightness of surface and of the lattice paravent.

LATTICE FURNITURE: 1999 the lattice idea carried into a family of furniture.

12. Alison Smithson, "A History of Three Natures of Layering," 3NL 3–4.
13. Ibid., 3NL 1.
14. Ibid.
15. Ibid., 3NL 2.
16. Ibid.
17. Ibid., 3NL 3.
18. Ibid.
19. Ibid., 3NL 4.
20. Ibid., 3NL 7.
21. Ibid., 3NL 6.
22. Ibid., 3NL 5.
23. Ibid., 3NL 8.
24. Alison and Peter Smithson, *The Shift*; Alison and Peter Smithson, *Italian Thoughts*.
25. Alison and Peter Smithson, *Italian Thoughts*, 1.
26. Ibid., 23.
27. Ibid., 22.
28. Ibid., 101–102.
29. Alison and Peter Smithson, *The Shift*, 9.
30. Ibid., 61.
31. Ibid., 22.
32. Alison and Peter Smithson, *Italian Thoughts*, 30.
33. The question mark appears in the original statement. Alison and Peter Smithson, *The Shift*, 12.
34. Alison and Peter Smithson, *Italian Thoughts*, 18.
35. Ibid., 20.
36. Ibid., 24.
37. Ibid., 25.
38. Ibid., 68.
39. Ibid., 25.
40. Alison Smithson, "City Centre Full of Holes," in Alison and Peter Smithson, "The Space Between" (prepared for publication, 1995), 12CCFH: 71–72. Smithson Family Collection. As this book was going to press, an edition of this manuscript was published: Alison and Peter Smithson, *The Space Between* (Cologne: Verlag der Buchhandlung Walther König and Simon J. B. Smithson, 2017).
41. Peter Smithson, "The Slow Growth of Another Sensibility: Architecture as Town Building," in *A Continuing Experiment* (1965); quoted by Peter Cook, "Time and Contemplation: Regarding the Smithsons," *AD* 172 (July 1982), 41.

42. Alison Smithson, "Places Worth Inheriting," in "The Space Between," 13PWI: 75–76.
43. Alison Smithson, "City Centre Full of Holes," 12CCFH: 70–71.
44. Alison Smithson, "The Wider Role of the Architect" (1984), WIDR 1–30: 6. BOX AMS LECTURES AS EVOLVED. Smithson Family Collection.
45. Alison and Peter Smithson, "The Heroic Period of Modern Architecture," *AD* 35 (December 1965), 590–643.
46. Alison and Peter Smithson, handwritten note on *The Shift* [probably P. S., conjectured from handwriting] (June 1977; Alison and Peter Smithson, April and September 1978; Spring 1980 and 1981). TTEN0004 BOX TEAM 10 SMITHSON, Folder 31. NAi.
47. Peter Smithson, letter to Jaap Bakema (July 12, 1973), about possible Team 10 meeting in Holland around April 11, 1974. TTEN0004 BOX TEAM 10 SMITHSON, Folder 28. NAi.
48. Alison Smithson, "Preface: The Architect as Witness," in Alison and Peter Smithson, "The Space Between," 01SP: 2–3, 01SP: 2. "For ourselves particularly as Team 10 became depleted." 001SP: 2.
49. Peter Smithson, letter to Bakema (March 5, 1974), "Concerning lecture at Delft (April 1974)." BAKE0152 BOX, folder g8. NAi.
50. Peter Smithson, "Concerning lecture at Delft (April 1974)."
51. Alison Smithson, "Last Thoughts on Team X" (1989, 1991), ARCH.ED: 1–5, ARCH.ED: 3. TTEN0004 BOX TEAM 10 SMITHSON, Folder 35. NAi.
52. Peter Smithson, "Concerning lecture at Delft (April 1974)."
53. Peter Smithson, "Work Presented at Team X; for Ankara, April 1989" (March 1989), ANKARA: 1–5; ANKARA: 4. TTEN0004 BOX TEAM 10 SMITHSON, Folder 35. NAi.
54. Alison Smithson, Asides to accompany Team 10 Seminar Session 1: ASIDES 1: 3. NAi.
55. Alison and Peter Smithson, letter to Bakema (August 26, 1975), BAKE0152 BOX, folder g8. NAi.
56. Alison and Peter Smithson, *Without Rhetoric: An Architectural Aesthetic 1955–1972* (Cambridge, MA: MIT Press, 1974), 79.
57. Ibid., 80.
58. This never-published collection of writings is given the working title *Initiators and Successors*. But iterations of the manuscript were variously titled *Urbalm*; or, *Initiators and Successors: Rebuilding the Meaning of Cities*; or, *The Founding and Renewal of Urban Nerve: Initiators and Successors*. The first draft had the title "Urbalm: Rebuilding the Meaning of Cities," and contained the following essays:

    "Introduction: The Founding and Renewal of Urban Nerve."
    "Ruminations on Founder's Court" (*AD*, August 1973).
    "The Good Tempered Gas Man" (*AD*, March 1975).
    "The Violent Consumer" (*AD*, May 1974).
    "A Change of Vision" (*AD*, July 1974).
    "Making the Connection" (*AD*, May 1975).
    "Collective" (*AD*, November 1974).
    "Lightness of Touch" (*AD*, June 1974).

No publisher was found for "Urbalm" (1978). Versions between 1978 and 1981 dropped the last two chapters and added "Graphics of Movement," "Structuring of Spaces," and "In Pursuit of Lyrical Appropriateness." A 1983 manuscript was sent to Delft University Press in 1984, but returned in 1985. Its content was rearranged to include the following items:

Ruminations.

The Good Tempered Gas Man.

The Violent Consumer.

Preparation of the Mind: toward an understanding of the Fabric of Place (Oxford and Cambridge Walks).

A Change of Vision.

Garden City/City in Garden.

In Pursuit of Lyrical Appropriateness.

The Landscape of Lyrical Appropriateness.

Graphic of Movement.

In Praise of Cupboard Doors.

A shorter manuscript of 1990 contains the following:

Ruminations.

The Good Tempered Gas Man.

The Violent Consumer.

Garden City/City in the Garden.

Lightness of Touch.

Collective Quality—the Pieter de Hooch Game.

Mat Building [a new addition].

Materials were sent to *Croquis* (Spring 1991) and later to Lars Lerup at Rice University with a chapter on "Interaction and Transformation" inserted after "Garden City/City in the Garden." Again, nothing came of their various attempts to publish the collection.

The original list of *AD* articles to which others have been added over time comes from BOX AS & PS INITIATORS AND SUCCESSORS, Folder 4. BOX AS & PS INITIATORS AND SUCCESSORS, Folder 5 contains the manuscript of 1983 sent to Delft for publication. Additional information is from Max Risselada's list of various manuscripts of "Initiators and Successors." Max Risselada, "Chronology of Unpublished Manuscripts" (unpublished, May 2008).

59. Peter Smithson, "Contributions to a Fragmentary Utopia," *AD* 36 (February 1966), 64–67.
60. Alison Smithson, "Introduction to Places Worth Inheriting," (1983): 1. AMS BOX LECTURES AS EVOLVED. Smithson Family Collection.
61. Ibid.
62. Ibid.
63. Ibid., 2.
64. Ibid.

65. Alison Smithson, "Quality of Place" (n.d.), 1. Her letter to Bakema told him "to make use of it [the manuscript she sent him] as you want." Alison Smithson, letter to Jaap Bakema (June 9, 1976), BAKE0152 BOX, folder g8. NAi.
66. Alison Smithson, "Quality of Place" (n.d.), 2.
67. Ibid., 3.
68. Ibid., 36.
69. Alison and Peter Smithson, "Initiators and Successors: Introduction: The Intention of the Document" (April and September 1978, Spring 1980, 1981). From Max Risselada's photocopy (May 2008). Smithson Family Collection.
70. Alison and Peter Smithson, "Introduction: The Founding and Renewal of Urban Nerve: Initiators and Successors," 3, 4. From Max Risselada's photocopy (May 2008). Smithson Family Collection.
71. Alison Smithson, "An Architecture of Response," 3.
72. Alison and Peter Smithson, "Collective Design: Signs of Occupancy," *AD* 42 (mislabeled 43) (February 1972), 91–97. The "Collective Design" articles are: Peter Smithson, "Collective Design: Initiators and Successors," *AD* 43 (October 1973), 621–623; Alison Smithson, "Collective Design: The Violent Consumer, or Waiting for the 'Goodies'," *AD* 44 (May 1974), 274–279; Peter Smithson, "Collective Design: Lightness of Touch," *AD* 44 (June 1974), 377–378; Alison Smithson, "Collective Design: Reappraisal of Concepts of Urbanism," *AD* 44 (July 1974), 403–406; Alison Smithson, "Collective Design: Collective Quality," *AD* 44 (November 1974), 719–721; Alison Smithson, "Collective Design: The Good Tempered Gas Man," *AD* 45 (March 1975), 163–168; Peter Smithson, "Collective Design: Making the Connection," *AD* (May 1975), 271–274.
73. Alison and Peter Smithson, "Collective Design: Signs of Occupancy," 91. (Republished in Alison and Peter Smithson, *Without Rhetoric*, 69–70.)
74. Ibid.
75. Ibid., 95.
76. Peter Smithson, "Collective Design: Initiators and Successors," 621–623.
77. Ibid., 621.
78. Ibid., 623.
79. Peter Smithson, "A Sense of Unfolding," 20SU: 120, in Alison and Peter Smithson, "The Space Between."
80. Peter Smithson, "A Sense of Unfolding," 20SU: 121.
81. Peter Smithson, "Collective Design: Lightness of Touch," 377–378.
82. Alison and Peter Smithson, "Transformations of the City," 20UNFTC:VI: 122, in Alison and Peter Smithson, "The Space Between."
83. Peter Smithson's reply, when asked in the 1990s why Robin Hood Gardens had failed. "Rebuilding Britain for the Baby Boomers," introduced by Maxwell Hutchison. BBC Radio 4 (November 26, 2011). At http://en.wikipedia.org/wiki/Robin_Hood_Gardens (accessed August 8, 2013).
84. Alison Smithson, "The City Centre Full of Holes," 12CCFH: 66.

85. Ibid.
86. Ibid., 12CCFH: 67.
87. Alison Smithson, "Collective Design: The Violent Consumer," 274–278.
88. Ibid., 276.
89. Ibid., 274.
90. Ibid.
91. Ibid.
92. Ibid., 276.
93. Ibid., 277.
94. Ibid.
95. Ibid.
96. Ibid.
97. Ibid., 278.
98. Alison Smithson, "Collective Design: Reappraisal of Concepts of Urbanism," 404–405.
99. Ibid., 403.
100. Ibid., 404.
101. Ibid., 405.
102. Alison Smithson, "Collective Design: Collective Quality," 719–721.
103. Ibid., 719.
104. Ibid.
105. Ibid., 721.
106. Alison Smithson, "Collective Design: The Good Tempered Gas Man," 163–168.
107. Ibid., 166.
108. Ibid., 167.
109. Ibid., 168.
110. Peter Smithson, "Collective Design: Making the Connection," 271–274.
111. Ibid., 271.
112. Ibid.
113. Ibid., 272.
114. Ibid.
115. Ibid., 274.
116. Peter Smithson, "Walk within Walls—A Study of Bath as a Built-Form Taken Over by Other Users," *AD* 39 (October 1969), 554–564; Peter Smithson "Oxford and Cambridge Walks," *AD* 46 (June 1976), 346–354; Peter Smithson, "Bath: Walks within the Walls," 06Bath W: 28–35; Peter Smithson, "Oxford Walks," 07OX.W: 36–44, and "Cambridge Walks," 08CAMB.W: 45–50, in Alison and Peter Smithson, "The Space Between."
117. Peter Smithson, "Bath: Walks within the Walls," 06Bath W: 28.
118. Peter Smithson, "Oxford Walks," 07OX.W: 36.

119. Peter Smithson, "Cambridge Walks," 08CAMB.W: 45.
120. Ibid.
121. Alison Smithson, "Preface: The Architect as Witness," 01SP: 2–3.
122. Ibid.
123. Alison Smithson, "Wider Role of the Architect," WIDR: 1–20.
124. Ibid., WIDR: 8.
125. Ibid., WIDR: 2.
126. Ibid., WIDR: 5.
127. Ibid., WIDR: 7.
128. Ibid., WIDR: 13–14.
129. Ibid., WIDR: 16.
130. Ibid., WIDR: 18.
131. Ibid., WIDR: 19.
132. Ibid.
133. Alison and Peter Smithson, *Italian Thoughts*, 102.
134. Alison and Peter Smithson, "New Introduction" and "Initiators and Successors." Manuscript (1983). BOX INITIATORS AND INHERITORS, Folder 5. Smithson Family Collection.

Chapter 9

1. Attributed to Nikolaus Pevsner by Paul Crossley, "Introduction," in Peter Draper, *Reassessing Nikolaus Pevsner* (London: Ashgate, 2004), 12. Footnote 17 on page 24 states that this quotation comes from a BBC radio broadcast given by Stephen Games on "Pevsner: The Necessity of Art" (November 1983).
2. Alison and Peter Smithson, quoted by John A. Walker in "The ICA, The IG and America during the 1950s," *Cultural Offensive: American's Impact on British Art since 1945* (London: Pluto Press, 1998), 28.
3. Alison and Peter Smithson, *The Shift* (London: Architectural Monographs and Academy Editions, 1982). For Pevsner's culminating thoughts on the "Englishness of English Art," see Nikolaus Pevsner, *The Englishness of English Art* (London: Architectural Press, 1956).
4. Reyner Banham, "Revenge of the Picturesque: English Architectural Polemics, 1945–1965," in John Summerson, ed., *Essays on Architectural Writers and Writing Presented to Nikolaus Pevsner* (London: Allen Lane, Penguin Press, 1968), 265–273.
5. Alison and Peter Smithson, *The Shift*, 36.
6. Peter Smithson, "Introduction," in Alison and Peter Smithson, "The Space Between" (prepared for publication, 1995), 01SB.V–VI. Smithson Family Collection.
7. Peter Smithson, "Building for Furniture" (extract from The Set of Mind lecture given in Lund, Peter Smithson, January–October 1991, edited March 1992, March 1999), BUILD.FUR:2. BOX AS & PS UNPUBLISHED PAPERS + CURRENT LECTURES. Smithson Family Collection.

8. Alison Smithson, "Growing a Landscape of Lyrical Appropriateness" (March 1984), GLL.5. BOX AMS LECTURES AS EVOLVED. Smithson Family Collection.
9. Ibid., GLL.1.
10. Ibid., GLL.3.
11. Ibid., GLL.2.
12. Ibid., GLL.3.
13. Ibid., GLL.1.
14. Ibid.
15. Ibid., GLL.2.
16. Ibid.
17. Alison Smithson, "A Fragment of an Enclave" for Barcelona, November 1985 (AMS Autumn 1985, November 1985), 3PAV: 1–7. BOX AMS LECTURES AS EVOLVED. Smithson Family Collection.
18. Alison Smithson, 3PAV: 1.
19. Ibid.
20. Ibid., 3PAV: 2.
21. Ibid., 3PAV: 7.
22. Alison Smithson, "The Territory of the Pavilion," T.P.1–4 (1984). Harvard University, Graduate School of Design, Special Collection, Smithson Archive, Folder E076.
23. Ibid., T.P.2.
24. Ibid., T.P.3.
25. Peter Smithson, "Territorial Imprint" (European Conference on Architecture, April 1987), in Alison and Peter Smithson, "The Space Between," 24TI: 139.
26. Peter Smithson, "Le Corbusier: First Confrontations with the Work of the Master" (9.1.87), CORB.DLF: 2. AS & PS MAGIC BOX. Smithson Family Collection.
27. Ibid., CORB.DLF: 5.
28. Peter Smithson, "Territory," 23T: 134.
29. Alison Smithson, "Paradis Eloigne" (Paradise Fiction), 116 pages (1975–1986), handwritten note AMS PARADIS.E. Unpaginated. Harvard University, Graduate School of Design, Special Collection, Smithson Archive, Folder F006.
30. Alison Smithson, "Paradis Eloigne," handwritten note AMS PARADIS.E. Unpaginated.
31. Alison Smithson, "Paradis Eloigne," ELO3 outline1987. Photocopy. Smithson Family Collection.
32. Alison Smithson, "Paradis Eloigne," ELO2 outline 1988. Photocopy. Smithson Family Collection.
33. Ibid.
34. Ibid.

35. Peter Smithson, "Just a Few Chairs and a House: An Essay on the Eames-Aesthetic," Special Issue on the Eames Celebration *AD* 36 (September 1966), 445.
36. AMS PARADIS.E. Unpaginated.
37. Alison Smithson states in the outline that each theme will be introduced by a black-and-white photograph. Alison Smithson, "Paradis Eloigne," ELO2 outline.
38. AMS PARADIS.1: SCENE: 1.
39. AMS PARADIS.1: SCENE: 2.
40. AMS PARADIS.1: SCENE: 4.
41. AMS PARADIS.1: SCENE: 8.
42. AMS PARADIS.1: SCENE: 6–7.
43. AMS PARADIS.1: SCENE: 7.
44. AMS PARADIS.3: PERSONS: 14–24.
45. AMS PARADIS.5: OCCUPATIONS: 54.
46. AMS PARADIS.4: THE SENSE OF THE YEAR: 25–44.
47. AMS PARADIS.2: TRACKS: 10.
48. AMS PARADIS.9: POLIS: 83.
49. AMS PARADIS.9: POLIS: 87.
50. AMS PARADIS.6: WALLS: 55–64.
51. AMS PARADIS.6: WALLS: 64.
52. AMS PARADIS.9: POLIS: 86.
53. AMS PARADIS.11: PAIRIDEZA IN LANDSCAPE: 101.
54. AMS PARADIS.11: PAIRIDEZA IN LANDSCAPE: 100.
55. Ibid.
56. Peter Smithson, "Bibliotheca Alexandrina," ARCH.ALX.BARC.PS: 1. Harvard University, Graduate School of Design, Special Collection, Smithson Archive, Folder BB664.
57. Alison Smithson, "Toward a Garden Appropriate to the Mat-Building: 1968–70," FTKG.91: 15. BOX AMS LECTURES EVOLVING. Smithson Family Collection.
58. Alison Smithson, "Mat Tradition Recognised" (1974), MAT AA: 2–15. BOX AMS LECTURES EVOLVING. Smithson Family Collection.
59. Alison Smithson, "How to Recognize and Read Mat-Building," *AD* 64, no. 9 (1974), 573–590.
60. Ibid., 573.
61. Peter Smithson, "Mat-Building Again" (March 13, 1999). BOX AS & PS UNPUBLISHED PAPERS + CURRENT LECTURES. Smithson Family Collection.
62. Alison and Peter Smithson, "Urban Form Study Old City of Kuwait" (1968), KU1–KU5. Harvard University, Graduate School of Design, Special Collection, Smithson Archive, Folder BB201.
63. Ibid.
64. Alison Smithson, "How to Recognize and Read Mat-Building," 580.

65. Ibid., 576.
66. Alison Smithson, inserted "Introduction" (1991), in "Mat Tradition Recognised," Mat AA: unpaginated.
67. AMS MAT AA: 3.
68. Ibid.
69. Alison Smithson, "The Hole in the City" (August 1980; edited version of transcript off tape: Glasgow Lecture, May 16, 1980), 1–4. Harvard University, Graduate School of Design, Special Collection, Smithson Archive, Folder BB307.
70. AMS MAT AA: 4.
71. AMS MAT AA: 5.
72. Alison Smithson, "The Functional Tradition in Islamic Architecture/Urbanism," FTKU.91: 2–19. BOX AMS EVOLVING. Smithson Family Collection.
73. AMS MAT AA: 5.
74. AMS MAT AA: 7.
75. Alison Smithson, "The Hole in the City," 1–4.
76. Ibid., 2.
77. Ibid., 3.
78. Ibid., 4.
79. Alison and Peter Smithson, *Italian Thoughts* (Stockholm: Alison & Peter Smithson, 1993), 60.
80. Ibid., 70.
81. Alison Smithson, "Mat Tradition Recognised," MAT AA: 2–16.
82. Alison Smithson, "Team X Preparation Meeting: London October 26–27 1980," TTEN0004 BOX TEAM 10 SMITHSON, Folder 33. NAi.
83. Alison and Peter Smithson, *Italian Thoughts*, 68.
84. Alison Smithson, "The Maintenance of Cities" (begun 1990, revised 1992), MAINT.CIT: 2. AMS BOX LECTURES EVOLVING. Smithson Family Collection.
85. Alison and Peter Smithson, *Italian Thoughts*, 31.
86. Ibid., 39.
87. Alison Smithson, "The Landscape of Lyrical Appropriateness Made Manifest" (Le Parc de la Villette: Paris: 1982, final 1984), 1, BOX AMS LECTURES AS EVOLVED. Smithson Family Collection.
88. Alison and Peter Smithson, "The Park de la Villette: 1982," 1. Harvard University, Graduate School of Design, Special Collection, Smithson Archive, Folder BB529.
89. Ibid., 4.
90. Alison Smithson, "Noah's Ark 'Futures'," Part 1 and Part 2 (Munich: Programme for students 1984), 1. BOX AMS LECTURESAS EVOLVED. Smithson Family Collection.
91. Alison Smithson, "Noah's Ark: On the Occasion of the Barcelona Seminar: A Fragment of an Enclave: The Equivalent for the Late 'Eighties of the Barcelona Pavilion," NOASARC: 1–21. BOX AMS LECTURES AS EVOLVED. Smithson Family Collection.

92. Max Risselada, "Another Shift," in Max Risselada and Dirk van den Heuvel, *Alison and Peter Smithson—From a House of the Future to a House of Today* (Rotterdam: 010 Publishers, 2004), 54.
93. Alison Smithson, "Noah's Ark 'Futures,'" 1.
94. AMS NOASARC, 1.
95. Alison Smithson, "Noah's Ark … Le Corbusier's Wood Sculpture," AMS NOA.LEC: 2. Photocopy. Smithson Family Collection.
96. AMS NOA.LEC: 1.
97. AMS NOA.LEC: 4.
98. Alison and Peter Smithson, *Italian Thoughts*, 32.
99. Alison Smithson, *Hieronymus Die Wüste Das Studierzimmer / St. Jerome: The Desert and the Study* (Lauenforde, Germany: TECTA, 1990), unpaginated.
100. Ibid.
101. Ibid.
102. Ibid.
103. Ibid.
104. Ibid.
105. Ibid.
106. Alison Smithson, "On Climbing Ground: or Not on the Level" (Lecture Stockholm, RISD Summer 1991), CLMBGND, unpaginated. BOX AMS LECTURES EVOLVING. Smithson Family Collection.
107. At the time of the publication of Le Corbusier's "The Poem of the Right Angle" in the mid-1950s, the Smithsons thought it merely an expensive book, really an illustrated poem that did not make clear the need for "thinking-otherwise." Alison Smithson, "On Climbing Ground," CLMBGND.
108. Ibid.
109. Peter Smithson, "On Climbing Ground: Thinking towards the Acropolis Place" (2:7:91 revised 9:10:91): CGND.US: 1–4. BOX AS & PS UNPUBLISHED PAPERS + CURRENT LECTURES. Smithson Family Collection.
110. Peter Smithson, "On Climbing Ground," CGND.US: 2; Alison Smithson "Acropolis Place" (May 1990), ARCH:ACROP.PL: 1–2 Harvard University, Graduate School of Design, Special Collection, Smithson Archive, Folder BB702.
111. Peter Smithson, "On Climbing Ground," CGND.US: 3.
112. Ibid., CGND.US: 4.
113. Alison and Peter Smithson, "Acropolis Place: A Protected Place Looking at Fragments of Buildings," 4. Harvard University, Graduate School of Design, Special Collection, Smithson Archive, Folder B704.
114. Alison Smithson, "Acropolis Place" (May 1990), ARCH:ACROP.PL: 1.
115. Alison and Peter Smithson, "The Acropolis Place: A Synopsis of Museum Proposal" (n.d.): ACROP, 1–3. Graduate School of Design, Special Collection, Smithson Archive, Folder BB702.

116. Alison and Peter Smithson, "Acropolis Place: A Protected Place Looking at Fragments of Buildings/Reports," 1. Graduate School of Design, Special Collection, Smithson Archive, Folder BB704.

117. Alison Smithson, "With Green in Mind" (for Syracuse, Philadelphia) (AMS Summer 1991). GREEN.MND: 1–9. BOX AMS LECTURES EVOLVING. Smithson Family Collection.

118. Alison Smithson, "With Green in Mind," 1.

119. Lorenzo Wong and Peter Salter, eds., *Climate Register: Four Works by Alison and Peter Smithson*, Works V Architectural Association (London: E. G. Bond, 1994).

120. Ibid., 9.

121. Ibid., 8.

122. Ibid., 9.

123. Alison and Peter Smithson, *Italian Thoughts*, 31.

124. Alison and Peter Smithson, *The Shift*, 32.

125. Ibid., 40.

126. Alison and Peter Smithson, *Italian Thought*s, 28.

127. Ibid.

128. Ibid., 29.

129. Peter Smithson, "Territorial Imprint" (European Conference on Architecture, April 1987), in Alison and Peter Smithson, "The Space Between," 24TI: 138.

130. Alison and Peter Smithson, *Italian Thoughts*, 34.

131. These thoughts on Edinburgh are taken from Alison Smithson, "Alison's Last Thoughts on Team X 1989 and 1991" (October 2, 1991), AMS ARCH.ED: 1–5. TTEN0004 BOX TEAM 10 SMITHSON, Folder 30. NAi. This is repeated with additions as Alison Smithson, "Edinburgh," in Alison and Peter Smithson, "The Space Between", 09ED: 51–59. Additional thoughts taken from Alison Smithson, "Edinburgh: New Town," in Alison and Peter Smithson, "The Space Between,"10ED.NT: 60–61.

132. Alison Smithson, "Alison's Last Thoughts on Team X," ARCH.ED: 5. Alison Smithson, "Edinburgh: New Town,"10ED.NT: 61.

133. AMS ARCH.ED: 2; 10ED.NT: 61.

134. Alison and Peter Smithson, *Italian Thought*s, 2; repeated, 34–35.

135. Ibid., 30–31.

136. There were other connections to be made as well. Theo Crosby introduced Peter Smithson to the writings of Rex Martienssen, specifically his 1942 article "Space Construction in Greek *Architecture*." Martienssen became the link to Le Corbusier's "Towards a New Architecture" and thus to the Smithsons' own looking at classical sites beginning in 1951. And so, many years later, the "Anthology of Classical Sites" was developed to accompany seminars on the invention of a language of urban form offered in South Africa at the University of Witwatersrand and at Cape Town. "Prospectus" for "Speaking into the Sky" (undated); Alison Smithson, "The Wit's Anthology of Classical Sites" (August 1990), WITSANTH.CS: 1–3. Photocopy.

137. Alison Smithson, "Preface: The Intention of the Document" (February 1990), INITSUC. PRE.4 (Initiators and Successors). Photocopy.
138. Alison and Peter Smithson, *Italian Thoughts*, 101.
139. Pevsner, *The Englishness of English Art*.
140. They included Newcastle in this list. Alison and Peter Smithson, *Italian Thoughts*, 28.
141. Ibid., 44.

Chapter 10

1. There is no attribution for the quote that Peter inserts. Peter Smithson, "The Writings of Alison Smithson, Q.F.K.; 1916 A.S.O., A.S. in D.S.: a general description" (15.9.72/ 2.10.72). Photocopy. Smithson Family Collection.
2. Ibid.
3. Ibid.
4. Ibid.
5. Alison Smithson, "BREATH OF INDIA 1916 A.S.O." (September 1987), BI.aso: 1–2. Photocopy. Smithson Family Collection.
6. Alison Smithson, "BREATH OF INDIA 1916 A.S.O." BI.aso: 1–2.
7. Alison Smithson, "Writing of the 'As Found,'" ASFND.WRT1 (undated). Photocopy.
8. Kester Rattenbury, "Think of It as a Farm! Exhibitions, Books, Buildings: An Interview with Peter Smithson" (interview before January 12, 2001; text of interview February 28, 2001), 1–11:1. BOX PS PUBLICATIONS PENDING. Smithson Family Collection.
9. Peter Smithson, "Building for Furniture" (extract from "The Set of Mind," lecture given in Lund. P.S. January–October 1991, edited March 1992, March 1999), BUILD.FUR: 1–2, BUILD.FUR: 2. BOX AS & PS UNPUBLISHED PAPERS + CURRENT LECTURES. Smithson Family Collection.
10. Alison Smithson, "BREATH OF INDIA 1916 A.S.O." (September 1987), BI.aso: 1–2. Photocopy. Smithson Family Collection.
11. Alison Smithson, "Quiet Flows the Kamasutra," first version (January 15, 1966; March 15, 1966; heavily revised 1968; restructured Spring 1970–June 1973). Henceforth referenced as Alison Smithson, QFK (date): page. Smithson Family Collection.
12. Page of graphic illustration. Alison Smithson, QFK (15.1.66/25.8.72): 3. Photocopy.
13. Alison Smithson, QFK (15.1.66/25.8.72): 4.
14. Alison Smithson, "Interpretation of Q.F.K.: India," Alison Smithson, QFK (Spring 1971), 2. Photocopy.
15. Alison Smithson, QFK, "Preface" (1970): 0. Photocopy.
16. Alison Smithson, QFK, "Preface" (1970): 0.
17. Alison Smithson, QFK, "Indian Publishing Notes" (15.1.66/25.8.72): 4. Photocopy. A slightly different paragraph appears in Alison Smithson, QFK, "Preface" (1970): 0.
18. Alison Smithson, QFK, "Life-style: The British in India" (15.1.66/25.8.72): 5. Photocopy.
19. Alison Smithson, QFK, "Preface" (1970): 0.

20. Alison Smithson, QFK, "Breath of India: Outline" (November 1987), B.I: 2. Photocopy.
21. Alison Smithson, QFK, "Preface" (1970): 0.
22. Alison Smithson, "Interpretation of Q.F.K.: India … ," in "Collective Design Sensibility Primers" (Spring 1971): 2. Photocopy. Smithson Family Collection.
23. Alison Smithson, QFK, "Built Place" (15: 1:66, 25:8:72): 6. Photocopy.
24. Alison Smithson, QFK, "Indian Publishing Notes": 4.
25. Alison Smithson, "Breath of India: Outline" (1987), B.I: 1. Photocopy.
26. Alison Smithson, "Breath of India: Outline," B.I: 1.
27. Alison Smithson, QFK, "Lifestyle: The British in India" (15: 1:66, 25:8:72), 5A. Alison Smithson, "Breath of India: Points of Departure" (undated): 2.
28. Urquart, Urguhart, and Urquhart are used interchangeably. Alison Smithson, *Imprint of India* (London: AA Publications, 1994): 19.
29. Alison Smithson, "Indian Connection" (May 1981). Photocopy.
30. Alison Smithson, "Indian Connection."
31. Alison Smithson, "Morning Tea, Afternoon Tea," in "Imprint of India" (various dates): 4. Photocopy.
32. Ibid.
33. Alison Smithson, "Scents of India," in "Imprint of India" (n.d.): 6.
34. Alison Smithson, "Horse Drawn," in "Imprint of India" (n.d.): 6.
35. Alison Smithson, "Exit from India," in "Imprint of India" (n.d.): 6.
36. Alison Smithson, "Layers of Occupation," in "Imprint of India" (n.d.): 4–5.
37. Ibid.
38. Alison Smithson, QFK, "Outdoor Place," (15.1.66; 25.8.72): 8.
39. Alison Smithson, "Work in Alien Climate," in "Imprint of India" (n.d.): 3.
40. Alison Smithson, *Imprint of India*.
41. Alison Smithson, "Prologue," ibid., 3.
42. Alison Smithson, ibid., 7.
43. Ibid., 18.
44. Ibid., 7.
45. Ibid.
46. Ibid., 11.
47. Ibid., 14.
48. Ibid., 8.
49. Ibid., 17.
50. Ibid., 37.
51. Ibid., 46.
52. Ibid., 12.
53. Ibid., 11.

54. Ibid., 32.
55. Ibid., 39.
56. Ibid., 43.
57. John Dixon Hunt, *Gardens and the Picturesque: Studies in the History of Landscape Architecture* (Cambridge, MA: MIT Press, 1994).
58. The Smithsons first visited India at Easter time, 1960. Alison Smithson's notes on QFK acknowledge that she drew inspiration from the writings and lectures of Mildred Archer, who worked for the Oriental and India Office Collection at the British Library. Archer lectured and wrote about British artists who traveled to India in the eighteenth and nineteenth centuries.
59. *Climate Register: Four Works by Alison & Peter Smithson. Selected and interpreted by Lorenzo Wong and Peter Salter. Works V Architectural Association* (London: E. G. Bond, 1994), 7.
60. Alison Smithson, "With Green in Mind," GREEN.MND: 1–9, October 1991; quotation from Alison and Peter Smithson, *Italian Thoughts* (Stockholm: Alison & Peter Smithson, 1993), 101.
61. Peter Smithson, "Territorial Imprint," in Alison and Peter Smithson, "The Space Between" (prepared for publication, 1995), 24TI: 138–141, 24TI: 140. Smithson Family Collection.
62. Alison Smithson, "1916 A.S.O." (n.d.): 00. Photocopy.
63. Alison Smithson, "1916 A.S.O.—at the time of writing" (March 1969), 10. Photocopy of one page.
64. Peter Smithson, "The writings of Alison Smithson, Q.F.K., 1916 A.S.O., A.S. in D.S.: a general description" (15:9:72/ 30:7:73), 1. Photocopy.
65. Alison Smithson, "1916 A.S.O.—at the time of writing," 10.
66. Alison Smithson, "1916 A.S.O." (July 1989), 1. Photocopy.
67. Alison Smithson, "1916 A.S.O.—at the time of writing," 10.
68. Ibid.
69. Ibid.
70. Alison Smithson, untitled [about "1916 A.S.O."] (June 1989), 1. Photocopy.
71. Alison Smithson, untitled [about "1916 A.S.O."], 1.
72. Alison Smithson, "1916 A.S.O.," 1–2.
73. Alison Smithson, handwritten note card in Folder "1916 A.S.O. Diverse Notes" (1989), unpaginated. "1916 A.S.O." Box 14 version AS sent to Book manuscript Sellerio 1993.
74. Alison Smithson, "1916 A.S.O. Preface" (undated), 1. Photocopy.
75. Alison Smithson, untitled [about "1916 A.S.O."], 1.
76. Le Corbusier, "Letter to CIAM 10, Dubrovnik," in Oscar Newman, ed., *CIAM '59 in Otterlo* (Stuttgart: Karl Krämer Verlag, 1961), 16.
77. In 1916, Ford actually uttered the less succinct phrase: "History is more or less bunk." See Alfred Borcover, "History Is Bunk? Ford had 2d [sic] Thoughts," *Chicago Tribune* (July 27, 1986), at http://articles.chicagotribune.com/1986-07-27/travel/8602240577_1_greenfield-village-bunk-history (accessed August 25, 2013). In 1921, the *New York Times* quoted him

as saying the shorter and more famous phrase, "History is bunk": see "History Is Bunk, Says Henry Ford," *New York Times* (October 29, 1921), at http://query.nytimes.com/gst/abstract.html?res=990CE3D8103CE533A2575AC2A9669D946095D6CF (accessed August 25, 2013).

78. Alison Smithson, "1916 A.S.O. The Earth of the Modern Movement" (1989 manuscript, the version sent to Sellerio, 1993). Henceforth referenced as Alison Smithson, "1916 A.S.O." Smithson Family Collection.
79. Ibid., 2.
80. Ibid., 3.
81. Ibid., 5.
82. Ibid.
83. Ibid., 7.
84. Ibid., 16.
85. Ibid., 24.
86. Ibid., 27.
87. Ibid., 24–25.
88. Ibid., 45.
89. Ibid., 59.
90. Ibid., 60.
91. Ibid.
92. Ibid., 84.
93. Ibid., 118.
94. Ibid., 124–125.
95. Ibid., 129.
96. Ibid., 241.
97. Ibid., 133.
98. Ibid., 135.
99. Ibid., 136.
100. Ibid.
101. Ibid.
102. Ibid., 157.
103. Ibid., 166.
104. Ibid., 175.
105. Ibid., 180.
106. Ibid., 200–201.
107. Ibid., 222.
108. Ibid., 266.

109. Alison and Peter Smithson, "The Heroic Period of Modern Architecture," *AD* 35 (December 1965), 590–635.
110. Ibid.
111. Ibid.
112. Ibid.
113. Note there are 7 boxes of material pertaining to Maigret's Map. Alison Smithson, "Paris: Maigret's Map" (1989), MMAP.91.1–181, MMAP.91.1: 1. Maigret Box 2. Smithson Family Collection.
114. Alison Smithson, "Maigret's Map: Preface follows PMM.OUT: 0-4. Without notation. Smithson Family Collection.
115. Alison Smithson, "Paris: Maigret's Map Outline of an Unpublished Writing," PMM.CB: 2.
116. Ibid., PMM.CB: 4.
117. Ibid., PMM.CB: 2.
118. Alison Smithson, "Paris: Maigret's Map: Outline," PMM.OUT: 4.
119. Alison Smithson, "Paris: Maigret's Map Outline of an Unpublished Writing," PMM.CB: 1–2.
120. Alison Smithson, "Paris: Maigret's Map," MMAP.91.1.13.
121. Alison Smithson, "The Patience of Maigret," MMAP.91.2: 21–41, MMAP.91.2: 39.
122. Ibid., MMAP.91.2: 40.
123. Alison Smithson, "Maigret Stonewalled," MMAP.91.5: 42–45, MMAP.91.5: 43.
124. Alison Smithson, MMAP.91.5: 36.
125. Alison Smithson, "Paris: Maigret's Map: Outline," PMM.OUT: 4.
126. Ibid., PMM.OUT: 0.
127. Frances Yates, "Architecture and the Art of Memory," *AD* 38 (December 1968), 573–578.
128. Ibid., 573.
129. Reyner Banham, "Revenge of the Picturesque: English Architectural Polemics, 1945–1965," in John Summerson, ed., *Essays on Architectural Writers and Writing Presented to Nikolaus Pevsner* (London: Allen Lane, Penguin Press, 1968), 265.
130. Reyner Banham, "Stocktaking 1960/1," *AR* 127 (February 1960).
131. Reyner Banham, *The New Brutalism: Ethic or Aesthetic?* (New York: Reinhold, 1966), 12, 14, 43.
132. Ibid.
133. Alison and Peter Smithson, "Banham's Bumper Book on Brutalism, discussed by Alison and Peter Smithson," *Architects' Journal* 144 (December 28, 1966), 1590.
134. Alison Smithson, "Paris: Maigret's Map Outline of an Unpublished Writing," PMM.CB: 5.

Chapter 11

1. Peter Smithson, "Many Meanings, Many Times," ARCH.MMT: 1 (27.2.98). BOX AS & PS UNPUBLISHED PAPERS + CURRENT LECTURES. Smithson Family Collection.

2. Rhona and Robert Rapoport, "The Bensons, Architects," *Dual-Career Families* (Harmondsworth, UK: Penguin, 1971), 84–137; Valerie Grove, "Alison Smithson, Architect," in *The Compleat Woman* (London: Chatto and Windus, 1987), 259–270.

3. Rhona and Robert Rapoport, *Dual-Career Families*, 88.

4. Ibid., 95.

5. Ibid., 91.

6. Ibid., 133.

7. Valerie Grove, "Alison Smithson, Architect," 269.

8. Rhona and Robert Rapoport, *Dual-Career Families*, 98.

9. Ibid.

10. Kester Rattenbury, "Think of It as a Farm! Exhibitions, Books, Buildings: An Interview with Peter Smithson" (interview before January 12, 2001; text of interview February 28, 2001), 1–11, 11. BOX AS & PS UNPUBLISHED PAPERS + CURRENT LECTURES. Smithson Family Collection. This interview is also published in Kester Rattenbury, "Think of It as a Farm! Exhibitions, Books, Buildings," in Kester Rattenbury, ed., *This Is Not Architecture: Media Constructions* (London: Routledge, 202), 9–98.

11. Ibid., 9.

12. Valerie Grove, "Alison Smithson, Architect," 265.

13. Rhona and Robert Rapoport, *Dual-Career Families*, 128.

14. Ruth Drake, review, "A Portrait of the Female Mind as a Young Girl," *AD* 37 (February 1967), 103.

15. Alison Smithson, *Portrait of the Female Mind as a Young Girl* (London: Chatto and Windus, 1966), 20.

16. Ibid., 11, 13.

17. Ibid., 30.

18. Ibid., 31.

19. Ibid., 32.

20. Ibid., 225–226.

21. Ibid., 272.

22. Ibid., 208.

23. Ibid., 208–209.

24. Ibid., 8–9.

25. Ibid., 24.

26. Ibid., 107.

27. Ibid., 212–213.

28. Ibid., 72.

29. Ibid., 219.

30. Conversation with Soraya Smithson, May 2011.

31. Alison Smithson, *Portrait of the Female Mind*, 215.

32. Conversation with Soraya Smithson, May 2008.
33. Alison Smithson, *Portrait of the Female Mind*, 223–224.
34. Ibid., 250.
35. Ibid., 265.
36. Ibid., 270.
37. Ibid., 271.
38. Ibid., 223.
39. Ibid., 286–287.
40. Ibid., 288.
41. Rattenbury, "Think of It as a Farm!," 9.
42. Ibid., 10.
43. Peter Smithson, "Toy Towns … Cradles of Authenticity," in Nicholas Olsberg, curator, *La Ville en Jeu Toy Town*, exh. cat. (Quebec: CCA/Canadian Centre for Architecture, 1998), 7–13.
44. Ibid., 7.
45. Ibid., 13.
46. Peter Smithson, Notes for Art Net Tram Lecture, "Keeping on the Right Lines," AA (1976). BOX PS PUBLICATIONS PENDING. Smithson Family Collection.
47. Ibid.
48. Alison and Peter Smithson, *The Tram Rats* (private publication, n.d.) (unpaginated).
49. Peter Smithson, "Notes for ArtNet Tram Lecture."
50. Alison and Peter Smithson, *Italian Thoughts* (Stockholm: Alison & Peter Smithson, 1993), 39–39.
51. Alison Smithson, "1916 A.S.O." (unpublished manuscript), 27.
52. Ibid., 151.
53. Alison and Peter Smithson, *The Tram Rats* (unpaginated).
54. Ibid.
55. Ibid.
56. Rattenbury, "Think of It as a Farm!," 7.
57. Ibid., 8.
58. Ibid., 9.
59. "Arch Criminals," referenced in Alison Smithson, "Making Ideas Manifest and So Introducing a Sensibility to Car Movement" (May 7, 1983), 1–8, 1. BOX AMS LECTURES AS EVOLVED, Smithson Family Collection; Alison and Peter Smithson, *The Euston Arch and the Growth of the London, Midland & Scottish Railway* (London: Thames and Hudson, 1968), unpaginated.
60. Notes accompanying folder for the spiral bound edition of Alison and Peter Smithson, *The Euston Arch*. "The Alison and Peter Smithson Archive," Harvard University, Graduate School of Design, Special Collection, Loeb Library, J073. Also appears in Alison and Peter Smithson, *The Euston Arch*.

61. Alison Smithson, in Alison and Peter Smithson, *The Euston Arch*.
62. Peter Smithson, "Postscript," in Alison and Peter Smithson, *The Euston Arch*.
63. Nikolaus Pevsner, "Foreword," in Alison and Peter Smithson, *The Euston Arch*.
64. "History of the Euston Arch," http://www.eustonarch.org/history.html (accessed August 16, 2012; site has since been taken down).
65. Alison Smithson, "Making Ideas Manifest."
66. Pevsner, "Foreword."
67. Alison Smithson, "Making Ideas Manifest."
68. Alison Smithson, in Alison and Peter Smithson, *The Euston Arch*.
69. Ibid.
70. Ibid.
71. Alison Smithson, "Preface," *Team 10 Primer* (Cambridge, MA: MIT Press, 1968), 7.
72. Ibid.
73. Ibid.
74. Ibid.
75. Alan Powers, "Houses in Children's Books," in Alan Powers, *Houses in Children's Books*, exh. cat. (London: Prince of Wales's Institute of Architecture, 1999), "The Alison and Peter Smithson Archive," Harvard University, Graduate School of Design, Special Collections, Loeb Library, J098, 3–8.
76. Alison Smithson, "Beatrix Potter's Spaces," *AD* 37 (December 1967), 573.
77. Ibid.
78. Ibid.
79. Ibid.
80. Ibid.
81. Peter Smithson, "Think of It as a Farm" (undated), BOX PS PUBLICATIONS PENDING, 4–5. Smithson Family Collection.
82. Ibid.
83. Ibid.
84. Alison Smithson, "Responsibility for the Renewal of Places" (November 1, 1984), RRP: 1. BOX AMS LECTURES AS EVOLVED. Smithson Family Collection.
85. Alison and Peter Smithson, *The Shift* (London: Architectural Monographs and Academy Editions, 1982), 72.
86. Ibid., 56.
87. "The Christmas Tree," material collected and edited by Alison Smithson (25-page booklet), "The Alison and Peter Smithson Archive," Harvard University, Graduate School of Design, Special Collection, Loeb Library, J005.
88. Alison Smithson, "Anthology of Christmas" (1979), "The Alison and Peter Smithson Archive," Harvard University, Graduate School of Design, Special Collection, Loeb Library, J007.

89. "24 Doors to Christmas" (1979), referenced in Alison Smithson, "A History of Three Natures of Layering" 3NL, 1–9 (December 1981), BOX AMS LECTURES AS EVOLVED. Smithson Family Collection.
90. Alison Smithson, "Exhibition in Edinburgh—Hogmanay Exhibition 1980–1981" (1981). CHRISTMAS BOXES. Smithson Family Collection.
91. Alison and Peter Smithson, "Gouda" (unpublished, n.d.), unpaginated. Smithson Family Collection.
92. Alison Smithson, "The Crone Calls," 1–8. "The Alison and Peter Smithson Archive," Harvard University, Graduate School of Design, Special Collection, Loeb Library, F012.
93. Alison Smithson, "The Crone Calls," 2.
94. Ibid., 6.
95. Ibid., 8.
96. Alison Smithson, "You Meet the Robin," "The Alison and Peter Smithson Archive," Harvard University, Graduate School of Design, Special Collection, Loeb Library, F012. See also for information: "How the Robin got its Red Breast (an Irish Tale)," at http://www.hnet.org/~nilas/seasons/robin.html; "How the Robin got its Red Breast … And other fascinating Christmas facts," at http://www.lady.co.uk/people/features/1529-how-the-robin-got-his-red-breast (both accessed April 2, 2014; sites have since been taken down).
97. Alison Smithson, "Making Ideas Manifest."
98. Ibid., 2.
99. Ibid., 2–3.
100. Alison Smithson, "The Wider Role of the Architect," WIDR, 1–30: 2. BOX AMS LECTURES AS EVOLVED. Smithson Family Collection.
101. George Lakoff and Mark Turner, *More than Cool Reason: A Field Guide to Poetic Metaphor* (Chicago: University of Chicago Press, 1989), 3–4.
102. Alison and Peter Smithson, *Italian Thoughts*, 12.
103. Attributed to Peter Smithson, an untitled two-page manuscript, written originally at Tisbury (1970s); typed (February 1985). TTEN0004 BOX TEAM 10 SMITHSON, Folder 35. NAi.
104. Ibid.; Alison Smithson, "A History of Layers," 3NL.4; Alison Smithson, "A Family of Exhibitions," AMS 1980, edited and added to by PS 1994, February–November 1997, February 1999. BOX AS & PS UNPUBLISHED PAPERS + CURRENT LECTURES. Smithson Family Collection.
105. Alison Smithson, "The City Centre Full of Holes," in Alison and Peter Smithson, "The Space Between" (prepared for publication, 1995), 12 CCFH: 67. Smithson Family Collection.
106. Alison and Peter Smithson, *Italian Thoughts*, 80.
107. Peter Smithson, "Many Meanings, Many Times" (27.2.98): ARCH.MMT.1. BOX AS & PS UNPUBLISHED PAPERS + CURRENT LECTURES. Smithson Family Collection.
108. Ibid.
109. Bakema likened his concept of "visual group" to "a family holding hands." Quoted by Peter Smithson, "Some thoughts for the Team X Book Launch, Delft," June 25, 1992. BOX AS & PS UNPUBLISHED PAPERS + CURRENT LECTURES. Smithson Family Collection.

110. Catherine Spellman and Karl Unglaub (eds.), *Peter Smithson: Conversations with Students A Space for Our Generation* (New York: PAP, 2005), 48.

111. Alison and Peter Smithson, *Italian Thoughts*, 100.

112. Ibid., 34–35.

113. Alison and Peter Smithson, "The Space Between" (prepared for publication, 1995); notes on the back of a photograph, Alison Smithson, "Smithsons Gone Swimming" (July 2, 1972); Peter Smithson, "Wallpaper 1959" (7.3.79).

114. Rem Koolhaas wrote: "Maybe Team X and Archigram were, in the sixties, the last real 'movements' in urbanism, the last to propose with conviction new ideas and concepts for the organization of urban life." Rem Koolhaas, "City of Exacerbated Difference ©," in *Great Leap Forward*, Harvard Design School Project on the City (Cambridge, MA: Harvard Design School, 2001), 27.

115. Walter Benjamin, "Unpacking My Library," in *Illuminations*, ed. Hannah Arendt, trans. Harry Zohn (New York: Schocken Books, 1969), 61.

116. Ibid., 66.

Index

Page numbers in italics refer to figures.

Abercrombie, Patrick, 2
Acropolis Museum, 319
Acropolis Place (A. and P. Smithson), 319–320
AD. See *Architectural Design*
Addison, Joseph, 14
Advertisements, 9, 32, 52–53, 66, 89–90, 93, 95, 115, 118–119, 120, 122, 133, 142, 143, 144, 145, 153, 154, 157, 159, 161, 164, 165–168, 185, 186, 190, 195, 197, 199, 210, 212, 216–217, 331, 352, 371
Aerial bombing. See Blitz
Aerial photography, 108, 345, 353, 354
Airplanes, 343–345, 346, 348, 351, 352
Alberti, Leon Battista, 43, 373
Alexander, Christopher, 240, 241, 242
Algeria. See Bidonvilles
Alloway, Lawrence, 113, 122, 125, 129, 132–133, 135, 142, 143–145, 157, 164, 188, 422n46
    America as anti-British, 154
    on American cities, 149, 152
    Ark, 183–185
    "Arts and the Mass Media, The" (1958), *146–147*, 148
    "City Notes" (1959), 149, *150–151*
    "Development of British Pop, The" (1966), 122
    on editorial policy of *Architectural Review*, 148
    "Long Front of Culture, The" (1959), 144
    on Paolozzi in *Architectural Design*, 145
    Pop Art, 113, 120, 122, 149, 152, 179, 421n25, 425n97
    "Toys and Films of Charles Eames, The" (1956), 135
American-style, 32, 113
Anti-picturesque generation, 41
"Appliance House" (A. and P. Smithson), 212, 214
AR. See *Architectural Review*
Arch Criminals of the Euston Arch, The. See *Euston Arch and the Growth of the London, Midland & Scottish Railway, The*
Archer, Mildred, 456–457n58
Archigram, 464n114
"Architect as Witness" (A. Smithson), 270, 288
Architects' Journal, 30, 168
Architectural Association, London, 231, 247, 322, 337
Architectural Design (*AD*), 92, 107, 113, 169, 231, 234, 240, 259, 366
    Alloway articles in, 145–148
    CIAM, critique of, 47
    Frampton as technical editor, 39
    history, 404n7
    Middleton as technical editor, 39
    modernism and tradition, debate between, 3
    New Brutalism, 89–92
    "Open Letter" (Giedion, Gropius, Le Corbusier, and Sert), 50–51
    "Opinion" pieces, 91–92, 415n53
    on postwar planning, 48
    preferred mouthpiece of the younger generation, 39
Architectural journals and magazines, 3, 8–9, 13
Architectural pattern-books and the contemporary picturesque, 13
Architectural Principles in the Age of Humanism (Wittkower), 43, 44
Architectural Review (*AR*), 90, 95–96, 118–119, 152, 215

American cities and culture, critique of, 113–115, 118, 152–153
American design, editor's critique of, 114–115
architectural ideals, changing world of, 8
editorial policy, 1940–1970s, 5, 33
editorial policy on Modernism, shift in, 32
editorial policy, self-censorship, and British propaganda, 11
English modernism, mouthpiece for, 3
Euston Arch, 380
Functional Tradition, 7
"Machine Made America" (1957), 113, *116*, 118
"Man Made America" (1950), 113–115, 149, 152
"Manplan" (1969), 12
modernism and the English Picturesque tradition, blending of, 6
modernism and tradition, debate between, 3
Pevsner's critique of Townscape Analysis, 40
picturesque urban design methodology, 1
Piper's topographical essays, 7
pseudonyms, use of, 3
Richards as editor, 3–7
Rykwert's critique of, 9, 11, 17
Townscape Analysis Casebooks, 159, 161, 208, 394
Townscape and the English Picturesque, 38–39
Townscape policy and the Festival of Britain, 32
visual reeducation, 5, 13, 20–21, 23
Ark, 157, 162, 165, 171, 174, 179, 183–184, 188, 190, 427–428n32
Art brut. See New Brutalism
Art of Memory, The (Yates), 356
Arts and Crafts movement, 273, 286
"Arts and the Mass Media, The" (Alloway), *146–147*, 148
"As found" aesthetic, 2, 53, 57, 75, 87, 97, 122, 127, 215, 260, 267, 302, 317
AS in DS: An Eye on the Road (A. Smithson), 85, *86*, 87, 201, *220*, 221, *222*, 223–228, 330
ATBAT-Afrique, 419n127

ATBAT-Afrique housing project, Casablanca (1953), 109
Athens Charter. *See Charte d'Athènes*
Austen, Jane, 329, 330
Automobile Parade (Edison), 206
Automobiles, 99, 195–199, 201, 203–204, 206, 208, 210, 214–217, 219, 221, 223–228, 302, 366, 368, 369, 373
"Avant-Garde and Kitsch" (Greenberg), 148

Bakema, Jaap, 70–71, 235, 241, 252, 272, 274, 393
on automobiles, 203, 219
CIAM, rejection of the name, 51
CIAM 6, 47
CIAM 10, 48–49, 57, 59, 60–61, 62
on growth and change, 251
"Open Letter" (January 1961), reply to in *Architectural Design*, 51
Team 10, 72, 249, 250, 253, 257
Banham, (Peter) Reyner, 38, 77, 142, 157, 165, 183, 235
advertisements, 115
anti-picturesque generation, 41
"Appliance House," critique of, 214
and *Architectural Review*, 12, 32, 215
Ark, 183
automobiles, 195–199, 201, 203, 210, 215–216, 228
Bartlett School of Architecture, 12, 400n49
Bristol Aeroplane Company, 12
"Brutalism," anecdotal etymology, 88
"Cluster City," critique of, 33
"Design by Choice" (1961), 192
Hauptstadt Berlin road system project, critique of, 208
historian, role as, 215
historical inaccuracy, 33–34
"House of the Future," critique of, 210
Italian influence on design, fashion, style, and taste, 169–170
New Brutalism, 1, 88, 90
"New Brutalism" (1955), 41
New Brutalism, The (1966), 94, 95, 199, 208
Picturesque, critique of, 34, 208, 356–357
polemical tracts and later works, 33

    on Pop Art, 179
    RIBA lecture (1959), 235
    Smithsons, critique of, 94, 215, 294
    "Stocktaking" (1960), 215
    "Vehicles of Desire," 197
Barry, Gerald, 30
Bartlett School of Architecture, 12
Bartram, Alan, 183
Bass, Saul, 179
Bates House. *See* "Burrows Lea Farm"
Bauhaus, 24, 40, 83, 197, 341, 343, 344
Baynes, Ken, 188–189
Benjamin, Walter, 395
Berlin. *See* Free University of Berlin; Hauptstadt Berlin
Bertalanffy, Ludwig von, 125. *See also* Systems analysis
Bethnal Green, 53, 104, 105, 108
Betjeman, John, 3, 6, 33, 380
Béton brut. *See* New Brutalism
"Better and Worse Dreams (some ideas about design)" (Baynes), 189
Beveridge Report, The (1942), 2
Bibliotheca Alexandrina (A. and P. Smithson), 308, 322–323
Bidonvilles, 75, 108
Bisley, A. J., 183
Black, Misha, 190–192
Blake, Peter, 154
Blitz, 2, 3, 11, 32, 101
Blom, Piet, 241
Bodiansky, Vladimir, 248, 254
Boelcke, Oswald, 345
Bowen, Denis, 188–189
Boyne, Colin, 89
Brasília. *See* British Embassy at Brasília
British Embassy at Brasília (A. and P. Smithson), 250, 323, 342–343, 365, 380
Brutalism. *See* New Brutalism
Building and Town Construction (B.T.C.), 70
Buildings of England (Pevsner), 12
Burleigh Lane Houses (A. and P. Smithson), 365
"Burrows Lea Farm" (A. and P. Smithson), *63*, 66, 298
Butor, Michel, 353

"But Today We Collect Ads" (A. and P. Smithson), 88, 153, 165

Calvino, Italo, 353
Cambridge Opinion, 133
Candilis, Georges, 47, 62, 235, 238, 253
    CIAM 10, 48–49
    Habitat du plus grand nombre, 108
    Team 10, first meeting, 249
Caravans (travel trailers), 214–215
Carré Bleu, 270
Cars. *See* Automobiles
Carter, E. J., 152
Case Study House No. 8 (C. and R. Eames), 133
Casson, Hugh, 30, 31
Castles on the Ground, The: The Anatomy of Suburbia (Richards), 7, 11
Causey Arch, 373
Censorship. *See* Self-censorship
Chandigarh, 109, 157–158, 335
Charte d'Athènes (1933), 48, 58
Charte de l'Habitat (1953), 48, 58, 62, 252, 407n64, 419n128. *See also* CIAM 9
Charte de l'Habitation. *See Charte de l'Habitat*
Charter of Habitat. *See Charte de l'Habitat*
Cherry, Colin, 129, 132
Children's books and stories, 359, 373, 382–384, 386, 388–389
Churchill College (A. and P. Smithson), 298–299, 323
CIAM (Congrès International d'Architecture Moderne), 31, 37, 68, 72, 231–234, 244, 247, 250–252, 254–255, 276
CIAM 6 (Bridgwater, 1947), 37, 47
CIAM 7 (Bergamo, 1949), 47, 62, 406n50
CIAM 8 (Hoddesdon, 1951), 31, 37, 47, 254
CIAM 9 (Aix-en-Provence, 1953), 89, 96, 157, 254–255
    aftermath, 52
    Charte de l'Habitat, 48, 252
    generational divide, 46–47, 48, 49, 52
    "How Other Peoples Dwell and Build" (Gutkind), 107–108
    "Man and His Dwelling," 48
    Smithsons and, 246–248

CIAM 10 (Dubrovnik, 1956), 49, 50, 59, 407n64
   cluster (A. and P. Smithson), 98
   collapse, 50
   functional city, 50
   generational divide, 61–62, 249
   "habitat," postwar concentration on, 107
   Le Corbusier's letter to attendees, 62, 231, 344
   organizing committee, 57
   Team 10 debates, 49, 57, 250
"CIAM Reorganization or Dissolution?" (A. and P. Smithson), 68
"CIAM Team 10" (A. Smithson), 52, 166, 231, 232
"CIAM Team 10 Meetings" (A. Smithson), 206
CICON (CIAM Continuity/Continuità/Contuit), 69
CIRPAC (Comité International pour la Résolution des Problèmes de l'Architecture Contemporaine), 47–48, 407n65, 409n89
"City Notes" (Alloway), 149, *150–151*
"Civilia, the End of Sub Urban Man" (1971), 13
Climate register, 323
"Climate Register" (A. and P. Smithson), 322–323, 337
Climate Register: Four Works by Alison and Peter Smithson (Wong and Salter), 322, 337
Clothes and clothing, 157–158, 163–164, 168–169
Cluster, 93, 206, 212, 214, 247
   Gutkind and, 107
   Smithsons at CIAM 10, 67–68, 98, 249, 276
   Smithsons on, 53, 75, 79, 99, 103, 208, 281, 357, 389
Cluster city, 98, 103
"Cluster City" (A. and P. Smithson), 33, 208, 294
"Cluster Diagram of Association" (A. Smithson), 79
"Cluster Diagram of involuntary/voluntary Association" (A. Smithson), 79
Cobbett, William, 227, 323, 332, 339
Cohn, Stephen, 188
Cold War, 24, 154, 170

Coleman, Roger, 170, 183–186, 188
Collage, 121–122, 125, 127, 141, 174, 179, 267. *See also* Scrapbooks
   associated ideas, 170
   collage thinking, 145, 158–159
   Eameses' aesthetic, 137
   Smithsons' collage writing, 157, 166, 261, 369, 394–395
"Collective Design" (A. and P. Smithson), 257, 259, 272, 274, *275*, 277, 279–281, *282*, 283, *284*, 285–290
Collins, David, 183
Colonial modernism, 109. *See also* Orientalism
Colquhoun, Alan, 38, 40, 43
Commercial art, 148, 159, 161–162, 166, 179. *See also* Mass arts
Communications Primer, A (C. and R. Eames), 113, 135, 154
Communication theory. *See* Information theory
Community and Environment: A Discourse on Social Ecology (Gutkind), 107
Congrès International d'Architecture Moderne. *See* CIAM
Conservative government, 97
Constructivism, 377
"Conversations on Brutalism" (A. and P. Smithson), 92, 94
Cordell, Frank, 165, 206
Cordell McHale, Magda, 38, 121, 250
Core of the city, 31
Costa, Lúcio, 70, 71
Council of Industrial Design, 32
"Counter-attack" (Nairn), 11
"Crone Call, The" (A. and P. Smithson), 359, 386, 388
Crosby, Theo, 38–39, 41, 73, 83, 120–121, 404n9
   at *Architectural Design*, 39
   "This Is Tomorrow" (1956), 120, 127, 129, 132, 161, 263
Cullen, Gordon, 3, *4*, 9, *10*, 15, 22–23, 24
Cut-ups. *See* Collage
Cybernetics, 120, 123, 125, 133. *See also* Wiener, Norbert
Cybernetics (Wiener), 123

Damascus Gate, Jerusalem (A. and P. Smithson), 308, 310–311
Davies, J. H. V., 91
De Carlo, Giancarlo, 233, 234, 238, 240
Dedalus, Stephen (fictional character), 367. *See also* Joyce, James
De Hooch, Pieter, 66, 67, *282*, 285
Dell, M. O., 3
Del Maré, Eric, 161
Del Renzio, Toni, 143, 164–165, 171, 173, 185, 186
    Alison Smithson on, 142
    pro-Americanism, 122–123
    "Shoes Hair and Coffee" (1957), 171, *172*, 183
    "This Is Tomorrow" (1956), 132
"Design by Choice" (Banham), 192
De Stijl, 271
"Development of British Pop, The" (Alloway), 122
"Document 53" (A. and P. Smithson), 53
Donner, Georg Raphael, 401n54. *See also* Donner, Peter F. R.; Pevsner, Nikolaus
Donner, Peter F. R. (pseudonym of Nikolaus Pevsner), 3, 13. *See also* Pevsner, Nikolaus
"Doorn Manifesto" (1954), 57–58, 257
Dorfles, Gillo, 165
Dorfsman, Lou, 179
"Dream Worlds, Associated" (Coleman), 184
Drew, Jane, 38, 92
Dubuffet, Jean, 88–89, 97
Dutch Group, 60–61
Dutch Group of 8. *See* Jeunes, Les

Eames, Charles, 119, 135
Eames, Charles and Ray, 71, 113, 133, 139, 154, 165, 254, 267, 305
    aesthetic, 137, 139, 141, 154, 158
    Alison Smithson on, 154–155
    Communications Primer, A (1953), 113, 135, 154
    Eames House (1947–1949), 137, 299, 302, 305
    "House of Cards" (1952), 137, 155
    pinboard work, 132
    reverence for objects and images, 141
    Santa Monica House (*see* Eames House)
Eames House (C. and R. Eames), 137, 299, 302, 305
Ecological thinking. *See* Environmentalism
Economist Building (A. and P. Smithson), 1, 33, 110, *110*, 269–270, 294–295, 322–323, 366
Edison, Thomas A., 206
Einstein, Albert, 45
Elgin Marbles, 320
Emergence of Team 10 out of CIAM (A. Smithson), 231, 247
Emery, Pierre-André, 248, 254
English Cities and Small Towns (Betjeman), 6
English Group, 58, 59, 60, 61
English landscape, art of, 14
English landscape garden (style), 223, 295, 324, 326, 329
Englishness, use of term, 398n1
English Picturesque, 12–17, 23, 27, 33–34, 38, 67, 115, 208, 215, 394. *See also* Picturesque
    Architectural Review, and propaganda, 11
    meaning and methodology, controversy, 1
    notions and concepts of, 2
    Pevsner on, 16–17, 41
    rejection by new generation, 32
    Smithsons and, 33–34, 226, 266, 272
    tradition, 8
"English Planning Tradition and the City, The" (Pevsner), 20
English Townscape Analysis. *See* Townscape Analysis
Environmentalism, 193, 221, 223, 228, 246, 294, 322, 339
Erskine, Ralph, 70, 71–72, 238, 249
Essays on the Picturesque (Price), 14–15
Euston Arch, 83, 377, 379–382
Euston Arch and the Growth of the London, Midland & Scottish Railway, The (A. and P. Smithson), 83, 325, 359, *378*, 379–382
Euston Station, 380. *See also* Euston Arch
"Exterior Furnishing or Sharawaggi: The Art of Making Urban Landscape" (Hastings), 16, 21

"Extracts from Talks to 5th Year Students on 'The Shape of Things'" (A. and P. Smithson), 46

Family and Kinship in East London (Willmott and Young), 104, 105
Farnsworth House (Mies van der Rohe), 299, 302–303
Fashion. *See* Clothes and clothing
Feedback. *See* Cybernetics
Festival of Britain (1951), 27, 30–32, 190
"50s Field of Enquiry" (A. Smithson), 72–73
"Fine and the Folk, The: An Essay on McKim, Mead and White and the American Tradition" (P. Smithson), 88, *138*, 366
Fixes (keyword), 205–206, 208, 210, 310, 381–382, 389
"Form and Mathematics" (Olitsky and Voelcker), 44
"Fragment of an Enclave" (A. Smithson), 318
Frampton, Kenneth, 39, 73
Freeman, Robert, 133, 163
Free University of Berlin (Candilis, Josic, and Woods), 240, 271, 308
"From the Astringency of Necessity to the Astringency of Choice" (P. Smithson), 97
Fry, Maxwell, 38, 92
Fry, Roger, 143
Functional city, 17, 50, 406n50
Functionalism, 17, 20, 26–27, 43, 75–76, 215, 216, 233
Functional Tradition, 7, 11, 21, 24–27, 28, 32, 34, 161, 312
  first use of term (1947), 399n28
  Richards and, 26, 31
"Function of Architecture in Cultures-in-Change, The" (A. and P. Smithson), 366
Futurism, 377

GAMMA, 108, 419n127
Garden City, 2, 22, 214, 273, 283, 285
Gate of Hell (Teinosuke), 96. *See also* Japanese architecture
Geddes, Patrick, 52, 57, 58, 60, 398n6
General Motors Technical Center (Saarinen), 173, 186
Gentry, 165
Giedion, Sigfried, 50, 61, 62, 67, 69, 72, 90, 249
  Mechanization Takes Command, 171
  new monumentality, 47
  "Open Letter" (January 1961), 50–51
  Space, Time and Architecture (1967), 171
Gill, Margaret (pseudonym of Alison Smithson), 168, 428n45
Glabrous, 173, 185, 195
Golden Lane Housing (A. and P. Smithson), 53, 101, *102*, 267, 298
Goldfinger, Ernö, 152
Goldsmith, Oliver, 223
Gombrich, Ernst, 161
"Gouda" (A. and P. Smithson), 359, 386, *387*
Grahame, Kenneth, 386
Graphics of communication, 75–76, 79, 83, 85, 389
Great Exhibition of 1851, 27
Greenberg, Clement, 148
Gropius, Walter, 50–51, 69, 242, 254
Group 12, 132
"Growing a Landscape of Lyrical Appropriateness" (A. Smithson), 295
"Growth and Form" (Independent Group and Richard Hamilton), 161, 260
Guedes, Amancio, 241
Guggenheim, Peggy, 76
Gül Baba Mat Mosque (A. and P. Smithson), 308, 319
Gustave, Flaubert, 344
Gutkind, Erwin Anton, 107–108
Gutmann, Rolf, 48–49
Guyatt, Richard, 179

Habitat, 107, 108
"Habitat" (A. and P. Smithson), *56*, 58
Habitat du plus grand nombre (Candilis and Woods), 108
Hamilton, Richard, 38, 120, 121, 125, 127, 250
  "Growth and Form" (1951), 260
  Pop Art collage, 145
Hardwick, Philip, 380
Hare, Augustus John Cuthbert, 332, 339
Harper's Bazaar, 171, 185
Hastings, Hubert de Cronin, 3, 7, 11, 12–13, 20–24
  Architectural Review, retires from (1973), 13

"Exterior Furnishing or Sharawaggi: The Art of Making Urban Landscape" (1944), 16, 21
  Lasdun, Susan, interview with, 401n73
  pseudonym, use of (Ivor de Wolfe), 3, 13
  Sharawaggi, 15–16
  "Townscape: A Plea for an English Visual Philosophy Founded on the True Rock of Sir Uvedale Price" (1949), 20, 22
Hauptstadt Berlin (Cordell, McHale, and A. and P. Smithson), 206
Hauptstadt Berlin road system project (A. and P. Smithson), 78, *98*, 99, 206, 208, 267, 365
Henderson, Judith, 105
Henderson, Nigel, 53, 67, 105, 125, 141, 142, 158–159, 260
  "Patio and Pavilion" (1956), 127, *128*, *262*, 263
  "Photo-Images" (1954), 161
  Pop Art, 129, 142
Heroic Period, 42, 89, 90, 96, 121, 251, 266, 267, 270–271, 298, 324, 325, 330, 352–353, 389
"Heroic Period of Modern Architecture" (A. and P. Smithson), 352–353
Hertfordshire Schools, 50
"History of Three Natures of Layering, A" (A. Smithson), 260
Holroyd, Geoffrey, 123, 132, 137, 139
Home storage design, 212. *See also* "Appliance House"
"House of Cards" (C. and R. Eames), 137, 155
"House of the Future" (A. and P. Smithson), 98, 129, 174–175, *176–177*, 178, 193, 210, 216, 267. *See also* Ideal Home Exhibition
"Housing for the greatest number." *See Habitat du plus grand nombre*
Hovens Greve, Hans, 57
Howard, Ebenezer, 2, 398n6
Howell, Gillian (Jill), 52, 249
Howell, William (Bill), 38, 47, 164, 249, 255, 357
  on CIAM 9, 52
  on CIAM 10, 50
  elected to MARS group, 48

"How Other Peoples Dwell and Build" (Gutkind), 107–108
Humanization, 27, 42, 44
Human Use of Human Beings, The (Wiener), 123, 171
Hunstanton Secondary Modern School (A. and P. Smithson), 88–89, 90, 91, 263, 265, *292*, 294, 323
  Boyne on, 89

ICA. *See* Institute of Contemporary Arts
Ideal Home Exhibition (1955–1956), 98, 129, 174, 210. *See also* "House of the Future"
Ideograms, 76, 77, 83, 179
IG. *See* Independent Group
Imprint of India (A. Smithson), 331, *333–334*, 337. *See also* "Quiet Flows the Kamasutra"
Independent Group, 39, 52, 53, 57, 76, 89, 120–123, 125, 129, 135, 142, 143, 153–154, 161–164, 171, 183–185
  "Growth and Form" (1951), 161
  members, notable, 421n32
  "Parallel of Life and Art (1953), 161
  "This Is Tomorrow" (1956), 161 (*see also* Crosby, Theo)
Information theory, 113, 120, 123, 125, 133. *See also* Shannon, Claude
"Initiators and Successors" (A. and P. Smithson), 259, 274, 445–446n58
Institute of Community Studies, 104
Institute of Contemporary Arts (ICA), 120, 121, 161, 162, 164, 183, 184, 210, 404n10, 420–421n24
  Communications Primer, A (C. and R. Eames), 135
  "Growth and Form" (1951), 260
  "Opposing Forces" (1953), 76
"Introduction to Places Worth Inheriting" (A. Smithson), 272
Istanbul, 103
Italian Thoughts (A. and P. Smithson), 266

Jacobsen, Arne, 79
James, Bill, 190–191
Japanese architecture, 96, 212. *See also* "Appliance House"

Jeunes, Les, 47. *See also* Dutch Group
Johansen, John, 70, 71
Johnson, Philip, 71
Johnson-Marshal, Percy, 31–32
Josic, Alexis, 235, 238
Joyce, James, 365, 367

Kahn, Louis, 70, 71, 72, 77–79, *78*, 217, *218*, 240, 254
    anecdotes about, 201
Kepes, György, 161
Klee, Paul, 76–77, 79, 85
Koolhaas, Rem, 464n114
Kurokawa, Kisho, 240
Kuwait Demonstration building (A. and P. Smithson), 308, 322–323
Kuwait Dune Gardens (A. and P. Smithson), 308
Kuwait Government offices (A. and P. Smithson), 310
Kuwait Urban Study (A. and P. Smithson), 308, 309–310

Ladies' Home Journal, 164, 165
Lancaster, Osbert, 3
Landau, Royston, 247
Langer, Suzanne, 123
Language of Vision (Kepes), 161
Lasdun, Denys, 38–39, 90–91, 415n53
Lasdun, Susan, 401n73
LCC. *See* London County Council
Le Corbusier, 38, 119, 234, 235, 249, 251, 254, 266, 373, 382–383, 389, 395
    Centrosoyus project, 40
    Chandigarh, 109, 157–158
    on CIAM, 231–232
    CIAM 10, letter to attendees, 62, 231, 344
    on clothes and clothing, 157–158
    on education, 157–158
    home storage design, 212
    house/city analogy, 101
    houses of, Peter Smithson on, 302–303
    Le Modulor (1948), 43, 44–45, 46
    Oeuvre Complète, 302–303
    "Open Letter" (January 1961), 50–51
    Propos d'Urbanisme, 99
    ramps, 320
    sculpture, 317
    Smithsons, influence on, 103
    Smithsons on, 41–42, 320
    St. Dié Reconstruction Project, 52
    St. Jerome, allegory of, 318
    Stuttgart houses, 40
    Towards a New Architecture (*see* Le Corbusier: *Vers une Architecture*)
    Unité d'Habitation (1947–1952), 38, 43, 48, 89, 95–96, 157, 248
    Vers une Architecture (1923), 89, 454n136
    Ville Radieuse, 49, 198
Léger, Fernand, 248, 254
Lethaby, William, 26
Life magazine, 157, 161
Lionni, Leo, 179
Llangennith Cluster Housing conglomerate (A. and P. Smithson), 319
Loewy, Raymond, 204
London & Birmingham Railway, 380
London County Council, 31, 38, 101, 104, 269–270
"London Roads Study" (A. and P. Smithson), 206
London Transport Commission, 380
"Long Front of Culture, The" (Alloway), 144
Los Angeles, 152, 208
Low, John Nicholson, 165
Lucas Headquarters (A. and P. Smithson), 265

"Machine Made America" (1957), 113, *116*, 118
Macmillan, Harold, 379, 380
MacQuedy, James (pseudonym of James M. Richards), 3
"Madame Representative—Woman Correspondent" (A. Smithson), 157, 166
Magazines. *See* Mass media
"Man and He-Man" (Smith), *181*, 183
"Man Made America" (1950), 113–115, 149, 152
"Manplan" (1969), 12
Marinetti, Filippo Tommaso, 377
MARS group, 37–38, 39, 48, 107
Martienssen, Rex, 454n136

Mass arts, 144, 148, 163. *See also* Commercial art
Massey, Anne, 421n25
Mass media, 7, 32, 93, 113, 120, 125, 127, 133, 135, 142–145, 148, 154, 155, 157, 159, 162, 168, 179, 184–185, 203, 214, 280, 354. *See also* Advertisements
Mass society, 97, 148, 270
Mat-building, 293, 308–311, 319, 322, 326, 389
Matthew, Robert, 38
Maude-Roxby, Ruddy, 184
McCallum, Ian, 118, 420n14
McHale, John, 38, 119, 120, 157, 164, 174–175, 250
   collage, 125
   Hauptstadt Berlin (1959), 206
   Pop Art, 145
McLaughlin, G. Harry, 165
McLuhan, Marshall, 171, 188
Mechanical Bride, The (McLuhan), 171, 188
Mechanization, 27, 119, 171, 205
Mechanization Takes Command (Giedion), 171
Media. *See* Mass media
Medium Is the Message, The (McLuhan), 188
Middleton, Robin, 39, 73
Mies van der Rohe, Ludwig, 91, 119, 212, 248, 254
   Farnsworth House, 299, 302–303
Milne, A. A., 386
"Miracle of Moderation, A" (Van Eyck), 244
Mobility (keyword), 50, 67, 72, 75, 79, 83, 97, 99, 103, 203–206, 214, 215, 226, 228, 256, 267, 276, 389
"Mobility" (A. Smithson), 366
Modern Architectural Research Group. *See* MARS group
Modern Architecture (Richards), 37
Modern Movement, 3, 23, 26, 40–41, 89, 90, 118, 228, 246, 251, 253, 255, 267, 270–271, 288, 343, 382–383, 392
Modulor, Le (Le Corbusier), 43, 44–45, 46
Moholy-Nagy, László, 161
Moholy-Nagy, Sibyl, 76
Mondrian, Piet, 204
Monumentality, 27
Moore, Gordon, 183

Mosque of Amr ibn al-As, Cairo, 310, 311
Motorcars. *See* Automobiles
Movement graphics, 76, 77, 78, 85, 217
Movement patterns. *See* Movement graphics

Nairn, Ian, 6, 11
Nash, Paul, 3, 22, 161
"Nautical Style, The" (Piper), 7
Neo-Palladian movement, 46
New Arts Building, Bath University (A. and P. Smithson), 322–323
New Brutalism, 1, 2, 33, 34, 39, 75, 88–97, 208, 210, 269, 294, 357, 365
   Alison Smithson and, 166
   art brut, 88
   Banham and, 41, 88, 90, 197, 215
   béton brut, 89
   materials, respect for, 96
   Peter Smithson and, 133, 199
   Pevsner and, 41
   Smithsons' 1955 definition of, 197
"New Brutalism" (Banham), 41
New Brutalism, The (Banham), 94, 95, 199, 208
New monumentality, 47
Newspapers. *See* Mass media
New Yorker, 165
"Next Step?, The" (Richards), 26
"1916 A.S.O.: The Earth of the Modern Movement" (A. Smithson), 330, 339, 341–353, 377, 379
"Not Quite Architecture" (A. Smithson writing as Gill), 168

Olitsky, Ruth, 44
"On Climbing Ground: or Not on the Level" (A. Smithson), 319
"On Climbing Ground: Thinking towards the Acropolis Place" (P. Smithson), 319–320
"On the Mat at Lime Grove" (Bisley), 183
"Open Letter" (Giedion, Gropius, Le Corbusier, and Sert), 50–51
"Opposing Forces" (1953), 76
Orczy, Emma, 354
Ordinariness and Light (A. and P. Smithson), 83, 88, 103, 159, 272

Orientalism, 307–312. *See also* Colonial modernism
"Outrage" (Nairn), 6, 11
Ozenfant, Amédée, 89

Paatelainen, Raili, 244–245
Pahlavi National Library, Tehran (A. and P. Smithson), 308, 319
"Painting and Sculpture of a Decade" (A. and P. Smithson), 267
Paolozzi, Eduardo, 38, 53, 105, 121, 141, 142
   on Alloway, 145
   art brut and Peter Smithson, 88
   automobiles, 201, 214
   collage thinking, 158–159
   "Patio and Pavilion" (1956), 127, *128*, *262*, 263
   Smithsons, influence on, 67, 76
"Paradis Eloigne" (A. Smithson), *162*, 293, 303, 305–308, 313, 322
"Parallel of Life and Art" (Independent Group and A. and P. Smithson), 53, 161, 267
Parc de la Villette, Paris, competition, 293, 312–313, 315
"Paris: Maigret's Map" (A. Smithson), 330, 353–356
Parker, Barry, 2
Parthenon Marbles. *See* Elgin Marbles
Pasmore, Victor, 77
"Patio and Pavilion" (Henderson, Paolozzi, and A. and P. Smithson), 127, *128*, *262*, 263, 267
Patterns of association (keyword), 66, 71, 72, 76, 105, 107, 206, 256, 280, 281, 298, 308, 309, 312, 357, 389
"Patterns of Association" (A. and P. Smithson), *84*
Patterns of movement, 206, 246, 312, 357
Peasant style, 46, 89, 91, 96
Pedagogical Sketchbook (Klee), 76–77
Perec, Georges, 353
Perriand, Charlotte, 212, 267
Pevsner, Nikolaus, 3, 5, 11, 24, 90, 157, 215, 293, 294, 326
   America, critique of, 114
   Buildings of England, 12
   English landscape, art of, 14
   "English Planning Tradition and the City, The" (1945), 20
   on Euston Arch, 380–381
   functional form, 20
   Le Corbusier, critique of, 40
   Modern Movement and the Picturesque, 14, 40
   "Picturesqueness of English Art, The," Reith Lectures (1955, published 1956), 41
   on Price, 14–15
   pseudonyms, 3, 13, 401n54
   rationalism, philosophy of, 14
   Sharawaggi, 15–16
   Townscape Analysis, critique of, 40
   "Treasure Hunt" (1942), 13
Philosophy in a New Key (Langer), 123
"Photo-Images" (Henderson), 161
Picasso, Pablo, 355
Piccadilly Circus, 152
Picturesque, 1–3, 5, 9, 14, 142, 189, 195, 199, 208. *See also* English Picturesque
   Banham's critique of, 33–34, 356–357
   Hastings on, 15, 20–22
   Pevsner on, 15, 16, 40–41
   Price on, 11, 14–15
   school of art, 11
   theory, Smithsons, 215, 219, 272, 293, 294, 298, 323, 329, 356–357
   Townscape, 159
"Picturesqueness of English Art, The" (Pevsner), 41
Pidgeon, Monica, 39, 73, 169, 404n7–n8, 408n75
Pietilä, Reima, 244–245
Piper, John, 3, 7, 9, 12, 22, 161
Pollock, Jackson, 67, 76, 97, 99, 119
Pologni, Charles, 238
Pop Art, 113, 120, 122, 129, 142, 145, 149, 152, 157, 179, 183–184, 216, 250, 425n97
Pop artists, 143, 157, 163, 198, 269
Pope, Alexander, 14, 223
Portrait of the Artist as a Young Man, A (Joyce), 365, 367
Portrait of the Female Mind as a Young Girl, A (A. Smithson), 359, 363, 365–372
Postarchitectural culture, 245

Postmodern architecture, 244, 245, 326
Postwar reconstruction, 2–3, 5–7, 9, 11, 13–17, 24, 40, 104. *See also* Bethnal Green
Potter, Beatrix, 359, 382–384
Powers, Alan, 399n17
Price, Sir Uvedale, 11, 14–15, 20, 22, 40
"Programme for London" (June 1945), 11
Propaganda, British, 11
Proportion theory, 43, 45–46
Propos d'Urbanisme (Le Corbusier), 99
Proust, Marcel, 354
Prouvé, Jean, 254
Pseudonyms, 3, 13, 168, 401n54, 428n45
Purism, 13, 89, 145, 197, 271

"Quality of Place, The" (A. Smithson), 274
"Quiet Flows the Kamasutra" (A. Smithson), *328*, 330, 331–332, 335–339, 456–457n58. *See also Imprint of India*

Radiant City. *See* Ville Radieuse
Radio. *See* Mass media
Railway, 370–371
Rand, Paul, 179
Randolph, Paul, 71
Rationing, 27, 30, 115, 205
Rattenbury, Kester, 373
RCA. *See* Royal College of Art
Read, Herbert, 121, 122, 143, 183
Realism, debates in England, 159
Reconstruction. *See* Postwar reconstruction
Re-Identification scroll (A. and P. Smithson), 79, *80–82*, 83
Revolution of Environment (Gutkind), 107
RIBA. *See* Royal Institute of British Architects
RIBA Journal, 39
Richards, James M., 3, 5, 7, 26–27, 31, 398n11
   architectural magazine, role of, 8–9
   Castles on the Ground, The: The Anatomy of Suburbia (1946), 7, 11
   Festival of Britain (1951), 30
   on Functional Tradition, 24, 26–27, 31
   Modern Architecture (1939), 37
   "Next Step?, The" (1950), 26
   pseudonym, use of (James MacQuedy), 3
   Townscape Analysis, English, 37

Riesman, David, 148, 171
Rietveld, Gerrit Thomas, 254
Rimmer, Angela, 183
Robin Hood Gardens (A. and P. Smithson), 240, 271, 279, 295, *296–297*
"Rocket, The" (P. Smithson), 366
Rogers, Ernesto, 71, 233, 254
Rosenberg, Harold, 171
Rowe, Colin, 43
Royal College of Art (RCA), 157, 161, 162–163, 165, 179, 183, 184, 188
   Charles Eames and, 135
   King's Road boutique, "Bazaar," 168
Royal Institute of British Architects (RIBA), 38, 45, 46, 135, 235
Rykwert, Joseph, 9, 11, 17, 43, 174

Saarinen, Eero, 173, 186
Salk Laboratory, 79, 240
Salon d'Automne Exhibition House of 1929, 212
"Scatter" (A. and P. Smithson), *210*, 366
Scharoun, Hans, 70, 71
Scrapbooks, 141, 305, 385
Self-censorship, 11
"Sensibility primers" (A. Smithson), 2, 223, 259, 267, 274, 322, 326, 329–332, 335–339, 341–357
Serial vision, 9, *10*. *See also* Cullen, Gordon
Sert, Josep Lluís, 50–51, 62, 69, 248, 254
Shannon, Claude, 113, 120, 132. *See also* Information theory
Sharawaggi, 15–16, 21, 22, 152
Shift, The (A. and P. Smithson), *262*, 266
"Shoes Hair and Coffee" (del Renzio), 171, *172*, 183
Sigmonde-Wonke, Peter, 206
Significant Image, 52, 57, 66, 67, 73, 90, 99
Simenon, Georges, 353, 354, 355
Skidmore, Owings and Merrill, 216
"Slow Growth of Another Sensibility, The" (P. Smithson), 269
Slums, 75, 108
Smith, Richard, 183
Smithson, Alison, 158–159, 163–165, 169, 192–193, 205, 249–250, 251, 268, 272–274

Smithson, Alison (cont.)
    advertisements, 157, 164–168, 331, 352, 371
    aerial combat, 345, 346, 348
    aerial photography, 345, 353, 354
    airplanes, 343–345, 346, 348, 351, 352
    America, critique of, 289
    on Arab urbanism, 309–310
    Archer, Mildred, influence of, 456–457n58
    "Architect as Witness," 270, 288
    Architectural Association, graduate seminars at, 231, 247, 251–252
    architect-urbanist, moral responsibility of, 281, 290
    on art and technology, 343–344, 353
    "as found" aesthetics, 330
    AS in DS: An Eye on the Road (1983), 85, 86, 201, *220, 221, 222*, 223–228, 330
    on Austen, 330
    automobiles, 201, 219, 221, 223–228, 368, 369
    on Bakema, 219
    Barcelona architectural seminar (1985), 315, 317–318, 322
    Bath University studio (1979), 385–386
    on books and building, 373
    British education system, critique of, 280
    on bureaucracy, 274, 342, 350, 385
    on caravans (travel trailers), 214–215
    Chandigarh, 335
    childhood and early life, 359, 366–367
    children's books and stories, 382–384
    CIAM, 370
    on CIAM 9, 247
    "CIAM Team 10" (May 1960), 52, 166, 231, 232
    "CIAM Team 10 Meetings" (1960), 206
    climate register, 323
    clothes and clothing, 164, 346, 349, 350
    cluster, 281
    "Cluster Diagram of Association" (1951), 79
    "Cluster Diagram of involuntary/voluntary Association" (1951), 79
    collage writing, 166, 261, 369
    on the collective, 285–286
    on conglomerate buildings, 312
    cultural fixes, 381–382 (*see also* Fixes)
    on Damascus Gate, Jerusalem, 310–311
    and de Hooch, 66–67, 285
    on the Eames aesthetic, 139, 141
    on the Eameses, 154–155
    on Eames House, 299, 302, 305
    on Edinburgh, 324, 335
    Emergence of Team 10 out of CIAM (1982), 231, 247
    on English landscape garden, 223–224, 324
    "Englishness" of their work, 293–294
    environmentalism, 223, 246
    on Euston Arch, 381
    fabric, 170, 259, 273, 279, 281, 283, 285, 290, 303, 305, 324, 349, 353–355
    on Farnsworth House, 299, 302–303
    fashion (*see* Smithson, Alison: clothes and clothing)
    "50s Field of Enquiry," 72–73
    form language, 283, 285
    "Fragment of an Enclave" (1985, rev. 1986), 318
    Garden City, critique of, 283
    "Growing a Landscape of Lyrical Appropriateness" (1984), 295
    "History of Three Natures of Layering, A" (1981), 260
    idylls, 299, 302–303
    Imprint of India (1994), 331, *333–334*, 337 (*see also* Smithson, Alison: "Quiet Flows the Kamasutra")
    India (colonial), picturesqueness of, 339 (*see also* Orientalism)
    "Introduction to Places Worth Inheriting" (1983), 272
    Italian influence on design, fashion, style, and taste, 170, 368
    Italy, visit to, 170–171
    Kuwait, urban form of, 309
    Ladies' Home Journal, 164, 165
    light touch (keyword), 386
    Liste Alphabétique des Rues de Paris, 354–355
    lyrical appropriateness (keyword), 293, 295, 303, 322

"Madame Representative—Woman Correspondent" (unpublished novelette), 157, 166
mat-building, 308, 309
on memory, 356
"Mobility" (1958), 366
on modern architecture, 270–271, 382–383
Munich architectural studio (1984), 315
New Brutalism, 359, 365
"1916 A.S.O.: The Earth of the Modern Movement," 330, 339, 341–353, 377, 379
Noah's Ark, 315, *316*, 317–318, 322
"Not Quite Architecture" (A. Smithson writing as Gill), 168
"On Climbing Ground: or Not on the Level" (1991), 319
"Paradis Eloigne" (1975–1986), *162*, 293, 303, 305–308, 313, 322
"Paris: Maigret's Map," 330, 353–356
on Picasso, 355
place-making, 354, 356
Plan de Paris, 354–355
Portrait of the Female Mind as a Young Girl, A (1966), 359, 363, 365–372
Potter, Beatrix, spaces of, 382–384
pseudonym, use of (Margaret Gill), 168, 428n45
"Quality of Place, The," 274
"Quiet Flows the Kamasutra," *328*, 330, 331–332, 335–339, 456–457n58 (see also Smithson, Alison: *Imprint of India*)
"sensibility primers," 2, 223, 259, 267, 274, 322, 326, 329–332, 335–339, 341–357
Simenon, use of, 353, 354, 355
Solar Pavilion (see Smithson, Alison: Upper Lawn Pavilion)
St. Jerome: The Desert and the Study, 317, 318–319
on Team 10, 52, 233, 234, 246–247, 251–254, 342
Team 10, role as editor, 232
"Team 10 at Royaumont 1962" (1975), 52, 231, 240–242, 437n32
Team 10 Meetings: 1953–1984 (1991), 231, 242, *243*, 256
"Team 10 Primer" (1962), 52, 78, 83, 166, 206, 231, 234–235, *236–237*
Team 10 Primer (1968), 217, 231, 238, *239*, 240, 252, 381
"24 Doors to Christmas" (1979), 385–386
on Upper Lawn Pavilion, 299, 302, 355, 363
urban theory, 354–357
on Volkswagen Beetle, 201
Welfare State, critique of, 269, 271, 273, 279–281, 289 (see also Smithson, Alison and Peter: conservatism, shift toward)
"With Green in Mind," 322
"Work of Team 10, The" (May 1960), 52, 166, 231, 232–233
World War I, 330, 341, 342, 344, 345, 352–353
World War II, 359
Smithson, Alison and Peter, 31–32, 38, 61, 62, 67, 69–71, 120, 142, 157–159, 198, 205, 217, 249, 250, 256–257, 266–267, 269–270, 325, 357
Acropolis Place (1990), 319–320
advertisements, 66, 89–90, 93, 95, 142, 153, 164, 210, 216–217
aerial photography, 353
"Appliance House" (1958), 212, 214
Arch Criminals of the Euston Arch, The (see Smithson, Alison and Peter: *Euston Arch and the Growth of the London, Midland & Scottish Railway, The*)
Architectural Design, 75
architect-urbanist, moral responsibility of, 389, 392, 395
Ark, 183
Arup and Partners, 267
"as found" aesthetic, 2, 53, 57, 75, 87, 97, 127, 215, 260, 267, 302, 317
automobiles, 195–199, 201, 203–204, 206, 208, 210, 214–217, 226–228, 366, 373, 432n23
Banham, response to, 94
Bates House (see Smithson, Alison and Peter: "Burrows Lea Farm")
Bibliotheca Alexandrina (1989), 308, 322–323

Index 477

Smithson, Alison and Peter (cont.)
   British Embassy at Brasília, 250, 323, 342–343, 365, 380
   British government, critique of, 271–272
   buildings, role of, 289–290
   building's effectiveness, measure of, 277–278
   Burleigh Lane Houses (1965–1966), 365
   "Burrows Lea Farm" (1953), *63*, 66, 298
   "But Today We Collect Ads" (1956), 88, 153, 165
   children's books and stories, 359, 373, 382, 386, 388–389
   Christmas ephemera, 359, 384–386
   Christmas Hogmanay exhibition (1975), 265, 385–386
   Christmas scrapbooks, *384*, 385
   Churchill College (1959), 298–299, 323
   on CIAM 9, 52, 108, 247, 248
   "CIAM Reorganization or Dissolution?" (1957), 68
   city elements, 101
   climate register, 2, 323
   "Climate Register" (1994), 322–323, 337
   climbing ground, 319
   Close Houses, *65*, 66, 79, 365
   cluster (keyword), 53, 67, 68, 75, 79, 93, 98, 99, 103, 208, 247, 276, 357, 389
   cluster city, 98, 103
   "Cluster City" (1957), 33, 208, 294
   collage, 137, 159, 259, 267, 380
   collage writing, 157, 394–395
   "Collective Design" (1973–1975), 257, 259, 272, 274, *275*, 277, 279–290, *282*, *284*
   conglomerate ordering, 17, 293, 308, 311–312, 389
   conservatism, shift toward, 273, 279, 289–290 (*see also* Smithson, Alison: Welfare State, critique of)
   "Conversations on Brutalism" (1959), 92, 94
   "Crone Call, The," 359, 386, 388
   Damascus Gate, Jerusalem (1979), 308, 310–311
   "Document 53" (1952), 53
   dressable assets, 278
   Eameses' influence on, 137, 155, 392

   Economist Building (1959–1962), 1, 33, 110, *110*, 269–270, 294–295, 322–323, 366
   Elgin Marbles, 320
   England's industrial past, 373, 377
   English Picturesque, 33–34, 266, 272, 394
   environmentalism, 193, 228, 294, 322, 339
   Euston Arch and the Growth of the London, Midland & Scottish Railway, The (1968), 83, 325, 359, *378*, 379–382
   exhibitions, chronological list of, 443n11
   "Extracts from Talks to 5th Year Students on 'The Shape of Things'" (1959), 46
   fabric, 178, 221, 255–256, 259, 266, 267, 268, 270, 271, 272, 274, 276, 279, 283, 290, 295, 303, 305, 308, 310, 311, 325–326, 389, 392, 393
   family and family farm, metaphor of, 392–393
   fixes (keywords), 205–206, 208, 210, 310, 381–382, 389
   Fold Houses, *64*, 66
   form language, 103–104, 225, 232, 276–277, 389 (*see also* Smithson, Alison and Peter: language of modern architecture)
   "Function of Architecture in Cultures-in-Change, The" (1960), 366
   Galleon Cottages, *64*, 66
   Golden Lane Housing (1952–1953), 53, 101, *102*, 267, 298
   "Gouda," 359, 386, *387*
   graphics of communication, 75–76, 79, 83, 85, 389
   growth and change, 97, 103, 289, 308
   Gül Baba Mat Mosque (1987–1988), 308, 319
   "Habitat," *56*, 58
   on Hamilton's "Growth and Form" (1951), 260
   Hauptstadt Berlin (1959), 206
   Hauptstadt Berlin road system project (1957–1958), 78, *98*, 99, 206, 208, 267, 365
   "Heroic Period of Modern Architecture" (1965), 352–353

Hogmanay exhibitions (*see* Smithson, Alison and Peter: Christmas Hogmanay exhibition)
home storage design, 212
"House of the Future" (1956), 98, 129, 174–175, *176–177*, 178, 193, 210, 216, 267 (*see also* Ideal Home Exhibition)
Hunstanton Secondary Modern School (1949–1954), 88–89, 90, 91, 263, 265, *292*, 294, 323
ideograms, 76, 83, 179
on industrialization, 373, 377
"Initiators and Successors," 259, 274, 445–446n58
Islamic architecture and urbanism, 293, 307–312
Italian Thoughts (1993), 266
Jenkins, Ronald, 267, 268
keywords, 75–76, 79, 97–101, 202–203, 269, 271, 289
on Klee, 77
Kuwait Demonstration building (Mat-Building, 1970), 308, 322–323
Kuwait Dune Gardens (1975), 308
Kuwait Government offices (1970), 310
Kuwait urban form proposal (1968–1970), 309, 310
Kuwait Urban Study (1969), 308, 309–310
language of modern architecture, 104, 247, 395 (*see also* Smithson, Alison and Peter: form language)
on Le Corbusier, 41–42, 320
Le Corbusier, influence of, 103, 373, 395
light touch (keyword), 228, 259, 265, 266, 277, 280, 294, 302, 319
Llangennith Cluster Housing conglomerate (1977), 319
"London Roads Study" (1959), 206
Lucas Headquarters (1973), 265
lyrical appropriateness (keyword), 2, 295, 303, 308, 313, 320, 324, 357
MARS group, elected to, 48
mat-building, 293, 308–311, 319, 322, 326, 389
mid-century Englishness, 34
Middle East, work in, 293, 307–312

Mies van der Rohe, influence of, 392
mobility (keyword), 50, 67, 72, 75, 79, 83, 97, 99, 103, 203–206, 214, 215, 226, 228, 256, 267, 276, 389
on Mosque of Amr ibn al-As, Cairo, 310, 311
New Arts Building, Bath University, 322–323
New Brutalism, 88–89, 90, 197, 210, 215, 269, 294, 415n46
"open" vs. "closed" (functionalist) aesthetic, 75–76
Ordinariness and Light (1970), 83, 88, 103, 159, 272
orientalism, 307–312
Pahlavi National Library, Tehran (1977), 308, 319
"Painting and Sculpture of a Decade" (1954–1964), 267
"Parallel of Life and Art" (1953), 267 (*see also* Smithson, Alison and Peter: "Sources")
Parc de la Villette, Paris, competition (1982), 293, 312–313, 315
"Patio and Pavilion" (1956), 127, *128*, *262*, 263, 267
patterns of association (keyword), 66, 71, 72, 76, 105, 107, 206, 256, 280, 281, 298, 308, 309, 312, 357, 389
"Patterns of Association" (1960), *84*
Picturesque theory, 215, 219, 272, 293, 294, 298, 323, 329, 356–357
place-making, 193, 267
platform network, 206, 208
politics, lack of interest in, 380
Potter, Beatrix, 359
pre-language of architecture, 295, 298
on process, 393–394
Re-Identification scroll (1956), 79, *80–82*, 83
revisionist history, 293–295, 298
Robin Hood Gardens (1966–1972), 240, 271, 279, 295, *296–297*
on ruins, 324–325
scatter (keyword), 389
"Scatter" (1959), 210, 366

Smithson, Alison and Peter (cont.)
  scrapbooks, 141, 385
  Shift, The (1982), *262*, 266
  socio-plastics, 103–105, 107, 108, 261
    (see also Socio-plastics)
  Solar Pavilion (see Smithson, Alison and Peter: Upper Lawn Pavilion)
  "Sources," 53 (see also Smithson, Alison and Peter: "Parallel of Life and Art")
  South Facing Terraced Houses, *65*, 66
  "Speaking to the Sky," 293, 325
  street-deck, 88, 107
  streets-in-the-air, 76, 101, 267
  system explanations, 353
  on Team 10, 47, 166, 242, 245, 256, 270, 392
  Team 10 England, 67, 68–69
  "Terraced Crescent Housing" (1955), 79
  toys, 155, 373
  Tram Rats, The (1968), 325, 359, 373, *374–376*, 377, 379, 380
  trams, 329, 346, 353, 359, 377, 379
  University College, London, seminar, 385
  Upper Lawn Pavilion (1959–1980), 268, 299, 302, 355, 363, 366, 415n52
  Urban Re-identification, *54–55*, 100, 103
  Urban Re-Identification (1966), 99, 159
  Urban Re-Identification Document (1952), 79, 107
  Urban Re-identification Project (1951–1952), 101
  Urban Structuring (1967), *74*, *100*
  "Urban Structuring" (1960), 83
  on weathering, 322–323, 339
  "Wedding in the City Milan Triennale" (1968), 267, 278, *278*
  Without Rhetoric: An Architectural Aesthetic 1955–1972 (1973), 83, 95, 96, 272
  on Wittkower, 43–44
  work ethic, 361
  written work, 1970–1980s shifts in, 259–260
  yard-garden, 88, 101, 107
  "You Meet the Robin," 359, 388–389
Smithson, Peter, 133, 189–190, 216–217, 225, 241–242
  on Acropolis Place, 320
  on Alberti, 373
  on Alison Smithson, 329–330
  on American civil engineering, 204
  on American urban landscape, 204–205
  on *AS in DS: An Eye on the Road*, 221
  on Austen, 329
  Bakema's influence on Team 10, 257
  on books and building, 373
  building, process of, 383–384
  CIAM 10, 48–49, 50, 57
  on cities of Bath, Oxford, and Cambridge, 287–288
  on the city, 111
  on "Doorn Manifesto" (1954), 257
  Eames, Charles and Ray, visits in California, 139
  on the Eames aesthetic, 141, 154
  on Eames House, 137
  on Economist Building, 294–295
  English landscape garden, 329
  on Euston Arch, 379
  fabric, 178, 221, 255–256, 271, 295
  family, uniqueness of, 361, 363
  family and family farm, metaphor of, 392–393
  "Fine and the Folk, The: An Essay on McKim, Mead and White and the American Tradition" (1965), 88, *138*, 366
  fixes (keyword), 205–206
  form language, 225, 286, 287
  on Free University of Berlin, 271
  "From the Astringency of Necessity to the Astringency of Choice" (1966/1999), 97
  ICA lecture topics, 1950s and 1960s, 142–143
  "Keeping on the Right Lines" (1976), 373, 377
  on language, 235, 245–246
  on language of classical architecture, 286–287
  on Le Corbusier, 198, 235, 302–303
  mat-building, 308, 309
  on modern architecture, 270–271
  New Brutalism, 133, 199
  on "1916 A.S.O.: The Earth of the Modern Movement," 341

"On Climbing Ground: Thinking towards the Acropolis Place" (1991), 319–320
  on picturesque theory, 329
  Pollock's spatter paintings, 76
  "Rocket, The" (1965), 366
  on Skidmore, Owings and Merrill, 216
  "Slow Growth of Another Sensibility, The" (1965), 269
  socio-plastics, 39, 69, 73, 75 (see also Socio-plastics)
  "Space Between, The," 287–288
  Summerson, response to, 45
  on Team 10, 245, 254–257, 271, 380
  on "Team 10 at Royaumont 1962," 240
  territorial acts, 302–303
  "Territorial Imprint," 339
  theory-practice cycle, 45
  on urban form, 178, 277
  on writing, 392–393
"Social Bias of Town Planning, The" (Taylor), 105
Socio-plastics, 39, 69, 73, 75, 103–105, 107, 108, 261
Solar Pavilion. *See* Upper Lawn Pavilion
Sołtan, Jerzy, 233
"Sources," 53. *See also* "Parallel of Life and Art"
"Space Between, The" (A. Smithson), 287–288
"Space Construction in Greek Architecture" (Martienssen), 454n136
Space, Time and Architecture (Giedion), 171
Spatial trajectory. *See* Serial vision
"Speaking to the Sky" (A. and P. Smithson), 293, 325
"Statement on Habitat," 57–58. *See also* "Doorn Manifesto"
St. Dié Reconstruction Project (Le Corbusier), 52
Stephenson, George, 379
Stephenson, Robert, 380
Steyn, Juliet, 159
Stirling, James, 38, 240, 241
St. Jerome: The Desert and the Study (A. Smithson), 317, 318–319
"Stocktaking" (Banham), 215
St. Paul's Cathedral, 16
Subtopia, 6, 11

Suburban style, 8, 32
Summerson, John, 45
Sunday Pictorial, 171
Sylvester, David, 77
Systems aesthetic, 125
Systems analysis, 123, 125. *See also* Cybernetics; Information theory
Systems of movement, 208. *See* Patterns of movement
Systems of proportion. *See* Proportion theory
Systems theory. *See* Systems analysis

Tange, Kenzō, 233, 240
Taylor, Basil, 183
Taylor, Rattray, 105
Team 10, 47, 49–51, 57, 60–62, 67, 68, 69–73, 75, 164, 231–235, 238, 240–242, 244–247, 249–257, 269–271, 276, 309, 342, 366, 408n75
  Alison Smithson's account of, 52, 166, 233, 234
  Alison Smithson's role as editor, 232
  first meeting, 249
  four processes, 50
  "Instructions for CIAM 10," 58
"Team 10 at Royaumont 1962" (A. Smithson), 52, 231, 240, 437n32
  archetypes vs. prototypes, debate, 241–242
Team 10 England, 67, 68–69
Team 10 Meetings: 1953–1984 (A. Smithson), 231, 242, *243*, 256
"Team 10 Primer" (A. Smithson), 52, 78, 83, 166, 206, 231, 234–235, *236–237*
Team 10 Primer (A. Smithson), 217, 231, 238, *239*, 240, 252, 381
Television. *See* Mass media
Temple, William, 14
"Terraced Crescent Housing" (A. and P. Smithson), 79
"Territorial Imprint" (P. Smithson), 339
"This Is Tomorrow" (Crosby), 120, 127, 129, 132, 161, 263
Time magazine, 165
Tinling, Teddy, 175
Towards a New Architecture. *See Vers une Architecture* (1923)

Town and Country Planning Ordinance (1945), 15
Towndrow, Tony, 39
Townscape, 3, 7, 11, 12, 15, 17, 20–24, 30, 32, 41, 118, 152, 161
"Townscape" (Hastings writing as Wolfe), 20–21
Townscape Analysis, 5, 9, 11–13, 20–24, 27, 37, 40, 92, 326, 394
    Townscape Casebooks, 12, 15, 22–23, 27, 32, 159, 161, 208
Townscape policy, 24, 215
Toys, 113, 135, 137, 141, 155, 302, 373, 383
Tram Rats, The (A. and P. Smithson), 325, 359, 373, *374–376*, 377, 379, 380
Trams, 329, 346, 353, 359, 377, 379
Travel trailers. *See* Caravans
Trease, Geoffrey, 165
"Treasure Hunt" (Pevsner writing as Donner), 13
Tunnard, Christopher, 114
Tyler, Parker, 171
Tyrwhitt, Jaqueline (Jackie), 69, 248, 249

Unité d'Habitation (Le Corbusier), 38, 43, 48, 89, 95–96, 157, 248
University College London, 385
Unwin, Raymond, 2
Uppercase magazine, 120
Upper Lawn Pavilion (A. and P. Smithson), 268, 299, 302, 355, 363, 366, 415n52
Urban Re-identification, *54–56*, 100, 103
Urban Re-Identification (A. and P. Smithson), 99, 159
Urban Re-Identification Document (A. and P. Smithson), 79, 107
Urban Re-identification Project (A. and P. Smithson), 101
Urban Structuring (A. and P. Smithson), *74*, 100
"Urban Structuring" (A. and P. Smithson), 83
Utzon, Jørn, 70

"Valley Section" (Geddes), 52, 57, 58, 60
Van Eesteren, Cornelis, 248, 254
Van Eyck, Aldo, 62, 72, 164, 235, 240–241, 242, 244, 249, 393, 407n64
    B.T.C. (Building and Town Construction), 70
    CIAM 6, 47
    CIAM 10, 57, 59
    "Miracle of Moderation, A" (1969), 244
Van Ginkel, Sandy, 10, 47, 57, 249
"Vehicles of Desire" (Banham), 197
Vehicular movement patterns. *See* Movement graphics
Vernacular architecture and objects, 5, 7–8, 13, 22, 24, 26, 92, 114, 118, 121, 357, 399n17
    functionalism, 17
    Piper and, 7
    rejection by new generation, 32
    Townscape design and, 11
Vers une Architecture (Le Corbusier), 89, 454n136
Ville Radieuse (Le Corbusier), 49, 198
Vision in Motion (L. Moholy-Nagy), 161
Visual planning. *See* Townscape Analysis
Vitruvius (Marcus Vitruvius Pollio), 43
Vitsur, John, 71
Voelcker, John, 38, 47, 233, 249, 250, 357
    CIAM 9, 52
    CIAM 10, 57
    "Form and Mathematics" (1954), 44
    MARS group, elected to, 48
Vogue magazine, 163, 173, 185, 186

Wainwright, H. L., 3
"Wedding in the City Milan Triennale" (A. and P. Smithson), 267, 278, *278*
Welfare State, 190, 191, 244, 269, 271, 273, 279–281, 289
Wiener, Norbert, 113, 120, 123, 132, 133. *See also* Cybernetics
    Cybernetics (1948), 123, 125
    Human Use of Human Beings, The (1950), 123, 171
Willmott, Peter, 104, 105
Wilson, Colin St. John, 38, 40, 121–122
"With Green in Mind" (A. Smithson), 322
Without Rhetoric: An Architectural Aesthetic 1955–1972 (A. and P. Smithson), 83, 95, 96, 272
Wittkower, Rudolf, 43, 44, 46

Wogenscky, André, 248
Wolfe, Ivor de (pseudonym of Hubert de Cronin Hastings), 3, 13, 20–21
Woman's Home Companion, 173
Wood, Christopher, 22
Woods, Shadrach, 47, 235, 238, 240, 249, 250, 270
   Habitat du plus grand nombre, 108
"Work of Team 10, The" (A. Smithson), 52, 166, 231, 232–233
World War I, 330, 341, 342, 344, 345, 352–353
World War II, 12, 39, 46, 121, 196, 201, 251, 359
Wright, Edward, 38
Wright, Frank Lloyd, 115, 254

Yale University, 179
Yates, Frances, 356
"You Meet the Robin" (A. and P. Smithson), 359, 388–389
Young, Michael, 104, 105
Young Group. *See* Independent Group
Yugoslavian Group, 61

Zodiac, 92, 94

PARALLEL of LIFE & ART

Alison & Peter Smithson.
46 LIMERSTON ST.
S·W·10·